Cultural Chronicle of the Weimar Republic

William Grange

THE SCARECROW PRESS, INC.
Lanham, Maryland • Toronto • Plymouth, UK
2008

SCARECROW PRESS, INC.

Published in the United States of America
by Scarecrow Press, Inc.
A wholly owned subsidiary of
The Rowman & Littlefield Publishing Group, Inc.
4501 Forbes Boulevard, Suite 200, Lanham, Maryland 20706
www.scarecrowpress.com

Estover Road
Plymouth PL6 7PY
United Kingdom

Copyright © 2008 by William Grange

All rights reserved. No part of this publication may be reproduced, stored in a retrieval system, or transmitted in any form or by any means, electronic, mechanical, photocopying, recording, or otherwise, without the prior permission of the publisher.

British Library Cataloguing in Publication Information Available

Library of Congress Cataloging-in-Publication Data

Grange, William, 1947–
   Cultural chronicle of the Weimar Republic / William Grange.
     p. cm.
   Includes bibliographical references and index.
   ISBN-13: 978-0-8108-5967-8 (hardcover : alk. paper)
   ISBN-10: 0-8108-5967-X (hardcover : alk. paper)
   eISBN-13: 978-0-8108-6261-6
   eISBN-10: 0-8108-6261-1
   1. Germany—History—1918–1933—Chronology. 2. Germany—Intellectual life—20th century—Chronology. 3. Popular culture—Germany—History—20th century—Chronology. I. Title.
   DD67.1.G73 2008
   943.085—dc22
2008008116

∞^{TM} The paper used in this publication meets the minimum requirements of American National Standard for Information Sciences—Permanence of Paper for Printed Library Materials, ANSI/NISO Z39.48-1992.
Manufactured in the United States of America.

for my father

JAMES MICHAEL GRANGE
pastor fides, patriae amans, pater familias

Contents

Acknowledgments	vii
Introduction	ix
1918	1
1919	21
1920	57
1921	81
1922	109
1923	137
1924	163
1925	189
1926	215
1927	247
1928	275
1929	297
1930	325
1931	355
1932	379
1933	403
About the Author	407

Acknowledgments

Rufe mich an, so will ich dir antworten und will dir kundtun große und unfaßbare Dinge, von denen du nichts weißt.

Jeremia 33:3

This book is a result of the author's long-standing interest in the culture of the Weimar Republic. It probably began with his first reading of German expressionist plays when he was college student at the University of Toledo, followed by a viewing of paintings by Ludwig Kirchner and drawings by Käthe Kollwitz at the Toledo Museum of Art. Seeing movies like *Metropolis* and *The Blue Angel* at the Westwood Art Theatre in Toledo helped the process along, as did a literature course with Prof. Herbert Schering in the university's German department. Prof. Schering introduced his students to novels by Alfred Döblin, Thomas Mann, Vicki Baum, and Erich Maria Remarque, while encouraging them all to study at German universities. His encouragement led to a generous stipend and a year in Heidelberg, where the author was able to immerse himself not only in the Weimar period, but also in the then-emerging recognition of just how innovative the Weimar years had actually been. Subsequent encounters with the music of Kurt Weill, Paul Hindemith, and Ralph Benatsky intensified the author's absorption with "the Golden Twenties" in Germany, while doctoral studies with Prof. Oskar Seidlin at Indiana University revealed that not everything was golden or even innovative in the Weimar Republic. Professor Seidlin, like Professor Schering, had attained young manhood during the Weimar Republic, and his remarkable, direct acquaintance with so many facets of Weimar culture promoted a sense of personal involvement with the Weimar Republic—both in its remarkable exceptionality but also in its sometimes pedestrian sordidness.

Several organizations as well as individuals contributed to the book's completion. My thanks first of all go to April Snider of Scarecrow Press, who almost single-handedly encouraged this book into existence and whose patience with me is greatly appreciated. The vice chancellor's Office for Research at the University of Nebraska provided much-needed funding for research and travel, as did the Austrian–American Educational Commission, the Dorot Foundation, and Dr. Patrice Berger of the Nebraska Honors Program. All of my colleagues in the Johnny Carson School of Theatre and Film have been enormously helpful, with Dr. Tice Miller and Prof. Harris Smith providing indispensable moral support during both the research and writing portions of the book. Dr. Marvin Carlson of the City University of New York, one of the academic world's premiere theater scholars, has likewise been unstinting in his advice—and very generous with his insights. To Dr. Elmar Buck and his colleague Dr. Hedwig Müller at the Theater Research Collection at the University of Cologne, I offer my sincere appreciation. Dr. Leigh Woods at the University of Michigan gave me several points of direction, as did Dr. Jürgen Ohlhoff and Frau Ulrike Münkel-Ohlhoff in Berlin. My wife Willa comes in for singular praise, not so much for scholarly guidance or tips in writing, but for her sheer stamina in putting up with me. Her patience is a thing of beauty.

Lincoln, Nebraska
Spring 2008

Introduction

The Weimar Republic got its name from the Thuringian town of Weimar, where delegates met in the municipal theater to write the new republic's constitution in 1919. Weimar already had a reputation as the German cultural mecca, because Goethe and Schiller had lived and worked there 120 years earlier. The foundations of what became "Weimar culture," however, lay within late 19th- and early 20th-century Wilhelmine culture. Remarkable innovations on those precedents thrived in the new dispensation proclaimed in the aftermath of Wilhelm II's abdication in 1918. Many scholars and historians consider the Weimar Republic the first "modernist" culture, largely because the republic itself was an experiment. Witnesses at the time marveled at the innumerable novelties springing up from the ruins of the Wilhelminian era, many with an unwonted, even frightening, intensity. Several observers in our own day remain convinced that "Weimar culture" and "innovation" are practically synonymous, usually with references to actress Marlene Dietrich, novels like *Berlin Alexanderplatz*, musical compositions by Paul Hindemith, the Bauhaus, Brecht and Weill's *The Threepenny Opera*, or film director Fritz Lang. These and other iconographic inscriptions of the Weimar Republic are legitimate artifacts of an unshackling process that began from the moment of the republic's birth. There was an exhilarating atmosphere of liberation at first, but it soon gave way to sobered anxiety. The German army returned home in defeat, the German economy entered a cataclysmic decline, and political violence erupted on an almost daily basis. Many began to regret the abruptness of Wilhelm's departure. Yet there was, in the early days of the republic at least, an undeniable sense that a new age had dawned. Or rather erupted, "lava-like," in the words of one direct participant,[1] inchoate and dangerous, manifesting a modernist tendency toward the fragmented, distorted, anecdotal, instinctive, and on nearly anything that was novel and authentic. The Weimar Republic thus became a kind of cultural laboratory, in which myriad artistic test trials took place in an effort to find the unique and unfamiliar, then revel in it.

The search for the exceptional and distinctive was, as Peter Gay has noted, a motor of modernism, because modernism was itself a call to reject formulas and a defiance of tradition. It was "a crusade in behalf of sincerity, in behalf of an expressive freedom that no establishment could command or in the long run frustrate."[2] The votaries among Weimar modernists proclaimed a new world open to artists, many of whom accepted the "eclipse of distance" as empirical fact. Perceptions that had been inexorably changing during the Wilhelmine years due to rapid advances in technology experienced wholesale transformation in the Weimar years. The opening salvo of the new order was literally a hail of unfriendly gunfire in the days immediately following the kaiser's abdication. The kaiser's government illegally turned over the reins of power to a de facto government, and the race was on to fill the power void. A republic came into being when politicians simply began proclaiming one, and revolutions broke out in many venues, especially in the former imperial capital, Berlin. With the disappearance of order, lawlessness enveloped the streets, theaters, museums, concert halls, and even churches. Much of the confusion turned violent, as a substantial minority of Germans hoped for a Bolshevik-style takeover that would institute a *juste milieu*, coercing a transformation of every German and his or her dealings with fellow Germans. Workers' and soldiers councils succeeded in taking over some cities, but the new rulers of the republic, however accidental their arrival in office, responded with equal violence and restored a semblance of stability. Most Germans resumed their accustomed habits of cultural consumption thereafter, as many new offerings appeared. The large majority of Germans continued to see boulevard comedies, attend light operas, watch detective movies, read romance novels, and go to orchestra concerts featuring the works of 18th- and 19th-century masters.

Signs of change, however, were unmistakable. Germans gawked in astonishment at previously unthinkable spectacles: Previously suppressed plays, films, and books flooded the market; choruses of protestors sang songs of disrespect for the defunct kaiser, and broadsheets calling for revolution were hawked openly on the streets. Along with the disturbing sounds of gunfire were the equally discomfiting presence of female proletarians taking part in street demonstrations, making street corner speeches, and getting killed in deadly revolutionary encounters with provisional government troops. Prostitutes likewise became a more obvious presence on urban streets throughout Germany, as police supervision of the sex trade dwindled in the face of general social upheaval. Revolutionary violence reached its explosive flashpoint in the "Spartacist" uprising of 1919, which attempted to take over lines of communication in Berlin and ultimately assume political power in the republic. The revolutionaries' attempts met with intense resistance from government troops and resulted in the murders of the Spartacist leaders, Karl Liebknecht and Rosa Luxemburg.

In the same year, what some pundits have termed the open and unbridled "commodification" of culture accelerated.[3] Images, books, musical compositions, plays, and especially films became subjects of relentless cultural commerce. Germans had engaged in the commerce of such artifacts within the patronage system that existed under the kaiser. However, accustomed patterns of marketing culture greatly intensified in the 1920s. Max Reinhardt had by 1911 established himself as one of the most successful theatrical entrepreneurs in Berlin's history, and by June 1930 his organization had presented more than 23,000 performances in Berlin alone, far more than any other manager in the city's history. Reinhardt had purchased additional venues and made extremely profitable tours of the United States, enabling him to remain profitable even in the midst of the German economy's complete collapse in 1923. His example encouraged other managers to imitate him, though they met with far less success. Henny Porten was perhaps the biggest film star in German films by 1916, and she founded her own company in 1921 to develop and produce vehicles to burnish her image as a film diva. She starred in more than forty films during the 1920s alone, producing 20 of them herself. Thea von Harbou had intended to become a novelist, hoping for a career like Ida Boy-Ed's or Carry Brachvogel's; after several of her novels became screenplays for successful movies, she devoted herself to motion pictures and became the German film industry's most prolific and celebrated screenwriter. Book production soared during the Weimar Republic as publishers sought to expand their markets among readers of all income and educational levels. Periodicals likewise proliferated, offering German readers a seeming limitless supply of political opinion, gossip, fashion, news summary, home decorating tips, literary effort, art appreciation, sports reportage, and advice for hobbyists. Musicians and composers benefited from a wide variety of new technologies, the most obvious of which was the silent film. Many of the large movie theaters in Berlin employed full-time orchestras, and composers vied with each others to arrange music that accompanied images flickering on the small screens inside mammoth movie palaces. The theaters were themselves objects of a vigorous competition among architects to create new and innovative building designs. The new technologies of recording and radio broadcasting also expanded markets for cultural consumption, providing new avenues of employment for various purveyors of cultural wares.

The increase in book readership, greater attendance at various performing arts productions, and an expansion of gallery showings were partly a result of lifting decades-old censorship restrictions. The republic began as one of the most restriction-free of any state in the world, because censorship had effectively ended with the fall of the kaiser. But old patterns to limit what readers could purchase and audiences could see and hear gradually began to insinuate themselves. Local police reclaimed authority over deciding whether or not words, images, or ideas presented a threat to public order and safety. By 1925 police in several local jurisdictions had established "arts committees" comprising lawyers, professors, and bureaucrats in departments for theater, literature, and pictorial arts. Such committees were to "counsel" authorities on maintaining order and "upholding public morality." Several artists were jailed in the Weimar Republic for violating bans that local committees had advised police to enforce.

Many painters, composers, playwrights, writers, and other artists organized vociferous objections to censorship; many were likewise vocal in their support of the republic itself. The whole idea of a republican form of government came under constant attack from both the extreme Right and Left; a noteworthy legacy of culture in the Weimar Republic is the way artists attempted to defend it, often at great peril to themselves. George Grosz, Paul Klee, László Moholy-Nagy, Oskar Schlemmer, Walter Gropius, and Kurt Weill were among those who formed the *Novembergruppe* (November Group) and publicly professed their political commitment to the republic. Other such organizations included the *Gruppe 1925* (Group 1925), which called for an end to reconstituted censorship.

The return of censorship notwithstanding, the years between 1925 and 1929 (from the death of President Friedrich Ebert in February 1925 to the economic collapse after the Wall Street crash in October 1929) witnessed an astonishing stretch of cultural productivity. In 1925 nearly 800 Berlin book and newspaper publishers operated at a profit. More than 200 films were produced and released in 1925, and by 1929 there were more than 5,000 movie theaters operating in Germany. Throughout the Weimar period Germans produced more films than all other European countries combined. Ownership of radio sets jumped from 100,000 in 1925 to 3.1 million by the end of 1929, and broadcasts of symphonies, plays, operettas, and readings of novels by their authors increased to a similar extent. But numbers alone are not barometers by which one might measure the culture of the Weimar Republic, though they certainly reveal a great deal about the catastrophes besetting it. Statistics attesting to the ruinous inflation in 1923 reveal unthinkable devastation, and the numbers of political murders that extremists perpetrated on their enemies are nothing short of appalling. Yet the Weimar Republic is best measured by the legacy it bequeathed to other cultures long after its death, "part murder, part wasting sickness, part suicide."[4]

Among the republic's most widely viewed legacies are its films, often those directed by Friedrich Wilhelm Murnau, Georg Wilhelm Pabst (though born in Bohemia), and Fritz Lang (born in Vienna). Other directors benefited from the film legacy of the Weimar period, one of whom was Alfred Hitchcock. He and many other non-Germans worked in the German film industry, and the cinematic techniques he witnessed in the Babelsberg studios near Berlin appeared years later in his own movies. Several German film artists (in addition to Murnau, Pabst, and Lang) went to Hollywood in the 1920s, vastly enriching the quality of American film. The most well known among them is probably Emil Jannings, winner of the first Academy Award for Best Actor. Americans also worked in German film during the Weimar period; best known among them is probably Louise Brooks, star of two Pabst films. Others were Mae Marsh, Imogene Robertson, and the redoubtable Fern Andra, who went to Germany in 1913 as a circus performer and competed with Henny Porten in the early 1920s to market herself as actress, screenwriter, and producer.

Expressionist theater and drama, like film, are closely identified in the public mind with Weimar culture, and like film they came into being before the republic did. Playwrights Georg Kaiser and Walter Hasenclever; actors Conrad Veidt, Ernst Deutsch, Agnes Straub, Werner Krauss, Fritz Kortner; and directors Leopold Jessner and Karl-Heinz Martin were well established by 1918. Yet they became identified as avatars of expressionism in the early 1920s. Many performers specializing in expressionism proved to be remarkably versatile, maintaining active careers long after the vogue for that style had passed. Pictorial artists such as Max Beckmann, Ernst Ludwig Kirchner, Emil Nolde, and Käthe Kollwitz had presented and sold their work under the Wilhelmine aegis and were for a time considered antiestablishment. By the end of the Weimar Republic many of them were members in good standing of the Prussian Academy of the Arts. Expressionist film, on the other hand, seemed to provide aesthetic departures closely identified with the republic itself. The acknowledged artificiality of settings, the steep angle of lighting, the distortions inherent to the mise-en-scène, and often the fractured psyches of many characters in the films, represented to some observers the fractures and distortions tormenting the republic's body politic. Nevertheless, although some of the expressionist films enjoyed popularity (e.g., *The Cabinet of Dr. Caligari*, *Nosferatu*, and *Metropolis*), the most popular films of the republic were detective thrillers with Max Landa or Harry Piel, or romantic comedies featuring attractive young performers like Ossi Oswalda, Oskar Karlweis, Erna Morena, Werner Fütterer, or Claire Rommer.

As it did in film almost everywhere, the advent of sound created an entirely new dimension in film attendance. German audiences were the first to benefit from the unique "sound-on-film" technology that technicians Josef Engl, Hans Vogt, and Joseph Massole had developed in 1919. The Tobis Klangfilm (Sound Film) company was founded in 1928 solely to create films employing the new technology. The Ufa Studio employed the technology in its global hit film, *Der blaue Engel* (*The Blue Angel*), in 1930. This film, directed by Joseph von Sternberg, made an international star of Marlene Dietrich and remains popular to this day.

The Blue Angel was based on a Wilhelmine novel by Heinrich Mann titled *Professor Unrat*. Both he and his younger brother Thomas were active novelists during the Weimar period, culminating with the award of the Nobel Prize for Literature to Thomas Mann in 1929. The novel may be the Weimar Republic's signal art form, for in fiction one may find the widest spectrum of cultural experimentation. German novels written during the Weimar years have also had a remarkable international readership. Thomas Mann's *Der Zauberberg* (*The Magic Mountain*) quickly became a best seller in Germany and has since become one of the most popular novels ever written in German. It has been translated into 28 languages and appears in the curricula of many schools and universities around the world. Hermann Hesse's *Demian* (1919), *Siddhartha* (1922), and *Der Steppenwolf* (1927) did not at first achieve the popularity of Mann's work, but like Mann, Hesse was awarded the Nobel Prize for Literature, and he remains widely read. Less popular, but no less significant, were the novels of Alfred Döblin, whose modernist experiments with narrative culminated in the monumental *Berlin Alexanderplatz* (1929). Perhaps the most popular and best-selling novels of the Weimar Republic were Erich Maria Remarque's *Im Westen nichts neues* (*All Quiet on the Western Front*, 1928) and Vicki Baum's *Menschen im Hotel* (*Grand Hotel*, 1929). Both were made into popular, Academy Award–winning American movies (the former in 1930, the latter in 1932). The most consistently popular novels, however, were rarely made into movies and seldom translated from German into other languages. They included the romance novels *Um Diamanten und Perlen* (*About Diamonds and Pearls*), *Duemmeine Welt* (*You—My World*), *Die Liebe höret nimmer auf* (*Love Shall not Cease*), and several others like them by the formidable Hedwig Courths-Mahler. To these one should add the children's novels of Waldemar Bonsels, the "novels of social consciousness" by Jakob Wassermann, the "novels of proletarian social criticism" by Hans Fallada, and novels that floated along in the Weimar "sex wave." Such novels featured narratives about the white slave trade, nights in a harem, women with whips, and exotic methods of sexual encounter. They competed with periodicals like *Free Love*, *The Grass Widow*, and *Woman without Man*.

Similar to the scores of then-popular but now dimly remembered novels were the dozens of operettas and operas that premiered during the Weimar period. In the midst of the Spartacist uprising in 1919, a time when the republic's very existence seemed to hang in the balance, provisional president Friedrich Ebert pleaded with managers of operetta houses to restrict their offerings to those that "represents the seriousness of the moment in German history." They ignored him, and the very evening Ebert made his plea saw the premiere of Walter Goetze's operetta *Ihre Hoheit, die Tänzerin* (*Her Majesty, the Dancer*). Dozens of other operettas premiered during the Weimar Republic; composers Eduard Künneke, Walter Kollo, Jean Gilbert, Leo Fall, Emmerich Kalman, and Karl Millöcker kept the German audience amply supplied with light, frothy entertainment. Operettas, like the cabaret, night club shows, dance reviews featuring naked women, musical vaudevilles, and variety shows, all thrived, particularly in Berlin.[5] Among the most well-known operettas premiering in Berlin were Franz Lehar's *Zarevich* (*The Heir-Apparent Czar*, 1927), followed by his *Friederike* in 1928 and *Land des Lächelns* (*Land of Smiles*) in 1929. Ralph Benatzky's *The White Horse Inn* premiered in 1930, and Paul Abraham's *Blume von Hawaii* (*Flowers from Hawaii*) in 1931. All were set before 1914, and none of their composers was Germans.

Adolf Hitler was not a German, either—and his career as a public personality, author, and politician is best understood within the context of cultural developments that emerged during the Weimar Republic. Hitler's career benefited from several factors, but he proved himself a master in the nuances of performance, exploiting innovations in technology and manipulating a burgeoning media environment in ways no other German politician had done. It is well known that Hitler was a superb orator, but speaking ability alone does not explain his skill in adumbrating a utopian dream that, he promised, would transform both Germany and Germans themselves. His many detractors dismissed him as a malignant caricature of Charlie Chaplin, and Chaplin himself described Hitler as "an imitation of me."[6] If Hitler was an imitation of Chaplin, it was to Hitler's advantage. Hitler embraced technology as did none of his contemporaries; he used radio broadcasts, gramophone recordings, and aircraft technology developed during the Weimar Republic in ways that enthralled growing numbers of Germans. But he also promised them that together they could liberate technology from capitalism's abuse, which the National Socialists, like their Marxist adversaries, termed "commodification." The difference between them was that the National Socialists identified "commodification" with Jewish oppression of Germans and control of German finance capital. Hitler, and later Joseph Goebbels, had an uncanny ability to see the emerging modernist culture in the Weimar Republic and turn it into a promise of an aesthetic experience for all Germans. For Hitler and Goebbels, "the modernist credo was the triumph of the spirit and will over reason and the subsequent fusion of this will to an aesthetic mode. Aesthetic experience alone justified life, morality was suspended, and desire had no limits."[7]

NOTES

1. Fritz Kortner, *Aller Tage Abend* (Munich: Kindler, 1969), 306.
2. Peter Gay, *Pleasure Wars* (New York: Norton, 1998), 195.
3. See Walter Benjamin, *Das Kunstwerk im Zeitalter seiner technischen Reproduzierbarkeit* [*The Work of Art in the Age of Mechanical Reproduction*] (Frankfurt am Main: Suhrkamp, 1963). Benjamin meditates extensively on his preoccupation with "commodification" in his *Das Passagen-Werk* [*The Arcades Project*].
4. Peter Gay, *Weimar Culture* (New York: Harper & Row, 1970), xii.
5. The most popular nude performer in Berlin was the American Josephine Baker; her dances had a sensational impact on Berlin audiences, though nude dancing was by no means a novelty in Berlin during the Weimar Republic. Count Harry Kessler confided to his diary that watching Baker perform was like witnessing a "beautiful predator" stalking her prey.
6. Charles Chaplin, *My Autobiography* (London: Penguin, 1964), 316.
7. Jeffrey Herf, *Reactionary Modernism* (New York: Cambridge, 1984), 25.

1918

NOVEMBER

9 In the early morning hours, at a Belgian hotel serving as headquarters for the German military, General Paul von Hindenburg and his field commanders vote to inform Kaiser Wilhelm II that they will lead all German armies on a retreat from the western front back to Germany. Those armies, Hindenburg notes, will not be under the kaiser's command.[1] There are 39 votes cast, with two dissenting. In their final communiqué, the generals urge the kaiser to depart immediately for Holland, where the Dutch royal family has offered him refuge. Wilhelm, residing in the Villa Fraineuse nearby, tells his generals that he will do as they advise, "But not before lunch."

Around 1:00 p.m. in Berlin, Reich Chancellor Max von Baden meets with leaders of the Social Democratic Party (SPD), the Catholic Center Party, and the German Democratic Party, who inform him that they will not tolerate the monarchy in any future form of the German government. By about 2:00 p.m., Chancellor von Baden announces Wilhelm II's abdication as both German kaiser and Prussian king. Wilhelm has signed no documents to that effect and accuses his confidantes of treason as he boards a train for Holland and makes his exit from the elaborate production that was the German Empire.[2]

In Berlin, Max von Baden resigns as Reich chancellor and illegally turns over the reins of government to Friedrich Ebert, head of the SPD; Ebert becomes the de facto Reich chancellor. Philipp Scheidemann of the "majority wing" of the SPD utters the first soliloquy of the German revolutionary drama by declaring from the sill of a second-story window in the Reich Chancellery the formation of a German republic. From a balcony at the City Palace at about the same time, "independent" Social Democrat (USPD) leader Karl

Liebknecht declares the formation of a "free, socialist republic of Germany." The republican era in Germany has accidentally begun. Soon other characters jostle Ebert, Scheidemann, and Liebknecht for the spotlight at center stage.

A huge chorus of political prisoners appears on the scene, released from prisons around the city at the command of Emil Eichhorn, who has assumed control of the Berlin police department. Among the many former prisoners is Rosa Luxemburg. Numerous "councils of workers and soldiers" call for a general strike throughout Germany, as heads of local governments abdicate. Economic activity in Germany comes to a brief standstill as a revolution in Berlin begins "to spread like an oil slick," according to Count Harry Kessler in his book *Tagebücher*.[3] Numerous violent encounters take place among armed groups with varying revolutionary and counterrevolutionary goals. Gunfire is heard in the middle of Berlin throughout the day. A council of workers and soldiers takes control of the Wolff Telegraph Bureau in Berlin. Stock exchanges close throughout Germany, as do most banks.

Performances in all the state theaters of Berlin are canceled. Private theaters and most movie houses remain open for business. At the Lessing Theater near the Reichstag, *Charley's Aunt*, by Brandon Thomas, is on the playbill. Most protest marches remain orderly, and gardeners in Tiergarten Park politely remind protesters to keep off the grass.

Premiering at the Cologne City Theater is Raoul Konen's *Der junge König* (*The Young King*), an ironic glorification of the Hohenzollern dynasty, of which Wilhelm II was the most dubious descendant. In Munich, despite the revolutionary outbreaks and the proclamation of a Soviet-style Bavarian republic two days earlier, the Volkstheater continues to present Arnold and Bach's *The Spanish Fly*, a wildly popular comedy about an exotic dancer who blackmails a shy professor. Johanna Spyri's *Heidi* series goes into its 45th printing, its popularity likewise unaffected by recent political and military events.

10 Ebert relinquishes the office of Reich chancellor and sets up an interim government entirely of SPD and USPD members, who insist on calling themselves the Council of Peoples' Representatives," with Ebert as chairman. Ebert telephones Army Chief of Staff Wilhelm Groener to appeal for military help in preserving civil order. Groener agrees to troop assignments, which patrol streets, railway stations, telegraph offices, electricity-producing facilities, and post offices. Groener swears loyalty to the new interim government—at least over the telephone—and claims that his primary objective is to prevent radical left-wing usurpation like the Bolshevik takeover in Moscow almost exactly one year earlier. The Ebert–Groener Pact becomes a source of bitter dispute in the upheavals to follow. Electricity, water, gas, telephone, telegraph, and public transport utilities continue uninterrupted.

Allied troops occupy Mainz, Cologne, and Koblenz according to the terms of the cease-fire. Activists throughout Germany declare former kingdoms, duchies, and even cities to be republics. In Berlin, a "council of intellectual workers" (*Politischer Rat geistiger Arbeiter*) forms under Kurt Hiller[4] to preserve the "cultural-political ideals" of the revolution. Similar councils spring up in Hannover, Hamburg, and Göttingen. In Königsberg, a group of writers, artists, and actors name theater director Leopold Jessner to head the local council. The Prussian Social Democratic Party assumes control of all Prussian ministries, including those with jurisdiction over cultural activities. One of its first decisions is to fire the superintendent of the Prussian Court Theater in Berlin, Count Georg Botho von Hülsen.

11 A council of soldiers assembles in the Reichstag. In Compiégne, France, Matthias Erzberger (representing the German interim government), Count Alfred von Oberndorff of the German Foreign Ministry, and army general Detlof von Winterfeldt initial the cease-fire agreement with the Allies. All fighting on the western front ceases on this 11th day of the 11th month, at 11:00 a.m.

Berlin city commandant Otto Wels invites 600 sailors from the port of Cuxhaven to form a reserve unit to defend the republic. They are to reside in the former Royal Stables; upon their arrival they call themselves the "Peoples' Naval Division." At the Excelsior Hotel, members of the Spartacus League rename themselves the Spartacus Group. Spartacus Group leader Karl Liebknecht refuses any role in the interim government. Rosa Luxemburg tells the Spartacus Group to prepare for armed and violent revolt: "Socialism does not mean getting together in parliament and passing laws. For us, socialism means overthrowing the ruling classes with all the brutality of which the proletariat is capable."[5] Luxemburg briefly surpasses actress Pola Negri as the most well-known Polish-born woman in Germany.

The king of Saxony and the grand duke of Oldenburg abdicate. The Hapsburg dynasty is officially dissolved.

Arthur Hoffmann's comedy *Fabrikgeheimnisse* (*Factory Secrets*) premieres at the Elberfeld City Theater.

12 Ebert and his Council of Peoples' Representatives, which assumes governmental authority, call for a national assembly to write a constitution that will guarantee female suffrage; an eight-hour day; freedoms of the press, assembly, and religion; and the elimination of all theater censorship. The new revolutionary government of Prussia expropriates all property of the Hohenzollern dynasty.

A new opera by Eugen d'Albert,[6] *Der Stier von Oliera* (*The Steer of Oliera*), opens at the Berlin City Opera; it had premiered earlier in Leipzig.

13 A nationalist militia called Stahlhelm (Steel Helmet) is formed. The first German translation of President Woodrow Wilson's 1913 book *The New Freedom* is released.

14 The Prussian state (formerly court) theaters in Berlin are reopened with Lessing's *Nathan der Weise* (*Nathan the Wise*), and the opera house is reopened with *Die Meistersinger von Nürnberg* (*The Meistersingers of Nuremberg*), by Richard Wagner.

SPD members assume direction of major national government offices, including the ministries of foreign relations, justice, treasury, and defense. Ebert announces plans to convene a national assembly to write a republican constitution. Baden becomes a "people's republic."

15 The romantic film *Sonnwendhof*,[7] with Fritz Kortner, premieres.

The new SPD government of Prussia warns all schoolteachers that any disparaging or contorted remarks to school pupils about the causes and results of the German revolution are henceforth forbidden.[8] The Berlin stock exchange reopens.

16 Administrators assigned to former Prussian court theaters and opera houses (in Kassel, Wiesbaden, and others cities under Prussian jurisdiction) are officially replaced with political appointees. Among the most important is Leopold Jessner, who transfers from Königsberg to Berlin.

Georg Kaiser's[9] *Der Brand im Opernhaus* (*Fire in the Opera House*) premieres at the Hamburg Kammerspiele (Chamber Theater). This production, starring Fritz Kortner,[10] probably qualifies as the first expressionist work of the revolutionary period, though it is set in Paris in 1763. It follows a bizarre series of incidents in the aftermath of the fire that destroyed the Paris Opera House, most of them motivated by extreme jealousy and despair.

17 At the first church services in the Berlin Cathedral since the establishment of the Council of Peoples' Representatives, Dada artist Johannes Baader stands up in response to the sermon topic of the day ("What is Jesus Christ to us?") to shout, "Christ is baloney!" Baader is quickly hustled out of the building.

18 The interim German government appeals to U.S. Secretary of State Robert Lansing for assistance in lifting the Allied embargo on German ports so that foodstuffs can be unloaded and distributed among the populace. Lansing does not respond.

The eleventh printing of Horst Wolfram Geissler's popular novel *Himmelstoss* appears in bookstores.[11]

Essays by Maxim Gorki titled "One Year of the Russian Revolution" are published in the literary journal *South German Monthly*. Germans read for the first time Gorki's condemnation of Lenin's ruthlessness, his blood thirst for power, his violent dissolution of Russia's Constituent Assembly, and his intention to make Russia an exporter of proletarian revolution throughout the world. The essays had appeared in Gorki's newspaper *New Life*, which Lenin shut down in July 1918.[12]

The *Arbeitsrat für Kunst* (Working Council for Art) is founded under Bruno Taut, an architect and city planner. The council produces a manifesto signed by 114 painters, architects, and museum directors, calling for a "socialist art" that will include and "benefit all people everywhere."[13]

The first issue of *Die rote Fahne* (*The Red Flag*) is published as the organ of the Spartacus Group, supervised by Karl Liebknecht and Rosa Luxemburg.[14] They invoke "the dissolution of capitalist control and the realization of a socialist order: that and nothing less is the historical theme of this revolution. [This revolution] is a mighty work, wrought not through hand-wringing nor decreed from above.... All power in the hands of the working masses, in the hands of the Councils of Workers and Soldiers can secure the revolution against enemies waiting in ambush to destroy it."[15] Both Liebknecht and Luxemburg are ambushed and murdered almost two months later.

19 The drama *Der Schöpfer* (*The Creator*), by Hans Müller, premieres at the Lessing Theater in Berlin, with Albert Bassermann in the title role, directed by Viktor Barnowsky. The comedy *Das Vertauer* (*The Confidante*), by Johannes Boldt, premieres at the Cottbus City Theater. The operetta *Sterne, die wieder leuchten* (*Stars that Shine Again*), by Sigmund Romberg and Walter Kollo,[16] resumes at the Berliner Theater.

For the first time, Franz Werfel's *Die Troerinnen des Euripides* (*The Trojan Women of Euripides*) appears in bookstores. Werfel's introductory essay to his adaptation of the Greek tragedy compares the Trojan queen Hecuba to a Christian saint, angering numerous German activists. Kurt Hiller declares that Hecuba's passive acceptance of fate "is a form of moral masochism."[17] Werfel responds by claiming that political activism is pointless and ultimately changes nothing.

Retreating German troops continue the evacuation of the western front at a rate of about 10 to 12 miles per day.

20 The detective comedy film *Der Fall Rosentopf* (*The Rosentopf Case*), written and directed by Ernst Lubitsch and starring Trude Hesterberg, premieres.

German troops west of the Rhine continue their disorganized retreat; many refuse to salute officers or obey orders. Some troops assault officers, and there are reports of soldiers killing their commanders. There are no reports of armistice violations.

21 The operetta *Drei tolle Tage* (*Three Crazy Days*), by Hans Hannes, resumes at the Berliner Theater.

22 Walter Hasenclever's expressionist drama *Der Sohn* (*The Son*) premieres at Max Reinhardt's Deutsches Theater, starring Ernst Deutsch, Werner Krauss, and Paul Wegener. The Czech-born Deutsch, in the title role of the play, sets a precedent for expressionist acting that many actors in the German theater subsequently attempt to emulate.

The films *Der Mandarin* (*The Mandarin*), directed by Fritz Freisler and starring Harry Walden, and *Tiefland* (*Lowlands*),[18] directed by Hans Rhoden and starring Josephine Josefi, are released.

Waldemar Bonsels's drama *Märztage* (*March Days*) appears in bookstores for the first time.[19] The German National Peoples' Party (DNVP) is formed; it calls for the union of all nationalist, anti-Semitic, and conservative groups. The Saxon government declares that the former Königliches Hoftheater (Royal Court Theater) is now the Sächsiches Landestheater (Regional Theater of Saxony), placed under the jurisdiction of the Saxon Cultural Ministry. The Grand Duke of Baden renounces claims to his throne.

23 Friedrich Kayssler stages Schiller's *Wilhelm Tell* at the Berlin Volksbühne with Jürgen Fehling, Adele Sandrock, and in the chorus an actress born Maria Magdelena von Losch but using the name "Mary Dietrich." She later becomes Marlene Dietrich. Theater director Leopold Jessner publishes "An die deutsche Theaterleiter" ("To All German Theater Directors") in the *Berlin Tageblatt* newspaper, urging individuals "called to perform the highest cultural tasks" to "march with a purpose to the beat of a new course."[20] The comedy *Die Erben* (*The Heirs*), by Wilhelm Hagen, premieres at the Munich Deutsches Theater.

Memoirs titled *Aus meinem Jugendland* (*From the Country of My Youth*), by poet and essayist Isolde Kurz (1853–1944), go into their second printing. The memoirs have been a surprise best seller since their initial publication in September 1918. Her poetry and novellas usually had Italian settings (she lived in Florence from 1877 to 1913), and she considered Italy the "country of her youth."

The enormously successful General Paul von Lettow-Vorbeck, who completely dominated the Zambian theater of war against the British and their allies from 1914 to 1918, surrenders in Kasama, Zambia. He is equally successful in arranging the repatriation of the approximately 10,000 troops under his command. In Germany itself, several divisions of retreating German infantry assemble on both shores of the Rhine River; regimental officers poll soldiers about their support of the new German republic and their willingness to defend it. Thousands of soldiers desert their units.

The Reich Office of Economic Demobilization issues 12 regulations setting forth rules governing length of the work day, paid holidays, sick leaves, and other aspects of labor relations within the German economy.

24 The Bavarian Middle Party, a middle-class, conservative, Protestant, nationalist organization is founded in Nuremberg, attempting to represent interests of the average citizen in Bavaria.

25 Delegates at the Reich Conference of German Republics vote to preserve a federal Germany and to call a national assembly. Delegates from the disparate states pledge to uphold the national unity of Germany and to oppose separatist movements.

Ernst Lothar's novel *Der Feldherr* (*The Field Commander*) is published.[21]

26 Georg Kaiser opens his play *Der Brand im Opernhaus* (*Fire in the Opera House*) at the Kleines Schauspielhaus in Berlin, timed to match the play's publication in book form. Critics expect something in the expressionist style from Kaiser and instead see a melodramatic treatment of clandestine love and fervid jealousy. Their reaction is lukewarm. The comedy *Von fünf bis sieben* (*From Five to Seven*), by Hans Brennert, premieres at the Hamburg Thalia Theater.

The Bavarian leader Kurt Eisner calls on the Berlin council of workers and soldiers to overthrow Ebert and his interim government.

27 The first in a group of 12 books titled *Die neue Reihe* (*The New Series*), by lyric poets and prose stylists, for example, Hermann Kasack, Arnold Zweig, and Heinrich Eduard Jacob, is published in Munich.

The German Democratic Party (DDP), claiming a western allied policy of hatred toward Germany appeals to President Woodrow Wilson for help. In Bremen, *Der Kommunist* (*The Communist*) newspaper is founded. The Düsseldorf stock exchange reopens.

The comedy *Heinrich der Beglücker* (*Henry the Happiness Man*), by Julius Mayergräfe, premieres at the Frankfurt am Main Schauspielhaus.

28 Kaiser Wilhelm II officially abdicates. He also renounces the kingdom of Prussia and releases all military and civil officials from their loyalty oaths. His son, the crown prince, also signs the instrument of abdication.

Georg Kaiser's *Gas I* premieres in Frankfurt, directed by Arthur Hellmer, and in Düsseldorf, directed by Gustav Lindemann. Critics hail it as a precedent-setting work of Germany's most significant contemporary playwright. Critic Hermann Esswein describes the play as "a gift to workers everywhere, though they will have no idea what it means."[22]

29 The films *Die Jüdin* (*The Jewess*), directed by Luise Kolm and Jakob Fleck,[23] and *Die blaue Laterne* (*The Blue Lantern*), directed by Rudolf Bierbrach and starring Henny Porten, premiere.

Arthur Schnitzler's novella *Cassanova's Journey Home*, featuring a young and beautiful Viennese woman from a privileged background who prostitutes herself in order to save her family from bankruptcy, is published.

The Ebert government urges the victorious Allied governments to form a neutral commission to study the "question of war debts" and the expectation of reparation payments from average German citizens.

The Prussian minister of culture decrees that student enrollment in religious instruction in Prussian schools must henceforth be only voluntary. The Hessian state government condemns Bavarian leader Eisner's demand for the overthrow of Ebert.

30 Elaborate 65-article, cross-referenced regulations for the election of a national assembly are published.

Two comedies premiere: *Feuerzauber* (*Fire Magic*), by Paul Frank and Siegfried Geyer, at the Hamburg Thalia Theater, and *Die grosse und die kleine Welt* (*The Big and Little World*), by Rudolf Eger, at the Munich Volkstheater.

DECEMBER

1 Ebert announces that his interim government will not be a dictatorship and will perform no socialist experiments on the German business community.

2 The Ebert government orders the minting of new coins; 50 pfennig pieces made from silver, 10 pfennig from zinc, 5 pfennig from steel, and 1 pfennig from aluminum. The American troops that will occupy German territory arrive in Bernkastel. Fabric stores in Berlin run out of red cloth, due to the home manufacture of revolutionary flags and banners among revolutionaries.

3 The *Novembergruppe* (November Group) of artists is formed under painter Max Pechstein, all professing political commitment to the November revolution in their work.[24] They include illustrator George Grosz; painters Paul Klee, Lionel Feininger, and Otto Freundlich; sculptor Rudolf Belling; sculptor and photographer László Moholy-Nagy; Dadaists Hans Arp and Raoul Hausmann; architects Erich Mendelssohn, Oskar Schlemmer, Ludwig Mies van der Rohe, and Walter Gropius; filmmakers Hans Richter and Viking Eggeling; composers Alban Berg, Paul Hindemith, and Kurt Weill; and the dramatist Bertolt Brecht.

A new production of Gerhart Hauptmann's drama *Michael Kramer* opens, directed by Felix Hollaender and starring Paul Wegener, Ernst Deutsch, and Max Gülstorff.

The king of Württemberg abdicates; a mob invades his palace in Stuttgart and hoists a red flag above the building.

4 Catholic Center Party chairman Carl Trimborn demands secession from Prussia of Cologne and the surrounding Rhineland. He makes "Rhenish separatism" a central plank in his party's platform, but Cologne mayor and fellow Catholic Center Party leader Konrad Adenauer[25] dismisses such separatist demands as nonsense.

6 The drama *Der Minister,* by Roda Roda (Sandor Friedrich Rosenfeld), premieres at the Munich Schauspielhaus, glorifying revolution. An exotic film about ancient Egypt is released, titled *Die Vase der Semirames* (*The Vase of Semiramis*), directed by Willi Grunwald, with Eva Speyer as Semiramis. The film *Das Mädel vom Ballett* (*The Girl from the Ballet*), directed by Ernst Lubitsch, premieres in Berlin.

In armed clashes between Spartacists and army regulars loyal to Ebert's interim government, troops open fire with heavy machine guns and kill 16 Spartacists.

7 Saladin Schmitt assumes leadership of the Bochum Schauspielhaus and remains at its helm for the next four decades, turning it into one of the leading German theaters.

8 Hindenburg demands that Ebert return sole authority to place troops in the field to the Reich officer corps, as well as that he dissolve all soldiers' councils. Ebert and his colleagues in the interim government denounce the "anarchism" of the Spartacists. They fear Hindenburg's threats from the right as much as they reject the lawlessness of the Spartacists. In the Spartacist newspaper *Red Flag*, Karl Liebknecht denounces them all and calls for a "world revolution."

Sculptor and print maker Käthe Kollwitz attends a performance of Beethoven's Ninth Symphony and writes in her diary that the experience was a rapturous departure from the partisan conflict around her, into the heights of joy. "In the Ninth there is the purest form of socialism. That is humanity, glowing like a rose at its fullest height, drenched in sunlight. A heavenly celebration of existence."[26]

9 Industrialist Oskar Münsterberg notes in his diary, "About 5,000 demonstrators march through the Brandenburg Gate as I was grocery shopping. They later listen to a speech by Karl Liebknecht. A remarkable revolution! Groups gather and ready themselves for a fight to the death for what may be

Germany's future. Nearby other people go about their business, seeking amusement. . . . To the superficial observer, there's not much difference between pre-revolutionary days and now."[27]

French troops occupy Mainz. The German university in Strasbourg closes; professors there are terminated and their pensions confiscated.

10 The German Fatherland Party (DVP) dissolves and joins the DNVP. Some newspapers call for the division of the present German Reich into a union of Soviet-style republics.

11 The Prussian Ministry of Culture issues a decree to the Prussian State Library to assemble a "Revolutionary Compendium" of books, documents, articles, and other archival materials relating to the German Revolution of 1918.

Albert Leo Schlageter, a foot soldier in the German Imperial Army, is demobilized.[28]

12 The dramatic film *Dida Ibsens Geschichte: Eine Finale zum Tagebuch einer Verlorenen von Margaret Böhme* (*Dida Ibsen's Story: A Finale to the Diary of a Lost Girl by Margaret Böhme*) is released.[29]

Max Planck, rector of the University of Berlin, is awarded the Nobel Prize for Physics for his research on quantum physics.[30]

13 The film *Lorenzo Burghardt*, directed by William Wauer[31] and starring Albert Basserman, premieres in Berlin.[32] The November Group issues a call to all like-minded "revolutionaries of the spirit, all artists who have broken with old forms"[33] to join with the group in creating works that support the revolution.

The victorious Allied countries refuse to recognize the governing councils of workers and soldiers, which the Allies refer to in their communiqués as "soviets." Allied authorities note that such councils simply appropriated power unto themselves in several German cities and provincial legislatures without the benefit of any legal procedure. German soldiers briefly occupy the editorial offices of *Red Flag*, the newspaper run by Liebknecht and Luxemburg.

14 The pro-revolution, antiwar drama *Freie Knechte*, by Hans Franck, premieres at the Kleines Theater in Berlin.

15 At a general assembly of the USPD, Rosa Luxemburg issues a four-point proclamation calling for the immediate withdrawal of all USPD members from the Ebert-Scheidemann interim government, the cancellation of plans for a national assembly to write a republican constitution, the seizure of all power by the councils of workers and soldiers, and the distribution of arms to all workers.

16 At the same general assembly of the USPD, Liebknecht rouses his hearers to defend the revolution, vanquish the counterrevolution, disarm all generals and officers. He also calls for the establishment of a Red Guard militia in order to carry out the social revolution, and eliminate the rest of the antirevolutionaries.

Piano virtuoso Wilhelm Kempff[34] makes his debut with the Berlin Philharmonic Orchestra, playing Beethoven's Piano Concerto no. 4 in G Major (op. 58), with Arthur Nikisch conducting.

17 Ernst Lubitsch's film *Carmen*, starring Pola Negri[35] (in the title role), Harry Liedtke, and Leopold von Lebedur, premieres in Berlin at the Kurfürstendamm Theater.

Streets in Berlin are decorated with garlands and laurel wreaths, intended as a happy greeting to homecoming soldiers, now beginning to arrive by the thousands. The decorations at semiofficial locations, such as Linden Boulevard, the City Palace, the Brandenburg Gate, and Potsdam Square, are also decked out with imperial colors (red, black, and white). The colors of the republic (black, red, and gold) are conspicuous by their absence. The red revolutionary banners, only days before seen in abundance, have likewise disappeared. Ebert addresses the troops at the Brandenburg Gate as "unconquered in the field of battle."[36]

18 Entire divisions of soldiers in full battle dress march down Linden Boulevard in Berlin; many wear garlands of flowers, laurel wreaths, and other decorations normally associated with victory. Officers ride alongside marching troops on horseback, likewise bedecked with garlands. Thousands line the avenue, some uttering weak shouts of praise, as military bands play. Numerous observers note the tragic irony of the spectacle, as one defeated cohort after another passes by in mock celebration—though nearly everyone agrees it is the best show Berlin has seen in weeks.

The Congress of the Councils of Workers and Soldiers passes a resolution that the German High Command must take an oath of loyalty to civilian governments. The congress meets in the Prussian House of Deputies, made available as a particularly auspicious showplace in the hope of conferring legitimacy.

19 The film *Der Rattenfänger* (*The Pied Piper of Hamelin*), with Paul Wegener directing himself in the title role, premieres.

Chief of General Staff Field Marshal Paul von Hindenburg informs all General Staff officers that he rejects the resolution of the Congress of the Councils of Workers and Soldiers; he furthermore rejects any loyalty oath to the Ebert interim government.

20 The historical drama *Hannibal*, by Christian Dietrich Grabbe, premieres at the National Theater Munich, with Albert Steinrück in the title role; *Die Büchse der Pandora* (*Pandora's Box*), directed by Carl Heine, opens at the Kleines Schauspielhaus in Berlin; *Die armseligen Besenbinder* (*The Poor Broom Makers*), by Carl Hauptmann, directed by Paul Legband, premieres. *Am Tor des Lebens* (*At the Threshold of Life*), directed by Conrad Wiene, with a screenplay by Robert Wiene, is released.

Cologne Mayor Konrad Adenauer calls for the reestablishment of the University of Cologne, which had been closed in 1798 during the Napoleonic invasions.

21 The revolutionaries return to center stage in the streets of Berlin, as funeral processions for the Spartacists killed on 6 December proceed through the city's center. The procession is timed to conclude the final plenary session of the Congress of the Councils of Workers and Soldiers. Coffins bedecked with red poppies and ribbons are carried on beer wagons and saluted as they pass by thousands of supporters in the bright sunshine. Liebknecht, who according to Harry Kessler has staged the entire affair, addresses the crowds in Tiergarten Park with promises of revenge against the killers of the comrades being laid to rest.

22 More parades and troop processions, featuring returning soldiers in full battle dress, beribboned and bemedaled, march down Linden Boulevard in Berlin. At the Wilhelm Strasse (about 400 yards east of the Brandenburg Gate), large numbers of wounded and disabled veterans, also in uniform, interrupt the parade. They carry placards that say, "Throw the guilty ones out," referring to the military leaders whom they hold responsible for their horrific injuries and disfigurements. Some of the war wounded attempt to mingle in the ranks of the returning troops, creating "an embarrassing show," reports Kessler.[37]

23 Members of the "Peoples' Naval Division" occupy the Hohenzollern Palace and Reich Chancellery in Berlin, making a hostage of Ebert and his staff. They demand back pay because Christmas is coming. Ebert orders them out of the building and back to Cuxhaven. They refuse to comply with Ebert's orders, abduct city commandant Otto Wels and beat him, and take over the Berlin central telephone exchange. Ebert uses a secret telephone line to the German Military Supreme Command in Kassel to request assistance. General Lequis mobilizes troops in Potsdam, and they set up a central command at the university on Linden Boulevard near the City Palace. Everyone in Berlin senses that a comedy has turned into a potential tragedy.

24 General Lequis finds the middle of Berlin an armed camp, with hundreds of armed revolutionaries in the streets; he sets up headquarters on the university grounds, on Linden Boulevard near the City Palace. He deploys platoons to engage revolutionaries, and skirmishes take place all day long.

Curious onlookers by the thousands mill about, seemingly oblivious to the danger of being caught in a crossfire. Many sing a parody of the Christmas song, "O Tannenbaum" ("O Christmas Tree, O Christmas Tree/The Kaiser's gone to take a pee"); organ grinders ply their trade among the crowds, as agitators from the Spartacus Group make speeches on street corners. Street peddlers offer wares from wagons; women offer traditional Christmas gingerbread cookies for 5 pfg. apiece; jewelry stores on Linden Boulevard remain open, lights blazing in showroom windows. Department stores like Wertheim accommodate thousands of customers doing last-minute shopping. In the Royal Stables lie the wounded and those men killed in bloody encounters with army regulars.

25 General Lequis orders artillery shelling of the Royal Stables, resulting in several killed; the surrender of the Peoples' Naval Division; and the release of Otto Wels. Spartacists and their sympathizers surround army regulars, many of whom disperse or simply desert. The revolutionaries occupy the headquarters of the *Vorwärts!* (*Forward!*) building, where the SPD newspaper of that name is published. They use the SPD printing press to publish and distribute on red paper their statement of solidarity with the Peoples' Naval Division and call for the overthrow of the Ebert-Scheidemann interim government.

In Magdeburg, Franz Seldte establishes *Stahlhelm* (Steel Helmet), an organization of soldiers who had served on the front lines.

The comedy *Um ein Kind* (*About a Child*), by Albert Matthei, premieres at the Chemnitz City Theater, and the comedy *Ihr Papa* (*Her Daddy*), by Leo Walter Stein, premieres at the Hannover Schauburg.

26 In the aftermath of the Christmas debacle, Ebert and his cabinet debate the possibility of leaving Berlin, realizing that they cannot depend on protection from regular army troops. Rumors fly that Liebknecht will declare himself head of a new government.

The drama *Legende eines Lebens* (*Legend of a Life*), by Stefan Zweig, premieres in Hamburg at the Deutsches Schauspielhaus.

27 Ebert and Scheidemann temporarily disappear from Berlin, seeking ways to safeguard their persons and the interim government. The comedy film *Das Baby*, produced by Arnold Pressburger, is released.

28 Otto Wels returns to his post as city commandant. Numerous militias are formed among volunteers, who reject the aims of Spartacus and other revolutionary groups. "Freikorps" begins to appear as the label for such groups.

29 Public funerals are held for members of the Peoples' Naval Division killed in the Christmas Day encounters. Thousands of people turn out, lining the streets; thousands of red banners, bouquets of red flowers, and songs are sung in honor of the dead. Fights break out among groups with various sympathies. Liebknecht's name is called out as the savior of the country by some, while others call for his immediate execution by a firing squad.

Ebert and Scheidemann reappear in Berlin and accept the resignations of USPD members from the interim government. They are replaced by SPD members, most notable among them Gustav Noske as commandant of Berlin. He agrees to play a new role in the revolutionary drama: "Bloodhound of the Republic."

30 Fritz von Unruh's *Ein Geschlecht* (*One Generation*), directed by Heinz Herald, premieres in Berlin at the Deutsches Theater. Delay in coal deliveries, along with a coal workers' strike in Silesia, renders most theaters, movie houses, concert halls, museums, and other public buildings unheated. Most audiences attend anyway, wearing heavy winter coats.

Eighty-five delegates of the Spartacus Group assemble in Berlin's Prussian House of Deputies; they establish the German Communist Party (KPD) and resolve not to participate in elections for the national assembly that will write a republican constitution.

31 Several German theater artists join the new German Communist Party, including the brothers John Heartfeld and Wieland Herzfeld, Erwin Piscator, and George Grosz. In Leipzig, Arthur Nikisch conducts Beethoven's Ninth Symphony for a sold-out audience of industrial workers in the city's Albert Concert Hall.

NOTES

1. Mathias Erzberger, leader of the Catholic Center Party, had led other German politicians the previous day (8 November) to a cease-fire meeting with French General Ferdinand Foch in a railway car near Compiègne, France. The Allies presented several non-negotiable demands to the German delegation, to take effect immediately and last for 30 days; until a formal peace treaty could be signed, the conditions of the cease-fire were to remain in place. Among the demands was that German armies must evacuate all occupied territory on the western front and west of the Rhine. The Allies were then to occupy those territories along, and several German cities on, the Rhine. The Germans were to turn over 5,000 railroad locomotives, 150,000 freight cars, 5,000 trucks, 160 submarines, and several warships to the Allies. They were also to destroy aircraft, tanks, artillery, and other materiel. The Allies were to maintain a

naval blockade of the German coastline until the conclusion of a peace treaty. The Germans agreed to the demands.

2. Warned that revolutionaries were prepared to abduct him near the Dutch border, Wilhelm and his small entourage left the train before it got to the border and proceeded by automobile to Doorn Huis, a manor house on a tiny estate outside Doorn, a small town near Utrecht. His asylum there was arranged by the Dutch royal family, to whom Wilhelm was related. The house was originally constructed in the 15th century, rebuilt in the late 18th century, and redecorated in the 19th century, and Wilhelm officially purchased it in 1919. By 1920, he had personally sawn down 12 thousand trees on the estate and split the trunks into firewood.

3. Harry Kessler, *Tagebücher* 1918–1937, Ed. Wolfgang Pfeiffer-Belli (Frankfurt am Main: Insel, 1982), 12.

4. Kurt Hiller (1885–1972) was considered by many on both the Right and the Left to be the most troubled and troublesome of all political agitators and self-promoters in the early days of the Weimar Republic. He had founded several political/satirical cabarets before the war and had numerous associations among antiestablishment groups, journals, and publications. He had been a leading member of the German Peace Movement in early 1918 and became chairman of the German Political Council of Intellectual Workers in November 1918. As a homosexual, Jew, political agitator, pacifist, and antinationalist, he aroused the ire of several groups throughout the Weimar period. Hiller edited *Das Ziel* from 1916 to 1924 and was a contributor to nearly all leftist reviews and periodicals, including *Die Aktion*, *Das Ziel*, and *Die Weltbühne*. He became a regular political contributor to *Weltbühne* after 1924. Also a member of the Council was Werner Richard Heymann, whose songs for Wilhelm Thiele's film comedy *Die drei von der Tankstelle* (1930), with Lilian Harvey, Willy Fritsch, and Heinz Rühmann, became one of the greatest movie musicals in German film history. Prior to that, he composed the incidental music for Toller's *The Transformation* (1919), a Communist propaganda piece premiered by Karlheinz Martin.

5. *Die Freiheit* (Berlin) 16, and 17 December 1918.

6. Eugen Francis Charles d'Albert (1864–1932) was a Scot by birth and attended the Royal College of Music in London. He wrote more than a dozen operas, eight of which premiered during the Weimar Republic.

7. Based on a comedy by Salomon Mosenthal (1821–1877) that premiered in 1857 at Vienna's Burg Theater. Sonnwendhof is the name of the remote farming village where the action takes place. It was subsequently adapted for the Danish stage by Hans Christian Andersen.

8. Manfred Overesch and Friedrich Wilhelm Saal, *Die Weimarer Republik* (Düsseldorf: Droste, 1982), 11.

9. Georg Kaiser (1878–1945) became the most prolific playwright of the Weimar Republic, writing more than 60 plays during the 1920s alone. He became closely identified with the expressionist movement in German drama, eschewing illusionism and making virtues of discontinuity, fragmentation, and the discordant.

10. Austrian-born Fritz Kortner (Nathan Kohn, 1892–1970) stated in his autobiography that expressionist productions broke out "like lava" during the early months

of the German revolution, many of them influenced by revolutionary rhetoric that actors felt compelled somehow to replicate. No actors had any training in expressionistic techniques, he noted, but none of the politicians had any training in dealing with a revolution, either. But "just as revolution is supposed to clear the way for a new form of government," expressionism was "the pioneer for a new meaningful realism [in the theater]."

11. Horst Wolfram Geissler (1893–1983) became a highly popular and frequently published novelist of the Weimar Republic, though his fiction had been published as early as 1909. His novels were humorous and accessible, finding a wide reading public. His most popular novel was *Der liebe Augustin* (*Sweet Augustine*), published in 1921. The 1960 film based on the novel, for which Geissler himself wrote the screenplay, was directed by Rolf Thiele.

12. Criticism of the Russian Revolution of 1917 did not always sit well with German revolutionaries. Many of them hoped to emulate the Russians and set up a "Republic of Councils" on Leninist precepts. Gorki's stock among German revolutionaries continued to fall when he later published appeals to European and American leaders for assistance in overcoming the famine that he believed Lenin's tactics had precipitated.

13. Bruno Taut, *Fruhlicht: Eine Folge für die Verwirklichung des neuen Baudenkens* (Berlin: Ullstein, 1963), 17.

14. The "Spartacists" took their name from the gladiator who led the Roman slave revolt in 73–71 BC. Leaders of the Spartacus Group had opposed Germany's entry into World War I; Liebknecht had been an SPD delegate to the Reichstag in 1914 and was its only member to vote against the war. Spartacist leaders had hoped to associate their antiwar agenda with the warlike Spartacus in an effort to draw historical parallels between the workers they claimed to represent and the slaves of Rome. Among the principal aims of the Spartacist movement was to turn working-class approval of the war prevalent in 1914 into revolutionary fervor. The Spartacists publicized their views surreptitiously until 1916, when they went public and organized a demonstration in Berlin against the war. They were arrested, tried, and convicted of treason. Liebknecht was released on 23 October 1918; Luxemburg made her reappearance, as noted above, two weeks later.

15. "Konstituierung der Kommunistischen Partei," *Die rote Fahe*, 31 December 1918, 3.

16. Walter Kollo (Walter Elimar Kollodziepski, 1878–1940) had written several popular operettas and continued to do so throughout the Weimar Republic. This particular show, a collaborative effort with Sigmund Romberg, transferred to the Broadhurst Theater on Broadway under the title *Springtime of Youth* in 1922, with lyrics in English by Harry B. Smith and Rollo Wayne.

17. *Vossische Zeitung* (Berlin), 19 November 1918.

18. *Tiefland* was based on an American movie of 1914 titled *Marta of the Lowlands*, which in turn was based on a play in the Catalan language by Angel Guimera that opened in 1896. Composer Eugen d'Albert used Guimera's melodrama as the basis for his opera *Tiefland*, which premiered in 1903 and remains popular in Germany to this day. In 1940, the director Leni Riefenstahl (1901–2003) used it as the basis of her last feature film, which she directed and which she played the leading role.

19. Waldemar Bonsels (1880–1952) became a popular writer of children's books, with translations of them in over forty languages. His most famous was *Die Biene Maja und ihre Abendteuer* (*Maya the Bee and Her Adventures*), written in 1912. In it, the adventurous Maya helped her community of honeybees and other insects organize and defend itself against a raid of marauding hornets. The disturbances prevalent in the revolution prompted Bonsels's publishers to reissue *Maya* and his other writings.

20. *Berliner Tageblatt*, 23 November 1918.

21. Ernst Lothar (Ernst Lothar Müller, 1890–1974) was a stage director and theater producer with a concomitant career as a novelist. Among his novels are *Macht über alle Menschen* (*Power over All People*), *Heldenplatz* (*Heroes' Square*), and *Der Engel mit der Pausane* (*The Angel with the Trumpet*).

22. The play formed the second part of Kaiser's *Gas Trilogy* and was a sequel to *Die Koralle* (*The Coral*), which had premiered in 1917. In *Gas I*, the Billionaire's Son runs the gas factory his father had founded, but with a mind toward running the place on a humane basis. When the gas factory explodes, the Billionaire's Son views the catastrophe as a fateful warning and refuses to rebuild the factory. His workers revolt and demand the factory's reconstruction. When the Billionaire's Son refuses to meet their demands, the state sends in troops to reestablish order. The Billionaire's Son shoots himself. The play seemed to many observers an uncanny reflection of what was transpiring on the streets outside the theater.

23. Luise Kolm (1873–1950) and Jakob Fleck (1881–1953) became known as "the directing couple" after they married in 1923 and Luise took Fleck's name. Her directorial career preceded his, beginning in 1908 with *Am Gänsehäufl* (*In the Goose Coop*) in 1908. In Berlin, they made more than 30 movies together. In 1940, Fleck managed to be released from the concentration camps at Buchenwald and Dachau, whereupon they both escaped to Shanghai. In China, they made three films together.

24. Before World War I, Max Pechstein (1881–1955) had been a member of a group of modernist painters known as "Die Brücke" (The Bridge). He and stage designer César Klein were most instrumental in recruiting members of the November Group. They organized numerous public exhibitions throughout the 1920s, but the group's significance lay in its subsequent influence. Because the group had a somewhat contradictory commitment to both socialist political goals and modernism in artistic endeavor, the ideals to which many members subscribed gained little immediate attention. But its ideal of unifying the arts for the benefit of society as a whole appealed to many influential leftists abroad. Among the institutions influenced by the November Group within the Weimar Republic itself was the Staatliches Bauhaus, which under Walter Gropius (1883–1969) combined the Weimar Academy of Arts with the Weimar School of Arts and Crafts; it came to be known simply as the Bauhaus. Almost as well known as the Bauhaus was Brecht and Weill's *Die Dreigroschenoper* (*The Three Penny Opera*).

25. Konrad Adenauer (1876–1967) is best known as West Germany's first chancellor, elected in 1949 and serving until 1963. During the 1920s, he supported expressionist theater productions when there was popular revulsion against them in Cologne. Under the Nazi regime, Adenauer was unceremoniously removed from office as

Cologne mayor and imprisoned. He was released in 1934 and spent the Nazi years in a monastery, but was arrested again in 1944 for suspicion of participating in the plot to assassinate Hitler in July of that year.

26. Käthe Kollwitz, *Die Tagebücher*, ed. Jutte Bohnke Kollwitz (Berlin: Siedler, 1949), 79.

27. www.dhm.de/lemo/forum/kollektives_gedaechtnis/051/index.html.

28. In 1923, French military units captured Schlageter as he participated in attacks on French installations in the Rhineland. After his execution he became a Nazi martyr, known as "the first soldier of the Third Reich."

29. This movie should not be confused with another Margaret Böhme screenplay of nearly the same title, *Tagebuch einer Verlorenen* (*Diary of a Lost Girl*), starring the American actress Louise Brooks. Böhme also wrote the novel on which that 1929 film was based, which in turn had been filmed earlier in 1918. *Dida Ibsen* featured Anita Berber in the title role, who like Brooks played an unwed mother.

30. Max Planck (1858–1947) was a superb musician with an abiding interest in the keyboard music of Schubert and Brahms. From his vantage point in Berlin, Planck was an eyewitness to the German revolution and its aftermath in the Weimar Republic. Later in life, he devoted much of his research and writing to artistic and philosophical concerns.

His work on thermodynamics preceded his theories of quantum physics, which earned him the Nobel Prize. Both research areas had a profound impact on 20th-century thinking, philosophy, and art. He completed a doctoral dissertation on thermodynamics at the age of 21 (in 1879, the year of Albert Einstein's birth in Ulm). Planck's research in Berlin led him to the discoveries that made him famous, and there is near-universal agreement among physicists that Planck's ideas completely altered the history of science in the 20th century. He was among the first to support Einstein's Theory of Special Relativity in 1905, stating that Einstein's work was as essential to understanding the nature of energy as was his own work in "quantifying" energy. His son, Erwin Planck, participated in the attempt to assassinate Hitler in 1944 and was executed in 1945.

31. William Wauer (1866–1962) was a Lutheran pastor's son who studied art at the Dresden Academy and worked in San Francisco and New York in the late 19th century. In 1900, he turned to the theater and studied directing in Berlin. In 1905, he staged a pantomime by Herwarth Walden (Georg Levin, 1878–1941) and became active in the German expressionist movement, of which Walden was a leading member. Wauer published articles in Walden's literary journal *Der Sturm* (*The Storm*), and by 1912 he had begun to direct short films. In 1913, he directed his first full-length movie, a biography of composer Richard Wagner. By the time *Lornezo Burghardt* premiered, he had directed 16 films. Wauer continued to exhibit his paintings, sculpture, and illustrations at the Sturm Galerie (Storm Gallery) concomitant with his film work. Among the most remarkable of the works that went on display at the gallery was his bust of Walden, which many consider exemplary of expressionist statuary. Wauer's other sculptures were also characteristic of expressionism, employing distortion and nonrealistic contours to create a sense of movement on the surface of the sculptive medium. Wauer also contributed essays to other journals, wrote books, and taught at

the "Storm" art school after his film career ended in 1921. In 1924, Wauer founded the artists' group called the International Union of Expressionists, Cubists, and Constructivsts.

32. This highly melodramatic but innovative film is noteworthy for the presence of Bassermann in the title role, but also because his wife Else wrote the screenplay. In it, Basserman (one of the few German actors ever to appear in a feature Hollywood movie with Ronald Reagan) plays a distraught and lonely young fisherman. One day, he rescues a young woman (played by Else Basserman) from drowning, and they fall madly in love. Soon, she must leave the sea and return to the city. Lorenzo follows her and discovers she is a slut who offers her charms to any available young man. Enraged, he strangles her. In court, Lorenzo receives the death sentence—but the judge grants him one last wish: to witness the waves crash one more time against the shoreline of his beloved Baltic coast. In the following scene, the camera finds him swirling in the sea waves, drawn below the verge to his death. It then becomes clear that he had imagined the entire movie's story line in the seconds before he drowned.

33. Helga Kliemann, *Die Novembergruppe* (Berlin: Deutsche Gesellschaft für bildende Kunst, 1965), 51.

34. Wilhelm Kempff (1895–1991) had one of the longest and most productive careers of any German piano virtuoso. A native of Potsdam, he studied in Berlin and began working professionally in 1916. As a soloist, Kempff specialized in the classical and romantic piano repertoire, particularly Beethoven sonatas and Chopin etudes, but his repertoire was as remarkably wide as his career was long. He gave his first American performance in 1964, and his last performance was in 1981. He thereafter continued his work as a composer, arranger, and teacher. Most of his recordings of Beethoven and Chopin, as well as Bach, Mozart, Schumann, Brahms, Schubert, and Liszt, are still in print.

35. Pola Negri (Barbara Appolonia Chalupek, 1894–1987) made six films in 1918; she was already (at age 24) an accomplished performer both in film and onstage. A native of Poland, Negri began her career as an actress in Warsaw, making her debut as a juvenile in Ibsen's *The Wild Duck*. Soon thereafter she changed her name to "Pola Negri," based supposedly on her nationality and her black hair. But "Pola" was actually derived from her middle name, Appolonia, and Negri was the name of a poet she admired. Max Reinhardt saw her in Warsaw, speaking Polish in German plays. She left Germany for Hollywood in 1922.

36. *Berliner Illustrierte*, 17 November 1918.

37. Count Harry Kessler, *Tagebücher, 1918 bis 1937* (Frankfurt am Main: Insel, 1983), 76.

1919

JANUARY

1 All films previously banned on grounds of "damage to public morale" are released for distribution for public presentation. The comedy *Der Mann mit 100 Köpfen* (*The Man with a Hundred Heads*), by Hans Gross, premieres at the Hannover Schauburg.

Strikes and other forms of labor unrest multiply; the eight-hour workday goes into effect throughout the country. Coal shortages increase, and in many areas food shortages are chronic. Industrial output wanes as a result of Allied occupation of the Rhineland. The decline in the value of German currency (the Reichsmark, or RM) against other Western currencies accelerates.

The Communist Party of Germany concludes its tumultuous, two-day congress in Berlin.

2 Bavarian provincial president Kurt Eisner and playwright Ernst Toller engage in an "artists' debate" in Munich before the provisional Peoples' Council in the Peoples' State of Bavaria. Archbishop Michael von Faulhaber condemns the new Bavarian government as secularist and anti-Catholic.[1]

The comedy *Badenreise wider Willen* (*Swimsuits under Protest*), by Hans Friedrof, premieres at the Hannover State Theater.

4 The Hamburg Volksbühne, a subscription-based theater dedicated to presenting plays from a socialist viewpoint, is renewed; the theater has 3,600 subscribers by the end of the year.

The University of Cologne is reestablished; originally founded in 1388, the university was abolished in 1798.[2]

Emil Eichhorn is replaced as Berlin chief of police. He refuses to relinquish his post and demands reinstatement. His sympathizers rally around him, and the Spartacist uprising begins.

5 Spartacus Group operatives occupy several Berlin newspaper offices in Koch Strasse as well as the Wolff Telegraph Bureau in Charlotten Strasse and attempt to monopolize information flow out of the city. Other revolutionaries set up barricades in adjoining streets, hoping to block or at least delay the arrival of troops sent in to reoccupy the buildings. Liebknecht addresses the revolutionaries, whose numbers increase by the hour as word spreads throughout Berlin that the possibility of overthrowing the Ebert interim government is at hand.[3]

Commandant of Berlin Gustav Noske assembles several platoons of volunteers, who come to be known as "Freikorps,"[4] in the suburb of Dahlem under the command and training of General Ludwig von Maercker. He issues them equipment to facilitate hand-to-hand combat. Noske assumes the unofficial portfolio of defense minister.

The German Workers' Party is formed in Munich; it later becomes the National Socialist German Workers' Party (NSDAP) under its new leader, an unremarkable Austrian veteran of the trenches in World War I who has remarkable gifts as an orator.

6 Opposing groups of demonstrators hurl insults and projectiles at each other; some groups support the Spartacist occupiers, others voice support for the interim government. Shots are fired. Ebert issues a plea to all veterans to come to the interim government's aid, and by midafternoon armed volunteers, many still in uniform, establish a front on Linden Boulevard opposing the Spartacists.

Thousands of workers join the ranks of Spartacists behind their lines in the newspaper district. Government offices in the Reich Chancellery empty as bureaucrats and officials prepare for a possible onslaught of Spartacists intent on taking over government buildings. Fighters set bonfires alight throughout central Berlin in preparation for what seems an inevitable armed confrontation.

At about 5:30 p.m., explosions of small arms fire, hand grenades, artillery, and mortar shells suddenly erupt. Just as suddenly, the firing ceases. The Berlin stock exchange closes for two weeks, as do most theaters (which refund ticket holders' money). Cafés, restaurants, and hotels remain open; prostitutes continue working in most streets; and streetcars and subway trains continue for the most part to run on schedule throughout Berlin.

7 Leaders of both the USPD and the newly formed KPD call for all workers to walk off their jobs and support the Spartacists. Thousands of workers and sympathizers occupy buildings in and near the newspaper district. In several German cities, revolutionaries in sympathy with the Berlin Spartacists occupy newspaper offices and attempt to publish revolutionary newspapers. Disturbances on the eastern border with Poland cause Ebert to dispatch volunteer troops there.

There are deadly encounters near the Brandenburg Gate as hand-to-hand combat ensues between Spartacists and Freikorps troops, whom Defense Minister Noske has stationed on the outskirts of the city. Some Spartacists make it to the top of the Gate and emplace a machine gun, with which they spray bullets over Linden Boulevard. Pedestrians dive for cover, but many are hit and lie bleeding in the street. The Spartacists soon run out of ammunition and abandon their position. Firefights break out in several squares in the middle of the city, killing and wounding several people. Gunfire and artillery reports sporadically punctuate the night air until morning.

A coal shortage prompts officials in many cities throughout Germany to ban delivery of coal orders to theaters, movie houses, meeting halls, and churches.

8 All public transport in Berlin comes to a halt because workers have not been paid; the stoppage spreads to several train lines leading into and out of the city.

There are continuous firefights between Freikorps and Spartacist groups as the latter attempt to take over railroad offices. Fighting intensifies in the newspaper district. Approximately 300 people are killed in fighting on this day alone.

The Palast Theater in Berlin opens a new production of *Die im Schatten leben* (*Those Who Live in the Shadows*), by Emil Rosenow, a drama featuring working-class heroes and heroines. Hundreds of shivering audience members watch the play in heavy winter overcoats.

9 Employees of the Berlin water works go on strike, causing water shortages throughout the city.

Sympathizers of the Spartacists in Berlin occupy newspaper offices in Hamburg, Dresden, and Stuttgart. They publish abridged editions proclaiming the victory of revolutionary socialism. In Berlin, more than 200 are estimated killed in clashes between partisans favoring the revolution and those favoring the interim government. Pleas are issued by all sides to stop the fighting immediately.

10 A new production of Henrik Ibsen's *Ghosts* is staged at the newly named Berlin State (formerly the Royal) Theater, the first Ibsen play to be mounted in that venue.

Konstanze von Franken's book on polite manners and refined behavior, *Der gute Ton*, goes into its 26th printing by the publisher Hesse.

During the night, militia units under the command of Major Franz von Stephani take up positions around the *Vorwärts* building, occupied by Spartacist partisans.

11 Freikorps militia use howitzers, trench mortars, heavy machine gun fire, and hand grenades against the Spartacists, who wave white flags and send seven men to discuss terms of a truce. Major von Stephani sends one of their number back into the building and executes the other six. Freikorps then storm the building and kill about 300 occupiers. Defense Minister Noske dispatches Freikorps units throughout the city to rout Spartacists from other occupied buildings.

12 Some Berlin newspapers resume publication. The rout of the Spartacists continues throughout the day, and *Spartakuswoche* (Spartacus week) comes to a bloody conclusion as Freikorps troops seal off streets. Defense Minister Noske declares a curfew and orders searchlights set up on rooftops; anyone caught in the light is shot on sight. Liebknecht and Luxemburg go into hiding.

An exhibition of collages by Kurt Schwitters opens in Hannover.[5]

13 Leopold Jessner[6] stages *Maria Magdalena,* by Friedrich Hebbel, with Gerda Müller in the title role, at the Berlin State Theater.

Elections in Bavaria give pluralities to the conservative Bavarian Peoples' Party and the SPD. Eisner's USPD party gets only three of a total 180 seats. In Baden elections, the USPD likewise wins a tiny fraction of seats in the provincial legislature.

In Berlin, nearly all violent encounters between Spartacist partisans and Freikorps militia troops cease, though Freikorps units continue searching for leaders of the recent uprising, particularly Liebknecht and Luxemburg.

14 The last Allied POWs leave Germany and are repatriated. Many workers call off strikes, although the transit workers in Berlin sporadically walk off their jobs.

15 Freikorps units locate Liebknecht, Luxemburg, Wilhelm Pieck, and others in their hiding places. Liebknecht and Luxemburg are taken to the Eden Hotel for questioning, where they are savagely beaten and later murdered.[7] Pieck is inexplicably released from the custody of the militias. They later deliver Liebknecht's body to a morgue in central Berlin and dump Rosenburg's in the Landwehr Canal, where it surfaces five months later.

A new production of Frank Wedekind's *King Nicolo* opens in Leipzig.

16 The comedy *Sohn der Excellenz* (*The Son of His Excellency*), by Emil Lorenz, opens at the Hamburg Thalia Theater. Frank Wedekind's drama *Music* opens at the Theater in der Königgrätzer Strasse in Berlin. Performances are sold out for weeks thereafter.

"Liebknecht was a character right out of a Wedekind play," notes Harrry Kessler in his diary. "He was the foolish revolutionary, the Don Quixote in jousting at windmills, genuinely humane, but at all times searching for the sensational. Even his death was a Wedekind ending."[8]

17 Two racist and anti-Semitic books are published, which later become popular: *Rasse und Nation* (*Race and Nation*), by Houston Stewart Chamberlain,[9] published in Munich by Lehmans; and a novel, *Die Sünde wider das Blut* (*Sins against the Blood*), by Arthur Dinter, published in Leipzig by Matthes and Thost.

18 Max Halbe's drama *Schloss Zeitvorbei* (*The Palace of Times Gone By*), which Halbe had completed in 1917, premieres at the State Theater in Munich.[10]

19 Elections are held throughout the country for delegates to a national assembly, which will write a constitution for the German republic. A large number of voters (83 percent of those eligible) select delegates along party lines, giving a plurality (39 percent) of delegates to the SPD. The Catholic Center Party (Zentrum) comes in second, with 19.7 percent.

Gustav Lindemann and Louise Dumont[11] are forced to resign as directors of the Düsseldorf Schauspielhaus, which they had founded in 1904.

20 The Gesellschaft für ältere deutsche Geschichtskunde (Society for Ancient Germanic History) produces a comprehensive catalogue of journals, book series, and other publications dealing with Germanic and Teutonic studies under the rubric *Monumenta Germaniae Historica* (*Monumental History of Germanica*). The society was founded exactly a century earlier under the leadership of Karl vom und zum Stein (1757–1831). Stein's goal, he said, was to recognize the importance of shared values and traditions among all Germans and to cultivate love of a shared homeland.

Ebert's interim government announces that the Weimar National Theater will be the site of the national assembly, set to convene on 6 February.

22 Occasional bursts of gunfire are heard in some Berlin neighborhoods. Spartacist sympathizers set up street barricades in Hamburg, engaging police and some military detachments in brief fire fights.

23 The world premiere of Carl Sternheim's *1913* takes place at the City Theater of Frankfurt am Main.[12]

24 The comedy film *Meine Frau, die Filmschauspielerin* (*My Wife, the Movie Star*), directed by Ernst Lubitsch and starring Ossi Oswalda, premieres.[13] Ernst Barlach and Käthe Kollwitz are elected to the Prussian Academy of the Arts, reflecting new control of that organization. Kollwitz is named honorary professor, allowing her to give lectures in Prussian universities.

25 Berlin police close off the inner city for public funerals for Karl Liebknecht, Rosa Luxemburg, and 37 other leaders killed in the Spartacist uprising. An empty casket is prepared for Luxemburg and placed alongside Liebknecht's; red roses are draped across Liebknecht's forehead to hide bullet holes.

Sternheim's political comedy *Tabula rasa* is staged at the Berlin Kleines Theater; critics praise the work as one of Sternheim's best. Several left-wing writers praise it, though the play is ironically, about a socialist glass blower who eventually becomes a highly paid artisan and then terminates all connections to socialism, including his membership in the Social Democratic Party.

26 The drama *The Fall of the Apostle Paul*, by Rolf Lauckner, directed by Felix Holländer, with Alexander Moissi in the title role, premieres at the Deutsches Theater in Berlin.

27 The 60th birthday of former Kaiser Wilhelm II goes largely unnoticed.

29 Wilhelm Speyer's drama *Der Revolutionär* (*The Revolutionary*), about the Russian Revolution of 1917, premieres at the Deutsches Schauspielhaus in Hamburg. The drama *Hölderlin*, by Walther Edlitz, premieres at the Kleines Schauspielhaus in Berlin. The comedy *Der rote Korah* (*The Rebel Korah*), by Richard Warmer, premieres at the Gera Provincial Theater. Its title character is an Old Testament revolutionary who led a revolt against Moses; the rebellion ends with Korah and his followers buried alive.

30 Emil Jannings joins Gertud Eysoldt[14] in the cast of Max Reinhardt's production of *Die Büchse der Pandora* (*Pandora's Box*), by Frank Wedekind.

31 *Von Morgen bis Mitternachts* (*From Morn to Midnight*), by Georg Kaiser, premieres in Berlin, with operetta comedian Max Pallenberg in the role of the cashier. The play had premiered at the Munich Kammerspiele in 1917. It becomes the most frequently performed of all Kaiser plays in the 1920s.[15]

FEBRUARY

1 Kaiser's *Der gerettete Alkibiades* premieres in Munich; it is a resounding flop with critics and audiences. The world premiere of Sudermann's comedy

Das höhere Leben takes place at the Residenz Theater in Berlin; critical response is lukewarm.

Rainer Maria Rilke gives a public reading of some of his recent works in Berlin. Ernst Rowohlt reestablishes his publishing business, which went bankrupt in 1913. He becomes one of Berlin's most important publishers of new fiction in the 1920s; his authors include Robert Musil, Hans Fallada, Ernest Hemingway, and Thomas Wolfe.

2 The Fox Trot Casino opens in Berlin near the Friedrich Strasse train station, catering to aficionados of American music and dance.

Ebert sends Freikorps troops to occupy Weimar in preparation for the arrival of the delegates to the National Assembly. He also dispatches troops to Bremen with orders to overthrow the Spartacus-led "Soviet Republic of Bremen."

The Kollwitz poster "Heraus mit unseren Gefangenen!" ("Release Our Prisoners of War!") is published and publicly circulated.

3 Trials of participants in the Spartacist uprising begin before special courts in Berlin. There is heavy fighting in Bremen between Spartacist loyalists and government troops.

4 The drama *Das Narrenspiel des Lebens* (*The Fool's Comedy of Life*), by Karl Schönherr, with Paul Wegener in the title role, premieres in Berlin.

Government Freikorps troops take over Bremen, occupy city offices, and arrest remaining Spartacist loyalists.

5 George Grosz displays his painting *Deutschland, ein Wintermärchen* (*Germany, a Winter's Fairy Tale*), prominently featuring army officers, pastors, and reactionary high school teachers as witless villains in a society built upon churches, cramped apartments, military barracks, and bordellos. His work uses a graphic style combining elements of expressionism, futurism, Dadaist caricature, and collage; he views himself as postwar Germany's Hogarth.

6 Ebert convenes the National Assembly in the Neues Theater of Weimar; various party factions vie for influence in the writing of the constitution.

At the Weimar National Theater, artistic director Ernst Hardt premieres his *Die Quelle* (*The Source*), a short verse drama that recalls the greatness of German culture and attempts to present ideals from classical antiquity (along with those of Goethe and Schiller) as guides for the concomitant creation of a German constitution. The play is a failure with both audiences and critics. The drama *Die Insel* (*The Island*), by Herbert Eulenberg, premieres in Dresden.

Dadaists in Berlin organize a competing convention of artists, who denigrate the National Assembly in Weimar. Johannes Baader is elected "Oberdada" as head of the "Dadaist Central Committee for World Revolution," whose members include George Grosz, Hans Arp, Richard Huelsenbeck, and Eugen Ernst. There is a call for a "Dadaist victory putsch," which they insist "will bury the unfortunate Weimar National Assembly in the Cemetery of Dada."[16]

8 The comedy *Ich, Theobald Blaschke*, by Hans Gans, premieres at the Guben City Theater.

Leo Löwenstein, an infantry captain in World War I, founds the League of German-Jewish Soldiers of the Front, comprising war veterans who served between 1914 and 1918. The organization lists 10,000 Jewish men killed in action on both the eastern and western fronts.

10 The drama *Christine*, by novelist and Hamburg native Otto Erich Kiesel, premieres at the Thalia Theater in Hamburg.

11 The National Assembly in Weimar names Friedrich Ebert "Reich president," even though the Reich is not officially a republic and the office of president does not officially exist. Ebert authorizes Philip Scheidemann to form a government.

12 Karl Radek, an agent in the employ of the Soviet Union, is arrested in Berlin as "an instigator of the Spartacus uprising" and is placed in "protective custody." Scheidemann announces the formation of a coalition government, composed of Social Democrats (SPD), German Democrats (DDP), and Catholic Center Party politicians.

14 The film *Irrungen* (*Errors*), starring Henny Porten, Ernst Deutsch, and Harry Liedtke, premieres at the Mozartsaal Theater in Berlin. The drama *Don Juan und Maria*, by Friedrich Sebrecht, premieres at the Court Theater of Reuss-Gera. The comedy *Nachtbeleuchtung* (*Night Lights*), by Kurt Götz,[17] reopens at the Künstler Theater in Berlin; Götz plays the leading roles in each of the four playlets that make up the evening's program. The comedy *Der dumme Jakob* (*Stupid Jacob*), by Thomas Rittner, premieres at the Deutsches Theater in Hannover.

15 The first and only issue of the illustrated bimonthly magazine *Jedermann sein it sein eigener Fußball* (*Everyone Is His Own Football*), edited by Julkian Gumperz and with illustrations by the brothers John Heartfield and Wieland Herzfelde, is published by the Dadaist Malik Press.

The comedy *Das freudige Ereignis* (*The Happy Occasion*), by C. K. M. Tressler, premieres at the Düsseldorf City Theater.

16 A 40-day sports festival begins in Berlin at the Sportpalast (Sports Palace).[18] Bicycle races, boxing matches, and events in track and field are scheduled.

18 In the first professional boxing match ever promoted in Berlin, Richard Naujoks knocks out Gustav Völkel in the seventh round at the Sports Palace.

20 S. Fischer publishing house buys publishing rights to *Vatermord* (*Patricide*) and *Geburt der Jugend* (*The Birth of Youth*), by Viennese warehouse clerk Arnolt Bronnen; the publication and later performances of the plays subsequently become occasions of public disgust and outcry.

Antigone, by Walter Hasenclever, opens at the Frankfurt/Main City Theater. Critics take notice of the actor playing Haemon, Heinrich George.[19]

21 Count Anton Arco-Valley (1897–1945) murders Bavarian minister-president Kurt Eisner on a Munich street. Arco-Valley is a war veteran recently returned from the front who had enrolled in university studies. He subsequently becomes a celebrity, is tried and convicted, and is later pardoned.

22 Funeral processions and demonstrations are staged by leftist organizations throughout Bavaria in honor of Kurt Eisner.

23 The Saxon State Provincial Theater opens, a touring company based in Dresden that presents theater productions in numerous Saxon towns and cities.

26 For the state funeral of Kurt Eisner, the Bavarian government orders church bells rung and black banners hung from church steeples throughout Bavaria; most parishes refuse to comply.

General strikes break out in several German cities in sympathy for Eisner and solidarity with the Bavarian leftists. Street demonstrations in Düsseldorf prevent the opening of a new production of Hugo Wolf's comic opera *Der Corregidor*.

27 Max Reinhardt's new production of Shakespeare's *As You Like It* opens at the Deutsches Theater. Critics heap praise on it, claiming that it "sheds light on the darkness of our days." Another critic says he left the theater with "distinct reluctance, returning to the bleak reality outside." "It would run at least 500 performances—unless we're all dead of starvation by then, or [have] been beaten to death."[20] The Hamburg opening of Fritz von Unruh's pacifist drama *Ein Geschlecht* provokes demonstrations outside the theater.

The film *Siegerin Weib* (*The Conquering Wench*), directed by Aruth Wartan, premieres.

28 The quarterly journal *Neue Rundschau* serially publishes the novel *Demian,* by "Emil Sinclair," who turns out to be Hermann Hesse. The novels *Christian Wahnschaffe*, by Jacob Wassermann, and *Die Junker* (*The Junkers*) by Fedor von Zobeltits, are published. *Geschichte als Sinngebung des*

Sinnlosen (*History as an Attempt to Give Meaning to the Meaningless*), by cultural pessimist Theodor Lesing (1872–1933), is published.

The comic film *Seine Majestät der Landstreicher* (*His Majesty the Goof-Off*), directed by Ludwig Stein, premieres.

Assembled delegates of the National Assembly in Weimar give the new republican constitution its first reading.

MARCH

1 East African troops under the command of General Paul von Lettow-Vorbeck stage a "victory" parade through Berlin, to the cheers of thousands. Hundreds of other returning soldiers with missing arms, legs, and hideous facial injuries beg passersby for pocket change.

2 Burglaries increase in cities throughout Germany as unemployment rates rise weekly. Strikes proliferate in many industries. Ebert's interim government announces plans to nationalize the coal industry.

Playwright Ernst Toller calls upon "the youth of all countries to join the fight for the victory of socialism and revolution" in Germany.

3 Several Freikorps officers are arrested for the murders of Karl Liebknecht and Rosa Luxemburg. Vandals destroy the printing presses of the Communist Party's newspaper, *Red Flag*. Posters proclaiming "Nationalization of Industry Marches Forward" appear throughout Berlin, sponsored by the interim government. Spartacists call a general strike in Berlin and take over police headquarters.

The crime film *Das Geheimnis des Amerika-Docks* (*The Secret of the American Docks*) premieres.

4 Dadaists in Cologne attempt to take over the offices of the City Theater and close Raoul Konen's drama *The Young King* for its monarchist "sympathies."

Czech and German troops clash on the Czech border with Germany.

5 There are outbreaks in Berlin of armed fighting between leftist militias calling for work stoppages and right-wing Freikorps groups.

The film *Der Spieler* (*The Gambler*), directed by Willy Zeyn and starring Käthe Haack, premieres in Berlin.

6 Government troops retake police headquarters in Berlin. There is heavy fighting in and near Alexander Square between Spartacists and government troops, both armed with machine guns, trench mortars, and artillery pieces.

The governments of France, Great Britain, and the United States reject efforts to lift port blockades and assist food deliveries within Germany.

A tragedy about schoolchildren, *Dies Irae* (*The Day of Judgment*), by Anton Wildgans, opens at the Saxon State Provincial Theater in Dresden.

7 The tragedy *Karl V*, by Wilhelm Speyer, premieres at the Darmstadt Regional Theater. The film *Hyänen der Lust: der Weg, der zur Verdammnis führt 2.* (*Hyenas of Lust: The Path That Leads to Damnation, Part 2*), directed by Otto Rippert and starring Käthe Haack, opens in Berlin. The comedy *Die verschwundene Pauline* (*Whatever Happened to Pauline?*), by Willi Wolff, premieres at the Potsdam Schauspielhaus.

Intermittent strikes in various labor sectors halt public transportation, newspaper publication, coal delivery, and utilities service.

8 Air mail service between Berlin and Frankfurt am Main is begun. Airplanes are also involved in attacking Spartacist positions in Berlin.

9 The first exhibition of the Hannover Secession, a group of avant-garde painters and sculptors, opens.

Defense Minister Noske declares martial law throughout Berlin and posts announcements that any civilian found with weapons will be executed on the spot.

10 Leo Jogiches,[21] editor of the Communist Party's newspaper, *Red Flag*, and former colleague of Liebknecht and Luxemburg, is apprehended. Government paramilitary troops remand him to Moabit prison, where he is murdered.

11 The world premiere of the comedy *Der blinde Gott,* by Viktor Georgen, takes place at the Munich Kammerspiele.

Paramilitary troops capture and execute 30 members of the "Peoples' Marine Division."

13 The Armistice Commission in Brussels approves the monthly release of 300,000 metric tons of bread flour, along with 70,000 metric tons of lard and cooking oil, for distribution in German cities. The Commission notes the widespread starvation throughout Germany, resulting in hundreds of deaths among children.

Defense Minister Noske appears in Weimar and assures members of the National Assembly that Berlin is secure and that domestic enemies of the republic have been liquidated.

Kurt Tucholsky's *Fromme Gesänge* (*Pious Songs*), a volume of poetry, is published.[22]

14 The drama *Die Verführung* (*The Seduction*), by Paul Kornfeld, opens at the Albert Theater in Dresden.

15 Piscator founds his first theater, Das Tribünal (The Tribunal), in Königsberg; he intends to stage "proletarian drama" to serve Communist Party propaganda efforts. In Berlin, Viktor Barnowsky stages a revival of Gerhart Hauptmann's comedy *Der rote Hahn* (*The Red Rooster*) at the Lessing Theater, starring Ilka Grüning and and Emil Lind.

Renewed encounters between government paramilitary troops and heavily armed Spartacists rage throughout the night in central Berlin.

16 Defense Minister Noske rescinds the order of martial law in Berlin.

Novelist Heinrich Mann leads a memorial service for Kurt Eisner at the Munich Odeon.

The comic fragment *Elins Erweckung*, by Frank Wedekind, premieres at the Kammerspiele in Hamburg.

17 Alfons Paquet[23] reads from his *Der Geist der russischen Revolution* (*The Spirit of the Russian Revolution*) in Heidelberg.

The film *Stahl und Stein* (*Steel and Stone*), directed by Hans Rhoden, opens.

18 Paul Büttner's Fourth Symphony premieres in Dresden, played by the Saxon State Orchestra under the direction of Herrmann Kutschbach.

20 The film *Die Reise um die Welt in 80 Tagen* (*Around the World in 80 Days*), based on the Jules Verne novel, directed by Richard Oswald and starring Conrad Veidt, premieres.

The drama *Der arme Vetter* (*The Poor Cousin*), by sculptor Ernst Barlach, premieres in Hamburg.

The Cologne City Council agrees to fund the reestablishment of the University of Cologne.

21 The Bauhaus[24] school of design and architecture opens in Weimar under the leadership of Walter Gropius, who establishes the school from a merger of the Grand Ducal Art Academy and the Grand Ducal Vocational Crafts Training Institute.

The drama *Das Ende der Marienburg* (*The Destruction of the Marienburg Fortress*), by Herbert Eulenberg, premieres in Weimar. The crime film *Das Auge des Buddha* (*Eye of the Buddha*), directed by Maurice Mondet and starring Fritz Kortner, opens. The horror film *Die Spinne* (*The Spider*), directed by Conrad Wiene and starring Robert Wiene, also opens.

22 Nikolai Gogol's comedy *Die Heirat* (*The Marriage*), directed by Jürgen Fehling and starring Lucie Mannheim, is revived at the Berlin Volksbühne.

23 The drama *Die Vorhölle* (*The Anteroom of Hell*), by Rudolf Leonhard, premieres at the Kleines Schauspielhaus in Berlin.

25 Sculptor Wilhelm Lehmbruck commits suicide.

The symbolist drama *The Four Horsemen of the Apocalypse*, by Leo Weismantel, premieres in Würzburg.

26 The comedy film *Karussell des Lebens* (*Carousel of Life*), starring Pola Negri, premieres.

29 The drama *Brüder* (*Brothers*), by Emil Sandt, premieres at the Altona City Theater.

30 The Prussian Cultural Ministry announces plans to transform the Princess Palace in Berlin into the Museum of Modern Art.

31 *Der Geist der neuen Volksgemeinschaft* (*The Spirit of the New Peoples' Community*), a collection of essays on "what it means to be German" from the viewpoints of numerous well-known authors (Arnold Zweig, Kasmir Edschmidt, Gustav Radbruch, and others), is published by the firm of S. Fischer in Berlin.

APRIL

2 Gropius publishes the "Bauhaus Manifesto," describing the curriculum of the Bauhaus school, and introduces its principal teachers.

The socialist satirical bimonthly journal *Die Pleite* (*Bankrupt*) makes its first appearance, featuring cartoons and illustrations by George Grosz; it is published by Malik Press.

Der Jäger aus Kurpfalz, by Ferdinand Bonn, premieres at the Walhalla Theater in Berlin.

3 Rudolf Pechel assumes editorship of the cultural journal *Deutsche Rundschau* (*German Review*). Alfred Rosenberg begins work for the anti-Semitic scandal sheet *Auf gut deutsch* (*In Good German*), edited by Dietrich Eckart in Munich.

4 The three-and-a-half-hour historical film trilogy *Veritas vincit* (*Truth Triumphs*), directed by Joe May, premieres, with a cast that appears in all three periods covered in the film: ancient Rome, a small German town at the beginning of the 16th century, and shortly before the outbreak of World War I in a ducal palace. The romantic film *Halbblut* (*Half Caste*), directed by Fritz Lang and starring Ressel Orla in the title role, premieres in Berlin.

5 The exhibition Unfamiliar Architecture, by Walter Gropius and Bruno Taut, opens in Berlin.

The operetta *Das Dorf ohne Glocke* (*The Village without a Clock*), by Eduard Künneke, premieres in Berlin.

6 The comedy *Spielereien einer Kaiserin* (*Escapades of an Empress*), by Max Dauthendey and starring Tilla Durieux and Albert Steinrück, opens at the Residenz Theater in Munich.

8 The Bühnenvolksbund (Peoples' Theater League), an organization of amateur theater groups that unites hobbyists in other artistic fields, is founded.

12 Hermine Körner assumes directorship of the Schauspielhaus in Munich, where a "Soviet Republic of Bavaria" has been declared, although the Communist Party refuses to participate in it.

The comedy film *Ihr Sport* (*Her Sporting Event*), directed by Rudolf Biebrach and starring Henny Porten, premieres. The comedy *Die Dame ohne Beruf* (*The Lady's Lost Her Profession*), by Ludwig Kirchfeld, premieres at the Theater in der Friedrichstadt in Berlin.

17 The Hungarian film *Alraune* opens in Berlin; it is the first film directed by Manó Kertész Kaminer to appear there. The director, Michael Curtiz, later becomes one of Hollywood's greatest directors, with films like *Casablanca* (1942) and *Mildred Pierce* (1945), among dozens of others, to his credit.

The Berlin Volksbühne's production of *Penthesilea,* by Heinrich von Kleist, opens, starring Mary (later Marlene) Dietrich, Heinz Hilpert, and Adele Sandrock.

18 *Der feurige Weg* (*The Fiery Path*), Alfons Petzold's novel about the Russian revolution, is published. In it, he maintains that socialism is a form of messianic religion.

19 The Paul Stegman Press is founded in Hannover; it becomes, with the Malik Press, a leading publisher of Dadaist writers, journalists, and graphic artists. Hermine Körner inaugurates her directorship of the Munich Schauspielhaus with *Die gefesselte Phantasie* (*The Enchained Imagination*), by Ferdinand Raimund. Anton Wildgans's tragedy about schoolchildren, *Dies Irae* (*The Day of Judgment*), directed by Viktor Barnowsky, premieres at the Lessing Theater in Berlin.

20 The Alfred Flechtheim Gallery opens in Düsseldorf, dedicated to exhibiting expressionist and Dadaist painting, sculpture, and photography.

23 The film *Anders als die Anderen* (*Different from the Others*), directed by Richard Oswald and starring Conrad Veidt as a homosexual violin virtuoso driven to suicide, premieres. It is among the first German films to confront Paragraph 175 of the German Penal Code, which criminalized male homosexual activity. The film is denied release for public viewing but permitted for viewing among psychologists, social workers, and clergymen.

27   *Die Wupper* (*The River Wupper*), by Else Lasker-Schüler, premieres in a showcase production staged at the Deutsches Theater in Berlin.

29   *Das Spielzeug der Zarin* (*The Czarina's Plaything*), directed by Rudolf Meinert and starring Ellen Richter as the Czarina, is the first movie filmed at the former Hohenzollern palaces in Potsdam.

30   The comedy *Die Kabarettdiva* (*The Cabaret Diva*), by Kurt Kraatz and Richard Kessler, premieres at the Potsdam Schauspielhaus.

A Dadaist exhibition of artworks and photography ends in a near-riot in Berlin as police confiscate several works. George Grosz is charged with blasphemy for depicting Christ crucified in a gas mask with the heading, "Keep your mouth shut and do your duty."

MAY

1   The first issues of the illustrated weekly *Freie Welt* (*Free World*) is published; it is the "official organ" of the Independent Social Democratic Party's (USPD). Klara Zetkin begins publication of her women's weekly newspaper, *Die Sozialistin* (*The Woman Socialist*).

The film *Die Prostitution* (*The Madam*), directed by Richard Oswald and starring Kissa von Sievers (in the title role), Conrad Veidt, Werner Krauss, Ferdinand Bonn, and Anita Berber, premieres in Berlin. The title is later changed to *Das gelbe Haus* (*The Yellow House*). The comedy *Die ewige Braut* (*The Eternal Bride*), by Robert Liebmann, premieres at the Munich Volkstheater.

2   Government paramilitary troops enter Munich and break up the "Soviet Republic of Bavaria," imprisoning several government leaders.

4   The comedy *Liselotte von der Pfalz* (*Liselotte of the Palatinate*), by Toni Impekoven and Carl Mathern, premieres; a satire on French sensibilities and manners, *Liselotte* becomes enormously popular throughout Germany in the immediate postwar period.

7   The German delegation receives Allied demands for a peace treaty at the Versailles Palace in Paris.

8   Ebert denounces the Allied conditions for peace; dozens of politicians throughout Germany echo Ebert's fulminations against the Allies. Government urges all public performance facilities, such as theaters, operas, operettas, and movie houses, to restrict their fare to that which represents the seriousness of the moment in German history.

The operetta *Ihre Hoheit, die Tänzerin* (*Her Majesty, the Dancer*), by Walter Goetze (1883–1961), premieres in Stettin; it becomes Goetze's most popular operetta, with more than 700 performances throughout the 1920s.

10 The newly established University of Hamburg is dedicated.

The drama *Der Kinderfreund* (*The Children's Friend*), by Mechthilde von Lichnowsky, premieres at the Deutsches Theater in Berlin.

11 Government paramilitary troops occupy government offices in Leipzig, declare martial law, and disband the municipal government.

12 Referring to the Treaty of Versailles, Prime Minister Scheidemann utters his widely repeated rhetorical question, "What hand must not wither, that binds both it and us within these chains?"[25]

13 President Ebert calls upon the people of the United States to recognize the injustice being done to Germany in the Treaty of Versailles and to insist upon President Wilson's "Fourteen Points" as a basis for European reconciliation.[26]

14 The week-long criminal proceedings against nine officers accused in the murder of Liebknecht and Luxemburg end. Three are given light sentences; six are exonerated.

The political drama *Summa Summarum*, by Hermann Kessler, premieres at the National Theater in Mannheim.

15 The thriller film *Der Diamant des Todes* (*The Diamond of Death*), directed by Leo Stoll and starring Fritz Strassny and Joseph Schildkraut, is released.

20 The drama *Fröhliche Wiederkunft* (*Happy Return*), by Franz Kaibel, premieres at the Weimar National Theater.

23 The comedy film *Zwei Welten* (*Two Worlds*), directed by Robert Wiene and starring Harry Walden, premieres.

The Berlin Academy of the Arts initiates exhibitions of modernist painters and sculptors for the first time, including works by Lovis Corinth, Max Liebermann, Emil Orlik, Georg Kolbe, Käthe Kollwitz, and Wilhelm Lehmbruck.

24 The inaugural issue of the satirical weekly *Der blutige Ernst*, edited by Carl Einstein and George Grosz and with drawings by Grosz, is published.

25 Two dramas by painter Oskar Kokoschka, *Der brennende Dornbusch* (*The Burning Thornbush*) and *Hiob* (*Job*), premiere at the Deutsches Theater in Berlin.

29 During a six-minute solar eclipse on Principe Island off the African coast, British astrophysicist Arthur Eddington validates Albert Einstein's General Theory of Relativity. In Eddington's photographs, images of known stars appear in new locations, proving that the sun's gravity deflects light from those stars. Einstein's concept of a universe in which humans can measure only relative motion displaces the Newtonian concept of a universe in which space and time are absolute.

30 The drama *Sonnenfinsternis* (*Eclipse of the Sun*), by Arno Holz, premieres at the Berlin State Theater.

31 The body of Rosa Luxemburg is discovered in the Landwehr Canal in Berlin.

JUNE

1 The comedy *Die Rutschbahn* (*The Toboggan Run*), by Heinz Gordon and Curt Goetz, premieres at the Künstler Theater in Berlin.

2 The first issue of the weekly *Der Dada*, edited by Raoul Hausmann, who also illustrates the paper with his own woodcut prints, is published.

The comedy *Weibchen* (*Little Wench*), by Ernst von Wolzogen, premieres at the Breslau City Theater.

3 *Die Kernpunkte der sozialen Frage in den Lebensnotwendigkeiten* (*The Central Points of the Social Question in the Necessities of Life*), by Rudolf Steiner,[27] is published.

5 The comedy *Die Marquise von Arcis* (*The Marquise of Arcis*), by Carl Sternheim, premieres at the Frankfurt am Main City Theater.

Painter Max Liebermann declares his allegiance to the Ebert government.

Paramilitary troops in Munich carry out numerous summary executions, including of Eugen Levine and other leaders of the "Soviet Republic of Bavaria."

6 The Bauhaus School mounts its first exhibition of student work in Weimar.

The film drama *Die Schuld* (*Guilt*), directed by Rudolf Biebrach and starring Henny Porten, premieres.

7 Orchestra conductor Otto Klemperer converts to Roman Catholicism and begins rehearsals for his *Missa sacra* (sacred mass).

12 Some 1,300 students enroll for classes at the newly reestablished University of Cologne.

The comedy *Das Jubiläum*, by Franz Arnold and Ernst Bach,[28] premieres at the Hannover Residenz Theater.

13 The comedy film *Wie werde ich mein Geld los?* (*How Can I Get Rid of My Money?*), directed by Walter Schmidthässler and starring Oslar Linke and Helene Voss, premieres.

An estimated 20,000 people attend Rosa Luxemburg's burial in the Central Cemetery in Friedrichsfelde, Berlin.

14 Food riots occur in several cities and towns throughout Germany because of shortages and spoilages.

15 The comedy *Bettys Talent* (*Betty's Talent*), by Hans L'Arronge, premieres at the Union Theater in Celle.

18 Hermine Körner stages *Die Büchse der Pandora* (*Pandora's Box*) at the Munich Schauspielhaus.

20 The entire national government resigns in protest against the conditions set forth in the Treaty of Versailles.

The pacifist drama *Die Krise* (*The Crisis*), by Karl Röttger, premieres at the Kassel State Schauspielhaus.

21 The German admiralty orders the sinking of 51 naval ships in Scapa Flow, a body of water surrounded by the Orkney Islands off the coast of Scotland. Nine German sailors are killed in the exercise, which is intended to avoid surrendering the ships to the British. Documentary films of the exercise are shown that evening in Berlin movie houses.

22 The Allies refuse to consider any German objections to the provisions for reparation payments or repatriation of German prisoners of war.

25 The social satire film *Die Austerprinzessin* (*The Oyster Princess*), directed by Ernst Lubitsch, with Ossi Oswalda in the title role (as the daughter of America's most successful oyster-fishing businessman) and Viktor Janson as her father, the "oyster king," premieres in Berlin.

26 Prussian authorities order the removal of all portraits of the former kaiser and members of his family from Prussian schools "for the purposes of safekeeping."

27   The drama *Mammon*, by Waldfried Burggraf, premieres at the Nuremberg City Theater.

28   The German delegation signs the Treaty of Versailles in Paris.

29   The Berlin newspaper *Vossische Zeitung* publishes the pacifist poem "Friedenslitanei" ("The Litany of Peace"), by Ina Seidel (1884–1975). Seidel later becomes the second woman (Ricarda Huch was the first) elected to the Prussian Academy of the Arts (in 1932). The expressionist journal *Der Sturm* (*The Storm*) publishes the first reproductions of Kurt Schwitters's *Merz* collages.

JULY

1   Max von Schillings is named director of the Berlin State Opera; Schillings immediately signs his future wife, soprano Barbara Kemp, to a lengthy contract. Playwright and opera lyricist Hugo von Hofmansthal condemns the move as a sign of a growing "Soviet Republic of the Arts." Leopold Jessner officially assumes directorship of the Berlin State Theater.
   The Institute for Sexual Rescarch opens in Berlin under the direction of neurologist Magnus Hirschfeld, an outspoken advocate of easing legal restrictions against male homosexuals.
   The war film *Ikarus, der fliegende Mensch* (*Icarus, the Flying Man*), directed by Carl Froelich and starring Ernst Hofmann, premieres in Berlin. The war drama *Urlaub* (*On Leave*), by Lola Landau, premieres in Breslau.

3   The comedy *So ein Mädel* (*Such a Girl*), by Hans Sturem, premieres at the Berlin Lustspielhaus. The film drama *Der ledige Hof* (*The Empty Court*), directed by Max Neufeld, opens.

5   The comedy film *Ein Hochzeitsmorgen* (*A Wedding Morning*), directed by Franz Seitz and starring Rolf Pinegger and Magda Simon, premieres. The film drama *Wenn Freunde zu Rivalen werden* (*When Friends Become Rivals*), directed by Paul von Worringen, opens.

7   Musarion Press in Munich rejects Bertolt Brecht's play *Baal* for publication.

8   The comedy film *Verlorenes Spiel* (*Lost Game*), directed by Franz Seitz and starring Lili Domenici and Fritz Kampers, premieres in Munich.

9   The National Assembly in Weimar ratifies the Treaty of Versailles by a vote of 208 to 115.

12 The comedy film *Stiefkinder des Glück* (*Stepchildren of Fortune*), directed by Arthur Wellin and starring Theodor Loos, Ethel Scharo, and Eva Richter, premieres in Berlin.

The Allies lift the blockade of German ports, allowing food shipments to begin; German shipping is allowed to resume across the Atlantic Ocean and in the Mediterranean Sea.

Writer Erich Mühsam is sentenced to a15-year prison term for his participation in the "Soviet Republic of Bavaria."

14 The comedy *Charley's Aunt*, by Brandon Thomas and starring Guido Thielscher, is revived at the Lessing Theater in Berlin; over the next four seasons it runs more than 1,000 performances.

15 The comedy *Konstantin Strobel*, by Georg Kaiser, premieres at the Munich Schauspielhaus.

An exhibition of paintings by Christian Rohlffs opens at the Alfred Flechtheim Gallery in Düsseldorf, if one marking the rise of Rohlffs to prominence in the 1920s.

16 Playwright Ernst Toller is sentenced to a five-year prison term for treason for his participation in the Soviet Republic of Bavaria.

As "Oberdada" and head of the "Dadaist Central Committee for World Revolution," Johannes Baader distributes flyers to members of the National Assembly in Weimar proclaiming himself president of "this terrestrial ball."

17 The comedy film *Die beide Gatten der Frau Ruth* (*Mrs. Ruth and Her Two Husbands*), directed by Rudolf Briebach and starring Henny Porten and Curt Goetz, premieres in Berlin.

Student representatives from 74 German-speaking universities assemble in Würzburg; they send a telegram of allegiance to General Paul von Hindenburg, pledging their devotion to him. They call for the establishment of a national ministry of culture in Germany and write a set of by-laws for all student governments in universities "wherever the German language is spoken."

24 The largest exhibition of modernist paintings, graphics, and sculpture in Berlin's history opens; several organizations of artists are represented, featuring many works never before seen in public. Among the artists whose works are shown are Anna Costenoble, César Klein, Conrad Felixmüller, Emil Orlik, Erich Heckel, Ernst Barlach, Ewald Mataré, Franz Skarbina, Hans Baluschek, Käthe Kollwitz, Maria Slavona, Fritz Klimsch, Max Klinger, Julie Wolfthorn, Otto Griebel, Bernard Hoetger, Georg Kolbe, Rudolf Belling, and Max Slevogt.

27 The detective thriller film *Die Apachen* (*The Apache of Marseilles*), directed by E. A. Dupont and starring Max Landa and Hanni Weisse, premieres in Berlin.

29 The film drama *Die Frau im Käfig* (*The Woman in a Cage*), directed by Hanns Kolbe and starring Ernst Deutsch and Maria Leiko, premieres in Berlin.

30 A new world record for altitude is set when a German airplane carrying eight passengers and powered by two Mercedes 260-horse power engines reaches an altitude of 6,100 meters (20,013 feet, or 3.8 miles).

AUGUST

1 A film adaptation of Shakespeare's *King Lear*, titled *König Krause* (*King Krause*), premieres in Max Reinhardt's Kammerspiele in Berlin; it is directed by Heinrich Bolten-Baeckers, with Conrad Dreher as Krause. The film melodrama *Das törichte Herz* (*The Foolish Heart*), directed by Erik Lund and starring Eva May, Hermann Thimig, and Leopold von Lebedur, also premieres in Berlin.

The first public art exhibition featuring wholly modernist works opens in Munich at the Glass Palace.

2 The film melodrama *Rausch* premieres at the Kurfürsten Film Palace in Berlin. Based on Swedish playwright August Strindberg's play *Advent*, it is the first postwar film appearance of Asta Nielsen.[29] It is directed by Ernst Lubitsch, with Alfred Abela as a playwright intoxicated (hence the German title) with a friend's wife (Nielsen); a stunning performance by Nielsen.

3 The University of Bonn awards novelist Thomas Mann an honorary doctorate; his novel *Buddenbrooks* enters its 100th printing.

The comedy film *Wenn Männer streiken* (*When Husbands Go on Strike*), directed by Edmund Edel and starring Paul Westermeier and Lotte Werkmeister, premieres in Berlin.

4 A new state art gallery opens at the former Crown Prince Palace in Berlin; paintings that the kaiser had labeled "art of the gutter" predominate.

6 New paintings by Max Liebermann, Lovis Corinth, Otto Freindlich, and Erich Heckel open at the new Fritz Gurlitt Gallery in Berlin.

8 *Die lebende Tote* (*A Woman Dead and Alive*), directed by Rudolf Biebrach, with Henny Porten in the title role, premieres in Berlin.[30]

Street riots in Chemnitz leave 29 dead and scores wounded. Among the slain are paramilitary Freikorps troops singled out for particularly gruesome killings.

11 President Ebert signs the new German Constitution of the Republic. It contains more than 180 articles, with a preamble that reads: "The German people, united in their ethnic origins and with a will to renew their commonwealth in both freedom and justice, have promulgated this Constitution to preserve domestic tranquility and peace abroad, and to promote social progress."

13 The exotic romantic film *Indische Nächte* (*Indian Nights*), directed by Richard Löwenbein and starring Rudolf Klein-Rohden, Gustav Adolf Semmler, and Leonore Oppermann, premieres in Berlin. The film melodrama *Seelenverkäufer* (*Sellers of Souls*), directed by Carl Boese and starring Lore Hillebrand, Toni Tetzlaff, and Josef Peterhans, also premieres in Berlin.

14 The Constitution of the Republic is officially published in the national legal code, thus taking effect.

The film drama *Maria Pawlowna*, based on the diplomatic career and remarkable exploits of Grand Duchess Maria Pavlova Romanoff-Holstein of Saxony-Weimar, daughter of the Russian Czar Paul I, premieres in Berlin. It is directed by Emil Justitz and stars Maria Fein in the title role.

15 The slave melodrama *Die Tochter des Mehemed* (*The Daughter of Mehemed*), directed by Alfred Halm, with Ellen Richter in the title role, premieres in Berlin, one of several films with "exotic" themes beginning to appear in German movie houses. This one deals with Leila, bought from slavery and presented as a gift to a Dutch doctor. The man who purchases her freedom, played by Emil Jannings, later goes bankrupt and commits suicide.

16 In response to demands by the Polish National Workers' Party in western Germany, a Polish "people's university" is established in Bochum.

20 Two movies premiere in Berlin: the comic film *Die Diplomatensäugling* (*The Apprentice Diplomat*), directed by Erich Schönfelder and starring Max Zilzer and Mabel May-Young; and the detective film *Das Geheimnis der alten Truhe* (*The Secret of the Old Chest*), directed by Robert Leffler and starring Sybil Smolowa and Hans Adalbert.

21 President Ebert swears in the new constitutional government in Weimar; delegates to the National Assembly adjourn and depart for Berlin, where they will henceforth meet in the Reichstag building.

23 The operetta *Die Frau im Hermelin* (*The Lady in Ermine*), by Jean Gilbert (Max Winterfeld), premieres at the Theater des Westens in Berlin.

25 The film melodrama *Vendetta*, directed by Georg Jacoby and starring Pola Negri, Emil Jannings, and Harry Liedtke, premieres in Berlin.

29 The new Leipzig Kammerspiele (Chamber Theater) opens with *The Pelican*, by August Strindberg.

SEPTEMBER

1 The comedy *Der ehemalige Leutnant* (*The Former Lieutenant*), by Gustav Kadelburg and Heinz Gordon, premieres at the Brelau Lobe Theater.

German universities in Posen (Poland), Prague, and Czernowitz (Romania) are closed, and their faculty members are fired and replaced by Polish-, Czech-, and Romanian-speaking faculty, respectively. German Catholic bishops in Alsace and Lorraine are forced out of office, to be replaced by French-speaking prelates.

2 In Leipzig, President Ebert declares that work "is the source of all culture." He assures his hearers that "the world will soon recognize the cultural achievements of which Germany is capable."

4 The film drama *Die Liebschaften der Käthe Keller* (*The Love Affairs of Kathy Keller*), directed by Carl Froelich and starring Hermine Körner and Paul Hartmann, premieres in Berlin.

5 The comedy film *Die Dame im Pelz* (*The Lady in Fur*), directed by Fred Preuss and starring Ellen Ullrich and Charles Willy Kayser, premieres in Berlin. The film drama *Göttin, Dirne, und Weib* (*Goddess, Whore, and Wife*), directed by Walter Schmidthässler with Hanni Weisse, Olga Desmond, and Rita Essermont in the title roles, also premieres.

7 At the Berlin International Youth Day Conference, several fist fights break out, followed by shootings. Several young people are taken to hospitals, but no deaths are reported.

9 An unprecedentedly early snowstorm sweeps through Berlin, disrupting traffic and food deliveries. Food riots break out in Breslau.

12 The film melodrama *Die Rose von Stambul*, directed by Arthur Wellin and starring Fritzi Massay Felix Basch, and Ernst Pittschau, premieres in Berlin.

The Berlin State Theater and Opera are subsumed organizationally under the Prussian Ministry of Culture.

In Munich, a local paramilitary commander hires a war veteran named Adolf Hitler to observe a meeting of the German Workers' Party (DAP). He becomes a member of the party six days later.

13 The comedy *Die letzten Ritter* (*The Last Knights*), by Heinrich Pfieffer, premieres at the Deutsches Künstlertheater in Berlin.

15 The Berlin Philharmonic Orchestra presents "Max Reger Week," performing many of the composer's works on successive evenings.

18 The film melodrama *Der Sohn der Magd, die Liebe des Bastards* (*The Son of a Maid, the Love of a Bastard*), directed by Max Mack with Rose Veldtkirch, Ludwig Hartau, and Hermann Thimig, premieres in Berlin. The historical epic film *Madame Dubarry*, directed by Ernst Lubitsch and starring Pola Negri (in the title role), Emil Jannings (as Louis XV), Harry Liedtke, and Eduard von Winterstein, also premieres in Berlin. Based on a historical personage, a seamstress's illegitimate daughter who became the French king's mistress, Negri played the character with characteristic passion and ardor. She was particularly effective when begging the executioner on the guillotine, "Please monsieur, just one moment more!" The film became a worldwide hit.

19 The expressionist drama *Im dritten Jahr* (*In the Third Year*), by Otto Flake, premieres at the Altes Theater in Leipzig.

20 The Tribüne Theater in Berlin opens with two political plays by Walter Hasenclever, a drama, *Der Retter* (*The Savior*), and a comedy, *Die Entscheidung* (*The Decision*).

23 The comedy film *Ich oder Du* (*Me or You*), directed by Albert Lastmann and starring Rita Parsen and Ingo Brandt, premieres in Berlin.

24 The comedy film *Prinz Kuckuck* (*Prince Cuckoo*), directed by Paul Leni and starring Conrad Veidt and Olga Limburg, premieres in Berlin.

25 An exhibition of wood sculptures by painter Josef Ebers (1880–1942) opens in Munich.

26 The drama *Christa, die Tante* (*Aunt Christa*), directed by Viktor Barnowsky and starring Ilka Grüning and Senta Bré, premieres at the Lessing Theater in Berlin.

30 The political drama *Die Wandlung* (*The Transformation*), by Ernst Toller (who is unable to attend the opening because he is imprisoned in Munich), directed by Karl-Heinz Martin and starring Fritz Kortner, premieres at the Tribüne Theater in Berlin.

OCTOBER

1 The new Detmold Regional Theater opens.
The German currency continues to decline in value against other currencies.

3 The adventure film *Der goldene See* (*The Golden Sea*), directed by Fritz Lang and starring Lil Dagover and Carl de Vogt, opens in Berlin. Dagover plays an Inca princess who helps a European adventurer find buried treasure. Many of the settings and props are authentic, supplied by the Hamburg Natural History Museum, where Lang shot many of the film's interior scenes.

4 The film *Der Galeerensträfling* (*The Galley Slave*), based on materials by Honoré de Balzac, directed by Paul Wegener and starring Ernst Deutsch, Lothar Müthel, and Adele Sandrock, opens in Berlin.

5 The film *Rose Bernd* (based on the popular play of the same name by Gerhart Hauptmann), directed by Alfred Halm and starring Henny Porten (in the title role), Emil Jannings, Paul Bildt, and Werner Krauss, opens in Berlin.

8 An assassination attempt is made on the steps of the Reichstag against Hugo Haase, chairman of the Independent Social Democratic Party (USPD); it leaves him severely wounded, and he dies a month later.

9 The drama *Das bist Du* (*It's You*), by Friedrich Wolf, premieres at the Dresden Regional Theater, with expressionist-style scenery and costumes by Conrad Felixmüller.

10 A new production of Shakespeare's *Cymbeline*, directed by Ludwig Berger, opens at the Deutsches Theater in Berlin. The drama *Die Trösterin* (*Consolation*), by Bruno Frank, opens at the Munich Schauspielhaus. The new Figaro Theater opens in Breslau.

The comic historical film *Kaiser Wilhelms Glück und Ende* (*The Rise and Fall of Kaiser Wilhelm II*), directed by Willy Achsel and starring Ferdinand Bonn[31] in the role of Kaiser Wilhelm II and as the Captain of Köpenick, opens at the Berlin Sportpalast, with seating for more than 6,000 viewers.

11 The comedy *Er kann nicht befehlen* (*He Can't Give Orders*), by Wilhelm Speyer, premieres at the Munich Residenz Theater.

A new production of the "musical legend" *Palestrina*, by Hans Pfitzner (it had premiered in 1912), with baritone Heinrich Schlusnus in the title role, opens at the Berlin State Opera.

16 In the newly constituted Reichstag, conservative parties call for tightening censorship of movies shown in Germany; liberal parties, especially the SPD, call for national control of schools and universities.

17 The detective film *Die Spione* (*The Spy*), directed by E. A. Dupont and starring Max Landa and Hanni Weisse, premieres in Berlin.

19 The romantic film *Der ewige Rätsel* (*The Eternal Mystery*), directed by Josef Coenen and starring Carola Toelle and Werner Krauss, premieres in Berlin.

21 Frederick Delius's opera *Fennimore and Gerda* premieres at the Frankfurt am Main Opera House. In Augsburg, the local USPD newspaper publishes Bertolt Brecht's first theater review (of *Ghosts*, by Henrik Ibsen).

22 Richard Strauss's opera *Die Frau ohne Schatten* (*The Woman without a Shadow*), with text by Hugo von Hofmannsthal, makes its German premiere at the Dresden Opera House.

23 The historical film *Die Pest in Florenz* (*The Plague in Florence*), directed by Otto Rippert, starring Theodor Becker and Marga Kierska and with a screenplay by Fritz Lang, opens in Berlin.

28 The Belgian government bans German children from attending Belgian schools.

29 The U.S. Supreme Court upholds a ban on opera performances in the German language.

30 The Munich publishing firm of Kurt Wolff markets first editions of numerous modernist writers, among them Franz Kafka, Karl Kraus, Carl Sternheim, and Franz Werfel.

31 The comedy *Der Grossstadtkavalier* (*The Big City Cavalier*), by Georg Okonkowsky, premieres at the Berlin Lustspielhaus.

NOVEMBER

1 The comedy *Der Ex-Herzog* (*The Ex-Duke*), by Albert Matthei, premieres at the Chemnitz City Theater.

3 Erich Mendelsohn submits a design for a solar observatory known as the "Einstein Tower" in the style of "architectonic expressionism," in honor of Albert Einstein, to be erected in Potsdam. The Royal Art Academy in Düsseldorf is rechristened the State Academy of Art.

A double bill of the drama *Miss Julie*, by August Strindberg, and the comedy *Der grüne Kakadu* (*The Green Cockatoo*), by Arthur Schnitzler, directed by Viktor Barnowsky and starring Tilla Durieux, Eugen Klöpfer, Ilka Grüning, and Conrad Veidt, opens at the Lessing Theater in Berlin.

4 The comedy film *Das fidele Gefängnis* (*The Faithful Prison*), directed by Ernst Lubitsch (filmed in in 1917) and starring Harry Liedtke, Kitty Dewall, and Ossi Oswalda, is released. The romantic film *Der Fürst der Diebe und seine Liebe* (*The Prince of Thieves and His Love*), directed by Viggo Larsen and starring Franz Derdier and Erra Bognar in the title roles, premieres in Berlin.

The drama *Die Richterin* (*The Woman Judge*), by Herbert Kranz, premieres at the Düsseldorf Schauspielhaus.

7   The biblical drama *Jaakobs Traum*, by Richard Beer-Hofmann, directed by Max Reinhardt and starring Alexander Moissi, Paul Hartmann, Eduard von Winterstein, Else Heims, and Ernst Deutsch, premieres at the Deutsches Theater in Berlin.

Kaemmerer Press in Dresden publishes two volumes of poetry by Klabund (Alfred Henschke), *Die gefiederte Welt* (*The Feathered World*) and *Montezuma*.

8   The drama *Predigt in Litauen* (*Sermon in Lithuania*), by Rolf Lauckner, directed by Paul Legband and starring Jürgen Fehling, Friedrich Kayssler, and Eugen Eisenlohr, premieres at the Berlin Volksbühne.

9   On the first anniversary of the German capitulation in World War I, several SPD leaders declare that the socialists did not want a revolution and have furthermore fought against revolution in both word and deed.

The drama *Die Totengräber* (*The Gravediggers*), by Klabund, premieres at the Hamburg Kammerspiele.

The thriller film *Das Ritualmord* (*The Ritual Murder*), directed by Joseph Delmont and starring Alfred Abel and Sybil Morel, premieres in Berlin.

10   The biblical drama *Esther*, by Adolf Goetz, premieres at the Hamburg Kammerspiele. On the occasion of Schiller's 140th birthday, scores of theaters present *William Tell*, many in new productions. Most other theaters present one of his other major plays.

11   The thriller film *Der Dolch der Malayen* (*The Dagger of the Malays*), directed by Leo Lasko and starring Carl Auen, Bernhard Goetzke, and Blandine Ebinger, premieres in Berlin.

14   The comedy *Albine und August*, by Max-Hermann Neisse, premieres at the Kleines Schauspielhaus.

16   The Western film *Bull Arizona und der Wüstenadler* (*Bull Arizona and the Desert Eagle*), starring Hermann Basler (in the title role) and Sonya Bernini, premieres in Munich.

18   The romantic film *Lili*, directed by Jaap Speyer and starring Leopoldine Konstantin (in the title role) and Ernst Stahl-Neubaur, premieres in Berlin.

In Essen, law professors and students lodge charges that judgeship appointments are contingent upon political party affiliation.

19   The drama *Robert Frank*, by Sigurd Ibsen, directed by Viktor Barnowsky, is revived at the Lessing Theater in Berlin.

21 The film melodrama *Die Fahrt ins Blaue* (*A Journey into the Blue*), directed by Rudolf Biebrach and starring Henny Porten, Georg Alexander, and Jacob Tiedtke, opens in Berlin. The thriller film *Vom Schicksal erdrosselt* (*Strangled by Fate*), directed by Carl Niesser and starring Heinz Herald, Ernst Deutsch, and Marianne Jugel, also opens in Berlin.

The drama *Brabach*, by Heinrich Mann, premieres at the Munich Resdenz Theater.

22 The drama *Der tote Tag* (*The Dead Day*), the first play by expressionist sculptor Ernst Barlach, premieres in Leipzig.

23 A Day of Remembrance is observed throughout Germany for soldiers killed in action and other fatalities in German military service; estimated totals exceed five million men.

26 The comic film *Madeleine*, directed by Siegfried Philippi and starring Ria Jende (in the title role), Eduard von Winterstein, and Hans Albers, premieres in Berlin.

28 Max Reinhardt stages *The Oresteian Trilogy*, by Aeschylus, in the former Renz Circus Arena, which Reinhardt has transformed into the Grosses Schauspielhaus (Big Theater). With seating for more than 3,800 patrons, it becomes the largest venue for live theater performance in Germany.

The detective film *Das Derby*, directed by E. A. Dupont and starring Max Landa,[32] Hermann Picha, Hanni Weisse, and several thoroughbred racing horses, premieres in Berlin.

The SPD and USPD introduce a bill in the Reichstag to commemorate 9 November as a national holiday; conservative parties denounce the bill and insist the date remain an unofficial day of mourning.

29 The comedy *Drei Frauenhüte* (*Three Ladies' Hats*), by Anna Brentano, one of the few female comic playwrights in the 1920s, premieres at the Theater in der Friedrichstrasse in Berlin.

30 The November Group installs its first exhibition of paintings at the Paul Cassirer Gallery, featuring works by its members, such as George Grosz, Paul Klee, Lionel Feininger, Otto Freundlich, Rudolf Belling, and Erich Mendelsohn.

DECEMBER

1 Richard Strauss resigns as director of the Berlin State Opera and assumes a similar position at the Vienna State Opera.

2 The film melodrama *Der Tod aus Osten* (*Death from the East*), directed by Martin Hartwig and starring Hans Adalbert Schlettow and Margarethe Schön, premieres in Berlin. The film is a thinly veiled fictional account of the Spartacist uprising earlier in the year, with Spartacists portrayed from a profoundly negative angle. The title implies that Lenin and the Soviet Union were behind the uprising.

5 The expressionist drama *Hölle-Weg-Erde* (*Hell-Road-Earth*), by Georg Kaiser, directed by Richard Weichert, premieres at the Frankfurt am Main City Theater.

Soviet agent Karl Radek is released from protective custody and immediately sent to the Soviet Union.

6 The four-part adventure film *Die Herrin der Welt* (*The Mistress of the World*), directed by Joe May and Uwe Jens Krafft, premieres in Berlin. The feature-length parts, opening throughout the month, feature Mia May as Maud Gregaards, an innocent young teacher on her way to a school in China. Along the way she is sold into prostitution, learns from an aged rabbi about buried treasure, and discovers an ancient bejeweled city in Africa.

The drama *Das Gelübde*, by Heinrich Lautensack, starring Hermine Körner, premieres at the Munich Schauspielhaus. Also in Munich, a new production of *Schloss Wetterstein* (*Castle Wetterstein*), by Frank Wedekind, opens at the Kammerspiele. The fairy tale drama *Die sechs Schwäne* (*The Six Swans*) premieres at the Düsseldorf Schauspielhaus.

7 Dadaists transform the Tribüne Theater in Berlin into the "Institute for Socialist Heuchelei" for the afternoon to present a program of playlets, readings, and political satires.

8 The experimental theater Kestner Bühne opens in Hannover and stages *Der Besuch aus Elysium*, by Franz Werfel, starring Fritz Kortner. Max Reinhardt reopens his cabaret Schall und Rauch (Noise and Smoke) in the cellar of his Deutsches Theater and features poetry readings, songs, and a puppet show designed by George Grosz, titled *Simple Classic: The* Oresteia *with a Happy Ending: Orestes in a Freikorps Uniform.*

10 The poem "Vor der Entscheidung" ("Before the Decision"), by Fritz von Unruh, is published.

Professor Johannes Stark at the University of Greifswald is awarded the Nobel Prize in Physics and Professor Fritz Haber at the University of Berlin is awarded the Nobel Prize in Chemistry. A certain "Herr Hitler" is the announced speaker in Munich, on the subject "Germany before Its Deepest Humiliation."

11 The drama *Der Pfarrer von Kirchfeld* (*The Pastor of Kirchfeld*), by Ludwig Anzengruber (1839–1889), directed by Viktor Barnowsky, is revived at the Lessing Theater in Berlin.

12 A new staging of *Wilhelm Tell*, by Schiller, directed by Leopold Jessner, is performed at the Berlin State Theater; conservative critics react with outrage, accusing Jessner of politicizing a German cultural treasure.

13 A new staging of *Götz von Berlichingen*, by Goethe, directed by Paul Legband, is performed at the Berlin Volksbühne.

The Berlin Secession presents its 37th annual exhibition of modernist paintings, drawing, and sculptures.

14 The operetta *Die Vielgeliebte* (*The Much Beloved Lady*), by Eduard Künneke (1885–1953), with Claire Waldorf in the title role, premieres at the Theater am Nollendorfplatz in Berlin.

16 A new staging of the drama *Und Pippa tanzt!* (*And Pippa Dances!*), by Gerhart Hauptmann, directed by Felix Holländer, is performed at the Deutsches Theater in Berlin.

20 The Singspiel *Dichterliebe* (*The Love of a Poet*), by Julius Bramer and Alfred Grünwald and set to music by Felix Mendelssohn (1809–1847), premieres.

21 The opera *Magdalena*, by Fritz Könnecke, premieres. It creates substantial controversy because it presents Pontius Pilate in love with Maria Magdalena and Jesus of Nazareth as his rival. In the end, Pilate uses crucifixion to eliminate his romantic competition.

The film *Unheimliche Geschichten* (*Tales of Mystery*), based on works by Edgar Allan Poe, directed by Richard Oswald and starring Anita Berber, Reinhold Schünzel, and Conrad Veidt, premieres in Berlin at the new Lichtspiel Palast movie theater.

22 The Nietzsche Archive in Weimar awards its Prizes for Retaining the German Intellectual Position of Power; among the recipients is Oswald Spengler, for his *Der Untergang des Abendlandes* (*The Decline of the West*).

23 The drama *Livets Spil* (*The Game of Life*), by the Germanophile Norwegian playwright Knut Hamsun, directed by Berthold Viertel, makes its German premiere at the State Theater Dresden.

Various Jewish artists and writers (e.g., Ernst Deutsch, Else Lasker-Schüler, and Stefan Zweig) present readings from the Old Testament and Hebrew poetry in Berlin as a benefit to raise funds for Zionist settlements in Palestine.

25 The operetta *Fräulein Puck*, by Walter Kollo, premieres at the Central Theater in Berlin; comedy writers Franz Arnold and Ernst Bach provide the lyrics and libretto. The "family comedy" *Feuer im Haus* (*Warmth of the Fireplace*), by Paul Hartwig, premieres at the Albert Theater in Dresden.

26 A performance of *Die Hose* (*The Underpants*), by Carl Sternheim, is disrupted by right-wing agitators at the Kleines Schauspielhaus in Berlin; they object to the comedy's satirical view of the Wilhelmine period.

31 A year-end survey of German theaters reveals that all 264 professional theaters in Germany had done at least one Shakespearean play; nearly 1,400 performances were given, 300 in Berlin alone. *As You Like It* and *Othello* were the most frequently performed throughout the country.

NOTES

1. Michael von Faulhaber (1869–1952) had taught at German universities before assuming the mitre and crozier of a bishop, first in Trier (1911–1917) and then in Munich (1917–1952). In his condemnation of the socialist government in Bavaria, he warned that "Jehovah's wrath" might be visited upon Bavaria, a phrase that many construed as somehow anti-Semitic. Many of the Bavarian republic's leaders were Jews, and some felt that Faulhaber's invocation of the name Jehovah was misguided.

Faulhaber subsequently demonstrated his legitimacy as a defender of Jews when the Nazis assumed power in 1933. If he had regarded the socialist republic of Bavaria as secularist, he found National Socialism much worse. In his sermons that excoriated the Nazis (collected under the title *Judaism, Christianity, and Germany*) as pagans, racists, and idolaters, he consistently emphasized Christianity's Jewish heritage and the inextricable connections of the New Testament with the Jewish scriptures. Perhaps most significant was his asseveration that the Germanic tribes were completely barbaric prior to their acceptance of Christianity; Christian values, he insisted, had furthermore become fundamental to German culture.

2. The Cologne City Council reestablished the university by creating a faculty of Economic and Social Sciences from the College of Commerce, which had existed since 1901. Within six years, the university had grown to become the second-largest university in the state of Prussia.

3. Count Harry Kessler described Liebknecht as the "invisible priest" motivating the masses swarming through Berlin's newspaper district (an area bounded by Mauer Strasse, Linden Strasse, Bessel Strasse, and Schütenstrasse) during the Spartacist uprising. He preached to them in a "sing song voice filled with soothing pathos, conveying deep feeling in his words. It was half a mass, half a political convention," wrote Kessler. "It was a wave of bolshevism, sweeping over us from the east, something like the flood that Mohammed had instigated in the seventh century. Fanaticism and weapons in the service of an unclear new hope" (*Tagebücher*, 92). Many of the revolutionaries carried

small arms, but some had obtained heavy machine guns, which they mounted on the numerous barricades they set up at street intersections.

4. The term *Freikorps* (denoting "free" or "voluntary") dated from 1813, when calls for volunteers went out to all Germans in the fight against Napoleon and his armies. Within the context of attempts to overthrow the Ebert interim government, Freikorps denoted freestanding, independent militia groups. The first of them assembled in mid-December under General Ludwig von Maercker. Ebert officially recognized this militia unit because it swore an oath of allegiance to the interim government.

5. Kurt Schwitters (1887–1948) was born in Hannover and is best known for his collage art, consisting of mundane and mostly two-dimensional found objects (train tickets, pieces of string, cigarette butts) and printed ephemera. He referred to such work as *Merz*, a word based on the German *Kommerz* (commerce), though he rarely had any commercial goal in mind with his creations. He later began to refer to everything he did and even to himself as "Merz." In the 1920s he branched into three dimensions and began constructing a Merzbau ("Merz building"), best described as an assemblage. He made several of them, but only a remnant of his last one survives (in Newcastle upon Tyne, in Northumberland).

6. The Prussian Cultural Ministry's subsequent appointment of Leopold Jessner (1878–1945) to head the former Prussian Royal Theater on Gendarme Square near the Royal Palace was a conscious attempt to publicly repudiate Kaiser Wilhelm II and the Hohenzollern tradition of "royal" theatrical entertainment. The kaiser had often involved himself in the theater's play selection process and even the staging of some productions. Jessner's credo was "thinking a thought through to its conclusion," which meant that his political commitments infused his artistic aims. His choice of *Maria Magdalena* is a good example. Writing in 1844, Hebbel stated in his preface to the play that dramatic art "can no longer stand outside social concerns." Jessner's active engagement as a member of the Prussian SPD later led him, when he officially took over the Berlin State Theater, to stage classics by Shakespeare, Schiller, and others in ways that would highlight social and political preoccupations, stagings that often outraged his numerous adversaries and delighted his supporters among the ruling SPD.

7. Both Liebknecht and Luxemburg became literary and media icons soon after they were murdered. Alfred Döblin's five-part novel *November 1918* features an entire volume dedicated to them, titled *Karl und Rosa*. It is perhaps the most innovative. By far the most effective cinematic treatment of Luxemburg was the 1986 movie directed by Margarethe von Trotta, starring Barbara Sukowa as Luxemburg and Otto Sander as Liebknecht. Sukowa won the Best Actress Award at the 1986 Cannes Film Festival for her portrayal of the doomed revolutionary.

8. Count Harry Kessler, *Tagebücher* (Frankfurt am Main: Insel, 1982), 107.

9. Houston Stewart Chamberlain (1855–1927) was a British-born teutonophile who became a devotee of composer Richard Wagner. He married Wagner's only daughter in 1908. Beginning with books such as *Die Grundlagen des neunzehnten Jahrhunderts* (*The Foundations of the Nineteenth Century*) in 1911, he posited the genetic superiority of the "Nordic peoples" in general and European culture as a prod-

uct of the "Aryan" peoples in particular. He received the German Military Cross in 1915, and in 1916 he became a naturalized German citizen.

10. Max Halbe (1865–1944) had been one of the Wilhelmine period's most successful playwrights. After the premiere of *Jugend* (*Youth*), his most successful play, in 1893 he created a theater in Munich called the Intimate Theater for Dramatic Experiments. He had little success in the Weimar period, however, largely because his plays were considered tediously old-fashioned and formulaic.

11. Louise Dumont (1862–1932) not only cofounded the Düsseldorf Schauspielhaus, she established its school and the monthly magazine *Die Masken* (*The Masks*), which chronicled the work she and Gustav Lindemann (1872–1960) were doing. After their forced removal as directors of the theater, Lindemann and Dumont concentrated on the school, which aimed at "the complete education of the body as an obligatory field of study." Their curriculum emphasized lessons in fencing, juggling, circus techniques, and movement, along with various kinds of dance classes. It was a training program unmatched among German acting schools at the time.

12. Sternheim's comedy *1913* was the last in his trilogy about the Maske family, whose members were largely poseurs and ruthless social climbers. His other comedies, such as *Bürger Schippel* (*Citizen Schippel*) and *Tabula rasa* (*A Blank Slate*), featured characters skilled in conformist language, using jargon common to bureaucratic "legalese" or in civil court proceedings where the petit bourgeoisie sued each other for restitution. Sternhcim (1878–1942) called these plays "Scenes from the Heroic Life of the Middle Class."

13. Ossi Oswalda (Oswalda Stäglich, 1899–1948) became known as the "German Mary Pickford" for her ability to project juvenile innocence in 40 silent films between 1916 and 1929. Like Pickford, she enjoyed enormous popularity and founded her own film company; the advent of sound in films effectively terminated her career, as it did Pickford's. Both actresses also found it difficult to play adolescents as they matured. Unlike Pickford, Oswalda died forgotten and in abject poverty.

14. Gertrud Eysoldt (1870–1950) was nearly 50 years old when she played Lulu in this production, though she had played the role 15 years earlier for Reinhardt. At that time she projected the gaunt figure of a teenaged boy with Julius Bab called "the volatile, menacing mien of a cat." Perhaps most significant was her portrayal of temptresses in ways diametrically opposed to the traditional coquette. According to Reinhardt's son Gottfried, she "reminded men of their impotence."

15. Georg Kaiser (1878–1945) was among the most prolific of German playwrights, with several plays in the repertoires of most German theaters in the 1920s. *From Morn to Midnight* was his most popular, and it remains among the most frequently performed of all Kaiser works. Other popular Kaiser plays were *Die Bürger von Calais* (*The Burghers of Calais*); *Hölle, Weg, Erde* (*Hell, Road, Earth*); and a trilogy consisting of *Die Koralle* (*The Coral*), *Gas I*, and *Gas II*.

16. Manfred Overesch and Friedrich Wilhelm Saal, *Die Weimarer Republik* (Düsseldorf: Droste, 1982), 32.

17. Kurt Götz (1888–1960) began his career while a schoolboy, performing self-written sketches for the patients of his mother's nursing home in Mainz. He later changed the spelling of his name to Curt Goetz, giving it a more international cachet.

His career both as a playwright and an actor progressed under the tutelage of director/ producer Viktor Barnowsky in Berlin. Goetz ultimately became known as "Germany's Noël Coward," writing clever fabrications of superficial middle-class dilemmas, amusing Berlin audiences with "polished manifestations of itself as a cultured and sophisticated caste." Volker Klotz, *Bürgerliches Lachtheater* (Munich: DTV, 1980), 183.

18. The Berlin Sports Palace opened in 1910. Its seating capacity of over 10 thousand made it one of the largest indoor sports arenas in the world, and it regularly featured not only bicycle races and track events (for which it was originally intended), but also ice hockey, ice skating races, indoor term sport competitions, and as noted, boxing matches. It enjoyed its prime as a boxing venue in the 1920s, when Max Schmeling was one of its most famous attractions. Promoters also occasionally transformed the Sports Palace into the world's largest movie theater. By the mid-1920s, it had become a significant venue for political rallies. The National Socialists, among many other organizations that held meetings and rallies there, were especially fond of the arena. National Socialist propaganda director Joseph Goebbels termed it "our tribunal."

19. Heinrich George (Georg August Hermann Schulz, 1893–1945) became one of the most popular actors of the 1920s. He began his career as a violinist in 1912 but developed a reputation as an actor capable of "volcanic outbursts," according to one critic. Max Reinhardt put George under contract in 1922, casting him in Bertolt Brecht's *Drums in the Night*, a play about the Spartacist uprising. George subsequently played leads in several other Brecht plays and established himself as a gifted film actor in 1927 in Fritz Lang's *Metropolis*.

20. *Die Weltbühne* (Berlin), 28 February 1919.

21. Leo Jogiches (1867–1919) was a Lithuanian national who was active in numerous Eastern European revolutionary circles prior to his arrival in Germany sometime in 1914. He and Luxemburg were lovers until 1906, and he was instrumental in founding the Spartacus movement.

22. Kurt Tucholsky (1890–1935) used several pseudonyms in his work as an essayist, poet, political pundit, and satirist. These included Ignaz Wrobel, Kaspar Hauser, and Peter Panther. He published his *Pious Songs* under the name Theobald Tiger. In December 1918, he became editor of the literary magazine *Ulk* (roughly translated as "Prankster"), delivered with Sunday editions of the *Berliner Tageblatt*. As a teenager he had published his initial efforts in *Ulk*. He moved to Paris in 1924, and in 1926 he briefly took over the editorship of *Die Weltbühne* (*The World Stage*). He relinquished that position soon thereafter and returned to reporting and contributing essays to it and other Berlin publications, in which his frequent targets were the German justice system, the military, and the burgeoning National Socialist Party. He moved to Sweden in 1930, where he committed suicide in 1935. The Swedish PEN Society established its Tucholsky Award in 1984, granted to a writer or publisher who has experienced persecution or is in exile.

23. Alfons Paquet (1881–1944) was primarily a journalist, but his plays (primarily in the Berlin productions of Piscator) attracted sensational publicity. He was born to a Baptist family in the Rhineland, but as an adult he embraced the Quaker faith and

became a confirmed pacifist. His religious faith took him frequently to the United States, and his 1925 book of poems, *Hymnen*, is a moving testimony of his affection for America. He was named to the Prussian Academy of the Arts in 1932 and in the same year received the City of Frankfurt am Main's Goethe Prize.

24. The Bauhaus quickly became an influential force in many areas of aesthetic education, including architecture, industrial design, typography, the graphic arts, sculpture, and even painting. It was among the first such institutions with a distinctly modernist curriculum that espoused abstraction, functionality, and self-referentiality. Many of the well-known Bauhaus modernist principles ironically had their roots in the 19th-century arts and crafts movement, which posited the idea that distinctions between practical craftsmanship and the aesthetics of fine arts were arbitrary. The Bauhaus curriculum gave such ideas a political slant by insisting that modern art and architecture should contribute to social progress. The Bauhaus moved from Weimar to a Dessau campus in 1926, composed of rectilinear glass and concrete structures that bespoke practices associated with the school. Bauhaus principles became most authoritative in the United States, largely because Bauhaus founder Walter Gropius (1883–1969) led Harvard University's architecture faculty from 1938 to 1952.

25. Quoted in Peter Gay, *Weimar Culture* (New York: Harper and Row, 1970), 15.

26. President Woodrow Wilson's speech on 8 January 1918, before the U.S. Congress had outlined "Fourteen Points" as the basis for peace in Europe at the conclusion of World War I. There seemed to be general agreement among the Allies at the time that the Fourteen Points would be implemented. The Germans mistakenly took the Fourteen Points for Allied policy and had signed an armistice on 9 November 1918, with the Allies on that basis. In the end, only three of Wilson's points were implemented.

27. Rudolf Steiner (1861–1925) was a Goethe scholar who became best known and widely influential as a spiritualist. He founded an esoteric discipline called anthroposophy, which he described as "a path of knowledge to guide the spiritual in the human being to the spiritual in the universe." He described anthroposophists as individuals who "experience as an essential need, certain questions on the nature of the human being and the universe, just as one experiences hunger and thirst." He published several books on the subject, the most influential of which was *Die Philosophie der Freiheit* (*The Philosophy of Freedom*, 1894).

28. The work of Franz Arnold (1878–1960) and Ernst Bach (1876–1929) became known as "the firm of Arnold and Bach" during the 1920s, turning out hit plays season after season. In every season except 1923–1924, their plays were usually the most often performed of all playwrights in any genre. Among their stupendously successful comedies were *Der keusche Lebemann* (*The Reluctant Playboy*, 1921), *Der kühne Schwimmer* (*The Intrepid Swimmer*, 1922), *Die vertagte Nacht* (*The Night of the Following Day*, 1923), *Der wahre Jakob* (*The Genuine Jacob*, 1924), *Stöpsel* (1926), *Hurra—ein Junge!* (*Hurray—It's a Boy!* 1927), *Unter Geschäftsaussicht* (*Business Looks Good*, 1928), and *Week-end im Paradies* (*Weekend in Paradise*, 1929).

29. Asta Nielsen (1881–1972) was a Danish actress who had career ambitions for the stage in Copenhagen but whose brilliance in German films, beginning in 1910,

made her arguably the first German movie star. She was known as "the silent muse," not because the films were themselves silent but for her eschewal of the overwrought histrionics common among her contemporaries.

30. This film was among the first in Germany to make dramatic use of a train wreck. Porten (1890–1960) plays the young wife of a professor, with whom she has a young daughter. She employs the ruse of a train journey to spend the night with her young lover. During the night, the train derails and several people are killed. Everyone presumes the young wife is among the dead, and she cannot return home without revealing here true whereabouts on the fateful night. She becomes a performer in a variety show, becomes addicted to cocaine, longs to see her daughter, and commits suicide.

31. This movie certainly qualifies as an artistic oddity, as did its leading actor, Ferdinand Bonn (1861–1933). It features the historical incident in which a homeless cobbler's mastery of military jargon prompted every German he met to knuckle under in servile obedience. Newspapers called him the "Captain of Köpenick," named for the Berlin suburb where he successfully commandeered an infantry platoon to assist in his robbery of a bank. Kaiser Wilhelm II found the episode hilarious, noting that a "Captain of Köpenick" could emerge only in Germany. Bonn played both Kaiser and Captain in the film. In the 1890s, Bonn was the first German Sherlock Holmes, and in 1905 he opened Ferdinand Bonn's Berliner Theater, where Kaiser Wilhelm II came to see him in the German premiere of *The Hound of the Baskervilles*.

32. Max Landa (Max Landau, 1880–1933) originally wanted a career in the legitimate theater, but the only jobs he could find were with third-rate touring companies. His film work began in 1915, and when he initiated the detective series (of which *Das Derby* was one of 12 films) with director E. A. Dupont, his acting career prospered greatly.

1920

JANUARY

1 Two periodicals debut: *Der Ararat*, a monthly journal dedicated to modern and contemporary art, edited by Hans Goltz and published in Munich; and *Das Tage-Buch*, a weekly magazine covering art and politics in Germany, edited by Stephan Grossmann and published in Berlin.

The Berlin Workers' Council for Art opens its first workers' art exhibition.

2 The detective film *Die Würger der Welt* (*World by the Throat*), directed by E. A. Dupont and starring Max Landa and Hanni Weisse, premieres in Berlin.

Cassirer Press publishes *Unser Weg* (*Our Path*) *1920*, with original woodcuts by Ernst Barlach. Director of the Stuttgart Art Collection Edwin Redslob is named director of fine arts in the Reich Home Office, a post he holds until 1933. Dr. Cora Berliner is named councillor in the Reich Finance Ministry, the first woman to hold such a post in German history.

3 The first issue of the weekly *Völkischer Beobachter* (*Popular Observer*, though the name has been translated as *Ethnic Observer* and sometimes *Racial Observer*) is published in Munich. The Dadaist weekly *Die Pleite* (*Bankrupt*) is banned from future publication.

4 S. Fischer Press publishes *Herr und Hund* (*A Man and His Dog*) and *Gesang vom Kindchen* (*Song of the Little Child*), by Thomas Mann. Martin Breslauer publishes the first Gerhart Hauptmann bibliography.

5 *Pfarrhauskomödie* (*Parish House Comedy*), by Heinrich Lautensack and starring Lucie Höflich and Ilka Grüning, premieres at the Kleines Theater Berlin. Catholic leaders denounce it as "insulting."

Anton Drexler becomes chairman of the German Workers' Party (DAP), headquartered in Munich; Adolf Hitler is named director of propaganda.

6 The film drama *Verlorene Töchter, 3: Die Menschen nennen es Liebe* (*Lost Daughters, Part 3: People Call It Love*), directed by William Kahn and starring Manja Tzatscheschewa and Karl Falkenberg, premieres in Berlin.

8 The comedy *Die Kokotte Phyllis* (*Phyllis the Coquette*), by C. P. van Rossem, premieres at the Schwerin Regional Theater.

9 The horror film *Der heulende Wolf* (*The Howling Wolf*), directed by Leo Lasko and starring Carl Auen and Meinhart Maur, premieres in Berlin. The science fiction film *Nachtgestalten* (*Creatures of the Night*), directed by Richard Oswald and starring Paul Wegener and Erna Morena, also premieres in Berlin.[1]

10 A drama about the Russian Revolution, *Das letzte Gericht* (*The Final Judgment*), by Julius Becker, premieres at the Darmstadt Regional Theater.

The Treaty of Versailles goes into effect, separating many cities and territories from German territorial sovereignty; Rhineland territories and cities remain German but fall under Allied High Command occupation and jurisdiction. German prisoners of war in French custody are released.

11 The Tribunal Theater in Königsberg, founded by Erwin Piscator and dedicated to presenting modernist or overtly political plays, stages Strindberg's *The Ghost Sonata*.

13 Street protests in Berlin leave 42 dead and scores wounded; the newspapers of the Communist Party, *Red Flag*, and the USPD, *Freedom*, are ordered closed until the end of February.

Catholic protestors interrupt performances of *Pfarrhauskomödie* (*Parish House Comedy*) in Berlin, Hannover, and Frankfurt am Main.

14 The drama *Unschuld* (*Innocent*), by Fritz Droop, premieres at the Hannover State Theater. The tragedy *Das Paradies* (*Paradise*), by Hans José Rehfisch, premieres at the Halle State Theater. The comedy film *Das Ski-Girl*, directed by Adolf Engl and starring Lia Ley and Hans Albrecht, premieres in Munich.

Bishop Karl Josef Schulte is named archbishop of Cologne.

16 Count Anton Arco-Valley is sentenced to death by hanging for the murder of Bavarian Minister-President Kurt Eisner; he is sent to Landsberg Prison to await execution.[2]

17 Max Reinhardt stages *Hamlet* at the Grosses Schauspielhaus, with Alexander Moissi in the title role.

20 *Hölle-Weg-Erde* (*Hell-Road-Earth*), by Georg Kaiser, directed by Viktor Barnowsky and starring Tilla Durieux and Eugen Klöpfer, premieres in Berlin.

The opera *Die Schatzgräber* (*The Treasure-Seekers*), by Franz Schreker, premieres in Frankfurt am Main.

25 The historical film *Satanas* (*Satanas, the Fallen Angel*), directed by F. W. Murnau, with Fritz Kortner as Pharaoh Amenhotep, Margit Barnay as his daughter, Nouri, and Ernst Hofmann as Jorab the Shepherd, premieres in Berlin. The detective film *Die Schlange mit dem Mädchenkopf* (*The Snake with the Girl's Head*), directed by Rudolf Walther-Fein and starring Hans Albers,[3] Josef Reithofer, and Ria Ende, premieres in Berlin.

The operetta *Die kleine Hoheit* (*Her Little Highness*), by Martin Knopf, premieres at the Neues Operettenhaus in Berlin.

27 The drama *Scapa Flow*, by Reinhard Goering, directed by Richard Weichert, premieres at the Frankfurt am Main City Theater.

29 The expressionist drama *Der gerettete Alkibiades* (*Alcibiades Saved*), by Georg Kaiser, premieres at the Munich Residenz Theater. The historical drama *Der Kronpriz* (*The Crown Prince*), by Hermann von Boetticher, premieres at the Berlin State Theater.

The drama *Indiphodi*, by Gerhart Hauptmann, is published in the monthly magazine *Die neue Rundschau.*

30 The comedy *Exzellenz*, by Heinrich Schmitt, premieres at the Deutsches Schauspielhaus in Hamburg.

The comedy film *Lo, die Kokotte* (*Lola, the Coquette*), directed by William Karfiol and starring Hedy Ury (in the title role) and Emil Sondermann, premieres in Berlin. The film melodrama *Die Liebe einer Sklavin* (*The Love of a Slave*), directed by Eugen Illés and starring Esther Carena, also premieres in Berlin. *Prinzesschen* (*The Little Princess*), directed by Alfred Halm and starring Lotte Neumann and Adolf Klein, also premieres in Berlin.

31 Rowohlt Press publishes *Menschheitsdämmerung* (*Twilight of Mankind*), an extensive volume of expressionist poetry edited by Kurt Pinthus, in Berlin.

FEBRUARY

3 An exhibition of sculptures by Wilhelm Lehmbruck opens at the Cassirer Gallery in Berlin.

Wilhelm Furtwängler agrees to present a ten-symphony season at the Berlin State Opera featuring the company's much-acclaimed orchestra, creating an unprecedented competition with the Berlin Symphony Orchestra.

The mystery film *Angelo, das Mysterium des Schlosses* (*Angelo, the Enigma of the Castle*), directed by Robert Leffler and starring Ernst Dernburg and Lina Salten, premieres in Berlin.

4 Albert Einstein begins a series of lectures on movement and gravitational balance at the Volkshochschule (Communal University) in Berlin.

5 Berlin police officials and government leaders hold open discussions about the growing problem of theater performance disruptions in the city.

6 Four films premiere in Berlin: the crime film *Die Spinnen* (*The Spiders*), directed by Fritz Lang and starring Reiner Steiner and Thea Zander; the comedy *Die Wohningsnot* (*The Housing Shortage*), directed by Ernst Lubitsch and starring Ossi Oswalda and Victor Janson; the detective film *Erpresst* (*Blackmailed*), directed by Carl Boese and starring Gertrud Welcker and Ernst Deutsch; and the melodrama *Das Lied der Tränen* (*The Song of Tears*), directed by Fritz Bernhardt and starring Maria Widal and Max Wogritsch.

8 The third exhibition in Hannover of Kurt Schwitters's collage works is held, and prints of his collages go on sale for the first time at the exhibition. In Berlin, the initial sale of his "Merz Pictures" is made. Several critics write that "his works belong in a garbage can," and Schwitters notes that most of the materials in his works initially came from garbage cans.

Kurt Wolff Press publishes Ruth Schaumann's first volume of lyric poetry, *Die Kathedrale* (*The Cathedral*).[4]

12 The operetta *Der letzte Walzer* (*The Last Waltz*), by Oscar Strauss, starring Fritzi Massary, premieres at the Berliner Theater.

13 Two films premiere in Berlin: the romance *Die Marchese d'Armiani* (*The Marquise of Arminiani*), directed by Alfred Halm, with Pola Negri in the title role; and the comedy *Mascotte*, directed by Felix Basch and starring Grete Freund and Felix Basch.

14 Max Reinhardt stages *Dantons Tod* (*Danton's Death*), by Romain Rolland, at the Grosses Schauspielhaus in Berlin, with a cast of hundreds, featuring Paul Wegener in the title role and Werner Krauss as Robespierre. The drama *Das grüne Haus* (*The Green House*), by Herbert Eulenberg, premieres in Meiningen.

The film drama *Wie das Schicksal spielt* (*The Wiles of Fate*), directed by Paul von Woringen and starring Theodor Burghardt and Hilde Wolter, premieres in Berlin.

15 The drama *Segen des Irrtums* (*The Blessing of Error*), by Ludwig Gagnhofer, premieres at the Hanau City Theater.

The opera *Der Fremde* (*The Stranger*), by Hugo Kaun,[5] premieres at the Dresden State Opera.

An exhibition of paintings, drawings, theater designs, and porcelain works by Paul Scheurich (1883–1945) opens at the Stuttgart Museum of Applied Art.

16 Alexander Granach[6] plays Shylock in *The Merchant of Venice* at the Munich Schauspielhaus; he becomes identified with the role in numerous productions throughout the 1920s.

17 The tragicomedy *Die Gabe Gottes* (*The Gift of God*), by Mortiz Goldstein and starring Albert and Else Bassermann, premieres at the Berlin State Theater.

23 The expressionist drama *Hexensabbath* (*Witches' Sabbath*), by Hermann Boetticher, premieres at the Weimar National Theater.

24 In Munich's Hofbräuhaus tavern, members of the German Workers' Party (DAP) announce a new name for their organization, the National Socialist German Workers' Party (NSDAP); their spokesman, Adolf Hitler, later presents the party's platform at a public gathering.

25 Dada on tour reaches Leipzig, where Richard Huelsenbeck and Raoul Hausmann entertain more than 2,000.

The National Gallery in Berlin opens a Christian Rohlffs exhibition in honor of the painter's 70th birthday .

27 The expressionist film *Das Kabinett des Dr. Caligari* premieres in Berlin and creates a sensation among critics and audiences. It is directed by Robert Wiene and stars Werner Krauss (in the title role), Conrad Veidt, Friedrich Feher, Lil Dagover, and Hans Heinrich von Twardowski. Several reviews and essays during the following weeks agree that German film "has become an art form."

28 The drama *Godiva*, by Hans Franck, premieres at the Düsseldorf Schauspielhaus.

The film *Der Reigen* (*La Ronde*), loosely based on the controversial play by Arthur Schnitzler and starring Asta Nielsen, Conrad Veidt, and Eduard von Winterstein, premieres.

29 Defense Minister Noske announces the dissolution of several Freikorps militias instrumental in terminating the Spartacus movement.

MARCH

1 Arthur Nickisch celebrates his 25th year as conductor of the Berlin Philharmonic with a concert featuring his son as piano soloist with the orchestra. The Freie Volksoper opens in Berlin.

4 The Kleist Society is established in Berlin; its officers include Gerhart Hauptmann, Ricarda Huch, Max Liebermann, and Hans Pfitzner.

6 The comedy *Der Herr Minister*, by Paul Schirmer, premieres at the Berlin Komödienhaus.

Prince Albrecht Joachim of Prussia attacks members of the French Allied Commission at dinner in the Hotel Adlon in Berlin; the German government issues an official apology and arrests Prince Albrecht.

7 A "futuristic" drawing by Josef Raderz displayed in the window of the Goltz Gallery in Munich ignites a public uproar against the drawing's perceived pornographic tendencies.

9 *Kohlhiesels Töchter* (*Kohlhiesel's Daughters*), an adaptation of Shakespeare's *The Taming of the Shrew* directed by Ernst Lubitsch and starring Emil Jannings and Henny Porten as a rustic Petruchio and Katherine, premieres in Berlin.

10 General Walther von Lüttwitz refuses to disband his Freikorps militia battalions as ordered by Defense Minister Noske; he furthermore demands a new Reichstag election and a popularly elected Reich president.

11 General von Lüttwitz is relieved of his authority over all militias.

12 The drama *Der ewige Mensch*, by Alfred Brust, premieres at the Halberstadt City Theater. The drama *Der Marquis von Keith* (*The Marquis of Keith*), by Frank Wedekind, directed by Leopold Jessner, and starring Fritz Kortner and Tilla Durieux, premieres at the Berlin State Theater.

Troops loyal to General von Lüttwitz and other militia units gather near Berlin for a planned Putsch (takeover) of the national government.

13 With former chairman of the Fatherland Party Wolfgang Kapp, troops under the command of General von Lüttwitz begin a takeover of the German government; Reichstag members and the presidential cabinet flee Berlin and gather in Dresden.

14 The Kapp Putsch is condemned in newspapers and in public proclamations from political parties. A general strike is declared by many labor unions in protest against the takeover.

15 Ebert, the government ministers, and members of the Reichstag gather in Stuttgart to set up an organized resistance to Kapp and Lüttwitz. The general strike spreads throughout Germany, and armed clashes occur among militia units in Hannover, Kiel, Schwerin, Leipzig, Dortmund, Duisburg, and Essen.

The adventure film *Ferreol ein Kampf zwichen Liebe und Pflicht* (*Ferreol: A Struggle between Love and Duty*), directed by Franz Hofer and starring Max Laurence and Margit Barnay, premieres in Berlin.

16 All theaters, concert halls, museums, and movie houses in Berlin are closed. Most others in German cities likewise close.

17 The takeover of the government ends as Kapp flees to Sweden and von Lüttwitz to Austria. Most strikes are called off, and government officials begin to make their way back to Berlin.

18 Defense Minister Gustav Noske is forced to resign.

19 Theater and music performances resume throughout the country; movie houses reopen and orchestra concerts resume. An exhibition of graphics by Max Beckmann opens in Darmstadt.

25 A national appeals court upholds the government decision to confiscate the property of participants in the recent Putsch.

26 The film drama *Die Stimme* (*The Voice*), directed by Adolf Gärtner and starring Else and Albert Bassermann, premieres in Berlin.

The drama *Die Schwestern* (*The Sisters*), by Arthur Schnitzler, premieres at the Vienna Burgtheater.

27 The drama *Hirtenlied* (*Pastoral*), by Gerhart Hauptmann, premieres at the Weimar National Theater.

28 The "dramatic fantasy" *Der weisse Heiland* (*The White Redeemer*), by Gerhart Hauptmann, directed by Karlheinz Martin and starring Alexander Moissi and Emil Jannings, premieres at the Grosses Schauspielhaus in Berlin. The dramatic fragment *Woyzeck* by Georg Büchner, directed by Viktor Barnowsky, with Eugen Klöpfer in the title role, is revived at the Lessing Theater in Berlin.

The comedy film *Romeo und Julia im Schnee* (*Romeo and Juliet in the Snow*), directed by Ernst Lubitsch and starring Lotte Neumann and Gustac von Wangenheim, premieres in Berlin.

29 New defense minister Otto Gessler cashiers several army generals whose loyalty to the national government he deems doubtful.

30 The drama *Gaukler, Tod, Juwelier* (*Impostor, Death, Jeweler*) premieres at the Düsseldorf Schauspielhaus.

31 Police confiscate drawings by Bauhaus professor Walter Klemm, titled *Erbsünde* (*Original Suns*).

APRIL

1 *Glanz und Elend der Kurtisanen* (*Splendor and Misery of the Courtesans*), directed by Conrad Wiene and starring Louis Ralph and Marietta Palto, premieres in Berlin. The comedy *Das Lied der Liebe* (*The Song of Love*), by Wismar Rosendahl, premieres at the Rose Theater in Berlin.

2 The film drama *Können Gedanken töten?* (*Can Thoughts Kill?*), directed by Alfred Tostary and starring Käthe Dorsch and Olga Engl, premieres in Berlin. *Die Tänzerin der Barbarina* (*Barbarina the Dancer*), based on the novel by Adolf Paul, directed by Carl Boese, and starring George de Georgetti, Franz Gross, Grete Hollmann, and Otto Gebühr, premieres in Frankfurt am Main.[7]

Wilhelm Furtwängler conducts Beethoven's Third Symphony (*Eroica*) with the State Opera of Berlin orchestra, to wildly enthusiastic acclaim by critics.

3 *Dame Kobold*, by Hugo von Hofmannsthal, based on Calderon de la Braca's comedy *La dama duende*, directed by Max Reinhardt, premieres at the Deutsches Theater in Berlin; the production helps to solidify groundwork for the revival of the Salzburg Festival. The comedy *Zwangseinquartierung* (*Forced Emergency Housing*), by Franz Arnold and Ernst Bach, premieres at the Lustspielhaus in Berlin; it becomes the most frequently performed play during the 1919–1920 and 1920–1921 seasons.

4 The 20th-century treatment of the Eastertide passion play *Vom Tode und von der Auferstehung des Herrn* (*The Death and Resurrection of the Lord*), by Franz Herwig, premieres at the Weimar National Theater.

The comedy film *Die Lissy vom Tietz* (*Lizzy from Tietz's Department Store*), directed by Adolf Engl and starring Lia Ley and Joe Stöcke, premieres in Munich. *Rafaelo, das Mysterium von Kopenhagen* (*Rafaelo, the Mystery of Copenhagen*), directed by Wolfgang Neff and starring Oskar Marion and Trude Hoffmann, premieres in Berlin.

6 Waldemar Bonsels's novel *Indienfahrt* (*India Journey*) reaches the top of most best-seller lists; it has more than 300 new printings during the 1920s.

8 Kiepenheuer Press publishes the nonfiction book *Die Heimsuchung* (*Searching for Home*), by Hermann Kasack; the drama *Der König* (*The King*), by Hanns Johst; and the novel *Der junge Goedeschal* (*Young Mr. Goedeschal*), by Hans Fallada.

9 The fantasy film *Ewiger Strom* (*The Eternal River*), directed by Johannes Guter and starring Werner Krauss and Marija Leiko, premieres in Berlin.

12 The drama *Der Geschlagene* (*The Defeated*), by Wilhelm Schmidtbonn, premieres at the Deutsches Schauspielhaus in Hamburg.

13 The drama *Stella*, by Johann Wolfgang Goethe, directed by Max Reinhardt and starring Agnes Straub and Helene Thimig, is revived at the Deutsches Theater in Berlin.

15 Violin virtuoso Georg Kuhlenkampf plays works by Beethoven and Schubert with the Berlin Philharmonic.

18 Karlheinz Martin stages *Antigone*, by Sophocles, at the Grosses Schauspielhaus in Berlin, with Gertrud Eysoldt in the title role and Emil Jannings as Creon, with scores of performers in the chorus.

19 Erich Mühsam completes his drama *Judas* in his prison cell at the Ansbach Penitentiary. Kurt Wolff Press publishes Mühsam's volume of poetry, *Brennende Erde* (*Burning Earth*).

20 The Dada Exhibition in Cologne (Dada Early Spring) is shut down by the police; protests force Cologne police to reopen the exhibition, which Richard Huelsenbeck later documents in his *Dada siegt!* (*Dada Wins!*).

21 The tragedy *Himmel und Hölle* (*Heaven and Hell*), by Paul Kornfeld, directed by Ludwig Berger and starring Agnes Straub and Werner Krauss, premieres at the Deutsches Theater in Berlin.

The film *Die Brüder Karamasoff*, based on Fyodor Dostoevsky's novel *The Brothers Karamazov*, directed by Carl Forelich, with Werkner Krauss as Karamazov, Berhard Goetke as Ivan, Emil Jannigs as Dimitri, and Hermann Thimig as Alexei, premieres in Berlin.

22 The tragedy *Alkestis* (*Alcestis*), by Robert Prechtel, based on Euripides's satyr play, premieres at the Berlin State Theater. The comedy *Der Lump* (*The Good-for-Nothing*), by Adolf Wittmack, premieres at the Hannover Deutsches Theater.

24 The first-ever exhibition of drawings by George Grosz opens in Munich.

Mrs. Warren's Profession, by George Bernard Shaw, directed by Viktor Barnowsky, is revived at the Lessing Theater in Berlin. The comedy *Der*

Trostpreis (*The Consolation Prize*), by Otto Stockhausen, premieres at the Darmstadt Regional Theater.

27 The Prussian Parliament creates "Greater Berlin," incorporating all of the city's suburbs into a metropolis covering 339 square miles, with 3.8 million inhabitants.

28 The opera *Schirin und Gertaude*, by Paul Graener, premieres at the Dresden State Opera.

30 The largest modern painting exhibition in Berlin's history opens in galleries along the city's Kufürstendamm Boulevard; artists represented include Heinrich Campendonk, August Macke, Conrad Felixmüller, Max Liebermann, Erich Heckel, Franz Marc, Marc Chagall, Ewald Mataré, Paula Modersohn, Emil Orlik, Max Slevogt, and many others.

MAY

1 Architect Hans Poelzig assumes directorship of the architecture studio at the Berlin University of Fine Arts.

3 The film melodrama *Das Mädchen aus der Ackerstrasse* (*The Girl from Acker Strasse*), directed by Reinhold Schünzel and starring Lilly Flohr and Otto Gebühr, premieres in Berlin.

4 The drama *Der junge Mensch*, by Hanns Johst, premieres at the Tribüne Theater in Berlin.

5 Three film melodramas premiere in Berlin: *Die Söhne des Grafen Dossy* (*The Sons of Count Dossy*), directed by Adolf Gärtner and starring Albert and Else Bassermann; *Johannes Goth*, directed by Karl Gerhardt and starring Carola Toelle and Werner Krauss; and *Das grosse Licht* (*The Great Light*), directed by Hanna Henning[8] and starring Emil Jannings and Frida Richard.

7 The drama *Die Nachtwandler* (*The Somnambulists*), by Klabund, premieres at the Hannover State Theater.

12 The revised national film censorship law goes into effect.[9]

15 The national government disbands all Freikorps paramilitary units. The Allgemeiner Studenteausschuss (AstA), the national organization of university students, is formed in Dresden. The Roman Catholic monthly *Hochland* describes cultural pessimist Oswald Spengler as merely the latest "meteor streaking across the skies of trendy philosophy."

The comedy film *Die graue Elster* (*The Gray Magpie*), directed by Max Obal and starring Ernst Reicher and Grete Jacobsen, premieres in Munich.

17 The comedy film *Der Knabe Eros* (*The Boy Cupid*), directed by Paul Legband and starring Erhard Siedel and Lia Borré, premieres in Berlin.

19 An exhibition of works by artisans along with expressionist paintings, sculptures, drawing, lithographs from the Mathildenhöhe Artists' Colony opens in Darmstadt.

20 The historical drama *Der König* (about the "mad king of Bavaria," Ludwig II), by Hanns Johst, premieres at the Dresden State Theater.[10]

21 President Ebert opens the Greater Berlin Art Exhibition, featuring works by artists of numerous styles, treatments, tastes, and political persuasions, hoping to signal the government's openness to all artistic endeavor.

22 The pacifist drama *Die Gewaltlosen* (*Without Violence*), by Ludwig Rubiner, premieres at the Neues Volkstheater in Berlin.

25 The tragedy *Fuhrmann Henschel* (*Teamster Henschel*),[11] by Gerhart Hauptmann, starring Lucie Höflich, is revived at the Berlin State Theater.

28 Max Reinhardt stages Shakespeare's *Julius Caesar* at the Grosses Schauspielhaus, with Werner Krauss in the title role and scores of extras as the Roman mob.

JUNE

2 The scenario *Die Passion* (*The Passion*), by Wilhelm Schmidtbonn, directed by Hermine Körner, premieres at the Munich Künstlertheater.

3 The expressionist drama *Platz* (*Place*), by Fritz von Unruh, directed by Gustav Hartung and starring Heinrich George and Gerda Müller, premieres at the Frankfurt am Main City Theater. The comedy *Die Köpfe des Hydra* (*The Heads of the Hydra*), by Bernhard Rehse, premieres at the Dresden State Theater.

5 The first nationwide Dada exhibition opens at the Berlin International Trade Fair.

10 The film melodrama *Der Gefangene: Sklaven des XX. Jahrhunderts* (*The Prisoner: Slaves of the 20th Century*), directed by Carl Heinz Wolff and starring Harry Liedtke and Käthe Dorsch, premieres in Berlin.

11 The police lift a ban on the comedy *Hahenkampf* (*Cockfight*), by Heinrich Lautensack, allowing its premiere at the Munich Kammerspiele.

The detective film *Die Augen als Ankläger* (*The Eyes as the Acuser*), directed by Fritz Bernhardt and starring Evi Eva and Henrich Schroth, premieres in Berlin.

13 The detective film *Das ausgeschnittene Gesicht* (*The Face Removed*), directed by Franz Seitz and starring Anton Ernst Rückert and Carla Ferra, premieres in Munich.

14 The death of sociologist and political economist Max Weber prompts editorials and essays in dozens of German newspapers about his influence, especially his most famous work, *Die protestantische Ethik und der Geist des Kapitalismus* (*The Protestant Ethic and the Spirit of Capitalism*), published in 1904. Weber was a member of the constitution-writing committee at the National Assembly in Weimar.

19 Actress Elisabeth Bergner[12] debuts at the Munich Kammerspiele in a new production of Shakespeare's *A Midsummer Night's Dream*.

24 The biopic *Die Tragödie eines Grossen* (about the Dutch painter Rembrandt van Rijn), directed by Aurthur Günsburg, with Carl de Vogt as Rembrandt and Sybil Morel as his wife Saskia, premieres in Berlin.

26 The opera *Rodelinde*, by Georg Friedrich Händel, makes its German premiere at the Göttingen City Theater, laying the groundwork for the Händel Festival in that university town and for a Händel revival throughout Germany.

The thriller film *Das Geheimnis der Mitternachtstude* (*The Secret of the Midnight Hour*), directed by Wolfgang Neff and starring Harry Frank and Trude Hoffmann, premieres in Berlin.

30 Carl von Ossietzky (1889–1938), a future Nobel Peace Prize winner, is named editor of the newspaper *Berliner Volkszeitung*.

JULY

2 Two films premiere in Berlin: the adventure film *Brigantenliebe* (*The Love of a Thief*), directed by Martin Hartwig and starring Emil Rameau and Tilly Wötzel; and the comedy *Die Frau im Doktorhut* (*The Woman in Doctor's Garb*), directed by Rudolf Biebrach and starring Lotte Neumann and Felix Basch.

6 The comedy film *Aus den Akten einer anständigen Frau* (*From the Files of a Respectable Woman*), directed by Franz Hofer and starring Margit Barnay and Fred Immler, premieres in Berlin.

8 The fantasy film *Der Bucklige und die Tänzerin* (*The Hunchback and the Dancer*), directed by F. W. Murnau and starring Sascha Gura and John Gottow, premieres in Berlin.

The operetta *Die Strohwitwe* (*The Grass Widow*), by Leo Blech, premieres at the Berlin State Theater.

9 Members of the Thuringian Provincial Legislature attack the Bauhaus School and its modernist guiding principles, threatening to cut off funding.

The film drama *Niemand weiss es* (*Nobody Knows*), directed by Lupu Pick and starring Lupu Pick and Eduard Rothauser, premieres in Berlin.

14 Mobs gather at the French embassy in Berlin on Bastille Day and tear down the French flag; the German government issues an official apology and posts a military guard around the embassy.

15 Theologian Fredrich Heiler's *Das Wesen des Katholizismus* (*The Essentials of Catholicism*) is published in Munich; Heiler (1892–1967) had earlier published *Jesus and Socialism* in an attempt to foster an ecumenical movement in Germany.

The film drama *Der Feuerreiter* (*The Fire Rider*), directed by Erik Lund and starring Bruno Kaster and Käte Haack, premieres in Berlin.

17 The adventure film *Die Luftpiraten* (*The Air Pirates*), directed by Harry Piel and starring Harry Piel and Paula Barra, premieres in Berlin.

The Ministry of the Interior creates a commission to establish a Reich History Archive in Potsdam; Prince Joachim, youngest son of former German Kaiser Wilhelm II, commits suicide in Potsdam.

22 The tragedy *Die Wächter unter den Galgen* (*The Guards under the Gallows*), by Leo Weismantel, directed by Saladin Schmitt,[13] premieres at the Bochum City Theater.

30 Two films premiere in Berlin: *Figaros Hochzeit* (*The Marriage of Figaro*), directed by Max Mack, with Alexander Moissi as Figaro, Eduard von Winterstein as Count Almaviva, and Johanna Mund as Figaro's intended bride; *Kurfürstendamm*, directed by Richard Oswald, starring Asta Nielsen and Conrad Veidt, and accompanied by Hans May on piano, playing music he composed specifically for the film.

31 Hoffmann and Campe Press publishes *Golgatha*, by Paul Zech.

AUGUST

3 The film drama *Sieger Tod* (*Death the Victor*), directed by Nils Chrisander and starring Uschi Elleot and Werner Krauss, premieres in Berlin.

4 The film drama *Die goldene Krone* (*The Golden Crown*), directed by Alfred Halm and starring Hugo Pahlke and Maria Reisenhofer, premieres in Berlin.

8 The comedy *Neunzehn-hundert-neunzehn* (*Nineteen-Hundred-Nineteen*), by Toni Impekoven[14] and Carl Mathern, premieres at the Frankfurt City Theater.

12 The film melodrama *Der weisse Pfau* (*The White Peacock*), directed by E. A. Dupont and starring Hans Mierendorff and Grit Hegesa, premieres in Berlin. The peacock of the title refers to the character Lord Cross (Mierendorff), who falls in love with a gypsy dancer (Helgesa) at a London variety show. He marries her and hopes his peers will overcome their racial prejudice against her. When his peers reject her, she leaves him and returns "to her own kind" somewhere in Eastern Europe.

13 Munich newspapers carry articles about the National Socialist German Workers' Party (NSDAP) and its leading spokesman, Adolf Hitler. His speech at the Munich Hofbräuhaus, "Why We Are Anti-Semites," attracts large crowds.[15]

22 Max Reinhardt revives the Salzburg Festival with a new production of *Everymann*, by Hugo von Hoffmansthal, on the city's Cathedral Square. Alexander Moissi plays the title role, with Werner Krauss as Death.

26 The horror film *Der Januskopf* (*The Split Personality*), based on Robert Louis Stevenson's novel *Dr. Jekyll and Mr. Hyde*. directed by F. W. Murnau, premieres in Berlin, with Conrad Veidt in the title role and Bela Lugosi as his butler.

28 The New Goethe Society is founded in Berlin.

SEPTEMBER

1 The exotic film *Sumurun*, directed by Ernst Lubitsch and starring Pola Negri and Paul Wegener, premieres in Berlin.

2 The drama *Reine Farbe* (*Pure Colors*), by Julius Meier-Graefe, premieres at the Dresden State Theater.

The film drama *Genuine*, directed by Robert Wiene and starring Fern Andra and Hans-Heirich von Twardowski, premieres in Berlin.

3 The drama *Die Freundin* (*The Girlfriend*), by Hermann Sudermann, with Tilla Durieux in the title role, premieres at the Residenz Theater in Berlin. The operetta *Wenn die Liebe erwacht* (*When Love Awakens*), by Eduard Künneke, premieres at the Theater am Nollendorfplatz in Berlin.

Two films premiere: the science fiction film *Algol*, directed by Hans Werckermeister and starring Emil Jannings and Hanna Ralph; and the historical biopic *Katharine die Grosse* (*Catherine the Great*), directed by Reinhold Schünzel, with Lucie Höflich in the title role and Gertrud de Lalsky as Empress Elizabeth.

10 Two films premiere in Berlin: the fantasy *Das fliegende Auto* (*The Flying Car*), directed by Harry Piel and starring Piel and Tilly Thönnesen; and the trilogy *Drei Masken* (*Three Masks*), directed by William Wauer and starring Albert and Else Bassermann. The trilogy consists of three films: *Mister Rex*, about a man who is cuckolded by his wife; *Varieté*, about an aging clown; and *Trappistenkloster* (*The Trappist Monastery*), about an old monk and his temptations.

14 The first congress of the Christian Art League meets in Würzburg.

18 The film melodrama *Anständige Frauen* (*Respectable Women*), directed by Carl Wilhelm and starring Ressel Orla and Olga Limburg, premieres in Berlin.

23 The Western *Das Gesetz der Wüste* (*The Law of the Desert*), directed by Friedrich Zelnik and starring Bernhard Goetzke and Emil Mamelok, premieres in Berlin.

24 The detective film *Abend-Nacht-Morgen* (*Evening-Night-Morning*), directed by F. W. Murnau and starring Conrad Veidt and Gertrud Welcker, premieres in Berlin.

25 The operetta *Der Geiger von Lugano* (*The Fiddler from Lugano*), by Jean Gilbert, premieres at the Wallner Theater in Berlin.

27 The film melodrama *Darwin: die Abstammung des Menschen von Affen* (*Darwin: The Evolution of Man from Apes*), directed by Fritz Bernhard and starring Alf Blütecher and Ria Jende, premieres in Berlin.

28 Kurt Wolff Press publishes the novel *Berlin, oder Juste milieu*, by Carl Sternheim.

OCTOBER

1 Max Liebermann is elected president of the Prussian Academy of the Arts, a post he remains in until 1933.

2 The drama *Der Kreis* (*The Circle*), by Kurt Heynicke, premieres at the Frankfurt am Main City Theater.

3 Reich president Ebert guarantees to provide the Schiller Foundation with a yearly subsidy. Numerous well-known authors gather in Berlin to form the

Union of German Fiction Writers, hoping to stem the rapid decline in book publication in Germany.

4 Composer Franz Schreker (1878–1934) conducts the Berlin Philharmonic Orchestra in a program entirely of his own symphonic works.

5 The drama *Godiva*, by Hans Franck, premieres at the Berlin State Theater.

8 The drama *Die Nacht* (*The Night*), by Hellmuth Unger, premieres at the Dresden Friedrich Theater.

The religious film *Die Legende von der Heiligen Simplicia* (*The Life of St. Simplicia*), directed Joe May and starring Eva May and Alfred Gerasch, premieres in Berlin.

9 Max Reinhardt relinquishes artistic control of his Berlin theaters in view of the worsening economic situation in Germany and announces the departure of touring productions, which he hopes will raise enough money for him to return to Berlin.

Der König (*The King*), by Hanns Johst, directed by Otto Falckenberg, premieres at the Kammerspiele in Munich.

11 The Berlin Philharmonic Orchestra premieres *Fantastic Appearances of a Theme by Hector Berlioz*, by Walter Braunfels, with Arthur Nickisch conducting.

The adventure film *Auf den Trümmern des Paradieses* (*On the Ruins of Paradise*), directed by Josef Stein and starring Gustav Kirchberg and Berate Herwigh, premieres in Berlin; it is the first film treatment of material by the popular writer Karl May, in a screenplay by Marie-Louise Droops.

12 The detective film *Karo 10*, directed William Kahn and starring Carl Auen and Edith Posca, premieres in Berlin.

15 Two comedy films premiere in Berlin: *Die Dame in Schwarz* (*The Lady in Black*), directed by Victor Janson and starring Curt Goetz and Gertrud Welcker and *Die Scheidungs-Ehe* (*The Divorce Marriage*), directed by Eugen Burg and starring Karl-Heinz Klubbertanz and Hilde Hildebrand.

Erwin Piscator opens his Proletarisches Theater in Berlin with his production of the drama *Der Krüppel* (*The Cripple*), by Karl August Wittfogel. The tragicomedy *Trieb* (*The Urge*), by Herwarth Walden, premieres at the Albert Theater in Dresden.

17 The antiwar drama *Am Glockenturm* (*At the Clock Tower*), by René Schickele, premieres at the Saarbrucken Regional Theater.

20 The film *Anna Karenina* , directed by Friedrich Zelnik and adapted for the screen from Tolstoy's novel by Fanny Carlsen, premieres in Berlin, with

Lya Mara as Anna, Johannes Riemann as Count Vronsky, and Heinrich Peer as Karenin.

21 The drama *Der Weg zur Macht* (*The Road to Power*), by Heinrich Mann, premieres at the Munich Residenz Theater.

22 Scenes from Goethe's original treatment of Faust material, titled *Urfaust*, are staged, directed by Max Reinhardt, at the Deutsches Theater Kammerspiele in Berlin, with Paul Hartmann as Faust, Ernst Deutsch as Mephisto, and Helene Thimig as Gretchen.

The film *Die Jagd nach dem Tode* (*The Hunt for Death*), directed by Karl Gerhardt and starring Nils Chrisander and Lil Dagover, premieres in Berlin.

23 Two films premiere in Berlin: the comedy *Die Sache mit Lola* (*The Business with Lola*), by Rudolf Bernauer and Rudolph Schanzer, at the Lustspielhaus; and the drama *Die Flamme* (*The Flame*), by Hans Müller-Einingen, at the Lessing Theater.

The Union of German Volksbühne Organizations is created in Berlin, with numerous government officials in attendance. Although officials voice support for such theater organizations, they reject an entertainment tax on tickets.

26 Mohr Press in Tübingen publishes *Gesammelte Aufsätze zur Religionssoziologie* (*Collected Essays on the Sociology of Religion*), by Max Weber.

28 The drama *Jenseits* (*The Other Side*), by Walter Hasenclever, premieres at the Dresden State Theater.

The film drama *The Mayor of Zalamea* (based on the play by Calderon de la Barca), directed by Ludwig Berger and starring Heinrich Witte, Albert Steinrück, and Lil Dagover, premieres in Berlin.

29 Berlin-Welt Press in Berlin publishes *Das ostjüdische Antlitz* (*The Face of East European Jewry*), by Arnold Zweig.

The film *Der Golem, wie er in die Welt kam* (*The Golem: How He Came into the World*), directed by Paul Wegener and Carl Boese, premieres in Berlin, with Wegner in the title role, Albert Seinrück as Rabbi Loew, and Lydia Salmonowa as the rabbi's daughter.

30 The opera *Das Spielwerk* (*The Plaything*), by Franz Schreker, premieres at the Munich National Theater.

31 The opera *Ritter Blaubart* (*Captain Bluebeard*), by Emil Nikolaus von Reznicek, premieres at the State Opera in Berlin.

NOVEMBER

2 The comedy *Mutter und Sohn* (*Mother and Son*), by Hellmuth Unger, premieres at the Rose Theater in Berlin.

4 Two films premiere in Berlin: the adventure *Der verfluchte Hunger nach Gold* (*The Curséd Hunger for Gold*), directed by Leo Lasko and starring Werner Funck and Rosa Porten; and the comedy *Das Chamäleon* (*The Chameleon*), directed by Carl Müller-Hagens and starring Max Landa and Hilde Wörner.

5 The drama *Europa*, by Georg Kaiser, directed by Karlheinz Martin, premieres at the Grosses Schauspielhaus in Berlin. An expressionist-style production of Shakespeare's *Richard III*, directed by Leopold Jessner, opens at the Berlin State Theater. The production creates an uproar among traditionalists, who stage large and noisy protests outside the theater.[16] Shortly afterward, the electricity system fails in both the Berlin State Theater and Opera; the houses remain dark for five days.

The film drama *Das Blut der Ahnen* (*The Blood of the Ancestors*), directed by Karl Gerhardt and starring Robert Scholz, Lil Gagover, and Harald Paulsen, premieres in Berlin.

6 The film melodrama *Eines grossen Mannes Liebe* (*The Love of a Great Man*), directed by Rudolf Biebrach and starring Lotte Neumann and Felix Basch, premieres in Berlin.

8 Prussian Culture and Education Minister Konrad Haenisch bans the display of swastikas in any Prussian school; he says the sight of the symbol may disturb some students.

9 S. Fischer Press publishes *Der neunte November* (*The Ninth of November*), Bernhard Kellermann's novel about the German revolution and its aftermath. It quickly becomes a best seller and is reprinted several times throughout the 1920s.

10 The Kleist Prize is awarded to Hanns Henny Jahn for his play *Ephraim Magnus*. Hermann Hesse rejects the Fontane Prize for his novel *Demian*. The Schiller Prize is not awarded.

11 The film melodrama *Das Tagebuch meiner Frau* (*My Wife's Diary*), directed by Paul Ludwig Stein and starring Erra Bognar and Alfred Abel, premieres in Berlin.

12 The film drama *Christian Wahnschaffe*, based on the novel of the same name by Jakob Wassermann about the 1905 Russian revolution, directed by Urban Gad and starring Conrad Veidt, Lillebil Christensen, Fritz Kortner, and Theodor Loos, premieres in Berlin.

13 The drama *Gas II*, by Georg Kaiser, premieres at the Frankfurt am Main Neues Theater. The play concludes Kaiser's *Gas Trilogy*, in which the central figure is the "Billionaire Worker," who pleads for peace and brotherhood among all mankind.

Bondi Press in Berlin publishes Friedrich Gundolf's monograph on Stefan George, *George*. S. Fischer Press publishes Jakob Wassermann's novel *Der Wendekreis* (*The Turning Point*). The Jewish Press in Berlin publishes Martin Buber's collected essays from 1910–1920 under the title *Die jüdische Bewegung* (*The Jewish Movement*).

15 The drama *Masse Mensch* (*Masses and Man*), by Ernst Toller, premieres at the Nuremberg City Theater.

16 The Czech government expropriates from its owners the Prague Deutsches Theater, an outpost of German theater culture since 1783, and rules that all plays in Prague must henceforth be presented in the Czech language.

20 The anti-Bolshevik film *Die entfesselte Menschheit* (*Humanity Unchained*), based on the novel by the same name by Max Glass, directed by Joseph Delmont and starring Eugen Klöpfer and Paul Hartmann, premieres in Berlin.

24 The historical drama *Sturmbraut* (*Bride of the Storm*), by Richard Volley, premieres at the Freiburg City Theater; the play is ostensibly about the French Revolution of 1789, but draws distinct parallels between the French Terror and Russian Bolshevism.

25 The Hans Goltz Gallery in Munich displays 362 works by Paul Klee, the largest exhibition of a single painter in Germany.

29 The Berlin Secession Movement opens its exhibition of featured painters of the year, Lovis Corinth and his wife Charlotte Berend-Corinth.

The comedy *Der grosse Augenblick* (*The Great Moment*), by Hellmuth Unger, premieres at the Gotha Regional Theater.

30 The drama *Musik* (*Music*), about the meeting of Beethoven and Goethe in 1812, by Carl Hauptmann, premieres at both the Leipzig Altes Theater and the Dortmund City Theater.

DECEMBER

1 The drama *Die Fälscher* (*The Counterfeiters*), by Max Brod, premieres at the Königsberg City Theater. *The King of the Dark Chamber*, by Nobel

Prize–winning Indian writer Rabindranath Tagore, directed by Richard Weichert, makes its European premiere at the Frankfurt am Main City Theater.

3 The historical film *Anne Boleyn*, directed by Ernst Lubitsch, premieres in Berlin, with Henny Porten in the title role and Emil Jannings as Henry VIII.

4 Continuing coal shortages close several Berlin galleries, museums, and theaters. The drama *Wahn* (*Delusion*), by Jakob Scherek, premieres at the Hamburg Kammerspiele.

5 The opera *Die tote Stadt* (*The Dead City*), by Erich Wolfgang Korngold, premieres at the Hamburg State Opera and Cologne City Opera.

A new dramatic adaptation of Upton Sinclair's 1903 novel *Prince Hagen*, directed by Erwin Piscator, premieres at the Proletarisches Theater in Berlin.

A film adaptation of Mark Twain's novel *The Prince and the Pauper*, directed by Alexander Korda and starring Tibi Lubinsky and Franz Erverth, premieres in Berlin.

6 Cotta Press in Stuttgart publishes Ernst Ludwig's biography of Goethe, *Goethe: Geschichte eines Menschen* (*Goethe: History of a Human Being*).

The film *Columbine*, directed by Martin Hartwig and starring Emil Jannings and Margarete Lanner, premieres in Hamburg.

7 The comedy *Ehelei* (*Wedlocking*), by Hermann Bahr, premieres at the Kleines Schauspielhaus in Berlin.

The horror film *Der Schädel der Pharonentochter* (*The Skull of Pharoh's Daughter*), directed by Otz Tollen and starring Emil Jannings and Erna Morena, premieres in Berlin.

9 The comedy *Der Amerikaner*, by Lion Feuchtwanger, premieres at the Munich Kammerspiele.

10 The drama *Kreuzweg* (*Crossroads*), by Carl Zuckmayer, premieres at the Berlin State Theater.

12 The crime film *Der Falschspieler* (*The Deceiver*), directed by Emil Justitz and starring Hans Albers and Anita Berber, premieres in Berlin.

The comedy *Der Skandal* (*The Scandal*), by Friedrich Eisenlohr, premieres at the Munich State Theater.

13 An exhibition of paintings by Ewald Materé and busts by the Chilean-born sculptress Totila Albert opens, sponsored by the Berlin Academy of the Arts. Totila Albert's bust of Albert Einstein attracts wide attention in the press.

16 On the occasion of Beethoven's 150th birthday, numerous concerts of his work take place throughout Germany. In Berlin, Ferruccio Busoni plays

Beethoven's Piano Concerto no. 5 in E-flat Major (*The Emperor*) with the Berlin Philharmonic, with Arthur Nikisch conducting. Nikisch and the orchestra conclude the program with Beethoven's Third Symphony, *Eroica*.

17 Playwright Georg Kaiser enters a psychiatric clinic at the University of Munich after being convicted of embezzlement.

The NSDAP, or Nazi Party, assumes publication of the weekly newspaper *Völkischer Beobachter* in Munich as its official party organ.

19 Rütten and Luening Press publishes *Eros und die Evangelien: aus den Notizen eines Vangabunden* (*Eros and the Evangelists: From the Notebook of a Vagabond*), by Waldemar Bonsels.

The thriller film *Das Geheimnis von Schloss Totenstein* (*The Secret of Totenstein Castle*), directed by Rudi Bach and starring Emil Mamelok and Rita Parsen, premieres.

20 Ravel's *Daphnis and Chloé,* Ballet Suite no. 2, makes its German premiere with the Berlin Philharmonic Orchestra, with Arthur Nikisch conducting.

22 The German Post Office transmits the first German live broadcast of an orchestral concert from its studios in Königswusterhausen, southeast of Berlin.

A film adaptation of Charles Dickens's novel *Oliver Twist*, titled *Die Geheimnisse von London* (*The Secrets of London*), directed by Richard Oswald and starring Manci Lubinsky and Louis Ralph, premieres.

23 The first German public performance of the drama *Reigen* (*La Ronde*), by Arthur Schnitzler, directed by Gertrud Eysoldt, takes place at the Kleines Schauspielhaus in Berlin. The drama *Caesar and Cleopatra*, by George Bernard Shaw, is revived at the Deutsches Theater in Berlin.

Rosa Valetti opens her cabaret, Café Grossenwahn, in Berlin.

24 The film drama *Arme Violetta*, loosely adapted from the play *The Lady of the Camelias*, by Alexandre Dumas fils, directed by Paul Ludwig Stein, premieres in Berlin, with Pola Negri in the title role and Michael Varkonyi as her love object.

25 The operetta *Schwan von Siam* (*The Swan from Siam*), by Victor Holländer, premieres.

29 Four related short films premiere in Berlin under the title *Verbrechen aus Leidenschaft* (*Crimes of Passion*), directed by Alfred Halm and Emmerich Hanus, with Eduard von Winterstein and Lilly Alexander leading a different cast in each of the films.

31 The film melodrama *Menschen im Rausch* (*People under the Influence*), directed by Julius Geisendörfer and starring Conrad Veidt and Aenne Ullstein, premieres in Berlin.

The German currency (the Reichsmark) drops to its lowest postwar exchange point against the U.S. dollar, at RM 74.50 per $1.00.

NOTES

1. In *Creatures of the Night*, Wegener plays a mad scientist whose son lives in an enormous cage as an orangutan, swinging from enormous artificial trees. Wegener's daughter is a nymphomaniac whose boyfriend discovers a formula to restrict the supply of oxygen around the world. He convinces Wegener that the formula will enable them to blackmail the global population and become fabulously wealthy.

2. Arco-Valley (Anton von Padua Alfred Emil Hubert Georg Graf von Arco auf Valley) was forced to give up his cell at Landsberg Prison in 1924 to a prisoner named Adolf Hitler. Arco-Valley was released in 1925 and two years later was granted a full pardon for murdering Eisner.

3. Hans Albers (1891–1960) had light blue eyes, which gave him additional appeal among German audiences as a villain in movies like *The Snake with the Girl's Head*. Like most films at the time, it was shot with orthographic film stock. His blue eyes printed as white, which gave him a particularly horrifying aspect.

4. Ruth Schaumann (1899–1975) was a prolific writer not only of poetry; she wrote more than 90 books of fiction, fairy tales, short stories, and essays. Her books often featured her own graphic designs, drawings, and woodcuts. She became completely deaf at age six; her deafness, she said, contributed enormously to her work as a writer. Her books and drawings were among the most widely purchased in the 1920s, and in 1932 she was awarded the Munich Poets' Prize and later the Bavarian Service Cross. She married editor and writer Peter Fuchs in 1924; together they had five children.

5. From 1887 until 1900, Hugo Kaun (1863–1932) worked as a conductor, composer, and teacher in Chicago and Milwaukee. Both cities in those years had large German-speaking populations, and Kaun was active in both. In 1901, he returned to Berlin, where in 1912 he was named professor of composition at the Royal Academy of the Arts.

6. Alexander Granach (Jessaja Szajko Gronach, 1890–1945) was known for his fiery portrayals of other "conflicted" character types as well. He had little formal training. Just as he was beginning to get work in Berlin, he was drafted into the Austro-Hungarian army in 1914. His performance as Shylock in Munich won him national attention, as did his subsequent film work in F. W. Murnau's *Nosferatu* (1922). Granach immigrated to New York and in 1939 played a Soviet apparatchik in the romantic comedy *Ninotchka*, directed by Ernst Lubitsch and starring Greta Garbo and Melvyn Douglas.

7. This film marks the first instance in which Otto Gebühr (1877–1954) appeared as the Prussian king Friedrich II, known as Frederick the Great (albeit in a distinctly minor role). Gebühr went on to make 11 subsequent movies playing Frederick (usually as a major character) over a 30-year period. He began his career as a comic actor and started playing character parts for Max Reinhardt in 1917. He was cast as Frederick the Great largely because of his stunning similarity to many portraits of the king.

8. Hanna Henning (Johanna Julie Adelheid von Koblinski, 1884–1925) became one of the first important German female film directors, with over 20 features to her credit, along with several short films. Among the latter was *Mutter* (*Mother*, 1917), which was an appeal for donations to help ease childhood hunger during the last year of World War I. That film won her the Reich Merit Cross for War Aid.

9. Censorship of movies had ended with the fall of the kaiser in 1918. The new *Reichslichtspielgesetz*, or National Motion Picture Law, employed some features of the old censorship law, including three principal grounds for banning a film. Local police had jurisdiction in deciding whether a film presented a threat to public order and safety, if it promoted immoral behavior, or if it undermined Germany's relations with other countries. Other provisions of the law were intended to protect youths under age 18. Local authorities generally enjoyed wide leeway in making decisions about the appropriateness of a film in their communities.

10. King Ludwig II of Bavaria (1845–1886) has been the subject of numerous treatments in drama, fiction, and the popular media. A 1972 film directed by Luchino Visconti, *Ludwig*, with Helmut Berger in the title role and Trevor Howard as the composer Richard Wagner, is among the best known. During his lifetime, Ludwig was known for his devotion to and liberal patronage of Wagner. Ludwig was also well known for his eccentricities, which culminated in several expensive building projects, the most well known of them being the fairy-tale castle Neuschwanstein.

11. Hauptmann's tragedy, set in his native Silesia, was one of the most riveting in the German naturalist movement during the 1890s. Henschel is a teamster whose freight delivery business requires his frequent absence from home. His wife contracts septicemia during childbirth, and her dying wish is that her husband dismiss their housemaid, Hanne Schäl. The wife's death causes hardship for Henschel, and he marries Hanne anyway, hoping she will manage his house and children. She does so initially, but soon takes a lover and abuses the children. Henschel begins a downward spiral that ends in his suicide. Hanne Schäl is one of the premier villain roles for German actresses, and Höflich received extensive praise for her performance.

12. After her breakthrough performance in Munich, Elisabeth Bergner (Elisabeth Ettel, 1897–1986) became one of the most sought-after actresses in the Weimar Republic. She often played trouser roles in Shakespearean plays because her legs were so shapely. In Berlin, she worked for several major directors and began film work in 1923. She played Nina in the German-language version of O'Neill's *Strange Interlude* and made more than 30 films, culminating in an Oscar nomination for *Escape Me Never* in 1935.

13. Saladin Schmitt (1883–1951) had one of the longest tenures of any director of a German theater. He began at the Bochum City Theater in 1919 and remained there

for the next 30 years, dedicating the place as a kind of temple to the classics. His productions of Shakespeare, Schiller, Goethe, Lessing, and Kleist always espoused exactitude in vocal delivery and restraint in gesture.

14. Anton "Toni" Impekoven (1881–1947) became one of the most frequently performed playwrights in the Weimar Republic, one of few based outside Berlin. Like most successful comedy writers in the 1920s, he frequently wrote with partners. His work with Carl Mathern (1887–1960), a former newspaper staff writer, was the most successful. Together they wrote *Liselotte von der Pfalz* (*Liselotte of the Palatinate*), *Die drei Zwillinge* (*The Three Twins*), *Luderchen* (*The Tart*), and *Junggesellendämmerung* (*Twilight of the Bachelors*), all of which remained in the repertoires of most German theaters throughout the 1920s and into the early 1930s. Impekoven spent his entire career in Frankfurt am Main.

15. In his speech, the decorated war veteran Hitler claimed that Judaism was a "racial tuberculosis among nations." German Jews had been granted full emancipation with the creation of the Weimar Republic; formal barriers to their participation in German political, cultural, and academic life were removed. The influx of *Ostjuden* (Jews from Eastern Europe, usually far more orthodox in their beliefs than were German Jews and more easily identified by their manner of dress), however, bolstered remaining prejudices. Authorities in many jurisdictions deported *Ostjuden* back to their countries of origin, much as authorities under the kaisers had done.

16. Protestors found much to dislike in this production, not the least of which was the fact that director Jessner and leading actor Fritz Kortner were Jews. In such a "Jewified" (a term that became increasingly commonplace through the 1920s to describe modernist techniques) production, there was a premium on abstraction instead of accessibility. Chief among the abstractions were the "Jessner steps," which designer Emil Pirchan created as a large scenic unit to dominate the stage space for the entire production. Actors spoke their lines at a rapid tempo, or at least it seemed that way to audiences accustomed to the declamatory style of German Shakespearean productions since the 1860s. The costumes bespoke no specific time period, and the lighting was likewise nondecorative. In this production, Jessner showed himself to be a master of compaction, reducing everything to basic elements.

1921

JANUARY

1 The comedy *Meine Frau, das Fräulein* (*My Wife, the Bachelorette*), by Helmuth Unger, premieres at the Baden Baden City Theater.

The comedy film *Opfer der Keuschheit* (*Victims of Chastity*), directed by Manfred Noa and starring Manja Tzatschewa and Charles Willy Kayser, premieres in Berlin.

3 Schuster and Loeffler Press publishes *Gustav Malers Sinfonien* (*Gustav Mahler's Symphonies*), by musicologist Paul Bekker. Cotta Presses publishes *Ursprung und Anfänge des Christentums* (*Origin and Beginnings of Christianity*), by Eduard Meyer. Rothbart Press publishes *Arbeit adelt* (*Work Ennobles*), a novel by Hedwig Courths-Mahler.[1]

4 The drama *Der Ketzer* (*The Heretic*), by Paul Bourfeind, premieres at the Cologne City Theater. Bourfeind's drama treated the life of Giordano Bruno (1548–1600), burned at the stake in Rome and later valorized among free thinkers as a martyr.

Georg Müller Press publishes the novel *Vampir*, by Hanns Heinz Ewers.[2]

5 Karlheinz Martin stages Gerhart Hauptmann's epic historical drama about the German Peasants' War, *Florian Geyer* (with Eugen Klöpfer in the title role) at the 3,800-seat Grosses Schauspielhaus in Berlin.

The opera *Die Gezeichneten* (*The Marked Ones*), by Franz Schreker, makes its German premiere at the State Opera House.

6 The exotic intrigue film *Das Geheimnis von Bombay* (*The Secret of Bombay*), directed by Artur Holz and starring Conrad Veidt and Lil Dagover, premieres in Berlin.

7 Cassirer Press publishes *Die Radierung* (*The Drawing*), by art historian Max Friedländer.

The comedy film *Der Dummkopf* (*The Fool*), directed by Lupu Pick and starring Max Adalbert and Paul Heidemann, premieres in Berlin.

A drama about Galileo, *Die Sterne* (*The Stars*), by Hans Müller, premieres at the Berlin State Theater.

8 Strache Press publishes *Sodom*, a novel by Egmont Colerus. S. Fischer Press publishes drawings and stories by Arthur Holitscher in *Drei Monate im Sowjet-Union* (*Three Months in the Soviet Union*).

The romantic film *Der Tempel der Liebe* (*The Temple of Love*), directed by Paul Ludwig Stein and starring Lia Eibenschütz and Erich Kaiser-Titz, premieres in Berlin.

12 The "dramatic poem" *Kain* (*Cain*), by Anton Wildgans (based on the biblical story of the brothers Cain and Abel), premieres at the Rostock City Theater, with Alexander Granach in the title role. The comedy *Die Eheringe* (*The Wedding Rings*), by Alexander Engel, premieres at the Hanau City Theater.

Ullstein Press publishes the novel *Der Stern von Afrika* (*The Star of Africa*), by Bruno Bürgel. Staackmann Press publishes the novel *Eiserne Jugend* (*Iron Youth*), by Paul Schreckenbach, about fraternity boys at the University of Jena. Seemann Press publishes *Von Corinth über Corinth* (*By and about Corinth*), a book of watercolors with commentary by the artist Lovis Corinth[3] and editor Wilhelm Hauenstein.

13 Schroedel Press publishes *Bauerngeschichten* (*Rural Tales*), featuring stories by authors Ludwig Thoma, Hermann Kurz, Jeremias Gotthelf, and Peter Dörfler.

14 Taxpayers in Hamburg grant their newly established University of Hamburg legal status by approving its by-laws.

A new production of Goethe's *Torquato Tasso*, directed by Ludwig Berger and designed by Emil Pirchan, opens at the Berlin State Theater.

The film dramas *10 Milliarden Volt* (*10 Billion Volts*), directed by Adolf Gärtner and starring Arthur Somlay and Ellen Richter; and *Die Dreizehn aus Stahl* (*Thirteen Men of Steel*), directed by Johannes Guter and starring Carl de Vogt and Claire Lotto, premiere in Berlin.

15 Ullstein Press publishes the novel *Kuriose Geschichte* (*A Curious Story*), by Fedor von Zobeltitz.

16 The "dramatic legend" *Die Heimkehr* (*The Journey Home*), by Karl Röttger (based on the New Testament parable of the prodigal son), premieres at the Gera-Reuss Regional Theater. August Strindberg's drama *Lucky Pehr* (written in 1883) makes its German premiere at the Frankfurt City Theater.

The Frankfurt Press Institute publishes *Anarchie im Drama* (*Anarchy in the Drama*), by critic Bernhard Diebold, one of the first authors to examine the theoretical bases of German expressionist drama.

17 Cassirer Press publishes the 12-volume edition of Ferdinand Lassalle's *Gesammelte Reden und Schriften* (*Collected Speeches and Writings*), edited by Eduard Bernstein.

The drama *Die Überlebenden* (*The Survivors*), by Heinrich Lilienfein, premieres at the Hannover Residence Theater.

18 Communist Party members stage noisy protest demonstrations in the Reichstag during ceremonies to commemorate the founding of the Wilhelmine Reich in 1871.

21 The comedy *Der pathetische Hut* (*The Pathetic Hat*), by Carl Rössler, premieres at the Kammerspiele of Deutsches Theater in Berlin.

The film tragedy *Der Gang in die Nacht* (*The Path into Night*), directed by F. W. Murnau and starring Olaf Fönss, Conrad Veidt, and Erna Morena, premieres in Berlin.

22 Right-wing activists set off stink bombs during performances of Arthur Schnitzler's *Reigen* (*La Ronde*) at the Kleines Theater in Berlin, protesting against a play they regard as "an insalubrious concoction by a Viennese Jew."

Theodor Lesing is awarded the August Strindberg Prize for the contributions of his book *Geschichte als Sinngebung des Sinnlosen* (*History as an Attempt to Give Meaning to the Meaningless*) to reconciliation among nations.

25 S. Fischer Press publishes the novel *Wallenstein*, by Alfred Döblin.

27 The National Socialist Party newspaper *Völkischer Beobachter* publishes for the first time an essay by Adolf Hitler as its front-page article. Duncker Press publishes *Die Geschichte des Judentums* (*The History of Judaism*), by historian Otto Hauser.

The film melodramas *Die Diktatur der Liebe: Die böse Lust* (*The Dictatorship of Love: Evil Desire*), directed by Willy Zeyn and starring Esther Carnea and Heinrich Schroth; and *Die Diktatur der Liebe: Die Welt ohne Liebe* (*The Dictatorship of Love: The World without Love*), directed by Fred Sauer and starring Esther Carena and Ilka Grüning, premiere in Berlin.

28 The pacifist drama *Deserteure* (*Deserters*), by Walter Wassermann, premieres at the Rose Theater in Berlin.

A film adaptation of Shakespeare's *Hamlet* premieres in Berlin, directed by Sven Gade and Heinz Schall, with Asta Nielsen[4] as Hamlet, Eduard von Winterstein as Claudius, Mathilde Brandt as Gertrude, Hans Junkermann as Polonius, and Lily Jacobsson as Ophelia. The film drama *Das Haus zur Mond* (*The House on the Moon*), directed by Karlheinz Martin and starring Erich Pabst, Fritz Kortner, and Leontine Kühnberg, also premieres in Berlin.

Langen Press in Munich publishes the novel *Ararat*, by Arnold Ulitz.

29 Ullstein Press publishes the novel *Fasching* (*Shrovetide*), by Paul Oskar Höcker. Drei Masken Press in Munich publishes the song book *Lautenlieder*, with words by Frank Wedekind set to "original and foreign melodies," edited by Emil Preetorius.

30 The film drama *Aschermittwoch* (*Ash Wednesday*), directed by Otto Rippert and starring Hella Moja and Ernst Winar, premieres in Berlin.

31 The drama *Die jüdische Witwe* (*The Jewish Widow*), by Georg Kaiser, premieres at the Meiningen Regional Theater.

The adventure film *Friedericus Rex: Sturm und Drang* (*Frederick the Great: Storm and Stress*), directed by Arsen von Cserépy and starring Otto Gebühr as Frederick the Great, Albert Steinrück, Gertrud de Lalsky, and Erna Morena, premieres in Berlin.

FEBRUARY

1 S. Fischer Press publishes Jakob Wassermann's *Mein Weg als Deutscher und Jude* (*My Life as a German and a Jew*). The Social Studies Press publishes Philipp Scheidemann's *Der Zusammenbruch* (*The Collapse*). The Communist Party (KPD) begins publication of its monthly magazine devoted to Marxist childrearing and political activism in schools, *Das proletarische Kind* (*The Proletarian Child*).

2 The comic Opera *Gianni Scicci*, by Giacomo Puccini, makes its German premiere in Hamburg.

The drama *Orpheus und Eurydike*, by painter Oskar Kokoschka, with Heinrich George and Gera Müller in the title roles, premieres at the Frankfurt am Main City Theater.

The film romance *Begierde: Das Abenteuer der Katja Nastjenko* (*Desire: The Adventure of Katia Nastyenko*), directed by Franz Hofer and starring Margit Barnay (in the title role) and Olaf Storm, premieres in Berlin.

3 The comedy *Das Krokodil* (*The Crocodile*), by Alfons Strecker, premieres at the Harburg City Theater.

The first "mass assembly" of the National Socialist German Workers' (Nazi) Party, at the Krone Circus Arena in Munich, attracts more than 6,000 people to hear Adolf Hitler's speech "The Future or the Downfall."

Three film dramas premiere in Berlin: *Die Blitzzentrale* (*Lightning Command*), directed by Valy Arnheim and starring Valy Arnheim and Marga Lindt; *Das Haus der Qualen* (*The House of Torment*), directed Carl Wilhelm and starring Fritz Kortner and Charles Willy Kayser; and *Kämpfende Herzen* (*Opposing Hearts*), directed by Fritz Land and starring Carola Toelle and Hermann Boettcher.

4 The dance theater production *Josephslegende* (*The Legend of Joseph*), by Count Harry Kessler and Hugo von Hofmannsthal, with music by Richard Strauss, makes its Berlin premiere at the State Opera.

Three comedy films premiere: *Die Gassenkönigin* (*The Back-Street Queen*), directed by Ernst Mölter and starring Gerturd de Lalsky and Traute Trauneck, in Hamburg; *Hannerl und ihre Liebhaber* (*Hannah and Her Lovers*), directed by Felix Basch and starring Grete Freund and Felix Basch, in Frankfurt am Main; and *Der Liebeskorridor* (*The Love Corridor*), directed by Emil Albes and starring Adolphe Engers and Erika Glässner, in Berlin.

7 The crime film *Haschisch, das Paradies der Hölle* (*Hashish, the Paradise of Hell*), directed by Reinhard Bruck and starring Tilla Durieux, Fritz Kortner, and Paul Hartmann, premieres in Berlin.

8 The drama *Die Schlacht der Heilande* (*The Battle of the Redeemers*), by Alfred Brust, premieres at the Halberstadt City Theater.

Rösl Press in Munich publishes *Irrfahrten eines Humoristen* (*The Erroneous Journeys of a Humorist*), by Roda Roda (Sandor Rosenfeld, 1872–1945). The Jewish Press in Berlin publishes Martin Buber's *The Jewish Movement*.

9 S. Fischer Press publishes the drama *Indiphodi*, by Gerhart Hauptmann.

10 The drama *Das Antlitz des Todes* (*The Countenance of Death*), by Karl Röttger, premieres at the Düsseldorf City Theater.

The comedy film *Die drei Tanten* (*The Three Aunts*), directed by Rudolf Biebrach and starring Lotte Neumann, Olga Limburg, and Josefine Dora in the title roles, premieres in Berlin.

11 The crime film *Das Geheimnis der Spielhöhle von Sebastopol* (*The Secret of the Gambling Pit in Sebastopol*), directed by Eugen Klöpfer and starring Klöpfer and Sybil Morel, premieres in Berlin. The mystery film *Das Medium* (*The Medium*), directed by Hermann Rosenfeld and starring Werner Krauss and Lil Dagover, also premieres in Berlin.

12 The biblical comedy *In Kanaan* (*In Canaan*), by Walter Harlan, premieres at the Hannover Deutsches Theater.

14 Rösl Press in Munich publishes the crime novel *Praschnas Geheimnis* (*Prashna's Secret*), by Friedrich Freksa. Callwey Press in Munich publishes the novel *Deutsche Braut* (*German Bride*), by Albert Trentini.

The drama *Armand Carrel* premieres at the Dresden Regional Theater.

15 The drama *Die Brüder* (*The Brothers*), by Hermann Kesser, premieres at the Wiesbaden State Theater.

17 The comedy *Der entfesselte Zeitgenosse* (*The Unchained Contemporary*) premieres.

Kiepenheuer Press publishes a volume of novellas by Hans Fallada, Hermann Hesse, Robert Musil, and Stefan Zzweig, *Die Einsamen* (*The Lonely Ones*).

18 The film *Die Bestie im Menschen* (*The Beast in Man*), based on the Emile Zola novel *La Bête Humaine*, directed by Ludwig Wolff and starring Maria Orska and Eduard Rothhauser, premieres in Berlin.

The operetta *Die Tanzgräfin* (*The Dancing Countess*), by Robert Stolz, premieres at the Wallner Theater in Berlin.

20 The science fiction film *Ein Tag auf dem Mars* (*A Day on Mars*), directed by Heinz Schall and starring Lilly Flohr and Hermann Picha, premieres in Berlin.

21 Schiller's drama *Die Jungfrau von Orleans* (*The Maid of Orleans*),[5] directed by Karlheinz Martin, is revived at the Deutsches Theater in Berlin.

22 The film melodrama *Die Liebschaften des Hektor Delmore* (*The Love Affairs of Hector Delmore*), directed by Richard Oswald, with Conrad Veidt as Hector Delmore and Erna Morena, and Kitty Moran, Helene Ford, Maja Savos, Sascha Gura, and Anenne Ullstein as the objects of his desire, premieres in Berlin.

23 Strache Press publishes a collection of Albert Ehrenstein's poetry, *Die Gedichte von Albert Ehrenstein* (*The Poetry of Albert Ehrenstein*). Georg Müller Press publishes a collection of plays, *Das Mädchen von Shalott und andere Dramen* (*The Lady of Chaillot and Other Plays*), by Hanns Heinz Ewers.

24 *Jenseits* (*Beyond This Life*), by Walter Hasenclever, premieres at the Kammerspiele of the Deutsches Theater in Berlin.

The crime film *Der Streik der Diebe* (*The Thieves Go on Strike*), directed by Alfred Abel and starring Maria Orska and Alfred Abel, premieres in

Berlin. A film adaptation of Schiller's play *Fiesko, Die Verschwörung zu Genua* (*The Conspiracy in Genoa*), directed by Paul Leni and starring Wilhelm Diegelmann, Maria Fein, Fritz Kortner, and Hans Mierendorff as Fiesko, premieres in Berlin.

26 The first sound film is developed by the Tri-Ergon Company in Berlin, using a light "reader" to translate sound waves into light waves and print them on a film sound track. The light waves are then retranslated into sound waves when the film is projected. Sound engineers Jo Engl, Joseph Massole, and Hans Vogt develop the technology in the Tri-Ergon laboratories and attempt to refine and market it, which ultimately revolutionizes the film industry around the world.

The revival of *Captain Brassbound's Conversion*, by George Bernard Shaw, at the Berlin Volksbühne marks the breakthrough of director Jürgen Fehling. Cast members include Heinz Hilpert, Helene Fehdmer, Friedrich Kayssler, and Guido Gerzfeld.

28 The film drama *Das Brandmal der Vergangenheit* (*Branded by the Past*), directed Erwin Baron, written by Georg Kaiser, and starring Bruno Kastner and Fritz Kampers, premieres in Munich.

MARCH

1 Wolff Press publishes the "Dadaist novel" *Dr. Billig am Ende* (*Dr. Cheap Bites the Dust*), by Richard Huelsenbeck, with illustrations by George Grosz.

2 Welcher Press publishes *Die Berechtigung des Antisemitismus* (*Entitled to Anti-Semitism*), by Adolf Bartels.

The comedy *Die ewige Braut* (*The Eternal Bride*), by Alexander Engel, premieres at the Munich Volkstheater.

3 The operetta *Der Günstling der Zarin* (*The Czarina's Minion*), by Robert Winterberg, premieres at the Hamburg Operetta Theater.

The comedy film *Die Geliebte des Grafen Varenne* (*Count Varenne's Lover*), directed by Friedrich Zelnik and starring Lya Mara and Johannes Riemann, premieres in Berlin.

Rothbarth Press publishes *Die Stiftssekretärin* (*The Monastic Secretary*), by Hedwig Courths-Mahler.

4 The film melodrama *Das Floss der Toten* (*The Raft of the Dead*), directed by Carl Boese and starring Aug Egede Nissen and Otto Gebühr, premieres in Munich.

7 Pope Benedict XV names Archbishop of Munich Michael von Faulhaber to the Sacred College of Cardinals.

8 Seifert Press publishes *Die Welt des Tänzers* (*The World of the Dancer*), by Rudolf von Laban.[6] Rascher Press publishes *Psychologische Typen* (*Psychological Types*), by Carl Gustav Jung.

10 The adventure film *Brennendes Land* (*Burning Country*), directed by Heinz Herald and starring Marie Wismar and Ernst Deutsch, premieres in Berlin.

11 The comedy film *Der Liebling der Frauen* (*The Ladies' Man*), directed by Carl Wilhelm and starring Olga Limbur and Ernst Winar, premieres in Berlin. The first installment of the *Mann ohne Namen* (*Man without a Name*) detective film series, *Der Millionendieb* (*The Gentleman Burglar*), directed by Georg Jacoby and starring Harry Liedtke, Mady Christians, and Jakob Tiedtke, premieres in Berlin.

12 The drama *Opfernacht* (*Night of the Victims*) by Hans Franck, premieres at the Frankfurt am Main Schauspielhaus. The operetta *Der Marmorgraf* (*The Marble Count*), by Viktor Hollaender, premieres at the Wiesbaden Residenz Theater.

15 An Armenian gunman murders a Turkish diplomat in Berlin, claiming it was "an act of revenge for the sufferings of my people at the hands of the Turks."[7] He is tried, found innocent of all charges, and released.

The drama *Die Welt ist krank* (*The World Is Sick*), by Herbert Eulenberg, premieres at the Bochum City Theater.

The University of Königsberg awards painter Lovis Corinth an honorary doctorate.

16 International Psychoanalytical Press publishes *Jenseits des Lustprinzips* (*Beyond the Pleasure Principle*), by Sigmund Freud.

18 The second installment of the *Man without a Name* detective film series, *Der Kaiser der Sahara* (*The Emperor of the Sahara*), again directed by Georg Jacoby and starring Harry Liedtke, Mady Christians, and Jakob Tiedtke, premieres in Berlin. The comedy film *Exzellenz Unterrock* (*Her Excellency in Petticoats*), directed by Edgar Klitsch, with Ellen Petz as Madame de Pompadour and Jürgen Fehling as King Louis XV, premieres in Berlin.

22 The comedy *Der Frauenmut* (*The Courage of Women*), by Hermann Essig, premieres at the Lessing Theater in Berlin. The drama *Louis Ferdinand, Prinz von Preussen* (*Louis Ferdinand, Prince of Prussia*) by Fritz von Unruh,[8] premieres at the Darmstadt Regional Theater.

23 Communist-led strikes bring Hamburg's waterfront activity to a halt; Party activists occupy several docks in an attempt to stop incoming ship traffic.

The drama *Kleist*, by Friedrich Sebrecht, premieres at the Mannheim National Theater. The tragicomedy *Die echten Sedemunds* (*The Real Members of the Sedemund Family*), by sculptor Ernst Barlach, premieres at the Hamburg Kammerspiele.

24 The adventure film *Die goldene Kugel* (*The Golden Bullet*), directed by Robert Wuelner and starring Gerturd Welcker and Erich Kaiser-Titz, premieres in Berlin.

26 The comedy *Rugby*, by Wilhelm Speyer, premieres at the Theater in der Königgrätzer Strasse in Berlin.

29 The third and final installment of the *Man without a Name* detective film series, *Gelbe Bestien* (*Yellow Beasts*), again directed by Georg Jacoby and starring Harry Liedtke, Mady Christians, and Jakob Tiedtke, premieres in Berlin.

Army units are sent to quell labor unrest in Hamburg.

30 The Berlin Philharmonic Orchestra provides musical accompaniment at the premiere of the film *Die Flucht aus dem goldenen Kerker* (*Escape from the Golden Prison*), directed by Urban Gad and starring Conrad Veidt, Ilka Grüning, and Werner Krauss.

31 Strikes and disturbances on the Hamburg waterfront end.

APRIL

1 The *Lichtspiel Opus 1* (*Play of Light, Opus 1*), the first color animated film in Germany, premieres; Walther Ruttmann creates the 12-minute film from more than 10,000 hand-tinted images, which create the illusion of moving geometric shapes.

Die echten Sedemunds (*The Real Members of the Sedemund Family*), by sculptor Ernst Barlach, directed by Leopold Jessner and starring Fritz Kortner and Lothar Müthel, premieres at the Berlin State Theater.

Staackmann Presses publishes the novel *Der Bauernstudent* (*The Peasant Student*), by Hans Sterneder.

2 The operetta *Onkel Muz*, by Jean Gilbert, premieres in Halle.

The comedy film *Großstadtmädels* (*Bog City Girls*), directed by Wolfgang Neff and starring Colette Corder and Clementine Plessner, premieres in Leipzig.

5   Max Reinhardt stages a new production of *Woyzeck*, by Georg Büchner, at the Deutsches Theater in Berlin, with Eugen Klöpfer in the title role.

7   The film drama *Schloss Vogelöd* (*The Vogelöd Palace*), based on the popular novel of the same name by Rudolf Stratz, directed by F. W. Murnau and starring Paul Hartmann, Paul Bildt, and Olga Chekhova, premieres in Berlin.

9   In an attempt to raise needed funds for its operations, the Berlin State Theater stages a "Strauss Evening" at Max Reinahrdt's Grosses Schauspielhaus, featuring scenes from *Die Fledermaus* and *The Gypsy Baron*.

The tragicomedy *Mückentanz* (*Mosquito Dance*), by Herbert Eulenberg, premieres at the Rostock City Theater.

10   The drama *Die Kanaker* (*The Wogs*), by Franz Jung, premieres at the Proleterian Theater Berlin, under the direction of Erwin Piscator. Several critics condemn the play's overtly provocative political ideology. Among the most powerful critics are the Berlin police, who close down Piscator's theater as a "disturbance of the peace" 10 days later.

The film drama *Die Amazone* (*The Amazons*), directed by Richard Löwenbein and starring Eva May and Adolf Klein, premieres in Berlin.

12   The drama *Kräfte* (*Powers*), by August Stramm, premieres at the Kammerspiele of the Deutsches Theater in Berlin, under the direction of Max Reinhardt. Playwright Stramm had visited several German American communities in the United States before World War I, in which he served as an officer and was killed in hand-to-hand combat with Russian forces in 1915.

14   The drama *Von morgens bis Mitternacht* (*From Morn to Midnight*), by Georg Kaiser, premieres at the Lessing Theater in Berlin; the play subsequently becomes Kaiser's most popular, with hundreds of performances throughout Germany, Austria, the United States, and Canada.

The "grotesque comedy" film *Die Bergkatze* (*The Mountain Pussycat*), directed by Ernst Lubitsch and starring Pola Negri (in the title role) and Victor Janson, premieres in Berlin.

15   The operetta *Der Vetter aus Dingsda* (*The Cousin from Whatchacallit*), by Edayd Künneke, premieres at the Theater am Nollendorf Platz in Berlin and the Düsseldorf Schauspielhaus.

The thriller film *Die Apotheke des Teufels* (*The Devil's Apothecary*), directed by Bruno Eichgrün and starring Kurt Gerron (as the Apothecary) and Leonore Oppermann, premieres in Berlin.

The drama *Die Geächtete* (*The Outlaws*), by Hellmuth Unger, premieres at the Eisenach City Hall.

16 The Berlin Philharmonic Orchestra presents a rare program of music by composer Arnold Schönberg, featuring the string sextet *Verklärte Nacht* (*Transfigured Night*) op. 4 and the "symphonic poem for orchestra" *Pelleas und Melisande* op. 5, inspired by the drama of Maurice Maeterlinck.

18 The film melodrama *Wie das Mädchen aus der Ackerstrasse die Heimat fand* (*How the Girl from the Acker Strasse Found Her Way Home*), directed by Martin Hartwig and starring Antonie Jaeckel (in the title role) and Hans Renfer, premieres in Berlin.

19 The comedy *Der grüne Lapilazuil* (*The Green Lapus Lazuli*), by Heinrich Berges, premieres at the Hamburg Thalia Theater. Max Reinhardt stages Shakespeare's *A Midsummer Night's Dream* at the Grosses Schauspielhaus.

20 Dada artists Johannes Baader (as "Oberdada"), Georg Grosz, Richard Huesenbeck, and Wieland Herzfeld face charges in Berlin district court for "defamation of the German armed forces" and are each fined RM 300.

21 The historical film *Kaiserin Elisabeth aus Österreich* (*Empress Elisabeth of Austria*), directed by Rolf Raffé, with Carla Nelson as Elisabeth (known popularly as "Sissi") and Nils Jensen as Emperor Franz Josef, premieres in Munich.

22 The film drama *Landstrasse und Großstadt* (*Country Road and Big City*), directed by Carl Wilhelm and starring Carola Toelle and Fritz Kortner, premieres in Berlin. The film melodrama *Vergiftetes Blut* (*Poisoned Blood*), directed by Fred Sauer and starring Aenderli Lebius and Käte Haack, premieres in Berlin.

27 The comedy *Die selige Exzellenz* (*His Blissfully Ignorant Excellency*), by Leo Walther Stein, premieres at the Deutsches Künstler Theater in Berlin.

29 The film drama *Die verbotene Frucht* (*Forbidden Fruit*), directed by Rudolf Biebrach and starring Lotte Neumann and Hans Riemann, premieres in Berlin.

30 The drama *Die helle Nacht* (*The Bright Night*), by Walter von Molo, premieres at the Leipzig Schauspielhaus.

MAY

1 The film melodrama *Aus den Tiefen der Großstadt* (*From the Depths of the Big City*), directed by Fred Sauer and starring Ilka Grüning and Ernst Hofmann, premieres in Berlin.

The comedy *Götterprüfung* (*Testing the Gods*), by assassinated Bavarian premier Kurt Eisner, premieres at the Berlin Volksbühne. The Deutsches Theater in Berlin presents a Russian-language production of Leonid Andreyev's drama *Days of Our Life*, directed by Ivan Schmith.

4 An exhibition opens at the Prussian Academy of the Arts in Berlin featuring works done only in black and white; prominent are drawings by Lovis Corinth and Käthe Kollwitz.

The historical film *Danton*, based on the play by Georg Büchner, directed by Dimitri Buchowetski, with Emil Jannings as Danton, Werner Krauss as Robespierre, and Robert Scholz as St. Just, premieres in Berlin.

6 The drama *Die Verschwörung des Fiescos zu Genua* (*Fiesko's Conspiracy in Genoa*), by Friedrich Schiller, directed by Leopold Jessner, starring Arthur Kraussneck, Ernst Deutsch, and Fritz Kortner and with music composed for the production by Ernst Krenek,[9] is revived at the Berlin State Theater.

Two crime films premiere in Berlin: *Der Mann im Schrank* (*The Man in the Closet*), directed by Gernot Bock-Schieber and starring Alexander von Atalffly and Magnus Stifter; and *Ein Erpressertrick* (*A Blackmailer's Trick*), directed by Erich Schönfelder and starring Ferdinand von Alten and Willy Schaeffers.

11 The film melodrama *Loge No. 11* (*Box Seat No. 11*), directed by Arsen von Cserepy and starring Ludwig Hartau and Sascha Gura, premieres in Berlin.

12 The crime film *Hochstapler* (*The Con Man*), directed by Werner Funck and starring Paul Hartmann and Olga Chekhova, premieres in Berlin.

13 The film drama *Um den Sohn* (*About the Son*), directed by Frederik Larsen and starring Carola Toelle and Ernst Hofmann, premieres in Berlin.

14 Two new productions of important plays open in Berlin: at the Volksbühne, the comedy *Der Bauer als Millionär* (*The Peasant as Millionaire*), by Johann Nepomuk Nestroy, directed by Jürgen Fehling; and at the Lessing Theater, the military tragedy *Rosenmontag* (*The Day Before Mardi Gras*), by Otto Erich Hartleben, directed by Viktor Barnowsky.

15 The comedy *Cassanova in Spa*, by Arthur Schnitzler, premieres at the Königsberg Neues Schauspielhaus.

The thriller film *Der Friedhof der Lebenden* (*The Cemetery of the Living*), directed by Gerhard Lamprecht and starring Peter Esser and Hanni Weisse, premieres in Berlin.

16 The dramatic poem *Der abtrünnige Zar* (*The Renegade Czar*), by Carl Hauptmann, premieres at the Gera-Reuss Regional Theater.

The opera *Scirocco*, by Eugen d'Albert, premieres at the Darmstadt Regional Theater.

18 Two new productions of works by Ferruccio Busoni open at the Berlin State Opera: *Turandot* and *Arlecchino*.

19 Two film dramas premiere in Berlin: *Das Spiel mit dem Feuer* (*Playing with Fire*), directed by Georg Kroll and starring Diana Karenne and Wassily Kronsky; and *Mann Überbord* (*Man Overboard*), directed by Karl Grune and starring Grit Hergesa and Erich Kaiser-Titz.

20 *Am Webstühl der Zeit* (*At the Loom of Time*), directed by Holger Madsen and starring Erich Kaiser-Titz and Käte Haack, premieres in Berlin.

21 The drama *Der Irrgarten* (*The Labyrinth*), by Herbert Eulenberg, premieres at the Oldenburg Regional Theater.

29 A new production of the operetta *Die spanische Nachtigall* (The Spanish Nightingale) by Leo Fall and starring Fritzi Massary, premieres at the Düsseldorf Opera House.

JUNE

2 The film drama *Der Schwur des Peter Hergats* (*The Oath of Peter Hergats*), directed by Alfred Halm and starring Emil Jannings (in the title role) and Stella Harf, premieres in Leipzig.

The comedy *Die goldene Freiheit* (*Sweet Liberty*), by Theodor Gehr, premieres at the Theater in der Kommandanten Strasse in Berlin.

3 The comedy *Stroh* (*Straw*), by Hanns Johst, premieres at the Berlin State Theater.

4 Two one-act operas by Paul Hindemith premiere with the Württemberg State Orchestra, directed by Fritz Busch, at the Württemberg State Theater in Stuttgart: *Mörder, Hoffnung der Frauen* (*Murderer, Hope of Women*), based on the play by painter Oskar Kokoschka; and *Das Nusch-Nuschi*, based on a "play for the Burmese marionette theater" by Franz Blei.

6 The film melodrama *Das Achtgroschenmädel* (*The Eight-Penny Girl*), Parts 1 and 2, directed by Wolfgang Neff and starring Edith Posca (in the title role) and Conrad Curt Cappi, premieres in Berlin.

7 The comedy film *Das Gelübde* (*The Solemn Oath*), based on the stage comedy by Heinrich Lautensack, directed by Rudolf Biebrach and starring

Lotte Neumann and Theodor Loos, premieres in Berlin. The film drama *Die Fremde aus der Alstergasse* (*The Stranger from Alster Street*), directed by Alfred Topstary and starring Margit Bartnay and Olaf Storm, premieres in Berlin. *Teufel und Circe* (*The Devil and Circe*), directed by Adolf Gärtner, with Walter von Allwörden and Sascha Gura in the title roles, premieres in Munich.

8 The German Post Office transmits its first broadcast of an opera (*Madame Butterfly*, by Giacomo Puccini), from its studios in Königswusterhausen near Berlin.

9 Bavarian USPD chairman Karl Gareis is assassinated on the street in Munich.

10 Thousands of workers walk off their jobs in Munich to protest the murder of Karl Gareis; USPD members vote to grant Gareis's seat in the Bavarian legislature to playwright Ernst Toller, who remains imprisoned at Niederschönenfeld.

11 The premiere of Arthur Honegger's opera *King David* in Switzerland helps to introduce the composer's work to opera managers and audiences in Germany.

15 Playwright Paul Gurk is awarded the Kleist Prize for his tragedy *Thomas Münzer*.

16 The Potsdam Schauspielhaus is named "Theater of the Fatherland" to serve as a locale for companies touring from other German theaters.

17 The drama *Geständnis* (*Confession*), by Ernö Vajda,[10] makes its German premiere at the Deutsches Künstler Theater in Berlin.

20 New Fatherland Press publishes an account of the German revolution, *Zwei Jahre Mord* (*Two Years of Murder*), by legal historian Emil Julius Gumbel.

21 A massive new production of the drama *Die Weber* (*The Weavers*), by Gerhart Hauptmann, opens at the Grosses Schauspielhaus in Berlin.

23 The Bavarian Cultural Ministry establishes the Bavarian Regional Theater in Munich.

The film drama *Die Furcht vorm Weibe* (*The Fear of Women*), directed by Hanna Henning and starring Bernd Aldor and Maria Leiko, premieres in Berlin.

24 The crime film *Das Haus in der Dragonergasse* (*The House in Dragoon Street*), directed by Richard Oswald and starring Edmund Löwe, Lily Flohr, and Werner Krauss, premieres in Berlin.

29 Construction of a new 1,000-seat Metropol Operetta Theater in Cologne is completed.

30 German currency hits new lows against the U.S. dollar and other European currencies. One dollar now buys 75 RM.

JULY

1 Erich Kleiber is named musical director of the Düsseldorf orchestra and opera company.

The film drama *Der Perlenmacher von Madrid* (*The Pearl Maker of Madrid*), directed by Eberhard Frohwein and starring Hermann Wlach and Herma van Delden, premieres in Berlin.

2 The drama *The Swan*, by Ferenc Molnar, makes its German premiere at the Dresden State Theater.

12 The melodrama *He Who Gets Slapped*, by Leonid Andreyev, makes its German premiere at the Kammerspiele of the Deutsches Theater in Berlin.

The film melodrama *Jim Cowrey ist tot* (*Jim Cowrey Is Dead*), directed by Edmond Gottschalk Stratton and starring Hedda Vernon and Otto Flint, premieres in Berlin.

19 A summer production of the comedy *The Guardsman*,[11] by Ferenc Molnar, at the Künstler Theater in Berlin creates a sensation, due in part to the performance of Otto Gebühr in the role of The Actor.

20 The crime film *Das Rattenloch* (*The Rat's Hole*), directed by Ernst Reicher and Max Obal and starring Ernst Reicher and Grete Reinwald, premieres in Munich.

21 The comedy film *Trix, der Roman einer Millionärin* (*Trixie, the Story of a Millionairess*), directed by Friedrich Zellnik and starring Lya Mira (in the title role) and Ilka Grüning, premieres in Berlin.

22 The film drama *Der Flug in den Tod* (*The Flight into Death*), directed by Bruno Ziener and starring Ernst Winar and Gerturd Welcker, premieres in berlin.

29 The film drama *Die Erben von Tordis* (*Inheritors of the Tordis Estate*), directed by Robert Dinesen and starring Ica von Lenkeffy and Paul Hartmann, premieres in Berlin. A film adaptation of Gerhart Hauptmann's urban tragedy *Die Ratten* (*The Rats*), directed by Hans Kobe, with Emil Jannings as the pimp Bruno, Lucie Höflich as the landlady Frau John, Eugen Klöpfer as the landlord Herr John, and Maria Leiko as the would-be actress Pauline Pieperkarcka, premieres in Berlin.

Adolf Hitler is elected chairman of the National Socialist Workers' Party after tumultuous party meetings in Munich.

30   The University of Prague awards playwright Gerhart Hauptmann an honorary doctorate.

AUGUST

4   The opera *Liebelei* (*Loving*), by Franz Neumann, based on the play by Arthur Schnitzler, premieres at the Berlin Volksbühne.

The film drama *Ehrenschuld* (*A Debt of Honor*), directed by Paul Ludwig Stein and starring Olaf Fönss and Gertrud Welcker, premieres in Berlin.

8   The horror film *Die schwarze Spinne* (*The Black Spider*), directed by Siegfried Philippi and starring Lissy Lind and Max Ruhbeck, premieres in Berlin.

12   The adventure film *Die Perle des Orients* (*The Pearl of the Orient*), directed by Karlheinz Martin and starring Viggo Larsen and Carola Toelle, premieres in Berlin.

Käthe Kollwitz's lithograph *Helft Russland* (*Help Russia*) is offered for sale.

13   The thriller film *Das tote Hotel* (*The Hotel of the Dead*), directed by Martin Hartwig and starring Albert Steinrück and Fritz Beckmann, premieres in Berlin. The adventure film *Im Kampf um Diamantenfelder* (*At War in the Diamond Fields*), directed by Hans Schomburgk and starring Meg Gehrts and Oskar Marion, premieres in Berlin.

14   The comedy *Die Nacht der Jenny Lind* (*Jenny Lind's Night*), by Robert Prechtl, opens at the Munich Schauspielhaus.

17   Two film dramas premiere in Berlin: *Der Herr der Bestien* (*The Lord of the Beasts*), directed by Ernst Wendt and starring Carl de Vogt and Claire Lotto; and *Die Nacht ohne Morgen* (*Night and No Morning*), directed by Karl Grune and starring Eugen Klöpfer, Hans Mierendorff, and Hanni Weisse.

18   The drama *Notruf* (*Emergency*), by Hermann Sudermann, premieres at the Theater in der Königgrätzer Strasse in Berlin.

20   The comedy *Wem gehört Helene?* (*Who Does Helene Belong To?*), by Eberhard Buchner, premieres at the Künstler Theater in Berlin.

24 The biographical drama *Kean* (based on the life of the English actor Edmund Kean), by Kasimir Edschmid, premieres at the Deutsches Theater in Berlin.

26 Former finance minister Matthias Erzberger is murdered in the Black Forest by right-wing nationalists and former members of the Erhardt Brigade militia, who call themselves "Organization Consul"; they later escape across the Austrian border and avoid prosecution.

28 Two thrillers films premiere in Berlin: *Grausige Nächte* (*Gruesome Nights*), directed by Lupu Pick and starring Edith Posca, Adele Sandrock, and Alfred Abel; and *Der Leidensweg eines Achtzehnjährigen* (*The Miserable Life of an Eighteen-Year-Old Boy*), directed by Eberhard Frowein and starring Ria Jende and Ernst Laskowski.

31 Widespread demonstrations erupt in response to the murder of Matthias Erzberger; political leaders in many cities make speeches accusing right-wing fanatics of waging a terror campaign against democracy in Germany.

SEPTEMBER

1 A new theater opens in Bochum, dedicated to the production of operettas.
Three films premiere in Berlin: the melodrama *Das Kind der Strasse* (*The Child of the Streets*), directed by Wolfgang Neff and starring Harry Nestor and Anna von Palen; the comedy *Die Abenteuer der schönen Dorette* (*Dorette's Adventures*), directed by Otto Rippert and starring Hella Moja and Arnold Czempin; and the romance *Schöne Nacht* (*Beautiful Night*), directed by Manfred Noa and starring Manja Tzatschewa and Hans Albers.

2 At the Twelfth Zionist Congress in Carlsbad, Martin Buber,[12] in support of a non-nationalistic form of Zionism, calls for cooperation between Jews and Arabs in Palestine.

3 A new theater opens in Cologne, called the Theater am Friesenplatz, dedicated to producing nonelitist fare intended for ordinary working people.
The romantic film *Die Geliebte Rosowskys* (*Rosowsky's Lover*), directed by Felx Basch and starring Paul Wegener and Asta Nielsen, premieres in Berlin.
The comedy *Der Grosse Moritz und die kleine Justine* (*Big Mortiz and Little Justine*), by Robert Walter, premieres at the Hamburg Komödienhaus.

4 As part of the Nordic Week Festival in Lübeck, novelist Thomas Mann delivers a speech, "Goethe and Tolstoy."

7 The comedy *Jonnys Busenfreund* (*Johnny's Bosom Friend*), by Walter Ellis, premieres at the Komödienhaus in Berlin.

9 Three films about love premiere in Berlin: the comedy *Das Handicap der Liebe* (*The Handicap of Love*), directed by Martin Hartwig and starring Ferdinand von Alten, Trude Hoffmann and Magnus Stifter; the melodrama *Die kleine Dagmar* (*Little Dagmar*), directed by Alfred Halm and starring Grete Reinwald and Albert Bassermann; and the revenge tragedy *Sappho*, directed by Dimitri Buchowetski and starring Pola Negri and Johannes Riemann.

11 Operetta star Trude Hesterberg opens her cabaret Wilde Bühne (Wild Stage) in the basement of the Theater des Westens in Berlin.

12 The drama *Alles um Geld* (*It's All about Money*), by Herbert Eulenberg, at the Schlosspark Theater in Berlin.

The film drama *Die Geier-Wally* (*Wally of the Vulture Cave*), based on the popular 1875 novel by Wilhelmine Hillerns, directed by E. A. Dupont and starring Henny Porten, Albert Steinrück, and Wilhelm Dieterle, premieres in Berlin.

14 Nazi Party operatives set off a bomb at a meeting of the Bavarian League in Munich; the Party's *Sturmabteilung*, or Storm Troopers, later boast of their "battle readiness."

15 The drama *Die Spielereien der Kaiserin* (*The Czarina's Diversions*), by Max Dauthendey, premieres at the Lessing Theater in Berlin.

The musical film *Trick-Track*, directed by Emil Albes and starring Charlotte Ander and Rita Burg, premieres in Berlin. The figure of an orchestra conductor was printed into the film at the lower end of the screen, in an attempt to help the conductor in the movie theater's orchestra pit synchronize the music and image.

16 A new theater opens in Hamburg, called the Freie Bühne (Free Stage), dedicated to producing plays of interest to ordinary working people.

Three film dramas premiere in Berlin: *Das Geheimnis der Santa Margherita* (*The Secret of Satana Magarita*), directed by Rolf Randolf and starring Albert Steinrück and Maria Zalenka; *Der lebende Propeller* (*The Living Propeller*), directed by Richard Eichberg and starring Aruth Wartan and Felix Hecht; and *Die eiserne Acht* (*The Iron Outlaw*), directed by Emil Justiz and starring Ludwig Rex and Tatjana Irah.

19 Director Otto Falckenberg of Munich makes his directorial debut in Berlin with the drama *Herodes and Marianne*, by Friedrich Hebbel, at the Deutsches Theater, starring Werner Krauss, Wilhelm Dieterle, and Agnes Straub.

20 The remodeling of the Munich Lustspielhaus is completed, expanding the theater's seating capacity to 700.

21 The film drama *Der Spielmann* (*The Gambler*), directed by Karl Otto Krause and starring Sadjah Gezza and Carola Toelle, premieres in Berlin.

22 The documentary film *Im Kampf mit dem Berge* (*In Conflict with the Mountain*), directed by Arnold Fanck[13] and with music by Paul Hindemith, premieres in Berlin. The film drama *Aus den Memoiren seiner Filmschauspielerin* (*From the Memoirs of a Film Actress*), directed by Friedrich Zelnik and starring Lya Mara and Ernst Hofmann, premieres in Berlin. The film melodrama *Der heilige Hass* (*The Holy Hatred*), directed by Manfred Noa and starring Walter Wolff and Adolf Hille, premieres in Munich.

24 The comedy *Die Schauspieler* (*The Actors*), by Wolfgang Schmidtbonn, premieres at the Komödienhaus in Berlin.

25 The exhibition Ältere und Neue religiöse Kunst (Religious Art, Ancient and Modern) opens in the Cologne Schnütgen Museum.

The film drama *Die Frau von Morgen* (*The Woman of Tomorrow*), directed by Hans Oberlander and starring Maria Leiko and Poldi Langora, premieres in Munich.

26 The crime film *Das Verbrechen von Houndsditch* (*The Outrage at Houndsditch*), directed by Arthur Wellin and starring Sascha Guras and Hans Adalbert, premieres in Berlin.

27 The thriller film *Die Schreckensnacht in der Menagerie* (*The Night of Terror in the Menagerie*), directed by Ernst Wendt and starring Carl de Vogt and Claire Otto, premieres in Berlin.

29 The drama *Masse Mensch* by Ernst Toller, directed by Jürgen Fehling, premieres at the Berlin Volksbühne with an enormous cast that includes Heinz Hilpert, Veit Harlan, Heinz Bernecker, Walter Buhse, and Hanns Neussing.

30 The adventure film *Der Schatz der Azteken* (*The Treasure of the Aztecs*), directed by Heinz Carl Heiland and starring Loo Hall, Theodor Loos, and Otto Gebühr, premieres in Berlin.

OCTOBER

1 German currency hits unprecedented lows; one U.S. dollar now buys 125 RM.

3 The comedy *Das Loch in der Hecke* (*The Hole on the Hedgerow*), by Hans Müller Schlosser, premieres at the Stuttgart Regional Theater.

6 The fantasy film *Der müde Tod* (*Behind the Wall*), directed by Fritz Lang and starring Lil Dagover and Walter Janssen, premieres in Berlin.

7 The comedy film *Amor am Steuer* (*Love at the Wheel*), directed by Victor Janson and starring Ossi Oswalda and Josef Rehberger, premieres in Berlin.

8 The comedy *Ingeborg*, by Curt Goetz, premieres at the Theater am Kurfürstendamm in Berlin.

14 Three films premiere in Berlin: *Das kommt von der Liebe* (*It Comes from Love*), directed by Heinrich Bolten-Baeckers and starring Arnold Rieck and Leona Bergere; *Der Wahn der Philipp Morris* (*The Delusion of Phillip Morris*), directed by Rudolf Biebrach and starring Erich Kaiser-Titz and Lyda Salmonova; and *Die schwarze Pantherin* (*The Black Pantheress*), directed by Johannes Guter and starring Elena Polewitzkaja and Xenia Desni.

15 The dramatic verse trilogy *Der Spiegelmensch* (*The Man in the Mirror*), by Franz Werfels, premieres at the Leipzig Altes Theater.

17 The crime thriller *Marodeure der Großstadt* (*Marauders in the Big City*), directed by Peter Paul Felner and starring Maria Ley and Isa Marsen, premieres in Berlin.

18 The comedy *Der lasterhafte Herr Tschu* (*The Lascivious Mr. Chu*), by Julius Berstl, is revived at the Lessing Theater in Berlin.

The film drama *Der vergiftete Strom* (*The Poisoned Stream*), directed by Urban Gad and starring Wilhelm Diegelmann and Emmy Denner, premieres in Berlin.

20 The film epic *Lady Hamilton*, based on the historical novel *Leben und Liebe der Lady Hamilton* (*The Life and Loves of Lady Hamilton*), by Heinrich Schumacher, directed by Richard Oswald, with Liane Haid in the title role and Conrad Veidt as Lord Nelson, premieres in Berlin.

21 Two comic films premiere in Berlin, both of which feature music written for them by Max Graf: *Die Bettelgräfin von Kurfürstendamm* (*The Beggar-Countess of Kurfürstrendamm Boulevard*), directed by Richard Eichberg and starring Aruth Wartan and Toni Tetzlaff; and *Verlogene Moral* (*Dishonest Morality*), directed by Hanns Kobe and starring Eugen Klöpfer and Adele Sandrock.

22 The exotic film drama *Die Sendung des Yoghi* (*The Yogi's Mission*), directed by Joe May and starring Conrad Veidt and Mia May, premieres in Berlin.

24 The film drama *Die rote Nacht* (*The Red Night*), directed by Jaap Speyer and starring Mia Pankau and Hermann Wlach, premieres in Hamburg.

26 The thriller film *Satansketten* (*The Chains of Satan*), directed by Leo Lasko and starring Ressel Orla, Alfred Haase, and Margarete Kupfer, premieres in Berlin.

27 The drama *Spiel der Schatten* (*Play of Shadows*), by Hellmuth Unger, premieres at the Karlsruhe Regional Theater. The drama *Armand Carrel*, by Moritz Heiman, premieres at the Saxon State Theater in Dresden.

29 The drama *Caesars Stunde* (*Caesar's Last Hours*), by Friedrich Freksa, premieres at the Munich Schauspielhaus.

30 The film drama *Der ewige Kampf* (*The Eternal Struggle*), directed by Paul Ludwig Stein and starring Lotte Neumann and Alfons Fryland, premieres in Berlin.

31 The drama *Vom anderen Ufer* (*From the Other Shore*), by Hedwig Courths-Maler, premieres at the Luisen Theater in Berlin.

NOVEMBER

1 The film drama *Merista, die Tänzerin* (*Merista the Dancer*), directed by Julius Herzka, with Maria Minzenti in the title role, Max Devrient as Pope Alexander VI, and Oscar Gergei as Cesare Borgia, premieres in Berlin.

The tragicomedy *Peter Brauer*, by Gerhart Hauptmann (who is present in the audience), premieres at the Lustspielhaus in Berlin.

2 The adventure film *Eine Weisse unter Kannibalen* (*A White Woman among Cannibals*), directed by Hans Schomburgk and starring Meg Gehrts and Lely Duperrex, premieres in Berlin.

3 The "comedy with music" *Der Heilige Ambrosius* (*St. Ambrose*), by A. M. Willner and Arthur Rebner, premieres at the Deutsches Künstlertheater in Berlin.

4 Adolf Hitler's speech "Wer sind die Mörder?" ("Who Are the Murderers?") at the Munich Hofbräuhaus is interrupted by Communists and socialists, who confront him and his Storm Troopers. A pitched battle ensues, with dozens wounded.

The film melodrama *Violet, der Roman einer Mutter* (*Violet, the Story of a Mother*), based on the novel by Kurt Aram, directed by Artur Holz, and starring Olga Chekhova and Eugen Burg, premieres in Berlin.

5   The trial of actress/director Gertrud Eysoldt and her company from the Kleines Theater in Berlin ends in acquittal of everyone accused. Eysoldt had staged Schnitzler's play *La Ronde*, for which she and performers in the production were arrested on charges of "arousing a public scandal." Playwright Schnitlzer later bans all future performances of the play on the grounds of anti-Semitic hatred directed against him.

6   The film melodrama *Das Mädchen aus dem Sumpf* (*The Girl from the Swamp*), directed by Bruno Eichgrün and starring Elsa Schartner (in the title role) and Erwin Fichtner, premieres in Berlin.

7   The comedy film *Die Ehe der Hedda Olsen oder dir brennende Akrobatin* (*The Marriage of Hedda Olsen, or the Burning Acrobat*), directed by Richard Eichberg and starring Lee Parry (in the title role) and Oskar Sima, premieres in Berlin.

8   The comedy *Der Schwierige* (*The Difficult Man*), by Hugo von Hofmannsthal, premieres at the Munich Residenz Theater.

9   The adventure film *Zwischen Flammen und Feuer* (*Between Flames and the Fire*), directed by Carl Heinz Wolf and starring Ludwig Trautmann and Ernst Rotmund, premieres in Berlin.

11   Leopold Jessner's new staging of Shakespeare's *Othello* at the Berlin State Theater, starring Fritz Kortner, outrages many right-wing cultural critics; they argue that no Jew should play Othello.

12   The film drama *Der Galiläer* (*The Galilean*), directed by Dimitri Buchowetzki, with Adolf Fassnacht as Jesus of Nazareth,[14] premieres in Berlin.
   The comedy *Der Hühnerhof* (*The Chicken Coop*), by Wilhelm Neubauer, premieres at the Leipzig Schauspielhaus.

15   The comedy *Der Sprung ins Paradies* (*The Leap into Paradise*), by Sigmund Neumann, premieres at the Hamburg Thalia Theater.

17   The adventure film *Der Tiger von Eschnapur* (*The Tiger of Anantapur*), part 3 of the *Indian Grave* series written by Thea von Harbou, directed by Joe May and starring Conrad Veidt and Mia May, premieres in Berlin.

18   The film drama *Der Fürst der Berge* (*The Prince of the Mountains*), directed by Harry Piel and starring Friedrich Berger and Maria Asti, premieres in Berlin.

19   The opera *Das Christelfein*, by Heinz Pfitzner, with the composer himself conducting the orchestra, premieres at the Berlin State Opera.

21 The science fiction film *Die Insel der Verschollenen* (*The Island of Dr. Moreau*), based on the novel by H. G. Wells, directed by Urban Gad and starring Alf Blütecher and Hans Behrendt, premieres in Berlin.

23 The film melodrama *Die Beichte einer Gefallenen* (*The Confession of a Fallen Woman*), directed by Franz Hofer and starring Grita van Ryt (in the title role) and Fritz Beckmann, premieres in Berlin.

24 The comedy film *Die Abenteuerin von Monte Carlo* (*The Adventuress of Monte Carlo*), directed by Adolf Gärtner and starring Ellen Richter (as the Shah of Iran's mistress in the title role) and Anton Pointner, premieres in Berlin.

25 The film melodrama *Die Jagd nach Wahrheit* (*The Hunt for the Truth*), directed by Karl Grune and starring Erika Glässner and Fritz Kortner, premieres in Berlin.

DECEMBER

1 A new 1,400-seat operetta theater opens in Frankfurt am Main.

The film drama *Das begrabene Ich* (*The Buried Ego*), directed by Leo Lasko and starring Albert Patry and Lia Eibenschütz, premieres in Berlin.

2 The comedy *Der Wohltätigkeitsverein* (*The Charity Club*), by Oskar Pietschel, premieres at the Lichterfeld Theater in Berlin.

Two thriller crime films premiere in Berlin: *Das zweite Leben* (*The Second Life*), directed by Alfred Halm and starring Erner Hübsch and Grete Reinwald; and *Der Gang durch die Hölle* (*The Road to Hell*), directed by Carl Boese and starring Otto Gebühr and Rose Veldtkirch.

3 The opera *Die Hochzeit des Fauns* (*The Faun's Wedding*), by Bernhard Sekles, premieres at the Düsseldorf Opera House.

A "magical comedy with music," *Der böse Geist Lumpazivagabundus* (*The Evil Spirit Lumpazivagabundus*), by Johann Nepomuk Nestroy,[15] is revived at the Berlin State Theater.

4 The comedy *Luderchen* (*The Tart*), by Toni Impekoven, premieres at the Frankfurt am Main Neues Theater.

Kurt Wolff Press publishes *Heidentum, Christentum, Judentum* (*Paganism, Christianity, and Judaism*), by Max Brod.[16]

7 The comedy *Napoleon mit der Warze* (*Napoleon with Warts*), by Herbert Schönlank, premieres at the Hamburg Thalia Theater.

8 Four films premiere in Berlin: the comedies *Das Mädel von Piccadilly* (*The Girl from Piccadilly*), directed by Friedrich Zelnik and starring Lia Mara (in the title role) and Erich Kaiser-Titz, along with *Papa kann's nicht lassen* (*Papa Can't Allow It*), directed by Erich Schönfelder and starring Annemarie Korff, Lotte Neumann, and Hans Junkermann; the detective drama *Das Souper um Mitternacht* (*Supper at Midnight*), directed by Hans Werckmiester and starring Hans Winkelmann and Sybil Morel; and the melodrama *Die Schuldige* (*The Guilty Woman*), directed by Fred Sauer and starring Esther Carena and Maria Zalenka.

10 Albert Einstein officially receives the Nobel Prize in Physics from King Gustav V of Sweden in Stockholm.

12 The drama *Friedrich und Anna*, by Georg Kaiser, premieres at the Leipzig Kleines Theater.

The expressionist drama film *Die Hintertreppe* (*The Back Stairs*), directed by Leopold Jessner and starring Henny Porten, Wilhelm Dieterle, and Friz Kortner, premieres. This is the film directorial debut of Jessner; critics are nearly unanimous in their condemnation of it, accusing Jessner of not knowing the difference between theater and film.

13 A new staging by Max Reinhardt at the Deutsches Theater in Berlin of *The Dream Play*, by August Strindberg, starring Hermann Thimig, Helene Thimig, Werner Krauss, and Eugen Klöpfer, receives extraordinary praise from critics; the production is sold out for weeks thereafter.

Thomas Mann publishes an essay condemning interest in the racist novel *Die Sünde wider das Blut* (*Sins against the Blood*), by Arthur Dinter. Mann makes no assertion that such books should be banned, but insists on calling the author to account.

The Reichsbank reports that German gold reserves, which back the German currency, are rapidly dwindling.

15 Two film melodramas premiere in Berlin: *Die Hafenelore* (*Laurie of the Docks*), directed by Wolfgang Neff and starring Maria Zelenka (as Laurie) and Fred Immler; and *Zirkus des Lebens* (*Circus of Life*), directed by Johannes Guter and starring Werner Krauss and Greta Schröder.

16 The film drama *Die Todesleiter* (*The Ladder to Death*), directed by Joseph Delmont and starring Luciano Albertini, Linda Albertini, and Alfred Haase, premieres in Berlin.

17 The film drama *Die Brillantenmieze* (*The Diamond Girl*), directed by Wolfgang Neff and starring Ria Aldorf (in the title role) and Karl Falkenberg, premieres in Berlin.

18 The film version of *Kean* (based on the life of the English actor Edmund Kean), directed by Rudolf Biebrach and starring Heinrich George (as Edmund Kean) and Carola Toelle, premieres in Berlin.

21 The comedy film *Pariserinnen* (*Parisian Women*), directed by Leo Lasko and starring Ressel Orla, Xenia Desni, and Ralph Arthur Roberts, premieres in Berlin.

22 The film drama *Die minderjährige* (*The Under-Age Girl*), directed by Alfred Totary and starring Magda Madeleine and Grete Maria Markstein, premieres in Berlin.

23 The drama *The Red Robe*, by Eugene Brieux, premieres at the Lessing Theater in Berlin.

The thriller film *Die Liebesabenteuer der schönen Evelyne oder die Mordmühle auf Evanshill* (*Evelyn's Love Adventures, or the Murder Mill of Evanshill*), directed Richard Eichberg and starring Lee Parry as Evelyne, Oskar Sima, Max Worgritsch, and Aruth Wartan, premieres.

25 The comedy *Der Vulkan* (*The Volcano*), by Ludwig Fulda, premieres at the Dresden Neustädter Schauspielhaus.

27 The thriller crime film *Der Mord der Greenstreet* (*The Murder in Green Street*), directed by Johannes Guter and starring Wassily Wronski and Edwin Baron, premieres in Berlin.

28 The romantic film *Des Lebens und der Liebe Wellen* (*Waves of Life and Love*), directed by Loren Batz and starring Toni Tetzlaff and Fern Andra, premieres in Berlin.

29 The film drama *Der Eisenbahnkönig* (*The Railroad King*), directed by Eugen Illés and starring Fritz Kortner and Hermann Vallentin, premieres in Berlin.

30 Two film dramas premiere in Berlin: *Der Verfluchte* (*The Cursed Man*) directed by Franz Osten and starring Fritz Greiner, Violette Napierska, and Ila Loth; and *Kinder der Finsternis* (*Children of Darkness*) directed by E. A. Dupont and starring Hans Mierendorff, Sybil Smolowa, and Adele Sandrock.

NOTES

1. Hedwig Courths-Mahler (Ernestine Maler, 1867–1950) was one of the most popular and widely published fiction writers in the German language in the first decades of the 20th century with more than two hundred titles to her name between 1905 and

1940. Her fiction appealed to a broad, mostly female reading public. Her first hit was *Die wilde Ursula* (*Wild Ursula*, 1912), followed by a series of best sellers, among them *Der Scheingemahl* (*The Trophy Husband*, 1919), *Glückshunger* (*Hunger for Happiness*, 1921), and *Des Herzens süße Not* (*Sweet Needs of the Heart*, 1932), and many other novels and plays, usually dismissed by critics as kitsch or "trivial literature."

2. Hanns Heinz Ewers (Hans Heinrich Ewers, 1871–1943) wrote *Vampir* in the United States during World War I, where he worked as a propagandist for the German cause among many of America's German communities. In 1918, he was arrested as a German agent and imprisoned in Fort Oglethorpe, Georgia. He returned to Germany in July 1920.

3. Franz Heinrich Louis "Lovis" Corinth (1858–1925) became an important member of "secessionist" movements in both Berlin and Munich, which had an enormous impact on painting, sculpture, drawing, and lithography in the Weimar Republic. "Secession" artists are perhaps best described as those who felt their work could survive on the open art market without depending on art academies for commissions. They generally presented their work in large exhibitions and hoped in this fashion to attract buyers. Corinth in particular was noted for his work in various styles and genres, from landscapes to nudes, from the religious and mythic to still life, and particularly self-portraits.

4. In this adaptation written by Erwin Geppard, Nielsen played Hamlet as a woman, the daughter of her murdered royal father. Her mother Gertrude had reared her as a boy, hoping somehow that her daughter Hamlet would inherit the Danish throne. Nielsen produced the film herself. In 2005, a color version of this film was discovered in Frankfurt am Main, and in 2007 it was shown at the Berlin Film Festival as part of its retrospective exhibition, City Girls.

5. Friedrich Schiller's verse tragedy about Joan of Arc took substantial liberties with historical events, although since its premiere in 1801 it had remained a standard in German repertoires. It offered numerous German actresses a vehicle for career advancement, and any new production of the play usually attracted attention. This production starring Agnes Straub in the title role, was no exception.

6. Jean-Baptiste Attila Laban (1879–1958) became an extraordinarily influential figure in dance, beginning in Munich. He subsequently created a means of dance notation, allowing choreographers and dance teachers to make a record of choreography for use among dance and ballet companies long after the initial work for the stage was completed. He based the notation system on an ingenious comprehension of the human body's relationship to stage space, identifying specific directions in space into which the figure might move. One of his students, Mary Wigman (1886–1973), used his system to develop a dramatic, highly expressive form of dance movement.

7. *BZ am Mittag* (Berlin), 16 March 1921.

8. Fritz von Unruh (1885–1970) often wrote about Prussian themes, largely because he was the son of a Prussian general, graduated from the Prussian military academy (where his classmates were the sons of Kaiser Wilhelm II), and became a member of the Prussian officer corps. Many of his plays, including the aforementioned *Louis Ferdinand, Prinz von Preussen*, featured the Prussian military. Unruh broke

with his family's tradition, however; severely wounded in 1916, he resigned his commission and became a devoted pacifist. "I had a right do so," he later said. "I earned it on the blood-soaked battlefields of the Marne and Verdun."

9. Ernst Krenek (1900–1991) became one of the 20h century's most eclectic composers, writing works in styles that ranged from imitations of Gustav Mahler, to dissonant operas that mixed expressionism with American jazz idioms, to 12-tone symphonies in the style of Arnold Schönberg, to "serial music" (employing pitch, rhythm, and other musical patterns arranged in repetitive series). He immigrated to the United States in 1938, where he remained for the rest of his life, composing and teaching at numerous American colleges and universities. By the end of his career, he was using electronically produced sound in mathematically ordered sequences. In between such experiments, he composed traditional works employing melody and accessible rhythm.

10. Ernö Vajda (1886–1954) was born in Hungary and had a distinguished career as a Hollywood screenwriter (usually under the name Ernest Vajda) in the 1930s and 1940s. Among his notable screen credits were *Marie Antoinette* starring Norma Shearer and Tyrone Power; *Reunion in Vienna* starring John Barrymore and Diana Wynyard; *The Merry Widow* starring Jeanette MacDonald and Maurice Chevalier, directed by Ernst Lubitsch; and *The Great Garrick* starring Brian Aherne, Lana Turner, and Olivia de Havilland.

11. *The Guardsman* (originally *Testör* in Molnar's native Hungarian) was adapted for the movies by Molnar's fellow Hungarian Ernö Vajda and was released in 1931, starring Alfred Lunt and Lynn Fontanne in the only film they ever made together. The plot concerns a husband-and-wife acting team. The husband tries to test his wife's capacity for infidelity by disguising himself using a costume, makeup, and a thick accent. He successfully seduces her, but the implication remains that the wife knew all along who her lover really was. To humor her insecure husband, she may have played along with the trick. Lunt and Fontanne gave the play its Broadway premiere in 1924.

12. Philosopher, historian, and teacher Martin Buber (1878–1965) became a Zionist in 1898, but he favored a form of Zionism that emphasized spirituality and embraced the moral values of Judaism rather than the establishment of a European-style nation-state. Buber insisted on the inclusion of truth and justice in all institutions and activities of Jewish settlements in the Middle East, convinced that Judaism could thus contribute to human civilization as a whole. In 1921, he proposed a federation of Middle Eastern states that would include Jews and Arabs in a community that might have united the entire Middle East.

13. Arnold Fanck (1889–1974) invented the "German mountain film," born of his interest in geology, in which he had an earned doctorate. He later directed sport and ski films. A notable member of his crew was Leni Riefenstahl, who later became infamous for her work as "Adolf Hitler's favorite director," creating both *Triumph of the Will* (1934), thought to be a masterpiece of propaganda film making, and *Olympia*, a documentary of the 1936 Berlin Olympics. She also appeared as an actress in Fanck's *Die weisse Hölle von Piz Palü* (*The White Hell of Piz Palu*, 1929). The distinguishing characteristics of this and other mountain films were their authentic locales. Fanck shot towering peaks, glaciers, and steep slopes with aerial cameras,

shooting granite rock faces, limestone karsts, and steep crevasses with handheld equipment that he often designed himself. Fanck also created narratives around his filmed material, often resulting in dramatic confrontations between the forces of nature and his human protagonists.

14. The earliest known "Jesus movie" on record was *The Passion Play at Oberammergau* (1898), staged and filmed on the rooftop of the Grand Central Palace Theatre in New York City. Also in 1898, the French movie pioneer Louis Lumiére filmed a short movie titled *The Life and Passion of Jesus Christ*. It was essentially a tableaux of familiar incidents, introduced by captions identifying the action. In *Der Galiläer*, Adolf Fassnacht as Jesus is a curiously passive figure, but one who inspires compassion among those who encounter him.

15. This production was one of the few instances in which a play by Nestroy enjoyed a long run (102 performances) in Berlin during the Weimar Republic. Johann Nepomuk Nestroy (1801–1862) had been Vienna's most popular playwright and actor during the 1840s and 1850s, though he thereafter was generally ignored. The main action of this particular comedy involves three shiftless wastrels, to each of whom a mysterious spirit figure named Lumpazivagabundus gives a winning lottery number. They buy lottery tickets the next day and become instantly wealthy. Two of them go through their money quickly, but the third (played by Nestroy in the original production) reforms himself and marries his sweetheart. Nestroy now ranks among the most successful and noteworthy of the German-language theater's comic playwrights, whose plays are performed regularly throughout the German-speaking world. He is best known in America as the author of the comedy on which the musical *Hello, Dolly!* was based.

16. Max Brod (1884–1968) is perhaps best known as Franz Kafka's literary executor, but Brod was an accomplished and highly successful writer of both fiction and nonfiction in his own right. Brod and Kafka became close friends when both were students at the University of Prague. Brod escaped from Prague after the Nazi takeover there in 1939 and settled in Palestine, where he worked with the Habimah Theater in Tel Aviv.

1922

JANUARY

1 The film melodrama *Tanz der Leidenschaften* (*Dance of Passions*), directed by Charles Willy Kaiser and starring Rita Clermont and Fritz Falckenberg, premieres in Berlin.

The remodeled Chamber Theater of the Hessian Regional Theatre in Darmstadt opens as the 850-seat Kleines (Small) Theater.

The value of the German currency sinks to an exchange rate of RM 190 to one U.S. dollar.

2 An exhibition of the works of Paula Modersohn-Becker opens at the Flechtheim Gallery in Berlin.

3 The Moscow Art Theater begins a 45-day tour of Germany, with a residence in Berlin.

Steegemann Press publishes Melchior Vischer's "grotesque" novel *Sekunde durch Hirn* (*Seconds through the Brain*).

4 The drama *Elga*, by Gerhart Hauptmann, premieres at the Trianon Theater in Berlin.

The romantic film *Die Tigerin* (*The Tigress*), directed by Ernst Wendt and starring Margit Barnay (in the title role) and Carl de Vogt, premieres in Berlin.

5 The film melodrama *Der Fluch des Schweigens* (*The Curse of Silence*), directed by Felix Basch and starring Grete Freund and Hermann Thimig, premieres in Berlin. The historical film *Louise de Lavalliere*, directed by Georg Burghardt and starring Eva Speyer and Fritz Delius, premieres in Munich.

6 Thomas Mann's novella *Tod in Venedig* (*Death in Venice*) goes into its fifth printing since its original publication in 1912 by Fischer Press. Cassirer Press publishes Rosa Luxemburg's translation from the Russian of *The History of My Contemporaries*, by Vladimir Korolenko.

Three films premiere in Berlin: *Der Abenteurer* (*The Adventurer*), directed by Lothar Mendes and starring Michael Bohnen and Rudolf Forster; *Seine Exzellenz von Madagascar* (*His Excellency from Madagascar*), directed by Georg Jacoby and starring Paul Biensfeldt and Ellen Plessow; and *Tanja, die Frau an der Kette* (*Tania, the Woman in Chains*), directed by Friedrich Zelnik and starring Lya Mara and Erich Kaiser-Titz.

8 Rohwolt Press publishes *Meine sämtliche Werke* (*My Collected Works*), by operatic tenor Leo Slezak.

The comic film *Die Trutze von Trutzberg* (*Trutzi from Trutzberg*), directed by Ernst B. Hey and starring Toni Wittels (in the title role), Franz Xaver Stury, and Curt Gerdes, premieres in Munich.

9 Arthur Nikisch[1] conducts his farewell concert as director of the Berlin Philharmonic.

11 *Libussa: Memoiren des Leibrosses Kaiser Wilhelm II* (*The Memoirs of Libussa, Kaiser Wilhelm's Favorite Stallion*) is published by the Communist satirical magazine *Die Aktion*.

12 Adolf Hitler is sentenced to three months in jail for disturbing the peace in Munich.

13 Kurt Wolff Press publishes a biography of painter and printmaker Emil Nolde written by Max Sauerlandt.

The romantic film *Lotte Lore*, directed by Franz Eckstein and starring Ilka Grüning and Alfred Abel, premieres in Berlin.

14 The comedy *Des Esels Schatten* (*The Shadow of the Ass*), by Ludwig Fulda, premieres at the Mannheim National Theater.

The Nietzsche Foundation awards its grand prize to two authors: Richard Müller-Freienfels (1882–1949) for philosophy and Martin Havenstein (1871–1945) for pedagogy.

16 More than 50,000 members of unions and civic groups in Dresden contribute to the formation of a Volksbühne[2] in Dresden, with plans to create a theater serving the needs of average working people.

The Goldschmidt Gallery in Berlin opens a new exhibition of paintings, watercolors, and drawings by Lyonel Feininger.[3]

17 Roland Press publishes *Der Kunterbuntergang des Abenlandes* (very loosely translated, "The Potpourri Decline of the West"), by Klabund.

The Gurlitt Gallery in Berlin presents an exhibition of paintings by Lovis Corinth.

The thriller film *Das Geheimnis der grünen Villa* (*The Secret of the Green Villa*), directed by Margaret Lander and Hermann Wlach, premieres in Hamburg.

19 Cassirer Press produces a new printing of the enormously popular *Galgenlieder* (*Gallows Songs*), by Christian Morgenstern.

20 The operetta *Tanz ins Glück* (*Dancing Your Way to Happiness*), by Robert Stolz, premieres at the Theater des Westens in Berlin.

The historical film *Die Intriguen der Mme. de la Pommeraye* (*The Intrigues of Mme. Pommeraye*), directed by Fritz Wendhausen and starring Grete Berger (in the title role) and Alfred Abel, premieres in Berlin.

21 Fischer Press publishes *Ausgewählte Briefe aus den Jahren 1883–1902* (*Selected Letters from the Years 1883–1903*), by Richard Dehmel.

22 The film drama *Das ungeschriebene Gesetz* (*The Unwritten Law*), directed by Carl Boese and starring Grete Hollmann and Marie Escher, premieres in Munich.

23 Conductor Arthur Nikisch dies in Leipzig, where he had been conductor of the Leipzig Gewandhaus Orchestra and with whom he performed a farewell concert.

24 The film melodrama *Die Asphaltrose* (*Rose of the Asphalt Streets*), directed by Richard Löwenbein and starring Charlotte Böcklin and Robert Leffler, premieres in Berlin.

25 The drama *Verklärung Falaises* (*Transfiguration of the Cliffs*), by Hellmuth Unger, premieres at the Nuremberg City Theater.

The film drama *Geld auf der Strasse* (*Money in the Streets*), directed by Reinhold Schünzel and starring Liane Haid and Eugen Klöpfer, premieres in Berlin.

The Dessau Friedrich Theater is badly damaged by fire.

27 The cantata *Von deutscher Seele* (*From the German Soul*), by Hans Pfitzner, is premiered by the Berlin Philharmonic; Pfitzner conducts the performance.

The drama *Gobseck*, by Walter Hasenclever, premieres at the Saxon State Theater in Dresden.

The film drama *Gelbstern* (*Yellow Star*), directed by Wolfgang Neff and starring Uschi Elleot and Robert Scholz, premieres in Berlin.

28 The drama *Vater und Sohn* (*Father and Son*), by Joachim von der Goltz, premieres at the Leipzig Altes Theater.

Lovis Corinth designs settings for a new production of *Faust I* by Johann Wolfgang Goethe at the Lessing Theater Berlin, starring Emil Jannings as Faust and Arthur Kraussneck as Mephisto.

31 The historical film *Fridericus Rex: Vater und Sohn* (*Frederick the King: Father and Son*), directed by Arsen von Cserepy, premieres in Berlin, with Albert Steinrück as Frederick William I, known as the "Soldier King," Gertrud de Lalsky as Sophie Dorothea, by whom Frederick William I had 14 children, and Otto Gebühr as his son Frederick II, later known as Frederick the Great.

President Ebert announces the appointment of financier and businessman Walther Rathenau as foreign minister.

FEBRUARY

1 Otto Falckenberg stages a new production of *The Game of Life* by Nobel Prize–winning Swedish playwright Knut Hamsun.

2 The film drama *Fräulein Julie*[4] (based on the August Strindberg play *Miss Julie*), directed by Felix Basch and starring Asta Nielsen and Wilhelm Dieterle, premieres in Berlin.

4 The first bust of Albert Einstein for which the physicist himself actually sat, for the sculptor (Kurt Kroner), goes on display in Berlin.

5 The expressionistic tragedy *Die Krönung Richard III* (*The Coronation of Richard III*) by Hans Henny Jahnn premieres at Leipzig Schauspielhaus.

6 Wilhelm Furtwängler named new director of the Leipzig Gewandhaus Orchestra and conducts a memorial concert featuring the music of Beethoven and Brahms in honor of his predecessor, the recently deceased Arthur Nikisch.

7 The comedy *Lolas Onkel* (*Lola's Uncle*) by Wilhelm Weigand premieres at Dresden Neustädter Schauspielhaus.

10 Felix von Weingartner, principal conductor of the Vienna Symphony Orchestra, conducts the Berlin Philharmonic in a program of Mendelssohn and Beethoven as part of his application for the post of the orchestra's directorship.

12 The adventure film *Das Ende des Abenteurers Paolo de Caspado* (*The End of the Adventurer Paolo de Caspado*), directed by Franz Seitz and starring Fritz Greiner and Carla Ferra, premieres in Berlin.

13 Leopold Jessner stages his third experimental Schiller production (*Don Carlos*), with Ernst Deutsch in the title role and Lothar Müthel as the Duke of Alba. Many critics again protest the casting of a Jew (Ernst Deutsch) in the leading role of a "German classic."

14 The tragicomedy *Kanzlist Krehler* (*Court Clerk Krehler*), by Georg Kaiser, with stage designs by Georg Grosz, premieres at the Kammerspiele of Deutsches Theater in Berlin.

The melodrama *Frauen Opfer* (*The Victim Woman*), directed by Karl Grune and starring Henny Porten and Wilhelm Dietlerle, premieres in Berlin.

17 Euphorion Press publishes a collection of drawings by Lovis Corinth, *Dance of Death*.

Two films premiere in Berlin: *Kinder der Zeit* (*Today's Children*), directed by Adolf Edgar Licho and starring Paul Hartmann and Mady Christians; and *Brigantenrache* (*Revenge of the Bandits*), directed by Reinhard Bruck and starring Asta Nielsen and Bruno Decarli.

20 Insel Press publishes *Die Sonette an Orpheus* (*Sonnets to Orpheus*), a book of lyrical poetry, by Rainer Maria Rilke.

21 The historical epic film *Das Weib des Phäro* (*The Pharaoh's Concubine*), directed by Ernst Lubitsch, premieres in Berlin; it stars Emil Jannings as Pharaoh Amenes, Dagny Servaes as his concubine Teonis, and Harry Liedtke as Amphiris, her unfortunate lover.

Kipenheuer Press publishes the novel *Mysterium der Leidenschaft* (*The Mystery of Passion*), by Max Glass.

22 The film melodrama *Ihr schlechter Ruf* (*Her Bad Reputation*), directed by Franz Eckstein and starring Werner Funck and Olga Engl, premieres in Berlin.

23 The dramatic poem *Indiphodi*, with playwright Hauptmann directing the production, premieres at the Saxon State Theater in Dresden.

24 The musical farce *Der geistige Verschwender* (*The Absent-Minded Spendthrift*), by Richard Kessler, premieres at the Künstler Theater in Berlin.

Three films premiere in Berlin: *Das Mädel mit der Maske* (*The Girl with the Mask*), directed by Victor Janson and starring Ossi Oswalda and Paul Biensfeldt; *Das verschwundene Haus* (*The Vanished House*), directed by Harry Piel and starring Piel and Emmy Sturm; and *Ihr Kammerdiener* (*Her*

Manservant), directed by Willy Achsel and starring Erika Glässner and Gerhard Ritterbrand.

25 Malik Press publishes a book of Marxist sermons by Oskar Kanhel, *Steh auf, Piolet!* (*Proletarian, Arise!*), with illustrations by Georg Grosz.

28 Malik Press publishes a series of lithographs by Georg Grosz, *Im Schatten* (*In the Shadows*).

MARCH

3 Two film sex melodramas premiere in Berlin: *Das Logierhaus für Gentlemen* (*The Gentlemen's Lodging House*), directed by Louis Ralph and starring Karl Etlinger and Ludwig Trautmann; and *Die Erlebnisse einer Kammerzofe* (*The Experiences of a Lady's Chambermaid*), directed by Gerhard Lamprecht and starring Ria Aldorf and Karl Hannermann.

7 The film drama *Der grosse Dieb* (*The Great Thief*), directed by Rudolf Walther-Fein and starring Heinz Bernecker and Claire Reigbert, premieres in Berlin.

9 Kösel and Pustet Press publishes *Die St. Blasianische Germania Sacra* (*The Sacred Manuscripts of the St. Blasius Monastery*), by Georg Pfeilschifter.

The film drama *Der brennende Acker* (*Fields Aflame*), directed by F. W. Murnau and starring Vladimir Gaidaraov, Werner Krauss, and Eugen Klöpfer, premieres in Berlin.

10 Rowohlt Press publishes the "fictional conversation" *Erlöserin* (Redemptress), by Max Brod. Langen Press publishes *Im Zwielicht der Zeit* (*In the Twilight of Time*), a memoir by Walter von Molo.

11 *Judith*, by Friedrich Hebbel, directed by Berthold Viertel, is revived at the Theater in der Kommandanten Strasse in Berlin.

The Congress of Progressive Artists opens in Weimar; its members include organizations such as the November Group, Das junge Rheinland (Young Rhineland), the Dresden Secession, and the Darmstadt Secession.

13 The film drama *Der Unheimliche* (*The Sinister One*), directed by Ernst Wendt and starring Heinrich Marlow and Margo von Hardt, premieres in Berlin.

14 Malik Press publishes *Hunger an der Wolga* (*Hunger on the Volga*), by Franz Jung, an account of the famine following the Soviet revolution.

15 The horror film *Nosferatu, eine Symphony des Grauens*[5] (*Nosferatu, a Symphony in Cruelty*), directed by F. W. Murnau and starring Max Schreck, Alexander Granach, and Grete Schröder, premieres in Berlin.

16 The film melodrama *Schande* (*Shame*), directed by Siegfried Dessauer and starring Lilly Flohr and Robert Scholz, premieres in Berlin.

17 A film adaptation of Shakespeare's *Othello*, directed by Dimitri Buchowetski, premieres in Berlin; it stars Emil Jannings as Othello, Ica von Lenkeffy as Desdemona, and Werner Krauss as Iago. This film closely followed Shakespeare's tragedy in plot and character. Unlike his Jewish colleagues, Heinrich George faced no critical or popular opprobrium as a "non-German" in the role, although he did play it in blackface, as all German actors of the period did.

18 The comedy *David und Goliath*, by Georg Kaiser, premieres at the Minden City Theater.

20 Fleischel Press publishes *Vom Geist der Erde* (*From the Spirit of the Earth*), by Ernst Heilborn. Müller Press publishes *Mimik in Film*, a book of instructions for would-be film actors and actresses, by Oskar Diehl.

21 The comedy *Die Frau mit der Maske* (*The Woman with the Mask*), by Rudolf Lothar, premieres at the Hamburg Thalia Theater.

23 Hirsel Press publishes *Einführung in die Theorie der Elektrizität und des Magnetismus* (*Introduction to the Theory of Electricity and Magnetism*), by Max Planck, in a simplified and readable edition intended for the general public.

24 The *Frauenverkäufer* (*The Vendor of Women*), by Lion Feuchtwanger (based on *Niña de Gomez Arias* by Pedro Calderon de la Barca), premieres at the Munich Kammerspiele.

The comedy *Improvisationen im Juni* (*Improvisations in June*), by Max Mohr, premieres at the Munich Residenz Theater; Mohr's comedy quickly becomes an audience favorite,[6] and directors stage scores of new productions in theaters throughout Germany over the next two years.

The historical film *Das Diadem der Zarin* (*The Diadem of the Czarina*), directed by Richard Löwenbein and starring Dora Bergner and Eduard von Winterstein, premieres in Berlin. The film melodrama *Das schwarze Gesicht* (*The Black Face*), directed by Franz Osten and starring Mara Tschuklewa and Fritz Greiner, premieres in Munich.

28 Schaffstein Press publishes *Die Geschichte der deutschen Dichtung* (*The History of German Poetry*), by Julius Wiegand.

29 The historical film *Der Schmied von Kochel* (*The Blacksmith of Kochel*), directed by Ernst Scheberg and starring Otto Kornburger and Adolf Satzenhofer, premieres in Munich.

30 The comedy *Die Flucht aus dem Himmel* (*The Flight from Heaven*), by Fritz Mack, premieres at the Altenburg Regional Theater.

The tragic love story *Das Spiel mit dem Weibe* (*The Game with Women*), directed by Adolf Edgar Licho and starring Lotte Neumann and Georg Alexander, premieres in Berlin.

31 Sibyllen Press publishes *Der Kampf ums Theater* (*The Battle for Theater*), by critic Herbert Ihering, one of the first books to attempt an analysis of the German theater's modernist tendencies.

APRIL

1 The costume film *Die Ehe der Fürstin Demidoff* (*The Marriage of Princess Demidoff*), directed by Friedrich Zelnik and starring Lya Mara and Charles Willy Kaiser, premieres in Berlin.

The comedy *Vivat Academia*, by Karl Schönherr, premieres at the Hamburg Thalia Theater.

German currency continues to decline; one U.S. dollar now buys RM 298.

2 The drama *Der Freier* (*The Suitor*), by Julius Maria Becker, premieres at the Düsseldorf Schauspielhaus.

3 Grethlein Press publishes the novel *Brüderlichkeit* (*Brotherliness*), by Walter Bloem.

4 The operetta *Die Czardasfürstin* (*The Csardas Princess*), by Imre Kalman, premieres at the Künstler Theater in Berlin.

Schnell Press publishes *Die Amsel* (*The Thrush*), a book of poetry by Ludwig Bäte.

5 Mittler Press publishes *Meine Kriegserinnerungen, 1914–1918* (*My War Memories, 1914–1918*), by General Erich Ludendorff.[7]

A costume film about a prince who falls in love with his half-sister, *Es waren zwei Königskinder* (*Once Upon a Time Two Royal Children*), premieres; it is loosely based on the German folk song of the same title, directed by Arthur Günberg and starring Wilhelm Kayser-Heil and Tatiana Irrah.

6 The film drama *Der Todesreigen* (*The Circle of Death*), directed by William Karfiol and starring Olga Chekhova and Albert Steinrück, premieres in Berlin.

7 The comedy *Soll man—soll man nicht?* (*Should I or Shouldn't I?*), by Jens Lorcher, premieres at the Braunschweig Regional Theater.

The film melodrama *Lüge und Wahrheit* (*Lies and Truth*), directed by Lupu Pick and starring Edith Posca and Ilka Grüning, premieres in Berlin.

8 The Prussian Cultural Ministry establishes the Prussian Regional Theater, intended to serve the less urbanized areas around Berlin.

Grote Press publishes the novel *Der Wald* (*The Forest*), by Ernst Wiechert.

10 The film tragedy *Hanneles Himmefahrt* (*Hannele's Assumption*), based on the play by Gerhart Hauptmann, premieres; it is directed by Urban Gad, with Margarete Schlegel in the title role and music by Max von Schillings.

Mosse Press publishes the novel *Das schöne Mädel* (*The Beautiful Girl*), by Georg Hirschfeld.

11 *Christ*, the third part of a "world historical trilogy" by August Strindberg (the first two parts were *Moses* and *Socrates*, as yet unperformed in Germany), makes its German premiere at the Hannover Schauspielhaus.

Cotta Press publishes *Erlebnisse und Gespräche mit Bismarck* (*Experiences and Conversations with Bismarck*), by Adolf von Scholz.

12 The largest movie theater in Germany, the 2,000-seat Schauburg, opens for business in Cologne.

14 Three films premiere in Berlin: *Der Mann aus Stahl* (*The Man of Steel*) directed by Joseph Delmont and starring Luciano Albertiji and Carola Toelle; *Brudermord* (*Fratricide*), directed by Wolfgang Neff and starring Robert Scholz and Lilly Flohr; and *Die Glocke* (*The Bells*), directed by Franz Hofer and starring Grita van Ryt and Gustav Adolf Semler.

15 Wolff Press publishes *Imaginäre Brücken* (*Imaginary Bridges*), a book of essays by Jakob Wassermann. Steegemann Press publishes a new translation of Robert Louis Stevenson's *Dr. Jekyll and Mr. Hyde* as *Der Mann mit den zwei Gesichtern* (*The Man with Two Faces*), by Wilhelm Süskind.

16 American playwright Avery Hopwood's comedy *Fair and Warmer*,[8] translated by Berta Pogson as *Der Mustergatte,* makes its German premiere.

17 Wolfgang Kapp, who lent his name to the ill-fated Kapp Putsch, returns to Germany.

22 The expressionistic tragedy *Vatermord* (*Patricide*), by Arnolt Bronnen, premieres at the Frankfurt am Main City Theater.

Käthe Dorsch stars in a new production of Sardou's comedy *Mme. Sans-Gene* as the eponymous heroine, at the Lessing Theater in Berlin; the production is sold out for weeks.

Diedrich Press publishes the novel *Das Labyrinth* (*The Labyrinth*), by Ina Seidel.

25 Cassirer Press publishes limited editions of the lithograph *Das Konzert* (*The Concert*), by Max Liebermann.

27 The comedy *Schöne Seelen finden sich* (*Beautiful Souls Find Each Other*), by Fritz Berend, premieres at the Kassel State Theater.

28 The thriller film *Dr Mabuse, der grosse Spieler: Ein Bild inserer Zeit* (*Dr. Mabuse, the Gambler: A Picture of Our Time*), directed by Fritz Lang and starring Rudolf Klein-Rogge (in the title role), Alfred Abel, Aud Egede Nissen, Bernhard Goetzke, and Gertrud Welcker, premieres in Berlin.

29 The film tragedy *Am roten Kliff* (*On the Red Cliff*), directed by Hanna Henning and starring Fritz Kortner and Agne Straub, premieres in Berlin.

30 The film melodrama *Das Strassenmädchen von Berlin* (*Girl of the Berlin Streets*), directed by Richard Eichberg and starring Lee Parry and Aruth Wartan, premieres in Berlin.

MAY

1 An abstract steel-plate sculpture designed by Walter Gropius, commemorating nine industrial workers killed during the Kapp Putsch of March 1920, is unveiled in a Weimar cemetery.

2 Rowohlt Press publishes the novella *Die Physiker von Syrakus* (*The Physicists from Syracuse*), by Heinrich Eduard Jakob.

The adventure film *Kapura, die tote Stadt* (*Kaopura, the Dead City*), directed by Heinz Carl Heiland and starring Loo Hall and Hugo Flink, premieres in Berlin.

3 Müller Press publishes the "fantastic novel" *Der Geisterseher* (*The Spirit Medium*), by Hanns Heinz Ewers. Fischer Press publishes a collection of poetry, *Die heimliche Stadt* (*The Secret City*), by Oskar Loerke.

4 Insel Press publishes the novel *Eine Kindheit* (*A Childhood*), by Hanns Carossa.

5 A revival of *Napoleon, oder die Hundert Tage* (*Napoleon, or the Hundred Days*), by Christian Dietrich Grabbe, is staged with a cast of more than 200 by Leopold Jessner at the Berlin State Theater. It is among the first Jessner productions in Berlin to win both critical and popular acceptance.

Maien Press publishes the novella *Schaffende* (*The Executors*), by Gertrud Prellwitz.

6 The comedy *You Never Can Tell*, by George Bernard Shaw, translated by Siegfried Trebitch,[9] premieres at the Künstler Theater in Berlin.

8 Tal Press publishes the drama *Die Maschinenstürmer* (*The Luddites*), by Ernst Toller.

10 An exhibition opens in Berlin presenting new paintings by members of the Berlin Academy of the Arts.

Vieweg Press publishes *Vier Vorlesungen* (*Four Lectures*), which discuss the Theory of Relativity, originally presented at Princeton University in 1921 by Albert Einstein.

The romantic film *Die Geliebte des Königs* (*The King's Lover*), directed by Friedrich Zelnik and starring Lya Mara (in the title role) and Erich Kaiser-Titz, premieres in Berlin.

12 Kaemmerer Press publishes the novel *Gestern und Heute* (*Yesterday and Today*), by theater critic Alfred Polgar. Rothbarth Press publishes the novel *Die Pelzkönigin* (*The Fur Coat Queen*), by Hedwig Courths-Mahler.

Two films premiere in Berlin: *Der Marquis von Bolibar* (*The Marquis of Bolibar*), directed by Friedrich Porges and starring Hanns Schindler (in the title role) and Ida Koor; and the circus film *Die vom Zirkus* (*Circus People*), directed by William Kahn and starring Tony Ebärg and Anita Berber.

13 The two-character opera *Herzog Blaubarts Burg* (*Bluebeard's Castle*), by Béla Bartók, makes its German premiere at the Frankfurt am Main City Opera House.

An exhibition featuring only drawings in pen and ink by Berlin Secession artists opens; Lovis Corinth is prominently featured.

14 Arnolt Bronnen's *Vatermord* (*Patricide*) premieres at the Deutsches Theater in Berlin, disrupted repeatedly by the audience protesting the play's portrayal of incest between son and mother. Police arrest disruptive audience members and Bronnen himself, who had confronted them in the street outside the theater.

17 *Des Esels Schatten* (*The Shadow of the Ass*), by Ludwig Fulda, premieres at the Deutsches Theater in Berlin; the actress Elisabeth Bergner is its star. She also appears prominently in the Deutsches Theater's controversial production of *Vatermord* (*Fratricide*).

18 The crime film *Betrogene Betrüger* (*The Betrayers Betrayed*), directed by Arsen von Cserepy and starring Harry Hart and Lilly Alexandra, premieres in Berlin.

19 The comedy film *Der Raub der Dollarprinzessin* (*The Rape of the Dollar Princess*), directed by Franz Seitz and starring Lotte Loring (in the title role) and Charles Willy Kayser, premieres in Munich.

20 The Greater Berlin Art Exhibition opens, featuring the work of both individuals and organizations, including the League of German Architects, the Düsseldorf Artists Union, the "Young Rhineland" group, and many others.

The farce *Der blaue Heinrich*, by Otto Schwartz and Georg Lenzbach, premieres at the Frankfurt City Theater.

22 Musarion Press publishes *Die Offenbarung der Musik: Eine Apotheose Friedrich Nietzsches* (*The Revelation of Music: An Apotheosis of Friedrich Nietzsche*), by Walter Armando.

25 Russian painter Wassily Kandinsky joins the faculty at the Bauhaus School in Weimar.

26 *Dr. Mabuse, der Spieler: Inferno, ein Spiel von Menschen unserer Zeit* (*Dr. Mabuse, the Gambler: Inferno, a Game of People in Our Time*) premieres in Berlin; it is a continuation of the initial *Mabuse* film that premiered one month earlier; likewise directed by Fritz Lang, with Rudolf Klein-Rogge as Dr. Mabuse.

27 Wolff Press publishes *Studien über die Bewegungesetze der menschlichen Gesellschaft* (*Studies in the Laws of Movement within Human Society*), a fragmentary manuscript by Karl Liebknecht.

29 The Oberammergau Passion Play, normally performed every 10 years but halted since 1910, is resumed. Approximately 340,000 spectators see the production and its 2,000 cast members over the summer months.

JUNE

1 The musical comedy *Die erste Nacht* (*The First Night*), by Hans Zerlett, premieres at the Künstler Theater in Berlin.

3 The classical Sanskrit play *Vantasena*, by Dudraka, translated by Lion Feuchtwanger, makes its German premiere at the Dresden State Theater.

4 An assassination attempt is made against former chancellor of the Weimar Republic Philipp Scheidemann in Kassel; Scheidemann, now the mayor of Kassel, is unhurt, and the perpetrators (members of the right-wing terrorist group Organization Consul) are apprehended.

5 The drama *Stürme* (*Storms*), by Fritz von Unruh, premieres at the Hessian Regional Theater in Darmstadt.

8 Tal Press publishes a collection of poetry, *Der schwermütige Musikant* (*The Melancholy Musician*), by Heinrich Leuthold, with illustrations by Leo Frank.

9 Four films premiere in Berlin: *Alexandra*, directed by Theo Frenkel and starring Margit Barnay (in the title role) and Paul de Groot; *Matrosenliebste* (*The Love of a Sailor*), directed by Hans Werckmeister and starring Clair Lotto, Carl de Vogt, and Hans Winkelmann; *Die Strandnixe* (*The Mermaid*), directed by Max Agerty and starring Lilly Flohr, Josef Commer, and Felix Hecht; and *Memoiren eines Kammerdieners* (*The Memoirs of a Valet*), directed by Arthur Teuber and starring Ernst Hofmann and Evi Eva.

10 Müller Press publishes two volumes: the historical survey *Die dreizehn Bücher der deutschen Seele* (*The Thirteen Books of the German Soul*), by Wilhelm Schäfer; and a collection of essays, *Zwischenreich* (*The Realm of the In-Between*), by Wilhelm von Scholz.

12 Beck Press publishes the second volume of the popular *Der Untergang des Abendlandes* (*The Decline of the West*), by Oswald Spengler, titled *Weltkritische Perspektive* (*Perspectives of World History*).

15 Reiss Press publishes a collection of poetry, *Helle Nacht* (*Bright Night*), by Emmy Hennings.

16 The comedy *Der Bigamist* (*The Bigamist*), by Otto Ernst Hesse, premieres at the Düsseldorf Schauspielhaus.

19 A federal court convicts publisher Paul Steegemann of distributing obscene literature (the publication of three volumes of poetry) by Paul Verlaine.

23 Attendees at a convention of German Volksbühne organizations in Bielefeld hear Social Democratic politician Carl Severing's call for more leftist political involvement in the German theater.

24 Foreign minister Walther Rathenau is assassinated in Berlin by members of the right-wing terrorist group Organization Consul. Its supporters celebrate in Berlin's streets with the chant "Auch Rathenau, der Walther/Erreicht kein hohes Alter!/Knallt ab den Walther Rathenau/Die gottverdammte Judensau!" (Now Walter, too, will never see old age! Down goes Rathenau, the God damned Jewish swine!)

26 President Ebert issues an emergency decree "for the defense of the Republic," permitting local officials to forbid expressions of menace or violence toward the republic or members of the government. Berlin police find evidence of a conspiracy to murder Rathenau and issue arrest warrants for members of Organization Consul.

27 A funeral is held for Walther Rathenau in the Reichstag; a full orchestra plays the overture to *Egmont* by Beethoven as several speakers eulogize the foreign minister; the occasion prompts outpourings of sympathy from thousands in Berlin streets, demonstrating against continued assassination attempts. Workers stage a general strike throughout Berlin to demonstrate "proletarian solidarity" with the republic.

28 Flechtheim Gallery presents an exhibition of new paintings by Rudolf Levy.

30 The drama *Die Maschinenstürmer* (*The Luddites*), by Ernst Toller, premieres at the Grosses Schauspielhaus in Berlin.

JULY

1 The satirical play *Das Christbaumbrettl* (*The Christmas Tree Show*), by comedian Karl Vallentin, premieres at the Hotel Germania in Munich.

The German currency exchange rate stands at RM 403 to one U.S. dollar.

2 Fischer Press publishes a two-volume set of Thomas Mann's novellas.

3 Insel Press publishes a collection of aphorisms, character sketches, and observations by Hugo von Hofmannsthal, *Buch der Freunde* (*Book of Friends*).

Journalist Maximilian Harden[10] is attacked and badly beaten by right-wing activists in a pattern of violent assaults against prominent Jews.

5 The opera *Julius Cäsar*, by Georg Friedrich Händel, makes its German premiere at the Göttingen City Theater.

The comedy *Der Stiefel* (*The Boot*), by Carl Rössler, premieres at the Munich Kammerspiele.

7 The film melodrama *Der Roman einer Halbwelt Dame* (*The Story of a Woman from the Demi-monde*), directed by Siegfried Dessauer and starring Sascha Gura, Uschi Elleot, and Robert Scholz, premieres in Berlin.

9 The historical drama *Friedrich der Grosse* (*Frederick the Great*), by Hermann von Boetticher, premieres at the Bochum City Theater.

14 The adventure film *Die weisse Wüste* (*The White Wasteland*), directed by Ernst Wendt and starring Max Kronert and Maria Bauer, premieres in Berlin.

17 Erwin Kern and Hermann Fischer, accused in the murder of Walther Rathenau, commit suicide in their hideout at the ruins of Saaleck Fortress near Bad Kösen, about 30 miles northeast of Weimar.

18 Cassirer Press publishes the *Gesammelte Schriften* (*Collected Writings*) of painter Max Liebermann.

20 Müller Press publishes the novella *Die mächstigste Frau* (*The Most Powerful Woman*), by Josef Magnus Wehner.

AUGUST

2 There is panic in the Berlin Stock Exchange as the German Reichsmark suddenly falls to 860 to one U.S. dollar

4 Insel Press publishes the dramatic spectacle *Das Salzburger Grosse Welttheater*, by Hugo von Hofmannsthal.

6 The spectacle Bilder aus der grossen französischen Revolution (Pictures from the Great French Revolution) premieres at the Festival of Trade Unions in Leipzig, sponsored by the Independent Social Democratic Party (USPD).

9 The Ministry of the Interior issues curriculum guidelines to inculcate republican values in civics classes in German elementary and secondary schools.

10 The comedy film *Yvette, die Modeprinzessin* (*Yvette, the Fashion Princess*), directed by Friedrich Zelnik and starring Lya Mara (in the title role) and Erich Kaiser-Titz, premieres in Berlin.

11 The Gerhart Hauptmann Festival opens in Breslau with a new production of the playwright's historical drama *Florian Geyer*, starring Eugen Klöpfer.

The adventure film *Die sterbende Stadt* (*The Dying City*), directed by Holger Madsen and starring Henrik Galleen and Geddy Goodwin, premieres in Munich.

"Deutschland, Deutschland Über Alles" is designated the German national anthem.

12 This is the second day of the Gerhart Hauptmann Festival in Breslau, where a new production of the playwright's tragedy *Fuhrmann Henschel*, starring Eduard von Winterstein, is being presented. President Ebert attends. Ebert later speaks at Breslau's city hall in praise of Hauptmann. The playwright states that the occasion for the festival and for Ebert's presence is "Germany itself."

13 A new production of Hauptmann's comedy *Der Biberpelz* (*The Beaver Coat*), starring Lucie Höflich and Emil Jannings, is presented on the third day of the Hauptmann Festival in Breslau.

15 Rowohlt Press publishes *Die Septemberovelle* (*The September Novella*), by Arnolt Bronnen.

The German government announces its inability to make reparation payments to the victorious Allies as set forth in the terms of the Treaty of Versailles.

16 Adolf Hitler attracts 70,000 people to a Munich stadium to hear his speech condemning the Weimar Republic and its attempts to preserve itself.

17 The film melodrama *Die Dame und Ihr Friseur* (*The Lady and Her Hairdresser*), directed by Heinz Ullstein and starring Aenne Ullstein and Eugen Rex, premieres in Berlin.

The theater troupe Die junge Bühne (The Young Stage) is established as "a protest against the forces of show business." Theodor Tagger leases the Renaissance Theater in Berlin; Erwin Piscator and Hans José Rehfisch open their Proletarian Volksbühne at the Central Theater in Berlin.

19 The film melodrama *Das Spielzeug einer Dirne* (*The Strumpet's Plaything*), directed by Ernst Fiedler-Spies and starring Colette Corder and Heinrich Schroth, premieres in Munich. The historical tragedy *Luise Millerin* (*Luise Miller*), based on Schiller's drama *Kabale und Liebe* (*Intrigue and Love*), premieres in Berlin, directed by Carl Froelich, with Lil Dagover in the title role, Paul Hartman as Ferdinand, Fritz Kortner as Miller, Friedrich Kühne as the president, and Werner Krauss as Wurm.

23 The film melodrama *Im Glutrausch der Sinne* (*In a Raging Fever of the Senses*), directed by Willi Zeyn and starring Sascha Gura and Carl Auen, premieres in Berlin.

29 Lehmann Press publishes *Rassenkunde des deutschen Volkes* (*Racial Elements of the German People*), by Hans Günther.

SEPTEMBER

1 George Szell, later musical director of the Berlin State Opera, conductor of the Berlin Radio Orchestra, and director of the Cleveland Orchestra, assumes the musical directorship of the Düsseldorf Opera House.

Berthold Viertel becomes in-house director at the Deutsches Theater in Berlin.

Three films premiere in Berlin: *Erniedrigte und Beleidigte* (*Insulted and Humiliated*), directed by Friedrich Zelnik and starring Lya Mara and Erich Kaiser-Titz; *Der Passagier von Nr. 7* (*The Passenger in Compartment Number 7*), directed by Willy Zeym and starring Max Landa and Hanni Weisse; and *Der schlummernde Vulkan* (*The Sleeping Volcano*), directed by James Bauer and starring Hans Miererendorff and Margit Barnay.

2 President Friedrich Ebert authorizes the use of the national anthem, "Deutschland, Deutschland Über Alles," at all military functions.

3 National Netherlands Week begins, celebrating the close ties between Germany and Holland, which extended asylum to former German Kaiser Wilhelm II and refuses to recognize numerous demands for his extradition as a war criminal.

6 Engelhorn Press publishes two plays by Herbert Eulenberg, *Mückentanz* (*Mosquito Dance*) and *Der Übergang* (*The Transition*).

7 The comedy *Lissi die Kokotte* (*Lissi the Coquette*) premieres at the Trianon Theater in Berlin.

8 Osterheld Press publishes the four-volume *Die Chronik des deutschen Dramas* (*Chronicle of German Drama*), by Julius Bab.
 The historical film *Der Graf von Charolais* (*Count Charolais*), directed by Karl Grune and starring Eva May and Wilhelm Dieterle, premieres in Berlin. The detective film *Der Mann im Hintergrund* (a Dutch-German production), directed by Ernst Winar and starring Erich Walter and Herma van Delden, premieres in Berlin.

12 The comedy film *Der böse Geist Lumpazivagabundus* (*The Evil Spirit Lumpazivagabundus*), based on the comedy by Johann Nepomuk Nestroy, directed by Carl Wilhelm and starring Hans Albers, Otto Laubinger, Fritz Hirsch, and Karl Etlinger, premieres in Berlin.

14 The historical film *Der Graf von Essex* (*Count Essex*), directed by Peter Paul Felner and starring Eugen Klöpfer (in the title role) and Werner Krauss, premieres in Berlin. The adventure film *Praschnas Geheimnis* (*Prashna's Secret*), directed by Ludwig Baetz and starring Hermann Leffler and Fern Andra, premieres in Berlin.

15 Fischer Press publishes *Siddhartha*, a lyric novel about the early life of the Buddha, by Hermann Hesse.

16 The religious drama *Golgotha*, by Alexander Köhler, premieres at the Dresden Regional Theater.

17 The world's first exhibition of a sound film takes place at the Alhambra Lichtspiele (movie house) in Berlin, featuring sound-on-film technology developed by the Tri-Ergon Company. The film is essentially a program of music and voice-over narration.

18 Bavarian State Radio begins broadcasting in Munich.

20 Rowohlt Press publishes the novel *Cormick, der Spieler* (*Cormick the Gambler*), by Max Krell.

23 The drama *Trommeln in der Nacht* (*Drums in the Night*), by Bertolt Brecht, about the Spartacist uprising in January 1920, premieres at the Munich Kammerspiele. The drama fragment *Der Sonnenspektrum* (*The Solar Spectrum*), by Frank Wedekind, premieres at the Tribüne Theater in Berlin.

The comedy film *Miss Venus*, directed by Ludwig Czerny and starring Ada Svedin (in the title role) and Manny Ziener, premieres in Berlin.

25 Rowohlt Press publishes the comedy *Der ewige Traum* (*The Eternal Dream*), by Paul Kornfeld.

27 The Congress of Dadaists and Constructivists convenes in Weimar.

29 Erwin Piscator opens his new "proletarian theater" at the Central Theater in Berlin with *Summerfolk*, by Maxim Gorky.

30 The drama *Die Nächte des Bruder Vitalis* (*The Nights of Brother Vitalis*), by Dietzenschmidt (Franz Anton Schmid), premieres.

OCTOBER

1 The Reichsmark begins a precipitous slide in value against the U.S. dollar, trading at RM 1,658 to $1. The decrease in the Reichsmark's value means price inflation in nearly every sector of German life. Train tickets cost 4,500 percent more than they did in 1914; newspapers and magazine see similar price increases due to higher costs of raw materials and production.

A comedy with the somewhat prophetic title *Das kritische Jahr* (*The Critical Year*), by Rudolf Lothar and Hans Bachwitz, premieres at the Hamburg Thalia Theater.

2 Fatherland Press publishes a lavish leather-bound and gold-embossed book of pictures, testimonials, and biographical essays on Field Marshal Paul von Hindenburg, *Hindenburg Denkmal für das deutsche Volk* (*Hindenburg*

Memorial for the German People); it becomes an immediate best seller despite its high price.

6 Three films premiere in Berlin: the drama *Jugend* (*Youth*), directed by Fred Sauer and starring Grete Reinwald and Fritz Schulz; the comedy *Knoppchen und seine Schwiegermutter* (*Little Knopp and His Mother-in-Law*), directed by Heinrich Bolten-Baeckers and starring Frederik Buch and Grete Flohr; and the melodrama *Vanina*, based on the novella by Stendhal, directed by Arthur von Gerlach, and starring Asta Nielsen and Paul Wegener.

7 Langen Press publishes three novels: one about naval warfare, *Die Woge* (*The Sea Billow*), by Joachim Ringelnatz; *Die Liebes-Symphonie* (*The Symphony of Love*), by Walter von Molo; and *Der Mooshof* (*The Mossy Farmyard*), by Karl Friedrich Kurz.

9 Wilhelm Furtwängler conducts the Berlin Philharmonic for the first time as its musical director in a performance of Anton Bruckner's Symphony no. 7 in E Major.

Carl Sternheim directs the premiere of his comedy *Der Nebbich* (*The Simpleton*) at the Deutsches Theater in Berlin.

10 Rowohlt Press publishes the comedy *Die Excesse* (*The Excesses*), by Arnolt Bronnen. The German Publishing Institute issues the novel *Unter dem Freiheitsbaum* (*Beneath the Tree of Freedom*), by Clara Viebig, about the "Rhineland Robin Hood" named Schinderhannes.[11]

11 President Ebert issues an emergency decree aimed at halting currency speculation.

The comedy *Henne und Korb* (*The Caged Hen*), by Bruno Frank, premieres at the Komödienhaus in Berlin.

13 The drama *Vater und Sohn* (*Father and Son*), by Joachim von der Goltz, premieres at the Lessing Theater in Berlin.

Three films premiere: in Munich, the thriller *Das Auge des Toten* (*The Eye of the Dead*), directed by Carl Boese and starring Vilma Banky and Theo Schal; in Berlin, the melodrama *Die Macht der Versuchung* (*The Power of Temptation*), directed by Paul Ludwig Stein and starring Lil Dagover and Paul Otto; and also in Berlin, the Austrian-German coproduction of the quasibiblical epic *Sodom und Gomorrah*, directed by Mihaily Ketersz (later Michael Curtiz), with Lucy Doraine as Lot's wife and Michael Varkonyi as an Angel of the Lord.

14 In a desperate attempt to bring in foreign currency, Berlin theaters and concert halls raise ticket prices for foreigners to as much as five times what

Germans pay. Managers and producers have raised ticket prices three times this year. A ticket to the Berlin State Opera now costs (for Germans) RM 1,000.

18 The new Renaissance Theater in Berlin opens with a production of the tragedy *Miss Sara Sampson*, by Gotthold Ephraim Lessing.

Wolff Press publishes the novel *Franzi, oder eine Liebe zweiten Ranges* (*Franzi, or a Second-Class Love Affair*), by Max Brod.

19 Benziger Press publishes a collection of novellas, *Frauenland* (*Woman Country*), by Henriette Brey.

21 A Berlin appeals court approves the dramatization of contemporary figures and the appearance of same on Berlin stages.

The drama *Bockgesang* (*Goat Song*), by Franz Werfel, premieres at the Leipzig Schauspielhaus.

The period film *Lucrezia Borgia*, directed by Richard Oswald, with Liane Haid in the title role and Conrad Veidt as Cesare Borgia, premieres in Berlin.

22 The Exhibition of Revolutionary Artists opens in Berlin, featuring works by members of Die Kommune (The Commune) under the leadership of Polish painter/essayist Stanislaw Kubicki and painter/sculptor Otto Freindlich.

The comedy *Die siamesichen Zwillinge* (*The Siamese Twins*), by Karl Streng, premieres at the Sonderhausen Regional Theater.

23 The mountain film *Das Wunder des Schneeschuhs* (*The Miracle of the Snow Shoe*), directed by Arnold Fanck and starring Hannes Scyhneider and Lita Korff, premieres in Berlin.

24 The thriller crime film *Der Jagd nach dem Tode II: Die verbotene Stadt* (*The Hunt for Death, Part II: The Forbidden City*), directed by Karl Gerhardt and starring Lil Dagover and Nils Chrisander, premieres in Berlin.

27 Painter Max Pechstein and graphic artist Thomas Theodor Heine are named new members of the Prussian Academy of the Arts.

The romantic film *Es leuchtet meine Liebe* (*My Love Will Light the Way*), directed by Paul Ludwig Stein and starring Mady Christians and Theodor Loos, premieres in Berlin.

28 The period film *Marie Antoinette, das Leben einer Königin* (*Marie Antoinette, the Life of a Queen*), directed by Rudolf Meinert and starring Diana Karenne (in the title role) and Ernst Hofmann, premieres in Berlin.

30 The drama *Mutterlegende* (*Mother Legends*), by Hellmuth Unger, premieres at the Bremen City Theater.

NOVEMBER

1 Kösel Press publishes the novel *Der ungerechte Heller* (*Heller the Unjust*), by Peter Dörfler.

2 The drama *Propheten* (*Prophets*), by Hanns Johst, about the life of Martin Luther and other leaders of the Protestant Reformation, premieres at the Dresden State Theater.

A gathering of international financial experts in Berlin considers ways to stabilize the German currency; they reach no final conclusions or agreements.

Two film melodramas premiere in Berlin: *Die Tochter Napoleons* (*Napoleon's Daughter*), directed by Friedrich Zelnik, with Lya May in the title role and Ludwig Hartau as Napoleon; and *Wenn die Maske fällt* (*When the Mask Falls*), directed by Erik Lund and starring Mathilde Sussin and Carl Ludwig Achaz-Duisberg.

Engelhorn Press publishes the novel *Wir Zugvögel* (*We Migratory Birds*), by Herbert Eulenberg.

4 Paul Hindemith's Third String Quartet in C, op. 16 premieres at the Donaueschingen Music Festival.

6 The drama *Wie die Träumenden* (*Like the Dreamers*), by Hermann Sudermann, premieres at the Königsberg Neues Schauspielhaus.

10 Leopold Jessner stages a modernist rendition of Shakespeare's *Macbeth* at the Berlin State Theater, with Fritz Kortner as Macbeth and Gerda Müller and Lady Macbeth; both performers are condemned vigorously for sometimes shouting their lines at each other, alternating with saying their lines in whispers.

11 The film drama *Phantom*, based on a novel by Gerhart Hauptmann, directed by F. W. Murnau and starring Alfred Abel and Lya de Putti, premieres in Berlin.

13 Bertolt Brecht is awarded the Kleist Prize; critic Herbert Ihering, in presenting Brecht with award, repeats the phrase he had used earlier that year to describe Brecht as the playwright who "has altered the literary countenance of Germany."[12]

The drama *Geschlechstmoral* (*Sexual Morality*), by Franz Kaibel, premieres at the Weimar Residenz Theater.

14 A new staging of Shakespeare's *Richard II*, directed by Berthold Viertel, with Alexander Moissi as Richard and Heinrich George as Bolingbroke, wins wide praise from critics and audiences.

15 On the occasion of Gerhart Hauptmann's 60th birthday, dozens of theaters throughout Germany stage performances of his plays. A majority of students at the University of Berlin vote to absent themselves from any celebration of the playwright, given his outspoken support of the republic.

At the festival performance of Hauptmann's historical drama *Florian Geyer* in the 3,800-seat Grosses Schauspielhaus, Hauptmann views the production near the stage while a spotlight illuminates him throughout. At the end of each of the play's five acts, the playwright goes onstage to acknowledge applause from the audience.

17 The antiwar drama *The Time Will Come*, by Romain Rolland, directed by Erwin Piscator, makes its German premiere at the Central Theater in Berlin.

18 Two one-act dramas premiere at the Hannover Deutsches Theater: *Bauspiel* (*Construction Play*) and *Höllespiel* (*Hell Play*), by Alfred Brust.

The Prussian government forbids activity of the Nazi Party within its jurisdiction.

19 Rosa Valetti opens her cabaret in Berlin, called Die Rampe (The Ramp, although it can also be translated as "The Stage Apron"); it joins the 37 other cabarets operating in Berlin that present music, playlets, singers, comedy sketches, and dance routines.

20 Cotta Press publishes the novel *Der junge Tod* (*The Early Death*), by Fritz Demuth.

22 Drei Masken Press publishes the memoir and travel book *Delphische Wanderungen* (*Delphic Travels*), by Alfons Paquet.

24 The historical film *Sterbende Völker I: Heimat in Not* (*A Dying Nation, Part I: Homeland in Misery*), directed by Robert Reinert and starring Paul Wegener, Otto Gebühr, and Fritz Kortner, premieres in Munich.

25 Rütten und Loening Press publishes a poetry volume, *Stolz und Trauer* (*Pride and Mourning*), by Rudolf Binding.

The comedy *Die Geliebte* (*The Beloved*), by Ludwig Fulda, premieres at the Hamburg Thalia Theater.

27 Actors go on strike in Munich, halting all theatrical production in the city.

The romantic film *Du Mädel vom Rhein* (*The Girl from the Rhine*), directed by Hans Felsing and starring Mizzi Schütz, Melitta Klefer, and Anton Langbein, premieres in Berlin.

DECEMBER

1 Two comedies premiere: *Die Mohrenwäsche* (*Indecent Exposure*), by Toni Impekoven and Carl Mathern, at the Frankfurt am Main City Theater; and *Cagliosto*, by Carl Rossegger, at the Wissmar City Theater.

2 The Suite for Piano op. 26, *1922*, by Paul Hindemith, premieres in Hannover, performed by Walter Gieseking.

An Abstinence from Alcohol conference in Berlin employs a new Käthe Kollwitz poster that she created especially for the conference, sponsored by the German Temperance League.

The comedy *Der Liebhaber von Saturn* (*Saturn's Devotee*), by Robert Walter, premieres at the Königsberg Neues Schauspielhaus.

6 The comedy *Napoleon mit der Warze* (*Napoleon, Warts and All*), by Herbert Schönlank, premieres at the Hamburg Thalia Theater.

The historical film *Sterbende Völker II: Brennende Meer* (*A Dying Nation, Part II: The Sea Aflame*), directed by Robert Reinert and starring Paul Wegener, Otto Gebühr, and Fritz Kortner, premieres in Munich.

7 Weitbücher Press publishes a collection of aphorisms and scriptural passages, *Die Weisheit des Morgenlandes: Türkisch-arabisch-persich* (*The Wisdom of the East: Turkish, Arabic, Persian*), by Roda Roda.

The romantic film *Graf Festenberg* (*Count Festenberg*), directed by Friedrich Zelnik and starring Charles Willy Kayser and Maria Widal, premieres in Berlin.

8 The opera *Katja Kabanovna*, by Leos Janacek (which he based on the Russian drama *The Thunderstorm*, by Alexander Ostovsky), makes its German premiere at the Cologne City Opera.

Die Füchse Gottes (*The Divine Foxes*), by Otto Brües, premieres at the Essen City Theater.

A new staging, by Karl-Heinz Martin, of *Hidalla*,[13] by Frank Wedekind, premieres at the Berlin State Theater, starring Fritz Kortner and Gerda Müller.

Three film dramas premiere in Berlin: *Bigamie* (*Bigamy*), directed by Rudolf Walther Fein and starring Alfred Abel and Margit Barnay; *Das Feuerschiff* (*The Fire Ship*), directed by Richard Löwenbein and starring Camilla von Hollay and Eduard von Winterstein; and *Die Finsternis und ihr Eigentum* (*What Belongs to Darkness*), directed by Martin Hartwig and starring Karl Etlinger and Erra Bognar.

9 The comedy *Die schwarze Messe* (*The Black Mass*), by Rudolf Lothar, premieres at the Hamburg Thalia Theater.

10 The drama *Der Geschlagene* (*On the Mark*), by Wilhelm Schmidtbonn, premieres at the Frankfurt am Main Schauspielhaus.

Rikola Press publishes *Die Bekenntnisse des Hochstaplers Felix Krull* (*The Confessions of Felix Krull, Confidence Man*), by Thomas Mann.

The romantic film *Das hohe Lied der Liebe* (*The Anthem of Love*), directed by Heinz Schall and starring Johannes Riemann and Claire Rommer, premieres in Berlin.

12 The film *Am Rande der Großstadt* (*At the Edge of the Great City*), directed by Hanns Kobe and starring Evi Eva and Fritz Kortner, premieres in Berlin.

14 The comedy fim *Die Teppichknüpferin von Bagdad* (*The Carpet Weaver of Baghdad*), directed by Edmund Linke and starring Herbert Hübner and Alfred Schlageter, premieres in Leipzig.

The drama *Queen Christina*, by August Strindberg, premieres at the Lessing Theater in Berlin, with Elisabeth Bergner in the title role, for which she becomes well known internationally.

15 The comedy *Die Entlassung* (*Getting Fired*), by Emil Ludwig, premieres at the Leipzig Kleines Theater.

The historical film *Der falsche Dimitri* (*Dimitri the Duplicitous*), directed by Hans Steinhof, with Alfred Abel as Czar Ivan the Terrible and Eugen Klöpfer as Boris Godunov, premieres in Berlin.

20 Otto Falckenberg brings his production of *Trommeln in der Nacht* (*Drums in the Night*) to Berlin, at the Deutsches Theater.

The film melodrama *Tabea, steh auf!* (*Tabitha, Arise!*),[14] based on the novel by Margarete Böhme, directed by Robert Dinesen, and starring Lotte Neumann and Peter Nielsen, premieres in Berlin.

22 The comedy *Die Grossmama* (*The Grandma*), by Hans Müller, premieres at the Künstler Theater in Berlin.

23 The comedy *Der kühne Schwimmer* (*The Clever Swimmer*), by Franz Arnold and Hans Bach, premieres at the Munich Volkstheater.

25 The comedy *Der Lampenschirm* (*The Lamp Shade*), by Curt Goetz, premieres at the newly remodeled and refurbished Leipzig Altes Theater.

28 The film drama *Lola Montez*, directed by Willi Wolff, with Ellen Richter in the title role and Robert Scholz as Louis Napoleon, premieres in Berlin.

29 Steegemann Press publishes the novel *Raffke*, by Hans Riemann. Bircher Press publishes an investigation into the authorship of Shakespeare's plays, *Shakespeares Geheimnis* (*Shakespeare's Secret*), by Karl Bleibtreu.

31   The comedy *Speissgesellen* (*Blue Collar Bachelors*), by Heinrich Zschalig, premieres at the Dresden Neustädter Schauspielhaus.
One U.S. dollar buys 7,500 Reichmarks.

NOTES

1. Arthur Nikisch (Lébényi Szentmiklòs, 1855–1922) was the first conductor to record a full orchestral symphony; it was Beethoven's Fifth, in Berlin with the Berlin Philharmonic. He had previously served as director of the Leipzig Gewandhaus Orchestra and the Boston Symphony Orchestra.
2. The Volksbühne (peoples' stage) movement in Berlin had close connections to the Social Democratic Party (SPD), which supported an organization and later the construction of a theater building in Berlin designed to serve the cultural needs of the proletariat. Its motto was *Die Kunst dem Volke*, or "art to the people." The organization was founded in 1890s as a subscription system, providing members with discounted tickets to plays of social uplift, class consciousness, and political activism. Its idealism gave way to splits within the organizations, but a splendid new theater building, the Volksbühne, was erected in 1913 on Bülow Square (which became Horst Wessel Square during the Nazi years), renamed Rosa Luxemburg Square, the name it retains to this day. The Berlin prototype inspired dozens of other movements like it throughout the German-speaking world and in the United States.
3. Lyonel Feininger (1871–1956) was born in New York City and departed for Berlin in 1887 to study at the Royal Academy of Art in Berlin. There he became a bona fide modernist as a member of several secessionist art groups in the early part of the 20th century. He also taught at the Bauhaus School for several years during the Weimar Republic. His work is exhibited in several German museums and in the Metropolitan Museum of Art in New York.
4. This film took substantial liberties with the text of the original play; the film, in a screenplay by Max Jungk and Julius Urgiss, portrays the early years of Julie's life. It features her mother's hatred for Julie's father, her setting the family mansion house in flames, and the servant Jean saving the young Miss Julie from death in the fire. The film then takes up where the play begins: Julie's encounter with Jean, their sordid love affair, and her suicide.
5. *Nosferatu* set the precedent for vampire films. Screenwriter Henrik Galeen adapted material from the Bram Stoker novel *Dracula* (1897) and turned it into a particularly chilling central European tale of pestilence, mystery, and repulsion. For the film's opening in Berlin at the Primus Palast, composer Hans Erdmann conducted a large orchestra in musical compositions to accompany the film, beginning with his "Vampire Overture." Critics praised the ghostly, fragmented lighting of the film, along with its "nerve-shattering" images of the Munich actor Max Schreck in the title role. Nearly all the critics agreed that Schreck had brought a new kind of artistry to what was essentially a childlike obsession with cruelty; they were likewise in agreement that the film was "sensational" and would create numerous imitators in its

wake. They were correct; by conservative estimates at least six hundred "vampire films" have been made since *Nosferatu*'s release with scores of additional films featuring vampirelike characters. Several remakes of *Nosferatu* itself have also appeared, most notably in 1979 as *Nosferatu: Phantom der Nacht* (*Nosferatu: Phantom of the Night*), directed by Werner Herzog and starring Klaus Kinski.

6. It is difficult to determine exactly what German audiences found to like in this play. It has recognizable characteristics of a murder mystery, comedy, romantic love story, and political satire, and in some odd ways it bears resemblance to a fragmented work by the controversial Frank Wedekind. It also has some noteworthy metaphorical motifs. The plot consists of the suicide (or was it murder?) of an elderly couple, who may represent the abdicated Wilhelmine order of the German state. In their place come younger people, materialistic and idealistic, who purchase the couple's ancient manor house and set about refurbishing it. The results of their refurbishing are disastrous for all concerned.

7. In his memoirs, Erich Ludendorff (1865–1937) describes his successes on the eastern front, particularly at what came to be known as the Battle of Tannenberg in 1914. In 1917, he was instrumental in approving unrestricted submarine warfare against shipping in the North Atlantic, a step that many historians agree led the United States into the war. Ludendorff's is largely a self-serving chronicle, failing to note fully his many failures, including a massive offensive on the western front in 1917, hoping to destabilize Allied lines before the Americans arrived. When the offensive broke down, he suffered a complete nervous collapse and thereafter held civilian leadership responsible for the rapid decline of German forces in 1918, claiming that his strategies would have succeeded had not civilians behind the lines deprived him of victory. Such asseverations of betrayal led him to participate in the 1920 Kapp Putsch, the Hitler putsch attempt in 1923, and later to become an active Nazi Party member.

8. Avery Hopwood (1882–1928) is the only American playwright to have had four plays running simultaneously on Broadway in any one season (1920–1921). His best known plays are probably *The Bat* (1920) and *Getting Gertie's Garter* (1921). *Fair and Warmer* had opened in 1915 at the Eltinge Theatre in New York and ran for 377 performances. Nine road companies did the play in the United States from 1916 to 1920, and it opened in London in 1918, running for 497 performances. *Der Mustegatte* (*The Model Husband*) became an even bigger hit in Germany, staged in over 80 different theaters during the 1920s, making Hopwood by far the most popular American playwright in the Weimar Republic.

9. Siegfried Trebitsch (1868–1956) was largely responsible for Shaw's enormous popularity during the Weimar Republic, yet he referred to himself only as "the modest herald of a unique genius' great achievements." He not only translated Shaw's plays into highly stageworthy German, he also negotiated beneficial contracts on Shaw's behalf with individual producers. Shaw granted Trebitsch exclusive rights to negotiate with any German-language theater on his behalf, although there was never a written contract between them.

10. Maximilian Harden (Maximilian Witkowski, 1861–1927) was born in Berlin to a family of textile merchants. After brief training as an actor in the 1880s, he performed with touring troupes before turning his energies to theater criticism. He was a

founding member of the Freie Bühne association and later worked with Max Reinhardt when the director took over the Deutsches Theater in Berlin. Harden remained an influential critic, though his antiroyalist sentiments often colored his criticism. As early as 1908 he called for the abdication of the kaiser, based on the strong belief that Wilhelm II was homosexual. An ardent supporter of the republic, Harden's severe injuries after the attack by right-wing zealots achieved the goal his attackers sought, severely weakening him and impairing his critical faculties. He immigrated to Switzerland in 1923 for the sake of his physical safety.

11. Clara Viebig (1860–1952) was one of a few writers whose naturalistic portrayals of women as central characters consistently earned serious attention, and at times even praise among critics, both in the Wilhelmine era (when she began writing) and in the Weimar Republic. Her fiction writing was often characterized as clear and undecorative; she wrote 34 novels between 1897 and 1933.

12. *Berliner Börsen-Courier* (Berlin), 12 November 1922.

13. Kortner played the play's protagonist, Karl Hetmann, who establishes an "International League for the Breeding of Racially Superior Beings." The only international location in which the league prospers, however, is the United States. Wedekind's parents were naturalized Americans.

14. Although the title derives from a passage in Acts 9:40 in which St. Peter commands the deceased girl Tabitha to arise, the girl in both the Margaret Böhme novel and the film (played by Loni Nest as a child and later by Lotte Neuman) must arise not from the dead but from horrific social conditions. Left an orphan at age nine, she suffers through numerous misfortunes, until a strong man (played by Peter Nielsen) rescues her, offering her both love and security.

1923

JANUARY

2 Cotta Press publishes "four acts from the tragicomedy of a magician," titled *Cagliostro*, by Heinrich Lilienfein.

3 The drama *Feuer*, by Ernst Bendix, premieres at the Hamburg Schiller Theater.

5 The drama *Der holländische Kaufmann* (*The Dutch Merchant*), by Lion Feuchtwanger, premieres at the Munich Residenztheater.
One U.S. dollar is now worth RM 8,800.

6 The drama *Cagliostro,* by Heinrich Lilienfein, premieres at the Erfurt City Theater.

8 Cotta Press publishes *Wie die Träumenden* (*Like the Dreamers*), by Hermann Sudermann. Drei Masken Press publishes *Der Frauenverkäufer* (*The Vendor of Women*), by Lion Feuchtwanger, based on *Niña de Gomez Arias*, by Pedro Calderon de la Barca.

10 Koch Press publishes an illustrated lexicon of arts and crafts, *Das neue Kunsthandwerk in Deutschland und Oesterreich*, by Alexander Koch.

11 Insel Press publishes the theological treatise *Ich und Du* (*I and Thou*), by Martin Buber.
French and Belgian army divisions invade the Ruhr coal mining and industrial district of Germany in response to German failure to make scheduled reparations payments. Under the command of General Jean Degoutte, more than 60,000 heavily armed troops take over railroad stations, mines, and factories.

12 Strindberg's dramatic fragment *Moses* and his *Socrates* premiere at the Hannover Schauspielhaus.

Heinrich George wins acclaim among critics and audiences for his performance as the kaiser in a new production of *Kaiser Karls Geisel* (*Emperor Charles' Hostage*), by Gerhart Hauptmann, at the Deutsches Theater in Berlin.

The film drama *Das Komödiantenkind* (*The Comedian's Child*), directed by Fred Sauer and starring Grete Reinwald and Harry Hardt, premieres in Berlin.

13 The comedy *The Circle*, by W. Somerset Maugham, makes its German premiere at the Frankfurt am Main Neues Theater.

14 *Schweiger*, by Franz Werfel, makes its German premiere at the Stuttgart Schauspielhaus.

The romantic film *Der Liebe Pilgerfahrt* (*The Pilgrimage of Love*), directed by Jakov Protazanov and starring Grete Diercks and Gustav Wangenheim, premieres in Berlin.

17 The comedy *Seitensprünge* (*Dalliances*), by Curt Goetz, premieres at the Hamburg Thalia Theater.

18 Koehler Press publishes the travel book *Unter Brahmanen und Parias* (*Among the Brahmins and Pariahs*), by Johannes A. Sauter.

The drama *Die Fahrt nach Orplid* (*The Journey to Orplid*), by Wilhelm Schmidtbonn, premieres.

20 The comedy *Der ewige Traum* (*The Eternal Dream*), by Paul Kornfeld, premieres at the Frankfurt am Main Schauspielhaus. The drama *Die Kokotte* (*The Coquette*), by August Glogau, premieres at the Gera-Reussliches Regional Theater.

23 The drama *Mächtiger als der Tod* (*More Powerful Than Death*), by Herbert Eulenberg, premieres at the Dresden State Theater.

The medieval fantasy film *Der steinerne Reiter* (*The Stone Rider*), directed by Fritz Wendhausen and starring Erika von Thellmann and Rudolf Klein-Rogge, premieres in Berlin.

Kiepenheuer Press publishes a collection of stories by Josef Ponten, *Der Jüngling in Masken* (*The Young Lad in Masks*).

24 Rheinland Press publishes a collection of poetry by Adolf von Hatzfeld, *Jugendgedichte* (*Youth Poetry*).

26 Fischer Press publishes a collection of five plays by George Bernard Shaw, *Back to Methuselah: A Metabiological Pentateuch*, translated by Siegfried Trebitsch.

The film drama *Dämon Zirkus* (*Demon Circus*), directed by Emil Justitz and starring Gertrud Welcker and Eduard von Winterstein, premieres in Berlin.

27 A new translation of Shakespeare's *Twelfth Night* by Hans Rothe, premieres at the Leipzig Schauspielhaus.

The war drama *Trotzdem* (*Nonetheless*), by Hans Gustav Wagner, premieres at the Kassel State Theater; the audience responds with thunderous applause and calls for revenge against the current Franco/Belgian occupation of the Ruhr district; they sing the German national anthem ("Deutschland, Deutschland Über Alles") several times as the actors are repeatedly called back for curtain calls.

The comedy *Der Geliebte* (*The Beloved*), by Siegfried Trebitsch, premieres at the Munich Volkstheater.

28 Oesterheld Press publishes the comedy *Der Lampenschirm*, by Curt Goetz.

German political parties uniformly editorialize in their newspapers, from the Nazi *Völkischer Beobachter* on the right to the Communist *Die rote Fahne* on the left, for removal of French and Belgian occupying troops.

30 The tragedy *Magdalena*, by Ludwig Thoma, premieres at the Lessing Theater in Berlin.

31 The historical drama *Katte*, by Hermann Burte, premieres at the Theater in der Kommandanten Strasse in Berlin.

FEBRUARY

1 Two films premiere in Berlin: *Ein Glas Wasser* (based on the play *A Glass of Water*, by Eugene Scribe), directed by Ludwig Berger and starring Lucie Höflich, Rudolf Rittner, Mady Christians, Helga Thomas, and Hans Brausewetter; and *Das Mädel aus der Hölle* (*The Girl from Hell*), directed by Friedrich Zelnik and starring Lya Ara and Albert Patry.

2 The film drama *Nora* (based on the play *A Doll's House*,[1] by Henrik Ibsen), directed by Berthold Viertel, with Olga Chekhova as Nora, Carl Ebert as Torvald, Fritz Kortner as Krogstad, and Lucie Höflich as Christine, premieres in Berlin.

3 Wolff Press publishes a collection of short fiction, *Himmelsstrassen* (*Streets of Heaven*), by Alfred Brust.

French and Belgian troops expand their occupation of Ruhr district cities and towns; General Jean Degoutte orders forced removal of elected officials.

4 The 17-century comedy *Das Friede wünschende Deutschland* (*Peace-Loving Germany*), by Johann Rist, premieres at the Baden-Baden City Theater.

6 Ullstein Presses publishes the novel *Die Entthronten* (*The Dethroned*), by Fedor von Zobeltitz.

8 Piper Press publishes a dramatic poem based on Sanskrit legends, titled *Savitri*, translated by Christian Morgenstern.

The film drama *Stadt in Sicht* (*City in View*), directed by Henrik Galeen and starring Friedrich Traeger and Edith Posca, premieres in Berlin.

10 The Nazi Party newspaper *Völkischer Beobachter* goes into daily publication and is distributed in most major German cities.

9 The drama *Die Flucht nach Venedig* (*The Flight to Venice*), by Georg Kaiser, premieres at the Nuremberg Intimes Theater.

The historical film *Peter der Grosse* (*Peter the Great*), directed by Dimitri Buchowetski and starring Emil Jannings (in the title role), Cordy Millowitsch, and Fritz Kortner, premieres in Berlin.

10 At his funeral in Munich, Wilhelm Röntgen, discoverer of radiography (informally known as "X-ray photography") and winner of the first Nobel Prize in Physics, is hailed as a giant of German science.[2]

13 The comedy *Tibania*, by Alwin Römer, premieres at the Dresden Neustädter Schauspielhaus.

The comedy film *Der Schatz der Gesine Jakobsen* (*The Treasure of Gesine Jacobsen*), directed by Rudolf Walther-Fein and starring Maria Leiko (as Gesine) and Paul Wegener, premieres in Berlin.

President Ebert announces planned passive resistance to the Franco/Belgian occupation of the Ruhr district; education ministries in many German provinces announce cancellation of required French language instruction and establish English as the required foreign-language study.

14 Fischer Press publishes the travel book *New York und London: Stätten des Geschicks* (*New York and London: Sites of Destiny*), by drama critic Alfred Kerr.

15 The drama *Menchikov und Katharina*, by Hellmuth Unger, premieres at the Regional Theater of Baden in Karlsruhe.

Irene D'Or (*Golden Irene*), directed by Friedrich Zelnik and starring Elena Polewitzkaja and Hans Albers, premieres in Berlin.

16 The operetta *Der Fürst von Pappenheim* (*The Prince of Pappenheim*), by Hugo Hirsch, with book and lyrics by Franz Arnold and Ernst Bach, premieres at the Künstler Theater in Berlin.

Leopold Jessner's modernist staging of *Wilhelm Tell* at the Berlin State Theater, starring Fritz Kortner, sets off another round of protests against "Jewifying" German classics.

The film biopic *Christoph Columbus*, directed by Marton Garas, premieres in Berlin, with Albert Bassermann in the title role, Emmerich Pethes as King Ferdinand, and Tamara Duvan as Queen Isabella.

22 The comedy *Der Günstling wider Willen* (*The Minion in Spite of Himself*), by Erich Feldhaus, premieres at the Magdeburg City Theater.

The film drama *Erdgeist* (based on the play of the same name by Frank Wedekind), directed by Leopold Jessner, with Asta Nielsen as Lulu, Albert Bassermann as Dr. Schön, Gustav Rickelt as Dr. Goll, and Rudolf Forster as Alwa Schön, premieres in Berlin.

23 A six-day bicycle race begins in the Berlin Sports Palace.

The adventure film *Rivalen* (*Rivals*), directed by Harry Piel, with Piel in the starring role and Inge Helmgard as his love interest, premieres in Berlin.

26 The film drama *Der Schatz* (*The Treasure*), directed by G. W. Pabst and starring Albert Steinrück and Lucie Mannheim, premieres in Dresden.

28 The pantomime *Die Kaiserin von Neufundland* (*The Empress of Newfoundland*), by Frank Wedekind, premieres at the Munich Kammerspiele.

The exotic thriller film *Die Männer der Sybill* (*The Men around Sybill*), directed by Friedrich Zelnik and starring Lya Mara and Harald Paulsen, premieres in Berlin.

MARCH

1 The comedy *Die kleine Heilige* (*The Little Saint*), by Ernst Weiss, premieres at the Hamburg Kleines Schauspielhaus. The drama *Der Gast* (*The Guest*), by Wilhelm von Scholz, premieres at the Berlin City Theater.

Fischer Press publishes *Von deutscher Republik* (*On the German Republic*), by Thomas Mann.

2 The drama *Landesverrat* (*Treason*), by Franz Kaibel, premieres at the Altenburg Regional Theater. The comedy *Die Brücke* (*The Bridge*), by Karl Heintze, premieres at the Dortmund City Theater.

Franco/Belgian troops ban publication of more than 100 newspapers in the occupied Ruhr district; their commander, Jean Degoutte, issues an order of summary execution of any German involved in sabotage of or interference with the transport of coal and other materials from the occupied district back to France.

3 The drama *Thomas Müntzer*, by Paul Gurk, premieres at the Breslau Lobe Theater.

8 Scherl Press publishes the novel *Harte Probe* (*Difficult Test*), by Ida Boy-Ed.[3]

The film melodrama *Die Frau mit den Millionen* (*The Woman Worth Millions*), directed by Willi Wolff and starring Ellen Richter and Georg Alexander, premieres in Berlin; the film has three parts, shown in different theaters simultaneously: *Der Schuss in der Pariser Oper* (*The Shot in the Paris Opera*), *Der Prinz ohne Land* (*The Prince without a Country*), and *Konstantinopel-Paris* (*Constantinople-Paris*).

10 Two dramas premiere: *Das indische Spiel* (*The Indian Play*), by Alfred Brust, at the Königsberg Neues Schauspielhaus, and *Der Scharlatan* (*The Charlatan*), by Robert Overweg, at the Leipzig Schauspielhaus.

Alfred Rosenberg is named editor of the Nazi Party newspaper *Völkischer Beobachter*.

14 Kiepenheuer Press publishes the drama *Hinkemann*, by Ernst Toller.

15 The romantic film *Alt-Heidelberg* (based on the play by Wilhelm Meyer-Förster), directed by Hans Behrendt and starring Paul Hartmann and Eva May, premieres in Berlin.

Nazi Party activity is banned in Prussia, Saxony, Baden, Bremen, and Hamburg.

16 Piano Concerto in E flat Major op. 31, by Hans Pfitzner, is played by Walter Gieseking with the Berlin Philharmonic.

The satirical film *Die Meisterspringer von Kürnburg* (*The Master Springers of Kuremberg*), directed by Alfred Fekete and starring Paula Batzer and Oskar Marion, premieres in Berlin.

18 The drama *Olympia*, by Ernst Weiss, premieres at the Renaissance Theater in Berlin.

19 The comedy *Hexentanz* (*Witches' Dance*), by Gottfried Falkenhausen, premieres at the Leipzig Kleines Theater.

Two quasi-historical films premiere that exalt King Frederick the Great of Prussia: in Berlin, *Fridericus Rex III: Sanssouci* and *Fridericus Rex IV: Schicksalswende* (*Transformation of Fate*), directed by Arsen von Cserepy and starring

Otto Gebühr, Lothar Müthel, Eduard von Winterstein, Alexander Granach, and Erna Morena.

22 Fischer Press publishes the comedy *Die Geliebte* (*The Beloved*), by Siegfried Trebitsch.

23 The film drama *Der steinerne Reiter* (*The Stone Rider*), directed by Fritz Wendhausen and starring Erika von Thellmann and Rudolf Klein-Rogge, premieres in Berlin.

The adventure film *Der letzte Kampf* (*The Last Battle*), directed by Harry Piel and starring Piel (in the leading role), Inge Helgard, and Charly Berger, premieres in Berlin.

24 Leopold Jessner stages a new production of Ibsen's *John Gabriel Borkman*, at the Berlin State Theater, Fritz Kortner in title role; reviews are generally positive, a departure from the general practice of routine condemnation when Kortner appears in State Theater productions.

25 The romantic film *Boheme: Künstlerliebe* (*Bohemians: Love among Artists*), directed by Gennaro Righelli, premieres in Berlin; it stars Maria Jacobini as Mimi, Walter Janssen as Rudolfo, Elena Lunda as Musette, and Wilhelm Dieterle as Marcel.

27 Langen Press publishes the novel *Münchnerinnen* (*The Ladies of Munich*), by Ludwig Thoma.

29 The religious drama *Die Passion* (*The Passion*), by Wilhelm Schmidtbonn, premieres at the Oldenburg Regional Theater.

30 The film drama *Der Absturz* (*The Breakdown*), directed by Ludwig Wolff and starring Asta Nielsen and Albert Bozenhard, premieres in Düsseldorf.

31 Insel Press publishes a collection of nonfiction prose by Rudolf Kassner, *Essays aus den Jahren 1900–1922*.

APRIL

1 As German currency begins a precipitous slide in value in the aftermath of the Franco/Belgian invasion, one U.S. dollar buys RM 21,000; troops in the Ruhr district confiscate gold bullion from banks throughout the district, further weakening the Reichsmark.

2 The film melodrama *Die Tänzerin Navarro* (*Navarro the Dancer*), directed by Ludwig Wolff and starring Alexander Granach, Adele Sandrock, and Asta Nielsen (in the title role), premieres in Berlin.

3 The drama *Die Verfolgung* (*The Persecution*), by Dietzenschmidt (Franz Anton Schmid), premieres at the Königsberg Neues Schauspielhaus.

5 The film melodrama *Das Haus ohne Lachen* (*The House without Laughter*), directed by Gerhard Lamprecht and starring Henrik Galeen and Mathilde Sussin, premieres in Berlin.

At a national congress of the German Parents' Association in Braunschweig, delegates call for a national law guaranteeing a Christian education for all pupils in Germany.

7 The comedy *Dollar*, by Fritz Gottwald, premieres at the Königsberg Neues Schaupielhaus.

12 The film drama *Die Prinzessin Suwarin* (*Princess Suvarin*), starring Heinrich Schroth and Lil Dagover (in the title role), premieres in Berlin.

13 Langen Press publishes the comedy *Wechsler und Händler* (*Traders and Money Changers*), by Hanns Johst.

Leopold Jessner stages his first Goethe play at the Berlin State Theater: *Faust*, Part 1, with Carl Ebert in the title role.

The comedy film *Die Fledermaus* (*The Bat*), based on a stage comedy by Roderich Benedix, directed by Max Mack and starring Eva May, Lya de Putti, and Harry Liedtke, premieres in Berlin.

17 Duncker und Humboldt Press publishes *Wirtschaftsgeschichte* (*General Economic History*), by Max Weber.

18 Max Reinhardt departs for the United States with actors who will perform in New York and other American cities in an attempt to earn foreign currency; several film actors and directors have already left Germany for Hollywood.

21 The film drama *Der zweite Schuss* (*The Second Shot*), directed by Maurice Krol and starring Wilhelm Dieterle and Heddy Sven, premieres in Berlin.

22 The comedy *Gustaf Adolfs Brautfahrt* (*Gustav Adolf's Honeymoon*), by Henriette Förster, premieres at the Theater am Nollendorfplatz in Berlin.

24 International Psychoanalytic Press publishes *Das Ich und das Es* (*The Ego and the Id*), by Sigmund Freud.

Füssli Press publishes the autobiography *Lebenserinnerungen* (*Life Memories*), by conductor and composer Felix Weingartner.

25 The comedy *Die parfümierte Braut* (*The Perfumed Bride*), by Hans Zerlis, premieres at the Hannover Deutsches Theater. The comedy *The French Fool*, by Danish playwright Ludvik Holberg, makes its German premiere at the Hildesheim City Theater.

1923

The film drama *Der Menschenfeind* (*The Misanthrope*), directed by Rudolf Walther-Fein and starring Werner Krauss and Ilka Grüning, premieres in Berlin.

Societätsdrückerei Press publishes the travel book *Der Rhein, eine Reise* (*The Rhine Journey*), by Alfons Paquet.

Berlin police confiscate copies of *Ecce Homo*, a volume of drawings by George Grosz, published by Gumpert Press.

28 The performance piece *Totentanz 1921: Ein Spiel vom Leben und Sterben unserer Tagen* (*Dance of Death 1921: A Play of Life and Death in Our Time*), by Leo Weismantel, premieres at the Breslau Lobe Theater.

30 Kiepenheuer Press publishes the comedy *Der Geist der Antike* (*The Spirit of the Ancient World*), by Georg Kaiser.

MAY

1 Massive inflation begins to wreak havoc on the German economy. A loaf of bread costs RM 1,900.[4]

2 The German Press Institute publishes the novel *Die Welt ohne Sünde* (*A World without Sin*), by Vicki Baum.[5]

The comedy film *Bummelotte* (*Lotte on the Road*), directed by Wolfgang Neff and starring Maria Zelenka and Robert Scholz, premieres in Leipzig.

4 The comedy *Die drei Grazien* (*The Three Graces*), by Richard Wilde, premieres at the Bonn City Theater.

5 The Berlin Academy of the Arts opens its annual spring exhibition of new paintings by its members.

The comedy *Wechsler und Händler* (*Traders and Money Changers*), by Hanns Johst, premieres at the Leipzig Schauspielhaus.

6 The drama *Esther Gobseck* (based on the novel *The Splendors and Miseries of Courtesans*, by Honoré de Balzac), by Theodor Tagger, premieres at the Renaissance Theater in Berlin.

7 On the occasion of Johannes Brahms' 100th birthday, dozens of orchestras throughout German cities present "all-Brahms" programs throughout the week.

8 The tragicomedy *Die Rache des verhöhnten Liebhabers* (*The Revenge of the Ridiculed Lover*), by Ernst Toller, premieres at the Jena Volkshaus.

German newspapers regale readers with lurid accounts of the arrest and trial of Albert Leo Schlageter, accused by French forces of sabotage and other activities aimed at disrupting occupation of the Ruhr district.

9 The drama *Im Dickicht der Städte* (*In the Jungle of Cities*), by Bertolt Brecht, premieres at the Munich Residenz Theater; strong public protests against the play and its homoerotic content force the theater to fire its dramaturg, Jacob Geis, and close the production after six performances.

10 The film drama *Lydia Sanin*, directed by Friedrich Zelnik and starring Lya Mara and Hans Albers, premieres.

12 The film drama *Die Schlucht des Todes* (*Death Canyon*), directed by Francis A. Bertoni and starring Luciano Albertini and Lya de Putti, premieres in Berlin.

13 Broadcasting on AM radio of a program of regularly scheduled Sunday afternoon classical music concerts begins. From the postal broadcasting studio in Königswusterhausen, the program reaches approximately 1,700 AM radio receiver sets in the Berlin metropolitan area.

14 The film drama *Wettlauf ums Glück* (*Footrace to Fortune*), directed by Bruno Ziener and starring Colette Brettel and Ernst Winar, premieres in Berlin.

15 The newly reestablished University of Cologne becomes the largest university in Prussia, with more than 5,000 students enrolled full-time.

16 Beck Press publishes *Verfall und Wiederaufbau der Kultur* (*The Decay and Rebuilding of Culture*), by Albert Schweitzer. Fischer publishes two novels, *Phantom*, by Gerhart Hauptmann, and *Ulrike Woytich*, by Jakob Wassermann.

17 The drama *Columbus,* by Franz Johannes Weinrich, premieres at the Mannheim National Theater.

18 Cassirer Press publishes the philosophical treatise *Geist der Utopie* (*The Utopian Spirit*), by Ernst Bloch.

19 The drama *Julius Cäsar und seine Mörder* (*Julius Caesar and his Murderers*), by Martin Langen, premieres at the Theater in der Kommandanten Strasse in Berlin.

23 The drama *Der arme Vetter* (*The Poor Cousin*), by sculptor Ernst Barlach, premieres at the Berlin State Theater.

The comedy film *Adam und Eva* (*Adam and Eve*), directed by Friedrich Porges and starring Werner Krauss and Loni Pyrmont, premieres in Berlin.

24 The drama *Der tote Tag* (*The Dead Day*), by sculptor Ernst Barlach, premieres at the Berlin Volksbühne.

25 The film *Das Wirtshaus im Spessart* (*The Farmhouse in Spessart*), directed by Adolf Wenter and starring Alise Aulinger and Fritz Berger, premieres in Berlin.

26 Albert Leo Schlageter is executed[6] by a French firing squad near Düsseldorf, setting off anti-French street demonstrations and cries for revenge among several political party newspapers.

JUNE

1 The romantic film *Abenteuer einer Nacht* (*A Night's Adventure*), directed by Harry Piel and starring Piel and Lissy Arna, premieres in Berlin.

Ticket prices for movies, along with consumer prices of everything else, rise approximately 500 percent over prices for similar goods and services in the previous month. One U.S. dollar buys RM 100,000.

2 The drama *Gilles und Jeanne*, by Georg Kaiser, premieres at the Leipzig Altes Theater.

The pastoral comedy *Sylvia*, by Christian Furchtegott Gellert (1715–1769), premieres (178 years after it was written) at the Heidelberg City Theater.

5 The operetta *Der süsse Kavalier* (*The Sweet Cavalier*), by Leo Fall, premieres at the Berliner Theater.

Malik Press publishes a collection of Marxist analyses, *Geschichte und Klassenbewusstsein* (*History and Class Consciousness*), by Georg Lukács.

The unfinished verse tragedy *Der Tod des Empedokles* (*The Death of Empedocles*), by Friedrich Hölderlin, premieres at the Berlin State Theater. This version features a conclusion in imitation of Hölderlin by Wilhelm von Scholz.

7 Mosaik Press publishes the novel *Christophorus*, by Hans von Hülsen. Europäisch Press publishes the novel *Die schöne Hedy Herz* (*The Beautiful Hedy Herz*), by Roda Roda.

8 The film drama *Das fränkische Lied* (*The Franconian Song*), directed by Hubert Moest and starring Hedda Vernon and Eduard von Winterstein, premieres in Berlin.

10 Attacks against French military personnel increase in the occupied Ruhr district; French authorities declare martial law in Düsseldorf, Essen, and Dortmund and they execute 11 Germans accused of resistance

The arrival of Schlageter's body for burial in his hometown of Schönau (Baden) prompts an outpouring of both sympathy and outrage in street demonstrations and newspaper editorials; the Nazi Party, the German National

Peoples' Party, and the Fatherland Federation hold memorial services for Albert Leo Schlageter in Munich.

12 The film melodrama *Der Mensch am Wege* (*Man on His Path*), directed by Wilhelm Dieterle and starring Alexander Granach, Heinrich George, and Marlene Dietrich, premieres in Berlin.

13 The German Book Society publishes the novel *Sterne der Heimkehr* (*Stars of the Journey Home*), by Ina Seidel.

15 Four films premiere in Berlin: *Der rote Reiter* (*The Horseman in Red*), directed by Franz W. Koebner and starring Albert Steinrück and Fern Andra; *Das Licht um Mitternacht* (*The Light at Midnight*), directed by Hans von Wolzogen and starring Max Landa and Thea Sandten; *Das Mädchen ohne Gewissen* (*The Girl without a Conscience*), directed by William Kahn and starring Maria Zelenka and Viggo Larsen; and *Jimmy: Ein Schicksal von Mensch und Tier* (*Jimmy: The Tale of a Girl and Her Bear*), directed by Jaap Speyer and starring Mia Pankau and Ernst Hofmann.

16 Members of the Berlin State Opera depart on a Scandinavian tour in an effort to earn valuable foreign currency; in their repertoire are new productions of *Salome*, by Richard Strauss and *Mona Lisa*, by Max von Schillings.

17 Songs by Paul Hindemith set to lyrics by Rainer Maria Rilke premiere at the Donaueschingen Music Festival.

Mosaik Press publishes the novella *Himmel voller Geigen* (*A Sky of Violins*), by Otto Ernst.

18 The opera *The Golden Cockerel*, by Nikolai Rimsky-Korsakov, premieres at the State Opera in Berlin.

Schneider Press publishes a "speech to the youth of Germany" titled *Vaterland und Freiheit* (*Fatherland and Freedom*), by Fritz von Unruh.

20 The musical parable *A Soldier's Tale*, with music by Igor Stravinsky, makes its German premiere at the Frankfurt am Main Opera House.

German political parties angle for the most advantageous position on the Schlageter execution; nationalist parties publish encomia, while centrist parties praise Schlageter's "dedication to justice." Leftist parties keep their distance but denounce efforts by nationalists to capitalize on the public hysteria aroused by the execution. Communist Party leader Karl Radek declares Schlageter a courageous soldier of the counterrevolution.

22 The film drama *Der allmächtige Dollar* (*The Almighty Dollar*), directed by Jaap Speyer and starring Lena Amsel, Charles Willy Kayser, and Hugo Döblin, premieres in Berlin.

A convention of German Volksbühne organizations convenes at the Potsdam City Palace. The organization has 450,000 subscribers, who receive discount tickets to 88 participating dramatic and music theaters throughout Germany.

25 Rikola Press publishes the novella *Der Zauberkäfer* (*The Magic Beetle*), by Karl Hans Strobl.

27 Rikola Press publishes the "happy novel" *Das Haus mit der Pergola* (*The House with the Trellis*), by Georg Hirschfeld.

28 Gyldenalscher Press publishes the volume of poetry *Verwehende Lieder* (*Songs the Breeze Blew Away*).

JULY

1 The comedy *Wie man's macht ist richtig* (*How to Do It Right*), by Herbert Eulenberg, premieres at the Danzig City Theater.

One U.S. dollar buys RM 160,500.

3 Bremer Press publishes an anthology of prose works and literary analyses, *Deutsches Lesebuch* (*German Reading Book*), by Hugo von Hofmannsthal.

4 Insel Press publishes the historical analysis *Michael Bakunin und die Anarchie* (*Michael Bakunin and Anarchy*), by Ricarda Huch.[7]

6 The animated film *Film ist Rhythmus* (*Film Is Rhythm*), by Hans Richter, premieres in Berlin.

9 Author and theater director Georg Fuchs is found guilty in a Munich court of collaboration with agents of the French government, with direct ties to French prime minister Raymond Poincaré, who initiated the policy of Ruhr occupation. Fuchs is sentenced to 12 years at hard labor. During the trial, prosecutors note that 92 Germans have so far died as a result of the occupation, and 70,000 have been forced out of the Ruhr district and deported back to Germany. The French authorities have closed 170 schools, affecting 50,000 schoolchildren and 2,000 teachers.

11 Mosaik Press publishes the novella *Der Riesenspielzeug* (*The Giant Toy*), by Max Dreyer.

14 Mosaik Press publishes the novella *Die Ungeborenen* (*The Unborn*), by Walter Bloem. Engelhorn Press publishes the novel *Erscheinungen* (*Appearances*), by Herbert Eulenberg.

The comedy *Reliquien* (*Relics*), by Fred Ungermayer, premieres at the Weimar Residenz Theater.

15 The German National Turner Festival opens in Munich; its is a celebration of physical fitness and national pride.

17 A comedy film with an English title, *Time Is Money*, directed by Fred Sauer and starring Grete Reinwald and Heinz Salfner, premieres in Berlin.

Wolff Press publishes the novel *Leben mit einer Göttin* (*Life with a Goddess*), by Max Brod.

21 The Berlin National Gallery opens an exhibition dedicated exclusively to the work of Lovis Corinth, at the Palace of the Crown Prince.

Wegweiser Press publishes the novel *Die hässliche Herzogin* (*The Ugly Duchess*), by Lion Feuchtwanger.

22 Bergstadt Press publishes the novel *Ferien vom Ich* (*Vacation from the Ego*), by Paul Keller.

23 Food riots in several German cities break out as a result of vaulting prices for basic groceries like bread, milk, eggs, and butter.

Drei Masken Press publishes two novels by Alfons Paquet, *Fahnen* (*Flags*) and *Die Prophezeiungen* (*The Prophecies*).

24 Insel Press publishes the novel *Sendung des Künstlers* (*Mission of the Artists*), by Hermann Bahr.

25 Hirt Press publishes *Nietzsche als Richter unserer Zeit* (*Nietzsche as Judge of Our Times*), by Ernst Gundolf.

26 Hegner Press publishes the novel *Die goldenen Äpfel* (*The Golden Apples*), by Friedrich Schnack.

28 Klinkhardt und Biermann Press publishes the contemporary art history analysis *Marc Chagall*, by Karl With, featuring numerous color plates of the artist's work.

AUGUST

2 Teubner Press publishes *Psychologie der Kunst* (*Psychology of Art*), by Richard Müller-Freienfels.

4 Insel Press publishes *Jeremias: Eine dramatische Dichtung* (*Jeremiah: A Dramatic Poem*), by Stefan Zweig.

7 The outdoor drama *Krieg und Frieden* (*War and Peace*), by Ernst Toller, premieres at the Leipzig Labor Union Festival.

10 President Ebert issues an emergency decree banning newspapers, especially those published by political parties, from publishing editorials advocating the use of violence to change the Weimar Republic's constitution.

Rösel Press publishes *Geschichte der Musik* (*History of Music*), by Otto Keller.

11 Teubner Press publishes *Die dramatische Dichtung* (*Dramatic Poetry*), by Albert Ludwig.

Arnold Mendelssohn receives the first Georg Büchner-Hessian State Prize for Literature.

13 Strikes and food shortages spread throughout the country; many districts and cities release schoolchildren from school to harvest potatoes, as field workers are often not available.

15 A classical music concert is broadcast from a new Berlin radio station located in the Telefunken building.

Several newspapers accuse right-wing political parties of fomenting strikes among workers in protest against the Ebert government; other newspapers accuse the Communist Party of fomenting strikes among workers in an effort to weaken the German economy even further.

16 Oskar Schlemmer stages *Triadisches Ballett* (*Threefold Ballet*), portraying the "Unity of Color, Space, and Movement" for the first Bauhaus Week in Weimar.

18 Lohmann Press publishes a collection of novellas, *Menschen und Strassen* (*People and Streets*), by Clara Viebig.

Marienlieder (*Songs of Mary*), by Paul Hindemith, premieres at the Weimar National Theater.

24 The historical film *Wilhelm Tell* (based on the play by Friedrich Schiller), directed by Rudolf Dworsky, with Hans Marr in the title role, Xenia Desni as his wife Hedwig, and Conrad Veidt as the villainous Gessler, premieres in Berlin.

25 Post und Obermüller Press publishes the novel *Aus einer Wiege* (*From a Cradle*), by Ida Boy-Ed.

28 Musarion Press publishes the novel *Das älteste Ding der Welt* (*The Oldest Thing in the World*), by Willy Seidel.

SEPTEMBER

1 One U.S. dollar buys RM 53,000,000.

The comedy *An die Barriere* (*To the Barricades*), by Gustav Davis, premieres at the Hamburg Kleines Lustspielhaus.

The New Schiller Theater in Berlin (a bankrupt private theater taken over by the Prussian state) opens its season with Gotthold Ephraim Lessing's call for tolerance and understanding, the "dramatic poem" *Nathan der Weise* (*Nathan the Wise*).

A German Congress of Fatherland Organizations opens in Nuremberg, where more than 100,000 members of nationalist groups and political parties gather to hear condemnations of the Weimar Republic's government, its policies, and its leaders. One of the most popular speakers is Adolf Hitler from Munich, who joins with former army general Erich von Ludendorff in forming the Deutscher Kampfbund (German Battle League), devoted to "restoring German honor" and repudiating the Treaty of Versailles.

6 National government officials begin secret discussions about creating a new currency.

8 Reiss Press publishes a volume of political analysis, *Deutschland-Frankreich-England* (*Germany-France-England*), by Maximilian Harden. Rothbarth Press publishes the novel *Es gibt ein Stück Glück* (*A Piece of Happiness*), by Hedwig Courths-Mahler.

9 A congress of "defense organizations" opens in Dresden, where about 8,000 members of Communist and Social Democratic groups and political parties listen to speeches defending the Weimar Republic's government, its policies, and its leaders. Many speakers condemn the "Hitler gangs," active in Munich.

11 The film drama *Die Flamme* (*The Flame*), directed by Ernst Lubitsch and starring Pola Negri and Alfred Abel, premieres in Berlin.

12 Langen Press publishes three books: the novel *Auf der rollenden Erde* (*As the World Turns*), by Walter von Molo; a collection of stories, *Söhne* (*Sons*), by Arnold Zweig; and the treatise *Kultur und Ethik* (*Culture and Ethics*), by Albert Schweiter.

13 The comedy *Mein Vetter Eduard* (*My Cousin Eduard*), by Fred Robs, premieres at the Berlin Komödienhaus.

14 Two films premiere in Berlin: *Die Liebe einer Königin* (*The Love of a Queen*), directed by Ludwig Wolff and starring Henny Porten and Harry

Liedtke; and *Scheine des Todes* (*Certificates of Death*), directed by Lothar Mendes and starring Alfred Abel and Eva May.

16   One of the largest sports stadium in Europe, seating 100,000 spectators, opens in the Cologne suburb of Müngersdorf.

17   One U.S. dollar buys RM 200,000,000.

19   The drama *Hinkemann*, by Ernst Toller, premieres at the Leipzig Altes Theater.

21   The film melodrama *Tragödie der Liebe* (*Tragedy of Love*), directed by Joe May and starring Emil Jannings and Mia May, premieres.
   A liter of milk costs RM 5,400,000.

22   The comedy *Die Stubenfliege* (*The Barflies*), by Georg Britting, premieres at the Munich Residenz Theater. The drama *Die Riese gegen Gott* (*The Giants against God*), by Rolf Lauckner, premieres at the Karlsruhe Regional Theater.

23   The drama *Überteufel* (*Super Devil*), by Hermann Essig, premieres at the Berlin State Theater.
   Street protests in Cologne, Aachen, and other Rhineland towns and cities turn violent as partisans wishing to secede from the Weimar Republic clash with nationalists.

24   The first documentary sound film, *Das Leben auf dem Dorfe* (*Life in a Village*), is premiered by the Triergon Company. Film showings are sold out, the ticket price of RM 6,000,000 notwithstanding.
   The German Press Institute publishes a collection of novellas, *Jugendnovellen* (*Novellas of Youth*), by Waldemar Bonsels. Rikola Press publishes two books: a collection of prose work, *Letzte Worte* (*Last Words*), by Marie von Ebner-Eschenbach; and the two-volume biography *Deutsche Charakter und Begebenheiten* (*German Characters and Events*), by Jakob Wassermann.

26   Reissner Press publishes *Die Kultur der Ehe* (*The Culture of Marriage*), by Rudolf von Delius.

27   Two films premiere in Berlin: *Mutter, dein Kind ruft!* (*Mother, Your Child Is Calling!*), based on a novella by Stefan Zweig, directed by Rochus Gliese and starring Ernst Deutsch and Otto Gebühr; and *Tatiana*, directed by Robert Dinesen and starring Olga Chekhova and Paul Hartmann.

28   Kiepenheuer Press publishes the comedy *Nebeneinander* (*Next to Each Other*), by Georg Kaiser.

The national government bans the printing and distribution of the Nazi Party organ *Völkischer Beobachter*, on the grounds that it publishes "insulting remarks" aimed at government leaders.

30 Roman Catholic bishops send a letter to all Catholic parishes in Germany, warning of the danger to German life and society posed by National Socialism. The letter is read aloud at church services throughout the country.

OCTOBER

1 Two comedies premiere at the Hamburg Thalia Theater: *Meisen (Tomtits)*, by Alfred Kihn; and *Der Barbier von Pampelfort (The Barber of Pampelfort)*, by Hans Müller-Schlosser.

One U.S. dollar buys RM 242 million.

2 *Fanny's First Play*, by George Bernard Shaw, makes its German premiere at the Tribüne Theater in Berlin.

Cassirer Press publishes a collection of essays, *Durch die Wüste (Through the Wasteland)*, by Ernst Bloch.

3 The Württemberg provincial legislature imposes political instruction in schools to guard against future "Spartacist uprisings."

5 Munich Peoples Press publishes *Adolf Hitler: Sein Leben und seine Rede (Adolf Hitler: His Life and Speeches)*, by Adolf-Victor von Koerber.

6 The comedy *Der Sprung in die ehe (Dallying into Marriage)*, by Max Reimann and Otto Schwarz, premieres at the Frankfurt am Main Neues Theater.

9 Two significant dramas premiere in Berlin: *Anna Christie*, by Eugene O'Neill, with operetta star Käthe Dorsch[8] in the title role, at the Deutsches Theater; and the dramatic poem *Der abtrünnige Zar (The Renegade Czar)*, by Carl Hauptmann, at the Volksbühne.

10 The film melodrama *Die grüne Manuela (Manuela in Green)*, directed by E. A. Dupont and starring Lucie Labass and Angelo Ferrari, premieres in Berlin.

12 Rowohlt Press publishes a pastoral play written in Alexandrine verse, *Die geliebte Kleinigkeit (The Beloved Bagatelle)*, by Rudolf Borchardt.

One U.S. dollar buys RM 4 billion.

13 An exhibition of Käthe Kollwitz's latest work, including woodcuts and drawings, opens at the Prussian Academy of the Arts in Berlin.

The Reichstag (despite strong opposition from both Communist Party members and representatives of nationalist parties) approves an executive enabling act, allowing President Ebert and his government to intervene in economic affairs.

14 The film *Der Kaufmann von Venedig* (*The Merchant of Venice*), based on Shakespeare's play of the same title, premieres in Berlin, directed by Peter Paul Felner, with Werner Krauss as Shylock and Henny Porten as Portia.

15 The expressionistic terror film *Schatten: Eine nächtliche Halluzination* (*Shadows: A Nightly Hallucination*), directed by Artur Robison and starring Alexander Granach, Fritz Kortner, and Ruth Weyher, premieres in Berlin. The film's innovative use of shadows, double exposures, and superimposed images creates a sensation among audiences.

The Ebert government establishes a "Rentenbank" (security bank), which holds mortgages on land and nonperishable goods, such as industrial and public transport equipment, for the purposes of creating a new German currency.

17 The comedy *Still am Wrack* (*Quiet in the Torture Chamber*), by Max Mohr, premieres at the Frankfurt am Main Neues Theater.

19 The film melodrama *Seine Frau, die Unbekannte* (*His Wife, the Unknown Woman*), directed by Benjamin Christensen and starring Lil Dagover and Willy Fritsch, premieres in Berlin.

One U.S. dollar buys RM 12 billion.

21 Separatists in Aachen announce their independence from Berlin and proclaim a "Republic of the Rhine."[9]

22 The adventure film *Der Sieg des Maharadjahs* (*The Maharajah's Victory*), directed by Joseph Belmont and starring Lil Dagover and Willy Fritsch, premieres in Berlin.

23 The comedy *Die Perücke* (*The Toupée*), by Karl Tietsch, premieres at the Schlosspark Theater in Berlin.

The film drama *Die Austreibung, oder die Macht der zweiten Frau* (based on the play by Carl Hauptmann), directed by F. W. Murnau and starring Ilka Grüning and Carl Goetz, premieres in Berlin.

24 Scherl Press publishes the novel *Die Spur des Dschingis Khan* (*The Trail of Genghis Khan*), by Hans Dominik.

The film melodrama *Fräulein Raffke* (*Miss Raffke*), directed by Richard Eichberg and starring Werner Krauss, Hans Albers, and Lydia Potechina, premieres in Berlin.

27 Two comedies premiere: *Die Börse* (*The Stock Exchange*), by Melchior Vischer, at the Königsberg Neues Schauspielhaus; and *Tybbke*, by Karl Strecker, at the Deutsches Künstler Theater in Berlin.

29 The German radio broadcasting company Voxhaus goes on the air with its inaugural program, *Radio-Stunde-Berlin* (*The Berlin Radio Hour*).

Two films premiere in Berlin: the melodrama *Das alte Gesetz* (*The Ancient Law*), directed by E. A., Dupont and starring Ernst Deutsch and Henny Porten; and the social satire *Alles für Geld* (*All for Money*), directed by Reinhold Schünzel and starring Emil Jannings, Dagny Servaes, and Hermann Thimig.

31 The comedy *Der Arbeiter Esau* (*Esau the Worker*), by Max Mohr, premieres at the Cologne City Theater.

NOVEMBER

2 A new translation of Christopher Marlowe's *Edward II*, by Alfred von Heymel, premieres at the Wilhelmstädtisches Theater in Berlin

3 The comedy *Nebeneinander* (*Next to Each Other*), by Georg Kaiser, premieres at the Lustspielhaus in Berlin.

5 Actress Elisabeth Bergner continues her triumphal reign over Berlin critics and audiences with her performance of the title role in a new production of *Hanneles Himmelfahrt* (*Hannele's Assumption*), by Gerhart Hauptmann, at the Schauspiel Theater in Berlin.

6 The drama *Das Fossil* (*The Fossil*), by Carl Sternheim, premieres at the Hamburg Kammerspiele.

Kiepenheuer Press publishes the comedy *Der entfesselte Wotan* (*Wotan Unchained*), by Ernst Toller.

One U.S. dollar buys RM 650 billion.

9 On the anniversary of German capitulation at the end of World War I, Adolf Hitler and members of his Nazi Party stage an attempted overthrow of the Bavarian government in Munich (popularly known as the Beer Hall Putsch).[10]

The drama *Not in Calais* (*Emergency in Calais*), by Hans Havemann, premieres at the Hildesheim City Theater.

10 The Bavarian government bans the Nazi Party. German radio reports on events in Munich, the first time radio is used to report news events.

11 Munich police arrest Adolf Hitler.

12 Separatists in Speyer announce their independence from Berlin and proclaim a "Republic of the Palatinate."[11]

13 The drama *Menschen ohne Tragödie* (*People without Tragedy*), by Carl Haensel, premieres at the Heidelberg City Theater.

15 The national government begins distribution of the new German currency, called the "Rentenmark." Its value as legal tender is secured by the newly established Rentenbank and retains the initials "RM," with its value pegged at one U.S. dollar to RM 4.2. The "great inflation" begins to slow down; German consumers conclude that the new currency may actually be worth something.

16 The drama *Karneol*, by Hellmuth Unger, premieres at the Halle City Theater.

17 Two foreign plays make their German premieres: *The Teacher*, by Dario Nicodemi, in a translation from the Italian by Harry Kahn, at the Frankfurt am Main Neues Theater; and *Candida*, by George Bernard Shaw, in a new translation by Siegfied Trebitsch, at the Berlin State Theater.

20 The drama *Die Denkmalsweihe* (*Dedication of the Memorial*), by Hermann Sudermann, premieres at the Cologne City Theater.

21 The comedy *Der Verführer* (*The Seducer*), by Rudolf Lothar and Alfred Hahn, premieres at the Altenburg Regional Theater.

Two films premiere in Berlin: the romance *Daisy, das Abenteuer einer Lady* (*Daisy: The Adventures of a Lady*), directed by Friedrich Zelnik and starring Alfons Fryland and Lyua Mara; and the melodrama *Die Strasse* (*The Street*), directed by Karl Grüne and starring Eugen Klöpfer, Aud Egede Nissen, and Max Schreck.

22 Fischer Press publishes the travel book *O Spanien! Eine Reise* (*O Spain! A Journey*), by drama critic Alfred Kerr; and the novel *Berge, Meetre, und Giganten* (*Mountains, Seas, and Giants*), by Alfred Döblinn.

26 Steegmann Press publishes the memoir *Mein Kabarettbuch* (*My Cabaret Book*), by Hans Reimann; and the short story collection *Liebesgeschichte des Orients* (*Love Stories of the Orient*), by Franz Blei.

27 The German Union Press Society of Stuttgart publishes two novels: *Das Wunderbare* (*The Miraculous*), by Jakob Schaffner; and *Die Mauer* (*The Wall*), by Georg Engel.

29 Two films premiere in Berlin: the comedy *Die närrische Wette des Lord Aldini* (*The Foolish Wager of Lord Aldini*), directed by Luigi Romano

Borqnetto and starring Carlo Aldini and Violette Napierska; and the comedy *So sind die Männer* (*Men Are Like That*), directed by Georg Jacoby and starring Harry Liedtke and Alice Hechy.

30 The comedy *Dachvögel* (*Rooftop Birds*), by Erich Marsen, premieres at the Wismar City Theater.

The adventure film *Im Schatten der Moschee* (*In the Shadows of the Mosque*), directed by Walter Richard Hall and starring Aruth Wartan and Dora Bergner, premieres in Berlin.

DECEMBER

4 The comedy *Vinzenz, oder die Freundin bedeutender Männer* (*Vincent, or the Girlfriend of Important Men*), by Robert Musil, premieres at the Lustspielhaus in Berlin.

5 The romantic film *Die verlorne Schuh* (*The Lost Slipper*), adapted from the fairytale Cinderella, directed by Ludwig Berger, and starring Helga Thomas and Paul Hartmann, premieres in Berlin.

6 Rowohlt Press publishes the novel *Anton und Gerda*, by Hanns Fallada. Rikola Press publishes three stories by Jakob Wassermann in *Der Geist des Pilgers* (*The Pilgrim's Spirit*).

8 The drama *Baal*, by Bertolt Brecht, premieres at the Leipzig Altes Theater; public reaction to the production is extraordinarily negative, and the mayor of Leipzig orders the theater to cease performances of the play.

10 Steffler Press publishes the memoir *Aus einem engen Leben* (*From a Narrow Life*), by Rudolf Huch.

11 The drama *Dubereau*, by Melchior Vischer, premieres at the Frankfurt am Main City Theater.

12 The film drama *Qurantäne* (*Quarantine*), directed by Max Mack and starring Rudolf Lettinger and Helena Makowska, premieres in Berlin.

13 Rütten und Loening Press publishes a volume of poetry, *Tage* (*Days*), by Rudolf Binding.

14 Koesel and Pustit Press publishes the novel *Die Hexe* (*The Witch*), by Leo Weismantel.

15 The operetta *Señora*, by Rudolf Pressler, premieres at the Künstlertheater in Berlin.

21 The Russian revolutionary drama *Emigrants*, by Fyodor Karpoff, starring Rosa Valetti, makes its German premiere at her new Theater Comedia Valetti in Berlin.

The adventure film *Vineta, die versunkene Stadt* (*Vineta, the Sunken City*), directed by Werner Funck and starring Gustav Diessl and Evi Eva, premieres in Berlin.

22 Director Erich Engel makes his Berlin debut with the staging of Christian Dietrich Grabbe's *Scherz, Satire, Ironie, und tiefere Bedeutung* (*Jest, Satire, Irony, and Deeper Significance*) at the Theater in der Kommandanten Strasse.

24 The drama *Utopia*, by Hanna Rademacher, premieres at the Königsberg Neues Schauspielhaus.

25 The religious film epic *I.N.R.I.* (*Iesus Nazarenus Rex Iudaeorum*, the words Pontius Pilate is said to have ordered nailed to the cross of the crucified Christ), based on the novel by Robert Rossegger and directed by Robert Wiene, premieres, with Gregri Chmara as Jesus, Werner Krauss as Pilate, Asata Nielsen as Maria Magdalena, and Alexander Granach as Judas Iscariot.

26 The detective film *Das Geheimnis von Brinkenhof* (*The Brinkenhof Secret*), directed by Sven Gade and starring Henny Porten and Paul Henckels, premieres in Berlin.

NOTES

1. This film marked the cinematic directing debut of Berthold Viertel. It also had two endings, both of which Ibsen originally wrote; the original one had Nora deserting her husband and family. The second was a "happy ending" primarily intended for the play's Berlin premiere at the Lessing Theater. In this version, Nora, overcome with guilt at the sight of her sleeping children, remains with her family. The actress who played Nora in its Berlin premiere in 1880, Hedwig Niemann-Raabe (1844–1905), refused to do the play with its original ending (which she termed "barbaric") and told Ibsen that she would herself write a new ending if he did not. Thereafter, the play appeared in the repertoires of German theaters with both endings available. In like manner, German cinema owners were permitted to show the film with the ending that seemed most appropriate for their audiences.

2. "X-rays" are called "Röntgen rays" in German, and German-speaking Europe uses his name to describe nearly all aspects of radiology to this day. Though he was awarded numerous prizes and honors in his lifetime, Röntgen donated nearly all his awards to the University of Munich, which had named him to a professorship in 1900. He strongly objected to the use of his name for his discovery and refused to patent

any of the processes he discovered, and upon his death he was bankrupt. His will stipulated that his correspondence, research notes, and other written ephemera be destroyed. In 2004, the International Union of Pure and Applied Chemistry renamed the element unununium "roentgenium" in his honor.

3. Ida Boy-Ed (Ida Cornelia Ed, 1852–1928) was, until the rise of Thomas and Heinrich Mann, the most well-known and popular author from Lübeck. She published more than 70 novels and encouraged writers, musicians, and artists in her informal circle, which came to be known as the "Lübeck Salon." The group met in a large apartment that the city placed at her disposal in 1904.

4. The macroeconomic causes of what came to be known as "hyperinflation" in Germany from late 1922 through 1923 were numerous, but essentially it occurred because the German government printed money in the belief that inflation could wipe out the burden of debt for reparation payments to the victorious Allies, especially France. German government leaders maintained that the increasing decline in the Reichsmark's value against the U.S. dollar "proved" how impossible it was for Germany to pay the reparations. They somehow convinced themselves and many of their constituents that the destruction of the Reichsmark was a form of retaliation against the French, who resolutely insisted on strict adherence to monthly reparation payments. John Maynard Keynes noted, "There is no subtler, no surer means of overturning the existing basis of society than to debauch the currency" (*The Economic Consequences of the Peace*, 1919), but few in the German government realized the destructive extent of their decision to print worthless money, contracting over 150 printing companies to turn out bogus currency around the clock.

5. Vicki Baum (Hedwig Baum, 1888–1960) was born in Vienna, where she was a serious student of music. She became a regular harpist for the Vienna Concert Union at the age of 22 and from 1912 to 1916 was a member of the Darmstadt Orchestra. She became an extraordinarily successful writer of novels in the "potboiler" genre (of which *A World without Sin* is a good example), employing a structural formula that featured a diverse set of characters who have no previous contact, then encounter each other in a series of seemingly random happenstances during a single day. This formula became a widely used basis for films, such as *Grand Hotel*, starring John Barrymore and Joan Crawford, based on Baum's novel *Menschen im Hotel*. Baum was the first writer to portray the "worldly young woman" in the Weimar Republic, independent and self-confident, unafraid to take risks, and sexually liberated.

6. The details surrounding the death of Albert Leo Schlageter (1894) are easily ascertained. Much less accessible are facts about his life. The son of poor Catholic parents in the Black Forest, Schlageter became the subject of much mythmaking soon after his execution, and his memory took pride of place within the pantheon of recently fallen heroes. Schlageter had an outstanding war record as a combatant at Ypres, the Somme, Verdun, and several other lesserknown battles. Having enlisted as a private, he rose in rank to second lieutenant. After the war he joined a Freikorps unit and took part in several bloody encounters with Communist militias in 1919, and his presence was significant in the Kapp Putsch of 1920. When his Freikorps unit was disbanded along with most others, he briefly attempted university study. The Franco/Belgian occupation of the Ruhr district, however, rekindled his desire to combat enemies of Ger-

many. He is thought to have slipped across the Rhine with others in his "battle platoon" and helped to derail trains taking German goods back to France. French troops captured him on 7 April 1923. Shortly before his execution he wrote his parents that his were acts of sacrifice for the Fatherland, conducted solely in the spirit of German loyalty. Such sentiments helped usher Schlageter into the realm of nationalist apotheosis, where he was memorialized (in the last lines of Hanns Johst's drama *Schlageter*), "not as the last soldier of the war, but as the first soldier of the Third Reich."

7. Ricarda Huch (1864–1947) was one of the first German women to earn a doctorate in history, which she completed at the University of Zurich in 1892. By the time she wrote the book on Bakunin, she had already published 30 books, many historical monographs. She was also the author of several volumes of poetry and fiction.

8. Käthe Dorsch (1890–1957) made her operetta debut as a teenager in Mainz and was soon performing regularly in the works of Offenbach, Lehar, Suppé, Millöcker, and Fall. When she played the former prostitute Anna Christie in O'Neill's play, she was already a well-established star at the Admiral's Palace Theater in Berlin. She began taking on serious roles in plays by Gerhart Hauptmann, George Bernard Shaw, and Henrik Ibsen, and at one point did a much-admired Queen Elisabeth in Schiller's *Maria Stuart*. Her film career began later, culminating in the 1941 film *Komödianten* (*The Comedians*), a biography of the legendary 18th-century theater reformer Caroline Neuber.

9. The proclamation of the "Rhineland Republic" was a result of longstanding animosity toward the government in Berlin among many Rhinelanders (especially in Cologne and Aachen), the German economic collapse, and the French occupation of the Ruhr. Separatists advocated a permanent break with the Weimar Republic and integration into France, which French generals of the occupation forces did nothing to prevent; nor did they dissuade separatists from gaining public sympathy. There was nevertheless significant resistance to separatism, and numerous outbreaks of violence occurred in Essen, Koblenz, and Mainz. The "Rhineland Republic" lasted until the French occupation ended, and its principal German advocates sought asylum in France.

10. Hitler was attempting to emulate the methods of Benito Mussolini a year earlier, who with his "blackshirts" successfully took over the reins of national government by means of intimidation. In this instance, Hitler and his men intruded on a meeting of other right-wing fanatics on 8 November at a beer hall in Munich; they all agreed on an armed march toward the city center of Munich the next day and from there to march onward to Berlin. They numbered about 3,000 men, but the Munich police force engaged them in a fire fight as soon as they reached the Feldherrnhalle, killing 16 Nazis. Hitler and his followers quickly ran for cover, and Hitler was arrested the next day.

11. Western parts of the Palatinate (*Pfalz* in German) had already been separated from the Palatinate proper according to the terms of the Treaty of Versailles. The treaty then attached those western districts to the newly established Saarland, which the League of Nations was supposed to govern. As they had done earlier, French occupation forces intervened and sought to encourage German separatist movements. The result was a growing sense of outrage among most Germans.

1924

JANUARY

3 The comedy *Der Halbgott* (*The Demigod*), by Friedrich Walter, premieres at Schlosspark Theater in Berlin.

The film drama *Sylvester* (*New Year's Eve*), directed by Lupu Pick and starring Eugen Klöpfer and Edith Posca, premieres in Berlin.

4 Three films premiere in Berlin: *Der falsche Emir* (*The Phony Emir*) and *Ein gefähliches Spiel* (*A Dangerous Game*), both directed by Harry Piel and starring Hermann Leffler, Claire Rommer, and Piel; and *Der Evangelimann* (*The Evangelist*), directed by Holger-Madsen, with Paul Hartmann in the title role, Hanni Weisse in her film debut, and Elisabeth Bergner.

5 Engelhorn Press publishes the novel *Der Leibhaftige* (*Man in the Flesh*), by Frank Thiess.

6 *The Rivals*, by Richard Brinsley Sheridan (which premiered in London 1776), makes its German premiere at the Dresden State Theater.

7 The ballet music *The Rite of Spring*, by Igor Stravinsky, is premiered by the Berlin Philharmonic, conducted by Wilhelm Furtwängler.

The film *Die Finanzen des Grossherzogs* (*The Archduke's Finances*), directed by F. W. Murnau and starring Harry Liedtke, Alfred Abel, and Mady Christians, premieres in Berlin.

8 *The Emperor Jones*, by Eugene O'Neill, makes its German premieres at the Lustspielhaus in Berlin.

9 The film drama *Die Marionetten der Fürstin* (*Marionettes of the Princess*), directed by Friedrich Zelnik and starring Gertrud Welcker and Erich Kaiser-Titz, premieres in Berlin.

10 The drama *Prozess Bunterbart* (*The Bunterbart Trial*) premieres at the Königsberg Schauspielhaus.

11 The film drama *Die letzte Maske* (*The Final Mask*), directed by Emmerich Hanus and starring Alf Blütcher and Margarete Lanner, premieres in Berlin.

Cassirer Press publishes limited editions of Max Pechstein's drawings *Die Fischerfamilie* (*Fisherman's Family*) and *Landschaft* (*Landscape*).

12 The drama *Kaiser Maxens Brautfahrt* (*The Honeymoon of Emperor Max*), by Gerhart Hauptmann, premieres at the Leipzig Schauspielhaus.

13 Director Leopold Jessner completes his first staging at the new Schiller Theater in Berlin: *Maria Magdalena*, by Friedrich Hebbel, with Gerda Müller in the title role.

The musical parable *A Soldier's Tale,* with music by Igor Stravinsky, premieres at the Berlin Volksbühne.

15 The comedy film *Die Fahrt ins Glück* (*The Happy Journey*), directed by Heinrich Bolten-Baeckers and starring Leo Peukert, Camilla Spira, Willy Fritsch, and Olga Chekhova, premieres in Berlin.

Max Reinhardt opens *Das Mirakel* (*The Miracle*), with Eugen Klöpfer, at the Century Theatre in New York City; American critics wax ecstatic over the production, which eventually runs for 298 performances. It earns hundreds of thousands of dollars, helping Reinhardt to finance his operations in Berlin.

16 The comedy *Der verschnorkelte Gitte* (*The Crooked Screen*), by Leo Feld, opens at the Chemnitz City Theater.

17 Insel Press publishes *Die gesammelten Gedichte* (*Collected Poetry*), by Stefan Zweig.

There are demonstrations and protests in front of theaters where Ernst Toller's drama *Hinkemann*[1] opens; police are sent to protect actors in Dresden and Berlin.

18 A full-length operetta is broadcast by radio from Berlin for the first time.

The film drama *Die grosse Unbekannte* (*The Great Unknown*), directed by Willi Wolff and starring Lydia Potechnina, Leopold von Ledebur, and Ellen Richter, premieres in Berlin.

19 The drama *Der Brief des Urias* (*Uriah's Letter*), by Emil Bernhard, premieres at the Koblenz City Theater.

21 The epic film *Helena* (based on Homeric passages about Helen of Troy and her abduction by Paris), directed by Manfred Noa, with Edy Darlea as Helen and Vladimir Gajdarov as Paris, premieres in Berlin.

23 The comedy *Mr. Pim Passes By*, by A. A. Milne, makes its German premiere at the Tribüne Theater in Berlin.

24 Ullstein Press publishes the novel *Garragan*, by Ludwig Wolff.

25 The inaugural winter Olympic games begin in France, excluding German competitors. Protests in sporting organizations around the country accuse French organizers of having a belligerent anti-German bias.

26 An exhibition of paintings by Paul Klee[2] opens at the Jena Artists' League.

27 Amelang Press publishes a collection of novellas, *Deutsche Frauen im Kampfe des Lebens* (*German Women in the Struggle of Life*), by Thea von Harbou.

30 Steegemann Press begins publishing the monthly literary magazine *Störtebeker*[3] and publishes a volume of Rhineland comedies, *Tünnes* (roughly translated as "whitewash"), by Hans Müller-Schlösser.

31 The comedy *Barbara Stossin*, by Ernst Bacmeister, premieres at the Gotha Regional Theater.

FEBRUARY

1 Recently appointed Berlin State Opera music director Erich Kleiber makes his first appearance as conductor with the Berlin Philharmonic.

The melodrama *Die Vergeltung* (*The Payback*), directed by Serge Liepski and starring Otto Gebühr and Charles Willy Kayser, premieres in Berlin.

Architect Oswald Eduard Bickler and graphic artist Heinrich Zille are named members of the Prussian Academy of the Arts.

2 There are two theatrical premieres: the comedy *Razzia* (*The Raid*), by Paul Rosenhayn, at the Hamburg Lustspielhaus; and the drama *Die Empörung des Lucius* (*The Outrage of Lucius*), by Carl Thedor Bluth, at the Berlin State Theater.

4 The comedy *Die vertagte Nacht* (*Evening Adjourned*) premieres at the Breslau Thalia Theater.

The melodrama *Der Spring ins Leben* (*Leap into Life*), directed by Johannes Guter and starring Xenia Desni and Paul Heidemann, premieres in Berlin.

8 The drama *Thou Shalt Not Kill*, by Leonid Andreyev, makes its German premiere at the Deutsches Theater in Berlin.

10 The comedy *Der Schiessbude* (*The Shooting Gallery*), by Wilhem Lichtenberg, premieres at the Kattowitz Deutsches Theater.

11 Rowohlt Press publishes the novella *Drei Frauen* (*Three Women*), by Robert Musil.

14 The epic film *Die Nibelungen: Siegfried*, directed by Fritz Lang,[4] premieres in Berlin, with Paul Richter as Siegfried, Maragrethe Schön as Kriemhild, Hanna Ralph as Brunhild, Theodor Loos as Günther, and Hans Adalbert as Hagen.

15 A new Berlin cabaret, named Tü-tü and operated by Wilhem Bendow, opens.

The District Court in Berlin convicts George Grosz, Wieland Herzfeld, and their publisher, Julian Gumpert, of distributing obscene materials; each is fined RM 500.

17 Fischer Press publishes the novel *Der Zauberberg*[5] (*The Magic Mountain*), by Thomas Mann.

19 The drama *Columbus*, by Franz Weinrich, premieres at the Schiller Theater in Berlin.

20 Kiepenheuer Press publishes a volume of poetry, *Geheimes Kinder-Spiel-Buch* (*The Secret Book of Children's Games*), by Joachim Ringelnatz.

23 Rowohlt Press publishes the comedy *Palme, oder der Gekränkte* (*Palme, or The Sorehead*), by Paul Kornfeld.

The drama *Regiswindis*, by Dietzenschmidt (the pen name of Anton Franz Schmid), premieres at the Meissen City Theater.

24 The film drama *Carlos and Elizabeth* (loosely based on Schiller's drama *Don Carlos*, but with emphasis on Elizabeth of Valois), directed by Richard Oswald, premieres in Berlin, with Conrad Veidt as Don Carlos and Aud Egede Nissen as Elizabeth of Valois.

26 The widely publicized trial of Adolf Hitler and Erich von Ludendorff begins in Munich; they and nine others are accused of leading the "Beer Hall Putsch" on 9 November 1923. The presiding judges allow Hitler to speak at the opening session, and he wonders that, "as a man who as a soldier was for six years accustomed to blind obedience, I should suddenly come into conflict with the State."[6]

27 The comedy *En brav Frau* (*A Well-Behaved Woman*), written in a local Cologne dialect, called "Kölsch" by Jakob Rasquin, premieres at the Cologne Metropol Theater.

29 The comedy *Duellen der Heiligen Helene* (*Dueling Saints Helen*), by Emilia Bock, premieres at the Essen City Theater.

MARCH

1 Spiertz Press publishes *Anti-Ford, oder von der Würde der Menschheit* (*Anti-Ford, or The Dignity of Humankind*), by Robert Mennicken.

2 Fischer Press publishes two novels: *Der Amerikaner* (*The American*), by Gabriele Reuter; and *Der Narr in Christo: Emanuel Quint* (*The Fool in Christ: Emanuel Quint*), by Gerhart Hauptmann.

3 Horen Press publishes the novel *Peter Brindeisner*, by Hermann Stehr.

6 Löwitt Press publishes *Die Stadt ohne Juden: Roman von Übermorgen* (*The City without Jews: A Novel from the Day after Tomorrow*), by Hugo Bettauer.

7 Ullstein Press publishes the novel *Der rote Kaschgar* (*The Red City of Kashgar*), by Fedor von Zobeltitz. Frankfurt Press Institute publishes the monograph *Der Denkspieler Georg Kaiser* (*Georg Kaiser, the Thinking Playwright*), by drama critic Bernhard Diebold.

8 The comedy *Mächte* (*Powers*), by Karin Smirnoff, premieres at the Hamburg Deutsches Schauspielhaus.

The German-Austrian Press in Leipzig publishes the treatise *Der sichtbare Mensch, oder die Kultur des Films* (*The Visible Man, or The Culture of Film*), by Bela Balazs.

9 The German Press Institute publishes the novel *Tochter der Hekuba* (*Daughter of Hecuba*), by Clara Viebig.

12 The comedy *Palme, oder der Gekränkte* (*Palme, or The Sorehead*), by Paul Kornfeld, premieres at the Deutsches Theater Kammerspiele in Berlin.

13 The comedy *Der Aal* (*The Eel*), by Robert Schein, premieres at the Reichenberg City Theater.

Two comedy films premiere in Berlin, both directed by Friedrich Zelnik: *Der Matrose Perugino* (*Perugino the Sailor*), starring Anton Pointner and Hans Brausewetter; and *Nelle, die Braut ohne Mann* (*Nelle, the Bride without a Husband*), starring Lya Mara and Erich Kaiser-Titz.

14 The comedy *Die Gegenkandidaten* (*The Opposition Candidates*), by Ludwig Fulda, premieres at the Hamburg Deutsches Schauspielhaus.

15 The drama *Opfernacht* (*Night of Sacrifice*), by Hans Franck, premieres at the Schwechten Theater in Berlin. The comedy *Der Skandal mit Molly* (*The Scandal with Molly*), by Hans Zerlitt, premieres at the Hamburg Kleines Lustspielhaus.

17 The opera *Jenufa*, by Leos Janacek (in a translation from the Czech by Max Brod), premieres at the State Opera in Berlin.

16 The comedy *Die heilige Untreue* (*Sacred Infidelity*), by David Niccodemi, premieres at the Deutsches Künstler Theater in Berlin.

18 *Leben des Eduard des Zweiten von England* (*The Life of King Edward II of England*), by Bertolt Brecht (based on the play by Christopher Marlowe) and directed by Brecht, premieres at the Munich Kammerspiele.

Rütten Press publishes a collection of fiction, *Wunderstunden* (*Providential Hours*), by Felix Braun.

19 The Greater Berlin Art Exhibition opens at the Glass Palace; more than 40 artists' groups are represented.

Kiepenheier Press publishes a volume of poetry, *Das Schwalbenbuch* (*The Book of Swallows*), by Ernst Toller.

20 Staackmann Press publishes the novel *Ein Volk* (*One People*), by Friedrich von Gagern.

22 Scholze Press publishes a modern mystery play "with a prologue and 12 stations," *Päpstin Jutte* (*Madame Pope Jutta*), by Georg Reinicke.

Knorr and Hirth Press publishes a collection of daily news accounts, *Der Hitler-Prozess vor dem Volksgericht in München* (*The Hitler Trial in the Peoples' Court of Munich*), by a staff of reporters.

The comedy *Die Wette* (*The Wager*), by Carl Sloboda, premieres at the Hamburg Thalia Theater.

24 Two books by Albert Schweitzer are published by Beck Press: *Aus meiner Kindheit und Jugendzeit* (*From My Childhood and Youth*) and *Das Christentum und die Weltreligionen* (*Christianity and the Religions of the World*).

25 Two one-act plays premiere at the Berlin Lustspielhaus: *Traumtheater* (*Dream Theater*) and *Traumstück* (*Dream Play*), by Karl Kraus.

26 Two comedies premiere: *Das Recht auf dem Vater* (*The Right to a Father*), by Rud Klutman, at the Hamburg Thalia Theater; and *Der Jungfernvater* (*The Virginal Father*), by Erwin Hahn, at the Greifswald New City Theater.

The Berlin police department institutes a new "artistic committee" to provide advice on "artistic questions" about which performance works, art exhibitions, and publications should be suppressed.

27 The comedy *Kolportage* (*Pulp Fiction*), by Georg Kaiser, premieres at the Lessing Theater in Berlin. The play becomes Kaiser's most popular to date, performed hundreds of times in dozens of German theaters.

Adolf Hitler gives what observers call a first-rate performance during closing arguments at his trial for leading the Beer Hall Putsch in Munich; the presiding judges allow him to denounce the national government.[7] Dozens of German newspapers print Hitler's speech in their next-day editions, giving him unprecedented national publicity.

28 The romantic film *Das Haus am Meer* (*The House by the Sea*), directed by Erich Kaufmann and starring Grigori Chmara and Asta Nielsen, premieres in Berlin.

31 Wasmuth Press publishes a photographic album, *Deutschland: Baukunst und Landschaft* (*Germany: Architecture and Landscape*), with an introduction by Gerhart Hauptmann.

APRIL

1 Malik Press publishes the novel *Der Bürger* (*The Middle Class Man*), by Leonhard Frank.

Adolf Hitler is sentenced to five years' confinement at Landsberg Prison in Bavaria; Erich von Ludendorff is released.

2 The Social Sciences Press publishes *Der Hitler-Ludendorff Prozess* (*The Hitler-Ludendorff Trial*).

3 Cotte Press publishes the novel *Befehl des Kaisers!* (*By Order of the Kaiser!*), by Karl Rosner.

4 The comedy *Die Raubritter vor München* (*The Robber Barons before the Gates of Munich*), by Karl Vallentin, premieres at the Munich Kammerspiele.

5 The comedy *Das schwache Geschlecht* (*The Weak Sex*), by Frank Stayton, premieres at the Hamburg Thalia Theater.

6 The Frankfurt am Main Book Fair includes for the first time a "Radio Section," exhibiting the latest in transmitters, broadcast/receiving equipment, and possible future uses for radio.

7 The Junge Bühne (Young Stage) organization, formed to introduce the work of new playwrights in Berlin, begins the season at the Deutsches Theater with the premiere of the drama *Anarchie in Sillian*, by Arnolt Bronnen. Three plays make their German premiere at the Lessing Theater in Berlin: the dramatic fragment *A Florentine Tragedy*, by Oscar Wilde; the one-act comedy *The Music Cure*, by George Bernard Shaw; and *Varieté*, by Heinrich Mann.

8 Jürgen Fehling's new production of the drama *Die Nibelungen*, by Friedrich Hebbel, at the Berlin State Theater, wins wide acclaim among critics.[8]

9 Max Reinhardt's new production of Schiller's tragedy *Kabale und Liebe* (*Intrigue and Love*) at the Komödie Theater in Berlin attracts unusual attention, largely because the Komödie Theater is located in the fashionable west end of Berlin and normally stages boulevard fare.

12 Two dramas premiere: *Vaterland* (*Fatherland*), by Emil Strauss, at the Karlsruhe Regional Theater; and *Der tote Tag* (*The Dead Day*), by sculptor Ernst Barlach, at the Aachen City Theater.

The opera *Die tote Stadt* (*The Dead City*), by Erich Wolfgang Korngold, premieres at the Berlin State Opera.

14 The film drama *Steuerlos* (*Rudderless*), directed by Gennaro Righelli and starring Charles Willy Kayser and Heinrich George, premieres in Berlin.

17 The film drama *Horrido*, directed by Johannes Meyer and starring Robert Lefler and Rudolf Forster, premieres in Berlin.

20 A convention of more than 50 local Immanuel Kant Societies begins in the philosopher's native Königsberg in observance of his 200th birthday (on 22 April).

There are several boisterous celebrations of Adolf Hitler's 35th birthday in Munich streets, beer halls, and parks.

22 A drama about the 1862 French intervention in Mexico, *Juarez und Maximilian*, by Franz Werfel, premieres at the Magdeburg City Theater.

Swastika Press publishes *Unberühmte Frauen berühmter Männer* (*Nonfamous Wives of Famous Men*), by Askan Schmitt.

23 The comedy *Der Liebenstrank* (*The Elixir of Love*), by Fritz Rumpf, premieres at the Munich Kammerspiele.

The film drama *Gobseck*, directed by Preben Rist and starring Otto Gebühr and Clementine Plessner, premieres in Berlin.

24 Kiepenheuer Press publishes the drama *Leben des Eduard des Zweiten von England* (*The Life of King Edward II of England*), by Bertolt Brecht, based on the play by Christopher Marlowe. Rowohlt Press publishes the drama *Napoleons Fall* (*The Case of Napoleon*), by Arnolt Bronnen. Kampmann und Schnabel Press publishes *Das ekstatische Theater* (*The Ecstatic Theater*), by Felix Emmel.

25 The German government accepts the basic tenets of the Dawes Plan, aimed at ridding Germany of Franco-Belgian troops in the Ruhr district and standardizing reparation payments to the victorious Allies.[9]

26 The second part of the epic film *Die Nibelungen*, titled *Kriemhilds Rache* (*Kriemhild's Revenge*), premieres in Berlin; it is directed by Fritz Lang and stars Margarete Schön as Kriemhild, Rudolf Klein-Rogge as King Etzel, Theodor Loos as King Gunther, and Hans Adalbert as Hagen.

Langes Press publishes the novella *Der Jüngling* (*The Stripling*), by Heinrich Mann. Kiepenheuer Press publishes the novel *Die sieben Schwestern* (*The Seven Sisters*), by Karin Michaelis.

27 The melodrama *Mater Dolorosa*, directed by Joseph Delmont and starring Ilka Grüning, Paul Bildt, and Margarete Kupfer, premieres in Berlin.

28 The film drama *Oberst Rokschanin* (*Colonel Rokschanin*), directed by Otto Linnekogel and starring Erwin Kalser and Fritz Greiner, premieres in Berlin.

30 A new arts and crafts college is dedicated in Cologne.

MAY

1 The film drama *Zalamort*, directed by Emilio Ghione and starring Fern Andra and Robet Scholz, premieres in Berlin.

Transmare Press publishes the novel *Babbitt*, by Sinclair Lewis, translated by Daisy Brody.

The first issue of the monthly *Gewerkschafts-Archiv* (*Arts and Crafts Archive*), dedicated to fostering support for the arts and crafts movement in Germany, is published.

2 A new production of *Paracelsus*, by Arthur Schnitzler, starring Grete Mosheim and Alexander Moissi,[10] opens at the Deutsches Theater in Berlin.

The radio station Nordische Rundfunk AG (Northern Radio Corp.), known as "Norag," begins broadcasting from studios in Hamburg.

4 Zsolnay Press publishes *Verdi*, "a novel about opera," by Franz Werfel. Reitzner Press publishes *Das Erwachen der Frauen: Neue Ausblicke ins*

Geschlechtliche (*The Awakening of Women: New Views of the Sexual*), by Rudolf von Delius

5 The film drama *Die Stadt ohne Juden* (*The City Without Jews*), based on a novel by Hugo Bettauer, directed by Hans Karl Brelauer and starring Johannes Riemann and Anna Milety, premieres in Berlin.

6 The Young German Press publishes a collection of poems, *Gekreuzigt Volk* (*A Nation Crucified*), by Hitler sympathizer Maria Kahle.

10 The "mountain film" *Der Berg des Schicksals* (*The Fateful Mount*), directed by Arnold Fanck and starring Erna Morena and Luis Trenker, premieres in Berlin.

The comedy *Der Pirat* (*The Pirate*), by Friedrich Eisenlohr, premieres at the Hamburg Thalia Theater. Eugen Klöpfer makes his Berlin comedy debut in Ludwig Anzengruber's *Der G'wissenswurm* (*The Worm of Conscience*) at the Lessing Theater in Berlin.

13 The drama *Simson*, by Karl Röttger, premieres at the Bonn City Theater.

14 Müller Press publishes the festival play *Der Stein im Schwarzwald* (*The Stone in the Black Forest*), by Baron Joachaim von der Goltz.

15 Dieck Press publishes the first German introduction to radio broadcasting aimed at the popular market, *Das Radiobuch* (*The Radio Book*), by Hans Günther.

16 Tagewerk Press publishes the novel *Der Richter* (*The Judge*), by Rudolf Stammler. Rowohlt Press publishes a poetry collection, *Vermischte Gedichte* (*Jumbled Poems*), by Rudolf Borchardt.

17 A new translation of Aeschylus's *Prometheus Bound*, by Carlo Phillips, premieres at the Deutsches Theater in Berlin.

19 Philo Press publishes *Der Judenhass: Ein Beitrag zu seiner Geschichte und Psychologie* (*The Hatred of Jews: A Study of Its Psychology and History*), by Ismar Freund.

22 The thriller film *Der Klabautermann* (*The Hobgoblin*), directed by Paul Merzbach and starring Evi Eva and Wilhelm Diegelmann, premieres in Berlin.

Jungbrunnen Press publishes the treatise *Neue Menschen: Gedanken über sozialistische Erziehung* (*The New Man: Thoughts on Socialist Education*), by Max Adler.

25 The radio station Schlesische Funkstunde AG (Silesian Radio Corp.) begins broadcasting from studios in Breslau.

26 The "documentary drama" *Fahnen* (*Flags*), by Alfons Paquet, directed by Erwin Piscator, premieres at the Berlin Volksbühne; the production is Piscator's first to attract wide critical and popular acclaim.

The comedy *Herzlich Wilkommen!* (*You're Welcome!*), by Aaron Hofmann, premieres at the Hamburg Thalia Theater.

27 The film drama *Der Weg zu Gott* (*The Path to God*), directed by Franz Seitz and starring Eduard von Winterstein and Agnes Straub, premieres in Berlin.

28 The comedy *Die Karawane* (*The Caravan*), by Max Mohr, premieres at the Braunschweig Regional Theater.

31 The Greater Berlin Art Exhibition opens, featuring new areas of design and architecture for the first time; also represented for the first time are members of the League of German Architects and the Organization of German Garden Designers.

JUNE

1 Carl von Ossietzky is named editor of *Tagebuch* (*Diary*), a weekly magazine of news and commentary.

3 Grethlein Press publishes the novel *Das Land unserer Liebe* (*The Land of Our Love*), by Walter Bloem.

Franz Kafka dies of tuberculosis at a sanatorium near Vienna.

4 Stuttgart Polytechnical University awards automobile designer and manufacturer Ferdinand Porsche an honorary doctorate.

5 Rowohlt Press publishes *Dichtungen* (*Poetry*), by Carl Ludwig Schleich.

The melodrama *Die Herrin von Monbijou* (*The Mistress of Monbijou*), directed by Friedrich Zelnik and starring Lya Mara and Hermann Böttcher, premieres in Berlin.

7 The adventure film *Taras Bulba*, based on a short story by Nikolai Gogol, directed by Vladimir Strizhevsky, and starring J. N. Douvon-Tarzow and Clementine Plessner, premieres in Munich.

9 The comic opera *Der Sprung über die Schatten* (*Leap over the Shadows*), by Ernst Krenek, premieres.

Nazi Party members and sympathizers begin a nationwide petition drive to free Adolf Hitler from prison.

10 The detective film *Auf gefährlichen Spuren* (*Dangerous Clues*), directed by Harry Piel and starring Esther Carena and Henrik Galeen, premieres in Berlin.

11 Rothbarth Press publishes the novel *Der verhängnisvolle Brief* (*The Ominous Letter*), by Hedwig Courths-Mahler.

13 Die rote Gruppe (The Red Group), an organization of Communist artists, painters, and sculptors, is formed; George Grosz is named chairman.

14 The radio station Ostmarken Rundfunk AG (Eastern Marches Radio Corp.), known as "Orag," begins broadcasting from studios in Königsberg.

16 The film drama *The Power of Darkness* (based on the play by Leo Tolstoy), directed by Conrad Wiene, premieres in Berlin. The film is a German production but features a cast made up entirely of actors from the Moscow Art Theater, filmed with a German crew and edited in Berlin.

20 The comedy *Das Heimatstück* (*The Stay-at-Home Play*), by Hans-Otto Merz, premieres at the Bonn City Theater.

21 The comedy *Das eheliche Verhältnis* (*The Marriage-like Affair*), by Ladislas Sakatos, premieres at the Hamburg Thalia Theater.

23 Kabitzsch Press publishes a translation by Helmut Müller of *Die Homosexualität* (*Homosexuality*), by Havelock Ellis.

24 The film *Der geheime Agent* (*The Secret Agent*), directed by Erich Schönfelder and starring Eva May and Carl Lamac, premieres in Berlin.

27 Trowitzsch Press publishes the novel *Die Liebe durch die Luft* (*Love through the Air*), by Georg Engel.

30 The operetta *Polenblut* (*Polish Ancestry*), by Oscar Nedball, premieres at the Königsplatz Oper in Berlin.

JULY

1 Approximately 100,000 Germans hold licenses to own radio sets; to purchase a radio, customers are required to pay a license fee and register the license with local authorities.

DeGruyter Press publishes the memoir *Errinerungen an Korfu* (*Memories of Corfu*), by former German emperor Wilhelm II.

3 Schmiede Press publishes the novel *Hotel Savoy*, by Joseph Roth.

5 The opera *Xerxes*, by Georg Friedrich Händel, makes its German premiere at the Göttingen City Theater.

The summer Olympic games open in Paris; German athletes are excluded.

6 Steegemann Press publishes the memoir *Kindheit: Erinnerungen aus meinen Kadettjahren* (*Memories of My Years as a School Cadet*), by Leopold von Wiese.

The operetta *Die Frau ohne Kuss* (*The Woman Without a Kiss*), by Walter Kollo, premieres at the Komische Oper in Berlin.

7 Hitler begins dictating his "political testimony" to Nazi Party colleague Rudolf Hess; the dictations are later published in *Mein Kampf* (*My Struggle*).

10 The comedy film *Das Mädel von Capri* (*The Girl from Capri*), directed by Friedrich Zelnik and starring Lya Mara and Ulrich Bettac, premieres in Berlin.

11 The Bavarian provincial legislature in Munich strips Ernst Toller of permission to live in Bavaria upon his release from Niederschönenfeld prison.

14 The Thuringian Press Institute publishes three racist treatises by Otto Hauser: *Rassezucht* (*Race Cultivation*), *Rasselehre* (*Race Instruction*), and *Die Menschenwerdung* (*On Becoming a Human Being*).

16 Gottschalk Press publishes the musical review *Europäische Nächte* (*European Nights*) "in three acts and twenty pictures," by Walter Mehring.

17 Eysler Press publishes the novel *Frau Befrords Tränen* (*Mrs. Bedford's Tears*), by Margarete Böhme.

22 The Bayreuth Festival reopens after a 10-year hiatus with Wagner's opera *Die Meistersinger von Nürnberg* (*The Mastersingers of Nuremberg*), conducted by Fritz Busch.

23 The operetta *Das Fürsentkind* (*The Maids of Athens*), by Franz Lehar, premieres at the Königsplatz Oper Berlin.

25 Renaissance Press publishes *Sexualität und Kriminalität: Ueberblick über Verbrechen geschlechtlichen Ursprungs* (*Sexuality and Criminality: A Review of the Sexual Origins of Crime*), by Magnus Hirschfeld.

AUGUST

2 The first live broadcast of the Berlin Philharmonic Orchestra is made from the Philharmonic concert hall.

The first public display (in the form of several dozen posters) of Käthe Kollwitz's lithograph *Nie wieder Krieg!* (*End All War!*) appears at the Socialist Worker Youth Convention in Leipzig.

3 The first official and public Day of Memorial and Mourning for German soldiers killed in World War I is observed in front of the Reichstag building. In his speech to an audience of thousands, President Ebert calls for a permanent memorial to be erected in Berlin for those who died to create "a free Germany."

4 The first public display (in the shop windows of the Malik Press bookstore) of a Johnny Heartfield "pacifist photomontage," entitled *Nach zehn Jahren–Väter und Söhne 1924* (*Ten Years Later—Fathers and Sons, 1924*), juxtaposes images of the former kaiser and young boys marching off to war, backed by a row of skeletons.

5 The German Press Institute publishes the novel *Die Wacht am Rhein* (*Watch on the Rhine*), by Clara Viebig.

11 Official celebrations of the Weimar Constitution begin throughout Germany, with speeches, parades, and concerts observing the republic's fifth birthday.

12 The historical film *Neuland* (*The New Land*), directed by Otto Gebühr and starring Gebühr as Christopher Columbus, premieres in Berlin.

13 Fischer Press publishes the historical treatises *Die Insel der grossen Mutter* (*The Island of the Great Mother*), by Gerhart Hauptmann, and *Staat, Gesellschaft, Kultur und Geschichte* (*State, Society, Culture, and History*), by Felix Rachfahl.

14 Mohr Press publishes *Gesammelte Aufsätze zur Sozial- und Wirtschaftsgeschichte* (*Collected Essays on Social and Economic History*), by Max Weber, and the biography *Goethe als Psycholog* (*Goethe as Psychologist*), by Johannes von Kries.

17 A national meeting of the National Socialist Freedom Movement in Weimar is led by former general Erich von Ludendorff.

18 Teubner Press publishes the survey *Die Geschichte der Vereinigten Staaten von Amerika* (*History of the United States of America*), by Carl Brinkmann.

23 Two choral cantatas premiere at the Ninth Annual German Choir Festival: *Völkerwanderungen* (*Tribal Migrations*), by Hans Stieber; and *König*

Laurin's Rosengarten (*King Laurin's Rose Garden*), by Fritz Volbach. The composers conduct a choir of 40,000 singers.

26 The drama *Tanja* (*Tanya*), by Ernst Weiss, premieres at the Renaissance Theater in Berlin.

27 Springer Press publishes the survey *Der Cocainismus: Ein Beitrag zur Geschichte und Psychopathologie der Rauschgifte* (*Cocaine: A Study of the History and Psychopathology of the Drug*), by Ernst Joël.

28 Schmiede Press publishes four stories by Franz Kafka under the title *Der Hungerkünstler* (*The Artist of Hunger*).

29 Film actor Wilhelm Dieterle opens his Dramatic Theater in Berlin with the premiere of *Gilles und Jeanne*, by Georg Kaiser.

The comedy *Die Expedition ins Innere*, by Franz Raff, premieres at the Stuttgart Schauspielhaus.

SEPTEMBER

1 Malik Press publishes three new translations (by Hermynia zur Mühlen) of novels by Upton Sinclair: *Jimmie Jones*, *Samuel der Suchende* (*Samuel the Seeker*), and *Der Sumpf* (*The Jungle*).

The German government resumes reparation payments to the French and Belgians in accordance with the Dawes Plan.

3 The film drama *Die Andere* (*The Other Woman*), directed by Gerhard Lamprecht and starring Hildegard Imhoff, Xenia Desni, and Fritz Alberti, premieres in Berlin.

The inaugural issue of the monthly *Das Dreieck* (*The Triangle*) is published; it features articles on culture and the arts, as well as criticism. It is edited by Walter Gutkelch and Boris Wassermann.

4 The comedy *Die Komödienprobe* (*The Comedy Rehearsal*), by Ulrich von Trenck-Ulrici, premieres at the Karlsruhe Lustspiel Theater.

Cassirer Press publishes the religious drama *Die Sindflut* (*The Flood*), by sculptor Ernst Barlach.

The Darmstadt Regional Theater opens its season with concerts of symphonies, masses, and concertos by Anton Bruckner on the occasion of what would have been the composer's 100th birthday.

6 The film drama *Mister Radio*, directed by Nunzio Malasomma and starring Luciano Albertini, Magnus Stifter, and Evi Eva, premieres in Berlin.

8 The Ninth International Book Publishers Congress opens with several Hamburg-themed books from Hamburg publishers on display, including Friedrichsen, Boysen, and Alster.

9 Scherl Press publishes the novel *Das Eine* (*The One*), by Ida Boy-Ed.

12 Reiss Press publishes the novel *Der Mädchenhirt* (*The Shepherd of Girls*), by Egon Kisch.

15 Rothbarth Press publishes *Die schöne Melusine* (*Beautiful Melusine*), by Hedwig Courths-Mahler.
    The first radio commercials are broadcast on German airwaves.

16 French and Belgian troops begin their departure from selected areas of the Ruhr district, in accordance with the Dawes Plan.

17 Hirzel Press publishes *Geschichte des deutschen Reiches 1871–1924* (*History of the German Reich, 1871–1924*), by Johannes Hohlfeld.
    The comedy film *Maud Rockefellers Wette* (*Maud Rockefeller's Bet*), directed by Erich Eriksen, with Rita Clermont as Maud and Karl Elzer as John D. Rockefeller, premieres.

18 Max Reinhardt stages the Berlin premiere of the comedy *Der Schwierige* (*The Difficult Man*), by Hugo von Hofmannsthal, at the Komödie Theater in Berlin.

19 Fischer Press publishes *Komödie der Verführung* (*Comedy of Seduction*) and the novella *Fräulein Else* (*Miss Elsie*), by Arthur Schnitzler.

20 The comedy *Onkel Sam* (*Uncle Sam*), by Ernst Krohn, premieres at the Hamburg Thalia Theater.
    An exhibition of new drawings by Max Liebermann opens at the Cassirer Gallery in Berlin.

21 The comedy *Liebeskonzert* (*Concert of Love*), by Gabriele Eckehard, premieres at the Intimes Theater in Berlin.

22 Piscator creates the Revue Roter Rummel (Red Carnival Review) as a "portable political entertainment" at factory entrances, union halls, and other locations to drum up support for Communist Party candidates in upcoming Reichstag elections; the review is performed about two dozen times.
    Rowohlt Press publishes a collection of novellas, *Tage des Königs* (*Days of the King*), by Bruno Frent.

23 Langenscheidt Press publishes the novel *Stickstoff* (*Nitrogen*), by Ferdinand Runkel.

24 The historical film *Auf Befehl der Pompadour* (*By Order of Mme. Pompadour*), directed by Friedrich Zelnik and starring Lya Mara (in the title role) and Hans Albers and Alwin Neuss, premieres in Berlin.

25 The comedy *Heimliche Ehen* (*Secret Marriages*), by Wilhelm Backer, premieres at the Hamburg Thalia Theater.

The film tragedy *Michael*, directed by Carl Theodor Dreyer and starring Walter Slezak (in the title role) and Grete Mosheim, premieres in Berlin.

26 The Zeppelin airship *Los Angeles* makes a final flight over the city of Berlin before it is flown to the United States as part of war reparation payments.

27 The religious drama *Die Sintflut* (*The Flood*), by sculptor Ernst Barlach, premieres at the Württemberg Regional Theater in Stuttgart.

Louise Dumont and Gustav Lindemann renew their program of staging a repertoire of play productions at their Schauspielhaus in Düsseldorf.

29 The comedy *Mein Leopold* (based on the play by Adolph L'Arronge), directed by Heinrich Bolten-Baeckers, premieres in Berlin, with Arthur Kraussneck as Gottlieb Weigelt[11] and Käte Haack as his daughter, Klara.

30 The romantic film *Komödie des Herzens* (*Comedy of the Heart*), directed by Rochus Gliese and starring Lil Dagover and Nigel Barrie, premieres in Berlin.

OCTOBER

1 *Die Deutsche Fussball-Zeitung* (*German Soccer Newspaper*) begins publication; it is the first weekly newspaper in German devoted to sports reporting.

The comedy *Die tote Tante* (*The Dead Aunt*), by Curt Goetz, premieres at the Kammerspiele of the Deutsches Theater in Berlin.

The exhibition Form opens at the Arts and Crafts Museum in Frankfurt am Main. New paintings by members of the Berlin Secession go on sale at the Arnold Gallery in Dresden.

2 Wöhrle Press publishes the novel *Der Schauspieler* (*The Actor*), by dramaturg, critic, and director Arthur Kahane.

The film drama *Arabella, der Roman eines Pferdes* (*Arabella, the Story of a Horse*), directed by Karl Grune and starring Alfons Fryland and American actress Mae Marsh (making her German film debut), premieres in Berlin.

3 The dramatic trilogy *Tolkenning* (consisting of three plays, *The Wolves*, *The Worms*, and *The Phoenix*), by Alfred Brust, premieres at the Dramatic Theater in Berlin.

Boxer Max Schmeling defeats British fighter Rocky Knight in Cologne in his first large indoor arena bout.

4 The comedy *Sam Fox, amerikanische Milliardär* (*Sam Fox, American Billionaire*), by Roland Frank, premieres at the Kiel Schauspielhaus.

Oldenburg Press publishes the novel *Mensch, nicht Jude!* (*A Man, not a Jew!*), by Johann Ferch.

6 The Chancellery Court in Munich rejects an appeal to release Adolf Hitler from prison.

8 The comedy *Die heimliche Brautfahrt* (*The Secret Honeymoon*), by Leo Lenz, premieres at the Hamburg Deutsches Schauspielhaus.

9 A congress of German student pacifist and antimilitarist organizations opens in Berlin.

10 The comedy *Der beliebte Beifu* (*Beifu the Beloved*), by Hellmuth Enger, premieres at the Mainz City Theater.

The comedy film *Mädchen, die man nicht heiratet* (*Girls You Don't Marry*), directed by Geza von Bolvary and starring Ellen Kürli, Clementine Plessner, and Henri-Peters Arnold, premieres in Munich.

11 The new Reichsmark (RM) is introduced and is accepted alongside the Rentenmark as legal tender throughout Germany.

Boxer Max Diekmann defeats Max Schmeling on points at Berlin Sportpalast. It is one of only 10 defeats for Schmeling in his entire career.

Jessner stages a new production of *Wallensteins Tod* (*Wallenstein's Death*) at the Berlin State Theater, with Werner Krauss in the title role, who receives lavish praise from most critics.

12 The drama *Janus-Opfer* (*The Victim of Janus*), by Otto Ernst Hesse, premieres at the Dortmund City Theater. The comedy *Die dritte Tasse* (*The Third Cup*), by Maria Ibele, premieres at the Constance City Theater.

13 George Bernard Shaw's *St. Joan* makes its German premiere at the Dresden State Theater.

Film actor Wilhelm Dieterle closes his Dramatic Theater in Berlin.

14 Max Reinhardt stages Shaw's *St. Joan*, starring Elisabeth Bergner, at his Deutsches Theater in Berlin; her performance creates a sensation and the show is sold out for weeks.

The International Communist Congress in Cologne denounces the "colonialization of Germany" by American capitalist interests; in New York, sales of bonds for loan aid to Germany sell out within 12 minutes.

15 The Zeppelin *Los Angeles*[12] arrives in Lakehurst, New Jersey, after an 81-hour flight across the Atlantic Ocean.

The tragedy *Titus Andronicus*, by William Shakespeare (translated by Count Wolf von Baudissin), makes its German premiere at the Munich Prinzregenten Theater.

Weltbund Press publishes *Der Kitsch: Eine Studie über die Entartung der Kunst* (*Kitsch: A Study in the Decay of Art*), by Fritz Karpfen.

17 The German Press Institute publishes *Architektur, die nicht bebaut wurde* (*Architecture That Was Never Built*), by Josef Ponten.

18 Bong Press publishes the historical biography *Nebukadnezar, der König der Könige* (*Nebuchadnezzar: King of Kings*), by Heinz Welten.

20 The film *Garragan*, directed by Ludwig Wolff (who wrote the novel on which the film is based) and starring Edward Burns and Carmel Myers, premieres in Berlin.

Violinist Alma Moodie makes her Berlin solo debut with Hans Pfitzner's Violin Concerto in B Minor, op. 34, with the Berlin Philharmonic Orchestra, conducted by Wilhelm Furtwängler.

21 The "scenic cantata" *Die Zwingburg* (*The Fortress*), by Ernst Krenek, with libretto by Franz Werfel, premieres at the State Opera in Berlin.

The musical review *An Alle* (*To Everyone*), by Ralph Benatsky, with lyrics by Eric Charrell, premieres at the Grosses Schauspielhaus in Berlin.

22 The film drama *Mutter und Kind* (*Mother and Child*), based on a poem by playwright Friedrich Hebbel, directed by Carl Froelich, and starring Henny Porten and Wilhelm Dieterle, premieres in Berlin.

Rowohlt Press publishes the drama *Katalaunische Schlacht* (*The Battle for Andorra*), by Arnolt Bronnen.

23 The dance pantomime *Der Dämon* (*The Daemon*), by Paul Hindemith, premieres at the Duisburg City Theater.

24 The comedy *Diplomaten* (*Recent Graduates*), by Georg Engel, premieres at the Hamburg Thalia Theater.

25 The comedy *Das Lächeln der Frau Staatsanwalt* (*The Smile of Mme. State's Attorney*), by Robert Grötsch, premieres at the Dresden Neues Theater.

29 *Im Dickicht der Städte* (*In the Jungle of Cities*), by Bertolt Brecht, premieres at the Deutsches Theater in Berlin; unlike the world premiere in Munich, there are few protests or government attempts to shut down the production.

31 *The Hairy Ape*, by Eugene O'Neill (in a translation by Frank Freund and Else von Lossow), premieres at the Tribüne Theater in Berlin.

NOVEMBER

1 Zsolnay Press publishes the letters of composer and conductor Gustav Mahler, edited by Mahler's widow, Alma.[13]

The comedy *David und Goliath*, by Georg Kaiser, premieres at the Wallner Theater in Berlin.

3 Bong Press publishes the novel *Der Brandstifter* (*The Arsonist*), by Hans Hyan.

4 The opera *Intermezzo*, by Richard Strauss, premieres at the Dresden State Opera.

7 The melodrama *Gräfin Donelli* (*Countess Donelli*), directed by G. W. Pabst and starring Henny Porten and Friedrich Kayssler, premieres in Berlin.

8 The comedy *Hannibals Brautfahrt* (*Hannibals' Honeymoon*), by Klabund, premieres at the Breslau Lobe Theater.

9 The comedy film *Zwischen Morgen und Morgen* (*Morning to Morning*), directed by Friedrich von Maydell and starring Heinrich George and Rosa Valetti, premieres in Berlin.

11 Max Reinhardt officially resumes control of his Berlin theaters (the Deutsches Theater and its adjoining Kammerspiele, the Grosses Schauspielhaus, the Komödie, and the Theater am Kufürstendamm).

12 The comedy *Der Glückspilz* (*The Lucky Devil*), by Gustav Rickelt, premieres at the Guben City Theater.

13 The fantasy film *Das Wachsfigurenkabinett* (*Waxworks*), directed by Leo Brinski, premieres in Berlin. It stars John Gottowt as the owner of the waxworks, a kind of carnival wax museum, Emil Jannings as Caliph Harun al-Rashid, Conrad Veidt as Ivan the Terrible, Werner Krauss as Jack the Ripper, and Wilhelom Dieterle as the writer whose imagination brings the figures to life.

14 Two films premiere in Berlin: a "musical idyll of the Black Forest," *Barfussele*, directed by Heinrich Lisson and starring Missi Schütz and Siegfried

Arno; and the drama *Die Schmetterlingsschlacht* (*Battle of the Butterflies*[14]), based on a play of the same name by Hermann Sudermann and directed by Franz Eckstein, with Asta Nielsen as Rosi, Lori Leux as Else, Mary Parker as Mary, and Adele Sandrock as their mother, Frau Hergentheim.

15 Three comedies premiere: *Gewalt* (*Violence*), by Ernst Lissauer, at the Frankfurt am Main Neues Theater; the musical *Don Gil von den grünen Hosen* (*Don Gil of the Green Trousers*), by Walter Braunfels, at the Munich State Opera; and *Der sprechende Schuh* (*The Talking Shoe*), by Rudolf Lothar, at the Hamburg Thalia Theater.

16 The film drama *Die Liebesbriefe der Baronin von S . . .* (*The Love Letters of Barnoness S.*), directed by Henrik Galeen and starring Mia May and Alfredo Bertone, premieres in Berlin.

17 Vobach Press publishes the novel *Seines Herren Sohn* (*Son of His Lordship*), by Agnes Harder.

19 The melodrama *Windstärke 9: Geschichte einer reichen Erbin* (*Storm Force 9: The Story of a Rich Heiress*), directed by Reinhold Schünzel and starring Maria Kamradek and Alwin Neuss, premieres in Berlin.

20 Rothbarth Press publishes the novel *Das ist der Liebe Zaubermacht!* (*That Is the Magic Power of Love!*), by Hedwig Courths-Mahler.

The melodrama *Nju* (*Husbands or Lovers*), based on a play by Ossip Dymow, directed by Paul Czinner and starring Elisabeth Bergner and Emil Jannings, premieres in Berlin.

26 The comedy *Otto der Treue* (*Otto the Faithful*), by Toni Impekoven and Carl Mathern, premieres at the Frankfurt am Main Neues Theater.

27 Spaeth Press publishes the drama *Der Kreidekreis* (*The Chalk Circle*), by Klabund.

28 The drama *Doktor Guillotin* (*Dr. Guillotine*), by Ludwig Winter, premieres at the Karlsruhe Regional Theater.

30 The comedy *Martha und Maria*, by Hans Franck, premieres at the Dortmund City Theater.

DECEMBER

1 The Kabarett der Komiker (Comedians' Cabaret) opens in Berlin, featuring founder Paul Morgan, Max Hansen, and Kurt Robitschek.

2 The film drama *Mensch gegen Mensch* (*Man against Man*), directed by Hans Steinhoff and starring Tullio Carmanati and Ferdinand von Alten, premieres in Berlin.

3 The film drama *Dreiklang der Nacht* (*The Third Watch*), directed by Karl Gerhard and starring Kurt Brenkendorf and Claire Rommer, premieres in Berlin.

4 Jürgen Fehling stages Bertolt Brecht's *Leben des Eduard des Zweiten von England* (*The Life of Edward II of England*) with Agnes Straub and Werner Krauss, the first time a Brecht production features star performers.

5 The detective film *Der Mann ohne Nerven* (*The Man without Nerves*), directed by Harry Piel and starring Marguerite Madys, Albert Paulig, and Piel, premieres in Berlin.

The first Radio Broadcast Convention in Germany opens in Berlin.

6 The comedy *Sie lässt sich nicht verkaufen* (*She Won't be Bought*), by Adolf Paul, premieres at the Berlin Trianon Theater.

7 Nationwide Reichstag elections result in gains for the Social Democrats (SPD) and losses for everyone else, particularly the Communists (KPD) and Nazis (NSDAP). In many local elections, however, the Social Democrats lose seats in regional legislatures.

8 The Concerto for Piano, Winds, Tympani, and Contrabass by Igor Stravinsky premieres in Berlin, played by the Berlin Philharmonic (Wilhelm Fürtwangler conducting), with the composer at the piano.

9 Rowohlt Press publishes the novella collection *Drei Frauen* (*Three Women*), by Robert Musil.

10 The comedy film *Moderne Ehen* (*Modern Marriages*), directed by Hans Otto Löwenstein and starring Fritz Kortner, Helena Markowska, Ernst Stahl Nachbauer, and Ellen Reith, premieres in Berlin.

11 Schöningh Press publishes the drama *Dorothea*, by Carla Sermes.

14 A new translation of the Sanskrit drama *Sakuntala*, by Rolf Lauckner, premieres at the Berlin Volksbühne.

The opera *Liebesgarten* (*Garden of Love*), by Hans Pfitzner, premieres at the Berlin State Opera.

16 Two films premiere in Berlin: *Der Fluch* (*The Curse*), directed by Robert Land and starring Albert Heine, Ferdinand Bonn, and Lillian Harvey; and *Ein Weihnachtsfilm für Grosse* (*A Christmas Film for Grown-Ups*), directed by Paul Heidemann and starring Reinhold Schünzel and Lya Mara.

17 The film drama *Die Liebe ist der Frauen Macht* (*Love Is the Power of Women*), directed by Georg Bluen and Erich Engel and starring Fern Andra and Henri Peters-Arnold, premieres in Berlin.

Oldenburg Press publishes the poem "Der ewige Jude" ("The Eternal Jew"), by Paul Mühsam.

18 The comedy *1913*, by Carl Sternheim, premieres at the Deutsches Theater Kammerspiele in Berlin, with the playwright himself directing the production.

19 Playwright and poet Erich Mühsam is released from a Bavarian prison after serving five years of his 15-year sentence for his participation in the Bavarian Soviet Republic of 1919.

20 Adolf Hitler is released from a Bavarian prison after serving eight months of his five-year sentence for his leadership of the Beer Hall Putsch of 1923.

21 The dramas *The Moon of the Caribbees*, by Eugene O'Neill (translated by Gustav Kauder with the title *Unterm Karibischen Mond*, or *"Under the Caribbean Moon"*), and *Südseespiel* (*South Sea Play*), by Alfred Brust, both directed by Erwin Piscator, premiere at the Berlin Volksbühne.

22 The romantic film *Das schöne Abenteuer* (*The Beautiful Adventure*), directed by Manfred Noa and starring Vilma Banky and Georg Alexander, premieres in Berlin.

23 The film drama *Der letzte Mann* (*The Last Laugh*),[15] directed by F. W. Murnau and starring Emil Jannings and Maly Delschaft, premieres in Berlin.

24 The number of radio owners in Germany now exceeds one million.

28 The film melodrama *Die Frau im Feuer* (*The Woman in Flames*), directed by Carl Boese and starring Asta Nielsen and Alfred Abel, premieres in Munich.

29 Portions of Gustav Mahler's 10 Symphony[16] are premiered by the Berlin Philharmonic, conducted by Otto Klemperer.

The film drama *Die Bacchantin* (*The Enchantress*), based on a novel by Ludwig Ganghofer, directed by William Karfiol, and starring Olga Chekhova and Hans Mierendorff, premieres in Berlin.

30 The comedy *Six Characters in Search of an Author*, by Luigi Pirandello, premieres at the Komödie in Berlin.

31 The operetta *Charleys Tante* (based on the comedy *Charley's Aunt*, by Brandon Thomas), premieres at the Berlin State Theater.

NOTES

1. Hinkemann is a German soldier who returns home to Germany without his testicles, a fact that many audiences found outrageous. That so many at home had deserted him while he was at the front (among them his wife, friends, and employer) critics found equally egregious. Most protestors found the play a defeatist screed, and many sought to extend Toller's term in prison, where he had written all his plays since 1919.

2. Soon after this exhibition, Klee joined with painters Vassily Kandinsky, Lionel Feininger, and Alexei von Jawalensky to form a partnership marketing their work and themselves as *Die blaue Vier* (The Blue Four). Klee was particularly effective in the United States, where he gave lectures explaining expressionist painting and the ideas behind his work. Sales of paintings by the Blue Four in America provided substantial amounts of much-needed foreign currency.

3. Like Spartacus, Störtebeker had a special place in the leftist lexicon. Klaus Störtebeker (1360–1401) was a pirate whose band supposedly shared equally in their booty. Many of the ships Störtebeker besieged were Hanseatic League merchant vessels, and leftists in the Weimar Republic regarded Störtebeker as a kind of 14th-century Robin Hood of the Baltic Sea, robbing the rich and giving to the poor. Right-wing activists paradoxically celebrated Störtebeker as well, viewing him as an early advocate of nationalist sentiments.

4. Many critics hailed this film not only as Fritz Lang's best movie, but also as the greatest achievement in German filmmaking to date. It was certainly impressive from a technical standpoint: It took two years to film in numerous locations, and the special effects were stunning. Among the most often cited effects were the dragon scene, which required a dozen crew members to operate the mechanical beast; Siegfried's cape, which renders him invisible; and the scene in which Hagen drives a spear through Siegfried. Some critics complained that the acting was as mechanical as the dragon, singling out Paul Richter's allowing Hagen to bore through his chest with little complaint. The shooting script by Thea von Harbou owed a lot to Friedrich Hebbel's 1862 play of the same title, and several showings of the film throughout Germany featured orchestras playing a score that Gottfried Huppertz had composed to accompany the film.

5. *The Magic Mountain* quickly became a best seller in Germany and has since become one of the most popular novels in the Thomas Mann *oeuvre*. It has been translated into 28 languages and appears in the curricula of many school and universities around the world in courses on German literature and culture.

6. *Münchener Zeitung* (Munich), 26 February 1924.

7. Eyewitness accounts report that Hitler brought the house down with his concluding remarks to the judges: "Gentlemen, it is not you who pronounce judgment upon us. Rather it is the eternal Court of History which will make that judgment. The judgment you will pass I already know. But that Court . . . will judge us as Germans [who] have wished the best for their people and their Fatherland, who wished to fight and to die. You may declare us guilty a thousand times, but the Goddess who presides over the Eternal Court of History will with a smile tear in pieces the charge of the Public Prosecutor and the court judgment, for she declares us innocent."

8. Jürgen Fehling (1885–1968) was known as the most "mystical" of the numerous outstanding theater directors in the 1920s, and this production in particular was marked by an emphasis on anti-illusionism. Fehling had directed several expressionist premieres by 1924, and this production of what had become a "standard" in the German repertoire seemed to awaken a new understanding of the play. Comparisons with Fritz Lang's popular film treating the same subject matter were inevitable, giving Berlin audiences a unique opportunity to contrast techniques in modernist mythmaking.

9. The Dawes Plan was named for American banker Charles G. Dawes (1865–1951), who helped devise it. According to the plan, foreign loans were made available at highly favorable rates for investment in Germany. Such investments were to promote increased economic activity, allowing the Germans to resume reparation payments, pegged initially at RM 1 billion per year and rising to a limit of RM 2.5 billion. The Dawes Plan provided temporary relief for the German economy, and Dawes was elected vice president of the United States in 1924. For the plan that bore his name, Dawes was named corecipient (with Sir Austen Chamberlain) of the 1925 Nobel Peace Prize.

10. This season at Max Reinhardt's Deutsches Theater also marked the return of Alexander Moissi (1879–1935) as the suicidal Fedya in Tolstoy's *The Living Corpse*. The role became Moissi's trademark in the 1920s in the same way that Charlie Chaplin's little tramp and Josephine Baker's banana costume became trademarks. Moissi played Fedya thousands of times all over the world, committing suicide in a courtroom at the play's conclusion with the words, "I feel so wonderful." Rarely was it performed anywhere in German without Moissi, and the actor himself claimed a close identification with the role. "I am always Moissi," he once said, "whether I'm slipping into the hell of a distraught, tortured Hamlet or of a weak, defenseless Fedya—both are a part of myself."

11. *Mein Leopold* (*My Son Leopold*) had been an extremely popular satire in the German theater since it premiered in 1873. It portrays a nearly illiterate yet prosperous entrepreneur named Gustav Weigelt in his misadventures as a real estate speculator in Berlin. His new wealth blinds him to the profligacy of his wastrel son Leopold, who has gone off to America to enjoy life as a gentleman in one of the numerous German-speaking communities there. Leopold embodied the "new" Germany, based on materialism, luxury, and pretentiousness. Weigelt himself embodied the German self-made man, proud owner of leather-bound collections of Schiller and Goethe, yet barely able to read a sales contract.

12. The *Los Angeles* could accommodate 30 passengers in a compartment that resembled a Pullman car used on American railroads. Passengers ate food prepared in a small kitchen facility and slept in beds prepared nightly for their convenience. The *Los Angeles* subsequently made more than 250 flights throughout the United States and the Caribbean.

13. Alma Mahler (Alma Schindler, 1879–1964) had three remarkable marriages: first to Mahler, then to architect Walter Gropius, and finally to novelist and playwright Franz Werfel. She bore children to all three men and also had liaisons with several prominent painters, composers, and writers. Her editing of the Mahler letters has

proved to be somewhat misleading, prompting some music scholars to doubt its accuracy altogether. Alma has nevertheless remained the subject of interest to subsequent generations of scholars and artists. Karen Monson's biography, *Muse to Genius*, was published in 1983; Françoise Giroud's *Alma Mahler, or The Art of Being Loved*, appeared in 1991, and Susanne Keegan's *Bride of the Wind* was published in 1992. Songwriter and satirist Tom Lehrer wrote a "singing obituary" after her death, which featured a lengthy list of her paramours. A 2001 film, directed by Bruce Bereford and titled *Bride of the Wind*, starred Sarah Wynter as Alma, Jonathan Pryce as Gustav Mahler, Vincent Perez as Oskar Kokoschka, Simon Verhoeven as Walter Gropius, Gregor Seber as Franz Werfel, and August Schmölzer as Gustav Klimt.

14. The "battle" refers to a design that Rosi Hergentheim (played by Nielsen) creates at her job as a fan painter in a ladies' dress shop. The play portrays the widow Hergentheim (Adele Sandrock) and her daughters barely able to eke out a living on their wages at the dress shop, exploited by the shop owner, and subject to sexual predation by salesmen who visit the shop. Playwright Hermann Sudermann (1857–1928) was for a time considered comparable to Gerhart Hauptmann, but during the Weimar Republic Sudermann's perceived sentimentality and acceptance of social conditions caused him to lose favor in the theater. His plays remained popular when adapted for films, however, for they resembled cinematic treatments of novels by Charles Dickens. Like Dickens, they often compensated "good" characters for their suffering and punished "bad" ones for their misdeeds.

15. *Der Letzte Mann* (literally "the last man"; its English-language title, *The Last Laugh*, is somewhat inapt) was popular with audiences from the beginning of its run in Berlin and later in dozens of German cities. From there it went on to worldwide popularity and is today hailed as one of the German cinema's landmark achievements. It is one of only a few silent films that eschewed title cards to explain the action or dialogue. Its remarkable editing and cinematography (by Karl Freund) embraced the modernist conventions of abstraction and fragmentation, but so had earlier German movies. What made this one so popular was Emil Jannings's performance, along with the screenplay by Carl Mayer. The surprise ending, allowing Jannings's character (named simply the "Hotel Doorman") to triumph over adversity and despair (granting Jannings the "last laugh" of the English-language title) found gratifying resonance among almost every audience that saw it, and among German audiences in particular.

16. Mahler attempted to compose his 10th and final symphony under the duress of recently discovering his wife Alma's numerous infidelities. He wrote numerous comments to Alma on the manuscript score, which he left unfinished at the time of his death in 1911. In the early 1920s, Alma asked Ernst Krenek to bring the manuscript into playable form. He did so with two movements (the first and the third), and in late 1923 Alma sent the manuscript to a publisher in Amsterdam, hoping that the Concertgebouw Orchestra in that city would perform it. It did so in November 1924; the Berlin Philharmonic performed that score as well for the German premiere of the work.

1925

JANUARY

2 Central Prussian Police Headquarters establishes an "Arts Committee" with departments for theater, literature, and pictorial arts in Berlin; the committee will "counsel" authorities on "the maintenance of the public peace, security and order" while "upholding public morality";[1] in other words, this is the reestablishment of official censorship.

3 Berlin Symphony director Wilhelm Furtwängler makes his American debut at Carnegie Hall, conducting the New York Philharmonic.

The drama *Der Kreidekreis* (*The Chalk Circle*), by Klabund, premieres at the Frankfurt am Main City Theater. The comedy *Die Göttin auf der Balz* (*The Goddess in Courtship*), by Hans Bachwitz, premieres at the Hamburg Kleines Lustspielhaus.

6 Fischer Press publishes the drama *Der Wiedertäufer von Münster* (*The Anabaptist of Münster*), by Bernhard Kellermann.

8 Wolff Press publishes the novel *Ein Erbe am Rhein* (*An Inheritance on the Rhine*), by René Schickele.

9 Two comedy films premiere in Berlin: *Der Aufstieg der kleinen Lilian* (*The Rise of Little Lillian*), directed by Fred Sauer and starring Maria Zelenka and Bruno Kastner; and *Lumpen und Seide* (*Sow's Ears and Silk Purses*), directed by Richard Oswald and starring Reinhold Schünzel and Mary Parker.

10 The drama *Die Gesteinigten* (*Death by Stoning*), by Karl Irmler, premieres at the Dortmund City Theater. The comedy *Durch den Rundfunk* (*On the Radio*), by Otto Schwarz and Max Reimann, premieres.

12 Biesenthal Press publishes *Kernworte und Aussprüche von Adolf Hitler* (*Key Words and Sayings of Adolf Hitler*), celebrating Hitler's release from prison.

13 The epic film *Die Rache der Pharaonen* (*The Revenge of the Pharaohs*), directed by Hans Theyer and starring Henry Roberts and Maria Palme, premieres in Berlin.

Actress Agnes Straub plays Katherina in Shakespeare's *The Taming of the Shrew* for the first time in Berlin, under the direction of Ludwig Berger at the Schiller Theater.

14 Celebrations in many German universities mark the 50th birthday of theologian, physician, and organist Albert Schweitzer.

15 Schmiede Press publishes a collection of essays, *Spiel mit dem Feuer* (*Playing with Fire*), by Willy Haas.[2]

The comedy *Die Bildungsdame* (*A Lady of Quality*), by Alice Warmbold, premieres at the Göttingen City Theater.

17 The drama *Die Erlösung des Johannes Parricida* (*The Redemption of John Parricide*), by Heinrich Lilienfein, premieres at the Weimar Deutsches National Theater.

The operetta *Riquette*, by Oscar Straus, premieres at the Deutsches Künstler Theater in Berlin.

18 The comedy *Cagliosto,* by Herbert Scheffer, premieres at the Halberstadt City Theater.

20 The comedy *Gust Botefür*, by Max Dreyer, premieres at the Hamburg Thalia Theater.

21 The drama *Sakuntala* (based on an ancient Sanskrit text of the same name), by Paul Kornfeld, premieres at the Cologne Schauspielhaus.

22 The romantic film *Die Motorbraut: Liebe, Leid, und Sport* (*The Motor Bride: Love, Sorrow, and Sport*), directed by Richard Eichberg and starring Lee Parry and Angelo Ferrari, premieres in Berlin.

23 The comedy film *Die Perücke* (*The Wig*), directed by Berthold Viertel and starring Otto Gebühr and Jenny Hasselqvist, premieres in Berlin.

24 The drama *Lebensballade* (*The Ballad of Life*), by Walther von Molo, premieres at the Leipzig Schauspielhaus. The comedy *Die Schlange* (*The Snake*), by Hans Bacmeister, premieres at the Constance City Theater.

The operetta *Uschi*, by Jean Gilbert, premieres at the Hamburg Deutsches Schauspielhaus.

26 Stravinsky's Pulcinella Suite makes its German premiere with the Berlin Philharmonic, Otto Klemperer conducting.

American investment credit begins flowing into Germany, beginning with a then-unprecedented $10 million loan from the J. P. Morgan investment bank in New York to the Siemens Corporation in Berlin.

27 The film drama *Kampf um die Scholle* (*Battle for the Soil*), directed by Erich Waschneck and starring Gustav Oberg and Ferdinand von Alten, premieres in Berlin.

28 The "modern mystery play," *Luzifer* (*Lucifer*), premieres at the Dresden State Theater.

The literary journal *Der Stachelschwein* (*The Porcupine*), edited by Hans Reimann, debuts.

30 The film drama *Der Turm des Schweigens* (*The Tower of Silence*), directed by Johannes Guter and starring Xenia Desni and Nigel Barrie, premieres in Berlin.

31 The drama *Wer weint um Juckenack?* (*Who Weeps for Juckenack?*), by Hans-José Rehfisch, premieres at the Berlin Volksbühne.

Voigtländer Press publishes *Die Biotechnik des Fliegens* (*The Biotechnology of Flight*), by Gustav Lilienthal.

FEBRUARY

3 DeGruyter Press publishes *Reallexikon der deutschen Literaturgeschichte* (*Current Lexicon of German Literary History*), edited by Paul Merker and Wolfgang Stammler.

5 The one-act comic opera *The Spanish Hour*, by Maurice Ravel, makes its German premiere at the Hamburg Deutsches Schauspielhaus.

6 The film drama *Aschermittwoch* (Ash Wednesday) in Berlin, directed by Wolfgang Neff and starring Bern Aldor and Sybill Morel.

8 The film drama *Wenn die Liebe nicht wär'!* (*If Only It Weren't Love!*), directed by Robert Dinesen and starring Jenny Jugo and Fritz Alberti, premieres in Berlin.

11 The film drama *Zur Chronik von Grieshuus* (*The Chronicle of Gray House*), based on a novel by Theodor Storm, directed by Arthur von Gerlach, and starring Henny Porten and Paul Hartmann, premieres in Berlin.

12 Insel Press publishes the biography *Freiherr vom Stein* (*Baron vom Stein*), by Ricarda Huch.

13 The film drama *Schicksal* (*Fate*), directed by Felix Basch and starring Lucy Doraine and Conrad Veidt, premieres in Munich. The comedy film *Niniche*, directed by Victor Janson and starring Ossi Oswalda and Livio Pavanelli, premieres in Berlin.

A new production of *Prinz Friedrich von Homburg* (*Prince Friedrich of Homburg*), in which Werner Krauss plays the title role for the first time in Berlin, opens at the Berlin State Theater.

The American comedy *The Boomerang*,[3] by Winchell Smith and Victor Mapes, premieres at the Schwerin City Theater.

14 Rombus Press publishes the satirical "handbook" *Die Kunst des Verführens: Ein Handbuch der Liebe* (*The Art of Seduction: A Handbook of Love*), by Rudolph Lothar.

15 The drama *Pankraz erwacht* (*Pankratz Awakens*), by Carl Zuckmayer, premieres at the Deutsches Theater in Berlin, sponsored by the Junge Bühne organization.

16 Two dramas premiere: *Der rote Mond* (*The Red Moon*), by Herbert Eulenberg, at the Weimar Deutsches National Theater; and *Untergang* (*Downfall*), by Hans Franke, at the Heilbronn City Theater.

18 *The Game of Love and Death*, by Romain Rolland, makes its German premiere at the Hamburg Deutsches Schauspielhaus.

19 The Prussian Academy of the Arts awards its State Prize in duplicate to painter Bernhard Dörries and sculptor Josef Henselmann. The Munich Academy of the Pictorial Arts names painter Lovis Corinth an honorary member.

The adventure film *Pietro der Korsar* (*Pietro the Corsair*), directed by Artur Robison and starring Paul Richter and Aud Egede Nissen, premieres in Berlin.

20 Dietz Press publishes a collection of essays, *Das törichte Herz* (*The Foolish Heart*), by Paul Zech. Insel Press publishes the philosophical treatise *Der Kampf mit dem Dämon* (*The Daemonic Battle*), by Stefan Zweig.

The comedy *Die weisse Weste* (*The White Vest*), by Otto Wrack, premieres at the Berlin Neues Theater am Zoo.

21 The film melodrama *Der Roman der Lilian Hawley* (*The Story of Lilian Hawley*), directed by Franz W. Koeber and starring Lotte Neumann and Livio Pavanelli, premieres in Berlin.

24 Arnold Press publishes a volume of drawings by Ernst Ludwig Kirchner, *Kirchner-Zeichnungen*, edited by Will Grohman; it is the first of many popular books about the artist by Grohman.

25 Keils Press publishes the novel *Atlantis*, by Hans Dominik.

26 The Nazi newspaper *Völkischer Beobachter* appears on newsstands for the first time since the release from prison of its publisher, Adolf Hitler.

27 Director Erich Engel stages his first production at the Lessing Theater in Berlin, Shakespeare's *Coriolanus*, starring Fritz Kortner and Agnes Straub.

28 Reich president Friedrich Ebert[4] dies at age 54 of infectious complications after an appendectomy in Berlin.

MARCH

1 There are 785 book and newspaper publishers in Berlin, a postwar high.
  Actress Hermine Körner assumes directorship of the Albert Theater in Dresden.

3 Two film melodramas open in Berlin: *Die Venus von Montmartre* (*The Venus of Montmartre*), directed by Friedrich Zelnik and starring Lya Mara and Jack Trevor;[5] and *Heiratsschwindler* (*Marriage Confidence Man*), directed by Carl Boese and starring Reinhold Schünzel Käte Haack, Evi Eva, Uschi Elleot, Erna Morena, and Rosa Valetti.
  Two comedies premiere: *Okkulte Geister* (*Occult Spirits*), by Lothar Schmidt, at the Magdeburg Wilhelminisches Theater; and *Der Galgenstrick* (*The Jailbird*), by Otto Erler, at the Dresden State Theater.

4 Funeral services for the late Reich president Friedrich Ebert are conducted in the presidential palace, Berlin; Ebert is laid to rest in Heidelberg.

6 The adventure film *Der Flug um den Erdball* (*Flight around the World*), directed by Willi Wolff and starring Ellen Richter and Reinhold Schünzel, premieres in Berlin.

7 The operetta *Bis hierher und nicht weiter* (*Thus Far and No Further*), by Peter Kreuder, premieres at the Munich State Theater.
  The comedy *Das Scheidungsessen* (*The Divorce Dinner*), by Wilhelm Mayer, premieres at the Munich Residenz Theater.
  The drama *Michael Hunderpfund*, by Eugen Ortner, premieres at the Leipzig Schauspielhaus.

9 The Bavarian government places a ban on public speaking by Adolf Hitler; most other regional governments follow suit.

The Reichstag debates the assumption of costs for Reich president Ebert's funeral; Communist deputies claim Ebert collaborated with bankers and financiers, as Social Democrats exit the chamber. Nazi deputies join the Communists in refusing to vote for state funds covering funeral costs, claiming Ebert rendered no service to the state.

10 Elisabeth Bergner plays the "Lady of the Camelias" (in Dumas fils' *Camille*) for the first time in Berlin, at the Deutsches Theater; the production is sold out for weeks.

The comedy *Die Blumenfrau von Potsdamer Platz* (*The Flower Girl from Potsdam Square*), directed by Japp Speter and starring Erika Glässner and Ralph Arthur Roberts, premieres in Munich.

The film *Ein Sommernachsttraum* (*A Midsummer Night's Dream*), based on Shakespeare's play, premieres in Berlin; it is directed by Hans Neumann and stars Theodor Becker as Theseus, Charlotte Ander as Hermia, André Mattoni as Lysander, Barbara von Annakoff as Helena, and Hans Albers as Demetrius.

12 Ullstein Press publishes the historical survey *Die Monarchie Wilhelms II*, by Erich Eyck.

Two film dramas premiere in Berlin: *Der Mann auf dem Kometen* (*The Man on the Comet*), directed by Alfred Halm and starring Luciano Alberttini and Elena Lunda; and *Der behexte Neptun* (*Neptune Bewitched*), directed by Willy Achsel and starring Paul Heidemann and Erra Bognar.

The comedy *Abenteuer in Moll* (*Adventure in a Minor Key*), by Hanns Braun, premieres at the Darmstadt Regional Theater.

Head of the Reich supreme court Walter Simons is appointed temporary Reich president of Germany.

14 The opera *The Love of Three Oranges*, by Serge Prokofiev, makes its German premiere at the Cologne City Opera; the opera had its world premiere four years earlier in Chicago.

15 The opera *Prince Igor*, by Alexander Borodin, makes its German premiere at the Mannheim National Theater; the opera had its world premiere in 1890 in St. Petersburg.

16 The documentary-dance-sport film *Wege zu Kraft und Schönheit*[6] (*Paths to Strength and Beauty*), directed by Wilhelm Prager premieres in Berlin. It features dancers, gymnasts, and athletes performing in the nude in an attempt to capture the aesthetics of the human form in movement. Mary Wigman choreographed some of the movement pieces, and Leni Riefenstahl appeared as a performer.

17 The film melodrama *Athleten* (*Athletes*), directed by Friedrich Zelnik and starring Asta Nielsen and Arnold Korff, premieres in Berlin.

19 The British-German film *Dekameron-Nächte* (*Decameron Nights*), based on two tales from Giovanni Boccaccio's 14th-century original collection, makes its German premiere in Berlin; its is directed by Herbert Wilcox and stars Lionel Barrymore, Werner Krauss, and Xenia Desni.

21 The comedy *Die Maske* (*The Mask*), by Otto Ernst Hesse, premieres at the Frankfurt am Main Neues Theater.

22 The first American exhibition of expressionist paintings by Heinrich Campendonk opens at the Daniel Gallery in New York.

24 The film melodrama *Kammermusik* (*Chamber Music*), directed by Carl Froelich and starring Henny Porten and Livio Pavanelli, premieres in Berlin.

25 Drei Masken Press publishes the historical account *Jüd Süss* (*Jew Suess*), by Lion Feuchtwanger.

The drama *Henry IV*, by Luigi Pirandello, translated by Hans Feist, makes its German premiere at the Hamburg Thalia Theater.

26 Two film dramas premiere in Berlin: *Zapfenstreich* (*Curfew*), directed by Conrad Wiene and starring Harry Nestor and Claire Lotto, in Berlin; and *Wetterleuchten* (*Heat Lightning*), directed by Rudolf Walther-Fein and starring Wilhelm Dieterle and Lia Eibenschütz.

The comedy *Der Harem* (*The Harem*), by Ernst Vajda, premieres at the Berlin Komödientheater.

27 Bondi Press publishes a book of prose sketches and essays, *Tage und Taten* (*Days and Deeds*), by Stefan George.

28 The comedy *Gummizeit* (*On a Flexible Schedule*), by Carl Händel, premieres at the Darmstadt Regional Theater Landestheater.

29 The drama *Fahrt nach der Südsee* (*Journey to South Seas*), by Bernhard Blume, premieres.

The first round of presidential elections, involving seven candidates, yields none with any hope of winning a majority of votes; political parties frantically attempt to find a candidate who can appeal across party lines.

30 The film *Hedda Gabler* (based on the play of the same title by Henrik Ibsen), directed by Franz Eckstein, with Asta Nielsen as Hedda, Paul Morgan as Tesman, Albert Steinrück as Judge Brack, Grigori Chmara as Lövborg, and Käte Haack as Thea, premieres in Berlin.

31 The drama *Oscar Wilde*, by Carl Sternheim, premieres at the Deutsches Theater in Berlin.

APRIL

1 The Thuringian legislature disbands the Bauhaus School and fires Walter Gropius; the faculty and Gropius attempt to find funding to move the school from Weimar to Dessau, rechristening it the Hochschule für Bau und Gestaltung (College for Construction and Design).

2 The film melodrama *Der Demütige und die Sängerin* (*The Suppliant and the Soprano*), directed by E. A. Dupont and starring Lil Dagover, Eberhard Leithoff, and Hans Mierendorff, premieres in Berlin.

The opera *The Gilded Cage*, by Emmano Wolf-Ferrari, makes its German premiere at the Dresden State Opera.

3 Zsolnay Press publishes the novel *Der Kopf* (*The Chief*), by Heinrich Mann.

4 The drama *Der Sündflut* (*The Flood*), by sculptor Ernst Barlach, premieres at the Berlin State Theater. The Munich Academy of the Arts names Barlach an honorary member—but for his sculptures, not his plays. The comedy *Der Geliebte* (*The Beloved Man*), by Siegfried Trebitsch, premieres at the Frankfurt am Main Neues Theater.

8 The French comedy *The Talking Ape*, by Rene Fauchois, translated by Julias Elias, makes its German premiere at the Berlin Komödie Theater.

Right-wing parties unite behind former field marshal Paul von Hindenburg, who subsequently agrees to stand for election.

9 The film drama *Die Stadt der Versuchung* (*The City of Temptation*), directed by Walter Niebuhr and starring Olga Chekhova and Malcolm Todd, premieres in Berlin.

Centrist parties nominate former Reich chancellor Wilhelm Marx as their candidate for Reich president.

11 The detective film *Face á mort* (a German-French coproduction), directed by Harry Piel and starring Dary Holm and Harry Piel, premieres in Berlin and Paris.

12 The film drama *Die Frau von vierzig Jahren* (*A Woman of Forty*), directed by Richard Oswald and starring Diana Karenne (who was not quite 40 at the time) and Siegfried Arno, premieres in Berlin.

14 Langen-Müller Press publishes the novel *Das dritte Reich des Paracelsus* (*The Third Reich of Paracelsus*), by Erwin Guido Kolbenhayer.

17 Two film dramas premiere in Berlin: *Der goldene Kalb* (*The Golden Calf*), directed by Peter Paul Felner and starring Henny Porten and Angelo Ferrari; and *Vater Voss: Um seines Kindes Glück* (*Father Voss and His Child's Happiness*), directed by Max Mack and starring Arthur Pusey and Mary Odette.

19 The drama *Die fröhliche Stadt* (*The Happy City*), by Hanns Johst, premieres at the Düsseldorf City Theater.

20 The comedy film *Luxusweibchen* (*Women of Luxury*), directed by Erich Schönfelder and starring Hans Albers, Lee Parry, and Lia Eibenschütz, premieres in Berlin.

22 Hindenburg employs radio broadcasts in an appeal to voters for their votes in the upcoming election, the first time radio is used in a German election.
  The film drama *Leidenschaft* (*Passion*), directed by Richard Eichberg and starring Lilian Harvey, Otto Gebühr, and Henri Peters-Arnold, premieres in Berlin.

25 Two comedies premiere: *Das Frühstück in Genoa* (*Breakfast in Genoa*), by Walter Harlan, at the Bremen Schauspielhaus; and *Eine Frau von Klasse* (*A Woman with Class*), by Hans Eisenzahn, at the Hannover Deutsches Theater.

26 Schmiede Press publishes the novel *Der Prozess* (*The Trial*), by Franz Kafka.
  The German electorate chooses former field marshal Paul Ludwig Hans Anton von Beneckendorff und von Hindenburg as the new Reich president, with a 90,000-vote plurality over Wilhelm Marx, in the first nationwide election of a German head of state in history. The French government reacts with alarm, and other European nations voice concern that a former warlord will now assume the duties of the German chief executive. Many right-wing Germans hope Hindenburg will overthrow the Weimar constitution and install an authoritarian regime; left-wing Germans see in Hindenburg's election a strengthening of the Prussian military caste and the growing influence of right-wing extremism.

28 The comedy film *Die gefundene Braut* (*The Unspoiled Bride*), directed by Rochus Gliese and starring Xenia Desni and André Matoni, premieres in Berlin.

29 The drama *Das Viergetier* (*The Four-Footed Creature*), by Albert Steffen, premieres at the Dortmund City Theater.

30 The film drama *Sündenbabel* (*Den of Iniquity*), directed by Constantin J. David and starring Reinhold Schünzel and Maly Delschaft, premieres in Berlin.

MAY

2 Three short black-and-white animated films by Walter Ruttmann premiere in Berlin: *Ruttmann Opus 2* (one minute), *Opus 3* (three minutes), and *Opus 4* (two minutes); Hanns Eisler composes music for the films, played at the showing of *Opus 2* by a small wind ensemble.

The comedy *Die Bräutigamswitwe* (*The Bridegroom's Widow*), by Walter Mycroft, translated by Bobby Lüthge, premieres at the Kiel City Theater.

5 The Academy for the Scientific Research and Promotion of Germanness is founded in Munich.

The film melodrama *Um Recht und Ehre* (*A Matter of Justice and Honor*), directed by Richard Löwenbein and starring Harry Liedtke and Mary Parker, premieres in Berlin.

The comedy *Dr. Knock*, by Jules Romains, translated by Benno Vigny, premieres at the Cologne Schauspielhaus.

6 The comedy film *Blitzzug der Liebe* (*Express Train of Love*), directed by Johannes Guter and starring Ossi Oswalda and Willy Fritsch, premieres in Berlin.

8 The comedy *Das weisse Kätchen* (*The Little White Cat*), by F. W. Ilges, premieres at the Krefeld City Theater.

9 The annual Spring Exhibition of the Prussian Academy of the Arts opens in Berlin.

11 The opera *Der ferne Klang* (*The Distant Sound*), by Franz Schreker, premieres at the Berlin State Opera.

12 The film drama *Lebende Buddhas* (*Living Buddhas*), directed by Paul Hartmann and starring Hans Sturm and Käte Haack, premieres in Berlin.

14 Paul von Hindenburg is sworn in as Reich president at the Reichstag; the ceremony is a study in modesty and the absence of pomp or circumstance. Communist Party deputies arrange themselves in a platoonlike formation as Hindenburg begins his speech and march in goose step out of the hall in protest.

15 The comedy *Der Ausländer* (*The Foreigner*), by Hanns Johst, premieres at the Baden-Baden City Theater.

16 The Grosse Berliner Kunstausstellung (Greater Berlin Art Exhibition, or "GroBeKa") opens, representing the works of more than 2,000 artists; it is the largest and most comprehensive art exhibition in Germany, organized by the Cartel of United Pictorial Artists' Organizations.

17 An exhibition in a "realistic modernist" style (as distinct from "expressionist" styles) opens at the Mannheim Kunsthalle (Hall of Art), organized by its director, Gustav Hartlaub. Hartlaub terms the style *Neue Sachlichkeit* ("new objectivity" or "new matter-of-factness"), which captures the imagination of German art critics and buyers. Among the artists in the exhibition are Otto Dix, Georg Schrimpf, Georg Scholz, Heinrich Davringhausen, Christian Schad, and Alexander Kanoldt.

18 The film drama *Die freudlose Gasse*[7] (*The Joyless Street*), directed by G. W. Pabst and starring Asta Nielsen, Greta Garbo, and Werner Krauss, premieres in Berlin.

19 The historical film *Wallensteins Macht* (*Wallenstein's Power*), loosely based on the trilogy by Friedrich Schiller, directed by Rolf Randolf, premieres, with Fritz Greiner as Wallenstein, Eduard von Winterstein as Terzky, Christian Bummerstedt as Max Piccolomini, Erna Morena as Isabella, and Wolfgang von Schwindt as Buttler.

20 The film *In den Sternen steht es geschrieben* (*Written in the Stars*), directed by Willy Reiber and starring John Mylong and Maria Mindzenty, premieres in Berlin.

21 The opera *Doktor Faust*, by Ferruccio Busoni, premieres at the Dresden State Theater.

22 Book Community Press publishes the novel *Die Heimsuchung* (*The Search for Home*), by Oskar Maria Graf.

24 The comedy *Amerikanische Frauen* (*American Women*), by Avery Hopwood, translated by Berta Pogson, premieres at the Karlsruhe Regional Theater.

25 The city of Dessau offers Walter Gropius funding to establish a College for Construction and Design along the lines of the Bauhaus in Weimar; some colleagues of the old Bauhaus, much less politically committed, remain in Weimar.

26 The comedy *Das grosse Erlebnis* (*The Great Experience*), by Heinrich Schmitt, premieres at the Schwerin Regional Theater.

29 The film drama *Le Comte Kostia* (*Count Costia*), a German-French co-production directed by Jacques Robert, with Conrad Veidt in the title role, premieres in Berlin.

30 An exhibition celebrating 100 Years of Rhineland Painting opens at the new Kunstpalast (Palace of Art) in Düsseldorf.

JUNE

2 Cassirer Press publishes *Die tapferen Zehntausend* (*The Courageous Ten Thousand*), with graphics by Max Slevogt and commentary by Karl Witt.

3 The comedy *Die blaue Stunde* (*The Blue Hour*), by Felix Josty, premieres at the Berlin Trianon Theater.

7 Two dramas premiere: *Die Exzesse* (*The Excesses*), by Arnolt Bronnen, at the Lessing Theater in Berlin; and *Heinrich aus Andernach* (*Henry of Andernach*), by Fritz von Unruh, at the Cologne City Theater.

The first "Stravinsky Program" is staged in Berlin at the State Opera, consisting of the theater piece *The Solder's Tale*, the ballet *Pulcinella*, and the burlesque *Reynard*.

9 Grunow Press publishes the novel *Pflüger* (*The Plowman*), by Adele Gerhard.

12 The city of Heidelberg names playwright Wilhelm Meyer-Förster an "honorary citizen" in gratitude for his extremely popular play *Alt-Heidelberg* and the operetta by Sigmund Romberg titled *The Student Prince*, which was based on the play.

14 Wolff Press publishes the novel *Babbitt*, by Sinclair Lewis, translated by Daisy Brody.

16 *The Pleasure of Honesty*, by Luigi Pirandello, translated by Emma Hecht, premieres at the Deutsches Theater Kammerspiele in Berlin.

17 Mosse Press publishes the travel book *Yankee-land: Eine Reise* (*Yankee-Land: A Journey*), by Alfred Kerr, which details the theater critic's travels in the United States.

19 The film drama *Der König und das Mädchen* (*The King and the Girl*), directed by Nuncio Malasomma and starring Hans Albers and Evi Eva, premieres in Berlin.

20 A new production of the "love drama" *Jugend*, by Max Halbe at the Berlin State Theater, starring Lucie Mannheim and Veit Harland, attracts large audiences and is sold out for weeks.

24 The German Press Institute publishes the novel *Der einsame Mann* (*The Lonely Man*), by Clara Viebig.

26 The documentary film *Der Film im Film* (*The Film within the Film*), directed by Friedrich Porges, premieres in Berlin, with numerous performers and directors appearing as themselves, including Ernst Deutsch, Emil Jannings, Werner Krauss, Fritz Lang, F. W. Murnau, Asta Nielsen, Lee Parry, Henny Porten, Robert Wiene, Paul Wegener, Harry Liedtke, and Hanni Weisse.

JULY

3 The Ethnic German Press Institute publishes the treatise *Die Arische Weltanschauung im Kampf mit dem Fremdtum* (*The Aryan World View in the Struggle against Foreignness*), by Arnold Wagemann.

4 The operetta *Annemarie*, by Jean Gilbert, premieres at the Schiller Theater in Berlin.

6 De Gruyter Press publishes the treatise *Grundzüge eine Metaphysik der Erkenntnis* (*Principle Bases for a Metaphysics of Perception*), by Nicolai Hartmann.

7 The film drama *Die Puppe vom Lunapark* (*The Doll of Luna Park*), directed by Jaap Speyer and starring Jenny Jugo and Fritz Rasp, premieres in Berlin.

8 The comedy *Die gestohlene Stadt* (*The Stolen City*), by Egon Kisch, premieres at the Stuttgart City Theater.

10 The detective film *Das Parfüm der Mrs. Worrington* (*Mrs. Worrington's Perfume*), directed by Franz Seitz and starring Ernst Reicher and Imogene Robertson,[8] premieres in Berlin.

11 Rütten und Loening Press publishes the retrospective *Waldemar Bonsels, sein Weltbild und seine Gestalten* (*The World and Characters of Waldemar Bonsels*), edited by Fritz Adler. Bruckmann Press publishes the biography *Luther: Gestalt und Symbol* (*Luther: Character and Symbol*), by Gerhard Ritter.

12 The Communist Party musical review *Trotz alledem!* (*Despite Everything!*) is staged by Erwin Piscator at the Grosses Schauspielhaus in Berlin.

The Prussian administrative court lifts the police ban on public singing of "The Borkumlied" ("Song of the Borkum Islands"); officials had claimed that the song's xenophobic lyrics[9] posed a threat to public order; court judges rule the lyrics were harmless.

14 French troops begin their long-delayed exit from the Ruhr district, defusing popular German protests against their continued presence.

15 The film melodrama *Frauen, die vom weg abirren* (*Women Who Fall by the Wayside*), directed by Geza von Bolvary and starring Georg Henrich and Lo Etthoff, premieres in Berlin.

17 Steegemann Press publishes *Berlin ohne Juden* (*Berlin without Jews*), by Artur Landsberger.

21 The comedy *Esther Labarre*, by Franz Schulz, premieres at the Stuttgart City Theater.

24 The "Workers' Olympic Games" open in Frankfurt am Main, sponsored in part by the Social Democratic Party.

25 The historical spectacle play *Anno 1634* (*The Year 1634*), by Wolf Meyer-Erlach, premieres at the Nördlingen Summer Theater Festival, near the historical site of the Battle of Nördlingen, which took place in 1634 during the Thirty Years' War (1618–1848).

27 The detective film *Zigano* (a German-French coproduction), directed by Harry Piel and Gerard Bourgeois and starring Dary Holm, Harry Piel, and Olga Limburg, premieres in Berlin.

The comedy *Die Familie Krull* (*The Krull Family*), by Edmund Paul, premieres at the Stuttgart City Theater.

29 "Über quantentheoretische Umdeutung kinematischer und mechanischer Beziehungen" ("On the Quantum-Theoretical Reinterpretation of Kinetic and Mechanical Relationships"), by Werner Heisenberg, is published in the *Zeitschrift für Physik* (*Journal of Physics*).

AUGUST

1 The film drama *Drei Portiermädel* (*Three Waiting Maids*), directed by Carl Boese, with Hanni Weisse, Marl Delschafft, and Helga Molander in the title roles, premieres.

6 Zsolnay Press publishes a collection of novels, *Die Forsyte-Saga*, by John Galsworthy, translated by Luise Wolf and Leon Shalit.

12 Buchenau und Reichert Press publishes the novel *Der Gott im Treibhaus* (*God in the Greenhouse*), by Willy Seidel.

14 Rombus Press sues the city attorney's offices in Bremen and Leipzig for banning sales of Rudolph Lothar's *Die Kunst des Verführens: Ein Handbuch der Liebe* (*The Art of Seduction: A Handbook of Love*), claiming that city officials have misunderstood the book's title, harming its opportunity for sale and distribution throughout Germany.

The romantic film *Liebe und Trompetenblase* (*Love and Fanfares*), directed by Richard Eichberg and starring Lilian Harvey and Harry Liedtke, premieres in Berlin.

17 Kösel und Pustet Press publishes the novel *Das Rosenwunder* (*The Miracle of the Rose*), by Enrica Händel-Mazzetti.

19 The musical review *Achtung Welle 505* (*This is Radio Channel 505 Calling*), by Willi Wolff and Walter Kollo, premieres at the Admiral's Palace Theater in Berlin.

21 The film drama *Des Lebens Würfelspiel* (*The Dice-Game of Life*), directed by Heinz Paul and starring Fritz Beckmann and Olga Engl, premieres in Berlin.

26 Müller Press publishes the collection *Jüdische Legenden* (*Jewish Legends*), by Emil Cohn.

27 The comedy film *Die Frau mit dem Etwas* (*The Woman with That Certain Something*), directed by Erich Schönfelder and starring Lee Parry and Bruno Kastner, premieres.

28 Two films premiere in Berlin: *Elegantes Pack* (*The Elegant Bunch*), directed by Jaap Speyer and starring Eugen Klöpfer and Hanni Weisse; and *Die Verrufenen* (*The Infamous*), directed by Gerhard Lamprecht and starring Aud Egede Nissen and Bernhard Goetzke.

29 The comedy *Die Expedition ins Innere* (*The Journey Inwards*), by Franz Raff, premieres at the Stuttgart City Theater.

31 The film drama *Das Abenteuer der Sybille Brant* (*The Adventure of Sybil Brant*), based on a novel by Hugo Bettauer, directed by Carl Boese, and starring Henni Porten and Rudolf Biebrach, premieres in Berlin.

SEPTEMBER

1 Viktor Barnowsky assumes the lease of the Theater in der Königgrätzer Strasse in Berlin and begins his tenure there with a production of Shakespeare's *As You Like It*, starring Elisabeth Bergner and Fritz Kortner.

3 The Bühnenvolksbund (Peoples' Theatre League) is founded in Frankfurt am Main, dedicated to fostering the Christian viewpoint in German plays and production.

Koehler and Amelang Press publishes a collection of stories, *Die Mundharmonika* (*The Mouth Harmonica*), by Walter Bonsels

4 The film drama *Die Prinzessin und der Geiger* (*The Princess and the Violinist*), directed by Graham Cuts, written by Alfred Hitchcock and starring Jane Novak[10] and Walter Rilla, premieres in Berlin.

5 The comedy *Great Catherine*, by George Bernard Shaw, translated by Siegfried Trebitsch, makes its German premiere at the Berlin State Theater.

The drama *Each in His Own Way*, by Luigi Pirandello, translated by Francesco von Mendelssohn, makes its German premiere at the Kleines Theater in Berlin.

7 Gruppe 1925 (Group 1925), an informal association of 39 leftist authors, theater director, and critics, is formed for the purpose of mutual support and organized resistance to growing governmental interference in artistic expression; leading members include Bertolt Brecht, Alfred Döblin, Willy Haas, Walter Hasenclever, Alfons Paquet, Erwin Piscator, and Ludwig Marcuse.

9 The comedy *Margarine*, by Georg Kaiser, premieres at the Komödienhaus in Berlin.

Reissner Press publishes *Gespräche und Briefe Walter Rathenaus* (*Discussions and Letters of Walter Rathenau*), edited by Max Scheler.

10 The film epic *Die vom Niederrhein* (*In the Valleys of the Southern Rhine*), adapted from the novel of the same name by Rudolf Herzog, premieres in several German cities simultaneously; it is directed by Rudolf Walther-Fein and stars Albert Steinrück and Erna Morena.

11 Cassirer Press publishes a collection of drawings, *Don Juan und Leporello*, by Max Slevogt.

The operetta *Die Teresina* (*Little Theresa*), by Oscar Straus, premieres at the Deutsches Künstler Theater in Berlin.

Two film melodramas premiere in Berlin: *Frauen, die man oft nicht grüsst* (*Women You Rarely Greet*), directed by Fredrich Zelnik and starring Lya Mara and Alfons Fryland; and *Liebesfeuer* (*Fire of Love*), directed by Paul Stein and starring Liane Haid and Paul Biensfeldt.

The five-play cycle *Zurück zu Methusalem* (*Back to Methuselah*), by George Bernard Shaw, translated by Siegfried Trebitsch, premieres at the Tribüne Theater in Berlin.

15 The Academy of Movement, Speech, and Music opens in Münster.

17 The film melodrama *Eifersucht* (*Jealousy*), directed by Karl Grune and starring Lya DePutti and Werner Krauss, premieres.

18 Steegemann Press publishes the novel *Berlin ohne Juden* (*Berlin without Jews*), by Artur Landsberger.

Two films premiere in Berlin: the melodrama *Die Anne-Lise von Dessau*, directed by James Bauer and starring Maly Delschaft and Hermann Böttcher; and the detective film *Der Schuss im Pavillon* (*The Shot in the Pavilion*), directed by Max Obal and starring Ernst Reicher and Margarete Schlegel.

19 Two dramas premiere: *Veland*, by Gerhart Hauptmann, directed by the playwright himself, at the Hamburg Deutsches Schauspielhaus; and *The Rules of the Game*, by Luigi Pirandello, at the Mannheim National Theater.

The comedy *Die Kavaliere der Herzogin* (*Cavaliers of the Duchess*), by Willy Kaufmann, premieres at the Hannover Deutsches Theater.

21 Fischer Press publishes two novels: *Laudin und die Seinen* (*Noël Laudin and His School*), by Jakob Wassermann; and *Der Schlangenmensch* (*The Snake Man*), by Alice Berend.

23 Rothbarth Press publishes the novel *Nur dich allein!* (*You and You Alone!*), by Hedwig Courths-Mahler.

25 The film drama *Das alte Ballhaus* (*The Old Ballroom*), Parts 1 and 2, premieres in Berlin, directed by Wolfgang Neff and starring Carl Auen, Olga Chekhova, and Sybill Morel.

26 The comedy *Garderobe Nr. 7* (*Dressing Room No. 7*), by Hans Witt-Ebernitz, premieres at the Frankfurt an der Oder City Theater.

28 The historical drama *Neidhardt von Gneisenau*, by Wolfgang Goetz, opens at the Stuttgart City Theater; overwhelmingly positive reaction from audiences and critics attracts national attention.[11]

29 The comedy film *O alte Burschenherrlichkeit* (*The Old Fraternity*), directed by Helene Lackner and starring Kurt Gerron, Charles Willy Kayser, Eugen Klöpfer, Hans Mierendorff, and Hilde Jary, premieres in Berlin.

30 A new production of Shakespeare's *The Merchant of Venice* premieres at the Berlin Volksbühne, starring Alexander Granach as Shylock; some critics describe Granach as "the most Jewish Shylock" yet seen in Berlin.

OCTOBER

1 Author Johannes R. Becher is arrested for the writing and publication of his book *Der Leichnam auf dem Thron* (*The Corpse on the Throne*).
 The first issue of the new theater journal *Die Premiere* is published. The first issue of the monthly journal *Abendland* (*The West*), dedicated to fostering a Christian-Catholic viewpoint, is published.

2 The first production in the Weimar Republic of the drama *Don Juan und Faust*, by Christian Dietrich Grabbe, takes place at the Theater in der Königgrätzer Strasse.
 The film drama *Liebe macht blind* (*Love Is Blind*), directed by Lothar Mendes with Lil Dagover, Emil Jannings, Conrad Veidt, and Georg Alexander, premieres.
 Prussian state and Cologne city authorities agree to establish a university-level academy of music in Cologne.

3 The comedy *Der Brief* (*The Letter*), by Friedrich Kanzler, premieres at the Hamburg Kammerspiele.

5 *Dance Suite*, by Béla Bartók, makes its German premiere in Berlin, played by the Berlin Philharmonic, with Wilhelm Furtwängler conducting.

6 The comedy *Kurve Links* (*Curve to the Left*), by Otto Palitzsch, premieres at the Cologne Kammerspiele.

9 The film melodrama *Briefe, die ihn nicht erreichten* (*Undelivered Mail*), directed by Friedrich Zelnik and starring Albert Bassermann and Marcella Albani, premieres in Berlin.

10 The epic film *Volk in Not* (*A People in Danger*), directed by Wolfgang Neff and starring Traute Gerlach and Wilhelm Diegelmann, premieres in Berlin.

11 A meeting at the Theater am Nollendorf Platz in Berlin of leading figures in German artistic and intellectual protests recent arrests of writers, performers, and painters. Several actors, playwrights, publishers, critics, and even scientists (including Albert Einstein) sign a petition titled "For the Freedom of Art."

The comedy *Bluff*, by Rudolf Schneider, premieres at the Stuttgart Regional Theater.

12 Luigi Pirandello[12] brings his company from the Teatro d'Arte di Roma to Berlin, where the troupe performs *Six Characters in Search of an Author*, *Henry IV*, and *Right You Are, If You Think You Are* at the State Theater.

The romantic film *Die vertauschte Braut* (*The Alternative Bride*), directed by Carl Wilhelm and starring Ida Wust and Bruno Kastner, premieres in Berlin.

13 The drama *Desire under the Elms*, by Eugene O'Neill, makes its German premiere at the Lessing Theater in Berlin. The comedy *Die Liebeslehre* (*The Lesson in Love*), by Otto Ernst Hesse, premieres at the Schwerin Regional Theater.

14 The epic film *Götz von Berlichingen* (based on the play by Johann Wolfgang Goethe), directed by Hubert Moest, with Eugen Klöpfer in the title role and Friedrich Kühne as Franz von Sickingen, premieres in Berlin.

15 The comedy film *Das Fräulein vom Amt* (*The Girl from the Office*), directed by Hanns Schwarz and starring Ellen Plessow and Karl Platen, premieres in Berlin.

17 Northern Rhine Radio in Dortmund makes its first broadcast.

The tragedy *Hannibal*, by Christian Dietrich Grabbe, is performed for the first time in the Weimar Republic at the Berlin State Theater.

19 Ullstein Press publishes the treatise *Die Sonderstellung des Menschen in der Natur* (*The Special Place of Man in Nature*), by Hans Friedenthal.

20 Two dramas premiere: *Der Kreidekreis* (*The Chalk Circle*), by Klabund, at the Deutsches Theater in Berlin; and *Anja und Esther*, by Klaus Mann, at the Munich Kammerspiele.

22 The comedy film *Der Farmer aus Texas* (*The Farmer from Texas*), based on the play *Kolportage*, by Georg Kaiser, directed by Joe May and starring Mady Christians and Edmund Burns, premieres in Berlin.

23 Three films premiere in Berlin: *Finale der Liebe* (*Love's Finale*), directed by Felix Basch and starring Nils Asther and Lia Eibenschütz; *Die Frau ohne Geld* (*The Woman without Money*), directed by Fritz Kaufmann and starring Blandine Ebinger and Alfons Fryland; and *Der Mann, der sich verkauft*

(*The Man Who Sells Himself*), directed by Hans Steinhoff and starring Olaf Fjord and Vivian Gibson.

25   The operetta *Der Zigeunerbaron* (*The Gypsy Baron*), by Johann Strauss, is performed for the first time at the Berlin State Opera.

27   The film *Geheimnis der alten Mamselle* (*The Old Lady's Secret*), directed by Paul Merzbac and starring Frida Richard and Hans Mierendorff, premieres in Berlin.

29   The film melodrama *. . . und es lockt ein Ruf aus sündiger Welt* (*The Sinful World's Seductive Call*), directed by Carl Boese and starring Fern Andra[13] and Otto Gebühr, premieres in Berlin.

30   The film melodrama *Die Moral der alten Gasse* (*The Morality of Street Life*), directed by Jaap Speyer and starring Werner Krauss and Evi Eva, premieres in Berlin.

NOVEMBER

2   Reissner Press publishes a collection of drawings, *Spiesser-Spiegel* (*Mirror of the Philistine*), by George Grosz.

3   The comedy *Der Wehrgreis* (*The Old Guard*), by Werner Schendell, premieres at the Breslau Thalia Theater.

4   The film drama *Schiff in Not* (*Ship in Danger*), directed by Fred Sauer and starring Gustav Fröhlich and Jenny Jugo, premieres in Berlin.

5   The drama *Maler Sandhaus* (*Sandhaus the Painter*), by Fritz Droop, premieres at the Dortmund City Theater.

The romantic film *Liebesgeschichten* (*Love Stories*), directed by Fritz Freisler and starring Olga Chekhova and Hans Unterkircher, premieres in Berlin.

6   Reudnitz Press publishes the romantic novel *Asiaten* (*Asians*), by Artur Landsberger. Quelle and Meyer Press publishes a history of the German navy, *Vom Segelschiff zum U-Boot* (*From Sailing Ship to Submarine*) by former admiral Reinhard Scheer.

The film melodrama *Der Tänzer meiner Frau* (*Dance Fever*), directed by Alexander Korda and starring Lea Seidl amd Willy Fritsch, premieres in Berlin.

7   The comedy *Das Frühstück in Genua* (*Breakfast in Genoa*), by Walter Harlan, premieres at the Bremen Schauspielhaus.

8 In his first public appearance in Berlin since his release from prison, Ernst Toller addresses an audience of nearly 3,000 people at the Grosses Schauspielhaus, on the failed revolution of 1919.

The comedy *Der Irrgarten der Liebe* (*The Labyrinth of Love*), by Hans Sturm, premieres at the Leipzig Schauspielhaus.

9 Two films premiere in Berlin: the drama *Der Trödler von Amsterdam* (*The Junk Dealer from Amsterdam*), directed by Victor Janson and starring Werner Krauss and Hilde Hildebrand; and the comedy *Wenn Du eine Tante Hast* (*If You Have an Aunt*), directed by Carl Boese and starring Maly Delschaft and Wilhelm Diegelmann.

On the second anniversary of the ill-fated Beer Hall Putsch, Adolf Hitler forms an elite guard unit for his personal protection, which he calls the *Schutzstaffel* (protective echelon) or "SS," with about 300 members.

11 The film drama *Der Herr ohne Wohnung* (*The Man without a Home*), directed by Heinrich Bolten-Baeckers and starring Georg Alexander and Margarete Lanner, premieres in Berlin.

12 The comedy *Der mutige Seefahrer* (*The Brave Traveler by Sea*), by Georg Kaiser, premieres at the Dresden State Theater.

14 The drama *Der Teufelspakt* (*Covenant with the Devil*), by Klabund, premieres at the Hannover Deutsches Theater.

16 The film drama *Varieté* (*Jealousy*), directed by E. A. Dupont and starring Emil Jannings and Lya De Putti, premieres in Berlin.

19 The film drama *Schatten der Weltstadt* (*Shadows of the Metropolis*), directed by Willi Wolff and starring Ellen Richter and Alfred Gerasch, premieres in Berlin.

The comedy *Die Galgenfrist* (*Date with the Hangman*), by F. A. Kerl, premieres at the Hildesheim City Theater.

20 The romantic film *Gräfin Mariza* (*Countess Mariza*), directed by Hans Steinhoff and starring Vivian Gibson and Harry Liedtke, premieres in Berlin.

24 Max Schillings resigns as director of the Berlin State Opera.

The film melodrama *Die Frau für 24 Stunden* (*A Woman for 24 Hours*), directed by Reinhold Schünzel and starring Lotte Neumann and Harry Liedtke, premieres in Berlin.

25 The film drama *Freies Volk* (*A Free People*), directed by Martin Berger and starring Albert Florath and Ellen Plessow, premieres in Berlin.

26 The film melodrama *Halbseide* (*Dubious*), directed by Richard Oswald and starring Mary Parker and Bernd Aldor, premieres in Berlin.

27 A drama about the Russian revolution, *Don Quixote Liberated*, by Soviet Education Commissar Anatoly Lunacharsky, premieres at the Berlin Volksbühne. The comedy *Captain Brassbound's Conversion*, by George Bernard Shaw, translated by Siegfried Trebitsch, premieres at the Schiller Theater Berlin.

30 Two films premiere in Berlin: *Tragödie* (*Tragedy*), directed by Carl Froelich and starring Walter Janssen and Henny Porten; and the comedy *Vorderhaus und Hinterhaus* (*Upstairs Downstairs*), directed by Richard Oswald and starring Max Adalbert and Trude Hesterberg.

DECEMBER

1 Heinz Tietjen is named the new director of the Berlin State Opera.

Two films premiere in Berlin: *Die eiserne Braut* (*The Iron Bride*), directed by Carl Boese and starring Claire Rommer and Otto Gebühr; and *Der Liebeskäfig* (*The Love Cage*), directed by Erich Schönfelder and starring Carl Auen and Maria Forescu.

The comedy *Klinkutsch* (*The Battered Coach*), by Otto Ernst Hesse, premieres at the Hamburg Kleines Lustspielhaus.

2 Spaeth Press publishes a collection of stories, *Regenbogen* (*Rainbows*), by Arnold Zweig.

4 Amsel Press publishes *Die Sonette an Orpheus* (*Sonnets to Orpheus*), by Rainer Maria Rilke.

5 The drama *Erde* (*Earth*), by Paul Zech, premieres at the Cologne Neues Schauspielhaus.

9 Union Press publishes *Der Glücksfischer* (*The Fisherman of Fortune*), by Jakob Schaffner.

8 The comedy *Muspilli, oder der Prinz von Oahu* (*Muspili, or The Prince of Oahu*), by Paul Josef Cremers, premieres at the Lübeck Stadttheater.

10 Two comedy films premiere in Berlin: *Die unberührte Frau* (*The Unruffled Wife*), directed by Constantin J. David and starring Imogene Robertson and Hans Junkermann; and *Die zweite Mutter* (*The Substitute Mother*), directed by Heinrich Bolten-Baeckers and starring Margarete Lanner and Hans Mierendorff.

12 The film drama *Schicksal* (*Fate*), directed by Felix Basch and starring Conrad Veidt and Lia Eibenschütz, premieres in Berlin.

The comedy *Die Dohle* (*The Grackle*), by Leonhard Adelt, premieres at the Dortmund City Theater.

13 The comedy *Geliebte Kleinigkeit* (*Beloved Bagatelle*), by Rudolf Borchhardt, premieres at the Düsseldorf Schauspielhaus.

14 The opera *Wozzeck* (based on the dramatic fragment *Woyzeck*, by Georg Büchner), by Alban Berg, premieres at the Berlin State Opera.

17 The film drama *Eine Minute vor Zwölf* (*One Minute to Noon*), directed by Nunzio Melasomma and starring Luciano Albertini and Charlotte Ander, premieres.

18 Two film dramas premiere: *Die Frau mit dem schlechten Ruf* (*The Woman with a Past*), directed by Benjamin Christensen and starring Gustaf Fröhlich, Lionel Barrymore, and Alexandra Sorina; and *Ein Walzertraum* (*A Dream Waltz*), directed by Ludwig Berger and starring Willy Fritsch and Mady Christians.

The comedy *Die Durchgängerin* (*The Casual Observer*), by Ludwig Fulda, premieres at the Residenz Theater in Berlin.

21 The film drama *Das Mädchen mit der Protektion* (*The Girl with Influence*), directed by Max Mack and starring Ossi Oswalda and Willy Fritsch, premieres.

22 The comedy *Der fröhliche Weinberg* (*The Merry Vineyard*), by Carl Zuckmayer, premieres at the Theater am Schiffbauerdamm in Berlin; overwhelmingly positive reaction from audiences and critics attracts national attention.[14]

24 The historical film *Bismarck*, directed by Enst Wendt, with Franz Ludwig as the "Iron Chancellor" Otto von Bismarck, and Erna Morena, premieres in Berlin.

25 Three films premiere in Berlin: *Abenteuer im Nachtexpress* (*Adventure on the Night Express Train*), directed by Harry Piel and starring Lissy Arna and José Davert; *Die Dame aus Berlin* (*The Woman from Berlin*), directed by Lorand von Kabdebo and starring Lia Eibenschütz and Werner Krauss; and *Hanseaten* (*The Hanseatics*), directed by Gerhard Lamprecht and starring Fritz Alberti and Hermine Sterler.

The comedy *Totenkopfhusaren* (*Skull and Crossbones Hussars*), by Leo Lenz, premieres at the Hamburg Deutsches Schauspielhaus.

30 The comedy film *Die Kleine von Bummel* (*The Little Girl on the Road*), directed by Richard Eichberg and starring Lilian Harvey (as "die Kleine") and Hans Brausewetter, premieres in Berlin.

NOTES

1. Manfred Overesch and Friedrich Wilhelm Saal, *Die Weimarer Republik* Düsseldorf: Droste, 1982, 242.
2. Willy Haas (1891–1973) first became prominent during the Weimar Republic as editor of the film journal *Filmkurier* (*Film Courier*) and as a screenplay writer. He later founded the literary journal *Die literarische Welt* (*The Literary World*).
3. This play was the basis of a 1925 silent film of the same title, directed by Louis Gasnier, and an early sound film titled *The Love Doctor*, directed by Melville Brown and starring June Collyer and Lawford Davidson.
4. Friedrich Ebert (born in 1871 in Heidelberg) left a mixed legacy. He had never been directly elected but instead had been chosen (albeit in a voting process) by the elected National Assembly. In many ways, he was as effective as any first president of the Weimar Republic could have been. He was unable, however, to bring the German army under his command and make it submissive to the will of a civilian government; he was likewise incapable of defusing leftist hatred of the military. Many still consider him a courageous advocate of German democracy, effectively preventing the creation of a German Soviet-style republic. Others maintain that he paved the way for National Socialism by using right-wing militias to suppress Communist-led uprisings. His was consistently a centrist position, yet he remains a controversial figure to this day, though many German cities and towns have streets named in his honor, and the Friedrich Ebert Foundation has offices in many cities around the world. The foundation supports efforts to promote participatory democracy and has provided thousands of fellowships to students who study at its various centers, archives, and libraries.
5. Jack Trevor (Anthony Cedric Sebastian Steane, 1893–1976) was one of a few wealthy British gentlemen-turned-actors who worked steadily in the German film industry, in both silent and sound productions. His first encounter with the German language came in 1916, when he was severely wounded in the trenches near Ypres. He began making films in London; this film was his first with a German director, costars, and crew. He subsequently appeared in more than 40 German productions. His private fortune (inherited from his Austrian wife, a baroness) gave him the freedom to work in films mostly as a hobby.
6. This film became extremely popular throughout Germany, hailed in many quarters as a worthwhile example of *Körperkultur* (body culture) in the idealized sense. Its use of nudity was distinct from that in feature films, which usually depicted decadence, drug use, and prostitution. The National Socialists in particular praised *Wege zu Kraft und Schönheit*, largely because they saw in it an exaltation of "German" youth, beauty, and health.
7. Many critics consider *The Joyless Street* a benchmark movie of the Weimar Republic, even though it is set in Vienna and features two Swedish actresses (Nielsen and Garbo). The movie's action focuses on the street (named Melchior Gasse) and its denizens. Chief among them are two women (Marie, played by Nielsen) and Greta (played by Garbo in her German film debut). They and women like them on the street

sink into prostitution, yet the movie avoids sensationalism or preachiness. Several critics claimed the movie was therefore *sachlich* (objective or matter of fact), but right-wing observers denounced its perceived cynicism and hopelessness. Leftist critics praised it as an authentic portrayal of powerless people caught in a maelstrom of economic, political, and social forces far beyond their control, emendable only through the ministrations of a compassionate state. The movie is essentially a manipulative melodrama, though extremely well made, boasting superb cinematography (by Robert Lach and Guido Seeber), lighting, editing, and acting. Although it was conceived of as an ensemble film, Werner Krauss (playing a butcher who trades bratwurst and pig's knuckles for sexual favors) dominates the film. *The Joyless Street* was enormously popular with German audiences in the mid-1920s and has remained a subject of fascination ever since. Although it was cut, censored, and reedited in many countries, it regularly appears on lists of "greatest movies of all time" in the popular media.

8. Imogene Robertson (1905–1948) was born in Louisville, Kentucky. As a teenager, she worked in New York as a chorus girl. She encountered legal troubles and in late 1924 left the United States for Berlin, where at age 20 she began working in films. She made 16 films in Berlin, often working with outstanding directors. Returning to the United States in 1927, she began working in Hollywood under the name Mary Nolan. Her German career was far more distinguished than her Hollywood one, although *Outside the Law* (1930) was a front-rank Universal Pictures production, directed by Tod Browning and costarring Edward G. Robinson.

9. Lyrics to the song included the verse

> On Borkum's strand the German reigns,
> And one who treads with fallen arches,
> Hookéd nose, or curly hair
> May not remain upon the shore!
> No, he must remove and then be seen no more!

10. Jane Novak (1896–1990) was born in St. Louis, Missouri, and began working at age 16 in Hollywood films with several notable stars, among them Tom Mix and Harold Lloyd. This was her only German movie; she returned to Hollywood in 1926 and continued working until the full implementation of sound ended her career. She then became a moderately successful real estate developer.

11. The election of former general and field marshal Paul von Hindenburg to the German presidency awakened in German audiences a renewed interest in military plays and a hunger for military heroes. Prussian Count August Wilhelm Anton Neidhardt von Gneisenau (1760–1831) had successfully defended the Kolberg fortress (on the Baltic Sea) against Napoleon's forces in 1807. In 1811, Gneisenau conducted secret negotiations with Prussia's allies to renew hostilities against Napoleon. In 1813, Gneisenau became chief battlefield strategist for Prussian forces (and sometimes for Russian forces as well); many historians credit him with the successful strategy at Waterloo, which led to Napoleon's final defeat. In the wake of defeat and humiliation after World War I, many Germans found a sense of redemption in heroes like Gneisenau.

Soon after the premiere, Reich Foreign Minister Gustav Stresemann held public discussions about the play's phenomenal audience appeal with the playwright Wolfgang Goetz (who at the time was president of the German Society for Theater History Research).

12. As a member of the Fascist Party, Pirandello received government sponsorship to form the Art Theatre of Rome. He and his company toured throughout Europe with productions of his plays. Because Pirandello had a doctorate in philology from the University of Bonn, he had numerous connections to the German language and with German theater personalities.

13. Fern Andra (Vernal Edna Andrews, 1894–1974) was among the most outstanding and successful film actresses, writers, and producers in the pre–World War I German film industry. Born in Illinois to a family of circus performers, she began making German films in 1913 while on tour in Europe. By the time German filmmaking began to recover from the devastating effects of the inflationary years, however, her German career was nearly over. She made more than 50 German films before returning to the United States in 1929.

14. The success of this comedy by Carl Zuckmayer (1896–1977) signaled a departure in comedic production toward what art and film critics were already calling *neue Sachlichkeit*. After its premiere, *Der fröhliche Weinberg* went on to more than 70 productions in provincial theaters and remained sold out in Berlin for the rest of the 1925–1926 season. Its popularity notwithstanding, the play's sexual "matter-of-factness" sparked controversy. Even in Zuckmayer's hometown of Mainz, protests delayed the planned opening at the local municipal playhouse for months. Rarely had a comedy engendered such disputes, but they became emblematic of the change in public attitudes taking place by late 1925 in the Weimar Republic.

1926

JANUARY

1 More than 1,100,000 radio owners are registered in Germany.
Erich Kleiber is named lead conductor of the Berlin State Opera orchestra.

2 Drei Masken Press initiates a contest among German readers to create a name for a new novel written by Roda-Roda (pen name for Sandor Erich Rosenfeld).

7 Publisher Paul Cassirer, whose publishing firm had produced more than 400 new titles since the founding of the Weimar Republic, commits suicide.

8 Rothbarth Press publishes the novel *Die Verbannten* (*The Ostracized*) by Hedwig Courths-Mahler.

9 Agis Press publishes the novel *As Levisite, der einzig gerechte Krieg* (*The Only Justifiable War*) by Johannes R. Becher; Ullstein publishes a cosmological study *Weltall and Weltgefühl* (*Outer Space and Worldliness*) by Bruno Bürgel.

10 The funeral for Paul Cassirer is attended by hundreds of novelists, dramatists, actors, designers, musicians, poets, and others whose work he had published; the Cassirer family refuses to allow actress Tilla Durieux, Paul Cassirer's estranged wife, to attend burial services.

15 The drama *Luise, Kronprinzessin von Preussen* (*Louise, Crown Princess of Prussia*), by Ludwig Berger, premieres at the Lessing Theater in Berlin; the "musical scenes" titled *Lusitania*, by Alfred Döblin, with music by Erich Riedel, premieres at the Darmstadt Regional Theater.

Propyläen Press publishes Carl Zuckmayer's comedy *Der fröhliche Weinberg* (*The Merry Vineyard*); Putmann Press publishes the first volume of *Geschlechtskunde* (*Study of Sexuality*) by Magnus Hirschfeld; Scherl Press publishes the novel *Entweder-oder* (*Either-Or*) by Horst Wolfram Geissler.

16 The drama *All God's Chillun Got Wings* by Eugene O'Neill, translated by Alfred Wolfenstein, has its German premiere at the Hamburg Kammerspiele; the adaptation of *The Bacchae* by Euripides titled *Die Bacchantinnen des Euripides*, by Berthold Viertel, premieres at the Mannheim National Theater.

The Prussian Academy of the Arts opens the first exhibition in German history of American architecture.

17 The drama *Michael Hundertpfund* (*Hundred-Pound Michael*), by Eugen Ortner, premieres at the Tribüne Theater in Berlin.

18 The drama *Die Jagd Gottes* (*God on the Hunt*), by Emil Bernhard, premieres at the the Frankfurt City Theater.

20 Dormach Press publishes the anthroposophic treatise *Wahrspruche* (*Proverbs*) by Rudolf Steiner; Fischer Press publishes the novel *Die Brüder Schellenberg* by Bernhard Kellermann.

22 The new 1600-seat movie theater Gloria-Palast opens in Berlin.

Prussian Academy of the Arts names three new members: sculptor Stanislaus Cauer, painter Hans Peter Feddersen, and architect Wilhelm Kries. The first retrospective exhibition of work by painter Lovis Corinth, who died six months earlier, is held in Berlin. Among the most striking is the 1906 portrait of actor Rudolf Rittner in the title role of Gerhart Hauptmann's drama *Florian Geyer*.

23 The drama *Triumph der Jugend* (*Triumph of Youth*), by Paul Zech, premieres at the Leipzig Schauspielhaus.

24 The drama *Die Schwester* (*The Sister*), by Hermann Kasack, premieres at the Heilbronn City Theater.

25 The drama *Gong*, by stage designer Emil Pirchan, premieres at the Magdeburg Wilhelminisches Theater.

Physicist Albert Einstein holds a lecture for the public at Humboldt University in Berlin explaining his theory of general relativity; thousands turn up at the university's Auditorium Maximum.

29 The drama *Ostpolzug* (*Train to the East*), by Arnolt Bronnen, premieres at the State Theater in Berlin.

30 The German operetta *Paganini¹*, by Franz Lehar, premieres at the Komische Oper Berlin.

FEBRUARY

1 Street festivals throughout the Ruhr district celebrate the final departure of allied occupation forces;² street theater performances parody French politicians and generals.

Rowohlt Press publishes a collection of essays titled *An den Rand geschrieben* (*Written on the Margin*) by theater critic Alfred Polgar. Rowohlt Press publishes a collection of poems titled *Menschen und Affen* (*Man and Apes*) by Albert Ehrenstein.

The film drama *Die Mühle von Sanssouci* (*The Mill at Sans Souci Palace*), directed by Siegfried Philippi, with Otto Gebühr as Frederick the Great and Lissi Lind as Wilhelmine of Bayreuth, premieres in Berlin.

4 A Reichsgericht (national court) in Berlin approves confiscation of all copies printed of the novel *As Levisite, Der einzig gerechte Krieg* (*The Only Justifiable War*) by Johannes R. Becher, on the grounds that the book poses a threat to national peace and stability.

6 German Publishing Institute Press publishes the pseudohistorical treatise *Die Geschichten von den unberührten Frauen* (*The History of Unmoved Women*) by Wilhelm Schidtbonn.

An essay by Bertolt Brecht appears in the *Berliner Börsen-Courier*, a business and stock-market newspaper, advocating more sportslike theater productions in order to attract a wider audience.

7 Elisabeth Bergner reads the entirety of the novella *Fräulein Elise* to an audience at the Deutsches Theater, with author Arthur Schnitzler in attendance; the controversial novella concerns a loyal daughter who becomes a prostitute in an effort to pay off her father's gambling debts.

8 Insel Press publishes a collection of four novellas titled *Erstes Erlebnis* (*First Experience*) by Stefan Zweig.

11 The film epic about the Rhineland *Die Anebenteuerer* (*The Adventurers*) based on a novel of the same name by Rudolf Herzog, on the occasion of the "liberation" of the Ruhr district and major Rhineland cities, in Berlin; directed by Rudolf Walther-Fein, with Harry Liedtke and Erna Morena

12 Two films premiere: *Gretchen Schubert*, directed by Karl Moos, with Ruth Beyer and Wilhelm Diegelmann; and *Der Mann ohne Schlaf* (*The Man*

without Sleep), directed by Carl Boese, with Harry Liedtke and Maly Delschaft.

13 American dancer Josephine Baker debuts occurs at The Harem nightclub on Pariser Platz in Berlin; several critics note that naked women had danced in Berlin before, but rarely had a headliner appeared in nothing more than a tiny diaphanous pink apron.[3]

14 The Berlin premiere of drama *Baal*, by Bertolt Brecht, occurs at the Deutsches Theater; though several notable actors and actresses participate (Oskar Homolka, Blandine Ebinger, Kurt Gerron, and Paul Bildt), audience and critical reaction is lukewarm and it soon closes.

15 Hackebeil Press publishes the novel *Die Frau des Schullehrers Tarnow* (*The Wife of the School Teacher Mr. Tarnow*), by Olga Wohlbrück.

The film drama *Manon Lescaut* premieres in Berlin, directed by Arthur Robison, with Lya De Putti and Vladimir Gajarov.

17 The drama *Luise, Königin von Preussen* (*Louise, Queen of Prus*sia), by Ludwig Berger, premieres at the Lessing Theater in Berlin.

19 The first in a series of cabaret revue productions by composer Friedrich Holländer at the Renaissance Theater in Berlin; this one titled *Laterna magica* (*The Magic Lantern*).

Langen Press publishes the fictionalized biography *Der Schiller Roman* (*The Schiller Novel*) by Walter von Molo; Fischer Press publishes two dramas *Der Gang zum Weiher* (*The Way to the Pond*) by Arthur Schintzler and *Demetrius* by Alexander Lernet-Holenia.

The film drama *Herrn Filip Collins Abenteuer* (Filip Collin's Adventure) premieres in Berlin, directed by Johannes Guter, with Georg Alexander and Ossi Oswalda.

20 Two dramas premiere in Berlin: *Duell am Lido* (*Duel on the Lido*) by Hans-José Rehfisch at the State Theater in Berlin (Marlene Dietrich has a small role, her first in a major production); and *Sturmflut* (*Storm Tide*) by Alfons Paquet at the Volksbühne in Berlin (the first major production in Berlin to employ a "mixed media" scenic design).

Max Liebermann presents a major retrospective exhibition of paintings by Lovis Corinth at the Prussian Academy of the Arts.

Berlin State Opera begins a week-long series of Richard Strauss operas, starting with *Salome*.

Productions of the comedy *Der fröhliche Weinberg* (*The Happy Vineyard*) set for Munich and Leipzig is ancelled by police, who cite threats of demonstrations and protests against the play.

23 Enoch Press publishes the novel *Der fromme Tanz* (*The Pious Dance*) by Klaus Mann.

24 Scherl Press publishes the novel *Die Insel der Unsterblichen* (*The Island of the Immortals*) by the extraordinarily successful and prolific screenplay writer Thea von Harbou.

25 The operetta *Die zehn Küsse* (*The Ten Kisses*), by Bernhard Sekles, premieres at Frankfurt City Opera.

The military film drama *Der Stolz der Kompagnie* (*The Pride of the Company*) premieres, directed by Georg Jacoby, with Reinhold Schünzel and Camilla Spira.

26 Zsolnay Press publishes the novella *Liliane and Paul* by Heinrich Mann; Scherl Press publishes the novel *Die Frau am Quell* (*The Woman at the Fountain*).

27 The drama *Der Stall des Augias* (*The Stable of Augias*), by Ivan Goll, premieres at the Kassel State Theater.

Fleischhauer and Spohn publish the novel *Tanzpause* (*Dance Break*) by Vicki Baum.

28 Adolf Hitler speaks for the first time in Hamburg; his subject: the prospects of National Socialist Party gains in upcoming elections.

MARCH

1 A national radio agency forms to supervise, censor, regulate, and administer radio broadcasts throughout the country.

A new publishing endeavor called the "Kampf Verlag" (Battle Press), which is intended to be the major print media enterprise of National Socialism is created.

Berlin Volksbühne assumes lease of the Theater am Schiffbauerdamm.

Police authorities release the film *Aus des Rheinlands Schicksalstagen* (*From the Fateful Days of the Rhineland*) for public distribution and exhibition.

2 The opera *Ivas Traum* (*Iva's Dream*), by Ernst von Dohnanyi, premieres at the Düsseldorf City Theater.

The German version of the drama *The Exchange*, by Paul Claudel, premieres at the Theater am Schiffbauerdamm in Berlin; the comedy *Der rote Mann* (*The Red Man*), by Gabriel Dragely and Emmerich Liplai, premieres at the Hamburg Thalia Theater.

4 Rudolf von Laban founds The School of Artistic Movement in Würzburg.

West German Radio Network broadcasts a six-day bicycle race, the first such athletic contest broadcast on German airwaves.

Eher Press publishes the political treatise *Die Südtiroler Frage und das deutsche Bündnisproblem* (*The South Tirolean Question and the Problem of German Alliances*) by Adolf Hitler.

The ballet *Achilles auf Skyros* (*Achilles on the Island of Skyros*) and the drama *Alcestis*, by Hugo von Hofmannsthal, premiere at Stuttgart City Opera; the former was composed and directed by Egon Wellesz; Wellesz also directed the Hofmannsthal play.

Two film comedies premiere in Berlin: *Der krasse Fuchs* (*The Clever Fox*) directed by Conrad Wiene, with Hans Brausewetter and Clementine Plessner; and *Warum sich scheiden lassen?* (*Why Get a Divorce?*), directed by Manfred Noa, with Andre Matoni and Vivian Gibson.

5 The German version of the comedy *Home and Beauty*, by W. Somerset Maugham, premieres at the Deutsches Theater in Berlin.

The film drama *Der Försterchristel* (*The Bohemian Dancer*) premieres in Berlin, directed by Friedrich Zelnik, with Lya Mara and Harry Liedtke.

7 Union Press publishes the literary monograph *Faust, das Werk des Goetheschen Lebens* (*Faust, the Life's Work of Goethe*), by Julius Bab.

8 The drama *Schutzengelspiel* (*Guardian Angel Play*), by Max Mell, premieres at the Düsseldorf Schauspielhaus.

The film drama *Der Rosa Diamant* (*Pink Diamond*) premieres in Berlin, directed by Rochus Gliese, with Xenia Desni and Rudolf Klein-Rogge.

9 Spaeth Press unsuccessfully sues Phoenix Film Studios in an attempt to halt filming of *Der Kreidekreis* (*The Chalk Circle*), based on the 13th-century Chinese drama, not on the Klabund play of the same title, published by Spaeth.

10 Union Press publishes the novel *Königin Luise* (*Queen Louise*) by Sophie Hochstetter.

The film romance *Der Geiger von Florenz* (*The Florentine Violinist*) premieres, directed by Paul Czinner, with Conrad Veidt in the title role and Elisabeth Bergner.

11 The film romance *Rosen aus dem Süden* (*Roses from the South*) premieres in Berlin, directed by Carl Froelich, with Henny Porten and Angeleo Ferrari.

The comedy *Der Gefallige* (*A Pleasing Manner*), by Albrecht Schäfer, premieres at Chemnitz City Theater.

12 The film comedy *Zwei und die Dame* (*Two and a Lady*) premieres in Berlin, directed by Alwin Neuss, with Agnes Esterhazy, Karl Platen, and Bernhard Goetzke.

The comedy *The Last of Mrs. Cheyney*, by Frederic Lonsdale, translated by Julius Berstl, premieres at the Theater in der Königgrätzer Strasse in Berlin.

14 Novelist Jakob Wassermann reads (at the invitation of some elected deputies) portions of his novella *Adam Urbas* in the main assembly hall of the Reichstag as part of the national government's program of fostering literary achievement.

15 Rowohlt Press publishes the biography *Bismarck: Geschichte eines Kämpfers* (*Bismarck: History of a Fighter*), by Emil Ludwig.

The film drama *Falsche Scham* (*False Shame*) premieres in Berlin, directed by Rudolf Biebrach, with Karin Soedenborg and Rudolf Biebrach.

18 Schmiede Press publishes the drama *Mord* (*Murder*) by Walter Hasenclever.

Two films premiere in Berlin: *Das Gasthaus zur Ehe* (*Accomodations for Marriage*), directed by Georg Jacoby, with Elga Brink and Georg Alexander; and *Das letzte Kutsche von Berlin* (*The Last Horse Carriage in Berlin*), directed by Carl Boese, with Maly Delschaft and Karl Falkenberg.

19 German version of the drama *The Tomb of the Unknown Soldier*, by Paul Raynal, translated by Hedwig von Gerlach, premieres at the Kleines Theater in Berlin; public response is surprisingly positive, initiating a wave of German plays about World War I over the next few months.

20 Rothbarth Press publishes the novel *Die Geheimnisse eines Seelenlosen* (*Secrets of a Soulless Man*).

21 President Paul von Hindenburg visits the formerly occupied cities of the Rhineland, and in Cologne, he witnesses a particularly large demonstration against the French.

22 The film drama *Die Brüder Schellenberg* (*The Schellenburg Brothers*) premieres in Berlin, directed by Karl Grune, with Conrad Veidt and Lil Dagover.

Hirzel Press publishes the autobiography of painter Lovis Corinth.

23 The drama *Mord* (*Murder*), by Walter Hasenclever, premieres at the Deutsches Theater in Berlin; the comedy *Fräulein Eulenspiegel*, by C. A. Rollinghoff, premieres at the Intimes Theater in Berlin.

Reissner Press publishes a book of illustrations titled *Dämonen und Nachtgesichte* (*Demons and Night Visions*) by painter Alfred Kubin.

Two film dramas premiere in Berlin: *Junges Blut* (*Young Blood*), directed by Manfred Noa, with Lya de Putti and Walter Slezak; and *Der siebente Jung* (*The Seventh Son*) directed by Franz Osten, with Maria Mindzenty and Ferdinand Martini.

24 The psychological film drama *Geheimnisse einer Seele* (*Secrets of a Soul*) premieres in Berlin, directed by G. W. Pabst, with Werner Krauss, Jack Trevor, and Ruth Weyher.

25 The film drama *Die Familie Schimeck* (*The Schimeck Family*) premieres in Berlin, directed by Alfred Halm, with Olga Chekhova and William Dieterle.

26 Reissner Press publishes a collection of short fiction and illustrations titled *Rings um den Alexanderplatz* (*In the Neighborhood of Alexander Platz*), by Heinrich Zille.

Writer Hans Fallada is sentenced to two and one half years imprisonment for drug dealing in Kiel.

27 The one-act opera *Der Protagonist* by Kurt Weill and libretto by playwright Georg Kaiser premieres at the Semper Opera House in Dresden.

29 The film drama *Fünf-Uhr-Tee in der Ackerstrasse* (*Tea Time in the Acker Strasse*) premieres in Berlin, directed by Paul L. Stein, with Reinhold Schünzel and Imogen Robertson.

30 The film melodrama *Unser täglich Brot* (*Our Daily Bread*) premieres in Berlin, directed by Constantin J. David, with Paul Hartmann and Imogen Robertson.

31 Braumüller Press publishes the sociological study *Geschlecht und Charakter* (*Sex and Character*), by Otto Weininger.

APRIL

1 There are now more than 1.2 million registered radio listeners in Germany, with the largest listening audience in Berlin (about 525,000). The broadcasting facilities in Königswusterhausen near Berlin are powerful enough (180,000 watts) to reach all of Germany on the AM band.

2 The first German radio transmission of photography is accomplished, between Berlin and Vienna; newspapers editorialize on "a new epoch in news reporting" as a result.

Bertolt Brecht publishes the essay "Kehren wir zu den Kriminalromanen zurück?" ("Are We Returning to the Crime Novel?") in the journal *Die literarsiche Welt*.

3 The *Menschen untereinander* (*Between Us*) premieres in Berlin directed by Gerhard Lamprecht, with Alfred Abel and Aud Egede Nissen.

4 In response to declining live theater attendance resulting from the growing popularity of radio and movies, the Berlin newspaper *Vossische Zeitung* asks several prominent Berlin theater artists to respond to the question, "Is drama dying?" There is no consensus among the artists questioned.

6 *Dürfen wir schweigen?* (*Should We Be Silent?*) premieres in Berlin, directed by Richard Oswald, with Conrad Veidt and Mary Parker.

7 Schmiede Press publishes a collection of poems titled *Maschinenrhythmen* (*Machine Rhythms*), by Johannes R. Becher.

8 The documentary film *Die Biene Maja* (*Maya the Bee*) premieres in Berlin, directed by Wolfram Junghans; a "dramatization" featuring live bees organizing and defending themselves against an invasion of marauding hornets; based on the popular children's books by Waldemar Bonsels.

Numerous leading German publishers inaugurate a policy of lowering book prices in hopes of stimulating sluggish sales.

9 The film drama *Die Wiskotten* (*The Wiscotte Family*) premieres in Berlin, directed by Arthur Bergen, with Gertrud Arnold and Ernst Behmer.

10 The drama *Sturm auf den Tod* (*Storm of Death*) by Alfred Wolfenstein premieres in Berlin at Mannheim National Theater.

The opera *Die Opferung des Gefangen* (*The Sacrifice of the Prisoner*, based on a Mexican dance drama), by Egon Wellesz, premieres at the Cologne Opera House.

12 Iris Press publishes the novellas *Das Räubermärchen* (*The Robber Fairy Tale*) and *Kind im grauen Haar* (*The Child with Gray Hair*), by Jacob Haringer.

15 The comedy *Zweimal Oliver* (*Oliver Twice Over*), by Georg Kaiser, premieres in seven German theaters simultaneously; Rowohlt Press publishes the play on this day as well.

The German version of the Russian film *Battleship Potemkin*, directed by Sergei Eisenstein, with Vladimir Barsky and Grigori Alexandrov, creates a sensation in Berlin and other cities. Officials in many localities ban its exhibition and the German General Staff forbid viewing of the film among the ranks.

Rowohlt Press publishes the novel *Ritter des Todes* (*The Death Knight*), by Albert Ehrenstein.

The film comedy *Prinzessin Trulala* (*Princess Tralala*) premieres in Berlin, directed by Erich Schönfelder and Richard Eichberg, with Lilian Harney and Dina Gralla.

16 Insel Press publishes the drama *Gudrun* by Ernst Hardt.

Two films premiere in Berlin: *Die Fahrt ins Abenteuer* (*The Trip to Adventureland*), directed by Max Mack, with Willy Fritsch and Ossi Oswalda; and *Frauen der Leidenschaft* (*Women of Passion*), directed by Rolf Randolf, with Fern Andra and Walter Janssen.

17 Three Berlin theater producers form a business partnership (called "ReiBarO"): Max Reinhardt, Viktor Barnowsky, and Robert Klein create the first-ever repertoire of interchangeable productions featuring mutual casts and crews at three Berlin venues: the Deutsches Theater, the Theater in der Königgrätzer Strasse, and the Berliner Theater.

The film comedy *Der Prinz und die Tänzerin* (*The Prince and the Dancer*) premieres in Berlin, directed by Richard Eichberg, with Hans Albers and Lucy Doraine in the title roles.

18 The first radio broadcast of an inter-European soccer game: Germany vs. Holland, with live commentary from the playing field in Düsseldorf.

19 An exhibition opens at Witschek Gallery in Berlin, featuring works by the poet Joachim Ringelnatz.

20 The German book dramatization *Children of the Ghetto*, by Israel Zangwill, translated Heinrich Fänkel, premieres at the Deutsches Theater in Berlin.

The first general exhibition opens in Berlin of works for sale by painter Egon Schiele at Gurlitt Gallery.

21 Actor Werner Krauss leaves the State Theater in Berlin and joins Max Reinhardt's permanent company at the Deutsches Theater.

Two dramas premiere: *Des Kaisers Soldaten* (*Soldiers of the Kaiser*), by Hermann Essig, at the Dresden State Theater; and *Brennende Erde* (*Burning Earth*) by Klabund at the Frankfurt City Theater.

Architect Otto Bartning is named superintendent of the new School for Crafts and Architecture, which replaced the controversial Bauhaus School (now located in Dessau).

22 The patriotic film drama *Deutsche Herzen am deutschen Rhein* (*German Hearts on the German Rhine*) premieres in Berlin, directed by Fred Sauer, with Hans Albers and Frida Lehndorf.

23 The comedy *Der Wundermann* (*The Miracle Man*), by Julius Maria Becker, premieres at the Dessau Friedrich Theater.

The film drama *Qualen der Nacht* (*Torments of the Night*) premieres in Berlin, directed by Curtis Bernhardt, with Claire Rommer and William Dieterle.

24 The comedy *Week-End*, by Noel Coward, translated by Hans Winter, premieres at the Deutsches Theater Kammerspiele in Berlin.

25 Junge Bühne (Young Theater) organization stages the premiere of *Fegefeuer in Ingolstadt* (*Purgatory in Ingolstadt*), by Marieluise Fleisser, at the Deutsches Theater in Berlin.

28 Serial publication of novel *Feme* by Vicki Baum begins in Berlin newspaper *Illustrierte Zeitung*; Reissner Press publishes a novel about Richard Wagner titled *Lohengrin* by Hans Reimann.

MAY

1 The comedy *Rebhuhn* (*The Partridge*), by Rudolf Schanzer and Ernst Walisch, premieres at the Theater am Kurfürstendamm in Berlin.
  Rowohlt Press publishes the novel *Treck* by Bruno Frank.
  For the annual May Day celebrations, Adolf Hitler makes an appeal to industrial workers at assemblies in Hamburg; newspapers there note the polished level of the speaker's performance skills, of which few other German politicians can boast.

2 State Opera House in Berlin closes for structural repairs; authorities claim the entire building poses hazards to both audiences and performers and requires complete reconstruction.

3 Ufa (Universum Film AG, or "Universal Film Corporation") Studios face bankruptcy again[4] and seek emergency funding to continue operations.
  Müller Press publishes the novel *Emil* by Arthur Landsberger.

4 Langen Press publishes the novel *Charlotte Löwensköd* by Swedish Nobel Prize-winning writer Selma Lagerlöf, translated by Pauline Klaiber-Gottschau.
  The tragedy *Medea*, by Hans Henny Jahnn, premieres at the State Theater in Berlin. The comedy *Der Ring des Polykrates* (*The Ring of Polycrates*), by Franz Cornelius, premieres at the Schwerin Regional Theater.

5 Reissner Press publishes a collection of unedited letters in two volumes titled *Briefe* (*Letters*), written by assassinated foreign minister Walter Rathenau.
  President Paul von Hindenburg decrees that German ships on the high seas docking in non-European ports must fly not only the republican flag (colors black, red, and gold) but also the imperial flag (colors of black, white, and red). There is an enormous outcry of protests from anti-imperial parties against the Reichstag.

6 Several German newspapers in their editorial pages denounce Hindenburg's flag decree.

The film drama *Fedora* (based on the play of the same title by Victorien Sardou) premieres in Berlin, directed by Jean Manoussi, with Lee Parry in the title role and Alfons Fryland.

7 The comedy *Gemeinde Schmuggeldorf* (*The Contraband Community*), by Karl Müller-Hoyer, premieres at Dresden Albert Theater.

Prussian Minister of Culture names new members of the recently created "Writers Section" of the Prussian Academy of the Arts: Thomas Mann, Ludwig Fulda, Arno Holz, Gerhart Hauptmann, and Hermann Stehr.

8 The newspaper *Vossische Zeitung* begins serialized publication of Maxim Gorky's autobiographical novel *My Universities*.

10 The German League of Women Academics in Berlin, dedicated to "protecting, fostering, and preserving the influence and legitimacy of the academically educated woman in German cultural life," is founded.

12 Almathea Press publishes the political history *Geist und Gesicht des Bolschewismus* (*The Mind and Face of Bolshevism*), by Rene Füllop-Miller.

13 Opening of first "ballet evening" ever presented at Berlin City Opera, featuring dances choreographed by Lizzie Maudrik.

The film drama *Der Dumme August des Zirkus Romanelli* (*The Silent Clown of the Romanelli Circus*) premieres in Berlin, directed by Georg Jacoby, with Reinhold Schünzel in the title role and Claire Rommer.

18 The detective drama *Einbruch* (*Break-in*), by Arthur Landsberger and Ralph Arthur Roberts, premieres at Hamburg Thalia Theater.

19 The novel *Das Fähnlein der Versprengten* (*The Little Flag of the Dispersed*) is serialized in the weekly feature magazine *Die Woche*.

20 The film drama *Wehe wenn sie losgelassen* (*The Agony of Her Departure*) premieres in Berlin, directed by Carl Froelich, with Henny Porten and Bruno Kastner.

The comedy *Unsterblichkeit* (*Immortality*), by Herbert Scheffler, premieres at Bremen Schauspielhaus.

21 The Greater Berlin Art Exhibition opens, featuring new works by faculty members of the Bauhaus School, now located in Dessau.

The drama *Das trunkene Schiff* (*The Sinking Ship*) by Paul Zech premieres at the Volksbühne in Berlin; the dance tragedy *Tanztragödie* by Kurt Joos premieres at the Münster City Theater.

25 The film comedy *Drei Kuckucksuhren* (*Three Cuckoo Clocks*) premieres in Berlin, directed by Lothar Mendes, with Nils Asther, Eric Barclay, and Paul Grätz in the title roles.

27 The film drama *Der Bergadler* (*The Mountain Eagle*) premieres in Berlin, directed by Alfred Hitchcock, with Bernhard Goetzke and Nita Naldi.

Two ballets premiere, *Don Morte* and *Die Vogelscheuche* (*The Bird Plague*) by Max Terpis at Berlin State Opera.

Playwright Gerhart Hauptmann refuses appointment to the "Writers Section" of the Prussian Academy of the Arts.

28 Two film comedies premiere in Berlin: *Der Provinzonkel* (*The Uncle from the Provinces*) directed by Manfred Noa, with Jakob Tiedtke and Margarete Kupfer; and *Trude, die Sechsenjährige* (*Trudy, the Sixteen-Year-Old*), directed by Conrad Wiene, with Olga Chekhova, Jack Trevor, and Max Landa.

JUNE

1 Rowohlt Press publishes the second volume of Alfred Polgar's essays on theater, titled *Stücke und Spieler* (*Plays and Players*).

A new ecumenical quarterly of research and opinion *Die Kreatur* (a title with ontological implications, meaning "man as creation") debuts, edited by Protestant, Catholic, and Jewish theologians, philosophers, and pundits.

An international art exhibition in Germany opens for the first time since World War I; Glass Palace in Munich displays paintings, sculptures, and drawing by artists of several countries through the summer.

3 The musical *Aus heiterem Himmel* (*Straight Out of the Blue*), by Friedrich Holländer, premieres at Lustspielhaus Berlin.

The German version of the choral work *König David* (*King David*), by Arthur Honnegger, premieres at Düsseldorf City Theater.

4 Schmiede Press publishes the drama *Bäume in den Himmel* (*Trees in the Heavens*), by Alfred Wolfenstein.

5 The first "German Theater Exhibition" featuring displays of designs for costumes and scenery from around the country premieres at Magdeburg City Theater.

Thomas Mann is named "honorary professor" by his native Lübeck, where he had been invited to speak on the city as a site of literary inspiration.

8 The comedy *Gelegenheitskavalier* (*Cavalier of Opportunity*), by Julius Witte and Heinz Friedrich, premieres at Zwickau City Theater.

Grunow Press publishes the novel *Weg ohne Ziel* (*Road without Destination*), by Reihold Muschler.

10 The comedy *Der deutsche Lelian* (*The German Lelian*), by Hans Schlesinger, premieres at the Teplitz-Schönau City Theater.

11 Reclam Press publishes the novel *Putsch auf Ithaka* (*Putsch in Ithaca*), by Friedrich Freksa.

The cabaret revue *Die fleissige Leserin* (*The Diligent Reader*), by Marcellus Schiffer, premieres at Catacomb Cabaret Berlin.

16 Reinhardt Press publishes the ecumenical treatise *Evangelische Katholizität* (*Evangelical Catholicity*), by Friedrich Heiler.

The drama *Der deutsche Michel* (*The German Michel*), by Fritz Stavenhagen, premieres at the Volksbühne in Berlin; the comedy *Der doppelte Moritz* (*Moritz Taken Twice*), by Toni Impekoven and Carl Mathern, premieres at the Frankfurt am Main City Theater.

17 Literary journal *Die neue Rundschau* publishes an issue devoted to George Bernard Shaw, with essays about the playwright and his works by several German critics; Shaw is the most frequently performed English-language playwright in German theaters besides Shakespeare.

21 The comedy *Das goldene Kalb* (*The Golden Calf*), by Otto Schwarz and Carl Mathern, premieres.

22 The film melodrama *Heimliche Sünder* (*Secret Sinners*) premieres in Berlin, directed by Franz Seitz, with Dorothea Wieck, Mary Kid, Margarete Kupfer, and Maria Kameradek in the title roles.

23 Drei Masken Press publishes *Das Nibelungenbuch* (the screenplay from the Fritz Lang film), by Thea von Harbou; New Berlin Press publishes the novel *Spaziergang in Potsdam* (*A Walk in Potsdam*).

26 The State Museum for Ethnology re-opens in Berlin.

28 Propyläen Press publishes a volume of poetry titled *Der Bann* (*The Proscription*), by Carl Zuckmayer.

29 The film comedy *Wir sind vom K. und K. Infanterie Regiment* (*We're from the Royal and Imperial Infantry Regiment*) premieres in Berlin, directed by Richard Oswald, with Paul Heidemann and Fritz Spira.

Director Berthold Viertel in the newspaper *Vossische Zeitung* calls for restrictions on film subject matter and what he terms theatrical conventions in film making; he advocates development of separate standards for film and theater, allowing the theater to regain part of its audience.

30 Ullstein Press publishes the novel *Das fiebernde Haus* (*The Feverish House*) by Walter Hollander.

JULY

1 The operetta *Die leichte Isabell* (*Light-Hearted Isabel*), by Robert Gilbert, premieres at City Opera Berlin.

The comedy *Der Held des Tages* (*The Hero of the Day*), by Leo Walter Stein, premieres at Dresden Neues Theater.

4 German version of the opera *Turandot*, by Giacomo Puccini, premieres at Semper Opera House Dresden.

Modernist German architects create a collective called "Der Ring," with the goal of promoting abstract yet functionalist designs and promoting them in Europe and America. They claim their work follows "newly discovered" laws of design, using the term "ring" as their motto because the figure of a ring unites a group within a collectivist mentality, a self-contained figure without a hierarchy.[6]

5 The comedy *Der Herr Monsieur* (*Mr. Monsieur*), by Hanns Johst, premieres at Krefeld City Theater.

6 The playwright and director of the Cologne City Theater, Ernst Hardt, is named director of new West German Radio Network based in Cologne.

7 National court in Leipzig convicts a Communist Party member of working for a renters' association, with the goal of organizing renters across the country to stage strikes against landlords.

8 The film comedy *Die Fürstin der Riviera* (*The Princess of the Rivera*) premieres in Munich, directed by Geza von Bolvary, with Hans Junkermann and Ellen Kürti.

Cassirer Press publishes the drama *Der blaue Boll* (*Blue Boll*), by Ernst Barlach.

10 Zsolnay Press publishes the biography titled *Ravaillac*, about the Roman Catholic zealot who assassinated French King Henri IV in 1610, by Paul Frischauer.

In Berlin, director Erich Engel leaves Max Reinhardt's Deutsches Theater and joins Leopold Jessner's staff at the State Theater.

11 Rudolf Carriciola wins the first German Grand Prix in Berlin, driving a Mercedes 8-cylinder Monza sport coupe at an average speed 81.1 miles per hour, the fastest ever recorded for a European Grand Prix race.

12 "Schwarze Reichswehr" (illegal paramilitary units of the German Army) increase the number and complexity of secret maneuvers in the Soviet Union, working with Red Army battalions in direct (though still secret) violation of Versailles Treaty.

13 A nationwide ban of the Russian film *Battleship Potemkin* goes into effect.

Engelhorn Press publishes the novel *Der Tor zur Welt* (*Gateway to the World*) by Frank Thiess.

The film melodrama *Ich hab' mein Herz in Heidelberg verloren* (*I Lost My Heart in Heidelberg*) premieres in Berlin, directed by Arthur Bergen, with Emil Höfer and Gertrud de Lalsky.

15 The comedy *Die Flucht ins Glück* (*The Escape into Happiness*), by Wilhelm Schmalfeldt, premieres at Bad Salzschlirf Spa Theater.

16 Author Leo Lania is sentenced to a 20-day jail sentence in Berlin for writing the political treatise *Gewehre auf Reisen* (*Weapons on Tour*).

17 German Festival Week begins in Weimar, with orchestral concerts of music by Richard Wagner, plays celebrating German ethnicity, and poetry readings in praise of historical German heroes and military figures.

28 The patriotic film melodrama *Deutsches Mutterz* (*Heart of a German Mother*) premieres in Berlin, directed by Geza von Bolvary, with Heinz Rühmann and Ellen Kürti.

30 German Colonial Week begins in Hamburg, glorifying Germany's colonial empire in Africa and the Pacific, featuring exhibitions of paintings, colonial army uniforms, and other memorabilia; highlight of the week: a showing of the film *Ich hatt' einen Kameraden* (*I Had a Comrade*, directed by Conrad Wiene, with Erich Kaiser-Titz, Otz Tollen, and Erwin Fichtner), a glorification of German military heroism in Africa, "a drama from the heroic days of the colonies."

AUGUST

1 The operetta *Yvonne*, by Hugo Hirsch, premieres at the City Opera in Berlin.

5 Actor Albert Bassermann (holder of the Iffland Ring as the German-language theater's most important actor) and his wife Else Schiff sign a lucrative one-year contract with commercial producer Heinz Saltenburg in Berlin, agreeing to appear in several of Saltenburg's theaters. Some critics accuse Bassermann and Schiff of "selling out" to mercantile interests.

Actress Asta Nielsen makes her Berlin theater debut with a sold-out four-week run in the title role of *Rita Cavallini* (based on the 1913 play *Romance* by American playwright Edward Sheldon) at Kleines Theater Berlin.

6 The film comedy *Kubinke der Barbier* (*Kubinke the Barber*, based on a novel by Georg Hermann) premieres in Berlin, directed by Carl Boese, with Werner Fütterer, Erika Glässner, and Käthe Haack.

Fischer Press publishes the memoir *Pariser Rechenschaft* (*Paris Account*), by Thomas Mann.

7 The musical revue *Der Zug nach dem Westen* (*Train to the West*), by Frede Mele, Willi Kollo, and Fritz Lehner, premieres at Theater des Westens Berlin.

Weimar National Theater threatens closure for the coming season unless financial assistance from the public is not forthcoming; local legislature (Thuringia) had cut subsidy for its operations.

German-American swimmer Gertrud Ederle becomes the first woman to swim across the English Channel; time: 14 hours 32 seconds.

8 *Die drei Mannequins* (*The Three Mannequins*) premieres in Berlin, directed by Jaap Speyer, with Grit Haid, Helga Molander, and Elisabeth Pinajeff in the title roles and Hans Albers.

13 The film drama *Die dritte Eskadron* (*The Third Cavalry Regiment*, based on the play by Bernhard Buchbinder) premieres in Berlin, directed by Carl Wilhelm, with Claire Rommer and Fritz Spira.

Bayreuth celebrates the 50th anniversary of the Bayreuth Festival and the opening of the Festspielhaus, a facility designed by Wagner and built to his specifications in 1876 for annual performance of the composer's operas.

Cassirer Press publishes two new collections of prints by painters Max Liebermann and Max Slevogt.

14 The first photography exhibition in Germany since World War I opens at Frankfurt am Main.

16 The film romance *An der schönen blauen Donau* (*On the Beautiful Blue Danube*) premieres in Düsseldorf, directed by Friedrich Zelnik, with Lya Mara and Harry Liedtke.

18 The musical revue *An und Aus* (*On and Off*), by Walter Kollo, premieres at the Admiral's Palace Theater in Berlin.

19 The film romance *Wie einst im Mai* (*Maytime*) premieres in Berlin, directed by Willi Wolff, with Adolf Klein and Ellen Richter.

Nuremberg district court finds that anti-Semitism can no longer be a factor in judicial decisions, citing conditions that have improved so markedly since the assassination of Walter Rathenau and attacks on other prominent Jews in 1923.

20 The film romance *Annemarie und ihr Uland* (*Anne Marie and her Lancer*) premieres in Berlin, directed by Erich Eriksen, with Coletta Bretl and Siegfried Arno.

Schneider Press publishes two religion treatises: *Rede über das Erzieherische* (*Speech on Educational Measures*), by Martin Buber, and *Die Schrift und Luther* (*Luther and Scripture*), by Franz Rosenzweig; Ullstein Press publishes the novel *Feme*, by Vicki Baum; the Frankfurt am Main newspaper *Illustiertes Blatt* serializes the novel *Metropolis*, by Thea von Harbou, based on her screenplay of the same title.

The drama *Die Marionetten der Zarin* (*The Czarina's Marionettes*), by Paul Hartwig, premieres at the Dresden State Theater; the drama *Vendt the Monk*, by Knut Hamsun, premieres in Germany at the Heidelberg Festival.

24 Boxer Max Schmeling wins German light-heavyweight championship by knockout over Max Diekmann in Berlin at the Sports Palace.

25 The comedy *O diese Bubiköpfe!* (*Oh These Flappers!*), by Curt Kraatz and Max Neal, premieres at Bad Nauheim Spa Theater.

26 The military film *Zopf und Schwert* (*Sword and Shield*, based on the play by Karl Gutzkow) premieres in Berlin, directed by Victor Janson, with Mady Christians and William Dieterle.

27 Three films premiere in Berlin: the military drama *Elf Schill'chen Offiziere* (*Eight Officers in the Style of Schill*), directed by Rudolf Meinert, with Rudolf Meinert as Major von Schill and Grete Reinwald as Queen Luise of Prussia; the comedy *Im weissen Röß'l* (*The White Horse Inn*, based on the play by Oskar Blumenthal), directed by Richard Oswald, with Liane Haid and Max Hansen; and the adventure drama *Jagd auf Menschen* (*Hunted People*), directed by Nunzio Malasomma, with Carlo Andini and Maly Delschaft.

28 The film romance *Der Kurier des Zaren* (*The Czar's Courier*, based on the novel *Michael Strogoff* by Jules Verne) premieres in Berlin, directed by Viktor Tourjansky, with Ivan Mozzhukhin and Nathalie Kovanko.

30 The film drama *Der goldene Schmetterling* (*The Golden Butterfly*) premieres in Berlin, directed by Michael Curtiz, with Lili Damita and Hermann Leffler.

SEPTEMBER

1 The newsreels produced by the Südfilm Corp. begin to appear in many German movie theaters on a weekly basis.

The musical revue *Vom Mund zu Mund* (*Word of Mouth*), by Erik Charell, premieres at the Schauspielhaus in Berlin.

Zsolnay Press publishes the drama *Paulus unter den Juden* (*St. Paul among the Jews*), by Franz Werfel.

2 The comedy film *Die Boxerbraut* (*The Boxer Bride*) premieres in Berlin, directed by Johannes Guter, with Xenia Desni and Willy Fritsch.

3 The new Berlin radio tower in Charlottenburg is dedicated as part of the Greater German Radio Fair.

Two films premiere in Berlin: the animated feature *Die Abenteuer des Prinzens Achmed* (The Adventures of Prince Ahmed), the first full-length (81 minutes) animated silhouette film, directed by Lotte Reiniger; and the comedy *Die Kleine vom Varieté* (*The Little Dance Hall Girl*, based on a comedy by Alfred Möller), directed by Hanns Schwarz, with Ossi Oswalda in the title role and Georg Alexander.

4 The drama *Cromwell*, by Klabund, premieres at the Lessing Theater in Berlin.

Insel Press publishes collection of novellas titled *Verwirrung der Gefühle* (*The Bafflement of Feelings*), by Stefan Zweig.

6 The film melodrama *Die Unehelichen* (*Unmarried*) premieres in Berlin, directed by Gerhard Lamprecht, with Ralph Ludwig and Margot Misch.

7 The European premiere of the American film epic *Ben-Hur* creates a sensation in Berlin.

8 The newspaper *Vossische Zeitung* begins serial publication of the novel *Der Aufruhr um den Junker Ernst* (*The Uproar about Squire Ernst*), by Jakob Wassermann; Fischer Press publishes a four-volume set of *Gesammelte Werke* (*Collected Works*), by novelist Hermann Bang.

9 The Prussian Academy of the Arts creates two new State Prizes, one for painting and another for architecture, for which applicants can receive substantial cash grants.

10 Germany is permitted to join the League of Nations.

The film drama *Spitzen* (*Pinnacle*) premieres in Berlin, directed by Holger-Madsen, with Olaf Fönss and Elisabeth Pinajeff.

Reissner Press publishes the first edition of Waldemar Bonsels' collected works.

11 Koehler Press publishes the novel *Teutonen* (*The Teutons*), by Walter Bloem.

An exhibition featuring the graphic work of film director Lotte Reiniger opens at the Neumann Gallery in Berlin.

The musical revue *Es geht besser* (*It's Getting Better*), by Rudolf Nelson, premieres at the Catacomb Cabaret in Berlin.

The residential apartments of the Bavarian royal family in the Munich Residenz (now a museum) opened to public viewing (apartments of Prussian royals opened in 1919).

12 The new production of *Die Räuber* (*The Robbers*), by Friedrich Schiller, directed by Erwin Piscator, features modern dress and contemporary scenery, opens at the State Theater in Berlin. Critics are divided in their estimation of such innovations with stage classics.

14 The detective film *Achtung Harry! Augen auf!* (*Eyes Open, Harry!*) opens in Berlin, directed by Harry Piel, with Eugen Burg and Colette Corder.

15 In a newly revived media presence, leaders of the National Socialists publish declarations that attempts by Communists to renew political unrest in the streets of Germany will be met with armed resistance.

The largest movie house opens in Berlin: the Mercedes Palace, with 2,300 seats; it surpasses the Ufa Palace Theater am Zoo, with 2,165 seats, as Berlin's largest.[7]

16 The musical revue *Wieder Metropol*, by Hugo Hirsch, with film actor Hans Albers, premieres at the Metropol Operetta Theater in Berlin.

The film melodrama *Wien, wie es weint und lacht* (*Vienna, Weeping and Laughing*, based on a story by Ludwig Anzengruber) premieres in Berlin, directed by Rudolf Walther-Fein, with Mady Christians and Erich Kaiser-Titz.

17 The film drama *Die Brandstifter Europas* (*The Arsonists of Europe*) premieres in Berlin, directed by Max Neufeld, with Charlotte Ander and Hermann Benke.

Hessel Press publishes the novel *Minnermann*, by Hans Franck; Cassirer Press publishes the literary biography *Sterblich Unsterblich* (*Mortally Immortal*), by Herbert Eulenberg; Cotta Press publishes the novel *Der tolle Professor* (*The Mad Professor*), by Hermann Sudermann.

18 Cassirer Press publishes the novel *Zwischen zwei Frauen* (*Between Two Women*), by Herbert Eulenberg.

The "Red Navy Congress" opens in Kiel, organized by the Red Front militia organization; it features numerous speeches about the growing threat of National Socialists and other right-wing organizations forming armed militias similar to their own.

20 The film comedy *Der Veilchenfresser* (*The Violet-Eater*, based on a comedy by Gustav von Moser) premieres in Berlin, directed by Friedrich Zelnik, with Lil Dagover and Harry Liedtke.

21 The comedy *Die Schule von Uznach* (*The School of Uznach*), by Carl Sternheim, premieres at Hamburg Deutsches Schauspielhaus, Cologne City Theater, and Mannheim National Theater simultaneously. The drama *Springtanz* (*Jumping Dance*), by Hermann Essig, premieres at the Essen City Theater.

23 The film drama *Der Mann im Feuer* (*The Man in the Fire*) premieres in Berlin, directed by Erich Waschneck, with Olga Chekhova and Jakob Tiedtke.

Eulenspiegel Press publishes a collection of satirical essays titled *Gift und Galle* (*Poison and Bile*), by Roda Roda (Sandor Erich Rosenfeld).

24 Cassirer Press publishes a two-volume historical survey *Die europäische Kunst im 19. Jahrhundert* (*European Art in the 19th Century*), by Karl Scheffler; Diedrich Press publishes a fiction anthology *Die Geschichten aus Altpreussen* (*Stories of Old Prussia*), by Agnes Miegel.

25 The satirical comedy *Mann ist Mann* (*A Man's a Man*), by Bertolt Brecht, premieres at the Darmstadt Regional City Theater and the Düsseldorf City Theater simultaneously.

The International Police Fair opens in Berlin, featuring exhibitions of new equipment and tactics, along with speeches and discussions of quelling riots, demonstrations, and techniques for maintaining public order.

The operetta *Lady Hamilton*, by Eduard Künnecke, premieres at the Breslau City Theater.

26 The new Hamburg State Opera opens with the opera *Die Meistersinger von Nürnberg* (*The Mastersingers of Nuremberg*), by Richard Wagner.

The ballet *Don Juan* by Rudolf von Laban, with music written for a ballet of that title in 1761 by Christoph Willibald Gluck, premieres at the City Opera in Berlin.

29 A series of "Sturm-Abende" (*Storm Evenings*), in which numerous well-known actors and actresses give public readings of poetry about storms, against a backdrop of paintings and/or graphic work depicting storms, opens at the Gurlitt Gallery in Berlin.

30 The adaptation of Aristophanes' comedy *Lysistrata*, by Leo Greiner, premieres at the Volksbühne in Berlin with Agnes Straub in the title role.

The detective film *Sein grosser Fall* (*His Toughest Case*) premieres in Berlin, directed by Fritz Wendhausen, with Carl Ebert and Olga Chekhova.

OCTOBER

1 Two films premiere in Berlin: the military drama *In Treue stark* (*Strong in Faith*), directed by Heinrich Brandt, with Otto Gebühr and Claire Rommer; and an abortion rights melodrama *Kreuzzug des Weibes* (*Pilgrimage of Woman*), directed by Martin Berger, with Conrad Veidt and Maly Delschaft.

Disciples of painter Lovis Corinth form a school in Berlin called "Freie Arbeitsstätte" (Open Workplaces) to inculcate techniques they had developed under Corinth's tutelage; among them are Anton Kerschbaumer and Martin Bloch.

Mary Wigman's solo works ("Witch's Dance," "Rhapsodic Dance," "Monotony I and II," and "Prelude") premiere at Trümpy-Güther School in Berlin.

Wunderlich Press publishes a memoir titled *Meine Mutter* (*My Mother*), by Isolde Kurz; Cassirer Press publishes a collection of drawings titled *95 Köpfe* (*95 Heads*), by Emil Orlik; Fischer Press publishes a volume of poetry titled *Der längste Tag* (*The Longest Day*), by Oskar Loerke.

2 Two comedies premiere: *Zeit auf Flaschen* (*Time in a Bottle*), by Friedrich Freksa at the Hannover Deutsches Theater; and *Die zwei Abenteurer* (*The Two Adventurers*) by Otto Zoff at the Frankurt am Main City Theater.

Rütten and Loening Press publishes the novel *Lukas Langkofler* and a book of lyrical poetry titled *Die Peitsche* (*The Whip*), both by Hermann Kesser.

Ban of the film *Battleship Potemkin* lifted; abridged versions permitted in nearly every German locality.

3 Marlene Dietrich joins the cast of the musical revue *Vom Mund zu Mund* (*Word of Mouth*), by Erik Charell, at Schauspielhaus Berlin.

The Mendelssohn Prize is awarded to composers Ignatz Stroszgel and Ernst Pepping.

The comedy *Die beste Polizei* (*The Best Police Force*), by Herbert Eulenberg, premieres at the State Theater in Berlin.

4 Actor Emil Jannings, agreeing to terms with Paramount Pictures in Hollywood, departs for California.

Oesterheld Press publishes biographical study titled *Schauspieler und Schauspielerinnen* (*Actors and Actresses*), by Julius Bab.

The film comedy *Die Königin von Moulin Rouge* (based on comedy *The Girl from Maxim's* by Georges Feydeau) premieres in Berlin, directed by Robert Wiene, with Mady Christians and André Roanne.

5 The drama *Das Weib das Akiba* (*The Wife of Rabbi Akiba*), by Moritz Heimann, premieres at Kiel City Theater; *Man and Superman* by George

Bernard Shaw, translated by Siegfried Trebitsch, premieres at the Lessing Theater in Berlin.

Controversial painter Otto Dix is named professor at the State Academic College of Art in Dresden.

7 Two films premiere in Berlin: the military melodrama *Der Feldherrnhügel* (*The Command Post*) directed by Hans Otto, with Harry Liedtke and Olga Chekhova; and *Das Mädel auf der Schaukel* (*The Girl on the Swing*, based on a novel by Werner Scheff), directed by Felix Basch, with Ossi Oswalda and Harry Liedtke.

8 Three films premiere in Berlin: *Die geschiedene Frau* (*The Divorcée*), directed by Victor Janson, with Mady Christians and Bruno Kastner; *Die Kleine und ihr Kavalier* (*The Little Lady and Her Cavalier*), directed by Richard Löwenbein, with Maly Delschaft and Hans Brausewetter; amd *Das süsse Mädel* (*The Sweet Girl*), directed by Manfred Noa, with Imogene Robertson and Paul Heidemann.

Reichl Press publishes the philosophical treatise *Menschen als Sinnbilder* (*Man as Image of the Senses*), by Count Hermann Keyserling.

9 The opera *The Love of Three Oranges*, by Serge Prokofiev, premieres at the Berlin State Opera.

President von Hindenburg names Lt. General August Wilhelm Heye as Chief of Army Command to replace Maj. Gen. Hans von Seeckt, forced to retire for allowing Crown Prince Wilhelm to participate in army maneuvers the preceding month.

10 The drama *Die Nadel* (*The Needle*), by Ernst Kaminitzer, premieres at the Neues Theater am Zoo in Berlin.

First International Congress for Sexual Research convenes at Reichstag in Berlin.

11 The comedy *Der verlorene Sohn* (*The Prodigal Son*), by Albrecht Schäfer, premieres at the Altona City Theater.

Rowohlt Press publishes comedy *Reparationen* (*Reparations*), by Arnolt Bronnen, and novella *Im letzten Wagen* (*In the Last Car Back*), by Leonhard Frank.

13 The drama *Der blaue Boll* (*Blue Boll*), by Ernst Barlach, premieres at the Stuttgart Regional Theater.

14 Two films premiere in Berlin: the drama *Faust* (loosely based on materials Goethe used in his play of the same title) in Berlin, directed by F. W. Murnau, with Gösta Ekman in the title role, Emil Jannings as Mephistopheles, and

Camilla Horn as Gretchen; and the comedy *Die kleine Inge und ihre drei Väter* (*Little Inge and Her Three Fathers*), directed by Franz Osten, with Mary Brandt, Harry Hardt, Oscar Marion, and Carl Walther Mayer in the title roles.

15 The comedy *Der Geist in der Flasche* (*The Ghost in the Bottle*), by painter Walter Tiemannn, premieres at the Leipzig Schauspielhaus.

16 The drama *Krankheit der Jugend* (*Illness of Youth*), by Ferdinand Bruckner, premieres at Dresden Albert Theater; the comedy *Küken* (*Sweet Young Things*), by Carl Jacoby, premieres at Frankfurt an der Oder City Theater.

Erwin Piscator secures funding from brewer Ludwig Katzenellenbogen for his planned "Piscator Bühne" at the Theater am Nollendorf Platz in Berlin.

Fischer publishes the novella *Unordnung und frühes Leid* (*Disorder and Early Sorrow*), by Thomas Mann.

17 Dancer and actress Valeska Gert premieres her solo program *Gesprochene und getanzte Grotesken* (*Spoken and Danced Grotesqueries*) at the Chat Noir cabaret in Berlin.

18 *Wenn das Herz für Jugend spricht* (*When the Heart Speaks to the Young*) premieres in Berlin, directed by Fred Sauer, with Albert Bassermann and Lee Parry.

19 Debut of novelist Thomas Mann on German radio; he reads an essay he has written about novelist Joseph Conrad.

20 Grote Press publishes the novel *Der Knecht Gottes, Andreas Nyland* (*God's Servant, Andreas Nyland*), by Ernst Wiechert; Torwohlt Press publishes a volume of short fiction titled *Erzählungen* (*Stories*), by Bruno Frank.

Two comedies premiere: *Das Testament* (*The Will*), by Bert Schiff, at Gera-Reuss Regional Theater; and *Rochus ist verloren* (*Rochus is Lost*), by Carl Sloboda, at the Hamburg Thalia Theater.

21 *Der gute Ruf* (*The Good Reputation*, based on 1913 drama of same title by Hermann Sudermann) premieres, directed by Pierre Marodon, with Lotte Neumann and Hans Mierendorff.

Kiepenheuer Press publishes the comedy *Volpone* (based on the comedy by Elizabethan playwright Ben Jonson), by Stefan Zweig.

22 The Kleist Prize is awarded to writer Alfred Neumann for his first novel, *Der Teufel* (*The Devil*).

Actors and actresses of Frankfurt am Main City Theatre refuse to perform as long as drama critic Ludwig Marcuse is present in the theater. A program of combined "Lulu plays" is performed: *Erdgeist* (*Earth Spirit*) and *Die*

Büchse der Pandora (*Pandora's Box*), by Frank Wedekind, under title *Lulu* at the State Theater in Berlin, with Gerda Müller as Lulu.

The film melodrama *Die Flammen lügen* (*The Flames Lie*) premieres in Berlin, directed by Carl Froelich, with Hans Adalbert Schlettow, Ruth Weyher, and Henny Porten.

The operetta *Jugend in Mai* (*Youth in May*), by Leo Fall, premieres at the Semper Opera House in Dresden.

23 The variety show *Alle Puppen tanzen* (*All the Puppets Dancing*) premieres at the Admiral's Palace in Theater Berlin.

The comedy *Schelmuffsky*, by Julius Havemann, premieres at the Lübeck City Theater.

The horror film *Der Student von Prague* (based on novel by Hanns Heinz Ewers) premieres in Berlin, directed by Henrik Galeen, with Conrad Veidt, Werner Krauss, and Elizza La Porta.

26 The Berlin premiere of military history drama *Gneisenau*, by Wolfgang Goetz, opens at the Deutsches Theater in Berlin, with Werner Krauss in title role; the German officer corps and the public hail Krauss' performance as a masterpiece of portraying German military valor.

The film drama *Kampf der Geschlechter* (*Battle of the Sexes*) premieres in Berlin, directed by Heinrich Brandt, with Aud Egede Nissen and Paul Richter.

Frankfurt Publishing Society publishes a travel book about Spain and Morocco titled *Basken/Stiere/Araber* (*Basques, Bulls, and Arabs*) by Kasimir Edschmid; Haessel Press publishes two books: a collection of essays titled *Der Mensch an der Waage* (*Man on the Scales*), by Rudolf Paulsen; and theatre history *Das neue Theater* (*The New Theater*), by Hans Brandenburg.

27 Munich district court sentences the editor of the newspaper *Münchener Zeitung am Abend* to three weeks' imprisonment for publishing the poem by playwright Carl Zuckmayer titled "Wenn der Wind in Frühling bläst" ("When the Spring Wind Blows"); the court decreed the poem constituted blasphemy.

German Publishing Institute publishes volume of fiction titled *Die siebzig Geschichten des Papageien* (*The Parrot's Seventy Stories*), by Wilhelm Schmidtbonn.

28 The film drama *Abenteuer eines 10-Mark Scheins* (*Uneasy Money*) premieres in Berlin, a German-American co-production; directed by Berthold Viertel, with Imogene Robertson and Oskar Homolka.

29 The comedy *Insel der Affen* (*Island of the Apes*), by Hellmuth Unger, premieres at the Bochum City Theater.

30 Two dramas premiere: *Bismarck*, by Frank Wedekind, at the Weimar National Theater; and *Paulus unter den Juden* (*St. Paul among the Jews*) at theaters in Breslau, Hamburg, Munich, and Cologne simultaneously.

Zsolnay Press publishes a collection of correspondence titled *Verdi Briefe* (*Letters of Guiseppe Verdi*), translated by Paul Stefan and edited by Franz Werfel.

NOVEMBER

1 Fischer Press publishes the drama *Dorothea Angermann*, by Gerhart Hauptmann, and the novel *Villa U.S.A.*, by Otto Flake.

National Socialist leader Adolf Hitler names Dr. Joseph Goebbels "Gauleiter" of Berlin and assigns him to use new media in winning over hundreds of thousands of workers in Berlin ("the reddest city in Europe west of Moscow") to the Nazi viewpoint.

Literary monthly *Die neue Rundschau* publishes a collection of verses by Hermann Hesse titled *Der Steppenwolf*.

2 The film drama *Überflüssige Menschen* (*Superfluous People*), a German–Soviet Union coproduction directed by Alexander Rasumnyi, with Eugen Klöpfer and Camilla von Hollay premieres.

The comedy *Kirschwasser* (*Cherry Liqueur*), by Fred A. Angermayer, premieres at the Kiel City Theater.

4 The operetta *Die Königin* (*The Queen*), by Oscar Straus, premieres at the City Opera in Berlin.

6 The comedy *Kilian, oder die gelbe Rose* (*Kilian, or the Yellow Rose*), by Paul Kornfeld, premieres at the Frankfurt City Theater.

The Deutsche Welle (German Wavelength), a privately financed broadcaster with programs aimed specifically at workers and common laborers throughout Germany, broadcasts its first radio transmissions from studios in Königswusterhausen, near Berlin.

Insel Press publishes the drama *Das Apostelspiel* (*Play of the Apostles*), by Max Mell.

Koehler Press publishes the novella *Der Bauernrichter* (*The Peasant Judge*), by Oskar Jellinek.

7 Heinrich Mann reads his novella *Der Jüngling* (*The Stripling*) at the Reichstag as part of the national government's program of fostering literary achievement.

8 German Press Institute publishes the novel *Die Hochzeit des Gaudenz Orell* (*The Marriage of Gaudenz Orell*), by Ernst Zahn.

9 The opera *Cardillac*, by Paul Hindemith, premieres at the Semper Opera House in Dresden.

The first issue of the National Socialist *Rundschreiben* appears in print, part of Dr. Joseph Goebbels' propaganda efforts to organize workers in Berlin.

10 The drama *Julchen und Schinderhannes* (*Julie and Schinderhannes*), by Wolfgang Hillers, premieres at Krefeld City Theater.

Schmiede Press takes over publication of the satirical monthly *Das Stachelschwein* (*The Porcupine*), retaining editor Hans Reimann.

11 The film comedy *Die keusche Susanne* (*Chaste Susanna*) premieres in Berlin, directed by Richard Eichberg, with Willy Fritsch and Lilian Harvey.

12 The film drama *Der Jäger von Fall* (*The Hunter of Fall*, based on a novel of same title by Ludwig Ganghofer) premieres in Munich, directed by Franz Seitz, with Grete Reinwald and William Dieterle.

Wolff Press publishes the novel *Maria Capponi* by René Schickele.

13 German Press Institute publishes a volume of verse titled *Neue Gedichte* (*New Poetry*), by Ina Seidel.

16 Williams Press publishes the biography *Elisabeth Bergner*, by Arthur Eloesser.

20 Wolff Press publishes the novel *Der Schloss* (*The Castle*), by Franz Kafka, edited by Max Brod; German Press Institute publishes the drama *Der Patriot* (*The Patriot*), by Alfred Neumann.

The drama *Dorothea Angermann*, by Gerhart Hauptmann, premieres at theaters in Munich, Leipzig, and Düsseldorf simultaneously; it is a complete flop with critics and audiences.

Newspaper *Berliner Tageblatt* publishes first accounts of secret German army maneuvers in the Soviet Union.

25 The comedy *Volpone* (based on the comedy by Elizabethan playwright Ben Jonson), by Stefan Zweig, premieres at theaters in Lübeck and Dresden; the drama *Das Friedenschiff* (*The Ship of Freedom*), by Julius Maria Becker, premieres at Gotha Regional Theater.

Eichblatt Press publishes the novel *Mann zwischen Frauen* (*Husband between Wives*), by The von Harbou.

27 The music to the ballet *The Miraculous Mandarin*, by Bela Bartok, premieres at Cologne City Opera.

The opera *Orpheus and Eurydice*, by Ernst Krenek (with libretto by painter Oskar Kokoschka), premieres at Kassel State Theater.

28 The drama *Der Kampf um Preussen* (*The Battle for Prussia*), by Kurt Heynicke, premieres at Hannover City Theater.

30 The first sound film program presented before an invited audience at Phöbus Film studios premieres in Berlin, featuring several cabaret acts.

DECEMBER

1 The film drama *Die lachende Grille* (*Fadette*, adapted from the novel by Georges Sand and drama by Charlotte Birch-Pfeiffer) premieres in Berlin, directed by Friedrich Zelnek, with Ly Mara as Fadette and Alfred Abel.

2 Langen Press publishes the ethnic study *Volk ohne Raum* (*A People without Living Space*), by Hans Grimm.

The film drama *Staatsanwalt Jordan* (*State Attorney Jordan*, based on the novel by Hans Land) premieres in Berlin, directed by Karl Gerhardt, with Alfred Gerasch and Mary Johnson.

Kurt Tucholsky is named editor of the literary journal *Die Weltbühne* to replace the recently deceased Siegfried Jacobsohn.

3 Leopold Jessner stages *Hamlet* by William Shakespeare in what critics term "another politicized classic," with Fritz Kortner in the title role; one critic condemns Kortner's performance of Hamlet as a misconceived "victim of circumstances."

4 The new Bauhaus School in Dessau is dedicated.

The film drama *Die Waise von Lowood* (*Jane Eyre*, adapted from the novel by Charlotte Brontë and drama by Charlotte Birch-Pfieffer) premieres in Berlin, directed by Curtis Bernhardt with Evelyn Holdt in the title role and Olaf Fönss as Rochester.

7 Fränkel Press publishes the newly discovered fairy-tale novel titled *Das Leben der Hochgräfin Gritta ovn Rattenzuhausebeiuns* (*The Life of High Countess Gritta Ratsinourhouse*), by Bettina von Arnim.

8 The theater troupe "Die junge Aktion" (Young Action), a group of actors and writers dedicated to making "Marxist theater," is created.

10 The film comedy *Die Königin des Weltbades* (*The Queen of the Baths*) premieres in Berlin, directed by Victor Janson, with Imogen Robertson and Walter Rilla.

Foreign Minister Gustav Stresemann and French foreign minister Aristide Briand are awarded the Nobel Peace Prize for their work in creating the Locarno Pact of 1925. "Locarno may be interpreted as signifying that the States of Europe at last realize that they cannot go on making war upon each other without becoming involved in common ruin," states Stresemann.

11 The comedy *Die Kleinbürgerhochzeit* (*A Petit Bourgeois Wedding*), by Bertolt Brecht, premieres at the Frankfurt am Main City Theater.

13 The film *Die Flucht in die Nacht* (*Flight into Night*, based on the drama *Enrico IV*, by Luigi Pirandello) premieres in Berlin, directed by Amleto Palermi, with Conradt Veidt as Enrico.

15 The film satire *Gern habe ich die Frauen geküsst* (*I Liked Kissing Women*) premieres in Berlin, directed by Bruno Rahn, with Alfons Fryland, Evi Eva, and Elisabeth Panajeff.

17 Dancer/filmmaker/actress Leni Riefenstahl presents her solo dance program at Ufa Palace movie house in Berlin, followed by the premiere of her latest "mountain film" *Der heilige Berg* (*The Holy Mountain*), directed by Arnold Fanck, with Luis Trenker.

The dance program *Tod des Empedokles* (*Death of Empedocles*), by Wilhelm Michel, premieres at the Darmstadt Regional Theater.

18 The three comedy films premiere in Berlin: *Als ich wiederkam* (*When I Returned*, based on a comedy of the same title by Oskar Blumenthal), directed by Richard Oswald, with Liane Haid and Max Hanson; *Nixchen* (*Little Nixie*), directed by Curt Blachnitzky, with Xenia Desni and Hans Albers; and *Die Warenhausprinzessin* (*The Warehouse Princess*), directed by Heinz Paul, with Hans Albers and Lotte Lorring.

At a Christmas celebration in Munich, among hundreds of admirers and followers, Adolf Hitler declares that Christ was a forerunner in the great struggle against world Jewry; to the acclaim of his hearers, he promises that he will complete the work Christ began.

19 The operetta *Spiel um die Liebe* (*The Game of Love*), by Jean Gilbert, premieres at the City Opera in Berlin.

20 Phöbus Film Studios open new movie theater in Berlin called the Phöbus Palace with film melodrama *Dagfin*, directed by Joe May, with Paul Bioensfeldt, Ernst Deutsch, and Marcella Albani.

21 The film melodrama *Die Strasse des Vergessens* (*The Street of Forgetfulness*) premieres in Berlin, directed by Heinz Paul, with Hella Moja, Ida Wüst, and Paul Otto.

22 The operetta *Die kleine Studentin* (*The Little Co-ed*), by Leon Jessel, premieres at the Stettin Bellevue Theater.

23 The drama *Der Diktator* (*The Dictator*), by Jules Romains, translated by Hans Feist, premieres at the Lessing Theater in Berlin.

Two operettas premiere: *Nur du* (*Only You*), by Walter Kollo, at the City Opera in Berlin; and *Die Nacht von Sebastian* (*Sebastian's Night*), by Ralph Benatzky, at the Leipzig Schauspielhaus.

Two films premiere in Berlin: *Ledige Töchter* (*Unmarried Daughters*), directed by Carl Boese, with Jenny Jugo, Charlotte Ander, and Ida Wüst in the title roles; and *Der Sohn des Hannibal* (*Hannibal's Son*), directed by Felix Basch, with Alfons Fryland and Liane Haid.

24 German premiere of the operetta *Die Zirkusprinzessin* (*The Circus Princess*), by Emmerich Kalman, premieres at the Künstler Theater in Berlin.

30 The film drama *Vater werden ist nicht schwer* (*Becoming a Father Isn't Difficult*, based on the novella by Ernst von Wolzogen) premieres in Berlin, directed by Erich Schönfelder, with Lilian Harvey and Harry Halm.

NOTES

1. *Paganini* differs from other Franz Lehar operettas by virtue of its serious tone, treating the love affair between violin virtuoso Niccolo Paganini (1782–1940) and Anna Elisa Bonaparte (1777–1820), who during her liaison with Paganini was Duchess of Lucca. Her brother Napoleon Bonaparte awarded her that title in 1805 and in 1809 presented her as "Grand Duchess of Tuscany." The problem with the operetta is its requirement of a violin virtuoso in the title role. The Vienna premiere in 1925 had suffered poor reviews, even though it featured the accomplished tenor Richard Tauber as Paganini. But the Berlin premiere (likewise with Tauber) proved to be an enormous success. Tauber could not play the violin, but he mimed the movements to music played offstage so well that several critics marveled at the tenor's previously unknown instrumental talents.

2. One of the few happy consequences of the French occupation was the birth to the family of French payroll officer Jean Giscard d'Estaing; the child, named Valery Giscard d'Estaing and born in Koblenz, later became president of France.

3. Count Harry Kessler noted in his diary that "This must have been the way girls danced in Solomon's court, or perhaps before King Tut-ankh-amun." Kessler noted that Baker's dancing was unique in its athleticism; she improvised movements that were both "grotesque and refined," but rarely erotic. Though she moved like "a beautiful predator" the whole experience was like finding oneself "between skyscrapers and a rain forest: ultramodern and ultra-primitive" (*Tagebücher* 485).

4. The Ufa Studios had nearly collapsed in late 1925, when the company's debts totaling $8 million forced it to look for American partnerships. Metro-Goldwyn-Mayer and Paramount loaned Ufa enough money to stay afloat, in exchange for distribution rights in Germany. The deal allowed far more American films than heretofore onto the German market, paradoxically complicating Ufa's already parlous financial situation.

5. The State Museum of Ethnology in Berlin housed a vast collection of ethnographic art, artifacts, and relics from around the world, based largely on the acquisitions of Adolf Bastian (1826–1905). His extensive travels took him around the world many times and his contributions to research on aboriginal peoples had a lasting impact through the 19th and 20th centuries. Bastian was a cofounder of the German Geographic Society and Ethnological Society of Berlin and was perhaps the first "structuralist," arguing that all mankind had similar structures of understanding the physical world. His ideas were singularly influential on the developing sciences of human culture, consciousness, and psychology.

6. Among the most prominent members of the group were Hugo Häring, Bernhard Pankok, Hans Poelzig, Walter Gropius, Richard Döcker, Arthur Korn, and Mies van der Rohe.

7. Berlin had far more large-capacity movie theaters than any other German city in the Weimar Republic; among the most important and capacious of them (showing first-run films on a regular basis) were the following: Marble House, 794 seats; Schaubühne am Lehniner Platz, 889; Titania Palace, 903; Alhambra, 950; Colosseum, 1,000; Gloria Palace, 1,144; Film Theater am Friedrichshain, 1,200; Babylon, 1,239; Capitol am Zoo, 1,284; Mozart Hall of the Theater am Nollendorf Platz, 1,364; and the Metropol, 1,438 seats. The number and size of these facilities explains in large part the prevailing tendency of German film producers to premiere their products almost exclusively in Berlin.

1927

JANUARY

3 The anti-Polish film *Brennende Grenze* (*Aftermath*) premieres in Berlin, directed by Erich Waschneck, with Hubert von Meyerink and Olga Chekhova.

6 The *Die Frau, die nicht nein sagen konnte* (*The Woman Who Could not Say No*) in Berlin, directed by Fred Sauer, with Lee Parry and Gustav Fröhlich.

7 Three films premiere in Berlin: the melodrama *Mädchenhandel—Eine internationale Gefahr* (*The White Slave Trade—An International Threat*), directed by Japp Speyer, with Trude Hesterberg, Mary Kid, Sophie Pagay, and Erich Kaiser-Titz; the detective drama *Piraten der Ostseebäder* (*Pirates on the Baltic Sea*), directed by Valy Arnheim, with Marga Lindt and Valy Arnheim; and the sequel to the historical film *Bismarck*, this time directed by Curt Blachnitzky but again with Franz Ludwig as Bismarck and Erna Morena. Right-wing pundits denounce the sequel as an attempt at "reducing a genius to the level of banality."

Max Schmeling defeats British boxer Jack Stanley in the eighth round at Sports Palace Berlin.

8 The drama *Penthesilea*, by Othmar Schöck, premieres at the Dresden State Theater.

Scherl Press publishes an illustrated edition of the novel *Metropolis*, by screenwriter Thea von Harbou.

10 The science fiction film *Metropolis*[1] premieres in Berlin, directed by Fritz Lang, with Gustav Fröhlich, Brigitte Helm, Alfred Abel, and Heinrich George.

Kiepenheuer Press publishes the comedy *Die Papiermühle* (*The Paper Mill*), by Georg Kaiser.

12 The comedy *Ein besserer Herr* (*A Better Sort of Gentleman*), by Walter Hasenclever, premieres at the Frankfurt am Main City Theater.

13 The opera *Judith*, by Arthur Honnegger, premieres at the Cologne City Opera.

Duncker and Humblot Press publish a history of dadaism titled *Die Flucht aus der Zeit* (*Flight Out of Time*), by Hugo Ball.

14 The detective film *Was ist los im Zirkus Beely?* (*What's Going On at the Beely Circus?*) premieres in Berlin, directed by Harry Piel, with Harry Piel and Eugen Burg.

15 The comedy *Geld* (*Money*), by Bernard Brentano, premieres at the Darmstadt Regional Theater.

Weber Press publishes the literary survey *Die Überseele* (*The Super Soul*), by Hermann Hamann; Langenscheidt Press publishes the novel *Die unbekümmerte Kläre* (*Carefree Lucidity*), by Hans Richter

Langenberg Radio makes its debut broadcast of a live orchestra concert from Dortmund.

17 The Berlin newspaper *Vossische Zeitung* publishes correspondence between composers Clara Schumann and Johannes Brahms, edited by Berthold Litzmann.

21 Lichtbildbühne Verlag (Motion Picture Stage Press) publishes comprehensive film lexicon on international film artists titled *Wie ich zum Film kam* (*How I Got into Movies*), featuring hundreds of entries on performers and directors.

The comedy *Das gastliche Haus* (*The Hospitable House*) by Heinrich Mann premieres at the Munich Kammerspiele.

The comedy film *Eine tolle Nacht* (*A Crazy Night*, based on the comedy of same title by Wilhelm Mannstaedt) premieres in Berlin, directed by Richard Oswald, with Harry Liedtke and Mira Hildebrand.

Graphic artist Hans Meid, painter Karl Walser, and architect Peter Behrens are named members of the Prussian Academy of the Arts.

23 The film romance *Die Villa im Tiergarten* (*The Villa in Tiergarten Park*, based on the novel by Artur Landsberger) premieres in Berlin, directed by Franz Osten, with Joe Stöckel and Aud Egede Nissen.

West German Radio broadcasts a full-length opera (*Fidelio* by Ludwig van Beethoven) performance from its studios in Cologne.

24 The film melodrama *Eine Dubarry von Heute* (*A Dubarry of Today*) premieres in Berlin, directed by Alexander Korda, with Hans Albers, Maria Corda, Friedrich Kayssler, and Marlene Dietrich.

26 The comedy *Die Papiermühle* (*The Paper Mill*), by Georg Kaiser, premieres at the Dresden Albert Theater.

27 The opera *Nikodemus,* by Hans Grimm, premieres at the Magdeburg City Theater.

Societät Press publishes the drama *Bonaparte* by Fritz von Unruh.

The film melodrama *Die Frau ohne Namen* (*The Woman with No Name*) premieres in Berlin, directed by Georg Jacoby, with Elga Brink in the title role and Jack Tevor.

28 The film romance *Wenn der junge Wein blüht* (*When the Young Wine Blossoms*, based on the play by Björnsterne Björnson) premieres, directed by Carl Wilhelm, with Robert Scholz and Lotte Lorring.

The German Press Institute publishes the memoir *Die Stabilisierung der Mark* (*The Stabilization of the Mark*), by former currency commissioner and president of Reichs Bank Hjalmar Horace Greeley Schacht; Schacht had been instrumental in the 1923 currency reform that ended inflation and renewed international confidence in the Reichs Mark.

29 The "Goldrausch-Fest" (Gold Rush Festival) of chorus lines, featuring precision dancing chorines, such as The Tiller Girls, the Admiral's Girls, and the Russian Ballet of the Haller Revue, opens at the Berlin Sports Palace.

Cotta Press publishes the drama *Der Hasenfellhändler* (*The Rabbit Fur Dealer*), by Hermann Sudermann.

The opera *Jonny spielt auf* (*Jonny Strikes Up the Band*), by Ernst Krenek, premieres at the Leipzig City Theater.[2]

The musical revue *Sünden der Welt* (*Sins of the World*), by James Klein, premieres at the Comic Opera in Berlin.

FEBRUARY

1 The film drama *Faschingszauber* (*Shrovetide Magic*) premieres in Berlin, directed by Rudolf Walther-Fein, with Grete Mosheim and Harry Liedtke.

Saxony joins Thuringia in lifting the ban on Adolf Hitler speaking within its borders.

2 The detective film drama *Der Mann mit den falschen Banknoten* (*The Man with the Counterfeit Money*) premieres in Berlin, directed by Romano Megnon, with Nils Asther, Siegfried Arno, and Vivian Gibson.

3 The film melodrama *Deutsche Frauen—Deutsche Treue* (*German Women—German Faithfulness*) premieres in Berlin, directed by Wolfgang Neff, with Solveig Hedengran, Sophie Pagay, and Gottfried Hagedorn.

Construction begins on a new regional theater for the North Sea island of Borkum.

4 The drama *Razzia* (*Raid*), by Hans-José Rehfisch, premieres at the Schiller Theater in Berlin.

5 The drama *Bonaparte*, by Fritz von Unruh, premieres at Frankfurt am Main City Theater; German premiere of *A Dream Play*, by August Strindberg, premieres at the Volksbühne in Berlin.

8 The film romance *Das war Heidelberg in blauer Sommernacht* (*That Was Heidelberg on a Twilight Summer Evening*) premieres in Berlin, directed by Emmerich Hanus, with Fritz Alberti and Olga Engl.

9 The military film drama *Der Feldmarschall* (*The Field Marshal*) premieres in Berlin, directed by Romano Megnon, with Harry Hardt and Cilly Feindt.

10 Two film melodramas premiere in Berlin: *Die Geliebte* (*The Beloved*), directed by Robert Wiene, with Olga Engl in the title role and Harry Liedtke; and *Die Tragödie einer Verlorenen* (*The Tragedy of a Lost Soul*) in Berlin, directed by Hans Steinhoff, with Alfred Abel and Sophie Pagay.

11 Engelhorn Press publishes the novel *Abschied vom Paradies* (*Farewell to Paradise*), by Frank Thiess; Zsolnay press publishes the novel *Der Traum* (*The Dream*), by H. G. Wells, translated by Otto Mandl, Helen Reiff, and Erna Redterbacher.

First mass rally of National Socialists in Berlin at Phärus Hall; Communist Party members attempt to break up meeting, leading to a full-scale riot that spills out into the adjoining streets.

12 The film drama *Schwester Veronika* (*Sister Veronica*) in Berlin, directed by Gerhard Lamprecht, with Aud Egede Nissen in the title role and Paul Richter.

14 Paul Hindemith is named professor of composition at the Berlin State College of Music.

16 The drama *Kaspar Hauser*, by Erich Ebermayer, premieres at the Munich Residenz Theater.

The operetta *Der Zarewitsch* (*The Czarevitch*) premieres at the Deutsches Künstlerhaus in Berlin.

17 The opera *Hanneles Himmelfahrt* (*The Assumption of Hannele*, based on the play by Gerhart Hauptamnn), by Paul Graener, premieres at the Semper Opera House in Dresden.

18 German radio networks broadcast readings from romance novels by Hedwig Courths-Mahler on the occasion of her 60th birthday.

The film melodrama *Die Insel der verbotenen Küsse* (*The Island of Forbidden Kisses*) premieres in Berlin, directed by Georg Jacoby, with Georg Alexander and Elga Brink.

19 Wolkenwanderer Press publishes the anthology titled *Das gesammelte Werk des Jean-Arthur Rimbaud* (*The Collected Work of Jean-Arthur Rimbaud*) in free-verse translations of Rimbaud's poems by Paul Zech.

The operetta *Pit-Pit*, by Robert Gilbert, premieres at the Dresden State Theater.

22 The drama *Der Patriot* (*The Patriot*), by Alfred Neumann, at the Lessing Theater in Berlin.

24 The film drama *Erinnerungen einer Nonne* (*Memories of a Nun*) premieres in Berlin, directed by Arthur Bergen, with Georg John, Ellen Kürti, and Imogen Robertson.

Gretlein Press publishes the novel *Der Engel vom westlichen Fenster* (*The Angel in the Western Window*), by Gustav Meyrink.

The film melodrama *Verbotene Liebe* (*Forbidden Love*) premieres in Berlin, directed by Friedrich Feher, with Evi Eva and Paul Otto.

27 Kiepenheuer Press publishes collection of three related plays titled *Bismarck: Trilogie eines Kämpfers* (*Bismarck: Trilogy of a Fighter*); the three related plays are *King and People*, *Union*, and *Dismissal*.

28 The one-act opera titled *Royal Palace*, by Kurt Weill, premieres at the State Opera in Berlin.

The film comedy *Meine Tante—deine Tante* (*My Aunt—Your Aunt*) premieres in Berlin, directed by Carl Froelich, with Henny Porten and Ralph Arthur Roberts.

MARCH

1 Zsolnay Press publishes the novel *Mutter Marie* (*Mother Maria*), by Herinrich Mann.

3 Two films premiere in Berlin: the adventure drama *Rinaldo Rinaldini*, directed by Max Obal, with Hans Albers and Eugen Burg; and the romantic drama *Das Rosapantöffelchen* (*The Pink Slipper*), directed by Franz Hofer, with Hanni Reinwald and Ernst Rückert.

4 Two film dramas premiere in Berlin: *Der Juxbaron* (*The Imaginary Baron*), directed by Willi Wolff, with Henry Bender, Teddy Bill, and Marlene Dietrich; and *Der Soldat der Marie* (*Marie's Solder*), directed by Erich Schönfelder, with Xenia Desni and Harry Liedtke

5 Bavaria lifts ban on Adolf Hitler speaking within its borders.

7 City of Frankfurt am Main establishes funding for its yearly "Goethe Prize," awarding RM 10,000 not necessarily to a writer but to any "personality" whose work honors Johann Wolfgang Goethe (1749–1832), who was born in Frankfurt.

9 Fischer Press publishes the novella *Spiel im Morgengrauen* (*Daybreak*), by Arthur Schnitzler; Curtius Press publishes the historical essay *Die weltgeschichtliche Bedeutung des Judentums und seine Zukunft* (*The Global Significance and Future of Jewry*), by Ernst Joerges; German Press Institute publishes the memoir *Erinnerungen und Dokumente* (*Memories and Documents*), by the last chancellor of imperial Germany, Maximilian von Baden.

11 Two films premiere in Berlin: *Klettermaxe* (*Up and Down the Staircase*), directed by Weilly Reiber, with Dorothea Wieck and Paul Heidemann; and *Der Zigeunerbaron* (*The Gypsy Baron*, based on novella *Saffi* by Mor Jokai), directed by Friedrich Zelnik, with Lya Mara and Michael Bohnen.

15 The romance film drama *Die Csardasfürstin* (*The Csardas Princess*, a German-Hungarian coproduction based on the operetta by Emmerich Kalman) premieres in Berlin, directed by Hanns Schwarz, with Liane Haid and Imre Raday.

16 Propyläen Press publishes two dramas by Bertolt Brecht: *Im Dickicht der Städte* (*In the Jungle of Cities*) and *Mann ist Mann* (*A Man's a Man*).

17 The comedy *Küsse in der Nacht* (*Kisses in the Night*), by Lothar Sachs and Louis Taufstein, premieres at the Wallner Theater in Berlin.

18 Schmiede Press publishes the novel *Jazz*, by Hans Janowitz.

The film comedy *Kopf hoch, Charly!* (*Head Held High, Charlie!*) premieres in Berlin, directed by Willi Wolff, with Michael Nohnen, Blandine Ebinger, and Marlene Dietrich.

19 An exhibition of paintings titled "Ostpreussenkunst" (The Art of East Prussia) premieres at the German Art Community Gallery in Berlin.

The German version of the comedy *Musotte*, by Guy du Maupassant, translated by Emerich von Bukovics, premieres at the Trianon Theater in Berlin.

20 Armed militia groups backed by the National Socialist and Communist Parties clash near Lichterfeld train station in Berlin, leaving dozens wounded.

21 The military action film *Prinz Luis Ferdinand* premieres in Berlin, directed by Hans Behrendt, with Hans Stüwe in the title role and Christa Tordy as Queen Luise.

22 Propyläen Press publishes a collection of poetry titled *Hauspostille* (*Manual of Piety*), by Bertolt Brecht; Wolff Press publishes *Das Schloss* (*The Castle*), by Franz Kafka, edited by Max Brod.

In preparation for observations of the 100th anniversary of Ludwig van Beethoven's death, Prussian Academy of the Arts establishes funding for its "Beethoven Prize" in the amount of RM 10,000. In Beethoven's birth city of Bonn, a German Beethoven Festival begins a succession of concerts along with the publication of a "Beethoven Almanac."

23 The drama *Gewitter über Gottland* (*Storm over Gottland*), by Ehm Welk, opens at the Volksbühne in Berlin; a 10-minute synopsis of a film by the same title, directed (as was the theater production) by Erwin Piscator, featuring the production's cast) premieres in Berlin in an attempt to stimulate interest in the Volksbühne.

The film drama *Einer gegen alle* (*One against All*) in Berlin, directed by Nunzio Malasomma, with Carlo Aldini, Michael Chekhov, and Inge Borg.

Kösel Press publishes the treatise *Rasse und Volk* (*Race and Ethnicity*) by Wilhelm Schmidt.

24 The film drama *Der Sohn der Hagar* (*Hagar's Son*) premieres in Berlin, directed by Fritz Wendhausen, with Mady Christians and Werner Füetterer.

25 Spaeth Press publishes the novel *Um den Rhein* (*Up and Down the Rhine*), by Herbert Eulenberg.

26 Hundreds of memorial concerts take place honoring the 100th anniversary of Beethoven's death.

The comedy *Das zweite Leben* (*The Second Life*), by Rudolf Bernauer and Rudolf Österreicher, premieres at the Komödienhaus in Berlin.

Schrag Press publishes *Das Amulett* (*The Amulet*), by Jakob Wassermann.

28 Piper Press publishes a volume of verse titled *Mensch Wanderer* (*Vagabond*), by Christian Morgenstern.

30 The drama *Thomas Paine*, by Hanns Johst, premieres at seven regional theaters, along with publication of the play by Langen Press.

APRIL

1 The musical revue titled *Halloh! Hier Republik* (*This is the Republic Calling*) premieres at the Neues Theater am Zoo in Berlin.

Alfred Hugenberg,[3] head of Scherl Press group, purchases a majority of Ufa film company stock.

The film melodrama *Das Meer* (*The Sea*) premieres, directed by Peter Paul Fellner, with Heinrich George and Olga Chekhova.

The comedy *Der Mann im Dunkel* (*The Main in the Dark*), by physician Friedrich Wolf, premieres at the Essen City Theater.

Knaur Press inaugurates new imprint called Novels of the World, a book series consisting of popular literature produced on cheap paper offered to mass audiences at low prices.

3 Two films premiere: *Walpurgisnacht* (*Witches' Night*), directed by James Bauer, with Gert Briese and Vivian Gibson; and *Laster der Menschheit* (*Guilty Pleasures of the Flesh*), directed by Rudolf Meinert, with Asta Nielsen and Werner Krauss.

4 The film comedy *Die Bräutigame der Babette Bomberling* (*The Bridegrooms of Babette Bomberling*), directed by Victor Janson, with Xenia Desni and Bruno Kastner premieres.

5 The comedy *Hexennacht* (*Night of the Witches*), by Wilhelm Poek, premieres at the Flensburg City Theater.

6 Klinkhardt and Biermann Press publishes the art history book titled *Die Entwicklung der modernen Malerei* (*The Development of Modern Painting*), by Helene Kröller-Müller.

7 The film melodrama *Die Achtzehnjährigen* (*The 18-Year-Old*) premieres, directed by Manfred Noa, with Andreé Lafayette in the title role and Paul Otto.

8 The drama *Agnes Bernauer*, by Eduard Reinacher, premieres at the Koblenz City Theater.

The film comedy *Die leichte Isabell* (*Isabell over Easy*, based on the operetta by Jean Gilbert) premieres, directed by Eddy Busch, with Lee Parry and Gustav Fröhlich.

9 Frank'sche Press publishes the architectural showcase *Ein Wohnhaus* (*A Family Residence*), by Bruno Taut.

The drama *Caesar's Wife* by W. Somerset Maugham, translated by Anna Kellner, premieres at Hamburg Thalia Theater.

10   The film drama *Die sieben Töchter der Frau Gyurkovics* (*Sister of Six*) premieres, directed by Ragnar Hylten-Cavallius.

13   Drei Masken Press publishes a biography of the participants in the Munich revolution of 1919 and the founders of the Bavarian Soviet Republic titled *Wir sind Gefangenen* (*We Are Prisoners*), by Oskar Maria Graf.

The film drama *Venus im Frack* (*Venus in Evening Wear*) premieres, directed by Robert Land, with Evi Eva and Georg Alexander.

14   Two films premiere: *Dirnentragödie* (presented in America as *Women without Men*, the German title means "A whore's tragedy"), directed by Bruno Rahn, with Asta Nielsen and Oskar Homolka; and *Hotelratten* (*Hotel Rats*), directed by Jaap Speyer, with Nils Asther and Ellen Kürti.

15   "Festival of *The Miracle*" opens in Düsseldorf, celebrating Max Reinhardt's 1911 epic production of Karl Vollmöeller's pantomime *Das Mirakel*.[4]

16   The comedy *Skandal in Amerika* (*Scandal in America*), by Hans-José Rehfisch, premieres at the Deutsches Künstler Theater in Berlin.

17   The comedy *Die bedrohte Unschuld* (*Threatened Innocence*), by Hilmar Rennspiess and Richard Rolland, premieres at the Theater in der Kommandanten Strasse in Berlin.

19   Cabaret performer and writer Joachim Ringelnatz exhibits artwork and gives readings from his cabaret sketches at the Flechtheim Gallery in Berlin.

20   The comedy *Die heisse Zone* (*The Hot Zone*), by Fritz Eckerle, premieres at the Kaiserslautern Regional Theater.

21   The film thriller *Ein Mordmädel* (*A Murderous Girl*) premieres, directed by Sidney Morgan, with Paul Conradi and Cilly Feindt.

Debut of the cabaret act "Revue zu Vieren" ("Revue of Four"), featuring Klaus Mann, Erika Mann, Pamela Wedekind, and most significantly, Gustaf Gründgens, premieres at the Altes Theater in Leipzig.

Cotta Press publishes the collected works volume titled *Jakob Christoph Heer: Romane und Novellen* (*Novels and Novellas*).

22   The documentary film *Der Weltkrieg: Des Volkes Heldengesang* (*The World War: A German Hymn to Heroes*) premieres, directed by Leo Lasko, whom the Reich Office of War Archives allowed access to its original films and still photographs.

The drama *Zwölftausend* (*Twelve Thousand*), by Bruno Frank, premieres at the Munich Kammerspiele.

25 Debut issue of the bimonthly journal of philosophy and art titled *Individualität* (*Individuality*).

26 The film thriller *Der Herr der Nacht* (*Lord of the Night*) premieres, directed by Carl Heinz Wolff, with Aud Egede Nissen and Kurt Brenkerhoff.

27 The film melodrama *Die Lorelei* (*The Lorelei*), directed by Wolfgang Neff, with Renate Brausewetter, Trude Hesterberg, Lotte Loring, and Maria Paudler in the title roles.

Fischer Press publishes the novel *Sommerroman* (*Summer Novel*), by Otto Flake.

28 Propyläen Press publishes the comedy *Ein besserer Herr* (*A Better Sort of Gentleman*), by Walter Hasenclever.

MAY

1 Cabaret performer Joachim Ringelnatz makes his radio debut by reading his cabaret sketches from the broadcast studio in Königswusterhausen.

Adolf Hitler makes his first speech in Berlin at the Clou Concert Hall; because Prussian police have banned his speaking in public, audience members are there by invitation only.

2 Two films premiere: the detective drama *Einbruch* (*Break-in*), directed by Franz Osten, with Erika Glässner and Kurt Gerron; and the intrigue melodrama *Mata Hari* directed by Friedrich Feher, with Magda Sonja in the title role and Fritz Kortner.

Kiepenheuer Press publishes the drama *Die Umkehr* (*The Reversal*), by Arnold Zweig. The Munich newspaper *Münchener Illustrierte* serializes the detective novel *The Terrible People*, by Edgar Wallace, translated by Fritz Pütsch.

4 Two films premiere: the comedy *Hallo Caesar!* directed by Reinhold Schünzel, with Imogen Robertson and Reinhold Schünzel; and the comedy *Wie heirate ich meinen Chef?* (*How Do I Marry the Boss?*), directed by Erich Schönfelder, with Dina Gralla and Henry deVries.

5 Opening of the "Congress of Reich Soldiers of the Front" sponsored by the paramilitary organization Stahlhelm (Steel Helmet) meets in Berlin for rallies and speeches denouncing the republic, its politicians, and its policies. More than 100,000 men converge on Berlin for the two-day event.

Berlin police ban the presence of National Socialists in Berlin until 31 March 1928 because of violent street altercations with Communist Party members in February and March.

6 German Press Institute publishes the novel *Unterm Kreuz des Südens* (*Under the Southern Cross*), by Heinrich Schüler

7 *Musik*, "a portrait of customs in four scenes," by Frank Wedekind, premieres at the Schiller Theater in Berlin; the Berlin newspaper *Vossische Zeitung* serializes the lengthy music history essay "Über die neue Sachlichkeit in der Musik" ("On the New Matter-of-Factness in Music"), by Hans-Heinz Stuckenschmidt.

12 The detective film drama *Sein grösster Bluff* (*His Greatest Bluff*) premieres, directed by Henrik Galeen, with Harry Piel, Toni Tetzlaff, and Marlene Dietrich.

13 Annual German Theater Exhibition opens in Magdeburg.

Reiss Press publishes the travel book *Zaren, Popen, Bolschwiken* (*Czars, Prelates, Bolsheviks*), by Egon Erwin Kisch; Keil Press publishes the novel *Der Brand der Cheopspyramide* (*Fire in the Pyramid of Cheops*), by Hans Dominik.

14 A film version of *Die Weber* (*The Weavers*, based on the play by Gerhart Hauptmann) premieres, directed by Friedrih Zelnik, with Wilhelm Dieterle, Paul Wegener, Dagny Servaes, and Hermann Picha.

16 The European Amateur Boxing Championships open at Berlin Sports Palace, featuring bouts among contenders from Austria, Belgium, Denmark, Estonia, France, Germany, Holland, Hungary, Italy, Lithuania, Norway, Poland, and Sweden; Germans win four championships.

17 Bock Press publishes *Kulturgeschichte der Neuzeit* (*Cultural History of the Modern Period*), by Egon Friedell.

The film melodrama *Die Jagd nach Braut* (*The Hunt for a Bride*), directed by Georg Jacoby, with Georg Alexander and Elga Brink, premieres.

19 The comedy *Ein Narr macht viele* (*A Fool Up to Something*), by Fritz Peter Buch, premieres at the Dresden State Theater; the drama *Das unsichtbare Mädchen* (*The Invisible Girl*), by Hans Kafka, premieres at the Theater am Zoo in Berlin.

The film drama *An der Weser* (*On the Banks of the River Weser*) premieres, directed by Siegfried Phillippi, with Carl Auen and Olga Engl.

21 American pilot Charles Lindbergh lands in Paris after his solo flight across Atlantic, creating a sensation in several German cities, with many newspapers devoting extra issues to the flight, the pilot, and his aircraft, *The Spirit of St. Louis*.

24 Ullstein Press resumes its "One Mark" series featuring paperback volumes costing one Reichsmark each, a book price not seen since World War I.

27 German dramatization of the detective novel *The Ringer*, by Edgar Wallace, premieres at the Deutsches Theater in Berlin.

28 The Leipzig Book Fair opens, with the exhibition of "special editions" of works by Gerhart Hauptmann; some volumes feature lithographs commissioned by Fischer Press, Hauptmann's main publisher.

30 The film drama *Valencia* premieres, directed by Jaap Speyer, with Maria Forescu and Oscar Marion.

Fischer Press publishes the novel *Der Steppenwolf*,[5] by Hermann Hesse.

JUNE

1 The Glass Palace Art Exhibition opens in Munich, featuring more than 1,500 works in various media, styles, and traditions, though the majority derive from the Munich area.

Approximately 1.6 million Germans hold licenses to own radio sets.

2 The Paula Modersohn Becker Museum opens in Bremen, featuring many of the paintings she created between 1900 and 1907.

Two films premiere: *Ehekonflikte* (*Conflicts in Marriage*), directed by Bruno Ran, with Werner Pittschau and Lydia Böttcher; and *Königin des Varietés* (*The Girl from Maxim's*, based on a play by Georges Feydeau), directed by Johannes Guter, with Ellen Kürti and Harry Halm.

Schmiede Press publishes a poetry collection titled *Die Harfenjule* (*The Girl with the Harp*), by Klabund.

3 The film melodrama *Primanerliebe* (*Schoolgirl Love*), directed by Robert Land, with Grete Mosheim and Matin Herzberg, premieres.

4 Engelhorn Press publishes the novel *Die Schauspielerin* (*The Actress*), by Carry Brachvogel.[6]

5 At Schiller Park Hall in Berlin, the Communist Party militia group Red Front declares its readiness to take on right-wing groups, such as the National Socialists, in street fighting.

12 All three opera houses in Berlin (the State Opera Unter den Linden, the City Opera, and the Kroll Opera House) agree to lower their ticket prices in the hope of attracting bigger audiences for the summer.

The Nuremberg soccer club defeats Berlin Hertha for the German national championship.

13 Propyläen Press publishes the drama *Trommeln in der Nacht* (*Drums in the Night*), by Bertolt Brecht, five years after its premiere in Munich.

16 The film comedy *Frühere Verhältnisse* (*Former Lovers*, based on a comedy of same title by Johann Nepomuk Nestroy) premieres, directed by Arthur Bergen, with Ossi Oswalda and Fritz Kampers.

Schneider Press publishes a poetry collection titled *Ruf aus der Zeit* (*Call from Times Past*), by Ludwig Strauss; Stackmann Press publishes the novella *Das Sympathiemittel* (*The Means of Sympathy*), by Max Dreyer; Scherl Press publishes the novel *Der Seelenverkäufer* (*The Seller of Souls*), by Kurt Faber.

19 Max Schmeling becomes the European cruiserweight boxing champion by knockout against Fernand Delarge of Belgium.

21 Ullstein Press publishes the novel *Das Erwachen des Donald Westhof* (*Donald Westhof's Awakening*), by theater director and producer Felix Hollaender.

22 The city of Berlin bans further licensing of horse-drawn carriages on the streets of Berlin, ending a tradition that began in 1793; more than 200 such carriages continue operation in the city, though their licenses will not be renewed upon expiration.

The film melodrama *Männer vor der Ehe* (*Men before Marriage*), directed by Constantin J. David, with Nina Vanna and Kurt Vespermann, premieres.

24 The film melodrama *Das Spielzeug einer schönen Frau* (*The Plaything of a Beautiful Woman*), directed by Fritz Friesler, with Evi Eva and Alfons Fryland, premieres.

27 Eysler Press publishes the novel *Donner und Doria* by Roda Roda.

28 Zsolnay Press publishes the short fiction volume *Die Dampfsäule* (*The Steam Columns*), by Hungarian playwright Ferenc Molnar.

JULY

1 *Ich war zu Heidelberg Student* (*I Was a Student in Heidelberg*), directed by Wolfgang Neff, with Charles Willy Kayser and Alice Kempen, premieres.

4 The monthly magazine *Der Angriff* (*The Attack*) debuts, a publication of news, opinion, and cultural commentary sponsored by the National Socialist Party, edited by Dr. Joseph Goebbels.

5 The German Press Institute publishes the novel *Der tolle Bomberg* (*Mad Bomberg*), by Josef Winckler.

7 The film melodrama *Glanz und Elend der Kurtisanen* (*Splendor and Misery of the Courtesans*),[7] directed by Manfred Noa, with Paul Wegener and Andreé Lafayette, premieres.

8 The film meoldrama *Mein Heidelberg, ich kann Dich nicht vergessen* (*Heidelberg, I Cannot Forget You*), directed by James Bauer, with Hans Adalbert Schlettowith and Dorothea Wieck, premieres.

Richter Press publishes the volume *Die Radierungen, Holzschnitte und Lithographien von Käthe Kollwitz* (*Drawings, Woodcuts, and Lithographs by Käthe Kollwitz*) as a celebration of the artist's 60th birthday.

9 Parey Press publishes a book of adventure stories celebrating American frontiersmen, Indians, mountain men, trappers, and hunters titled *Das Grenzerbuch* (*The Frontier Book*), by Baron Friedrich von Gagern.

11 Conservative Christian newspapers begin editorializing for a restoration of the monarchy in Germany; Goebbels editorializes that Germany has become "an exploitation colony of international Jewish finance capital;" he also notes that such a movement as National Socialism, which stands for the complete break-up of the German state, cannot "walk around in silk slippers" but must be prepared for violent conflict in the streets.

12 The film *Das Mädchen von der Heilsarmee* (*The Salvation Army Girl*), directed by William Kahn, with Camilla von Hollay in the title role and Ernst Rückert, premieres.

15 The German Chamber Music Festival opens in Baden-Baden, directed by composer Paul Hindemith.

18 An automobile race is broadcast for the first time in Germany, namely the Nürburgring, about fifty miles south of Cologne.

19 The Bayreuth Festival opens with a new production of *Parsifal*; productions of *Das Rheingold* and *Die Walküre* follow.

21 The musical revue *Das bist Du!* (*That's You!*), by Friedrich Hollaender, premieres at the Theater am Kurfürstendamm.

23 Comic actor Heinz Rühmann makes a national breakthrough in the performance of the American comedy *Fair and Warmer*, by Avery Hopwood, at the Munich Kammerspiele.

Eher Press publishes National Socialist economics treatise titled *Gold oder Blut* (*Gold or Blood*), by Otto Bangert.

25 The film comedy *Himmel auf Erden* (*Heaven on Earth*) premieres, based on the comedy by Wilhelm Jacoby, directed by Reinhold Schünzel, with Charlotte Ander and Erich Kaiser-Titz.

27 The Hamburg newspaper *Hamburger Illustrierte* serializes the novel about life in the theater titled *Baumeister Kessler* (*Kessler the Builder*), by Felix Hollaender.

German-American swimmer Johnny Weissmuller sets new world record in the 800-meter freestyle event, clocked at 10 minutes 22.2 seconds.

28 The comedy film *Die schönsten Beine von Berlin* (*The Most Beautiful Legs in Berlin*) premieres in Berlin, directed by Willi Wolff, with the Tiller Girls and the Dodge Sisters.

The film drama *Die Lindenwirtin am Rhein* (*A Small Hotel on the Rhine*) premieres, directed by Rolf Randolph with Iris Arland, Maly Delschaft, and Gert Briese.

29 The film melodrama *Regine, Tragödie einer Frau* (*Regine: A Woman's Tragedy*) premieres, directed by Erich Waschneck, with Lee Parry and Harry Liedtke.

AUGUST

1 Kampmann Press publishes the biography *Agnes Sorma* by Julius Bab.

2 The film melodrama *Ein rheinisches Mädchen beim rheinischen Wein* (*A Girl from the Rhine, with Rhenish Wine*) premieres, directed by Johannes Guter, with Xenia Desni and Jack Trevor.

9 The detective film *Ein schwerer Fall* (*A Difficult Case*) premieres, directed by Felix Brasch, with Ossi Oswalda and Alfons Fryland.

10 Eher Press continues its series of publications promoting National Socialist ideology with two new treatises: *Der Zukunftsweg einer deutschen Aussenpolitik* (*The Way of the Future in German Foreign Policy*), by Alfred Rosenberg and *Die jüdische Weltpest: Kann ein Jude Staatsbüger sein?* (*The Jewish World Plague: Can a Jew Be a Citizen of the State?*), by Hermann Esser. With such publications, Eher Press hopes to emulate Schmiede, Malik, and other Marxist-oriented publishing enterprises.

More than 10,000 protestors stage demonstrations in front of American Embassy in Berlin to protest conviction of Italian immigrants Fernandino Sacco and Bartolomeo Vanzetti on murder charges in Massachusetts.

11 A torch-light parade from the Radio Tower in the western part of Berlin to the Reichstag in the city's center concludes festivities celebrating "Constitution Day" throughout the Republic.

The film melodrama *Ihr letztes Liebensabenteuer* (*Her Final Romantic Adventure*), directed by Max Reichmann, with Gustav Fröhlich and Vera Schmiterlöw, premieres.

12 The film melodrama *Ein Tag der Rosen im August* (*A Day of the Roses in August*), directed by Max Mack, with Eduard von Winterstein and Margarete Schön, premieres.

15 Sponholte Press publishes a novel about fighter pilots titled *T 1000*, by Hans Richter.

16 Drei Eulen Press begins a series of film star biographies titled *Filmgesicht* (*Face of Film*), beginning with volumes on Emil Jannings (by Margarete Lang-Kosak) and Paul Wegener (by Wolfgang Martini).

The film melodrama *Ich habe in Mai von der Liebe geträumt* (*I Dreamed of Love in May*), directed by Franz Seitz, with William Dieterle and Margarete Lanners, premieres.

17 Insel Press publishes the novel *Agnes Altkirchner*, by Felix Braun.

18 *Die letzte Nacht* (*The Queen Was in the Parlour*, a British-German coproduction, based on a play by Noel Coward), directed by Graham Cutts, with Lili Damita and Paul Richter, premieres.

19 First Nuremberg congress of National Socialists is held; the highly theatrical features of the congress attract onlookers curious about Hitler and other leaders of the party; newspaper coverage is wider than for any other political party's yearly meetings, with some accounts publishing pictures of the congress.

Two film melodramas premiere: *Gehetzte Frauen* (*Female Freight*), directed by Richard Oswald, with Asta Nielsen and Gustav Fröhlich; and *Der letzte Walzer* (*The Last Waltz*), directed by Arthur Roboson, with Liane Haid and Willy Fritsch.

Langen Press publishes a novel about Jesus titled *Die Legende vom Herrn* (*The Legends of the Lord*), by Walter von Molo.

20 The film satire *Die Hose* (*The Underpants*, based on the comedy of the same title by Carl Sternheim) premieres, directed by Hans Behrendt, with Jenny Jugo and Werner Krauss.

23 The film drama *Feme* (based on novel of same title by Vicki Baum) premieres, directed by Richard Oswald, with Mathilde Sussin and Hans Stüwe.

24 Reiss Press publishes the biographical account *Briefe aus dem Zuchthaus* (*Letters from the Penitentiary*) premieres, by Max Hoelz.

The film drama *Die Vorbestraften* (*The Ex-Cons*) premieres, directed by Rudolf Meinert, with Henry de Vries and Julius Falkenstein.

26 The film drama *Der Fluch der Vererbung* (*The Legacy's Curse*) premieres, directed by Adolf Trotz, with Maly Delschaft and Carl de Vogt.

28 The Goethe Prize from the city of Frankfurt am Main is awarded to author Stefan George.

SEPTEMBER

1 Kiepenheuer Press publishes the political revue *Hoppla, wir leben* (*Hooray, We're Alive!*), by Ernst Toller, also the production of the new "Piscator Stage" company debuts at the Theater am Nollendorf Platz in Berlin.

The comedy film *Arme kleine Sif* (*Poor Little Sif*) premieres, directed by Arthur Bergen, with Paul Wegener and Olga Engl.

The German government announces it has paid RM 1.5 billion in reparation payments to the victorious World War I allies over the past three years; right-wing and nationalist newspapers denounce the payments as money extorted from the German people.

2 Knaur Press publishes the novel *Angst* (*Anxiety*), by Walter Harich; the novella *Das Traumhaus* (*The Dream House*), by Franz Werfel, is published in the literary journal *Die neue Rundschau*; Rowohlt Press publishes the satirical memoir *Die Reisebriefe eines Artisten* (*An Artists's Travel Letters*), by cabaret performer Joachim Ringelnatz.

Two films premiere: *Die heilige Lüge* (*The Holy Lie*), directed by Holger-Madsen, with Paul Bildt and Ortto Gebühr; and *Das Heiratsnest* (*The Marriage Nest*), directed by Rudolf Walther-Fein, with Harry Liedtke and Margarete Lanner.

5 *Standarte*, a right-wing, nationalist literary journal, debuts.

The film *Meister von Nürnberg* (*Master of Nuremberg*), directed by Ludwig Berger, with Rudolf Rittner as Hans Sachs and Gustav Fröhlich as Walter von Stolzing, premieres.

Reissner Press publishes memoirs titled *Erinnerungen und Dokumente aus meiner Londoner Mission* (*Memories and Documents of My Mission to London*), by Prince Karl von Lichnowsky, German ambassador to the United Kingdom from 1912 until the outbreak of World War I.

6 Zsolnay Press publishes the novella *Geheimnis eines Menschen* (*A Man's Secret*), by Franz Werfel and novel *Die Frau, nach der man sich sehnt* (*The Woman a Man Longs For*), by Max Brod.

7 The film comedy *Der Fürst von Pappenheim* (*The Masked Mannequin*) premieres, directed by Richard Eichberg, with Curt Bois and Mona Maris.
  Reissner Press publishes the novel *Meister Eckehart*, by Max Muchs.

8 The film drama *Svengali* (based on the novel by George Du Maurier), directed by Gennaro Righelli, with Paul Wegener in the title role and Anita Dorris as Trilby, premieres.

9 At the Berlin Sports Palace, boxer Max Schmeling retains the European cruiserweight title in a bout with Robert Larsen of Denmark, whom Schmeling knocked out in the fourth round.
  Reissner Press publishes memoirs titled *Kämpfe und Ziele* (*Struggles and Goals*), by Friedrich Ebert; Propyläen Press publishes an art history volume *Die Kunst des Realismus und des Impressionismus* (*The Art of Realism and Impressionism*), by Emil Waldmann.

12 *Nation und Staat*, a monthly publication dealing with the problem of minorities in Europe debuts.

13 German Press Institute publishes the novel *Mario und die Tiere* (*Mario and the Animals*), by Waldemar Bonsels.
  The film *Kleinstadtsünder* (*Small Town Sinners*, based on play by Hans Alftred Kihn), directed by Bruno Rahn, with Asta Nielsen and Hermann Picha, premieres.

14 Gutenberg Press publishes the novel *Der Schatz der Sierra Madre* (*The Treasure of the Sierra Madre*), by B. Traven.[8]

15 German Press Institute publishes the novel *Brettspiel des Lebens* (*The Board Game of Life*), by Ernst Zahn; Insel Press publishes the novel *Das Ochsenfurter Männerquartett* (*The Ochsenfurt Men's Quartet*).

16 Two films: *Die selige Exzellenz* (*His Late Excellency*), directed by Adolf Licho, with Olga Chekhova and Willy Fritsch; and *Das Frauenhaus von Rio* (*The Women's House in Rio*, based on a novel by Norbert Jacques), directed by Hans Steinhoff, with Vivian Gibson and Hans Stüwe.

18 The memorial to the Battle of Tannenberg in East Prussia at the beginning of World War I is dedicated; in prepared remarks, President Paul von Hindenburg refuses to acknowledge any German war guilt and claims that

Germany simply used war as a means toward self-determination in a world surrounded by enemies.

19 Two films premiere: *Alpentragödie* (*Alpine Tragedy*), directed by Robert Land, with Lucy Doraine and Fritz Kortner; and the war melodrama *Am Rande der Welt* (*At the Edge of the World*), directed by Karl Grune, with Albert Steinrück and Brigitte Helm.

20 Reissner Press publishes a photography collection titled *Das Berlin Bilderbuch* (*The Berlin Picture Book*), by Heinrich Zille.

21 The operetta *Eine Frau von Format* (*A Wife Made to Order*), by Rudolph Schanzer and Ernst Welisch, premieres at the Theater des Westens in Berlin.

22 Two films premiere: *Die Gefagene von Shanghai* (*The Prisoners of Shanghai*), directed by Geza von Bolvary, with Carmen Boni and Jack Trevor; and *Die weisse Sklavin* (*The White Slave*), directed by Augusto Genina, with Liane Haid and Harry Hardt.

23 The quasi-documentary film *Berlin: Die Sinfonie einer Großstadt* (*Berlin: Symphony of a Great City*), directed by Walter Ruttmann, premieres; a celebration of the German urban landscape is held, concentrating on rhythms of the workday world in Berlin, featuring a montage of exteriors, public transport, and street scenes.

24 Motion Picture Press publishes the extended essay *Hollywood, das Filmparadies* (Hollywood, Paradise of Film), by directors Ernst Lubitsch and E. A. Dupont.

25 Rowohlt Press publishes a volume of biographies titled *Kunst und Schicksal* (*Art and Destiny*) by Emil Ludwig, featuring Beethoven, Balzac, Rembrandt, and Carl Maria von Weber.

29 Reissner Press publishes two books: the biography *Walter Rathenau* by Etta Federn-Kohlhaas and a collection of drawing and graphic work titled *Das Käthe Kollwitz Werk* (*The Work of Käthe Kollwitz*), by Käthe Kollwitz, with an introductory essay by Arthur Bonus.

The film drama *Der Kampf des Donald Westhofs* (*The Trial of Donald Westhof*, based on a novel by Felix Hollaender) premieres, directed by Fritz Wendhausen, with Oskar Homolka and Karin Evans.

30 Two films premiere: the drama *Die Frau im Schrank* (*The Woman in the Closet*, based on a play by Souli Dussieux de Chennevières), directed by Rudolf Biebrach, with Käthe Consee in the title role and Willy Fritsch; and a comedy about radio, *Funkzauber* (*Radio Magic*), directed by Richard Oswald, with Werner Krauss and Xenia Desni.

OCTOBER

1 The political journal *Klassenkampf* (*Class Struggle*) debuts, a publication of news, opinion, and cultural commentary "from the Marxist Standpoint," sponsored by the Social Democratic Party.

Werner Heisenberg is named professor of physics at the University of Leipzig.

The film *Das tanzende Wien* (*Dancing Vienna*) premieres, directed by Fredrich Zelnik, with Lya Mara and Hermann Picha.

2 Eichblatt Press publishes the biography *Hindenburg: Ein Leben der Pflicht* (*Hindenburg: A Life of Duty*), by Hans von Zobeltitz, on the occasion of the Reich president's 80th birthday.

4 Reiss Press publishes the biography *Friedrich der Grosse* (*Frederick the Great*), by Veit Valentin.

The film *Liebesreigen* (*Circle of Lovers*, based on the novel by Ernst Klein) premieres, directed by Rudolf Walther-Fein, with Charlotte Ander and Wilhelm Dieterle.

6 Bergstadt Press publishes the novel *Titus und Timotheus und der Esel Bileam* (*Titus, Timothy, and an Ass Named Bileam*), by Paul Keller.

7 The film *Die Frau mit dem Weltrekord* (*The Woman with the World's Record*) premieres, directed by Erich Waschneck, with Lee Parry and Otto Kronburger.

8 Braumüller Press publishes the political treatise *Feminismus und Kulturuntergang* (*Feminism and Cultural Decline*), by Erhardt Eberhardt.

11 Hübsch Press publishes the architectural treatise *Bauten und Pläne* (*Constructions and Plans*), by architect Bruno Taut.

13 Two films premiere: *Das Erwachen des Weibes* (*The Awakening of Woman*), directed by Fred Sauer, with Margarete Kupfer, Frieda Lehnhoff, and Sybil Morel; and *Leichte Kavallerie* (*Light Cavalry*), directed by Rolf Randolph, with Alfons Fryland and Vivian Gibson.

14 The drama *Schinderhannes*, by Carl Zuckmayer, premieres at the Lessing Theater in Berlin.

Two films premiere: *Die Dame mit dem Tigerfell* (*The Lady in the Tigerskin Coat*), directed by Willi Wolff, with Ellen Richter and Georg Alexander; and film drama about soccer *Die Elf Teufel* (*The Demonic Eleven*), directed by Carl Boese, with Gustav Frölich, Lissy Arna, and Fritz Alberti.

15 The first Nietzsche Congress opens in Weimar, where the keynote speaker is popular author Oswald Spengler.

The drama *Die Wupper* (*The River Wupper*), by Else Lasker-Schüler, premieres at the Berlin State Theater.

Monthly magazine *Der Tanz* debuts, chronicling dance productions, dancers, and choreographers in Germany.

17 Reissner Press publishes *Volk in Not! Das Unheil des Abtreibungsparagraphen §218* (*Public Emergency! The Calamity of Abortion Law, Paragraph 218 in the German Penal Code*), by Carl Crede, with illustrations by Käthe Kollwitz.

18 Carl von Ossietzky is named editor of *Die Weltbühne* literary magazine; Westermann Press publishes the novel *Die Kinder Israel* (*The Children of Israel*), by Werner Jansen; Grethlein Press publishes a collection of fiction titled *Die Unsichtbaren* (*The Unseen*), by Isolde Kurz.

Author Heinrich Mann presents lecture at Theater am Nollendorf Platz denouncing the arrest of Germans on political grounds and demands the release of all those he terms political prisoners.

19 German version of the drama *Singing Jailbirds*, by Upton Sinclair, translated by John Heartfield, premieres at the Breslau City Theater.

20 The first German soccer film drama *Die Elf Teufel* (*The Eleven Devils*), directed by Carl Boese, with Gustav Fröhlich, Evelyn Holt, and Fritz Alberti, premieres.

21 The First Greater German Homeland Congress is held in Frankfurt am Main.

22 Wolff Press publishes the fragmentary novel *Amerika*, by Franz Kafka, edited by Max Brod.

24 Kösel und Pastet Press publishes the cultural treatise *The Jews*, by Hilaire Belloc, translated by Theodor Häcker-Hennich.

25 Kiepenheier Press publishes the novel *Pep: J. L. Wetcheeks amerikanisches Liederbuch* (*Pep: J. L. Wetcheek's American Songbook*), by Lion Feuchtwanger.

26 Union Press publishes the novel *Jesuiten des Königs* (*The King's Jesuits*), by Werner von der Schulenberg.

27 Two films premiere: *Die weisse Spinne* (*The White Spider*), directed by Carl Boese, with Maria Paudler and Walter Rilla; and *Die tolle Lola* (*Crazy Lola*), directed by Richard Eichberg, with Lilian Harvey and Harry Halm.

28 The film drama *Die Berühmte Frau* (*The Famous Wife*) premieres, directed by Robert Wiene, with Lissy Arna and Alexander Granach.

29 The detective film drama *Der Geisterzug* (*The Ghost Train*, based on the play by Arnold Ridley) premieres, directed by Geza von Bolvary, with Ilse Bois and Louis Ralph.

31 The drama *Die Petroleuminsel* (*The Petroleum Islands*), by Lion Feuchtwanger, premieres at Hamburg Deutsches Schauspielhaus.

NOVEMBER

1 Welt Press publishes the historical survey *Juden auf der deutschen Bühne* (*Jews on the German Stage*), by Arnold Zweig.[9]

The film drama *§182 minderjährig* (*Paragraph 182: Age of Consent*), directed by Ernst Winar, with Colette Brettel and Gerhard Ritterbrand, premieres.

2 Piper Press publishes a collection of parodies titled *Die Schallmühle* (*The Noise Mill*), by Christian Morgenstern.

The film drama *Die Ausgestossenen* (*Caught in Berlin's Underworld*) premieres, directed by Martin Berger, with Fritz Kortner and Maly Delschaft.

4 The drama *Revolte auf Höhe 3018* (*Revolt at Altitude 3,018 Meters*), by Ödön von Horvath, premieres at Hamburg Kammerspiele.

6 The weekly publication *Film-Magazin* debuts, aimed at the popular market of German film-goers.

7 The romantic film drama *Anwalt des Herzens* (*Attorney for the Heart*) premieres, directed by Wilhelm Thiele, with Lil Dagover and Ernst Stahl-Nachbaur.

8 Almathea Press publishes a two-volume history of World War I in the years 1916–1918 titled *The Crisis* by Winston Churchill, translated by Count Hans Czernin and Carl Zell.

The film melodrama *Hast Du geliebt am schönen Rhein* (*Did You Fall in Love along the Beautiful Rhine*) premieres, directed by James Bauer, with Dorothea Wieck and Oscar Marion.

9 Two films premiere: *Die grosse Pause* (*The Long Intermission*, based on the play by Oskar Blumenthal), directed by Carl Froelich, with Henny Porten and Walter Slezak; and *Wochenendzauber* (*Weekend Magic*), directed by Rudolf Walther-Fein, with Lissy Arna and Harry Liedtke.

12 The documentary theater piece *Rasputin, die Romanows, der Krieg, und das Volk, das gegen sie aufstand* (*Rasputin, the Romanovs, the War, and the People who Rose against them*), by Alexei Tolstoy at the Piscator Stage at the Theater am Nollendorf Platz in Berlin.

14 The pulp magazine *Wahre Geschichten* (*True Stories*) debuts, an imitation of the American publication *True Story Magazine*, featuring such stories as "Confessions of a Chorus Girl," articles about athletes and other prominent individuals, and advertisements for women's undergarments.

17 Director Max Reinhardt embarks on a second American tour featuring spectacular productions of *A Midsummer Night's Dream* and *Everyman*.

Meyer and Jessen Press publishes *Memoirs*, by Josephine Baker, translated by Lilly Ackermann.

18 The German premiere of the opera *The Sunken Bell*, by Ottorino Respighi, opens at Hamburg Deutsches Schauspielhaus.

Engelhorn Press publishes the novel *Die Streiche des Junkers Marius* (*The Escapades of Squire Marius*), by Roda Roda and the novella *Der Kampf mir dem Engel* (*The Battle with the Angel*), by Frank Theiss.

19 Otto Klemperer is named director of the Kroll Opera House in Berlin.

25 The film drama *Die Dollarprinzessin und ihr sechs Freier* (*The Dollar Princess and her Six Admirers*) premieres, directed by Felix Basch, with Liane Haid, Georg Alexander, Hans Albers, and Leopold von Ledebur.

Rowohlt Press publishes the comic novel *Mit fünf PS* (*On Five Horsepower*), by Kurt Tucholsky; Gretlein Press publishes the two-volume historical survey of German cities and towns titled *Im alten Reich*, by Ricarda Huch.

28 Zsolnay Press publishes the novel *Buschow* by Carl Sternheim; Langen Press publishes the drama *Ordnung im Chaos* (*Order in Chaos*), by Walter von Molo.

30 The film melodrama *Schwere Jungs–leichte Mädchen* (*Tough Guys, Easy Girls*, based on a novel by Felix Salten), directed by Carl Boese, with Gustav Fröhlich and Lissy Arna, premieres.

DECEMBER

1 Two films premiere: crime thriller *Der falsche Prinz* (*The Counterfeit Prince*), directed by Heinz Paul, with Harry Domela and Mary Kid; and *Das Mädchen mit den Fünf Nuller* (*The Girl and the Five Nobodies*), directed by Curtis Bernhardt, with Marcel Salzer and Viola Garden.

Eher Press publishes the two-volume compendium on National Socialism: *Die nationalsozialistische Bibliothek* (*The National Socialist Library*) and *Das Program des NSDAP und seine weltanschaulichen Grundlagen* (*The Program of the NSDAP and its Global Perspectives*), by Gottfried Feder.

2 Reissner Press publishes the photography volume *Bilder vom alten und neuen Berlin* (*Pictures of the Old and New Berlin*), by Heinrich Zille; Cassirer Press publishes a volume of new lithographs titled *Macbeth*, by Max Slevogt.

6 The film drama *Die Liebe der Jeanne Ney* (*The Lusts of the Flesh*) premieres, directed by G. W. Pabst, with Edith Jehanne and Vladimir Sokolov.

8 Avalun Press publishes a historical survey of the Wilhelmine Reich titled *Von Versailles nach Versailles* (*From Versailles to Versailles*), by Maximilian Harden.

Three films premiere: the drama *Dr. Bessels Verwandlung* (*Dr. Bessel's Transformation*), directed by Richard Oswald, with Jakob Tiedke and Sophie Pagay; *Eheskandal im Hause Fromont und Risler* (*Marriage Scandal in the Houses of Fromont and Risler*, based on the novel by Alphonse Daudet), with Lucy Doraine, Peter Leska, and Ivan Hedquist; and *Das Geheimnis des Abbey X* (*Behind the Altar*), directed by Wilhelm Dieterle, with Wilhelm Dieterle and Marcella Albani.

10 Pacifist and president of the German Peace Society Ludwig Quidde shares the Nobel Peace Prize with French pacifist Ferdinand Buisson.

13 Two films premiere: *Die Spielerin* (*The Lady Gambler*), directed by Graham Curtis, with Gerturd de Lalsky and Harry Liedtke; and *Die geliebte des Gouverneurs* (*The Governor's Lover*), directed by Friedrich Feher, with Fritz Kortner and Magda Sonja.

14 Schmiede Press publishes a collection of theater criticism titled *Die vereinsamte Theaterkritik* (*Lonely Theater Criticism*), by Herbert Ihering.

15 West German Radio broadcasts an entire evening of readings featuring the works of American novelist Jack London.

16 The film comedy *Eine Freundin braucht jeder Mann* (*Every Husband Needs a Girlfriend*) premieres, directed by Paul Hiedemann, with Paul Heidemann and Vera Schmiterlöw.

17 Fischer Press publishes the memoir titled *Es sei wie es wolle, es war doch so schön* (*Be What it May, It was Still so Beautiful*), by theater critic Alfred Kerr.

20 Two film comedies premiere: *Der fröhliche Weinberg* (*The Merry Vineyard*, based on the comedy by Carl Zuckmayer), directed by Jakob and Luise Fleck, with Rudolf Rittner, Camilla Horn, and Lotte Neumann; and *Der grosse Sprung* (*The Big Leap*), directed by Arnold Fanck, with Leni Riefenstahl and Luis Trenker.

23 The operetta *Evelyne*, by Bruno Granischstaedten, premieres at the Deutsches Künstler Theater in Berlin.

The comedy *Erotik*, by Alxeander Lertmet-Holena, premieres at the Komödie Theater in Berlin.

25 The musical revue *Bei uns um die Gedächtniskirche rum* (*At Our Place near the Memorial Church*), by Moriz Seeler and Friedrich Hollaender, premieres at the Berliner Theater in Berlin.

Two operettas premiere: *Heute nacht . . . eventuell* (*And Tonight . . . Sometime*), by Walter Bromme at the Neues Theater am Zoo in Berlin and *Die blonde Liselotte* (*Blonde Liselotte*), by Eduard Künneke at the Altenburg Regional Theater.

NOTES

1. *Metropolis* became a signal cultural accomplishment of the Weimar Republic (and a modernist emblem besides) because director Lang exploited the medium of film rather than create a conventional narrative. Lang's cinematographer Karl Freund and special effects director/designer Erich Kettelhut employed optics technology to allow human figures to mingle within miniature settings–thus avoiding re-editing in a laboratory–to achieve the desired distorted effect. The result depicts a hallucinatory dystopia that several scholars and critics consider the first great science-fiction film. It was certainly not the first science fiction film, but it was precedent-setting depiction of what a city of the future will be like: a Gomorrah of efficiency, redeemed only by a hero who somehow gets into the inner workings of the place and attempts to destroy it. Lang used more than 35,000 extras in a movie whose plot made little sense–but whose images were riveting to the point of hypnosis. Production costs for the movie far outstripped budgets and many observers later claimed that *Metropolis* drove the Ufa film studios into another round of bankruptcy negotiations.

2. *Jonny spielt auf* quickly became the biggest musical success of 1927, as 45 theaters did productions of the show; in the 1927–1928 season alone, the work was performed more than 400 times. It continued running in dozens of theaters through the life of the Weimar Republic, spurred by popular demand. The show's most familiar and popular tune, "Leb' wohl, mein Schatz" ("So long, darling") soon became a standard for dance hall orchestras under the title "Jonny's Blues" and was a best-selling record on 78-rpm discs. The opera became a benchmark for the popularity of the jazz idiom in German culture; it was also among the first to make a distinct "cross-over" into popular culture outlets, such as radio, newsreels, and movies. Orchestras in movie theatres, for example, often played music from *Jonny spielt auf* regardless of what film was to follow. Right-wing cultural defenders denounced the show, citing it as one more example of how "jungle music" was invading and degrading German culture.

3. Hugenberg's stated goal in taking over the Ufa company was to impose a more nationalistic mentality in the German film industry. He was a cofounder of the Pan-German League and an influential member of the right-wing German National Peoples' Party. Concerned that liberal and left-leaning publishers might attempt to take over German film-making enterprises, and likewise convinced of the growing power of new media to shape public opinion, he was determined to become a prominent player. He was also worried that American companies might again involve themselves in German film production; since nearly all American film companies were owned or operated by Jews, Hugenberg wanted to make sure that at least one prominent studio would remain in German hands. With the deal came 134 German movie theaters and two large production complexes in Tempelhof and Neubabelsberg.

4. Karl Vollmöller wrote *Das Mirakel* in 1911, but it is best known as the massive spectacle that saved Max Reinhardt from bankruptcy in 1924. It was based on a medieval legend about a nun who leaves her convent and runs away with an errant knight, only to experience several inexplicable events that she considers miracles. The people whom she encounters, however, accuse her of witchcraft and she returns to convent life. The real miracle occurs back in her monastery, where a statue of the Virgin Mary comes to life and takes the nun's place in the convent until she returns. Reinhardt staged it initially in Berlin and took it to London for a successful run in 1912. He revived it for an American tour in 1924, beginning with a six-month residence on Broadway with Werner Krauss; it then went on a limited tour of residences in Detroit, Milwaukee, and Dallas. In America, another miracle occurred: Reinhardt made so much money from the tour that he was able to refinance his Berlin properties and remain in business until the end of the Weimar Republic.

5. Many critics have argued that Hermann Hesse's *Der Steppenwolf* is a distinct cultural artifact of the Weimar Republic. Its structure as a literary collage is one manifestation of modernism's rejection of causal narrative, and the Weimar period is closely associated with the embrace of modernist tendencies in numerous fields of cultural activity. The fragmentation modernism espoused is also abundant in characters of *Der Steppenwolf*, who randomly appear and then depart with little evident motivation. Their identities furthermore shift according to a particular idea Hesse wants

to explore in different passages of the novel. But other aspects of the novel seem to operate in isolation, outside the Weimar era. There is little or no direct reference to the 1920s in the novel, to the great war that had preceded those years, the collapse of the "old order," the intolerable economic conditions in Germany, nor to the suicidal fractiousness of German politics that prevailed throughout the decade.

6. Carry Brachvogel (Caroline Hellmann, 1864–1942) was one of several female German writers whose careers began in the late 19th century and continued successfully well into the Weimar period and are today largely forgotten. The author of more than 40 books, plays, essays, and fiction works, her writing covered a wide spectrum of subjects and topics of interest.

7. This film had the same title as a 1920 film directed by Conrad Wiene. Both were based on a novel by Honoré de Balzac (1799–1850), titled *Splendeurs et misères des courtisanes*, sometimes translated as *The Harlot, High and Low*. Balzac's novels were extremely popular in the Weimar Republic, and not only as reading material. They, along with novels by Balzac's contemporary Eugéne Sue (1804–1854), often formed the basis of silent film melodramas, largely because their plot outlines were so accessible and because they frequently depicted crime, drugs, gambling, prostitution, and social disintegration. Those themes became more prevalent as subject matter in the Weimar Republic during the later 1920s.

8. Little is known about the novelist B. Traven. It is generally agreed that he was born in Germany in the 1880s and by the 1920s was living in Mexico. It is certain that he wrote originally in German and his novels about rural life in Mexico were first published in Germany; he refused to divulge personal details about himself. Among his most significant work published during the Weimar Republic besides *The Treasure of the Sierra Madre* (which subsequently became the basis of a Warner Brothers film directed by John Huston, with his father Walter Huston, Humphrey Bogart, and Tim Holt) were *Das Totenschiff* (*The Death Ship*, 1926), *Der Karren* (*The Tumbrel*, 1931), *Regierung* (*Government*, 1931), and *Die weisse Rose* (*The White Rose*, 1931). Most of his fictional works contained spare, undecorated descriptions of human suffering, often coupled with accounts of deceit and cruelty.

9. Zweig claimed in his 300-page survey that "the Jew" was not European but Mediterranean by nature, who, finding himself in a foreign environment, seeks to release his tension by means of theatrical performance. He also notes that Jewish actors in Germany were often from the farther reaches of the Austro-Hungarian Empire and thus present on the German stage by virtue of historical "anomaly." Yet many notable non-Jewish actors came likewise from provincial German-speaking enclaves; they had done so since the 18th century. Many prominent Jewish actors came furthermore from cosmopolitan centers, such as the Austro-Hungarian capital Vienna, while others hailed directly from major German cities. Right-wing and nationalist groups sometimes used Zweig's claims to bolster their own arguments that German culture was being "jewified," citing the prominence of Jewish directors and producers whose authority extended to casting, production formats, and repertoire selection.

1928

JANUARY

1 Approximately 2.1 million Germans hold licenses to own radio sets.

2 Gretlein Press publishes the memoir *Was mich das Leben lehrte* (*What Life Has Taught Me*), by poet Lisa Wenger.

6 A new production of Henrik Ibsen's *Peer Gynt* opens at the Deutsches Theater in celebration of the 100th anniversary of the Norwegian playwright's birth, featuring Werner Krauss in the title role.

Max Schmeling becomes the European heavyweight champion in a bout with Italian champion Michel Bonagila; Schmeling knocks out Bonagila in the first round.

8 Hundreds attend a program at the Volksbühne in Berlin in protest against the arrest and detention of author Johannes R. Becher for writing and publishing the books *Der Leichnam auf dem Thron* (*The Corpse on the Throne*) and *Der einzig gerechte Krieg* (*The Only Justifiable War*).

The drama *Heimweh* (*Homesick*), by Franz Jung, premieres at Piscator Stage of the Theater am Nollendorf Platz in Berlin.

10 Beltz Presses publishes a five-volume compendium titled *Handbuch der Pedagogik* (*Handbook of Pedagogy*), by Hermann Nohl and Ludwig Pallat.

The Prussian Academy of the Arts names writers Alfred Döblin and Fritz von Unruh as new members.

11 The German version of the opera *Antigone* (based on the tragedy by Sophocles, adapted by Jean Cocteau), by Arthur Honegger, premieres at Essen City Opera.

The film drama *Die Leibeigenen* (*The Serfs*) premieres, directed by Richard Eichberg, with Heinrich George and Mona Maris.

13 The Communist Party establishes its "Peoples' Film League," aimed at producing and exhibiting films that arouse the working class in Germany against capitalism and solidify class consciousness.

14 A film studio scandal results in resignation of Defense Minister Otto Gessler; he admits manipulating government funds to rescue the bankrupt Phöbus Film Corp. and using the money to finance illegal military exercises and weapons development.

Horen Press publishes the collected letters of Carl Hautpmann under the title *Leben mit Freunden* (*Life with Friends*).

15 The Reformation Party, a political party dedicated to opposing Marxism and forming a cultural counterweight to the Catholic Center Party, is formed.

16 The historical film drama *Königin Luise* (*Queen Luise*) Part II premieres, directed by Karl Grune, with Mady Christians as Queen Luise of Prussia and Mathis Wiemann as her husband King Friedrich Wilhelm II.

Playwright Gerhart Hauptmann changes his mind and accepts membership in the Prussian Academy of the Arts.

19 The film drama *Ich hatte einst ein schönes Vaterland* (*Once I Had a Beautiful Fatherland*) premieres, directed by Max Mack, with Alexander Granach and Charles Willy Kayser.

21 "All Comedy Night" premieres at the Berlin Sports Palace, as 100 comedians perform their work before thousands needing laughs. Headliners are Munich comedians Karl Vallentin[1] and Lisl Karlstadt.

Braun Press publishes a compendium titled *Internationaler Faschismus* (*International Fascism*) with chapters on the Fascist movement in Italy, Germany, Hungary, Spain, France, and Russia, with excerpts from speeches by Benito Mussolini.

The comedy *Das Haar in der Ehe* (*A Hair in the Marriage*), by Julius Knopf, premieres at Frankfurt am Main City Theater.

23 The multimedia antiwar performance piece *Die Abenteuer des braven Soldat Schwejks* (*The Adventures of Good Soldier Schweik*, based on the novel by Czech satirist Jaroslav Hasek) opens at Piscator Stage at the Theater am Nollendorf Platz in Berlin.

The film melodrama *Die Hölle der Jungfrauen* (*The Virgins' Hell*) premieres, directed by Robert Dinesen, with Werner Krauss and Dagny Servaes.

25 Eysler Press publishes the memoir *Die Berliner Schnauze* (*Berlin's Agreeable Bullshit*), by Paul Simmel; Rowohlt Press publishes the novel *Film und Lebern Barbara La Narr* (*The Film and Life of Barbara La Narr*), by Arnolt Bronnen.

26 Titania Film Palace opens in Berlin, featuring 2,000 seats and a futuristic 120-foot light spire that houses over 160,000 lightbulbs.

27 President Hindenburg declares to the Reichstag that under no circumstances is his Administration prepared to commemorate or even observe the Republic's 10th anniversary.

28 The comedy *Der Präsident* (*The President*), by Georg Kaiser, premieres at the Frankfurt City Theater.

The historical film drama *Der alte Fritz: Ausklang* (*Old Fritz: The Finale*) premieres, directed by Gerhard Lamprecht, with Otto Gebühr as Frederick the Great, nicknamed "Old Fritz" and Julia Serda.

FEBRUARY

1 Hugo Correll is named production chief of the newly reorganized Ufa Film Studios

The German Press Institute publishes the treatise *Ludendorff auf dem Kriegspfade gegen die deutsche Freimauerei* (*Ludendorff on the Path to War against German Freemasonry*), by German National Lodge of Freemasonry in Berlin.

The film *Schinderhannes* (*Prince of Rogues*, based on the play by Carl Zuckmayer), directed by Curtis Bernhardt, with Hans Stüwe and Lissy Arna, premieres.

2 Kiepenheuer Press publishes the drama *Toboggan* by Gerhard Menzel.

4 German premiere of drama *Der Turm* (*The Tower*), by Hugo von Hofmannsthal at Prince Regent's Theater in Munich.

Walter Gropius submits his resignation as director of Bauhaus School in Dessau.

5 The comedy *Leinen aus Irland* (*Irish Linen* by Stefan Kamare) premieres at Munich Residenz Theater.

8 The film *Die Pflicht zu schweigen* (*The Duty to Remain Silent*) premieres, directed by Carl Wilhelm, with Gustav Fröhlich and Vivian Gibson.

Zsolnay Press publishes the sports novel *Sport um Gagaly*, by Kasimir Edschmid.

10 Radio telephone interchange is established between Germany and United States.

14 The film *Ledige Mutter* (*Single Mother*) premieres, directed by Fred Sauer, with Lilian Hardt and Werner Füetterer.

Novelist and neurologist Alfred Döblin presents two lectures at the national assembly of Society for Sex Reform titled "Your Body Belongs to You, No One Else" and "The Class Conflict behind Anti-Abortion Laws."

15 Kolk Press publishes a book of cartoons by fighter pilot Ernst Udet titled *Hals- und Beinbruch!* (*Break a Leg!*); Udet was a member of Baron Manfred von Richtoffen's "Flying Circus" squadron and became the second-most decorated pilot in World War I.

16 The historical film *Luther*, directed by Hans Kyser, with Eugen Klöpfer as Martin Luther and Teodor Loos as Philipp Melanchton, premieres.

17 The film melodrama *Mädchen, hütet Euch!* (*Girls, Protect Yourselves!*), directed by Valy Arnheim, with Hanni Weisse and Gitta Ley, premieres.

18 The one-act opera *Der Zar lässt sich photographieren* (*The Czar Gets his Picture Taken*), by Kurt Weill, premieres at Leipzig City Opera.

The film comedy *Dragonerliebchen* (*Darling of the Dragoons*) premieres, directed by Rudolf Walther-Fein, with Maria Paudler and Harry Liedtke.

19 The opera *Armer Columbus* (*Poor Columbus*), by Erwin Dressel, premieres at Kassel State Theater.

20 Rowohlt Press publishes the *Politische Novellen* (*Political Novellas*), by Bruno Frank; Merlin Press publishes the political biography *Mussolini und sein Faschismus* (*Mussolini and His Fascism*), by Kurt Gutkind.

22 The film melodrama *Therese Raquin* (*Shadows of Fear*, a German-French coproduction) premieres, directed by Jacques Feyder, with Gina Manés and Wolfgang Zilzer.

23 The detective film *Panik* premieres, directed by Harry Piel, with Harry Piel and Dary Holm.

24 The world ice hockey tournament begins at the Berlin Sports Palace, one of the few venues in Germany with the capacity to accommodate large crowds for the sport.

Kiepenheuer Press publishes the autobiography *Mein Leben in dieser Zeit* (*My Life in These Times*), by Arthur Holitscher.

25 The German version of the oratorio *Oedipus Rex*, by Igor Stravinsky, premieres.

28 Ullstein Press publishes a novel about the Chinese Yüan Dynasty *Räuber und Soldaten* (*Robbers and Soldiers*, based on the novel by Guanzhong Luo), by Albert Ehrenstein.

MARCH

1 Scherl Press publishes the novel *Die Unbekannte* (*The Unknown Woman*), by Rudolf Stratz; Bong Press publishes the novel *Der hillige Ginsterbusch* (*The Crooked Broom Shrub*), by Felicitas Rose.

2 The German premiere of the opera *Das Märchen vom Zar Saltan* (*The Tale of Czar Saltan*), by Nikolai Rimsky-Korsakov opens at the Aachen City Theater.

The Volksbühne organization assumes the lease of the Lessing Theater in Berlin and names Erwin Piscator as its director.

7 Fischer Press publishes a poetry collection titled *Krisis* (*Crisis: Pages from a Diary*), by Hermann Hesse.

8 Two operettas premiere at the Mainz City Theater: *Der falsche Harlekin* (*The Counterfeit Harlequin*), by Gian-Francesco Malpiero, and *Die Prizessin auf der Erbse* (*The Princess and the Pea*), by Ernst Toch.

The film melodrama *Liebe und Diebe* (*Love and Thieves*), directed by Carl Froelich, with Henny Porten and Paul Bildt, premieres.

9 The German version of the comedy *Broadway*, by Philip Dunning and George Abbott, premieres at the Komödie Theater in Berlin.

The German premiere of the ballet *Liebeslist* (*The Art of Love*), by Alexander Glasunov, opens at the Chemnitz City Theater.

The film comedy *Der Biberpelz* (*The Beaver Coat*, adapted from comedy by Gerhart Hauptmann) premieres, directed by Erich Schönfelder, with Lucie Höflich and Ralph Arthur Roberts.

10 The Albrecht Dürer retrospective exhibition opens at the Prussian Academy of the Arts.

13 The drama *Oktobertag* (*One Day in October*), by Georg Kaiser, premieres at Hamburg Kammerspiele.

16 The detective film drama *Der grösste Gauner des Jahrhunderts* (*The Criminal of the Century*) premieres, directed by Max Obal, with Hans Albers and Vivian Gibson.

17 The film *Sechs Mädchen suchen Nachtquartier* (*Six Girls and a Room for the Night*) premieres, directed by Hans Behrendt, with Ilse Baumann,

Hilde Hildebrand, Jenny Jugo, Ilse Mindt, Ellen Plessow, and Else Wasa in the title roles.

19 Sieben Stäbe Press publishes the commemorative compendium *Zehn Jahre deutsche Republik* (*Ten Years of Republican Government in Germany*), by Anton Erkelnez.

20 Spaeth Press publishes the biography *Stefan Zweig*, by Erwin Rieger.

Reclam Press publishes a new edition of the complete works of playwright Henrik Ibsen, translated by Ludwig Passarge, on the occasion of the 100th anniversary of Ibsen's birth.

22 The opera *Schlag zwölf* (*At the Stroke of Twelve*), by Franz Ludwig, premieres at the Münster City Theater.

23 The operetta *Äffchen* (*Little Ape*), by Robert Gilbert, premieres at the Dresden Central Theater.

24 An exhibition of new work by architect Erich Mendelssohn (designer of the Einstein Tower in Potsdam) opens at the Neumann-Nierendorf Gallery in Berlin.

26 The comedy *Pioniere in Ingolstadt*, by Marieluise Fleisser, premieres at the Dresden Komödie Theater.

The Beethoven Prize is awarded to composers Arnold Ludwig Mendelssohn and Henrich Kaminski.

27 Fischer Press publishes the novel *Therese* by Arthur Schnitzler.

28 The drama *Schinderhannes*, by Joseph Velter, premieres at the Trier City Theater.

30 The German premiere of operetta *Rose Marie*, by Rudolf Friml, opens at the Admiral's Palace Theater in Berlin.

Kiepenheuer Press publishes the novel *Josef sucht seine Freiheit* (*Joseph Searches for His Freedom*), by Hermann Kesten.

APRIL

1 Hannes Meyer is named successor to Walter Gropius as director of the Bauhaus School in Dessau.

The operetta *Die grosse Kaiserin* (*The Great Empress*), by Walter Kollo, premieres at Theater der Komiker in Berlin.

2 The German premiere of the film *Ten Days that Shook the World*, directed by Sergei Eisenstein, creates a sensation among Communist Party members and leftist sympathizers in Berlin; a 70-piece orchestra plays the film's score by Dimitri Shostakovich at the luxurious Tauentzien Palace Film Theater.

4 Fischer Press publishes the novel *Daphne* by Annette Kolb.

The film melodrama *Evas Töchter* (*Daughters of Eve*) premieres, directed by Carl Lamac, with Anny Ondra, Steffi Vida, and May Manja.

11 The city of Nuremburg declares itself seat of "Dürer Year" with an exhibition of native son (born 1471 in Nuremberg, died 1528 in Nuremberg) Albrecht Dürer's work extant in the city.

13 First nonstop fixed-wing westbound flight across the North Atlantic takes place; German pilot Hermann Köhl, Irish copilot James Fitzmaurice, and navigator Baron Günther von Hünefeld fly single-engine Junkers aircraft from Ireland to Newfoundland in 36.5 hours; German newspapers celebrate the event for days.

14 The drama *Der letzte Kaiser* (*The Last Kaiser*) premieres, by Jean Richard Bloch at the Berliner Theater in Berlin.

The opera *Frühlings erwachen* (*Spring's Awakening*, based on the play by Frank Wedekind), by Max Ettinger, premieres at the Leipzig Neues Theater.

17 Weller Press publishes a collection of poetry titled *Herz auf Taille* (*Heart on His Sleeve*), by Erich Kästner, with illustrations by Erich Ohser.

19 The comedy *Gré*, by Hadrian Maria Netto, premieres at the Weimar National Theater.

Reissner Press publishes the biography *Stresemann* by Baron Rochus von Rheinbaben.

The film comedy *Die Durchgängerin* (*The Runaway Girl*, based on the comedy by Ludwig Fulda) premieres, directed by Hanns Schwarz, with Käthe von Nagy in the title role and Mathias Wiemann.

20 The two "Five Minute Operas," by Darius Milhaud, premiere at Wiesbaden State Theater: *Die verlassene Ariadne* (*Ariadne Abandoned*) and *Der befreite Theseus* (*Theseus Liberated*).

The Christian Service Party, a Lutheran political organization dedicated to opposing Hitler and National Socialism, is formed.

Zsolnay Press publishes a volume of poetry *Heimweh* (*Homesick*), by Jakob Haringer.

21 The German premiere of the opera *König Poros* (*King Pros*), by Georg Friedrich Händel, opens at the Braunschweig Regional Theater.

The drama *Der Frühling* (*Spring*), by sculptor Ernst Barlach, premieres at the Königsberg City Theater.

22   Lehmann Press publishes the treatise *Kunst und Rasse* (*Art and Race*), by Paul Schultze-Naumburg.[2]

23   The adventure film *Flucht aus der Hölle* (*Escape from Hell*) premieres, directed by Georg Asagaroff, with Fritz Alberti and Agnes Esterhazy.

25   Experimental school lessons are broadcast in the afternoon to children from radio studios in Königswusterhausen.

Rowohlt Press publishes a biography of Jesus titled *Der Menschensohn* (*The Son of Man*), by Emil Ludwig.

27   The jazz revue *Tempo Tausend!*, assembled by Friedrich Hollaender, premieres at the Renaissance Theater in Berlin.

The film melodrama *Die Dame in schwarz* (*The Lady in Black*) premieres, directed by Franz Osten, with Liane Haid and Erich Kaiser-Titz.

28   The State Opera in Berlin reopens after renovations and remodeling with a new production of *Die Zauberflöte* (*The Magic Flute*), by Wolfgang Amadeus Mozart.

The comedy *Arm wie ein Kirchenmaus* (*Poor as a Church Mouse*), by Ladislas Fodor, premieres at the Breslau Lobe Theater.

29   The drama *Judas*, by Erich Mühsam, premieres at Piscator Stage of the Theater am Nollendorf Platz in Berlin.

30   Cassirer Press publishes a collection of lithographs titled *Studien aus Spanien* (*Studies of Spain*), by Emil Orlik.

MAY

2   The German Press Institute publishes the memoir *Aus der Jugendzeit* (*From My Youth*), by Rudolf Presber.

5   Two short operas and one operetta by Ernst Krenek premiere at Wiesbaden State Theater; the former are *Das geheime Königreich* (*The Secret Kingdom*) and *Der Diktator* (*The Dictator*); the latter is *Schwergewicht* (*Heavyweight*).

9   Former Chancellor and Nobel Prize-winner, German Peoples' Party leader and Foreign Minister Gustav Stresemann is taken to the hospital in Berlin; mindful of the disruption in public life following the death of President Friedrich Ebert, many newspapers in Berlin publish extra editions covering his illness.

11 The first German television broadcast is transmitted from studios in Wilmersdorf to reception facilities in Charlottenburg, a distance of about four miles.

12 First international Press (print media) Exhibition opens in Cologne.

13 The drama *Der Schneesturm* (*The Snow Storm*), by Otto Zoff, premieres at the Theater am Schiffbauerdamm in Berlin.

15 The film *Cassanovas Erben* (*The Heirs of Cassanova*) premieres, directed by Manfred Noa, with Harry Hardt, Maly Delschaft, and Kurt Gerron.

21 The film melodrama *Die Sünderin* (*The Sinner*) premieres, directed by Mario Bonnard, with Elisabeth Pinajeff and Hans Stüwe.

Müller Press publishes the novel *Bankhaus Reichenbach* (*The Reichenbach Banking Firm*), by Artur Landesberger.

25 The novel *Sohn seines Landes* (*His Country's Son*), by Walter Bloem, is serialized in the Berlin newspaper *Illustriete Zeitung*.

26 Street fighting between members of the Red Front militia and Berlin police breaks out; later in the day, police ban the Red Front from meeting or organizing in Berlin.

31 Piscator Stage at the Theater am Nollendorfplatz declares bankruptcy.

JUNE

2 The opera *1000 Jahre Hamburg* (*Hamburg's Millenium*) premieres at the Hamburg Popular Opera House.

5 Gustav Hartman, a horse-drawn carriage driver in Berlin, arrives in Paris at the end of a protest journey in his carriage to demonstrate against termination of horse-drawn coach services in Berlin and against growing automobile traffic everywhere; Hartmann later becomes known as "Iron Gustav" in the novel of the same name by Hans Fallada.

6 The opera *Die ägyptische Helena* (*The Egyptian Helen*), by Richard Strauss (libretto by Hugo von Hofmannsthal), premieres at the Semper Opera House in Dresden.

8 The film prison drama *Notschrei hinter Gittern* (*Cry for Help behind Bars*) premieres, directed by Franz Hofer, with Hans Mierendorff and Theodor Loos.

9 The operetta *Die singende Venus* (*The Singing Venus*), by Eduard Künneke, premieres at the Breslau City Theater.

13 The German Peoples' Service Press publishes a treatise titled *Bismarcks Bündnissystem und seine Lehren* (*Bismarck's System of Foreign Relations and Its Lessons*), by Count Albrecht zu Stolberg-Wernigerode.

15 Reich Radio Corp. purchases a large tract of land for the construction of its broadcast offices and studios, a further indication of radio's ability to attract investment and bank financing.

Foreign Minister Gustav Stresemann enters convalescent hospital in the Black Forest, an occurrence many newspapers note with optimism.

20 Gretlein Press publishes the travel memoir *Weltgesicht* (*The Face of the World*), by Walter Bloem.

The film comedy *Fräulein Chauffeur* (*The Lady Chauffeur*) premieres, directed by Jaap Speter, with Mady Christians and Johannes Riemann.

22 The Reichstag stages a reception for the trans-Atlantic pilots Günther von Hünfeld and Hermann Köhl.

24 Klemm Press publishes the biography *Rathenau: Sein Leben und sein Werk* (*Rathenau: His Life and Work*), by Count Harry Kessler; the book renews contentious debate about Rathenau and the role of German Jews in high office.

28 The drama *Hinterhaus Legende* (*Legends of the Inner Courtyard*), by Dietzenschmidt, premieres at the Schiller Theater in Berlin.

30 The Karl May[3] Museum opens in Radebeul, Saxony.

JULY

1 The musical revue *Reise durch Berlin in 40 Stunden* (*A Trip through Berlin in 40 Hours*) premieres at the Lustspielhaus in Berlin.

3 Koehler and Amelang Press publishes the travel memoir *Seeteufel erobert Amerika* (*Sea Devil Conquers America*), by Count Felix Luckner; Luckner was a naval officer in World War I whose exploits earned him the sobriquet "Sea Devil."

The film comedy *Die Dame und ihr Chauffeur* (*The Lady and her Chauffeur*) premieres, directed by Manfred Noa, with Elisabeth Pinajeff and Jack Trevor.

8 Deutsche Luftschiffahrts-AG (German Airship Company, known as DELAG) completes construction LZ 127, its first dirigible airship since the war and christens it *Graf Zeppelin* in honor of the man who founded the company, Count Ferdinand von Zeppelin. It is the largest airship ever built, with an overall length of 776 feet and a capacity of 3 million cubic feet of hydrogen gas.

10 Steegemann Press publishes the satire *Die voll und ganz vollkommene Ehe* (*The Fully and Quite Fully Consummate Marriage*), by Hans Reimann.

11 The musical revue *Es kommt jeder dran* (*Everyone Gets a Turn*), by Fredrich Hollaender, premieres at the Deutsches Künstlerhaus in Berlin.

12 Ullstein Press publishes the novel *Wohin rollst Du, Äpfelchen?* (*Where Are you Rolling, Little Apple?*), by Leo Perutz.

16 Malik Press publishes the memoir *Nacht über Russland* (*Night over Russia*), by Vera Figner, one of the assassins of Czar Alexander II.

19 Bayreuth Festival opens with a new production of Wagner's *Tristan und Isolde*.

21 Haberlan Press publishes *Die Idee Mussolinis und der Sinn des Faschismus* (*The Mussolini Concept and the Idea of Fascism*), by Georg Mehlis.

24 The film comedy *Das Girl von der Revue* (*The Girl in the Chorus Line*) premieres, directed by Richard Eichberg, with Dina Gralla and Werner Füetterer.

26 Ullstein Press publishes the novel *Sybillenlust* (*Disintegration and Downfall*), by Wilhelm Speyer.

28 Olympic Games begin in Amsterdam; for the first time since World War I, German athletes are allowed to participate.

30 The film melodrama *Der Tanzstudent* (*Because I Love You*), directed by Johannes Guter, with Fritz Alberti and Valerie Boothby, premieres.

31 Emil Jannings wins the first Best Actor Award from Academy of Motion Picture Arts and Sciences in Hollywood; it later becomes the "Oscar." Jannings receives the award for two films: *The Way of All Flesh* (directed by Victor Fleming) and *The Last Command* (directed by Josef von Sternberg).

AUGUST

1 Conductor Heinz Tietjen is named general superintendent of the Prussian State Theater.

3 The film crime drama *Vom Täter fehlt jeder Spur* (*No Trace of the Perpetrator*), directed by Constantin J. David, with Hanni Weisse and Kurt Gerron.

6 Foreign Minister Gustav Stresemann suffers a mild stroke; brief panic ensues in German stock exchanges.

8 The film melodrama *Liebeshölle* (*Pawns of Passion*) premieres, directed by Wiktor Bieganski, with Olga Chekhova and Hans Stüwe.

9 Zsolnay Press publishes the comic novel *Das Mädchen mit dem blauen Hut* (*The Girl with the Blue Hat*), by Johan Fabricius.

The film crime drama *Der Henker* (The Executioner) premieres, directed by Theodor Sparkuhl, with Bernhard Goetzke and Max Landa.

10 The film drama *Abwege* (The Devious Path) premieres, directed by G. W. Pabst, with Brigitte Helm and Gustav Diessl.

13 Tobis Sound Film Syndicate Corp. is founded in Berlin with the intention of creating sound films only, employing the Tri-Ergon sound-on-film technology.

18 Malik Press publishes a 14-volume collection of the works of Leo Tolstoy on the occasion of the 100th anniversary of his birth, translated by Ilse Frapan, August Scholz, Arthur Luther, Erich Boehme, and Erich Müller.

21 The musical revue *Schön und Schick* (*Beautiful and Chic*), by Hermann Haller, premieres at the Admiral's Palace Theater in Berlin.

The film drama *Moulin Rouge* premieres, directed by E. A. Dupont, with Olga Chekhova and Marcel Vibert.

23 Rembrandt Press publishes an autobiography of Heinrich Heine, edited by Herbert Eulenberg.

28 The film melodrama *Ein besserer Herr* (*A Better Sort of Gentleman*, transformed from the comedy by Walter Hasenclever) premieres, directed by Gustav Ucicky, with Leo Peukert and Elisabeth Pinajeff.

30 The most intricately planned and monumentally executed amusement palace in the world, called "Haus Vaterland" ("Fatherland House"), opens on Potsdam Square in Berlin. Under one roof, the six-story facility houses an enormous restaurant seating 2,500 patrons, an opulent ballroom, a 2,000-seat motion picture theater, and 11 smaller concert cafés with raised stages to present all manner of musical entertainment. There are also seven "nationally themed" restaurants in the building: a Viennese wine garden, a "Rhine Terrace" bistro, a Turkish café, the "Löwenbrau" Bavarian beer hall, a Spanish bodega, a Hungarian peasant tavern, and an American "wild-west" saloon. Throughout the building, live music programs could simultaneously accommodate more than 8,000 guests.

31 The Greater German Radio Fair opens, which for the first time features special displays of new technologies: television, sound film, and magnetic recording devices; visitors to the fair witness television transmissions, many for the first time.

The musical *Die Dreigroschenoper* (*The Threepenny Opera*)[4], by Kurt Weill, with libretto and lyrics by Bertolt Brecht and Elisabeth Hauptmann, premieres at the Theater am Schiffbauerdamm in Berlin.

The film melodrama *Zuflucht* (*Escape*), directed by Carl Froelich, with Henny Porten and Carl de Vogt, premieres.

The city of Frankfurt am Main bestows the Goethe Prize to theologian, missionary physician, and organist Albert Schweitzer.

SEPTEMBER

1 The Rübsam Memorial bas-relief for the 39th Fuselier Regiment in Düsseldorf is dedicated; its use of modernist abstraction sets off a fury of debate about its appropriateness as a memorial to fallen German soldiers.

Two operettas premiere in Berlin: Ralph Benatsky's adaptation of *Casanova* by Johann Strauss at the Grosses Schauspielhaus, and *Killy macht Karriere* by Walter Kollo at the Theater der Komiker.

Phaidon Press publishes the novel *Borgia* by Klabund.

3 Köhler Press publishes the novel *Königskinder* (*Children of the King*, about the youthful years of Frederick the Great), by Sophie Höchstetter; Horen Press publishes the novel *Eine Tür fällt ins Schloss* (*Shutting a Door*), by actress Tilla Durieux.

4 Fischer Press publishes three plays: the drama *Krankheit der Jugend* (*Illness of Youth* by Ferdinand Bruckner and comedies *Leinen aus Irland* (*Irish Linen*), by Stefan von Kamare and *Parforce* by Alexander Lernet Holenia.

10 The German premiere of film romance *The Student Prince of Old Heidelberg* (given the German title *Alt-Heidelberg*) opens. It was shot in Heidelberg and based on the play *Alt-Heidelberg*, by Wilhelm Meyer-Förster, directed by Ernst Lubitsch, with Roman Navarro and Norma Shearer.

15 The drama *Der rote General* (*The Red General*), by Hermann Ungar, premieres at the Theater in der Königgrätzer Strasse in Berlin.

17 Zsolnay Press publishes two novels: *Der Sohn* (*The Son*), by Oskar Jellinek, and *Die neue Rasse* (*The New Breed*), by Egmont Colerus.

22 Hässel Press publishes nine novellas in one volume titled *Recht ist Unrecht* (*Justice is Injustice*).

25 Köhler and Amelang Press publish a lengthy summation and evaluation of modernist literary trends titled *Was bleibt?* (*What's Left?*), by Eduard Engel; German Press Institute publishes the novel *Der Mann im feurigen Ofen* (*The Man in the Fiery Furnace*), by Fedor von Zobeltitz.

The film comedy *Der erste Kuss* (*The First Kiss*), directed by Carl Lamac, with Anny Ondra and Werner Pittschau, premieres.

26 The film drama *Heut' spielt der Strauss* (*Strauss, the Waltz King*) premieres, directed by Conrad Wiene, with Alfred Abel as Johann Strauss, Jr., and Hermine Sterler.

28 Adolf Hitler resumes an intensive public speaking schedule after the Prussian police lift the ban on his appearances.

An innovative vocal group called the "Comedian Harmonists" debuts in Berlin at the Berlin Grosses Schauspielhaus as part of a variety show produced by Erik Charell. The Comedian Harmonists (five male vocalists plus a pianist) go on to a brief but spectacular career. Their jazz-inflected close harmony singing was unique, derived from similar groups in the United States.

The film melodrama *Die Dame mit der Maske* (*The Lady with the Mask*), directed by Wilhelm Thiele, with Gertrud Eysoldt and Heinrich George, premieres.

30 National Socialists hold a mass rally at the Berlin Sports Palace, where speakers demand an end to German reparation payments and an abrogation of the Dawes Plan; afterward violent encounters occur in the streets near the Sports Palace between Communist Party and National Socialist gangs.

OCTOBER

1 The governmental "television office" opens under the name *Bildrundfunkdienst* (*Image Radio Service*).

2 Cultural Politics Press publishes the memoir *Gedanken eines Soldaten* (*Thoughts of a Soldier*), by Gen. Hans von Seeckt.[5]

4 The operetta *Friederike*, by Franz Lehar, premieres at the Metropol Theater in Berlin.

8 Three major electronics manufacturers (Siemens, Telefunken, and AEG) form a partnership to manufacture sound film technology, called *Klangfilm*.

9 The Jewish Academic Theater of Moscow makes its first visit to Berlin, performing *Night in the Old Market* by Itzak Peretz at the Berliner Theater in Berlin.

Andermann Press publishes the memoir of World War I *Die Unvergessenen (The Unforgotten)*, by Ernst Jünger.

10 The film drama *Die Carmen von St. Pauli (The Docks of Hamburg)*, directed by Erich Waschneck, with Jenny Jugo and Willy Fritsch, premieres.

Reissner Press publishes the novel *Die unvollkommene Liebe (Unconsummated Love)*, by Rudolf von Delius; Wunderlich Press publishes the short fiction volume titled *Der Ruf des Pan (The Call of Pan)*, by Isolde Kurz.

11 The *Graf Zeppelin* airship makes its maiden voyage from Germany to its American landing dock in Lakehurst, New Jersey; the flight time is 111 hours, just over 4.5 days.

12 The comedy *Ehen werden in Himmel geschlossen (Marriages Made in Heaven)*, by Walter Hasenclever, premieres at the Kammerspiele in Berlin.

Kiepenheuer Press publishes two novels: *Jahrgang 1902 (The 1902 Generation)*, by Ernst Gläser, and *Der unsichtbare Gast (The Invisible Guest)*, by Felix Braun.

13 The Prussian Academy of the Arts opens its first Max Slevogt exhibition, displaying more than 200 works by the painter and illustrator.

14 The "Constructions of Technology" exhibition opens at the Folkwang Museum in Essen.

15 The film comedy *Die Republik der Backfische (The Republic of Teenagers)* premieres, directed by Constantin J. David, with Ruth Albu, Daisy Lorand, and Arthur Duarte.

16 The drama *U-boot S4 (Submarine No. S4)*, by Günther Weisenborn, premieres at the Volksbühne in Berlin; it is the first play to attempt an onstage portrayal of the inner workings of a submarine on duty.

17 The German version of drama *The Great God Brown*, by Eugene O'Neill, translated by Konrad Maril, premieres at the Cologne City Theater.

The opera *Hassan gewinnt (Hassan Wins)*, by Hans Schmidt-Isserstedt, premieres at the Elberfeld City Theater.

18 The Mendelssohn Prize is awarded to composers Hans Humpert and Grete von Zieritz.

20 Publisher Alfred Hugenberg is elected head of the German National Peoples' Party (DNVP); Hugenberg reiterates his opposition to the Weimar Republic, its constitution, and to parliamentary democracy altogether.

Reissner Press publishes the memoir*en eines Sozialdemokraten* (*Memoirs of a Social Democrat*), by Philipp Scheidemann, who had declared the formation of the German republic from a window in the Reich Chancellery in 1918. He soon thereafter became coleader, with Friedrich Ebert, of an interim German government. An opponent of the Versailles Treaty, he was best remembered in the 1920s for his reference to the Versailles Treaty with the rhetorical flourish, "What hand must not wither, that binds both it and us within these chains?"

The film melodrama *Liebe im Kuhstall* (*Love in the Cow Barn*) premieres, directed by Carl Forelich, with Henny Porten and Eugen Neufeld.

22 The Berlin weekly magazine *Die Woche* serializes the novel *Die Frau im Momd* (*The Woman in the Moon*), by screenplay writer Thea von Harbou.

The comedy with music titled *Bibi, Jugend 1928* (*Bibi, a Girl of 1928*), by Heinrich Mann, premieres at the Palm House of the Berliner Theater in Berlin.

23 The drama *Die Verbrecher* (*The Criminals*), by Ferdinand Bruckner, premieres at the Deutsches Theater in Berlin.

25 Müller Press publishes the tragedy about the life of Giordano Bruno titled *Heroische Leidenschaften* (*Heroic Passions*), by Erwin Guido Kolbenheyer.

29 Cassirer Press publishes an art history survey titled *Echt und Unecht* (*Genuine and Fake*), by Max Friedländer.

NOVEMBER

1 Adolf Hitler notes that the National Socialist German Workers' Party now enjoys the support of nineteen daily newspapers in Germany, while a dozen more are "sympathetic" to the Nazi cause.

List Press publishes a biography of 19th-century socialism activist Ferdinand Lasalle titled *Die Macht der Illusion, die Illusion der Macht* (*The Power of Illusion, the Illusion of Power*), by Arno Schirokauer; Fischer publishes the travel memoir *Die allgier Trieb nach Algier* (*Driven by Curiosity to Algiers*), by theater critic Alfred Kerr; Rowohlt Press publishes the novel *Das Lächeln der Mona Lisa* (*The Smile of Mona Lisa*), by Kurt Tucholsky; Hanseatic Press Institute publishes the novel *Land Not* (*The Land in Need*), by Gustav Schröer.

The film comedy *Saxophon-Susi* (*Saxophone Susie*) premieres, directed by Carl Lamac, with Anny Ondra in the title role and Hans Albers.

3 The drama *Krisis* (*Crisis*), by Rolf Lauckner, premieres at the Stuttgart Württembergisches Regional Theater.

Foreign Minister Gustav Stresemann returns to work in Berlin; stock prices rise and some newspapers run extra editions.

5 The airship *Graf Zeppelin* returns to Berlin from America and docks in Spandau to tumultuous welcome.

8 Zsolnay Press publishes the novel *Eugenie* by Heinrich Mann.

9 On the occasion of the tenth anniversary of the republic's existence, Stollberg Press publishes *Zehn Jahre deutsche Geschichte* (Ten Years of German History), by various politicians involved, edited by Hermann Oncken.

10 The Berlin newspaper *Vossische Zeitung* begins serializing the war novel *In Westen nichts neues* (All Quiet on the Western Front), by Erich Maria Remarque.[6]

11 The Social Democratic Party (SPD) holds a mass rally at the Schöneberg Sports Palace in Berlin to celebrate ten years of SPD governments in the republic.

12 The International Library Press publishes a memoir of seafaring life titled *Sailors* by cabaret performer Joachim Ringelnatz.

The historical film drama *Dornenweg einer Fürstin* (The Thorny Path of the Princess, also titled *Rasputin*), directed by Nikolai Larin, with Hedwig Wangel and Gregori Chmari as Rasputin, premieres.

13 Kiepenheuer Press publishes the novel *Familie Worm* (The Worm Family), by Karin Michaelis, translated by Klara Bade.

16 Adolf Hitler attracts 16,000 listeners to his first speech at the Sports Palace in Berlin.

The film drama *Der moderne Cassanova* (The Modern Cassanova) premieres, directed by Max Obal, with Harry Liedtke and Vivian Gibson.

17 List Press publishes the novel *My First Two Thousand Years: The Autobiography of the Wandering Jew*, by George Sylvester Viereck and Paul Eldridge, translated by Gustav Meyrink.

18 Alfred Hugenberg, head of the German National Peoples' Party, declares readiness of his party to form allegiances with right-wing militias for battles in the streets against left-wing militias.

The film documentary *Die Filmstadt Hollywood* (*Hollywood, Film City*), directed by Max Goldschmidt, with Charles Chaplin, Delores Del Rio, Emil Jannings, Conrad Veidt, and F. W. Murnau, premieres.

19 Kiepenheuer Press publishes the drama *Die Lederknöpfe* (*The Leather Buttons*), by Georg Kaiser.

20 Radio broadcasting studios in Königswusterhausen broadcasts a television signal for public reception.

23 European heavyweight champion Max Schmeling in his first American bout defeats Joe Monte in Madison Square Garden in the eighth round by a knockout.

24 The drama *Die Lederknöpfe* (*The Leather Buttons*), by Georg Kaiser, premieres at the Frankfurt am Main Neues Theater.

26 Safari Press publishes the novel *Der Tag der Untermenschen* (*The Day of the Sub-humans*), by Paul Rohrbach.

27 Meister Press publishes *Mata Hari*, a fictionalized life of Margarete Zelle, the Dutch exotic dancer whom the French executed as a spy in World War I.

28 Ernst "Teddy" Thälmann, head of the Communist Party, proposes more attacks against the "social imperialism and social fascism" of the Social Democrats; he also promises violence against Nazi militias.

The film melodrama *Weib in Flammen* (*Woman in Flames*) premieres, directed by Max Reichmann, with Olga Chekhova and Hans Albers.

30 Zsolnay Press publishes the novel *Das Zauberreich der Liebe* (*The Magic Kingdom of Love*), by Max Brod; Fischer publishes biography *Stendhal: Das Leben eines Egotisten* (*Stendhal: The Life of an Egotist*), by Rudolf Kayser.

DECEMBER

1 The opera *Die schwarze Orchidee* (*The Black Orchid*), by Eugen d'Albert, premieres at the Leipzig City Opera.

2 The drama *Revolte im Erziehungshaus* (*Revolt in the Reform School*), by Peter Martin Lampel, premieres at the Thalia Theater in Berlin.

4 Weibezahl Press publishes a biography of actor and Iffland Ring holder Albert Bassermann by Julius Bab.

5 The conductor of the Berlin Philharmonic Orchestra, Wilhelm Furtwängler, turns down an offer to become director of the Vienna State Opera and elects to remain in Berlin.

10 The opera *Der singende Teufel* (*The Singing Devil*), by Franz Schreker, premieres at the State Opera in Berlin.

Graphic artist George Grosz and publisher Wieland Herzfeld are found guilty of blasphemy (Grosz for portraying the crucified Christ in a military gas mask, and Herzfeld for distributing it); a Berlin court fines both men RM 2,000.

German chemistry professor (at University of Göttingen) Adolf Windaus is awarded the Nobel Prize in Chemistry for research on the properties of cholesterol and vitamin D.

13 The Berlin chief of police, citing the rising incidence of altercations between Communist and National Socialist partisans in street demonstrations, forbids demonstrations altogether in Berlin.

16 The German premiere of the opera *Schwanda, der Dudelsackpfeifer* (Schwanda the Bagpiper), by Jaromir Weinberger, premieres at the Breslau City Theater.

21 The drama *Katharina Knie*, by Carl Zuckmayer, premieres at the Lessing Theater in Berlin.

A retirement home for German actors opens in Berlin, operated by the German actors' union.

22 The Kleist Prize is bestowed on Anna Seghers for her novella *Aufstand der Fischer von Santa Barbara* (*Insurrection of the Santa Barbara Fishermen*).

The operetta *Jettchen Gebert*, by Walter Kollo, premieres at the Theater am Nollendorf Platz in Berlin.

23 A lengthy essay by Thomas Mann in the Berlin newspaper *Berliner Illustrierte* deliberates on the question of photography's status as an art form.

25 A lengthy article in a Berlin newspaper on "The Man of Today" features interviews with feminist writers Eugenie Schwazwald and Alice Salomon, along with actress Mady Christians.

NOTES

1. A good example of Karl Vallentin's characteristic brand of self-deprecating humor at this particular venue: an improvised curtain went up and revealed him under a street light, looking for his house key. As he walks around the light, he searches through his pockets a dozen or so times. A policeman appears and Vallentin tells him of his predicament. They both begin to look for the key, exchanging odd observations and commentary. Finally the policeman asks Valentin, "Are you sure you lost it here?" "Oh no," replies Valentin. I lost it over there" (pointing to the darkness). "Then why the hell are you looking for it here?" demands the policeman. "There's no light over there," replies Vallentin.

2. Schultze-Naumburg (1869–1949) was a well-known painter and architect and the author of several publications condemning modern art and architecture on the basis of ethnic identity. He insisted that classical Greece and the Middle Ages were sources of "true" German art and that only "racially unsullied" artists could produce art that embraced wholeness, interior unity, accessibility, and harmony. Modern art, with its inclusion of disharmony, fracture, distortion, decomposition, and despair was the product of racially "mixed" modern artists. In other words, Shulztze-Naumburg believed that much of modernist art and architecture was a disease, or at best a kind of cultural dysfunctionality. Many of Schultze-Naumburg's ideas began to find resonance in National Socialist ideology, which insisted that art must sustain people by reminding them of their ethnic authenticity.

3. The Karl May phenomenon ranks as one of the most idiosyncratic in the annals of popular German culture. Karl Friedrich May (1842–1912) became one of the best selling and widely read of all German writers with an *oeuvre* consisting largely of adventure books for adolescent readers about the American West. The books feature a German frontiersman named Old Shatterhand and an Apache warrior-chieftain named Winnetou; in 16 remarkable volumes, these two "blood brothers" have numerous adventures with various bad guys, and they almost always emerge victorious. May is thought to have made one brief trip to the United States, but he seems never to have gone any farther west than Lake Ontario. What makes his novels so convincing (to young German readers, at least) is their imaginative use of factual sources, American geography, landmarks, and native linguistics—all of them combined with an eerie, almost mystical German sensibility that informs character motivation. May's were the first "Euro-westerns" (as they came to be known in the 20th century), and many significant German personalities have admitted addiction to Karl May westerns in their youth, among them Bertolt Brecht, Albert Einstein, Hermann Hesse, Adolf Hitler, Karl Liebknecht, Heinrich Mann, and Carl Zuckmayer. Over 200 million copies of May's books have sold worldwide, translated into 32 languages. Eight movies featuring Old Shatterhand and Winnetou have been made (many starring Lex Barker at Old Shatterhand), along with dozens of television episodes and hundreds of radio shows.

4. *The Threepenny Opera* encountered some initial problems at the box office but then became a massive hit with audiences and ran for two years. Soon thereafter the show and its songs became an internationally recognized cultural emblem of the Weimar Republic and remains so to this day. It joined the ranks of films like *The Cabinet of Dr. Caligari*, *Metropolis*, and *The Blue Angel*, along with the Bauhaus School, the political cabaret, sculptures of Käthe Kollwitz, drawings by George Grosz, novels by Vicki Baum and Erich Maria Remarque, and perhaps the boxer Max Schmeling as global recognition points of modern German culture. The show was an adaptation of John Gay's *The Beggar's Opera*, which had premiered exactly two centuries previous, but Kurt Weill's stunningly innovative music figured most prominently in its popularity with audiences. His 19 songs and incidental music were precedent-setting in their originality. *The Threepenny Opera* has been translated into 18 languages and according to some estimates there have been 100,00 different productions of the show since its premiere. The most significant one among the seven done in New York took place off Broadway in 1954, in a version by Marc Blitzstein. Lotte Lenya ap-

peared in that production, as she did in the Berlin premiere. The first London production, staged in 1933, ran only a dozen times. Two other London productions have since then fared much better in lengthier runs.

5. The new republican government appointed Hans von Seeckt (1866–1936) head of the new Reichswehr in 1919, giving him responsibility for dismantling the old imperial army and forging a new Reichswehr in its place. Saddled with the restrictions on the German military set forth in the Versailles Treaty, von Seeckt successfully evaded many of those restrictions and was largely responsible for the secret military exercises with the Soviet Union confidentially negotiated in the early 1920s with Leon Trotsky, then head of the Soviet Red Army. He also fostered numerous new weapons programs *sub rosa*, employing many inventive (and totally surreptitious) sources for funding those programs. As a result, he perpetuated the culture of a German military outside and in many ways beyond civilian control.

6. *All Quiet on the Western Front* became a best seller soon after its serial publication, and it went on to enjoy wide popularity in several translations. The original German title *In Westen nichts neues* replicates a fairly routine report from the front lines, literally meaning "nothing new to report in the West." That phrase was a euphemism for "stalemate" and the title in English "All Quiet on the Western Front" is likewise somewhat euphemistic. What author Remarque wanted to convey in the title was the humdrum deadly existence of the average soldier in the trenches, something he personally experienced as a draftee, beginning in June of 1917. He was severely wounded twice, and his novel is based on his first-hand knowledge, which Remarque rendered in terse, understated prose. Because its tone was so matter-of-fact, the book outraged right-wing and nationalist readers, who felt that something heroic had been left out. The book's critics were right: Remarque concentrated on the mud, misery, loneliness, and death that was the average soldier's lot in the trenches. The book's popularity reached its height after the American movie (directed by Lewis Milestone, with Lew Ayres as Remarque's alter ego, named Paul Bäumer) premiered in 1930. It has remained a popular book for decades, and another film version of it premiered 1979, directed by Delbert Mann, with Richard Thomas as Bäumer.

1929

JANUARY

3 The Labor Ministry orders "official" work week reduced to 50 hours instead of the current 52 hours. Overtime pay is set at an additional 25 percent of regular wages.

4 An unprecedented Sophoclean "twin bill," featuring *Oedipus the King* and *Oedipus at Colonus*, with Fritz Kortner in the title role of both, opens at the State Theater in Berlin; the drama *Die Bergbahn* (*The Mountain Cable Car*), by Ödön von Horvath, premieres at the Theater am Bülow Platz in Berlin.

The "International Conference of Modern Methods of War" sponsored by the German Women's League for Peace and Freedom opens at Frankfurt am Main.

European heavyweight champion Max Schmeling defeats American Joe Seykyra by points in a 15-round decision at Madison Square Garden New York.

5 The German version of drama *Orpheus,* by Jean Cocteau, translated by Friedrich Hardekopf, premieres at the Theater am Schiffbauerdamm in Berlin.

Novelist Heinrich Hauser receives the Gerhart Hauptmann Prize.

7 Composer Lisa Maria Meyer leads the Berlin Philharmonic Orchestra in a performance of Beethoven's Fourth Symphony and her tone poem "Cocaine." Soon after the tone poem's conclusion, a man storms the podium and demands the conductor's hand in marriage; the man turned out to be her husband, and she faints. In the lobby, a riot ensues and police break it up. After the intermission, the conductor resumes her program and the orchestra performs the "Euryanthe Overture," by Carl Maria von Weber.

The comedy *Der himmlische Handelsmann* (*The Heavenly Tradesman*), by Herbert Eulenberg premieres at the Krefeld City Theater.

8   First American sound films begin to appear in some German theaters; their use of sound-on-disc technology,[1] inferior to the German sound-on-film technology, limits their exhibition.

10   The film epic *Waterloo*, directed by Karl Grune, premieres with Otto Gebühr as field marshal Gebhard Leberecht von Blücher and Charles Vanel as Napoleon Bonaparte.

12   The ballet *Fünf Wünsche* (*Five Wishes*), by Ralph Benatsky, premieres at the Berlin Philharmonic.

14   The Max Reinhardt Foundation begins awarding scholarships on a regular basis to acting students at the Max Reinhardt Seminar (acting school) in Berlin.

15   Albert Einstein presents his paper "Eine neue Feld-Theorie" ("A New Field Theory") at the Prussian Academy of Sciences in Berlin. Einstein claims to have worked on the five-page paper for a decade and regards it as more important that his Theory of Relativity.

16   The first German sound film *Das letzte Lied* (*The Last Song*, fourteen minutes in length), directed by German-American Frank Clifford, with Ludwig Hoffmann and Hermine Sterler, premieres.

The drama *Karl und Anna* by Leonhard Frank premieres at a dozen German theaters simultaneously.

17   The film *Ich küsse Ihre Hand, Madame* (*I Kiss Your Hand, Madame*), directed by Robert Land, with Marlene Dietrich and Harry Liedtke, premieres; it's a silent film, but with a sound segment featuring Harry Liedtke mouthing the words as the recorded voice of Richard Tauber provides the "singing." Theaters equipped for sound show the 14-minute *Das letzte Lied* (*The Last Song*) as an afterpiece.

Kiepenheuer Press publishes a volume of lyrics titled *Die Songs von der Dreigroschenoper* (*Songs from "The Three Penny Opera"*), by Bertolt Brecht.

19   The exhibition *Faust I auf der Bühne* (*Faust Part I on the Stage*) opens in Braunschweig, celebrating the 100th anniversary of the first complete professional performance of *Faust* Part I, which took place at the Braunschweig Court Theater.

Fischer Press publishes an illustrated volume titled *Rundherum* (*Round and About*), by Klaus and Erika Mann.

20   The exhibition "Contemporary Photography" opens at the Folkwang Museum in Essen.

21   Max Schmeling defeats American boxer Pietro Corri in a nontitle bout at Madison Square Garden, New York, after one minute in the first round by a knockout.

22   A direct communications cable opens between New York and Berlin, facilitating telegraph, telephone, and some photographic transmission.

23   The Bavarian Peoples' Party denounces a proposed national tax increase on beer consumption on both social and cultural grounds.

25   Several German regional theaters announce a reduction of the performance season from nine months to eight months in view of increasing financial shortfalls.

Cultural Policy Press publishes the treatise *Meine Vorfahren* (*My Ancestors*), by former Kaiser Wilhelm II, in which, on the occasion of his impending 70th birthday, he postulates the superiority of a hereditary monarchy over a republican form of government.

26   Prussian Academy of Sciences publishes a six-page article "Zur einheitlichen Feldtheorie" ("On a Unified Field Theory"), by Albert Einstein.

28   The Reich Finance Ministry warns that continued generous outlays for social and cultural spending by national government cannot be sustained; unemployment rates in Germany begin a steep increase throughout the country.

Callwey Press publishes the cultural treatise *Das Gesicht des deutschen Hauses* (*The Face of the German Domestic Residence*), by Paul Schultze-Naumburg.

The film drama *Mein Herz ist eine Jazzband* (*My Heart Is a Jazz Band*) premieres, directed by Friedrich Zelnik, with Alfred Abel and Hermann Böttcher.

29   Zsolnay Press publishes the novel *Der Hellseher* (*The Visionary*), by Ernst Lothar.

31   Ullstein Press publishes the war novel *In Westen nichts neues* (*All Quiet on the Western Front*), by Erich Maria Remarque. All available copies sell out at bookstores within three days as a result of advance purchases. By June, more than 640,000 copies have sold; selection by the Book of the Month Club in the United States prompts a quick translation into English by Arthur W. Wheen, which sells 60,000 copies.

FEBRUARY

2   Max Schmeling defeats American heavyweight Johnny Risco by a knockout in the ninth round before 15,000 spectators at Madison Square Garden, New York.

3 The Ernst Barlach Exhibition opens in Duisburg, featuring not only his sculptures but also his drawings and graphic prints.

4 Steegemann Press publishes a biographical account of Max Alsberg, a former penitentiary inmate, titled *Die Unterwelt von Berlin* (*Berlin's Underworld*), by Arthur Landsberger.

6 Klett-Cotta Press publishes a collection of "chronicles by day and night" titled *Das abenteuerliche Herz* (*The Adventurous Heart*), by Ernst Jünger.

9 The film drama *Die Büchse der Pandora* (*Pandora's Box*, based on the play of the same title by Frank Wedekind) premieres, directed by G. W. Pabst, with Louise Brooks as Lulu and Fritz Kortner as Dr. Schön.

10 The German national soccer teams defeats Switzerland in Mannheim, advancing in the European championship series.

11 The coldest winter on record with temperatures dropping below $-25°$ F. ($-35°$ C.) in many parts of Germany causes delayed heating fuel deliveries, particularly brown coal; for the first time since records have been kept beginning in 1791, the Rhine River freezes over at its widest point in Germany.

The German public is stunned by the sudden deaths of two cultural icons: actor Albert Steinrück (who had appeared in more than 70 films and in dozens of theatre productions since the founding of the republic) and navigator Baron Günther von Hünefeld (who had flown in the single-engine Junkers aircraft from Ireland to Newfoundland the previous year).

Discussions begin in Paris under the leadership of American businessman and diplomat Owen D. Young to renegotiate reparations payments from Germany to Allied victors in World War I.

14 The German premiere of the opera *The Makropulos Affair*, by Leos Janacek, based on a play by Karel Capek, opens at the Frankfurt am Main City Opera.

Munich police ban performances by American dancer and entertainer Josephine Baker; they cite fears of "injury to public decency," particularly in Baker's "Banana Dance," as a basis for the prohibition.

Propyläen Press publishes the drama *Katharina Knie* by Carl Zuckmayer.

15 The detective film *Indizienbeweis* (*Circumstantial Evidence*) premieres, directed by Georg Jacoby, with Fritz Alberti and Max Neufeld.

16 The drama *Dietrich: Der Morgen eines Volkes* (*Dietrich: Dawn of a People*), by Wilhelm Schmidtbonn, premieres at the Kassel State Theater; the military drama *Douamont*, by Eberhard Wolfgang Möller, premieres at the Dresden Komödientheater and the Essen City Theater.

The film romance *Das brennende Herz* (*The Burning Heart*) premieres, directed by Ludwig Berger, with Mady Christians and Gustav Fröhlich.

20 The drama *Verschwörer* (*Conspirator*), by Peter Martin Lampel, premieres at the Trianon Theater in Berlin.

21 Korn Press publishes the novel *Ulrichshof* (*Ulrich's Court*), by Paul Keller; Fischer publishes the poetry volume *Trost der Nacht* (*Consolation of Night*), by Hermann Hesse.

22 The drama *Kreuzabnahme* (*Descent from the Cross*), by journalist Ehm Welk, premieres at the Volksbühne in Berlin.

24 The opera *Der Tenor* (*The Tenor*, based on the comedy *Bürger Schippel* by Carl Sternheim), by Ernst von Dohnanyi, premieres at the Nuremberg City Theater.

25 Fischer Press publishes the novel *Es geschah in Moskau (It Happened in Moscow)*, by Arthur Holitscher.

26 Insel Press publishes new adaptations of Greek myths and legends titled *Griechische Helden-Sagen* (*Greek Heroic Sagas*), by Albrecht Schäfer; Langen publishes a collection of novellas titled *Menschendämmerung* (*Twilight of Humanity*), by Otto Stoessl.

28 The opera *Der betrogene Bräutigam* (*The Bridegroom Betrayed*, based on the opera *Lo sposo delusa* by Wolfgang Amadeus Mozart) premieres at the Gotha Regional Theater.

MARCH

1 The Reich Labor Ministry announces that unemployment rates have hit an all-time high, with 2.2 million Germans out of work.

2 Gretlein Press publishes a children's book titled *Puppenspiel* (*Puppet Play*), by Manfred Kyber.

3 The Reichstag celebrates the 100th birthday of German-American politician Carl Schurz, who was born near Cologne, studied at the University of Bonn, was a member of Abraham Lincoln's cabinet, and became a Senator from Missouri in 1869.

The German Press Institute publishes the novel *Die mit den tausend Kindern* (*The Woman with a Thousand Children*), by Clara Viebig.

The "Tanzdarbietungen in Verbindung mit Projektionen und Lichtspielen" ("Dance Work in Combination with Projections and Play of Light") in cooperation with the Dessau Bauhaus, staged by Oskar Schlemmer, premieres at the Volksbühne in Berlin.

5 The drama *Giftgas über Berlin: Drei Akte einer Diktatur der Zukunft* (*Poison Gas over Berlin: Three Acts of a Future Dictatorship*), by Peter Martin Lampel for invited audiences only, premieres at the Theater am Schiffbauerdamm in Berlin; police had refused permission for the production to be performed publicly.

Fischer publishes the drama *Die nächtliche Hochzeit* (*The Nightly Marriage*), by Alexander Lernet-Holenia.

7 Police close down the production of Lampel's *Giftgas über Berlin*, prompting protests in several newspaper editorials and vocal street demonstrations against the police action.

8 The film drama *Fräulein Else* (*Miss Else*, based on the novel by Arthur Schnitzler) premieres, directed by Paul Czinner, with Elisabeth Bergner as Else and Albert Bassermann.

The first regularly scheduled television broadcast is transmitted by the German postal service from studios in the Witzleben district of Berlin.

The drama *Die Ursache* (*The Cause*), by Leonhard Frank, premieres at Munich Kammerspiele.

9 The comedy *Halt–nicht weiter spielen!* (*Wait–Stop the Performance!*), by Emil Herfurth, premieres at Greifswald City Theater.

10 The automobile firm Horch begins an advertising campaign featuring theater actors endorsing the Horch 8; among the first is Werner Krauss, who claims to drive only German cars.

11 Enoch Press publishes a poetry collection titled *Anthologie jüngster Lyrik* (*Anthology of Recent Lyric Poetry*), by Willi Fehse, Erich Kästner, Klaus Mann, Hermann Kesten, and Rudolf Binding.

12 Articles in the literary journal *Die Weltbühne* magazine describe the illegal activities of the German army, the development of new weapons, and other rearmament operations; writer Walter Kreiser and editor Carl von Ossietzky are immediately arrested and imprisoned. They are later tried and sentenced to 18 months in prison.

The documentary travelogue film *Melodie der Welt* (*Melody of the World*), directed by Walter Ruttmann and billed as "the first German full-length sound film," premieres. It followed a newsreel format with clips of people talking to the camera. George Bernard Shaw appears near the end of the film.

13 The drama *Abschied* (*Farewell*), by Agnes Miegel, premieres at the Bad Godesberg City Theater.

14 Art historian Max Friedländer assumes directorship of the Kaiser Fredrich Museum in Berlin.

15 Rowohlt Press publishes the treatise *Reinhardt-Jessner-Piscator—oder Klassikertod?* (*Reinhardt-Jessner-Piscator—or Death of the Classics?*), by theater critic Herbert Ihering.

The detective film *Die Mitternachts-Taxe* (*The Midnight Taxi*) premieres, directed by Harry Piel, with Maria Asti and Hermann Böttcher.

16 Cassirer Press publishes the biography *Wilhelm Leibl* by Emil Waldmann.

General Motors Corporation buys German automobile manufacturer Opel for $30 million; newspapers and politicians publicly bemoan the growing influence of foreigners in the German automobile industry. Rumors already circulate that Ford Motor Co. is planning to build a manufacturing plant in the Cologne area.

18 In a lengthy article published in the newspaper *Berliner Tageblatt* novelist Heinrich Mann denounces the recent censorship of plays throughout the country.

19 The film melodrama *Hotelgeheimnisse* (*Hotel Secrets*) premieres, directed by Friedrich Feher, with Gertrud de Lalsky and Alfred Gerasch.

Zsolnay Press publishes a collection of novellas titled *Das Herz im Ausverkauf* (*The Heart on Clearance Sale*), by Paul Frischauer.

20 The German version of the war drama *What Price Glory?*, by Maxwell Anderson and Laurence Stallings, translated and adapted by Carl Zuckmayer, premieres at the Theater in der Königgrätzer Strasse in Berlin; the German version of drama *The Return of the Prodigal Son,* by André Gide, translated by Rainer Maria Rilke, premieres at the Stuttgart Regional Theater.

The film comedy *Die keusche Kokotte* (*The Chaste Coquette*) premieres, directed by Franz Seitz, with Maly Delschaft and Alfons Fryland.

21 The German version of *Arms and the Man*, by George Bernard Shaw, translated by Siegfried Trebitsch, premieres at the Berliner Theater in Berlin.

The Prussian government declares a complete ban on street demonstrations throughout cities of Prussia.

22 The film melodrama *Tagebuch einer Kokotte* (*Diary of a Coquette*) premieres, directed by Constantin J. David, with Mary Kid and Ernst Stahl-Nachbaur.

The German Stock Exchange and German League of Booksellers organize a "Day of the Book" throughout the country in an effort to stimulate book sales.

Fischer Press publishes a collection of autobiographical essays titled *Die Lebensalter* (*The Stages of Life*), by Jakob Wassermann.

23 Phaidon Press publishes a historical survey of the Bavarian royal family titled *Die letzten Wittelsbacher* (*The Last Wittelsbachs*), by Herbert Eulenberg; Fischer publishes a biography of the mysterious Greek weapons dealer, the "salesman of death" Sir Basil Zaharoff, titled *Der Mann im Dunkel* (*The Man in the Dark*), by Richard Lewinsohn.

26 The Prussian Academy of the Arts confers its Beethoven Prize on composers Paul Juon and Joseph Haas.

A higher quality (30 horizontal lines—900-pixel transmission)[2] television broadcast by the German postal service from studios in the Witzleben district of Berlin depict a man smoking his pipe and a woman looking at herself in a mirror.

27 Foreign minister Stresemann announces Germany's inability to maintain ruinous reparation payments called for in the Versailles Treaty; national government debts now total RM 8 billion.

28 Lavish funeral services are held in Berlin for deceased actor Albert Steinrück, who had died more than a month previous. Service consisted of a performance of Wedekind's *Marquis of Keith* to benefit Steinrück's widow and family, featuring numerous well-known actors and actresses.

29 The film melodrama *Möbliertes Zimmer* (*Furnished Room*), directed by Fred Sauer, with Hans Albers and Yvette Darnys, premieres.

30 Berlin police close down production of the drama *Pioniere in Ingolstadt* (*Pioneers in Ingolstadt*), by Marieluise Fleisser, at the Theater am Schiffbauerdamm in Berlin.

31 In the Berlin newspaper *Vossische Zeitung* author Lion Feuchtwanger denounces the practice of not paying screenplay writers royalties for their work in films.

APRIL

2 The 1550-seat Tauentzien Palace movie theater closes because it, like many other large-capacity film exhibition venues, experiences massive financial losses in the changeover to sound films.

4 The Berlin newspaper *Berliner Illustrierte* begins serial publication of the novel *Menschen im Hotel* (*Grand Hotel*), by Vicki Baum.

Ludwig Haymann becomes the German heavyweight boxing champion by defeating Rudi Wagner on points in a 15-round bout at the Berlin Sports Palace.

6 Twelve-year-old violin virtuoso Yehudi Menuhin debuts with the Berlin Philharmonic under the direction of Fritz Busch; after the concert, Professor Albert Einstein goes backstage to tell the boy, "Tonight you have proved once again to me that there is indeed a God in Heaven."

The drama *Trojaner* (*Trojans*), by Curt Corrinth, premieres at the Volksbühne in Berlin.

10 Playwright Bertolt Brecht marries actress Helene Weigel; their artistic partnership becomes one of the most powerful, influential, and financially successful in the history of German theater.

11 The Reich Foreign Ministry refuses to admit former Soviet Union official Leon Trotsky into Germany; Trotsky had wished to spend time at a German spa for rest and recuperation after his recent expulsion from the Soviet Union.

The film adventure *Auf der Reeperbahn nachts um halbeins* (*Red Light District, Half Past Midnight*), directed by Fred Stranz, with Inge Borg and Harry Nestor, premieres.

13 The opera *Machinist Hopkins*, by Max Brand, premieres at Duisburg City Theater; critics are initially bewildered by a "working class opera" in which machines sing along with a chorus of factory laborers.

17 The film romance *Maschotten* (*Mascots*) premieres, directed by Felix Basch, with Käthe von Nagy and Max Gülstorff.

19 An essay by author and pundit Friedrich Sternthal in the literary weekly *Die literarische Welt* titled "Die Ohnmacht der Geistigen in Deutschland" ("The Impotence of Intellectuals in Germany") stirs debate and consternation among the German intelligentsia.

21 The drama *Staatsräson: Ein Denkmal für Sacco und Vanzetti* (*State Security: A Memorial to Sacco and Vanzetti*), by Erich Mühsam, premieres at the November Studio of the Central Theater in Berlin

23 The film melodrama *Die Ehe* (*Marriage*) premieres, directed by Eberhard Frowein, with Lil Dagover and Gustav Diessl.

Violent street clashes ensue after a speech in Karlsruhe by Communist Party official Max Hölz, recently released from prison; his supporters fight with National Socialist partisans.

26 The film romance *Die weissen Rosen von Ravensberg* (*The White Roses of Ravensberg*) premieres, directed by Rudolf Meinert, with Diana Karenne and Jack Trevor.

27 The drama *Jürg Lanatsch*, by Heinrich Keminski, premieres at the Dresden State Theater.

28 Street riots break out as National Socialists disrupt performances of a Polish touring theater troupe in Oppeln, Upper Silesia.

The German national soccer team defeating Italian national team, is broadcast on radio live from Turin back to Germany.

30 The drama *Die Umkehr* (*The Reversal*), by Arnold Zweig, premieres at the Frankfurt City Theater.

MAY

1 Berlin police vigorously attack street participants in the May Day celebrations, assuming they are violating the ban on political demonstrations in the city; many of the celebrants carry placards with political slogans, along with large pictures of politicians such as Rosa Luxemburg and Karl Liebknecht. Seven participants killed and more than 100 wounded.

2 In the Reichstag, Communist Party deputies sing "The Internationale" in honor of celebrants injured in May Day activities, then stage a walkout in unison from the Reichstag into the street, daring the Berlin police to arrest them. Police ban publication of the Communist Party newspaper *Red Flag* for three weeks.

3 A new production of *King John*, by William Shakespeare, opens at the State Theater in Berlin, the first time the play has been staged at the State Theater in more than a century.[3]

The film comedy *Der lustige Witwer* (*The Merry Widower*) premieres, directed by Robert Land, with Harry Liedtke, La Jana, and Alice Roberts.

The German version of the detective drama *The Man Who Changed His Name*, by Edgar Wallace, translated by Hans Rothe, premieres at the Komödie Theater in Berlin.

4 Insel Press publishes a survey of "alternative medicine" by Franz Anton Mesmer, Mary Baker Eddy, and Sigmund Freud titled *Die Heilung durch den Geist* (*Healing with the Mind*), by Stefan Zweig; Langen Press publishes autobiographical essays titled *Der Schriftsteller und die Zeit* (*The Author and Time*), by Hans Grimm; Staackmann publishes the novel *Die Ehepause* (*Marriage Intermission*), by Max Dreyer.

5 The drama *Die Unüberwindlichen: Ein Nachkriegsdrama* (*The Unconquerable: A Postwar Drama*), by Karl Kraus, premieres at the Dresden State Theater.

6 The Prussian government bans Red Front militia from operating in any fashion anywhere within Prussian jurisdiction.

Zsolnay Press publishes the novel *Die Geliebte des Kaisers* (*The Emperor's Lover*), by Felix Salten; Kiepenheuer publishes the novel *Rechts und Links* (*Right and Left*), by Joseph Roth.

7 Horen Press publishes the novel *Im Schatten Shakespeares* (*In the Shadow of Shakespeare*), by Eduard Stucken.

11 Rowohlt Press publishes *Ungewöhnliche Menschen und Schicksale* (*Uncommon People and Destinies*), by Franz Blei; Tradition Press publishes *Hitler—eine Biographie in 134 Bildern* (*Hitler—A Biography in 134 Pictures*).

15 Professor Albert Einstein refuses the city of Berlin's testimonial and offering of a lifelong residence in the city.

16 The first Academy of Motion Picture Arts and Sciences Awards ceremony is held in Hollywood. The Best Actor Award winner, Emil Jannings, is absent, having departed for Germany months earlier.

The airship *Graf Zeppelin* departs for a second flight to United States, but engine malfunction requires an emergency landing in Toulon, France.

17 Fischer Press publishes the novel *Symphonie für Jazz* (*Symphony for Jazz*), by René Schickele.

18 Zsolnay Press publishes the novel *Die Scheidung: Ein Roman unserer Zeit* (*The Divorce: A Novel of Our Time*), by Walter von Molo.

22 Arturo Toscanini begins a six-week residence in Berlin, conducting German orchestras, and the production of Verdi's *Falstaff* premieres at La Scala opera house in Milan.

Kurt Weill premieres his cantata *Das Berliner Requiem* on radio, broadcast from Frankfurt am Main.

23 Fischer Press publishes the novel *Es ist Zeit . . .* (*It's time . . .*), by Otto Flake.

24 Foreign Minister Gustav Stresemann, theater director Eugen Robert, music historian Oskar Bie, and others form a committee to create the Bruno Walter Foundation, providing money to assist students at the Berlin College of Music.

The film drama *Großstadtjugend* (*Youth of the Big City*) premieres, directed by Rudolf Walther-Fein, with Helmut Gauer and Trude Lehmann.

25 The drama *Die Weiber von Weinsberg* (*The Wives of Weinsberg*), by Hermann Essig, premieres at the Oldenburg City Theater.

29 The cornerstone laid at the building site in the Charlottenburg district of Berlin for what will become the broadcast central headquarters of German Radio; the building is designed by Hans Poelzig.

31 The film drama about German abortion law *Der Sittenrichter* (*The Judge of Morals*) premieres, directed by Carl Heinz Wolff, with Margarete Schlegel, Margarete Kupfer, Rudolf Lettinger, and Erna Morena.

JUNE

1 The first meeting between the German and Scottish national soccer teams ends in a 1 to 1 tie before 40,000 fans in Berlin.

The film comedy *Ja, ja—die Frauen sind meine schwache Seite* (*Yes, yes—Women are My Weakness*) premieres, directed by Edmund Heuberger, with Hans Albers and Mary Parker.

Dorothea Freudenthal is named criminal detective inspector in the Berlin Police Department, the first German woman to hold such a post.

2 A convention of the right-wing militia group Stahlhelm (Steel Helmet) concludes in Munich, resolving the continued onslaught against "spiritually destructive cultural Bolshevism."

An outdoor festival of radio and film called "The New World" opens in Berlin's Hasenheide Park.

3 The American sound film *The Singing Fool*[4] premieres in Berlin, directed by Lloyd Bacon, with Al Jolson and Betty Bronson.

5 The comedy *Tumult*, by Alexander Lernet-Holenia, premieres at the Munich Kammerspiele.

The Reich Finance Ministry declares that reparation payments to the victorious Allies in World War I according to terms of the Versailles Treaty make it impossible for the national government to continue unemployment insurance benefits to German workers who have lost their jobs.

7 German officials approve the Young Plan in Paris, providing a new schedule of reparation payments; the Young Plan foresees continued annual reparation payments for the next 68 years, though in amounts that German officials hope the country can achieve.

A "Film und Foto" exhibition opens in Stuttgart. It is one of the first to present both motion and still pictures as expressions of the German artistic temperament.

The film *Das Recht der Ungeborenen* (*The Right of the Unborn*) premieres, directed by Adolf Trotz, with Maly Delschaft and Hans Adalbert Schlettow.

Playwright Carl Sternheim experiences profound depression in a Swiss sanatorium and is brought to a closed Berlin sanatorium for electroshock treatment.

8 The opera *Neues vom Tage* (*News of the Day*), by Paul Hindemith, premieres at Kroll Opera House in Berlin, conducted by Otto Klemperer.

The drama *Eleonora Duse*, based on the life of the Italian actress, by Alfons Paquet, premieres at Düsseldorf Schauspielhaus.

9 Director Leopold Jessner receives a five-year extension on his contract as head of the State Theater in Berlin from Prussian Cultural Ministry.

10 The adaptation of the Johann Strauss operetta *Die Fledermaus*, by Erich Wolfgang Korngold, premieres at the Deutsches Theater in Berlin, with Korngold conducting the orchestra for the production.

11 The manufacturing firms Bosch of Stuttgart, Baird Television of London, Zeiss-Ikon of Dresden, and Loewe of Berlin establish "Television Corporation of Berlin."

12 The Reichstag passes a non-binding resolution condemning the growing "decadence and barbarization of German literature and theater," along with a concomitant resolution for maintaining and assuring "the political and religious neutrality of German radio." Deputies of both the Social Democratic and Communist Parties denounce the resolutions and vote almost unanimously against them.

13 Playwright Alfred Unger receives the Schiller Prize and the Bochum-Duisburg "Best Play" Award for his "play of social consciousness" *Menschen wie Du und Ich* (*People Like You and Me*).

14 The American ambassador to Germany Jacob Schurmann unveils busts at the Reich Transport Ministry in Berlin depicting the three men who made the first nonstop fixed-wing westbound flight across the North Atlantic: Hermann Köhl, James Fitzmaurice, and Baron Günther von Hünefeld.

15 The Breslau Architecture Exhibition Wohnung und Werkraum (*Space for Living and Working*), opens featuring work by Mies van der Rohe and the work he exhibited in the German Pavilion at the Barcelona Architecture Fair.

17 The 11th World Congress of Suffrage Rights for Women opens in Berlin.

19 The Munich Theater Festival opens with several new productions of plays by Friedrich Schiller.

The Prussian Academy of the Arts begins a series of concerts and institutes master classes by composer Arnold Schönberg.

21 The retail firm Karstadt of Hamburg opens the largest department store[5] in Europe on Hermann Platz in the Neukölln district of Berlin.

23 The German national soccer team defeats the Swedish national team in Cologne by 3 to 1.

25 Extensive reports in the Berlin newspaper *Vossische Zeitung* on the implementation of the five-day work week in automobile plants of Detroit, where few unskilled workers belong to labor unions and there is little influence by socialist political parties; German labor union leaders defend their practices and ideology despite the much lengthier work week in Germany.

28 On the tenth anniversary of the signing of the Versailles Treaty in Paris, President Paul von Hindenburg declares an official day of mourning, marking "a decade of burden at every level of German society."

29 National Socialists form a school in Munich to train party members in public speaking, realizing that radio and new voice recording technology permits wide dissemination of the party's ideology.

Professor Albert Einstein receives the Max Planck Medal from the German Physics Society.

30 Thousands of German university students gather in Berlin for a day of protest demonstrations featuring banners that read "Against the Lie of German Responsibility for World War I!!!"

JULY

1 The musical drama *Hotel Stadt Lemberg* (*Lemberg City Hotel*), by Ernst Neuber, composed by Jean Gilbert, premieres at Hamburg Deutsches Schauspielhaus; the comedy *Im siebten Himmel* (*In Seventh Heaven*), by Hermann Burkhardt and Harry Waldau, premieres at Schlosspark Theater in Berlin.

2 The president of the Prussian Literary Academy in a speech at Heilbronn stuns his listeners by criticizing German theater directors and insisting that all subsidies to theater in Germany must cease.

The film melodrama *Sündig und Süss* (*Sinful and Sweet*), directed by Carl Lamac, with Anny Ondra and Teddy Bill, premieres.

3 The Prussian government bans all Prussian civil servants from membership in either Communist Party (KPD) or National Socialist German Workers' Party (NSDAP) organizations.

4 Ullstein Press purchases the Theater des Westens in Berlin from the Rotter Brothers producing firm, with the intention of opening a nonsubsidized "literary theater" on the premises.

Rudolf Laban moves his Choreography Institute from Berlin to Essen, where he will house it under the name "Dance Department" in the Essen Folkwang Museum.

University students (numbering in the thousands, according to Berlin police) stage a demonstration in central Berlin with placards reading "Germany Awake!" and "For Academic Freedom, against the Suppression of Freedom in Universities"; police permit the demonstration to proceed because the students have no ostensible political affiliation.

9 Right-wing political leaders Heinrich Class, Theodor Düsterberg, Adolf Hitler, Alfred Hugenberg, and Franz Seldte form a committee to organize a nationwide referendum to disavow the Young Plan and its revised schedule of reparation payments. They call for a law "Against the Enslavement of the German People," which would include long prison sentences for any German politician signing the Young Plan agreement in its present form.

11 The Prussian Cultural Ministry announces cuts in subsidies for Prussian city theaters by about 40 percent; subsidies to regional theaters in Prussian jurisdictions will receive increases in subsidy.

14 German national tennis team defeats British team for victory in European round of the Davis Cup championship.

15 Albert Schweitzer is named honorary member of the Prussian Academy of Sciences.

16 Phaidon Press publishes the poetry volume *Dichtungen aus dem Osten* (*Eastern Poetry*), by Klabund.

17 More than 100,000 participants converge on Nuremberg for the second annual Proletarian Turner Festival of gymnastics and fitness training.

18 Steamship *Bremen* begins its maiden voyage across the North Atlantic to New York; the ship features a steam catapult, allowing postal airplanes aboard the ship to take off midway across the ocean and deliver airmail in New York the next day.

The novel *Wilde Jugend* (*Wild Youth*), by Rudolf Herzog is serialized in the monthly general circulation magazine *Gartenlaube*.

19 The film *Der Teufelsreporter* (*One Hell of a Reporter*), directed by Ernst Laemmle, screenplay by Billy Wilder, with Eddie Polo and Gritta Ley, premieres.

20 The Heidelberg Festival opens, featuring productions of plays by new playwrights, invited from theaters around the country.

The German National Track and Field championship meet opens in Breslau.

22 The Charlottenburg Sport Club 400-meter relay team sets a world record of 40.8 seconds for the event at the Breslau Track and Field meet.

Steamship *Bremen* arrives in New York City after making passage from Bremerhaven in a record time of four days, 18 hours, and 17 minutes.

25 The annual Baden-Baden Chamber Music Festival features new works composed for radio and films by several contemporary composers. Among the premieres: *Der Lindberghflug* (*Lindbergh's Flight*) and *Das Badener Lehrstück* (*The Baden Didactic Play*), by Bertolt Brecht,[6] both with music by Paul Hindemith and Kurt Weill.

26 Fischer Press publishes the novel *Es geschah in Moskau* (*It Happened in Moscow*), by Arthur Holitscher.

28 Fürth soccer team defeats Berlin Hertha 3 to 2 for the German national championship.

30 The film *Flucht die Fremdenlegion* (*Escape into the Foreign Legion*) premieres, directed by Louis Ralph, with Hans Stüwe and Eva von Berne.

31 There are now more than 3 million licensed radio listeners in Germany.

AUGUST

1 The literary journal *Die Linkskurve* (*Curve to the Left*) premieres, published by League of Proletarian-Revolutionary Authors.

The fourth annual National Socialist German Workers' Party congress opens in Nuremberg, with more than 60,000 members of the brown-shirted *Sturmabteilung* (Storm Troopers) in attendance.

7 The airship *Graf Zeppelin* departs from Lakehurst, New Jersey, for a round-the-world journey, which the Zeppelin Airship Company in Friedrichshafen estimates will take about three weeks.

The crime film *Kolonne X* (*Column X*) premieres, directed by Reinhard Schünzel, with Ernst Stahl-Nachbaur and Grete Reinwald.

9 German stock exchanges react negatively to the decision by the United States Federal Reserve Bank to raise the prime interest rate from 5 to 6 percent, causing panic sell-offs of numerous shares.

10 The Exhibition of Advertising opens at Kaiserdamm Exhibition Hall in Berlin.

11 International Advertising Congress opens at the Wintergarden Convention Center in Berlin; about 5,000 people from Europe, the United States, and Canada attend.

Playwright Carl Zuckmayer is awarded the city of Darmstadt's Georg Büchner Prize.

12 Paula von Recznicek wins the women's German National Tennis Championship in Hamburg.

26 Helmut Körnig sets a new world record at the Bochum track and field competition of 21.0 seconds for the 200-meter dash.

29 The German version of the World War I drama *Journey's End*, by Robert Cedric Sheriff, translated by Walter Schönherr, premieres at Künstler Theater in Berlin.

The airship *Graf Zeppelin* returns to its docking station in Lakehurst, New Jersey, after a 21-day, seven-hour, 12-minute trip around the world.[7] Hearst-controlled newspapers and radio stations in America give extended accounts of the trip, promoting interest among Americans to travel more extensively aboard airships.

31 The comedy *Grand Hotel*, by Paul Frank, premieres at the Lustspielhaus in Berlin; the musical *Happy End*, by Kurt Weill and Bertolt Brecht, premieres at the Theater am Schiffbauerdamm in Berlin.[8]

SEPTEMBER

1 An attempt to blow up Reichstag building in Berlin is minimally successful; some structural damage but the building remains sound and usable; members of the peasant movement *Landvolk* (People of the Land) are suspected of planting the bomb.

The Young Plan officially goes into effect.

2 Köhler Press publishes the novel *Held seines Landes* (*Hero of His Country*), by Walter Bloem.

National Socialists devote an entire issue of their weekly *Angriff* to attacks on the Young Plan. "Down with this betrayal of German freedom!" says one headline. "Plant Flags of Resistance and Outrage!" says another.

3 The film romance *Ich lebe für Dich* (*The Triumph of Love*) premieres, directed by Wilhelm Dieterle, with Dieterle himself in the principal male role and Lien Deyers as his love interest.

Bonz Press publishes the novel *Muspilli*, by Wolfgang Goetz.

4 More than 200,000 people gather in Friedrichshafen to welcome the airship *Graf Zeppelin* back to Germany after circumnavigating the globe, covering a total of 30,800 miles.

5 The musical revue *Zwei Krawatten* (*Two Neckties*), by Michael Spoliansky and text by Georg Kaiser, starring Hans Albers, premieres at the Berliner Theater in Berlin.

The operetta *Marietta*, by Oscar Straus, premieres at the Metropol Theater in Berlin.

Bauhaus faculty members and artists Vassily Kandisnky and Oskar Schlemmer are awarded the Medal of Distinction by the city of Cologne at an exhibition of their work in the Rhineland city.

Zsolnay Press publishes the novel *Lord Byron* by Kasimir Edschmid.

6 The pro-abortion drama *Cynakali* (*Cyanide*), by physician Friedrich Wolf, premieres at the Lessing Theater in Berlin.[9]

Erwin Piscator is able to refinance his lease at the Nollendorf Platz Theater and reopen his Piscator Stage with the premiere of the drama *Der Kaufmann von Berlin* (*The Merchant of Berlin*), by Walter Mehring.

8 The newly constituted Berlin Radio Symphony Orchestra debuts, broadcasting live their performance of "Dance Suite for Jazz Band and Orchestra," by Eduard Künneke..

11 Foreign Minister Gustav Stresemann attempts to defuse growing enthusiasm for a popular referendum against the Young Plan: "Germany's burden is eased," he says. "We are once again master of our own house."

12 The Möller Gallery in Berlin opens an exhibition of paintings and drawings by Paula Modersohn-Becker.

Insel Press publishes the political biography *Joseph Fouché*, by Stefan Zweig.

14 Cassirer Press publishes the final volume of the Ernst Cassirer series[10] *Philosophie der symbolschen Formen* (*Philosophy of Symbolic Forms*) titled *Phänomenologie der Erkenntnis* (*Phenomenology of Recognition*).

15 German-American economist Richard Weidenhammer publishes an article in the Berlin newspaper *Vossische Zeitung* advocating new kinds of American-inspired economic activity intended to stimulate the German domestic economy, among them the retail chain store and the self-service store—both of which many Germans reject as dangerous and "typically American."

16 Reiss Press publishes the travel memoir *Paradies Amerika* (*Paradise America*), by Egon Erwin Kisch.

21 Andermann Press publishes the travel memoir *Deutschland, mein Deutschland* (*Germany, My Germany*), by Rudolf Herzog.

22 The right-wing militia group Steel Helmet practices "maneuvers" during a three-day meeting in the Rhineland; Crown Prince August Wilhelm participates as thousands of participants hear speeches and sing songs denouncing the republic and ridiculing the entire concept of democracy.

The liturgical chant cycle *Marianische Atiphonen* (*Marian Antiphonies*), by student composer Wolfgang Fortner at Lower Rhine Music Festival in Düsseldorf.

23 The Berlin newspaper *Neue Rundschau* begins serial publication of the novel *Narziss und Goldmund* (*Narcissus and Goldmund*), by Hermann Hesse.

25 The Berlin newspaper *Vossische Zeitung* begins serial publication of the novel *Bruder und Schwester* (*Brother and Sister*), by Leonhard Frank.

27 At a mass rally of National Socialists in Berlin's Sports Palace, "gauleiter" (a term Hitler has invented meaning "district leader") Joseph Goebbels claims that the drive for a popular referendum on the Young Plan is "simply the beginning of a wider peoples' revolution."

The cabaret performer and actor Gustaf Gründgens has his directorial debut at the State Opera in Berlin with the German premiere of three short operas: *The Spanish Clock* by Maurice Ravel, *The Poor Sailor* by Darius Milhaud, and *Angélique* by Jacques Ibert.

28 The drama *Die Präsidentenwahl* (*The Presidential Election*), by Max Halbe, premieres at the Munich Residenz Theater.

30 Fischer Press publishes the novel *Berlin Alexanderplatz*, by Alfred Döblin.[11]

Actress Brigitte Helm loses her suit against Ufa Film Studios for voiding her contract because she was overweight (more than 120 lbs).

OCTOBER

1 The drama *Stempelbrüder* (*Peas in a Pod*), by Richard Duchinsky, premieres at the Renaissance Theater in Berlin.

3 Foreign Minister Gustav Stresemann dies of a stroke in Berlin; Count Harry Kessler notes in his diary that Stresemann's death is the first note in the death knell for the Weimar Republic, as hatred toward the victorious Allies and the Versailles Treaty will increase and sentiment for a right-wing dictatorship will grow proportionately.[12]

4 The science fiction film *Die Frau im Mond* (*The Woman in the Moon*) premieres, directed by Fritz Lang, with Willy Fritsch and Gerda Maurus.

Economics Minister Julius Curtius is named Foreign Minister.

5 The dramatic adaptation by Arnolt Bronnen of the novella *Michael Kohlhaas* by Heinrich von Kleist premieres at the Frankfurt an der Oder City Theater; the pro-abortion drama *§218: Gequälte Menschen* (*Paragraph 218: Tormented People*), by Carl Crede, premieres at the Leipzig Komödienhaus Theater.

6 At the memorial service for Foreign Minister Gustav Stresemann, Reich Chancellor Hermann Müller states that the entire German nation mourns the loss "of one of its best sons, while the world has lost one of its greatest statesmen." Political pundit Carl von Ossietzky writes that in Stresemann, "Germany had, after decades of mediocrity, a truly gifted and above average political figure [on the stage]. There will now be a long intermission."[13]

Two dramas premiere: *Gerechtigkeit für Holubek* (*Justice for Holubek*), by Georg Röschel at Breslau Lobe Theater, and *Das kleine Welttheater* (*The Little Theater of the World*), by Hugo von Hofmannsthal at the Munich Residenz Theater.

7 The drama *Ächtung des Krieges* (*Proscription of War*), by Georg Kaiser, premieres at the Deutsches Künstlerhaus in Berlin.

10 The operetta *Land des Lächelns* (*Land of Smiles*), by Franz Lehar, premieres at Metropol Theater in Berlin.

11 The German Theater Club eulogizes its honorary member the late foreign minister Gustav Stresemann in a memorial service.

The drama *Die Königin* (*The Queen*), by Carl Sternheim, premieres at Görlitz City Theater.

13 The tragicomedy *Sladek der schwarze Reichswehrmann* (*Sladek the Militiaman*), by Ödön von Horvath, premieres at the Lessing Theater in Berlin.

Radio broadcasts are increasingly used both to advocate and condemn the planned popular referendum on the Young Plan; today Reich Justice Minister Theodor von Guérard gives a speech on the significance of the referendum for the Rhineland.

15 The film drama *Tagebuch einer Verlorenen* (*Diary of a Lost Girl*) premieres, directed by G. W. Pabst, with Louise Brooks and Sybille Schmitz.

16 Die Katakombe cabaret opens in the cellar of the Artists' Cultural League in Berlin with Werner Finck as "conferencier" (master of ceremonies).

Reich President von Hindenburg declares that he has no position regarding a popular referendum on the Young Plan and no one should use his name in attempts to advocate for or against the Young Plan.

The German version of the drama *The Fourteenth of July* by Roman Rolland, translated by Wilhelm Herzog, premieres at the Frankfurt am Main City Theater.

18 The operetta and musical revue star Fritzi Massary, in her first dramatic role as *The First Mrs. Selby*, by St. John Ervine, translated by Erich Glass, premieres at the Theater in der Königgrätzer Strasse in Berlin; the show becomes a popular hit among both audiences and critics.

19 Two foreign comedies premiere in Germany: *The Apple Cart*, by George Bernard Shaw, translated by Siegfried Trebitsch, at the Deutsches Theater in Berlin and *Marius*, by Marcel Pagnol, translated by Bruno Frank, at the Breslau Lobe Theater.

Albert Einstein debuts on the radio, as he extends congratulations to American inventor Thomas Alva Edison on the 50th anniversary of Edison's development of the incandescent light bulb.

20 The drama *Hellseherei* (*Clairvoyance*), by Georg Kaiser, premieres at Württemberg Regional Theater in Stuttgart.

24 The Kleist Prize is divided between novelist Alfred Brust and dramatist Eduard Reinacher.

The Wall Street stock market in New York collapses, with more than 12.9 million shares of stock sold.

25 Reports of a stock market crash in New York precipitates panic in German stock exchanges, as the value of shares drops and massive sell-offs accelerate.

26 The comedy *Das Parfum meiner Frau* (*My Wife's Perfume*), by Leo Lenz, premieres at Görlitz City Theater.

Construction begins on new university buildings and campus properties for the University of Cologne, overseen by Cologne mayor Konrad Adenauer.

28 The sound film *Atlantik* (a German-British production, dramatizing the sinking of the *Titanic*) premieres, shot with German- and English-speaking casts; both versions are directed by E. A. Dupont, with German-speaking actors Fritz Kortner, Heinrich Schroth, Elsa Wagner, Lucie Mannheim, and Hermann Valentin.

30 The drama *Pennäler* (*School Boys*), by Peter Martin Lampel, premieres at the Theater am Schiffbauerdamm in Berlin.

Kipenheuer Press publishes anthology *24 neue deutsche Erzähler* (*24 New German Authors*), with short fiction by Marieluise Fleisser, Franz Carl Weiskopf, Ödön von Horvath, Anna Seghers, Erich Kästner, Ernst Toller, and others.

31 The drama *Gesellschaft der Menschenrechte: Stück um Georg Büchner* (*Society of Human Rights: A Play about Georg Büchner*), by Franz Theodor Csokor, premieres at the Munich Prinzregenten Theater.

NOVEMBER

2 Referendum on the Young Plan gains enough votes to force introduction of a law in the Reichstag to rescind German agreement.

In reaction to the American stock market crash of the week previous, German banks begin lowering their prime lending rates of interest.

4 German version of drama *Strange Interlude*, by Eugene O'Neill, translated by Marianne Wentzel, premieres at the Deutsches Künstlerhaus in Berlin.

The *Der Günstling von Schönbrunn* (*The Minion of Schönbrunn*, directed as a silent film but later synchronized in some scenes with actors' voices), directed by Erich Waschneck, with Lil Dagover and Ivan Petrovich, premieres.

9 The sound film *Das Land ohne Frauen* (*Bride 68*) premieres, directed by Carmine Gallone, with Conrad Veidt and Elga Brink.

12 Thomas Mann is awarded the Nobel Prize for Literature.

13 The film drama *Giftgas* (based on material in the play by Peter Martin Lampel) premieres, directed by Mikhail Dubson, with Alfred Abel and Lissy Arna.

15 The adventure film *Die weisse Hölle von Piz Palü* (*The White Hell of Pitz Palu*) premieres, directed by Arnold Fanck and G. W. Pabst, with Leni Riefenstahl, Gustav Diessl, and fighter pilot Ernst Udet.

19 The drama *Die Brücke* (*The Bridge*), by Erwin Guido Kolbenheyer, premieres at Düsseldorf Schauspielhaus.

21 The sound-on-disc film *Königsloge* (*The Royal Box*, based on a play by Alexandre Dumas about the English actor Edmund Kean) premieres, directed by Bryan Foy, with Alexander Moissi and Camilla Horn.

22 The sound-on-disc film *Dich habe ich geliebt* (released as *Because I Loved You*, the first German sound film in the United States) premieres, directed by Rudolf Walther-Fein, with Mady Christians and Walter Jankuhn.

24 A wood sculpture by Ernst Barlach is unveiled Magdeburg Cathedral depicting a group of squashed, unheroic soldier-figures gathered symmetrically around a cross.

25 The drama *Die Affäre Dreyfus* (*The Dreyfus Case*), by Hans-José Rehfisch, premieres at the Volksbühne in Berlin.

28 The drama *Die gute Zeit* (*The Good Time*), by sculptor Ernst Barlach, premieres at the Gera Reussisches Theater.

29 The film drama *Das Mädel mit der Peitsche* (*The Girl with the Whip*) premieres, directed by Carl Lamac, with Anny Ondra in the title role and Werner Füetterer.

30 The comedy *Drei Herren im Frack* (*Three Gentlemen in Evening Wear*), by Hans Adler, premieres at the Tribüne Theater in Berlin.

A bill to rescind the Young Plan is defeated in the Reichstag; National Socialists and other right-wing parties promise vengeance against deputies who voted against it.

Several private banks in Germany announce liquidity failure.

DECEMBER

2 The German version of the opera *Christopher Columbus*, by Darius Milhaud, premieres at Mannheim National Theater; officials at the theater later announce its bankruptcy and need for emergency funding from the Mannheim city council to remain open.

3 The comedy *Abenteuer in den Pyranäen* (*Adventure in the Pyrenees*), by Hadrian Maria Netto, premieres at Saxon Regional Theater in Dresden.

4 The dramatization *Winnetou* by Hermann Dimmler and Ludwig Körner, based on fictional accounts of the American West, by Karl May, premieres for young audiences at the Theater in der Königgrätzerstrasse in Berlin.

5 The drama *Columbus*, by Hans Kyser, premieres at the Cologne City Theater.

6 The film *Ehe in Not* (*Ménage à trois*) premieres, directed by Richard Oswald, with Elga Brink, Walter Rilla, and Evelyn Holt.

7 The comedy *Der Lügner und die Nonne* (*The Liar and the Nun*), by Curt Goetz, premieres at Hamburg Thalia Theater.

Conductor Bruno Walter accepts the musical directorship of the Leipzig Gewandhaus Orchestra.

8 National Socialists for the first time make substantial gains in elections; their victories in Thuringia and Bavaria are most notable.

12 The drama *Die Gartenlaube* (*The Summer House*), by Hermann Ungar, premieres at the Theater am Schiffbauerdamm in Berlin.

15 The drama *Flieg, roter Adler von Tirol* (*Fly, Red Eagle of Tyrolia*), by Fred W. Angermeyer, premieres at the Munich Kammerspiele.

16 The sound film melodrama *Melodie des Herzens* (*Melody of the Heart*) premieres, directed by Hanns Schwarz, with Willy Fritsch and Dita Parlo.

17 The comedy film *Karl Valentin, der Sonderling* (*Karl Valentin, the Oddball*) premieres, directed by Walter Jervin, featuring many of Valentin's sketches and routines, with Liesl Karlstadt.

The city of Dresden declares itself insolvent but receives a last-minute loan from a consortium of banks to meet its payrolls through the end of December.

19 The sound film *Die Nacht gehört uns* (*The Night Belongs to Us*) premieres, directed by Carl Froelich, with Hans Albers and Charlotte Ander.

20 The city of Berlin declares itself insolvent and agrees to submit its budgets to state supervision; Reich finance minister Rudolf Hilferding is forced to resign after revelations that his deputies had engaged in secret negotiations with American banks to secure loans to finance government obligations.

21 The comedy *Hulla di Bulla*, by Franz Arnold and Ernst Bach, premieres at the Comic Opera in Berlin.

The Reichstag passes emergency legislation to allow measures to address the growing financial crisis.

23 Reich President von Hindenburg appoints new economics and finance ministers to the government of Chancellor Hermann Müller.

A group of banks enters agreement with the German Reichsbank to reschedule certain loans based on expected tax revenues, though revenue shortfalls are beginning to increase.

24 Numerous street demonstrations by unemployed workers occur throughout Berlin.

25 German national radio studios in Königswusterhausen send shortwave broadcasts directed to a chain of German-speaking AM radio stations in the United States, creating the first direct German-American radio hookup.

26 The musical *Ich tanze um die Welt mit Dir* (*I'll Dance around the World with You*), by Friedrich Hollaender, premieres at the Darmstadt Regional Theater.

30 The pseudodocumentary of proletarian life in Berlin *Mutter Krausens Fahrt ins Glück* (*Mother Krause's Journey to Happiness*) premieres, directed by Phil Jutzi, with Alexandra Schmitt in the title role and Ilse Trautschold.

31 The operetta *Mit dir allein auf einer Insel* (*All Alone on an Island with You*), by Ralph Benatzky, premieres at the Dresden Residenz Theater.

NOTES

1. The sound-on-disc technology developed by American Telephone and Telegraph Corporation was cheaper than the sophisticated sound-on-film technology of the German Tri-Ergon Corporation, but the discs delivered with the film had only four minutes of sound recording space. The Tri-Ergon system employed an optical "reader" within the film camera that could electronically convert sound waves into light waves and record them onto the film. Exhibitors wishing to employ the sound-on-film system, however, had to invest in new projection equipment that contained "playback" capacity; exhibitors using the sound-on-disc system had to invest in a turntable that played the discs accompanying the film and train a technician to play the disc in synchronization with actors' lip movements on the film. Neither system provided a solution to the rather primitive state of amplification technology in the late 1920s, and no loudspeakers were readily available to fill huge movie theaters convincingly with undistorted sound.

2. A comparison of horizontal lines and pixels found in that transmission with those currently in use reveals how murky that "higher quality" television transmission in Berlin must have been. Current television broadcast protocols in the United States employ 525 horizontal lines, according to the National Television Standards Committee (NTSC) system, while Europe uses 625 lines under Phase Alternate Line (PAL) protocols. Both display about 350,000 pixels on television screens. The new Advanced Television Systems Committee in the United States has defined High-Definition Television (HDTV) as having either 720 and 1080 horizontal lines, with between 921,600 and 2,073,600 pixels.

3. The most frequently performed Shakespearean plays at the State Theater (formerly the Court Theater) in Berlin over the past century were (in order of frequency) *Hamlet*, *The Merchant of Venice*, *King Lear*, *Richard III*, *The Comedy of Errors*, *Macbeth*, *Othello*, *Romeo and Juliet*, *Much Ado about Nothing*, and *As You Like It*.

4. This Warner Brothers film used the same clumsy sound-on-disc technology from Western Electric as had its predecessor, the Al Jolson film *The Jazz Singer*. Like

that film, *The Singing Fool* was not really a sound film at all: it had passages where a disc played vocalizations of both songs and spoken dialogue—synchronized with the film, depending on the skill of the turntable operator. *The Singing Fool* in Berlin used dialogue titles (not subtitles) to translate the dialogue in silent passages, just as all films before it had done. It was running to full houses nearly every night for seven weeks until the film exhibitors association in Berlin got a court injunction against it, successfully convincing a Berlin judge that Western Electric equipment was unlicensed for use in Berlin theaters.

5. The new department store had 72,000 sq. meters (775,015 sq. feet, a combined total area of approximately 13.5 American football fields) in nine floors of commercial floor space, featuring 24 escalators, 24 elevators, and a 43,000 sq. foot rooftop restaurant. Many German critics of the "department store concept" cited its glorification of consumerism and acquisitiveness; department stores not only glorified shopping, they attempted to make it culturally desirable. Compounding the misgivings of many critics was the "installment plan," which allowed Karstadt customers to purchase and even possess merchandise before they had fully paid for it. Making debt more easily accessible worked against thrift and promoted gratification of desire— though some economic theorists at the time contended that easier credit might help the German economy, which by 1929 was in a distinctly downward spiral. Opponents held that consumer spending could not possibly have a positive effect because it compromised long-cultivated traits among Germans of delayed gratification and strength of character.

6. *The Lindbergh Flight* was originally conceived as "a didactic play for boys and girls" to premiere on radio, not for live performance in a concert hall. Performers therefore gathered in a room that festival organizers agreed to transform into a temporary broadcast studio; the performers' vocal and instrumental efforts then were transmitted into several surrounding rooms–but not on public airwaves. Brecht's attempts to get radio broadcasters subsequently to repeat the work were largely unfruitful, though *The Lindbergh Flight* remains a pioneer effort in modernist performance art. At the "regular" concert performance on the following day, Brecht divided the performers on a concert stage into groups; they comprised "The Radio." In a downstage area, an actor called "The Listener" sat and read from a script. The other Brecht effort, officially titled *Das Badener Lehrstück vom Einverständnis* (*The Baden Didactic Play of Mutual Understanding*) featured a trans-Atlantic plane crew whose aircraft crashes. In the ensuing discussions they conduct about what to do next, two clowns entered and sawed off the legs of a stilt figure. This performance likewise proved unappetizing and few audience members (among them Nobel Prize laureate Gerhart Hauptmann, who exited the performance hall early) left with positive impressions of Brecht's experiments. Most of the other experiments carried out at the 1929 Baden-Baden festival proved likewise unsuccessful, contributing to the termination of Baden-Baden festival.

7. American media magnate William Randolph Hearst sponsored the globe-circling flight of the *Graf Zeppelin* in exchange for exclusive rights to report on its journey and anything connected with it, its crew, its flight path, and the airship itself throughout the endeavor. One of Hearst's conditions was that the flight begin and end

in Lakehurst, located about 70 miles south of New York City and about 10 miles inland from the Atlantic Ocean. From Lakehurst, the *Graf Zeppelin* flew to Germany, then northeast across the Asian landmass to Tokyo. From Tokyo, the airship made history's first trans-Pacific flight, landing in San Francisco. From San Francisco, the airship flew to Chicago, and from there back to Lakehurst.

8. Several sources list September 2 as the "official" date of *Happy End*'s premiere, largely because the show continued to change after it opened on August 31. Changes were needed because soon after opening, it was obvious the show had flopped with critics and audiences—even though it was conceived to run as a "sister act" with the enormously successful and popular *The Threepenny Opera* in the same theater. *Happy End* not only premiered in the same theatre under the same producer (Ernst Josef Aufricht); it had virtually the same cast as the earlier show. That Brecht, Weill, and Hauptmann had also written it seemed to augur similar success as the previous collaboration. Yet it ran for only six more performances after its opening. It remained unrevived on German stages until the mid-1950s, but since then there have been numerous outstanding productions. The most notable among them on Broadway occurred in 1977 in a translation by Michael Feingold, featuring Bob Gunton and Meryl Streep.

9. Three major feature films had already focused on the debate about legalized abortion in Germany before the opening of *Cyanide*. *Kreuzzug des Weibes* (*Pilgrimage of Woman*), *Der Sittenrichter* (*The Judge of Morals*), and *Das Recht der Ungeborenen* (*The Right of the Unborn*). None of those movies, however, provoked the public outcry and discussion that the play occasioned, largely because of the controversy surrounding the physician who had written *Cyankali*, Friedrich Wolf. Wolf was an active member of the German Communist Party, and soon after the play's premiere, he was briefly arrested and accused of running an abortion clinic; the charges were later dropped. According to one estimate of a physician's group in Germany, between 500,000 and 800,00 abortions were performed in the year 1926; in other years during the Weimar Republic, those figures were approximately similar. A woman could be sentenced to five years' imprisonment for having an abortion, according to Paragraph 218 of the German Penal Code.

10. Ernst Cassirer (1874–1945) had just been named rector of the University of Hamburg at the time of this publication. He was a member of the prominent Cassirer family from Breslau, whose members included his cousins Bruno and Paul Cassirer. The National Socialist Student League in Hamburg staged numerous protests against Ernst Cassirer's appointment as university rector, which was the first accorded to a Jew among Herman universities.

11. *Berlin Alexanderplatz* by physician Alfred Döblin (1878–1957) became emblematic of Weimar culture, largely because of its experimental structure, montage-like effects, and linguistic oddities. Döblin had begun a writing career before he graduated from medical school in 1905, though few publishers were interested in him until he won the Fontane Prize in 1915 with his novel *Die drei Sprünge des Wang-lun* (*The Three Leaps of Wang-lun*). He continued writing during his service as a medical officer during World War I and by the mid-1920s had produced three more novels. Critics and scholars have noticed similarities between *Berlin Alexanderplatz* and the work

of James Joyce, James T. Farrell, and John Dos Passos. Like Joyce, Döblin uses "interior monologue" as a narrative device and concentrates the novel's action within a tightly restricted geographical area (the densely urbanized confines of Alexander Square in central Berlin). Its central character Franz Biberkopf wanders through this wasteland, his senses assaulted by snatches from newspaper headlines, advertising slogans, popular song lyrics, weather forecasts, reports from sporting events, quotations from sex manuals, and other fragmentations of popular culture in Döblin's attempt to flesh out a montage of urban life. The first cinematic treatment of the novel appeared in 1931, directed by Phil Jutzi with Heinrich George as Biberkopf and Magarete Schlegel as his doomed girlfriend Mieze. A far more detailed version in 14 episodes made for televison appeared in 1980, directed by Rainer Werner Fassbiner, with Günther Lamprecht as Biberkopf and Barabra Sukowa as Mieze.

12. Count Harry Kessler, *Tagebücher* (Frankfurt am Main: Insel, 1982), 629.

13. *Die Weltbühne: vollständiger Nachdruck der Jahrgänge* 1918–1933 (Königstein: Athenäum, 1978), entry for 8 October 1929.

1930

JANUARY

1 1.9 million Germans lose their jobs in 1929 and join the ranks of the unemployed eligible for jobless benefits.

Tenor Richard Tauber forms the "Richard Tauber Sound Film Co." with the intent of making musical movies that showcase his unique vocal talents.

3 Playwright and director of Trianon Theater in Berlin Leo Walter Stein commits suicide in wake of his theater's bankruptcy and closure.

4 Exhibition of new paintings by Otto Pankok opens at the Düsseldorf Kunsthalle.

7 The beginning in *Die Weltbühne* literary journal of a discussion and essay series about radio's influence on German culture. Editor Carl von Ossietzky claims that Hitler is a mere puppet in the hands of other nationalist, right-wing party leaders such as Alfred Hugenberg. "Once [Hugenberg] no longer needs him, [Hitler and] the National Socialist movement will mysteriously disappear just as it has so mysteriously grown over the last two years."

8 A retrospective exhibition of work by sculptor Ernst Barlach is held (on the occasion of his 60th birthday six days earlier) at the Prussian Academy of the Arts in Berlin.

The film *Revolte im Erziehungshaus* (*Revolt in the Reform School*, based on the play of same title by Peter Martin Lampel) premieres, directed by Georg Asagaroff, with Carl Balhaus and Vera Baranovskaya.

9 The operetta *Das Spielzeug ihrer Majestät* (*The Plaything of Her Majesty*), by Josef Königsberger, premieres at the Cologne Opera House.

The drama *Apollo-Brunnenstrasse* (*Apollo of Brunnen Strasse*), by Stefan Grossmann and Franz Hessel, premieres at the Volksbühne in Berlin.

14 Communist militia members attack National Socialist militia member Horst Wessel in his apartment; Adolf Hitler declares Wessel's song *Die Fahne hoch* (*Hang High the Banner*) the official anthem of the National Socialists. His death gives the National Socialist German Workers' Party its first "Berlin martyr."

Oldenburg Press publishes the historical survey *Feinde Bismarcks* (*Bismarck's Enemies*), by Otto Westphal.

15 The German Association of Motion Picture Theater Owners meet at Schlaraffia Hall in Berlin to discuss strategies of covering costs for refurbishing their facilities and the extraordinary expenses of converting to sound film exhibition.[1]

The comedy *Ein hässliches Mädchen* (*An Ugly Girl*), by Felix Joachimson, premieres at the Hamburg Deutsches Schauspielhaus

16 The drama *Menschen im Hotel* (*Grand Hotel*), by Ladislas Fodor, based on the popular novel of the same title by Vicki Baum, premieres at the Theater am Nollendorf Platz in Berlin; an English translation of this adaptation opens later in New York City.[2]

The Prussian Interior Minister forbids all manner of outdoor demonstrations, gatherings, assemblies, or "mobilizations" throughout Prussia in an attempt to derail confrontations between Communist and National Socialist partisans.

17 The Communist Party organ *Red Flag* urges its readers to transform all workers in Berlin into a "red army" that will "turn the entire country into a Soviet Germany." Berlin police confiscate the party's printing presses, ink, and paper supplies.

18 The dance suite *Schwingende Landschaft* (*Swaying Landscape*), by Mary Wigman, premieres at the Düsseldorf Opera House.

Leopold Jessner resigns as director of the State Theater Berlin under pressure from right-wing activists in the Prussian legislature; his "Jewified" productions had been controversial since the early 1920s and many had accused him of "cultural Bolshevism."[3]

A French acting troupe from Lyons opens an "exchange tour" with Freiburg City Theater, the first French troupe to perform as guests of a German theater since World War I.

The musical farce *Der Walzer von heute nacht* (*Tonight's Waltz*), by Heinz Ilgenstein, with music by Franz Lehar, premieres at the Kleines Theater in Berlin.

The comedy *Was spät kommt, kommt doch* (*Better Late than Never*), by Hartwig Bonner, premieres at the Leipzig City Theater.

19 The opera *Das Leben des Orest* (*The Life of Orestes*), by Ernst Krenek, premieres at the Leipzig Opera House.

The Independent Turner Association stages a "proletarian sports festival" at Berlin Schöneberg Sports Palace attracting more than 1,500 participants, nearly all industrial workers who excel in gymnastics, wrestling, and some indoor track events.

Ernst Legal is named new director of the State Theater in Berlin.

The drama *Amnestie* (*Amnesty*), by Karl Maria Finkelburg, premieres at the Volksbühne in Berlin.

20 The drama *Kalifornische Tragödie* (*California Tragedy*, about the discovery of gold at Sutter's Mill near Sacramento and the gold rush that followed), by Eberhard Wolfgang Möller, premieres at the Erfurt City Theater.

Eden Press publishes the novel *The Cardinal's Mistress* by Italian dictator Benito Mussolini.

23 The comedy *Kuckuck und sein Kind* (*Cuckoo and His Child*), by Herbert Eulenberg, premieres at the Krefeld City Theater.

Thüringen becomes the first German province to install National Socialists as ministers in its government.

24 Much-publicized libel proceedings take place between the Munich newspaper *Telegrammzeitung* and National Socialist leader Hitler, as both had sued each other for defamation; the newspaper had accused Hitler of threatening Bavarian Crown Prince Rupprecht, while Hitler had referred publicly to the newspaper as a *Mistblatt* (shit sheet). The Munich court fines both parties RM 400.

25 The German premiere of the comedy *Tonight We Improvise!* by Luigi Pirandello, translated by Harry Kahn, opens at the Königsberg City Theater.

26 The one-act opera *Galatea*, by Walter Braunfels, premieres at the Cologne Opera House.

27 The drama *Gegenüber von China* (*Across from China*), by Klaus Mann, premieres at the Bochum City Theater.

28 The German premiere of ballet *Apollon Musagète*, by Igor Stravinsky, opens at the Königsberg Opera House.

Astrologer Willy Krone attracts an audience of 2,000 to his lecture "Astrology and Human Destiny," featuring photo projections and film clips.

29 The drama *Die Verräter Gottes* (*God's Traitors*), by Franz Anton Dietzenschmidt, premieres at the Ulm City Theater.

The film drama *Der weisse Teufel* (*The White Devil*) premieres in both silent and sound versions, directed by Alexandre Volkoff, with Lil Dagover, Fritz Alberti, and Peter Lorre.

30 The comedy *Reparationen* (*Reparations*), by Arnolt Bronnen, premieres at the Mannheim National Theater.

Ullstein Press publishes the novel *Charlotte von Weiss* by Clara Viebig.

31 Renaissance Theater in Berlin declares bankruptcy, joining six other private theaters in Berlin that have closed their doors and ceased operations; of the remaining Berlin private theaters attempting to produce "serious fare," only the Volksbühne (with support of Social Democratic Party) maintains a full performance schedule.

FEBRUARY

1 The one-act opera *Von Heute auf Morgen* (*From Today to Tomorrow*), by Arnold Schönberg, premieres at the Frankfurt am Main City Opera.

Fischer Press publishes a collection of reworked short fiction titled *Diesseits* (*This Side*), by Hermann Hesse.

3 The musical sound film *Ich glaub' nie mehr an eine Frau* (*Never Trust a Woman*), premieres, directed by Max Reichmann, with Richard Tauber, Maria Matray, and Gustaf Gründgens.

The drama *Im Namen des Volkes* (*In the Name of the People*), by Bernhard Blume, premieres at the Leipzig City Theater.

The tone poem *Variationenen über eine schottische Volksweise* (Variations on a Scots Folk Melody), by Günther Raphael, premieres at the Duisburg City Opera.

4 The Reich National Bank lowers its prime lending rate another 0.5 percent (to 6 percent), hoping to halt rapid slide in economic activity throughout Germany in wake of Wall Street stock exchange collapse.

5 The drama *Donautragödie* (*Danube Tragedy*), by Wilhelm von Schramm, premieres at the Augsburg City Theater.

Langen Press publishes the war novel *Sieben vor Verdun* (*Seven at Verdun*), by Josef Magnus Wehner.

6 The comedy *Frauenschuh* (*A Lady's Shoe*), by Alfred Neumann, premieres at the Hamburg Thalia Theater.

7 The sound film operetta *Liebeswalzer* (*Love Waltzes*), directed by Wilhelm Thiele, with Willy Fritsch and Lilian Harvey, premieres.

National Socialists attract an audience of 15,000 people to the Berlin Sports Palace to a program titled "So kann es nicht weitergehen!" ("It Cannot Continue This Way!"), with Gen. Karl Litzmann, Joseph Goebbels, and Hermann Goering as featured speakers.

8 Two comedies premiere: *Napoleon greift ein* (*Napoleon Gets Inovlved*), by Walter Hasenclever at the Frankfurt am Main Neues Theater and *Geschäft mit Amerika* (*Business with America*), by Paul Frank and Ludwig Hirschfeld at the Stuttgart Schauspielhaus.

Thuringian cultural minister Wilhelm Frick (and a National Socialist) bans reading of the "Marxist-pacifist propaganda" novel *All Quiet on the Western Front* in Thuringian schools.

9 The German national team defeats the Swiss national team for the European ice hockey championship at the Berlin Sports Palace.

In a race across a frozen lake in Bavaria pitting a single-engine airplane, race car, and specially outfitted motorcycle against each other, fighter pilot Ernst Udet defeats car and motorcycle to collect about RM 10,000 in wagers placed on the race.

10 The drama *Flieger auf dem Atlantik* (*Flyers on the Atlantic*), by Walter Erich Schäfer, premieres at the Coburg Regional Theater.

The Prussian Academy of the Arts confers its State Prize for Architecture on Rudolf Lodders.

Officials and faculty at the University of Cologne vote to ban the presence of the National Socialist German Student League from university property and activities.

12 Director Erwin Piscator attempts to raise money by taking his production of the drama *§218: gequälte Menschen* (*Paragraph 218: Tormented People*), by Carl Crede, on tour; first stop is a Düsseldorf movie theater.

Rowohlt Press publishes a biography of the 16th American president titled *Lincoln* by Emil Ludwig; Gretlein publishes an autobiography by European heavyweight boxing champion Max Schmeling titled *Mein Leben—meine Kämpfe* (*My Life—My Fights*).

15 Knaur Press publishes a two-volume collection titled *Oscar-Wilde-Werke* (*The Works of Oscar Wilde*), edited by and with an introduction by Arnold Zweig.

Thuringian cultural minister Wilhelm Frick (and a National Socialist) fires the superintendent of Weimar schools for banning membership in the right-wing school organization "Eagle and Falcon" among high school students.

16 The drama *Die Südpolexpedition des Kapitäns Scott* (*Capt. Scott's South Pole Expedition*), by Reinhard Goering, premieres at the State Theater in Berlin.

20 Cologne mayor Konrad Adenauer makes an unprecedented public appeal to the national government in Berlin for assisting regional governments in getting loans from banks for meeting payrolls and fulfilling other government obligations.

The war drama *Reims*, by Friedrich Bethge, premieres at the Osnabrück City Theater.

21 The musical sound film *Der unsterbliche Lump* (*The Immortal Vagabond*), premieres, directed by Gustav Ucicky, with Gustav Fröhlich and Liane Haid; the music is by Ralph Benatzky.

22 An exhibition opens sponsored by the Communist Community Center for Workers' Culture in Berlin of works by George Grosz; police confiscate lithograph of his drawing "Christ in a Gas Mask" and other works decreed blasphemous. At Folkwang Museum in Essen, a display opens featuring works by Bauhaus faculty members and associates Walter Gropius, Paul Klee, Vassily Kandisnky, Lyonel Feininger, and others.

23 The Berlin school system raises the maximum number of pupils per class to 36, allowing the system to release nearly 390 teachers as a money-saving measure; other school systems around the country begin putting similar measures into place.

27 The sound film *Der Weg zur Schande* (*The Road to Dishonor*), a German-British co-production directed by Richard Eichberg, with Chinese-American actress Anna May Wong in both English and German versions, premieres.

28 Albert Einstein performs duets for violin and organ at the Oranienburger Jewish Community Center in Berlin.

MARCH

1 The exhibition "Rhineland Art" opens in Berlin, an attempt to express solidarity with German territories west of the Rhine still occupied by Allied troops. The opening is preceded by a radio broadcast from Berlin to those territories by Joseph Wirth, cabinet minister responsible for welfare of German citizens in the territories.

An exhibition that showcases the paintings of the "Berlin Secession Movement opens at the Düsseldorf Kunsthalle.

2 The sound film melodrama *Alraune* (*Daughter of Evil*), directed by Richard Oswald, with Brigitte Helm and Albert Bassermann, premieres.

The German national soccer team loses to the Italian national team 2 to 0 in Frankfurt am Main.

4 The State Theater and Opera in Berlin furloughs dozens of workers in a cost-cutting measure; Heidelberg City Theater closes and the Heidelberg Festival featuring new plays is postponed indefinitely.

Berlin district court rules that a man may divorce his wife if she fails to reveal to him prior to their marriage the names of all her premarital lovers.

6 The drama *Ein Schatten fiel über den Tisch* (*A Shadow Fell over the Table*), by Max Dauthendey, premieres at the Würzburg City Theater.

7 The drama *Putsch* by Peter Martin Lampel, premieres at the Koblenz City Theater.

The operetta *Der doppelte Bräutigam* (*The Duplicated Bridegroom*), by Walter Kollo, premieres at the Theater am Schiffbauerdamm in Berlin.

8 Reich National Bank lowers the prime lending rate another 0.5 percent (to 5.5 percent), hoping to halt increasingly rapid decline in every sector of the German economy.

9 The opera *Aufstieg und Fall der Stadt Mahagonny* (*The Rise and Fall of the City of Mahogany*), by Kurt Weill and Bertolt Brecht, premieres at Leipzig Neues Theater. Most critics denounce it as a misbegotten experiment, and it closes after five performances.

The music revue *Einst und jetzt* (*Then and Now*), by Paul Linke, premieres at the Cologne Luisen Theater.

An exhibition featuring the sculpture and graphic work of Ernst Barlach opens at the Folkwang Museum in Essen.

10 The drama *Die Kreatur* (*The Creature*), by Ferdinand Bruckner, premieres at the Komödie Theater in Berlin.

The Oberammergau Passion Play begins performances in its new facility.

12 Tatania Press publishes the novel *Um Diamanten und Perlen* (*About Diamonds and Pearls*), by Hedwig Courths-Mahler.

13 The sound film operetta *Zwei Herzen im Dreivierteltakt* (*Two Hearts in Three-Quarter Time*), directed by Geza von Bolvary, with Oskar Karlweis and Gretl Theimer, and music by Robert Stolz, premieres.

Müller Press publishes a fictionalized account of a historical incident titled *Der Hauptmann von Köpenick* (*The Captain of Köpenick*), by Wilhelm Schäfer.[4]

14 The sound film *Die letzte Kompanie* (*The Last Company*, about the Napoleonic wars), directed by Curt Bernhardt, with Conrad Veidt and Karin Evans, premieres.

15 The drama *Das Lamm des Armen* (*The Poor Man's Lamb*), by Stefan Zweig, premieres in several theaters simultaneously.

16 Renewed street fighting between Communist and National Socialist militias breaks out in Chemnitz, as both groups, and the parties that support them, openly declare intentions to replace republican government.

17 The sound film *Liebe im Ring* (*Love in the Boxing Ring*), directed by Reinhold Schünzel, with Max Schmeling and Olga Chekhova, premieres.

18 Fischer Press publishes the treatise *Das Theater der Hoffnung* (*The Theater of Hope*), by drama critic Alfred Kerr.

19 The literary monthly *Monatshefte* publishes the novella *Mario und der Zauberer: Ein tragisches Reiseerlebnis* (*Maria and the Magician: A Tragic Travel Experience*), by Thomas Mann; the general-circulation magazine *Gartenlaube* begins serial publication of the novel *Die letzten Tage des Marschalls von Sachsen* (*The Last Days of the Saxon Marshal*), by Hermann Stegemann.

20 Rowohlt Press publishes a collection of essays, theater reviews, and short fiction titled *Auswahlband* (*Volume of Selected Writings*), by Alfred Polgar.

21 The dramatic adaptation *Haus Danieli* by Alfred Neumann (based on his novella *König Haber*), premieres at the Bochum City Theater; performances are disrupted by National Socialist operatives, who have begun a systematic program of performance spoliation throughout the country. Their attacks are aimed at both live performances and film exhibitions.

Fischer Press publishes the travel memoir *Wiedersehen mit Amerika* (*Reconnecting with America*), by Arthur Holitscher.

22 Mohr Press publishes the theological treatise *Die Mystik des Apostels Paulus* (*The Mysticism of the Apostle Paul*), by Albert Schweitzer.

24 The musical suite *Wunderuhr* (*The Magical Clock*), by Michael Taube, premieres at Beethoven Hall in Berlin.

25 The drama *Zuletzt bleibt Hiob* (*Here Job Will Remain*), by Paul Zech, premieres at the Zittau City Theater.

26 Paul Schultze-Naumburg is named director of Weimar College of Architecture, setting off protests against his theories of German ethnicity and his endorsement of the National Socialists.

27 The government of chancellor Hermann Müller collapses in the wake of mounting economic troubles and he resigns; Müller was the 11th chancellor of the Weimar Republic (he was also its third chancellor, serving for two months in 1920).

29 The musical *Meine Schwester und ich* (*My Sister and I*), by Ralph Benatzky, premieres at the Metropol Theater in Berlin.

Phaidon Press publishes a volume of fiction titled *Herr, erbarme Dich meiner!* (*Lord, Have Mercy on Me!*), by Leo Perutz.

31 The drama *Spiel um den Sergeanten Grischa* (*The Sgt. Grischa Play*), by Arnold Zweig, premieres at the Berliner Theater in Berlin.

APRIL

1 The sound film *Der blaue Engel* (*The Blue Angel*), directed by Josef von Sternberg, with Emil Jannings and Marlene Dietrich, premieres.[5]

The comedy *Die neue Sachlichkeit* (*The New Matter-of-Factness*), by Toni Impekoven and Carl Mathern premieres at the Frankfurt am Main City Theater.

Meteorologist Alfred Wegener, originator of the "Kontinetalverschiebungstheorie" (*Theory of Continental Drift*) departs for Greenland for continued research on the reason continents drift across the earth, a theory very few other scientists accept.

2 The opera *The Bandits* by Jacques Offenbach, with new libretto by Karl Kraus, premieres at the Stendal Altmärkisches Theater.

The first German full-length (one hour) radio play, *Fünf Sekunden* (*Five Seconds*), by Walther von Hollander, broadcasts over a network of several broadcast partners.

3 Director Erwin Piscator leases the Wallner Theater in Berlin, dubbing his troupe the "Piscator Collective."

5 The operetta *Majestät lässt bitten* (*It Pleases Her Majesty to Request*), by Walter Kollo, premieres at the Comic Opera in Berlin.

Junker and Dünnhaupt Press publishes an edition of wartime reminiscences titled *Krieg und Krieger* (*War and Warriors*) edited by Erst Jünger; Fischer publishes the novel *An der Leine* (*By the River Leine*), by Mechthilde Lichnowsky.

7 The exhibition titled "German Art of Our Time" opens featuring new works by contemporary artists at the Nassau Art League in Wiesbaden.

9 The radio literary monthly *Rundfunkschriftum* (*Writing for Radio*) debuts, featuring radio plays and critical commentary on radio.

Reich Economics Minister Hermann Robert Dietrich addresses a convention of the German Industry and Trade Congress, noting that accelerating difficulties of the German economy may be due to what is becoming a global economic crisis.

10 The opera *Die weisse Pfau* (*The White Peacock*) by Arthur Piechler debuts at the Munich National Theater.

12 The Thuringian culture minister and National Socialist Wilhelm Frick issues decree against "Negro culture"and other "racially foreign influences" in German cultural life.

14 The "swine comedy" *Krach um Iolanthe* (*Much Ado about Iolanthe*), by August Hinrichs, premieres at the Low German Theater in Oldenburg.

15 The Reich Labor Ministry announces that there are 2.9 million "officially unemployed" workers (i.e., entitled to received jobless benefits of RM 81 per month) in Germany.

The detective sound film *Der Tiger* (*The Tiger*), directed by Johannes Meyer, with Harry Frank and Charlotte Susa, premieres.

17 Ullstein Press publishes the literary survey *Geschichte der deutschen Literatur* (*History of German Literature*), by Paul Wiegler.

19 The sound film musical *Das lockende Ziel* (*The Alluring Goal*) debuts, directed by Max Reichmann, with Richard Tauber and Maria Elsner, and music by Paul Dessau.

20 Communist Party members stage "Communist Youth Day" in Leipzig; in the afternoon open street fighting with Leipzig police breaks out; about 20 people are reported killed.

24 The drama *Wird Hill Amnestiert?* (*Will Hill be Granted Amnesty?*), by Lion Feuchtwanger, premieres at the State Theater in Berlin.

27 Bavarian government officials and Cardinal Michael von Faulhaber dedicate the new structure in Oberammergau where performances of the town's decennial *Passion Play* will now take place.

29 Berlin police apprehend the city's most well-known and popular bank robbers, Franz and Erich Sass; the brothers were well known for sharing the money they had stolen with the poor in their native Moabit district.

30 The Berlin newspaper *Der Mittag* investigates and publishes salaries paid to entertainers: among highest-paid performers in Berlin are operetta tenor Richard Tauber at RM 2,7000 and American singer Al Jolson at RM 6,000 per performance respectively; actor Conrad Veidt, RM 130,000 per film. Topping the lists are Elisabeth Bergner and Emil Jannings, both of whom earn about RM 300,000 per film.[6]

MAY

1 Festivities in Würzburg open celebrating the 700th birthday of medieval poet Walther von der Vogelweide.
  Karl Barth is named professor of Protestant Theology at the University of Bonn.

2 The Congress of Psychotherapy convention in Baden-Baden chooses Carl Gustav Jung as its principal spokesman.

4 Erwin Piscator opens the "Piscator Collective" at Wallner Theater in Berlin with his touring production of *§218: gequälte Menschen* (*Paragraph 218: Tormented People*), by Carl Crede; Piscator stages a matinee performance for an invited-only audience of judges, prosecutors, lawyers, and government officials; the evening performance open to the general public prompts vigorous discussions of abortion in several Berlin newspapers.

5 The Berlin premiere of the opera *Christopher Columbus* by Darius Milhaud, is transferred from the financially strapped Mannheim National Theater to the State Opera in Berlin.

6 The sound film romance *Die Jungedgeliebte* (*Goethe's Young Love*), directed by Hans Tintner, with Hans Stüwe as Johann Wolfgang Goethe and Elga Brink as Friederike von Sesenheim, premieres.

7 Director Max Reinhardt purchases outstanding shares of stock in Terra Film Studios from the I. G. Farbenindustrie Corp. and forms a film company to produce sound movies of operas employing the Tri-Ergon sound-on-film technology.
  The opera *Die Richterin* (*The Woman Judge*), by Hermann Grabner, premieres at the Wuppertal Music Festival.

8 The sound film *Der Walzerkönig* (*The Waltz King*, a biography of Johann Strauss, Jr., with music by Eduard Künneke based on melodies by Strauss), premieres, directed by Manfred Noa, with Hans Stüwe in the title role and Claire Rommer.

9 Choreographer and dance theorist Rudolf von Laban is named director of ballet at the State Opera in Berlin.

10 The annual exhibition at Prussian Academy of the Arts, featuring work of its members, opens; this year's spotlighted artist is painter Ludwig Knaus.

12 The "Präludium für Orchester" ("Prelude for Orchestra"), by Ernst Pepping, premieres at the Frankfurt am Main Opera House.

13 The Deutsches Theater in Berlin celebrates a quarter century of director Max Reinhardt's ownership of the facility with a premiere of the drama *Phaea* (a parody of the motion picture industry), by Fritz von Unruh.

The Berlin Philharmonic Orchestra debuts on live radio, featuring pianist Edwin Fischer in a concert broadcast from Berlin studios.

14 The German comedy *Bitter Sweet*, by Noel Coward, premieres at the Theater am Schiffbauerdamm in Berlin.

15 The opera *Der Tag im Licht* (*By the Light of Day*), by Hans Grimm, premieres at the Nuremberg Neues Theater.

Fisticuffs break out at a Berlin City Council meeting, as newly elected National Socialist members of the council physically attack other representatives in a discussion of how the new schedule of Young Plan reparation payments will affect Berlin's expenditures for cultural activities.

16 The German Museum of Hygiene opens in Dresden; a discussion about a German Beer Museum and a German Bread Museum follows.[7]

18 The Congress of Pan-European Union opens in Berlin, where featured speaker Thomas Mann calls for a politically united Europe; other speakers during the week of meetings advocate the development of "fostering cultural ties" among European nations and ethnicities.

The airship *Graf Zeppelin* departs from Friedrichshafen on an inaugural South Atlantic crossing to Rio de Janeiro in Brazil.

20 The first exhibition of German architecture, interior, stage, and industrial design in Paris since before World War I opens.

A massive number of workers are laid off in the Ruhr industrial district; several coalmines, steel works, iron foundries, and machine tool firms reduce their work forces by 50 percent.

21 Broadcast from Berlin, "Acht Klavierstücke" ("Eight Pieces for Piano"), written by Hanns Eisler and performed by Hans Erich Riebensahm, premieres on the radio.

Piper Press publishes a retrospective volume titled *Max Reinhardt: 25 Jahre Deutsches Theater* (*Max Reinhardt: 25 Years at the Deutsches Theater*) edited by Hans Rothe.

22 *Requiem* by Lothar Windsperger premieres at the Düsseldorf Musikverein.

The Reich finance ministry announces unprecedented revenue shortfalls anticipated for the coming year; with few credit sources for government borrowing available, officials prepare for cutoffs in jobless benefits to unemployed workers.

23 Two sound films premiere: *Cyankali* (*Cyanide*, based on the pro-abortion drama of the same title by Fredrich Wolf), directed by Hans Tintner, with Grete Mosheim, Margarete Kupfer, and Paul Henckels), and the war film *Westfront 1918* (*Comrades of 1918*, based on the antiwar novel *Four from the Infantry* by Ernst Johanssen), directed by G. W. Pabst, with Fritz Kampers, Gustav Diessl, Hans-Joachim Möbis, Claus Clausen, and Hannah Hössrich.

24 The scenic cantata *Esau und Jakob* by Rudolf Wagner-Regeny, premieres at the Gera Reussliches Regional Theater.

25 The opera *Transatlantik* (*Trans-Atlantic*), by German-American composer George Antheil, premieres at the Frankfurt am Main Opera House.

The comedy *Wetten, dass . . . ?* (*Wanna Bet?*), by Hermann Richter, premieres at the Lessing Theater in Berlin.

The *Graf Zeppelin* arrives in Rio de Janeiro, completing the world's first trans-equatorial airship passage.

27 The Berlin Secession opens a new exhibition of paintings by Hans Purrmann, Leo Lesser Ury, and Rudolf Schlichter.

The first "post-synchronized" German films, *Die Jagd nach dem Glück* (*Chasing Fortune*), directed by scene designer Rochus Gliese as a silent film, is later synchronized with sound by Carl Koch, with performances by Catharine Hessling and Berthold Bartosch.

The Reich government issues details of its "Plan of Necessary Sacrifice," requiring a 10 percent increase on incomes of all German wage-earners whose jobs are not presently in danger.

28 Conductor Arturo Toscanini arrives in Berlin to begin his second guest residence among the city's orchestras and to present a series of concerts.

29 The first Ladies Flying Championship Derby opens at Hangelar in the Rhineland; German women pilots compete in aerial acrobatics and speed runs competing for cash prizes awarded by the Siebengebirgsflug Corp.

30 Director Max Reinhardt is awarded an honorary doctorate from the University of Kiel at the 3,600-seat Grosses Schauspielhaus in Berlin after a performance there of the operetta *Die Fledermaus* by Johann Strauss; the operetta is Reinhardt's "Jubilee Production," marking 23,374 performances in Berlin under Reinhardt's aegis.

31 Sales of *Nichts neues im Westen* (*All Quiet on the Western Front*), by Erich Maria Remarque top the 1 million mark, the first novel since World War I to achieve that level of sales in Germany.

National Socialist deputy to the Reichstag Joseph Goebbels is fined RM 800 for insulting President Paul von Hindenburg in a National Socialist newspaper editorial titled "Lebt Hindenburg noch?" ("Is Hindenburg Still Alive?").

JUNE

3 Hans F. K. Günther is named professor of Social Anthropology and Race Research at the University of Jena; faculty members protest his appointment in view of his numerous anti-Semitic publications.

4 The comedy *Wie wird man reich?* (*How Do You Get Rich?*), by Fritz Gottwald and Joe Gribitz premieres at the Leipzig Altes Theater.

5 The Bavarian provincial government forbids "political attire" or the costuming associated with political parties at any state function or in the performance of any state-related duty or occupation.

10 The Bildergalerie (Picture Gallery) opens in Potsdam after extensive renovations and is now accessible to the public as a museum; built in 1755 at the order of Frederick the Great, the gallery was the first to house a "national collection" of paintings.

11 The Prussian government bans the wearing in public of the National Socialist militia *Sturmabteilung* (*Storm Trooper*) uniform.

13 Max Schmeling becomes the world heavyweight boxing champion by defeating Jack Sharkey in a controversial match before 80,000 spectators at Yankee Stadium in New York City. Sharkey was winning on points but lost the bout in the fourth round on a disqualification, hitting Schmeling below the belt.

14 The drama *Krach um Leutnant Blumenthal* (*Much Ado about Lt. Blumenthal*), by Alfred Herzog, premieres at the Theater am Schiffbauerdamm in Berlin.

15 The World Theater Congress opens in Hamburg, displaying architectural plans for several planned theater buildings, among them the "Total Theater" of Walter Gropius.

16 Trustees of the Prussian Academy of the Arts name painter and graphic artist Max Liebermann to a third consecutive term as the Academy's director.

20 Foreign minister Julius Curtius makes a national radio address to the people of United States, thanking them for their assistance to Germany in the postwar years for their financial assistance, which often arrived through private channels.

21 The Prussian Cultural Ministry informs the Egyptian government that the Prussian State Museum will retain the limestone bust of Queen Nefertiti, who lived and reigned in 14th century Egypt of the Amarna Period. The Egyptian government had requested its return to Cairo and had offered two Amarna busts in exchange.

22 The Berlin Hertha soccer club defeats Kiel Holstein by 5 to 4 and wins the German national championship at Düsseldorf Stadium.

23 The "school opera" *Der Jasager* (*He Who Says Yes*, based on the Japanese Noh drama *Taniko*), by Kurt Weill with libretto by Bertolt Brecht, premieres at the Berlin College of Music.

24 The Congress of International Choreographers and Teachers of Dance opens in Munich; the many participants are introduced to the techniques and ideas of German choreographers Rudolf von Laban and Mary Wigman.

25 The comedy *Ich habe keine Zeit* (*I Don't Have Time*), by Carl Rossler, premieres at the Giessen City Theater.

28 The largest street brawl to date breaks out between militias of Communist and National Socialist parties, with more than 3,000 participants; police estimate that 30 are killed and dozens injured.

29 German National Folk Song Dayis held; local choirs, singing clubs, and vocal music organizations present hundreds of concerts throughout the country.

JULY

2 A convention titled "Against Persecution" is organized by the Reich League of Jewish Soldiers; the League publicizes numerous cases of personal assaults against Jewish citizens, acts of vandalism aimed at Jewish-owned businesses, and verbal attacks against Jewish political leaders and war veterans, most organized and perpetrated by National Socialists.

8 The largest motion picture theaters in Berlin are now equipped for exhibition of sound films; the German union of instrumental musicians reports that half of all musicians formerly employed by motion picture theaters are now jobless.

12 The sound film comedy *Hokuspokus* (based on a play of same title by Curt Goetz) premieres, directed by Gustav Ucicky, with Willy Fritsch, Lilian Harvey, and Gustaf Gründgens.

14 The comedy *Konto X* (*Account X*), by Rudolf Bernauer and Rudolf Östreicher, premieres at the Neues Theater in Berlin

16 The sound film drama *Nur am Rhein* (*Only on the Rhine*), directed by Max Mack, with Julius Falkenstein and Maria Reisenhofer, premieres.

20 Life-size wax figures of world heavyweight boxing champion Max Schmeling appear in display windows of several Berlin department stores, modeling the latest in men's fashions.

22 Conductor Arturo Toscanini debuts at the Bayreuth Festival, conducting the performance of *Tannhäuser*; he later conducts the performance of *Tristan und Isolde*.

24 In Frankfurt am Main, Nobel Prize-winning author Rabindranath Tagore gives the first public reading of his works to a German audience.

25 The sound film murder mystery *Der Schuss im Tonfilmatelier* (*Gunfire in the Sound Film Studio*), directed by Alfred Zeisler, with Gerda Maurus and Harry Frank, premieres.

Reich President Paul von Hindenburg issues a "Weapon Misuse Decree," barring any member of a militia organization from carrying a concealed weapon in public.

30 Private tutor Max Horkheimer named professor of social philosophy at the University of Frankfurt am Main and takes over directorship of the Marxist-oriented Institute for Social Research.

AUGUST

1 The director of the Bauhaus School in Dessau, Hannes Meyer, resigns under pressure.[8]

The sound film *Das Kabinett des Dr. Larifari* (*The Cabinet of Dr. Larifari*), directed by Robert Wohlmuth, with Max Hansen and Mariane Stanior, premieres.

4 Winifred Wagner is named the new director of the Bayreuth Festival; she replaces her recently deceased husband Siegfried, son of composer Richard Wagner.

6 The city of Frankfurt am Main awards its Goethe Prize to the founder of psychoanalysis, Sigmund Freud.

8 The left-leaning Berlin newspaper *Berliner Tageblatt* publishes a full-page poster portraying Adolf Hitler as a boxer, defeating his right-wing rival Alfred Hugenberg. The poster begins appearing on numerous billboards around the city of Berlin.

10 National Socialists stage a ceremony in central Berlin during which they trample the republican flag underfoot; police arrest participants caught wearing Storm Trooper uniforms.

11 Numerous politicians throughout the country speak at celebrations marking the 11th anniversary of the date on which the Weimar Republic's constitution went into effect; right-wing extremists denounce the Republic and its founders at rallies. The leader of the German National Peoples' Party, Alfred Hugenberg, declares that a "Third Reich" will soon displace the republic.

12 The city of Hamburg awards its first Lessing Prize to literary historian Friedrich Gundolf.

The sound film *Der Andere* (*The Other*, based on a play by Paul Lindau), directed by Robert Wiene, with Fritz Kortner and Käthe von Nagy, premieres.

13 Neufeld and Henius Press publishes the memoir *Das Antlitz des Weltkrieges* (*The Face of the World War*), by Ernst Jünger.

14 Ullstein Press publishes the children's book *Ich geh' aus und Du bleibst da!* (*I'm Going Outside and You Stay Here!*), by Wilhelm Speyer.

15 The French silent film *Under the Roofs of Paris*, one of the last silent films to be released in Germany for general exhibition, premieres in Germany.

16 The sound film drama *Dreyfus*, directed by Richard Oswald, premieres with Fritz Kortner in the title role and Grete Mosheim. National Socialists in their several publications denounce the film as "Jewish propaganda" as part of their campaign in the upcoming Reichtag elections.

18 Director Max Reinhardt is awarded an honorary doctorate from the University of Frankfurt am Main; National Socialists impugn Reinhardt's reputation, referring to him as a "Jewish low comedian."

19 Fischer Press publishes an autobiography of Bolshevik revolutionary Leon Trotsky, titled *Mein Leben* (*My Life*), translated by Alexandra Ramm.

22 The Radio and Phonograph Show opens in Berlin; the keynote speaker is Albert Einstein, who predicts that radio will be an instrument for greater understanding among peoples. The National Socialists announce they will use radio to "expose" the campaign among Jews to grant themselves celebrity status. Other political organizations announce similar plans to employ radio broadcasts for political purposes.

23 Bonn City Theater declares bankruptcy and ceases operation.

Street fighting between National Socialists and Communists in Hessia, Silesia, and Bavaria claims dozens of lives; other parties denounce the violence as tension mounts for upcoming national elections.

25 The sound film *Abschied* (*Farewell*) premieres, directed by Robert Siodmak[9], with Brigitte Horney[10] and Aribert Mog.

26 Kiepenheuer Press publishes the political treatise *Nationalsozialismus? Eine Diskussion über den Kulturbankrott des Bürgertums* (*National Socialism? A Discussion about the Cultural Bankruptcy of the Middle Class*), by playwright Ernst Toller and journalist Alfred Mühr.

29 The comedy *Sturm im Wasserglass* (*Tempest in a Teapot*), by Bruno Frank, premieres at the Dresden State Theater.[11]

The sound film comedy *Komm' zu mir zum Rendezvous* (*Come Meet Me for a Rendezvous*), directed by Carl Boese, with Lucie Englisch and Ralph Arthur Roberts, premieres.

31 The drama *Feuer aus den Kesseln* (*Draw the Fires*), by Ernst Toller, premieres at the Theater am Schiffbauerdamm in Berlin.

SEPTEMBER

1 Adolf Hitler inaugurates extensive use of the airplane and of phonograph recordings in the campaign for the upcoming Reichstag elections; he visits several cities per day and National Socialist operatives provide election volunteers with 78-rpm records of his speeches.

The sound film *Rosenmontag* (*The Monday before Mardi Gras*, based on a play by Otto Erich Hartleben), directed by Hans Steinhoff, with Lien Deyers and Mathias Wiemann, premieres.

The drama *1914* by Georg Wilhelm Müller, premieres at the Deutsches Theater in Berlin.

3 Playwright and actor Curt Goetz is named director of the Lustspielhaus Theater in Berlin.

5 The sound film romance *Nur Du* (*Only You*), directed by Hermann Feiner, with Charlotte Ander and Walter Janssen, premieres.

11 The editor of *Die Weltbühne* literary magazine, Carl von Ossietzky, maintains in an opinion essay, "The national socialist movement has a noisy presence, but absolutely no future."

12 Fox Movietone newsreels debut in German motion picture theaters under the rubric "Die Stimme der Welt" ("The Voice of the World").

14 Reichstag elections provide stunning successes for the National Socialists; they win 107 seats, making them the second-largest party (behind the Social Democrats) in the national legislature. In regional legislatures, National Socialists also make big wins, enabling them to take charge of several regional ministries. German foreign minister Julius Curtius describes the outcome as "a political earthquake."

15 The musical sound film *Drei von der Tankstelle* (*Three Guys from the Gas Station*), directed by Wilhelm Thiele, with Willy Fritsch, Heinz Rühmann, and Oskar Karlweis in the title roles, premieres; Lilian Harvey and the Comedian Harmonists also appear in the cast. The film becomes the most commercially successful of any film during the Weimar Republic.

16 The sound film war romance *Zwei Welten* (*Two Worlds*) premieres, directed by E. A. Dupont, with Teddy Bill, Julius Brandt, Friedrich Kayssler, and Maria Paudler.

17 The crime sound film *Der Greifer* (*The Snatcher*) premieres, directed by Richard Eichberg, with Hans Albers in the title role and Charlotte Susa.

The operetta *Das Mädel am Steuer* (*Girl at the Wheel*), by Jean Gilbert, premieres at the Comic Opera in Berlin.

18 The comedy *Tausend Dollars* (*One Thousand Dollars*), by Hans Müller-Schlösser, premieres at the Düsseldorf City Theater.

19 Kiepenheuer Press publishes the retrospective *25 Jahre Berliner Theater und Victor Barnowsky* (*Twenty-Five Years of Theater in Berlin with Victor Barnowsky*), by Julius Berstl.

The operetta *Eine Freundin—so goldig wie Du* (*A Friend So Lovely as You*), by Will Meisel, premieres at the Central Theater in Berlin.

20 The drama *Mississippi* by Georg Kaiser, premieres in 14 different theaters simultaneously throughout the country.

21 The new libretto by Erich Walther to operetta *Robinsonade* by Jacques Offenbach, premieres at the Leipzig Neues Theater.

23 Reich President Paul von Hindenburg decrees that no foreign newspapers, reporters, or press agents may report from Germany that after the recent Reichstag elections an overthrow of the national government is imminent.

24 The operetta *Der Gatte des Fräuleins* (*The Maiden's Husband*), by Paul Abrahamm, premieres at the Leipzig City Theater.

26 Six members of the Communist Party militias are sentenced to five-year prison terms for the murder of National Socialist militiaman Horst Wessel.

27   The broadcast premiere of the radio play *Der Minister ist ermordet* (*The Minister Has Been Murdered*)—Erich Ebermeyer's fictionalized account of the assassination of foreign minister Walter Rathanau in 1922—creates a sensation, as many listeners mistake it for a live news broadcast.

The drama *Irgendwie geht alles* (*Somehow It All Works Out*), by Wilhelm Speyer, premieres at the Württemberg Regional Theater in Stuttgart.

28   The German national soccer team defeats the Hungarian national team in Dresden by 5 to 3 before 44,000 spectators.

30   The adaptation for radio of the novel *Berlin Alexanderplatz* by physician Alfred Döblin, featuring Heinrich George as Franz Biberkopf and Hilde Körber as Mieze has its broadcast premiere.

OCTOBER

1   The number of licensed German radio listeners tops 3.7 million, which means that more than 25 percent of German households have a radio.

2   Prussia opens the new Pergamon Museum on the "Museum Island" of Berlin.[12]

American automobile manufacturer Henry Ford lays the cornerstone for the new Ford plant in Cologne.

3   The cantata *Vom Fischer un syner Fru* (*The Fisherman and His Wife*), by Othmar Schoeck, premieres at the Dresden State Opera.

4   Two dramatic works premiere: an adaptation by Klara Brauner of Fyodor Dostoyevsky's novel *The Idiot* at the Berliner Theater in Berlin and *Gott, König, und Vaterland* (*God, King, and Fatherland*) by Leo Lania at the Frankfurt am Main Neues Theater.

5   The "dance pantomime" *Offenbachiade* by Valeria Katrina, premieres at the Breslayu State Theater.

Reich Chancellor Heinrich Brüning meets with leaders of the National Socialists (Hitler, Goering, and Frick) for a "courtesy discussion" of their participation in the new government. They reject any notion of their participation as "bit players."

6   Painter George Grosz and publisher Wieland Herzfeld go on trial for the fourth time, charged with the same offense: insulting the Christian church in a lithograph depicting the crucified Christ wearing a gas mask.

Propyläen Press publishes the novel *Der ewige Spiesser* (*The Eternal Philistine*), by Ödön von Horvath.

7 The tragedy *Jüd Süss* (*Jew Suess*), by Paul Kornfeld, premieres at the State Theater in Berlin.

8 An exhibition organized by the Society of German and Austrian Women Artists opens featuring a show of paintings titled "Women Presenting Women."

10 The week-long "Frankfurt Opera Festival" opens featuring performances of invited productions from around the country; the festival celebrates the 50th anniversary of the Frankfurt Opera House's construction.

The drama *Brest-Litovsk*, by Hans José Rehfisch, premieres at the Theater des Westens in Berlin.

11 The drama *Besetztes Gebiet* (*Occupied Territory*), by Franz Theodor Csokor, premieres at theaters in Leipzig, Mannheim, and Erfurt simultaneously.

12 Cellist Ludwig Hoelscher receives the Mendelssohn Prize.

13 Ceremonies inaugurating the new session of the Reichstag are disrupted as the entire contingent of National Socialist deputies march into the hall wearing Storm Trooper uniforms.

14 The sound film Brand in der Oper (*Fire in the Opera Houses*) premieres, directed by Carl Froelich, with Alexa Engström, Gustav Fröhlich, and Gustaf Gründgens.

16 The sound film musical revue *Zwei Krawatten* (*Two Neckties*, based on the revue by Michael Spolianksy and text by Georg Kaiser), directed by Felix Basch, with Olga Chekhova and Michael Bohnen, premieres.

17 At a speech in Berlin's Phärus Hall condemning the National Socialists, Thomas Mann is shouted down and forced off the stage by a group led by playwright Arnolt Bronnen, who has recently become a follower of Hitler.

Fischer Press publishes the novel *Mord im Nebel* (*Murder in the Fog*), by George Bernard Shaw, translated by Siegfried Trebitsch.

18 The war drama *Wunder um Verdun* (*Miracle at Verdun*), by Hans Chlumberg, premieres at the Leipzig City Theater.

Playwright Reinhard Goering awarded Kleist Prize.

20 The first sound film treatment of the enormously popular comedy *Pension Schöller* (*The Schöller Boarding House*, originally written by Wilhelm Jacoby and Carl Lauffs), directed by Georg Jacoby, with Jakob Tiedtke, Josefine Dora, Paul Henckels, and Elga Brink, premieres.

23 The opera *Der tolle Kapellmeister* (*The Crazy Chamber Music Director*), by Benno Bardi, has German broadcast premiere.

Kiepenheuer Press publishes the novel *Die grosse Sache* (*An Important Business*), by Heinrich Mann.

24 The musical sound film *Dolly macht Karriere* (*Dolly's Way to Stardom*) premieres, directed by Anatole Litwak, with Dolly Haas and Oskar Karlweis.

25 The drama *Panama Skandal* (*Scandal in Panama*), by Eberhard Wolfgang Möller, premieres at the Frankfurt am Main Neues Theater.

Rowohlt Press publishes the treatise *Die getarnte Revolution* (*The Camouflaged Revolution*), by theater critic Herbert Ihering.

28 The musical sound film *Leutnant warst Du einst bei den Husaren?* (*Lieutenant, Were You Once in the Husar Regiment?*) premieres, directed by Manfred Noa, with Mady Christians and Gustav Diessl.

31 The Kleist Prize Foundation revokes its 1926 award of the Kleist Prize to Alexander Lernet-Holenia for what they consider his "ignoble comportment."

NOVEMBER

1 The drama *Elisabeth von England*, by Ferdinand Bruckner, premieres at the Deutsches Theater in Berlin.

The National Socialist weekly newspaper *Der Angriff* (*The Attack*) begins publishing biweekly; Joseph Goebbels and Adolf Hitler establish their party's own film production company, with a mind to exploit film as a propaganda medium in the manner they have successfully followed with phonograph production, the print media, and some radio broadcasting.

3 Scherl Press publishes a "novel of industrial life" titled *Kautschuk* by Hans Dominik; Kiepenheuer publishes a volume of short fiction title *Auf dem Wege zur amerikanischen Botschaft* (*On the Way to the American Embassy*), by Anna Seghers.

5 The sound film melodrama *Kohlhiesels Töchter* (*Kohlhiesel's Daughters*) premieres, directed by Hans Behrendt, with Henny Porten playing both daughters and Leo Peukert as their father.

6 The twelve-tone "Begleitmusik zu einer Lichtspielszene" Opus 34 ("Musical Accompaniment to a Film Scene"), by Arnold Schoenberg, premieres at the Berlin Philharmonie.

7 A public exhibition of paintings and drawing of George Grosz, in the private holdings of publisher Bruno Cassirer, opens at Cassirer Press headquarters in Berlin.

8 The musical *Im weiss'n Rössl* (*The White Horse Inn*, based on a comedy by Oskar Blumenthal), by Ralph Benatzky, premieres at the 3600-seat Grosses Schauspielhaus in Berlin; several of the show's tunes become popular hits, and the show itself becomes one of the most profitable musicals in Berlin theater history.[13]

9 The drama *Die Matrose von Cattaro* (*The Sailors of Cattaro*), by physician Friedrich Wolf, premieres at the Volksbühne in Berlin.

The opera *Soldaten* (*Soldiers*, based on the 18th-century play of the same title by Jakob Lenz), by Manfred Gurlitt, premieres at the Düsseldorf Opera House.

10 The military sound film comedy *Drei Tage Mittelarrest* (*Three Days in the Guardhouse*) premieres, directed by Carl Boese, with Max Adalbert, Paul Otto, Franz Schultz, Felix Bressart, and Lucie Englisch.

11 The opera *Vasantasena* by Hugo Herrmann, premieres at the State Theater Wiesbaden.

The comedy *Geld wie Heu* (*Money Like Hay*), by Peter Kreuder, premieres at the Neues Theater am Zoo in Berlin.

12 The drama *Wir sind Kameraden* (*We Are Comrades*), by Peter Martin Lampel, premieres at the Theater am Schiffbauerdamm in Berlin.

13 Malik Press publishes the novel *Des Kaisers Kulis* (*The Kaiser's Coolies*), by Theodor Plievier.

14 Actor Emil Jannings makes a triumphal return to live performance in Berlin after nearly three years and two Oscars in Hollywood with the comedy *Business is Business* by French playwright Octave Mirbeau. The comedy premieres at the Theater des Westens in Berlin, whereupon Jannings' first entrance, audience cheers and applause halts the performance for ten minutes until he acknowledges their greeting.

15 The comedy *Abschied von der Liebe* (*Farewell to Love*), by Hans Kyser, premieres at the Halberstadt City Theater.

16 The drama *Die Schule der Niedertracht* (*The School of Infamy*), by Rudolf Schneider-Schelde, premieres at the Görlitz City Theater.

17 The sound film operetta *Das Land des Lächelns* (*The Land of Smiles*), by Franz Lehar, directed by Max Reichmann, with Richard Tauber and Mara Loseff, premieres.

18 The Dresden Philharmonic Orchestra celebrates the 60th anniversary of its founding with a Beethoven Concert at Semper Opera House, featuring *Coriolan* Overture Opus 62, and Symphony No. 9 in D minor, Opus 125.

19 The war drama *Die endlose Strasse* (*The Eternal Road*), by Sigmund Graff, premieres at the Aachen City Theater.

20 The dramatic adaptation *Emil und die Detektive* (*Emil and the Detectives*) for children's audiences by Erich Kästner (based on his children's novel of the same title), premieres at the Theater am Schiffbauerdamm in Berlin.

21 The opening of new radio broadcast facilities in Stuttgart sends the most powerful signal (60,000 watts) of any in Germany.

22 The drama *Richter Feuerbach* (*Feuerbach the Judge*) by Walter Erich Schäfer, premieres at the Nurenberg City Theater.

The opera *Die Alpenhütte* (*The Alpine Cottage*), by Conradin Kruetzer, premieres at the Freiburg City Theater.

24 The musical sound film *The Love Parade* directed by Ernst Lubitsch (his first sound film), with Maurice Chevalier and Jeanette MacDonald, makes its German premiere.

Propyläen Press publishes the children's play *Kakadu-Kakada* by Carl Zuckmayer.

29 The drama *Die Ehe* (*The Marriage*), by physician Alfred Döblin, premieres at the Munich Kammerspiele; two weeks later, the Munich police close the production on the grounds that the play constitutes "communist poropaganda."

30 The German national field hockey team defeats the Australian team 3 to 2 in Cologne.

DECEMBER

3 The German welterweight boxer Gustav Eder defeats Belgian Gustave Roth on points in 12 rounds at the Frankfurt am Main Sports Palace to become the European welterweight champion.

4 Playwright Bertolt Brecht brings suit against Nero Film Studio (a subsidiary of the Hollywood studio Warner Brothers) for filming *Die 3groschenoper* (adapted from the 1928 *The Threepenny Opera*, a musical he had helped write) without his permission. Brecht demands that filming cease.

The German theater producers' publication *Deutsche Bühne* publishes an analysis of theatrical fare now offered in German theaters, concluding that the majority of tickets sold to performances of spoken drama reflect audience preference for "light entertainment," i.e., farce and light comedy. Audiences prefer grand opera, however, to other forms of musical production.

5 The American war film *All Quiet on the Western Front* (based on the novel by Erich Maria Remarque and adapted by Maxwell Anderson), directed by Lewis Milestone, with Lew Ayres and Louis Wohlheim premieres in Germany; National Socialists disrupt showings of the film by releasing mice in the theater. Joseph Goebbels promises to disrupt every showing of the film throughout Germany because of what he claims are insults to German military tradition.

The comedy *Dreick der Liebe* (*Triangle of Love*), by Erich Ebermayer, premieres at the Halberstadt City Theater.

7 Street battles between Communists and National Socialists in Bonn leave several dead and wounded; Goebbels proclaims the fallen Storm Troopers "martyrs to our movement."

10 The didactic play *Die Massnahme* (*The Disciplinary Measures Taken*), by Bertolt Brecht, with music by Hanns Eisler, premieres in cantata-like fashion at a labor union hall in Berlin.

11 Regional governments of Saxony, Bavaria, Baden, and Württemberg ban the exhibition of the film *All Quiet on the Western Front* for fear of disruptions and possible riots and in Thuringia for possible "assaults on the German character."

12 The comedy *Die Defraudanten* (*The Embezzlers*), by Alfred Polgar, based on a Russian novel by Valentin Katayev, premieres at the Volksbühne in Berlin.

13 On the occasion of the poet Heinrich Heine's birth in 1797, dozens of public readings of his works and concerts of songs set to his verses take place throughout Germany; National Socialists disrupt about half of them with protests against "the Jew Heine" and his influence on German culture.

15 The comedy with music, *Cocktail*, by Karl Vollmöller, music by Ralph Benatzky, premieres at Komödienhaus in Berlin.

The sound film melodrama *Boykott* (*Boycott*), directed by Robert Land, with Henny Porten and Ernst Stahl-Nachbaur, premieres.

16 The musical sound film *Einbrecher* (*Burglars*) premieres, directed by Hanns Schwarz, with Heinz Rühmann, Lilian Harvey, and Willy Fritsch.

17 Max Reinhardt cancels production of the opera *Mahagonny* by Brecht and Weill at the Deutsches Theater in Berlin, citing numerous recent attempts to sabotage performances and threats of violence against theaters that attempt to present it.

"Konzertmusik für Klavier, Blechbläser, und zwei Harfen," Opus 49 ("Concert Music for Piano, Brass Instruments, and Two Harps"), by Paul Hindemith, premieres in Germany at the Cologne Chamber Music Hall; the world premiere had taken place two months earlier in Chicago.

19 The historical sound film *Das Flötenkonzert von Sanssouci* (*The Flute Concert at Sans-souci Palace*), directed by Gustav Ucicky, with Otto Gebühr as King Frederick the Great and Renate Müller, premieres; Communists threaten to disrupt showings of the film because of what they claim is its glorification of Prussian militarism.

The opera *Die Gespenstersonate* (*The Ghost Sonata*, based on a play of the same title by August Strindberg), by Julius Weismann, premieres at the Munich National Theater.

22 Nero Film Studio agrees to pay Bertolt Brecht a RM 9,000 royalty fee for filming *Die 3groschen Oper* and accede to Brecht's demand that the phrase "freely adapted from the stage work of the same name by Brecht and Weill" appear under the film's title.

The opera *Peppina*, by Robert Stolz, premieres at the Comic Opera in Berlin.

23 The sound film drama *Hans in allen Gassen* (*Hans Is Everywhere*) premieres, directed by Carl Froelich, with Hans Albers as Hans and Camilla Horn.

25 The mountain sound film *Stürme über dem Mont Blanc* (*Storms over Mont Blanc*) premieres, directed by Arnold Fanck, with Leni Riefenstahl and Ernst Udet.

The Berlin newspaper *Vossische Zeitung* begins serial publication of the comedy *Der Hauptmann von Köpenick* (*The Captain of Köpenick*), by Carl Zuckmayer.

26 The comedy *Kavaliere* (*Cavaliers*), by Wolfgang Götz, premieres at the Hamburg Deutsches Schauspielhaus.

28 Dancer and choreographer Mary Wigman arrives in New York for residence and a series of performances.

29 The musical sound film *Tingel-Tangel* (*Honky-Tonk*) premieres, directed by Jaap Speyer, with Elisabeth Pinajeff and Fritz Kampers.

31 There are 3.97 million unemployed in Germany.

NOTES

1. The Association notes that approximately 4,000 cinemas are in active use throughout Germany, and about 2 million patrons watch movies every night in their

establishments. German film companies account for 12 percent of world production, but only 6 percent of all German film production is shown outside German-speaking Europe. German film studios and production companies invest about RM 1 billion yearly in film production.

2. The Berlin production was staged by actor and cabaret performer Gustaf Gründgens; the New York production titled *Grand Hotel* opened November 13, staged by Herman Shumlin in a translation by William A. Drake. It was a colossal success, running for 459 performances at the National Theater. A musical based Drake's translation opened in 1989 at the Martin Beck Theatre and was even more successful; it won 13 Tony Awards for more than 1,000 performances over a three-year period.

3. The National Socialists in particular were fond of the term "cultural Bolshevism," employing it to describe cultural activities that had arrived in Germany in the wake of the Bolshevik revolution in Russia. As the 1920s progressed, particularly after Hitler placed Joseph Goebbels in charge of Berlin operations, attacks against perceived "cultural Bolshevism" intensified. Nazi pundit Alfred Rosenberg was most responsible for bringing the term into mainstream currency with his book *The Myth of the 20th Century*, which he finished in 1925 (though it was not published until 1930). In May of 1929, Rosenberg had inaugurated a well-planned attack against theater directors Max Reinhardt and Leopold Jessner. Their "Bolshevistic, mollusk-like and neurasthenic aesthetics" (Hildegarde Brenner *Die Kunstpolitik des Nationalsozialismus* (Hamburg: Rowohlt Press, 1963, 116), Rosenberg insisted, were a direct threat to German culture as a whole. Rosenberg's alternative to cultural Bolshevism was German art that provided "direction for the driving German will, ending modern loneliness, chaos and confusion, protecting the racial insights of heroism and courage."

4. Schäfer's treatment of the "Köpenick escapade" was not the first; two others had previously appeared and others were to follow. The "escapade" was familiar to most Germans, although it had taken place in 1906. At its center was unemployed cobbler, ne'er do well, and ex-convict Wilhelm Voigt (1850–1922), who augmented his legitimate income with minor burglaries. His fortunes paradoxically improved when he received a lengthy sentence to Berlin's Moabit Prison, where he got an in-depth course in Prussian military history from an eccentric warden. Every Sunday afternoon, the warden arranged groups of prisoners in miniature military formations and called out their movements as if they were infantry, cavalry, and artillery divisions in the Franco-Prussian War. They in turn learned to respond with distinctly Prussian expressions of obedience. Armed with a thorough command of military jargon, Voigt managed to obtain a used Prussian captain's military uniform upon his release from prison in 1906. Soon thereafter, he commandeered a platoon by barking orders at them, which they instantly obeyed. They accompanied him via trolley car to Köpenick (a Berlin suburb), where he demanded the municipal strongbox from the mayor. The mayor and other Köpenick officials complied with the "Captain's" requests because Voigt blustered effectively with impressive Prussian bombast. He then made a clean getaway, though he turned himself in later. Kaiser Wilhem II was so impressed with the entire operation that he pardoned Voigt and granted him a lifetime pension. Voigt later supplemented his pension by selling autographed pictures of himself in uniform; business was brisk whenever and wherever he appeared, because he had become an authentic German folk hero.

5. *The Blue Angel*, perhaps best known as Marlene Dietrich's cinematic breakthrough, also became one of the most recognized of any movie shot during the Weimar Republic. Many critics claimed it offered proof (as if any were needed) that a German sound film could be a work of art, just as many of its silent predecessors had been. But *The Blue Angel* remained silent—and effective—in many scenes; though the music (a Friedrich Hollaender pastiche from several sources) was evocative, there was actually very little spoken dialogue. The result was a softened central character (Jannings' Immanuel Rath), transformed into a kind of pathetic plaything for Dietrich's Lola Lola. She provides the impetus for his descent into pitiable degradation, and Dietrich's portrayal was almost gruesome—the polar opposite of the glamor queen many believe she later became. Unglamorous or gruesome, Lola Lola provided Dietrich with a stunning calling card in Hollywood, where she began working immediately after her arrival at the Paramount studios. Within eight months of *The Blue Angel*'s release, she and director Sternberg had completed *Morocco* for Paramount, for which they both received Oscar nominations.

6. The Reichsmark (RM)–American dollar exchange rate in 1930 stood at 4.2 to 1, so Jannings earned about $71,428.00 for his work in *The Blue Angel*—far less than he was making in Hollywood, where his contract called for $10,000 per week. Bergner's earnings of the same amount as Jannings' per film gave her the highest salary among all German actresses.

7. The discussions went nowhere in the face of depressed economic conditions during the Weimar Republic, but the Ulm Museum of Bread Culture opened in 1955. Several beer museums opened in subsequent decades: the Georg Lechner Beer Museum in Olde, the Cologne Beer Museum, and the Kulmbacher Beer Museum in Bayreuth among many noteworthy examples.

8. Hannes Meyer (1889–1954) had replaced Walter Gropius as director of the Bauhaus School and Gropius had likewise resigned under political pressure. Many Bauhaus faculty members had a tendency toward allegiances with leftist parties, often to the consternation of government officials who provided generous subsidies to the School. Dessau city officials had provided RM 133,000 for the School's move from Weimar, and thereafter they designated a yearly subsidy of RM 167,000 to support the school. Yet the school never had more than 170 students, of whom about 40 were foreigners.

9. *Farewell* was the first sound film of director Robert Siodmak (1900–1973). During his career as a director in Hollywood, Siodmak made the first Technicolor horror film, titled *Cobra Woman* (1944). Two years later, he directed what many consider the first "film noir," titled *The Killers*, based on a short story by Ernest Hemingway.

10. Brigitte Horney made her movie debut in this film, having just been awarded the Max Reinhardt Prize at age 19 for her stage debut in Berlin at Reinhardt at the Lessing Theater. She was the first of a new generation of actresses in German sound films, one whose extraordinary photogenic qualities combined with subtle vocal talents to make her an ideal figure in the early years of sound film production. In the United States (of which she eventually became a citizen), her career failed to develop; she remained best known as the daughter of psychologist and author Karen Horney, who for many years was director of American Institute of Pscychoanalysis in New York.

11. *Tempest in a Teacup* became so popular after its premiere in Dresden that dozens of German theaters did productions of it in the next two months. By the end of the year, more than 1,000 performances of the comedy had taken place. Playwright Bruno Frank's combination of humor, astute political observation, and a happy ending within a plot that involved civic corruption, the media, and lost dogs proved irresistible to most German audiences. The clever arrangement of such ingredients seemed to assure gratifyingly long runs in several theaters, many of which were in desperate financial straits in the face of growing downturns in the German economy.

12. The Pergamon Museum was built to house the magnificent marble altar found in the city of Pergamum, mentioned in the New Testament book of Revelation as "Satan's seat." The altar is actually an enormous building, originally constructed sometime in the second century B.C. Pergamum was located in present-day northwestern Turkey, about 16 miles east of the Aegean Sea, and the altar was a site of worship and animal sacrifice. So many animals could be sacrificed on the altar, in fact, that the smoke rising from the roasting meat could be seen for miles at sea. A German archeological team excavated and removed the altar along with adjoining structures between 1879 and 1904 led by Carl Humann. Also located in the Pergamon Museum are the Market Gate of Miletus and the Ishtar Gate, both of which were originally found in ancient Babylon (present-day Iraq).

13. The original *The White Horse Inn* premiered in 1898 and was a transparently formulaic boulevard comedy that nearly every German-language theater had in its repertoire at one time or another. It takes place in the Salzburg Lake District in a modest little vacation resort on Lake Wolfgang; it makes fun of the Austrians who run the place and parodies without mercy the Berlin *nouveau riche* who come south and patronize such establishments. Leopold the headwaiter is a masterpiece of the headwaiter with ambitions; the object of his amorous and commercial desires is the inn's owner, a young widow named Josepha. A subplot centers two Berlin businessmen who hate each other—but whose teenage children fall in love with each other. Benatsky's superb music actually improved the play as agreeable entertainment and as a musical *The White Horse Inn* remains popular in the German-speaking world to this day. An enormously elaborate production of the musical opened on Broadway in 1936 (with lyrics by Irving Caesar) starring Kitty Carlisle as Josepha and ran for more than 200 performances.

1931

JANUARY

2 The Berlin newspaper *Vossische Zeitung* begins serial publication of the new novel by Erich Maria Remarque titled *Der Weg zurück* (*The Way Back*).

3 Two dramas premiere: *Talleyrand* by Carl Leyst at the Leipzig City Theater and *Die Nacht der Könige* (*The Night of the Kings*), by Julius Maria Becker at the Mainz City Theater.

Stalling Press publishes the biography *Hitler, eine deutsche Bewegung* (*Hitler, a German Movement*), by Erich Czech-Jochberg.

5 The film comedy *Schneider Wibbel* (*Wibbel the Tailor*, based on the comedy of the same title by Hans Müller-Schlösser) premieres, directed by Paul Henckels, with Henckels in the title role and Thea Grodyn.

6 Two comedies premiere: *Die Grosstante* (*The Great Aunt*, based on Fyodor Dostoevsky's novella *The Gambler*) by Willy Buschoff at the Saarbrücken City Theater and *Der Schlager der Saison* (*The Hit of the Season*) by Carl Rohde at the Stendal Regional Theater.

7 The cabaret *Tingel-Tangel-Theater* (*Honky-Tonk Theater*) premieres under the direction of composer Friedrich Hollaender in Berlin.

The drama *Um den König* (*Inside the Royal Court*), by Hans Fritz von Zwehl, premieres at the Potsdam City Theater.

9 The film comedy *Ihre Majestät die Liebe* (*Her Majesty the Barmaid*), premieres, directed by Joe May, with Käthe von Nagy and Francis Lederer.

Authors Hermann Hesse and Erwin Guido Kolbenheyer resign from the Prussian Academy of the Arts, noting increasing Marxist tendencies of Academy members.

10 The Thuringian court lifts the ban on pro-abortion drama *§218: gequälte Menschen* (*Paragraph 218: Tormented People*), by Carl Crede, allowing its performance in most theaters. The National Socialist culture minister Wilhelm Frick had banned the play throughout Thuringia.

12 Attempts to create a National Socialist Volksbühne (*Peoples' Stage*) at the Berliner Theater in Berlin result in the production of drama *Klaus von Bismarck* by Walter Flex. The production attracts little notice, even among Nazi party members.

15 The drama *Tai-yang erwacht* (*Tai-yang Awakens*), by Fredrich Wolf, premieres at the Piscator Stage of the Wallner Theater in Berlin; the drama *Amphytrion 38* by Jean Giraudoux, translated by Hans Feist, premieres at the Theater in der Stresemann Strasse in Berlin.

The crime film *Der Weg nach Rio* (*The Road to Rio*) premieres, directed by Manfred Noa, with Oskar Homolka and Maria Matray, and music by Friedrich Hollaender.

The Essen city council declares itself no longer capable of subsidizing the Essen City Theater; the facility will close at the end of the year's theater season, though the city will maintain subsidies for opera.

16 The musical film *Die Privatsekretärin* (*The Private Secretary*) premieres, directed by Wilhelm Thiele, with Renate Müller in the title role and Hermann Thimig; the music is by Paul Abraham.

A German-language theater is established in Paris.

17 Sales of Erich Maria Remarque's novel *Im Westen nichts Neues* (*All Quiet on the Western Front*) top 2 million copies, making it the fastest-selling novel in modern German publication history.

18 The opera *König Midas* (*King Midas*), by Wilhelm Kempff, premieres at the Königsberg Opera House.

German regular army regiments, military bands, flag and bugle corps, and patriotic organizations march through Berlin celebrating the 60th anniversary of German unification and the establishment of the Wilhemine Reich.

19 Voigtländer Press publishes the treatise titled *100 Autoren gegen Einstein* (*100 Authors against Einstein*), featuring essays by scientists and physicists who dispute the Theory of Relativity.

20 The historical film *1914: Die letzten Tage vor dem Weltbrand* (*1914: The Last Days before World War I*) premieres, directed by Richard Oswald, with

Albert Bassermann, Wolfgang von Schwindt, Reinhold Schünzel, and Oskar Homolka.

21 The film *Danton* (based on the play by Hans José Rehfisch) premieres, directed by Hans Behrendt, with Fritz Kortner as Danton and Gustaf Gründgens as Robespierre.

Rowohlt Press publishes the novel *Der Mann ohne Eigenschaften* (*The Man without Qualities*), by Robert Musil.

22 The executive director of the Bayreuth Festival, Winifred Wagner, names Hans Tietjen artistic director and Wilhelm Furtwängler musical director of the festival.

The one-act ballet opera for marionettes *Das Nusch-Nuschi* by Paul Hindemith premieres at the Köningsberg Opera House.

23 The film crime thriller *Der Mann, der den Mord beging* (*The Man Who Committed the Murder*) premieres, directed by Curtis Bernhardt, with Conrad Veidt and Trudo von Molo.

The drama *Legende in Mazedonien* (*Legends in Macedonia*), by theater professor Friedrich Schreyvogel, premieres at the Zwickau City Theater.

Manager Ernst Josef Aufricht of Theater am Schiffbauerdamm in Berlin cuts ticket prices in half, hoping to compete with prices to see movies.

24 The comedy *Liebe unmodern* (*Unmodern Love*), by Wilhelm Sterk, premieres at the Berlin Kleines Theater.

25 Propyläen Press publishes the novel *Katrin wird Soldat* (*Katherine Becomes a Soldier*), by Adrienne Thomas.

28 The comic opera *Don Diego* by Arthur Scholz, premieres at the Braunschweig Regional Theater.

Rothbart Press publishes the novel *Du—meine Welt* (*You—My World*), by Hedwig Courths-Mahler.

29 The Berlin city officials ban exhibition of the Social Democrat propaganda film *Ins Dritte Reich* (*Into the Third Reich*) on the basis of the film's likelihood to provoke renewed street combat among political party adherents.

30 Theater director Erwin Piscator arrested and jailed for delinquent entertainment tax payments on ticket sales totaling RM 16,000.

31 *Hamlet*, by William Shakespeare, premieres on German radio, in a 90-minute adaptation by Bertolt Brecht, with Fritz Kortner in the title role.

The drama *Jagt ihn—ein Mensch* (*Hunt Him Down—a Human Being*), by Erwin Guido Kolbenheyer, premieres.

FEBRUARY

1 The operetta *Kisses and Quarrels*, by Riccardo Pick-Mangiagalli, premieres at the Hamburg Opera House.

Boxer Hein Müller defeats Hans Schönrath on points in a 12-round bout in Dortmund to become German heavyweight champion.

Three books about National Socialism and Adolf Hitler join his own *Mein Kampf* on the German best-seller lists: Johannes Stark's *Adolf Hitlers Ziele und Persönlichkeit* (*Adolf Hitler's Goals and Personality*); Erich Czech-Jochberg's *Hitler, eine deutsche Bewegung* (*Hitler, a German Movement*); and Alfred Rosenberg's *Wesen, Grundsätze, und Ziele der Nationalsozialistischen Deutschen Arbeiterpartei* (*Character, Fundamentals, and Goals of the National Socialist German Workers' Party*).

2 Albert Einstein, Carl Zuckmayer, Käthe Kollwitz, Arnold Zwieg, and other prominent scientists, artists, writers, and journalists form the German League for Human Rights in an attempt to release the American film *All Quiet on the Western Front* from proscription and/or confiscation in nearly every police jurisdiction throughout Germany.

4 The drama *Der dunkle Kaiser* (*The Dark Kaiser*), by theater professor Friedrich Schreyvogel, premieres at the Augsburg City Theater.

Berlin police ban the publication and distribution of the National Socialist bi-weekly *Der Angriff* for two weeks.

5 The drama *Etienne und Luise*, by Ernst Penzoldt, premieres at the Mannheim National Theater.

Theater director Erwin Piscator is released from jail after he opens his account books to Berlin tax inspectors.

6 The of satirical comedy *Mann ist Mann* (*A Man's a Man*), by Bertolt Brecht, who stages the play himself at the State Theater, premieres in Berlin; critic Alfred Kerr condemns it as "intellectually backward," and most other critics reviewing the production agree.

The newly formed Berlin Radio Symphony Orchestra performs the German radio broadcast premiere of Violin Concerto No. 1, Opus 48, by Alfredo Casella.

7 The film operetta *Königin einer Nacht* (*Queen for a Night*) premieres, directed by Fritz Wendhausen, music by Otto Stransky, with Friedl Haerlin and Otto Wallburg.

National Socialist and Communist Party deputies join forces in an initial series of co-operative maneuvers to discredit what they term "the Weimar System."

8 Theater manager and director Robert Klein follows the precedent of Ernst Josef Aufricht and cuts admission prices in half at his Deutsches Künstler Theater in Berlin.

10 The comedy *Der stille Compagnon* (*The Silent Partner*), by Leo Lenz, premieres at the Frankfirt an der Oder City Theater.

11 The operetta *Der Mann im Frack* (*The Man in Evening Dress*), by Ralph Maria Siegel, premieres at the Oberhausen City Theater.

12 Stalling Press publishes the treatise *Deutschland in Ketten* (*Germany in Chains*, with the subtitle "from Versailles to the Young Plan"), by Werner Beumelburg.

13 The operetta *Das blaue Hemd von Ithaka* (*The Blue Shirt of Ithaca*), based on music by Jacques Offenbach, with libretto by Ernst Römer, premieres at the Admiral's Palace Theater in Berlin.

A majority of the Lübeck population votes against installing the Ernst Barlach modernist sculpture *Gemeinschaft der Heiligen* (*Communion of the Saints*) in the city's St. Catherine Church.

16 Fischer Press publishes the novel *Etzel Andergast*, by Jakob Wassermann.

17 The Württemberg culture ministry bans uniforms, symbols, images, or slogans of any political party in all Württemberg schools.

18 The film romance *Drei Tage Liebe* (*Three Days of Love*) premieres, directed by Heinz Hilpert (in his cinematic directing debut), with Hans Albers and Käthe Dorsch.

19 The musical film *Die 3groschen Oper* (*The Threepenny Opera*, based on the stage musical by Kurt Weill, Bertolt Brecht, and Elisabeth Hauptmann), directed by G. W. Pabst, with Rudolf Forster, Carola Neher, Reinhold Schünzel, Lotte Lenya, and Ernst Busch, premieres.

Kiepenheuer Press publishes the novel *Glückliche Menschen* (*Fortunate People*), by Hermann Kesten.

20 The film romance *Ariane* premieres, directed by Paul Czinner, with Elisabeth Bergner in the title role and Rudolf Forster.

21 The comedy *Liebe, Mord, und Alkohol* (*Love, Death, and Alcohol*), by Otto Bernhard Wendler, premieres at the Tribüne Theater in Berlin.

Physician and playwright Friedrich Wolf is arrested in Stuttgart for criminal violations of the antiabortion law Paragraph 218 of the German Penal Code.

22 The paramilitary organization Reichsbanner engages in Berlin street demonstrations; the group is affiliated with some centrist political parties in the Reichstag and supported by some members of the Social Democrats.

24 The circus film *Grock* premieres, directed by Carl Boese, with Grock the Clown and Liane Haid.

25 The Communist Party organizes "hunger marches" of unemployed workers in several German cities; riots break out in most of them, usually between workers and National Socialist Storm Troopers.

Fischer Press publishes *Die Geschichte der russischen Revolution* (*The History of the Russian Revolution*), by Leon Trotzky, translated by Arthur Müller.

28 Physician and playwright Friedrich Wolf is released on RM 10,000 bond pending trial for violations of Paragraph 218.

MARCH

1 Singer and dancer Marika Rökk debuts in Berlin at the Varieté Theater Scala.

The initial National Socialist "cleansing" of museums in Weimar is ordered at the behest of Thuringian culture minister Wilhelm Frick.

The drama *Der Graue* (*The Old Man*), by Friedrich Forster, premieres at the Cologne City Theater.

2 Fischer Press publishes song book *Arche Noah: Neues trostreiches Liederbuch* (*Noah's Ark, New Songs of Consolation*), by Walter Mehring.

3 The film comedy *Ihre Hoheit befiehlt* (*At Her Highness' Command*) premieres, directed by Hanns Schwarz, with Käthe von Nagy and Willy Fritsch.

5 The comedy *Der Hauptmann von Köpenick* (*The Captain of Köpenick*, subtitled "a German fairy tale"), by Carl Zuckmayer, premieres at the Deutsches Theater in Berlin.

6 The musical comedy film *Die lustigen Weiber von Wien* (*The Merry Wives of Vienna*) premieres, directed by Geza von Bolvary, with Lee Parry, Willi Forst, Irene Eisinger, and Paul Hörbiger.

A Communist Party faction in the Reichstag initiates a vote of no confidence against cultural policies of Reich home secretary Joseph Wirth; the vote is defeated by 75 percent of all deputies in the house.

National Socialist deputies in numerous regional legislatures introduce bills to ban the exhibition of the musical film *Die 3groschen Oper* (*The Threepenny Opera*) within their jurisdictions.

The operetta *Kalifornische Früchte* (*California Fruits*), by Max Hausler and Willy Prager, premieres at the Theater am Zoo in Berlin.

7 Roman Catholic bishops in the Rhineland send letters to be read in local churches admonishing parishioners of the dangers posed by National Socialism.

8 The Berlin Academy of the Arts opens an exhibition of work by architect Hans Poelzig.

9 Director and actor Charlie Chaplin arrives in Berlin for German premiere of his most recent silent film, *City Lights*; several critics note that Chaplin, and only Chaplin, can now make an effective and popular silent film.

The war drama *Bunker X*, by Henrik Herse, premieres at the Dessau Theater der Gegenwart.

10 The German premiere of the opera *Andromeda* by Pierre Maurice, opens at the Weimar National Theater.

12 The comic opera *Der Alchemist*, by Karl Friedrich Pistor, premieres at the Kiel City Theater.

13 The new Schinkel Museum opens in the former Palace of the Crown Prince in Berlin, on the occasion of the 150th anniversary of architect and stage designer Karl Friedrich Schinkel's birth.

14 Rowohlt Press publishes the quasi-biography titled *Adolf Hitler: Wilhelm III* by Weigand von Miltenberg.

15 The number of unemployed in Germany reaches 4.98 million, about 14 percent of the entire workforce.

The French national soccer team defeats the German team 1 to 0 in Paris.

Three National Socialists openly murder Communist Party member Ernst Henning, a Hamburg city council deputy, in a street near the city council chamber house.

16 The drama *Ein Volk ohne Heimat* (*A Homeless Nation*), by Hans Christoph Kaergel, premieres at the Leignitz City Theater.

The Hamburg city council bans meetings and newspapers of both National Socialists and Communists; Hamburg police arrest and jail three men accused of murdering Ernst Henning.

18 The historical drama about the university student who assassinated playwright August von Kotzebue titled *Der einsame Tat* (*The Lonely Deed*), by Sigmund Graff, premieres at the Gera Reussisches Theater.

Berlin police ban exhibition of the film *Das Lied vom Leben* (*The Song of Life*), directed by Alexei Granowsky, with Margot Ferra and Aribert Mog; police maintain that the film "insults the dignity of marriage."

19 The Prussian Academy of the Arts opens the exhibition of paintings and drawings Goethe und seine Zeit (Goethe and His Times).

20 The tragicomedy *Italienische Nacht* (*Italian Night*), by Ödön von Horvath, premieres at the Theater am Schiffbauerdamm in Berlin.

21 The comedy *Kommt ein Vogel geflogen* (*A Bird Overhead in Flight*), by Walter Hasenclever, premieres at the Komödie Theater in Berlin.

22 Ullstein Press publishes the first European weekly radio program guide, titled *Sieben Tage, Funkblätter* (*Seven Days of Radio*).

23 Kroll Opera House declares bankruptcy in the face of insurmountable financial losses; performances continue during the present season, after which the house will close indefinitely.

26 Financial straits force the city of Magdeburg to consolidate its opera and theater and reorganize its city theater as a venue concentrating on operetta.

Composer Hans Pfitzner is awarded the Beethoven Prize

The first American shortwave radio programs in German are broadcast from New York studios to Germany.

27 The German-speaking version of the Metro-Goldwyn-Mayer film drama *Anna Christie* (based on the drama by American playwright Eugene O'Neill) premieres, directed by Jacques Feder, with Greta Garbo, Theo Shall, and Hans Junkermann.

28 Reich president Paul von Hindenburg issues emergency decrees reducing the severity and length of bans against political party gatherings, street demonstrations, and publication that local jurisdictions have variously invoked to reduce street violence.

29 A national law banning use of or wearing concealed or unlicensed firearms in public goes into effect.

APRIL

1 Painter Paul Klee accepts appointment as professor of painting at the State Art Academy in Düsseldorf. He opens an exhibition dedicated to the work of painter Erich Heckels at the Kunsthütte in Chemnitz.

The Thuringian regional government is ousted by a vote of no confidence; National Socialists, including culture minister Wilhelm Frick, are forced to resign.

2 The detective film *Gassenhauer* (*Back Alley Inspector*) premieres, directed by Lupu Pick, with Ina Albrecht, Ernst Busch, and Albert Hoermann.

4 The film western *Die grossse Fahrt* (the German-language version of *The Big Trail*, directed by Raoul Walsh, with John Wayne) premieres, directed by Lewis Seiler and Raoul Walsh, with Theo Shall in the John Wayne role, and Marion Lessing.

Tobis Film Studio opens a film school in its new sound stage facilities in Berlin to train new actors, directors, and technicians.

5 Nierendorf Press publishes the poetry collection *Neue Herzlichkeit* (*New Joviality*), by Werner Finck.

8 The ballet *Josephslegende* (*The Legend of Joseph*), by Richard Strauss, premieres in Germany at the Berlin City Opera.

9 Zsolnay Press publishes the novel *Tycho Brahes Weg zu Gott* (*Tycho Brahe's Path to God*), by Max Brod.

10 The musical revue *Alles Schwindel* (*It's All Fake*), by Marcellus Schiffer with music by Michael Spoliansky, premieres at the Kurfürstendamm Theater in Berlin.

11 The drama *Kassandra*, by Paul Ernst, premieres at the Weimar National Theater.

The opening of the annual spring exhibition at the Berlin Secession of paintings by its members, features a lecture by physician and novelist Alfred Döblin, entitled "Artists among Us."

12 German driver Rudolf Carraciola wins the Mille Miglia sports car race in Brescia, Italy.

14 Universitas Press publishes the novel *Die weisse Rose*, by B. Traven.

15 The drama *Die Puppen von Poschansk* (*The Dolls of Poschansk*), by Robert Neumann, premieres at the Zwickau City Theater.

16 The film melodrama *Gefahren der Liebe* (*A Woman Branded*, the first German sound film to treat the subject of syphilis infection among women) premieres, directed by Eugen Thiele, with Toni van Eyck and Albert Bassermann.

17 The documentary film *Heilende Hände* (*Healing Hands*) premieres, directed by Eberhard Frowein, filmed in Berlin hospitals.

The drama *Die Ehe* (*Marriage*), by physician Alfred Döblin, premieres at the Volksbühne in Berlin.

19 The drama *Rosse* (*Stallions*), by Richard Billinger, premieres at the Munich Residenz Theater.

20 The film drama *Voruntersuchung* (*Inquest*) premieres, directed by Robert Siodmak, with Albert Bassermann and Charlotte Ander.

21 The Leipzig Komödienhaus Theater signs contracts with several "noncommercially viable" playwrights whose plays often encounter difficulty finding producers willing to stage them, granting the theater option rights to premiere their new plays.

22 After a sensational trial in Düsseldorf that attracted nationwide publicity, serial killer Peter Kürten ("The Vampire of Düsseldorf") is convicted of several sex crimes and murders, then given nine death sentences.[1]

23 The drama *Panama*, by Wilhelm Herzog, premieres at the Hamburg Deutsches Schauspielhaus

30 German unemployed tops 4.4 million.

MAY

1 The musical variety show from Moulin-Rouge in Paris, directed by Mme. Mistanguett, with a bevy of beautiful, mostly nude French women, opens at the Theater des Westens in Berlin.

Rowohlt Press publishes the autobiography *Mein Leben bis zum Kriege* (*My Life Up to the War*), by cabaret entertainer Joachim Ringelnatz; Der neue Geist (*The New Spirit*) Press publishes the treatise *Die Idee des Friedens und der Pazifismus* (*The Idea of Peace and Pacifism*), by Max Scheler.

2 The opera *Valerio*, based on dramatic fragments by Georg Büchner, by Hans Simon, premieres at the Darmstadt Regional Theater.

7 The 1913 parody on Wagner's opera *Tristan und Isolde* titled *König Hahnrei* (*King Cuckold*), by Georg Kaiser, premieres.

The annual Munich Museum Conference opens with an address by Oswald Spengler titled "Culture and Technology."

8 Adolf Hitler testifies at a court inquest that the Weimar constitution "is both false and corrupt. But I also know that an attempt to overthrow this constitution with violence would cost blood and would probably be futile."

9 "Astrological orchestral suite" titled "Die Planeten" ("The Planets"), by Gustav Holst, premieres at the State Opera in Berlin.

11 The film thriller *M* premieres, directed by Fritz Lang, with Peter Lorre, Gustaf Gründgens, and Theodor Loos.

The Bremen Music Festival opens, featuring premieres of new orchestral, choral, and operatic works.

13 The Berlin newspaper *Vossische Zeitung* begins serial publication of the novella *Flucht in die Finsternis* (*Flight into Darkness*), by Arthur Schnitzler.

The International Olympic Committee awards the 1936 Olympic Games venue to Berlin.

14 The drama *Auf Meineid steht Zuchthaus* (*Perjury Leads to the Penitentiary*), by Karl Lukas, premieres at the Hamburg Kammerspiele.

15 The opera *Komödie des Todes* (*Comedy of Death*), by Gian Francesco Malpiero, premieres at the Bavarian State Theater in Munich.

16 Kipenheier Press publishes a volume of unpublished work by Franz Kafka title *Die chinesische Mauer* (*The Great Wall of China*), edited by Max Brod and Joachim Schoeps.

17 The drama *Die heilige Elisabeth* (*St. Elizabeth*), by Margarethe von Gottschall, premieres.

Hamburg defeats Leipzig 4 to 2 to win the championship in the German Proletarian Soccer League at the Victoria Stadium in Hamburg.

20 The body of meterologist Alfred Wegener, originator of the "Theory of Continental Drift," is found in Greenland.

21 Conductor Wilhelm Furtwängler opens the Silesian Music Festival in Görlitz with a performance of orchestral works by Emanuel Aloys Förster.

22 The drama *Kampf um den Rhein* (*Campaign for the Rhine*), by Wilhelm Hendel, premieres at the Bochum City Theater.

24 The National Socialist League of Struggle for German Culture opens a conference in Potsdam with speeches denouncing "cultural Bolshevism," the Jewish dominance of German culture, and other perceived tendencies accelerating decline.

Novelist Vicki Baum signs a contract with Paramount Studios calling for three film adaptations of her fiction work.

27 The drama *Die Magd Gottes* (*The Maid of God*), by Franz Johannes Weinrich, premieres at the Cologne City Theater.

28 National Socialist and Communist partisans battle in the streets of Hagen; three are killed and about 20 wounded.

29 Communist partisans battle members of the Steel Helmet militia in the streets of Berlin; two are killed, six wounded.

JUNE

1 The theater management firm Rotter Brothers takes over Albert Theater in Dresden.

2 Huge sell-offs and stock price plunges at the New York Stock Exchange in New York the day previous causes panic in the German stock exchanges; many major German banks do not open for business.

6 Fire destroys the Glass Palace in Munich's Old Botanical Garden, and with it about 3,000 paintings and works of sculpture, many of which were assembled in Munich for the exhibition The German Romantics. Among the lost works were nine paintings by Caspar David Friedrich (1774–1840) and Josef Anton Koch (1768–1839), six by Moritz von Schwind (1804–1871), and four by Adrian Ludwig Richter (1803–1884).

The biographical drama *Cecil Rhodes*, by Hans Rehberg, premieres at the State Theater in Berlin.

8 The Berlin police grant limited release to the film *All Quiet on the Western Front* for private screenings to small audiences.

Director Gustav Hartung is named artistic manager of the Hessian Regional Theater in Darmstadt.

10 The combination travelogue and interview film *Wir schalten um auf Hollywood* (*We Take You Now to Hollywood*) premieres, directed by Frank Reicher and featuring many German actors, directors, and writers in casual situations and interviews; also appearing in the film are Buster Keaton, Joan Crawford, Adolphe Menjou, and Wallace Beery.

The drama *Die Reifeprüfung* (*The School Graduation Exam*), by Max Dreyer, premieres at the Dresden State Theater.

11 Communist Party officials stage "hunger marches" of unemployed workers in 15 German cities.

Rothbarth Press publishes the novel *Die Liebe höret nimmer auf* (*Love Shall Not Cease*), by Hedwig Courths-Mahler.

12 Zsolnay Press publishes the memoir *Ein Deutscher ohne Deutschland* (*A German without Germany*), by Walter von Molo.

14 The Berlin Hertha soccer club defeats Munich 1860 by 3 to 2 and remains the German national champion.

15 The film drama *Der Erlkönig* (*The Elf King*) premieres, directed by Peter Paul Brauer, with Otto Gebühr and Rosa Bertens.

16 The Bruckner Symphony Festival opens in Weimar, during which the Weimar Sate Orchestra will perform all nine of Anton Bruckner's symphonies.

17 An exhibition at the Academy of the Arts in Berlin opens featuring work by American architect Frank Lloyd Wright, the first American so honored.

18 Social Democrat chairman Hans Vogel explains his party's program in a broadcast titled "Our Fight against Chaos," the first time a political party is allowed to use government-regulated radio waves to promote its agenda.

20 German newspapers are filled with positive responses to American president Herbert Hoover's assertion that all German reparation payments should cease for one year in view of the mounting bank failures, food shortages, and unemployment in Germany.

Berlin police ban the National Socialist "sport festival" planned for Berlin; police later allow the Communist Party's "Spartacus Sports" event to take place, outraging National Socialists.

23 The crime film *Panik in Chikago* (*Panic in Chicago*) premieres, directed by Robert Wiene, with Olga Chekhova and Hans Rehmann.

24 The crime film *Menschen hinter Gitter* (*Men Behind Bars*, the German-language version of the Metro-Goldwyn-Mayer film *The Big House* starring Wallace Beery) premieres, directed by Paul Fejös, with Heinrich George in the Wallace Beery role and Gustav Diessl.

26 Playwright Gerhart Hauptmann makes a plea for "courage and continued work for a better future" on a nationwide radio broadcast.

27 The German League for Human Rights schedules three unpublicized showings of the American film *All Quiet on the Western Front*, open only to members of the League.

28 Fischer Press publishes the treatise in the form of "letters to young people" titled *Wissen und verändern!* (*Learn and Change!*), by physician Alfred Döblin.

29 The National Socialist Students' League stages protests against Versailles Treaty at the University of Berlin; afterward riots break out near the university among different student political factions.

30 Student riots in Hamburg and Munich break out after bans on protests against the Versailles Treaty are announced.

JULY

1 Communists in Cologne employ illegal radio broadcasting and cause interference with regularly licensed frequency.

3 Max Schmeling defeats American challenger William Stripling by technical knock-out in the 15th round of a scheduled bout in Cleveland, Ohio; Schmeling remains the world heavyweight boxing champion.

The All-England Lawn Tennis women's championships in Wimbledon features an all-German finale: Cilly Aussem defeats Hilde Krahwinkel 6:2 and 7:5 to become the first German to win a Wimbledon championship.

4 Actor and director Oskar Wallek is named artistic manager of the Coburg Regional Theater.

Propyläen Press publishes the tragicomedy *Italienische Nacht* by Ödön von Horvath.

5 The Kroll Opera House closes with a final performance of *The Marriage of Figaro* by Wolfgang Amadeus Mozart.

Rowohlt Press publishes the novel *Schloss Gripsholm* (*Gripsholm Palace*), by Kurt Tucholsky.

6 The first American Music Festival ever held in Germany begins at Bad Homburg with the work of composers Roger Sessions, Howard Hanson, Leo Sowerby, Quincy Porter, and others.

10 A three-way street riot breaks out among partisans of three different political parties (Social Democrats, Communists, and Social Democrats) in Heide, Holstein.

13 Darmstadt and National Bank (the fourth-largest bank in Germany) declares insolvency, setting off a panic run on banks and savings institutions throughout the country.

14 Reich president Paul von Hindenburg declares a bank holiday, allowing banks a respite from recent runs in depositor withdrawals; all German stock exchanges remain likewise closed.

15 Rothbarth Press publishes the novel *Des Schicksals Wellen* (*The Waves of Fate*), by Hedwig Courths-Mahler.

16 Banks reopen in Germany, but they allow depositors only limited withdrawals. Limited activity on stock exchanges resumes.

18 Reich president von Hindenburg issues several "emergency decrees," ordering closer supervision of newspapers, reduced or delayed pension payments, some suspension of government monetary liabilities, restriction of international currency exchange, limitations on German vacationers taking currency outside the country, among several others.

19 Sports car driver Rudolf Caracciola wins the German Grand Prix at Nüurburgring.

21 The Bayreuth Festival opens its first season under the musical direction of Wilhelm Furtwängler; productions this season are *Tannhäuser*, *Parsifal*, *Tristan und Isolde*, and the entire *Ring des Nibelungen* cycle; Adolf Hitler attends the festival as a guest of the festival's general director Winifred Wagner.

23 Hobbing Press publishes the memoir *Ich will leben* (*I Want to Live*), by Peter Flamm.

24 The operetta *Die Blume von Hawaii* (*The Flower of Hawaii*), by Paul Abraham, premieres at the Leipzig Neues Theater.

26 The film melodrama *Die Opernredoute* (*The Opera Ball*) premieres, directed by Max Neufeld, with Liane Haid and Georg Alexander.

27 Jess Press publishes a song and poetry collection titled *Gesänge gegen bar* (*Songs for Cash*), by Günther Franzke, with illustrations by George Grosz.

The musical comedy film *Nie wieder Liebe* (*No More Love*), directed by Anatole Litvak, with Harry Liedtke and Lilian Harvey, premieres.

30 The Berlin newspaper Illustrierte Zeitung begins serial publication of the novel *Mit dem Kopf durch die Wand* (*With Your Head through the Wall*), by Felix Hollaender.

The crime film *Der Zinker* (*The Informer*, based on a novel by Edgar Wallace) premieres, directed by Carl Lamac, with Lissy Arna and Karl Ludwig Diehl.

AUGUST

1 Ullstein Press publishes the novel *Ein Mensch geht seinen Weg* (*A Man Goes His Own Way*) with the new title of *Mit dem Kopf durch die Wand* (*With Your Head through the Wall*), by Felix Hollaender.

The Communist Party stages antiwar rallies in several cities, leading to numerous outbreaks of violence and several reports of injuries, though no deaths.

The Reich central bank raises its discount rate (the interest rate charged to banks for borrowing short-term funds from the central bank) to 15 percent, hoping to attract foreign investment in Germany.

4 The International Photography Fair opens in Dresden.

5 The Berlin newspaper *Vossische Zeitung* begins serial publication of the novel *Kingsblood Royal*, translated by Klaus Lambrecht, by Sinclair Lewis.

7 The film operetta *Die grosse Attraktion* (*The Big Attraction*) premieres, directed by Max Reichmann, with Riachard Tauber and Margot Lyon.

9 Communist partisans are accused in the murder of two Berlin policemen near the Volksbühne in Berlin; police shut down the Communist Party newspapers, close party headquarters, and seal off the area around the Volksbühne.

10 Modernist painters Emil Nolde and Ludwig Kirchner, sculptors Rudolf Belling and Edwin Scharff, and architect Mies van der Rohe are named members of Academy of the Arts; National Socialists react with outrage at the honors given artists whom they consider "decadent."

11 The film melodrama *Zwischen Nacht und Morgen* (*Between Night and Dawn*, based on a play by Wilhelm Braun depicting the world of prostitutes and pimps in Berlin) premieres, directed by Gerhard Lamprecht, with Aud Egede Nissen and Oskar Homolka.

12 Hesse Press publishes the treatise *Führung und Verführung* (*Leadership and Seduction*), by Fritz Brügel.

13 The quasi-documentary war film *Douaumont: Die Hölle von Verdun* (*Douaumont: The Hell of Verdun*) premieres, directed by Heinz Paul.

14 The musical comedy *Die Dubarry* (*Mme. Dubarry*), by Theo Mackeben based on the operetta *Countess Dubarry* by Karl Millöcker, premieres at the Admiral's Palace Theater in Berlin.

The film spy thriller *Im Geheimdienst* (*In the Secret Service*) premieres, directed by Gustav Ucicky, with Brigitte Helm and Willy Fritsch.

16 Grete Heublein sets the world record for the women's shot put event at the meet in Bielefeld with a distance of 13.7 meters (44 feet, 11? inches).

Drei Masken Press publishes the novel *Herzog Karl der Kühne* (*Duke Carl the Clever*), by Werner Bergengruen.

17 Conductor Karl Böhm debuts as music director of the Hamburg State Opera with a new production of *Die Meistersinger von Nürnberg* by Richard Wagner.

Crowds estimated at 23,000 turn out for funeral of two policemen slain on August 9.

18 Wilhelm Furtwängler conducts Wagner's *Tristan und Isolde* in the first live radio broadcast from the Bayreuth Festival.

21 German Radio Fair opens in Berlin, with exhibits featuring radio photography transmission, developments in television, and innovations in amplitude modulation (AM) broadcasts.

A Berlin newspaper begins serial publication of the novel *Georg Letham, Artzt und Mörder* (*George Letham, Physician and Murderer*), by Ernst Weiss.

25 The comedy *Affentanz* (*Ape Dance*), by Vera Bern, premieres at the Leipzig Komödienhaus.

The German stock exchanges cease operations and plan to reopen in two weeks.

27 The film comedy about bicycle racing *Um eine Nasenlänge* (*By a Nose-Length*) premieres, directed by Johannes Guter, with Sigfied Arno, Lucie Englisch, and Fred Louis Lerch.

28 The city of Frankfurt am Main awards its Goethe Prize to writer Ricarda Huch.

31 The film musical *Bomben auf Monte Carlo* (*The Bombardment of Monte Carlo*) premieres, directed by Hanns Schwarz, with Hans Albers, Heinz Rühmann, and Peter Lorre.

SEPTEMBER

1 The dramatic adaptation *Kat* (from the novel *A Farewell to Arms* by Ernest Hemingway), by Carl Zuckmayer and Heinz Hilpert, premieres at the Deutsches Theater in Berlin.

2 The German-American head of Paramount Studios Carl Laemmle assures police authorities in Berlin and other large urban jurisdictions that his company will edit its film *All Quiet on the Western Front* and exclude scenes that might offend nationalist-minded segments of the German audience.

3 The German Press Institute publishes the novels Das Kind Eva (*The Child Eva*), by Hermann Stegemann and *Föhn* by Helene Böhlau.

4 The weekly political journal *Die Fackel* (*The Torch*), which has a leftist editorial slant, debuts announcing "vigorous opposition to National Socialism and to cultural reactionaries."

5 The comedy Nina by Bruno Frank, premieres at the Dresden State Theater.

7 The drama *Die Entscheidung der Lissa Hart* (*Lissa Hart's Decision*), by Hermann Sudermann, premieres at the Bremen City Theater.

8 Mannheim police ban production of the comedy *Tartuffe* (written in 1664), by Moliére, after complaints from leaders of the local Catholic Center Party about the play's presumed anticlerical stance.

10 The managing director of the Berlin State Theater is named a member of the Prussian Academy of the Arts.

11 The drama *Vaterland* (*Fatherland*), by Peter Martin Lampel, premieres at the Mannheim National Theater.

14 Rowohlt Press publishes volume of essays titled *Lerne lachen ohne zu weinen* (*Learn to Laugh Without Crying*), by Kurt Tucholsky.

15 Buster Keaton makes his sound film debut in Germany with the premiere of *Free and Easy* directed by Edward Sedgwick, with Robert Montgomery and Lionel Barrymore.

17 The musical revue *Spuk in der Villa Stern* (*Ghost in the Stern Villa*), by Friedrich Hollaender, premieres at the Tingel-Tangel Theater in Berlin

Ufa Film Studio declares a profit for the first time in five years and pays a dividend to stockholders of 6 percent.

18 The war drama *Deutschland: Die Fahrt des Tauchboots UB 116* (*The Journey of Submarine #116*, the Deutschland).

The Berlin stock exchange ceases operation, with plans to reopen in four months.

20 Wunderlich Press publishes the novel *Vanadis* by Isolde Kurz.

21 The musical film comedy *Der ungetreue Eckehart* (*Eckehart the Unfaithful*), directed by Carl Boese, with Ralph Arthur Roberts, Lissy Arna, and the Comedian Harmonists, premieres.

Stock exchanges in Frankfurt am Main and Leipzig follow the lead of the Berlin stock exchange and close indefinitely.

24 Five banks declare insolvency—a new record for bank failures in one day.

25 Both major theaters in Breslau, the City Theater and the Lobe Theater, cease operations because of bankruptcy.

27 Recent elections give National Socialists big gains in Oldenburg and Hamburg; they become the ruling party in Braunschweig.

28 The adventure film *Berge in Flammen* (*Mountains on Fire*) premieres, directed by Luis Trenker, with himself and Lissy Arna.

30 The German Press Institute publishes the novel *Fabian* by Erich Kästner.

OCTOBER

1 Köhler Press publishes the novel *Faust in Montbijou* by Walter Bloem.

2 The musical film *So lang' noch ein Walzer von Strauss erklingt* (*As Long as Strauss Waltzes Are Heard*) premieres, directed by Conrad Wiene, with Gustav Fröhlich, Maria Paudler, and Valerie Boothby.

5 The drama *Kampf um Kitsch* (*Campaign for Kitsch*), by Robert Adolf Stemmle, premieres at the Volksbühne in Berlin.

6 Ehrenwirth Press publishes the novella *Die Letzte am Schafott* (*The Last One up the Scaffold*), by Gertrud von Le Fort.

8 The film drama *Berlin Alexanderplatz* (based on the novel by Alfred Döblin) premieres, directed by Phil Jutzi, with Heinrich George as Franz Biberkopf and Margarete Schlegel as Mieze.

9 Drei Masken Press publishes the novel *Bolwieser* by Oskar Maria Graf.

10 The drama *Rauhnacht* (*Bleak Night*), by Richard Billinger,[2] premieres.

Reich president Paul von Hindenburg and Reich chancellor Brüning agree to an official meeting with National Socialist leader Adolf Hitler; they reportedly discuss the disastrous economic situation in Germany.

11 The comedy *Der Reparationsagent* (*The Reparations Agent*), by Gustav Rickelt, premieres at Guben City Theater.

The "National Opposition" parties (National Socialists, German Nationalists, the Steel Helmet organization, and the Union of Fatherland Organizations), all of whom parade their various armed militias in Bad Harzburg, hold a conference; they form the "Harzburg Front" and dedicate themselves to replacing the present German government.

12 The film melodrama *24 Stunden aus dem Leben einer Frau* (*24 Hours in the Life of a Woman*, based on a novel by Stefan Zweig) premieres, directed by Robert Land, with Henny Porten and Friedrich Kayssler.

14 The operetta film *Viktoria und ihr Husar* (*Victoria and Her Hussar*, based on the operetta by Paul Abraham) premieres, directed by Richard Oswald, with Friedel Schuster as Victoria and Ivan Petrovich as her hussar.

15 The organization of Berlin motion picture theater owners agree to make a monthly allotment of 60,000 free tickets available to unemployed workers.

16 The comedy film *Reserve hat Ruh* (*Peace of Mind*) premieres, directed by Max Obal, with Fritz Kampers and Lucie Englisch.

17 Meiner Press publishes the memoir *Aus meinem Leben und Denken* (*Out of My Life and Thought*), by Albert Schweitzer, premieres.

18 The largest rally to date of National Socialist militia brigades is held in Braunschweig, where more than 100,000 uniformed militia members pass in review before Adolf Hitler. "This will be our final mass rally before we take over the reins of government!" proclaims Hitler. The National Socialist daily newspaper *Völkischer Beobachter* states, "Over 100,000 men in [public] review before Adolf Hitler, not any election, reveals the true face of the new Germany!"

20 The opera *The Mischievous Widow* by Ermanno Wolf-Ferrari, premieres at the Berlin City Opera.

22 Two film comedies premiere: *Hurra! Ein Junge* (*Hooray! It's a Boy*, based on a comedy by Franz Arnold and Ernst Bach), directed by Georg Jacoby, with Max Adalbert and Georg Alexander; and *Der brave Sünder* (*The Virtuous Sinner*, based on a comedy by Alfred Polgar, which in turn was based on a Russian novel by Valentin Katayev), directed by Fritz Kortner, with Max Pallenberg and Dolly Haas.

23 The musical film *Der Kongress tanzt* (*Dancing at the Congress of Vienna*) premieres, directed and choreographed by Erik Charell, with Willy Fritsch and Lilian Harvey.

"The Concerto for Violin and Orchestra in D Major" by Igor Stravinsky premieres at the Berlin Philharmonic Hall, with the composer conducting.

24 Playwright Ödön von Horvath and novelist Erik Reger are awarded the Kleist Prize.

The comedy *Sie und er* (*He and She*), by Phillip Moeller, premieres at the Leipzig City Theater.

29 The war film *Die andere Seite* (*The Other Side*, based on a play by R. C. Sheriff titled *Journey's End*; the film depicts English solders, as did the play, in the trenches before a battle near St. Quentin) premieres, directed by Heinz Paul, with Conrad Veidt, Theodor Loos, Friedrich Ettel, and Viktor de Kowa.

31 More than 1,500 business firms declare bankruptcy in the month of October; unemployment surpasses 4.6 million; eight banks declare insolvency.

NOVEMBER

2 The tragicomedy *Geschichten aus dem Wienerwald* (*Tales of Vienna Woods*), by Ödön von Horvath, premieres at the Deutsches Theater in Berlin.

3 Right-wing extremist student groups disrupt lectures of professors at the University of Halle with whose political views they disagree.

4 Kiepnheuer Press publishes *Junge Frau von 1914* (*Young Woman of 1914*), by Arnold Zweig.

5 The musical comedy film *Arm wie ein Kirchenmaus* (*Poor as a Church Mouse*, based on a play by Ladislas Fodor, with music by Ralph Benatzky) premieres, directed by Richard Oswald, with Grete Mosheim and Anton Edthofer.

Berlin school officials close 23 elementary schools in an effort to cut operating costs; most schools in Berlin are already overcrowded, many with 45–50 pupils per room.

12 The opera *Das Herz* (*The Heart*), by Hans Pfitzner, simultaneously premieres at the Berlin and Munich State Operas.

13 The opera *Friedemann Bach* (based on a novel by Emil Brachvogel, based on the the life of Johann Sebastian Bach's eldest son), by Paul Graener, premieres at the Schwerin City Theater.

14 The drama *Das Gesetz in Dir* (*The Law Within Thyself*), by Erwin Guido Kolbenheyer, premieres at the Munich Residenz Theater.

15 The first broadcast of an operetta over German airwaves occurs: *1001 Nights* by Johann Strauss, Jr., from the Kroll Opera House in Berlin; conductor Wilhelm Furtwängler in the Berlin newspaper *Vossische Zeitung* warns of damage to Berlin's concert-going tradition by recordings and radio broadcasts.

16 Police arrest former brewery executive Ludwig Katzenellenbogen, who had subsidized many of Erwin Piscator's experimental stage works at the Theater am Nollendorfplatz in Berlin; Katzenellenbogen is charged on suspicion of insider trading on the Berlin stock exchange.

17 Officials at the Reich cultural ministry implore regional security services to help put a stop to a recent spate of political murders, describing them as "a cultural catastrophe."

19 The film comedy *Der Bürovorsteher* (*The Office Manager*) premieres, directed by Hans Behrendt, with Felix Bressart and Maria Meissner.

21 The oratorio *Das Unaufhörliche* (*The Perpetual*), by Paul Hindemith, text by Gottfried Benn, premieres, by the Berlin State Choir at the Philharmonie.

23 The reich criminal court in Leipzig sentences editor Carl von Ossietzky and reporter Walter Kreiser of the literary journal *Die Weltbühne* to 18 months in prison for publishing military secrets, namely the co-operative maneuvers of the German armed forces with the Soviet Union's Red Army.

27 The film melodrama *Mädchen in Uniform* (*Girls in Uniform*, based on a play by Christa Winsloe) premieres, directed by Leontine Sagan, with Dorothea Wieck and Hertha Thiele.

28 The adaptation of the opera *Hoffmanns Erzählungen* (*Tales of Hoffmann*), by Jacques Offenbach, musically arranged by Leo Blech, with new libretto by Egon Friedell and Hanns Sassmann, premieres at the 3,800-seat Grosses Schauspielhaus in Berlin.

The children's play *Emil und die Detektive* (*Emil and the Detectives*, based on the children's novel by Erich Kästner) premieres at the Frankfurt am Main City Theater.

30 Nationwide unemployment reaches the 4.85 million mark.

DECEMBER

2 The film *Emil und die Detektive* (*Emil and the Detectives*, based on the children's novel by Erich Kästner) premieres, directed by Gerhard Lamprecht, with Rolf Wenkhaus as Emil, Käthe Haack, Fritz Rasp, and Rudolf Biebrach.

4 Adolf Hitler stages a press conference with foreign journalists, explaining the political goals and strategies of his party, emphasizing the formidable threat that Communism represents.

5 The Berlin police report outbreaks of National Socialist–instigated street violence in numerous neighborhoods throughout the city.

6 The *Weihnachstoratorium* (*Christmas Oratorio*) Opus 17, by Kurt Thomas, premieres at the Berlin Philharmonie with the Berlin State and Cathedral choirs.

9 Transmere Press publishes the first novel by playwright Georg Kaiser titled *Es ist genug* (*It Is Enough*).

10 The mountain skiing film drama *Der weisse Rausch* (*White Ecstasy*) premieres, directed by Arnold Fanck, with Leni Riefenstahl and Hannes Schneider.

11 Reich government officials attempt to block a planned radio address by Adolf Hitler to the United States; National Socialists plan a telephone linkup with the headquarters of the Columbia Broadcasting System in London, who then will broadcast the speech over shortwave radio.

16 The Vatican proclaims Cologne theologian and philosopher Albertus Magnus (ca. 1200–1280, beatified 1661) Doctor of the Church.

17 Müller Press publishes a volume of nonfiction work titled *Stimme* (*Voice*), by Erwin Guido Kolbenheyer.

21 The Berlin premiere of *Aufstieg und Fall der Stadt Mahagonny* (*The Rise and Fall of the City of Mahagonny*), by Kurt Weill and Bertolt Brecht, opens at the Kurfürstendamm Theater in Berlin.

22 The film comedy *Der Hauptmann von Köpenick* (*The Captain of Köpenick*, based on the play of same title by Carl Zuckmayer), directed by Richard Oswald, with Max Adalbert in the title role, and Käthe Haack, premieres.

23 The Napoleonic war film *Yorck* premieres, directed by Gustav Ucicky, with Werner Krauss as General Yorck von Wartenberg, Grete Mosheim, and Gustav Gründgens.

24 American president Herbert Hoover signs a law providing a one-year moratorium on German reparation payments.

31 Reich president Paul von Hindenburg attempts to make a nationwide New Year's Eve radio address to the German people, calling for "unity in a shared fate;" Communist Party operatives manage to tamper with transmission lines to the broadcast studio, jamming the frequency and making much of the speech unintelligible.

The year 1931 is the most economically catastrophic in modern German history: unemployment tops 5.6 million; 13,588 businesses declared bankruptcy; steel production operates at 20 percent of capacity, coal mining at almost 30 percent; and suicide rates are the highest since record-keeping began.

NOTES

1. Kürten was executed only once (by guillotine on July 2, 1931) and his head was sent to different university medical research laboratories where examiners attempted to find irregularities in his brain that might explain his homicidal tendencies. They found nothing of serious interest; Kürten's head was later mummified and sent to the United States, where it is currently on display at a museum in Wisconsin Dells.

2. The increasing popularity of plays by Austrian-born playwright Richard Billinger (1893–1965) is an indication of the rightward-shift in popular drama during the waning years of the Weimar Republic. His plays often evinced nationalist tendencies, and this particular play showed a pronounced distaste of African influences on European culture. The central character in *Bleak Night* is a Roman Catholic priest serving a small parish in Bavaria. In years previous, the priest was a missionary to Africa; there he fell in with a primitive tribe that practiced human sacrifice. The priest has been unable to shake off the effects of such practices in Bavaria, and in the final act of *Bleak Night*, he lures an innocent girl to his secret lair and subjects her to a grisly ritualistic ceremony that results in her death. His parishioners react with calculated fury against what they perceive to be tribalism in their midst and drive him to his death by drowning in a nearby river.

1932

JANUARY

1 The unemployment rate stands at roughly 24 percent of the German workforce; unemployment in the United States hovers at 20 percent.

4 The war comedy film *Der Stolz der 3. Kompanie* (*The Pride of Company Three*) premieres, directed by Fred Sauer, with Heinz Rühmann, Adolf Wohlbrück, and Viktor de Kowa.

5 The city governments of Dortmund and Dresden are no longer capable of paying interest on bonds or loans, essentially declaring themselves bankrupt.

Snow and ice storms plague much of Germany; flooding near Munich causes the Isar River to rise seven feet to flood stage in less than 48 hours; National Socialists exploit catastrophes in their newspapers to criticize the republican government's perceived incompetence in assisting those affected.

6 The Reich chancellor declares that the German central government can make no further reparation payments called for in the Versailles Treaty (and renegotiated in the Dawes and Young Plans) to the victorious World War I allies; the Germans have to date paid the French government a total of RM 21.3 billion ($5.1 billion).

8 The Aachen City Theater attempts to stir interest among audiences by transmitting the audio portion of performances via loudspeakers out onto the street in front of the theater; the attempt fails, and attendance continues to decline.

The Annette von Drost-Hülshoff Museum in Münster is dedicated and opens.

9 Cabaret performer Joachim Ringelnatz has his first hit song made popular by radio: "Die Flasche," ("The Bottle") a song about a drunken sailor.

12 The film comedy *Madame hat Ausgang* (*Madame Makes Her Exit*) premieres, directed by Wilhelm Thiele, with Liane Haid and Hans Brausewetter.

Fischer Press publishes two dramas: *Timon* by Ferdinand Bruckner and *Lukardis* by Jakob Wassermann.

13 Metzner Press publishes the monograph titled *Rassenforschung und Volk der Zukunft* (Race Research and Ethnicity of the Future), by the director of the Kaiser Wilhelm Institute for Anthropological and Eugenics Studies.

15 The German-language version of the comedy film *Spite Marriage* premieres under title *Cassanova wider Willen* (*Cassanova against His Will*), directed by Edward Brophy, with Buster Keaton, Egon von Jordan, Gerda Mann, and Marion Lessing.

16 The drama *Die Mutter* (*The Mother*), by Bertolt Brecht, premieres for a once-only performance at the Komödienhaus Theater in Berlin.

19 Numerous outbreaks in Berlin of public violence occur between National Socialists and partisans of other groups; street fighting with Communists in north Berlin districts leave two dead. Attacks against Jewish faculty members and students (or those thought to be Jews) leave several seriously injured; administrators order the university closed for two days.

20 The drama *Mata Hari*, by Karl Maria Becher, premieres at the Nuremberg City Theater.

21 The film drama *Nachtkolonne* (*Night Convoy*) premieres, directed by James Bauer, with Oskar Homolka and Olga Chekhova.

22 The film melodrama *Stürme der Leidenschaft* (*Storms of Passion*) premieres, directed by Robert Siodmak, with Emil Jannings and Trude Hesterberg.

24 The drama *Timon* by Ferdinand Bruckner premieres at the Deutsches Theater in Berlin.

26 Cotta Press publishes the drama *Es brennt an der Grenze* (*Fires Along the Border*), by Hans Kyser.

28 Fischer Press publishes the drama *Vor Sonnenuntergang* (*Before Sunset*), by Gerhart Hauptmann.

30 Cotta Press publishes the novel *Reiter in der deutschen Nacht* (*Rider in the German Night*), by Hanns Heinz Ewers, who dedicates the book to "all German university students."

31 Unemployed workers now total more than 6 million individuals.

FEBRUARY

4 Pianist Wilhelm Kempff is named a member of the Prussian Academy of the Arts.

5 The film comedy *Man braucht kein Geld* (*No Money Needed*), directed by Carl Boese, with Heinz Rühmann, Hans Moser, and Ida Wüst, premieres.

10 State theaters in Kassel and Wiesbaden close because of worsening financial straits; in Berlin Max Reinhardt relinquishes the lease on the Komödie Theater, sells the Grosses Schauspielhaus to Rotter Brothers, and retreats to the Deutsches Theater as his only remaining theatrical venue.

11 The comedy *Krieg über Sonja* (*War about Sonia*), by Peter Franz Stubmann, premieres at the Hamburg City Theater.

13 The film comedy *Ein steinrecher Mann* (*Filthy Rich*) premieres, directed by Steve Sekely, with Curt Bois and Dolly Haas.

The German national ice hockey team wins the bronze medal at the Olympic Winter Games in Lake Placid, New York.

16 The drama *Vor Sonnenuntergang* (*Before Sunset*), by Gerhart Hauptmann on the occasion of the playwright's 70th birthday, premieres at the Deutsches Theater in Berlin.

Berlin appeals court upholds a ban on the sale or distribution of the novel *Sturm auf Essen* (*The Storming of Essen*), by Hans Marchwitza, a fictional account of the Kapp Putsch in 1920.

17 By a narrow margin, Adolf Hitler is named "extraordinary professor" of social studies and politics at the Technical University of Braunschweig; he thus is accorded German citizenship by becoming a government official and may now run for presidency of the German republic.

Langen Press publishes the novella *Ave Eva* (*Hail to Eve*), by Hanns Johst.

18 Zsolnay Press publishes the biography *Schliemann: Geschichte eines Goldsuchers* (*Schliemann: History of a Treasure Hunter*), by Emil Ludwig.[1]

19 The history film *Rasputin* premieres, directed by Adolf Trotz, with Conrad Veidt in the title role and Hermine Sterler as Czarina Alexandra.

20 Langen Press publishes treatise *Von der bürgerlichen Ehre und bürgerlichen Notwendigkeit* (*On Middle Class Honor and Necessity*), by Hans Grimm.

22 To an overflow crowd of National Socialists at the Berlin Sports Palace, Joseph Goebbels announces the candidacy of Adolf Hitler for the German presidency.

23 The war drama *Die endlose Strasse*[2] (*The Eternal Road*), by Sigmund Graff, premieres in Berlin at the Schiller Theater.

The film operetta *Mamsell Nitouche* premieres, directed by Carl Lamac with Anny Ondra in the title role and Oskar Karlweis.

24 The National Socialists distribute more than 50,000 phonograph records containing speeches by Adolf Hitler to activists in dozens of German cities, where the records will be played on loudspeakers set up on street corners.

25 Propyläen Press publishes the novel *Narrenspiegel* (*Mirror of Fools*), by Alfred Neumann; S. Fischer publishes the novel *Treffpunkt im Unendlichen* (*Meeting Point in the Infinite*), by Klaus Mann.

28 The German-American runner Henry Ventzke sets the world indoor record for the 1500-meter event at 3:53.4 minutes in Chicago.

29 The film comedy *Drei von der Stempelstelle* (*Three Guys from the Unemployment Off*ice) premieres, directed by Eugen Thiele, with Fritz Kampers, Adolf Wohlbrück, and Paul Kemp.

Zsolnay Press publishes the novel *Die Macht* (*Power*), by Robert Neumann.

MARCH

1 Gerhart Hauptmann is named a member of the American Academy of Arts and Sciences (located in Cambridge, Massachusetts), the first German national so honored; German radio makes a national broadcast of his speech about the worldwide importance of Johann Wolfgang Goethe, given at the Columbia University in New York City.

The electoral campaign for the Reich presidency officially begins.

2 A labor survey of Europe and the United States reveals that Germany now has the highest unemployment rate in the industrialized world, with 28 percent of the work force idle; America's rate stands at 21 percent, Great Britain's at 19 percent.

Reclam Press publishes the patriotic novel titled *Horridoh Lützow!* (*Lützow the Fighter Pilot*), by Rudolf Herzog.

The steamship passenger liner *Bremen* sets new record for an Atlantic crossing from Bremerhaven to New York: four days, 17 hours.

5 The comedy *Dämmerung der Dollar* (*Twilight of the Dollar*), by Joachim Grübel, premieres at the Leipzig Komödienhaus.

8 Fischer Press publishes the novel *Giganten* (*Giants*), an adaptation and revision of an earlier fiction work titled *Berge, Meere, und Giganten* (*Mountains Seas, and Giants*), by physician Alfred Döblin.

9 German Press Institute publishes the treastise *Deutsche Geist im Gefahr* (*The German Mind at Risk*), by literature professor Robert Curtius (at the University of Bonn).

10 The opera *Die Bürgschaft* (*The Pledge*), by Kurt Weill, with libretto by stage designer Caspar Neher, premieres at the City Opera in Berlin.

In a nationwide radio address close to the first round of presidential elections, Reich president Paul von Hindenburg claims that Germany needs a leader not obligated to party interests nor the agenda of any specific party.

11 German Vereins Press publishes the novel titled *Elisabeth geht zum Tonfilm* (*Elisabeth Goes to the Talking Pictures*), by Melchior and Eva Vischer.

12 The comedy *Liebling der Kurve* (*Child of Fortune*), by Fred Antoine Angermayer, premieres at the Leipzig Kleines Theater.

State art academies in Kassel, Königsberg, and Breslau are closed, leaving only the Düseldorf art academy among Prussian-supported art academies in Germany.

13 The first round of presidential elections concludes, with incumbent Paul von Hindenburg winning the most votes—49.6 percent of the electorate—just short of the majority required for election. Adolf Hitler comes in second with 30.1 percent of the votes. Communist Party leader Ernst Thälmann is third, with 13.2 percent. The date for the final three-way runoff election among von Hindenburg, Hitler, and Thälmann is set for April 10.

16 The opera *Andromache* by Herbert Windt premieres at the State Opera in Berlin.

17 Two biographical films about Johann Wolfgang Goethe premiere, *Der Werdegang* (*The Rise to Prominence*) and *Die Vollendung* (*The Completion*) both directed by Fritz Wendhausen, with Theodor Loos and Luise Ullrich.

19 Ernst Legal, director of the Schiller Theater in Berlin, resigns in the midst of worsening financial conditions among Berlin's state-subsidized theaters.

The opera in five scenes *Claudine von Villa Bella* by Johann Wolfgang Goethe, set to new music by Alfred Irmler, premieres at the Weimar National Theater.

21 The film comedy *Der Sieger* (*The Victor*) premieres, directed by Hans Hinrich, with Hans Albers and Käthe von Nagy.

22 Several German newspapers note the worldwide observations of the 100th anniversary of poet, playwright, theater director, and diplomat Johann Wolfgang Goethe's death.

The film *Einmal möcht ich keine Sorgen haben* (*One of These Days I'd Like to be Free of My Troubles*) premieres, directed by Max Nosseck, with Max Hansen and Ursula Grabley.

23 The crime comedy film *Peter Voss, der Millionendieb* (*Peter Voss, the Thief who Stole Millions*) premieres, directed by E. A. Dupont, with Rudolf Anders and Therese Giehse.

24 Actress Leni Riefenstahl debuts as film director with *Das blaue Licht* (*The Blue Light*), with herself in a major role and Mathias Wiemann.

The Leipzig Komödienhaus Theater declares bankruptcy and ceases operations.

25 The drama *Thomas Müntzer*, by Herbert Eulenberg, premieres at the Hannover City Theater.

26 The film *Skandal in der Parkstrasse* (*Scandal on Park Street*) premieres, directed by Franz Wenzler, with Fritz Kampers, Fritz Odemar, and Rosa Valetti.

28 Malik Press publishes the novel *Der Kaiser ging–die Generäle blieben* (*The Kaiser Left—the Generals Remained*), by Theodor Plievier.

29 The opera *Die Zwillingsesel* (*The Jackass Twins*), by Erwin Dressel, premieres at the Dresden State Theater.

30 The comedy *Mary treibt Politik* (*Mary Goes into Politics*), by Stefan Salm, premieres at the Freiburg City Theater.

31 Berlin police ban exhibition and distribution of the film *Kuhle Wampe, oder wem gehört die Welt?* (*Kuhle Wampe, or Who Owns the World?*), directed by Slatan Dudow, written by Bertolt Brecht and Ernst Ottwald, with Ernst Busch and Hertha Thiele, on the grounds that it is "Communist Party agitation."[3]

The newly restored version of the opera *Ritter Roland* (*Knight Sir Roland*), by Franz Josef Haydn, premieres with a new libretto by Ernst Latzko.

APRIL

1 The comedy *Kamrad Kasper*, by Paul Schurek, premieres at the Volksbühne in Berlin; The German premiere of two one-act dramas, *Anatols Grössenwahn* (*Anatol's Delusions of Grandeur*) and *Die Gleitenden* (*The Floaters*) from the estate of Arthur Schnitzler, open.

Reich president von Hindenburg rejects the proposal to pardon editor and journalist Carl von Ossietzky, who was sentenced to 18 months in prison for publishing military secrets in the literary journal *Die Weltbühne*.

3 The campaign for Reich presidency officially begins; bloody encounters among partisans in several German cities leave a dozen dead and scores wounded. Adolf Hitler renews the innovative use of aircraft and media of radio and phonograph recordings to win votes: he speaks at mass rallies in three to four cities every day before the election.

6 The Prussian Academy of the Arts awards its Beethoven Prize to composer Max von Schillings.

Fischer Press publishes the novel *Der Widersacher* (*The Adversary*), by Joachim Maass; Rowohlt Press publishes a collection of poetry titled *Gedichte dreier Jahre* (*Poems of Three Years*), by Joachim Ringelnatz.

8 Langen Press publishes the novel *Lebenslauf eines dicken Mannes, der Hamlet hiess* (*Biography of a Fat Man Named Hamlet*), by Georg Britting.

9 The assassination attempt at the Potsdam train station on Reich bank director Hans Luther proves unsuccessful; two National Socialist partisans are arrested.

10 Paul von Hindenburg is elected to a second term of Reich presidency with 53.2 percent of the vote; Adolf Hitler wins 36.7 percent, Thälmann 10.1 percent.

11 The exhibition in Hannover of cartoonist, illustrator, satirist, poet, and graphic illustrator Wilhelm Busch opens on the 100th anniversary of his birth near Hannover.

The German premiere of the film romance *Shanghai Express*, directed by Josef von Sternberg, with Marlene Dietrich, Clive Brook, Anna May Wong, and Warner Oland, opens.

Radio Berlin premieres the broadcast version of the drama *Die heilige Johanna der Schlachthöfe* (*St. Joan of the Stockyards*), by Bertolt Brecht.

12 The musical film *Fünf von der Jazzband* (*Five Guys from the Jazz Band*) premieres, directed by Erich Engel, with Jenny Jugo, Rolf von Goth, and Fritz Klippel.

15 The Berlin Philharmonic Orchestra under the direction of Wilhelm Furtwängler premieres "Philharmonisches Kozert" ("Philharmonic Concerto"), by Paul Hindemith, at the Philharmonie in Berlin.

The film operetta *Es war einmal ein Walzer* (*Once There Was a Waltz*) premieres, directed by Victor Janson, music by Franz Lehar, screenplay by Billy Wilder, with Martha Eggert and Rolf von Goth.

20 The drama *Zero*, by Fritz von Unruh, premieres at the Frankfurt am Main City Theater.

The "Prolog und Epilog zu einem dramatischen Gedicht für Orchester" ("Prologue and Epilogue to a Dramatic Poem for Orchestra") composed by tenor Richard Tauber premieres at the City Orchestra of Freiburg; Tauber also conducts the orchestra.

21 Swimmer Lise Rocke from Magdeburg sets the world record for the 200-meter breaststroke in Leipzig with a time of 3:08.2 minutes.

22 The film comedy *Die Gräfin von Monte-Christo* (*The Countess of Monte Cristo*) premieres, directed by Karl Hartl, with Brigitte Helm in the title role, Rudolf Forster, and Gustav Gründgens.

24 Max Reinhardt's production of *Kabale und Liebe* (*Intrigue and Love*), by Friedrich Schiller opens at the International Theater Festival in Rome.

National Socialists make substantial gains during elections in Anhalt, Bavaria, Prussia, Württemberg, and Hamburg.

The operetta film *Melodie der Liebe* (*Melody of Love*) premieres, directed by Georg Jacoby, music by Fritz Friedmann-Frederich, with Richard Tauber and Petra Unkel.

30 The drama *Oedipus* (based on the tragedy by Sophocles), by Andre Gide, translated by Ernst Robert Curtius, has its German premiere at the Hessian National Theater in Darmstadt.

MAY

1 Composer Richard Strauss debuts on German radio, conducting a concert of his works on the *Berlin Radio Hour*.

May Day celebrations are held throughout Germany with the National Socialists and Communists vying with each other as "authentic" representation of workers; numerous partisans are killed and injured in major cities.

3 The Johann Sebastian Bach Festival opens in Heidelberg.

4 Propyläen Press publishes the novella *Die Affenhochzeit* (*The Wedding Present*), by Carl Zuckmayer.

6 The horror film *Vampyr* (*Castle of Doom*) premieres, directed by Carl Theodor Dreyer, with Julian West and Rena Mandel.

7 Three Rhineland theaters amalgamate in an effort to avoid bankruptcy: the Düsseldorf and Cologne City Theaters, along with the private Düsseldorf Schauspielhaus.

8 The gangster film *Scarface* (based on the life and career of Chicago crime boss Al Capone), directed by Howard Hawks, with Paul Muni and Ann Dvorak, has its German premiere. Many German critics cite similarities between Chicago gang wars and those taking place in the streets of German cities.

10 The city of Frankfurt am Main awards its Goethe Prize to playwright Gerhart Hauptmann.

12 Ullstein Press publishes the memoirs of former foreign minister Gustav Stresemann under title *Vermächtnis* (*Legacy*).

14 The German-Danish adventure film *Der weisse Gott* (*The White God*), directed by George Schneevoigt, with Paul Richter and Mona Martenson, premieres.

The newly renovated St. Hedwig's Cathedral in Berlin, seat of the Berlin Catholic bishop, opens with a ceremony of sanctification.

17 Two dramas premiere: *Haifische* (*Sharks*), by Theodor Plievier at Theater der Schauspieler in Berlin; and *Robinson soll nicht sterben* (*Robinson Should Not Perish*), by Friedrich Forster at the Leipzig Altes Theater.

18 The film romance *Der Prinz von Arkadien* (*The Prince of Arcadia*) premieres, directed by Karl Hartl, with Willi Forst in the title role and Laine Haid.

20 The drama *Ein Kind will helfen* (*A Child Wants to Help*), by Robert Kluttmann, premieres at the Hamburg Kammerspiele.

The naval quasi-documentary film *Kreuzer Emden* (*Cruiser Emden*) premieres, directed by Louis Ralph, with himself and Renée Stobrava.

Rowohlt Press publishes a collection of essays and poetry titled *Konzert* (*Concert*), by playwright Else Lasker-Schüler.

24 The opera *Grosse Katherina* (*Great Catherine*, based on the play by George Bernard Shaw), by Jakon Lilien, premieres at the Wiesbaden May Festival Theater.

25 Violent fisticuffs break out in the Prussian state legislature between National Socialist and Communist deputies; many are taken to hospitals after order is restored.

27 The film romance *Das Lied einer Nacht* (*Song in the Night*) premieres, directed by Anatole Litvak, with Julis Falkenstein and Magda Schneider.

28 Fischer Press publishes the biography *Bula Matari: Das Leben Stanleys, des Eroberers von Zentralafrika* (*Bula Matari: The Life of Stanley, Conqueror of Central Africa*), by Jakob Wassermann.

30 Berlin police lift the ban and allow the premiere of the quasi-documentary film *Kuhle Wampe, oder wem gehört die Welt?* (*Kuhle Wampe, or Who Owns the World?*), directed by Slatan Dudow, written by Bertolt Brecht and Ernst Ottwald, with Ernst Busch and Hertha Thiele.

Composer Max von Schillings is named the successor to Max Liebermann as director of the Prussian Academy of the Arts.

JUNE

2 The comedy *Engel* (*Angel*), by Melchior Lengyels, premieres at the Hamburg Thalia Theater.

3 The annual Munich Art Exhibition (which formerly took place in the now-destroyed Munich Glass Palace) opens at the library of the Deutsches Museum in Munich.

4 The drama *Kaiser Franz Josef I*, by Richard Duschinsky, premieres at the Coburg Regional Theater.

Zsolnay Press publishes a collection of speeches and essays titled *Die Zeit ist reif* (*The Time Is Ripe*), by novelist Frank Thiess.

6 German sprinter Arthur Jonath sets a world record for the 100-meter dash with a time of 10.3 seconds.

9 The one-act operatic drama *Der Kammersänger* (*The Court Singer*), by Frank Wedekind, with new music by Rudolf Hartung, premieres at the Braunschweig Regional Theater.

Rowohlt Press publishes the economic treatise *Der Niedergang des deutschen Kapitalismus* (*The Decline of German Capitalism*), by Fritz Sternberg.

10 Rowohlt Press publishes the novel *Kleiner Mann—was nun?* (*Little Man, What Now?*), by Hans Fallada.

12 The musical *Lais*, by Richard Enders, premieres at the Breslau City Opera.
The Munich soccer team Bayern München defeats Frankfurt am Main Eintracht by 2 to 0 to win the German national championship.

13 The Reich interior ministry decrees one hour per day on all radio frequencies in Germany be made available to government broadcasts aimed at informing the populace about efforts and programs designed to improve the economic situation in the country.

14 The crime comedy film *Der Flucht nach Nizza* (*The Escape to Nice*) premieres, directed by James Bauer, with Fritz Fischer and Else Elster.

15 The crime comedy film *Jonny stiehlt Europa* (*Johnny Steals Europe*) premieres, directed by Harry Piel, with himself, Alfred Abel, and Dary Holm.
The comedy *Die eiserne Jungfrau* (*The Iron Virgin*), by Julius Dernburg, premieres at the Rose Theater in Berlin.

17 Kiepenheuer Press publishes the novel *Quartett zu dritt* (*Quartet for Three*), by Hans Reimann.
The city orchestras of Essen, Duisburg, and Bochum amalgamate to form the Orchestra of the Ruhr.

19 The world's first clock museum opens in the Thuringian town of Laucha.
Werner Ladewig is named music director of the Dresden Philharmonic Orchestra.

21 World boxing heavyweight champion Max Schmeling loses his title to American Jack Sharkey in a controversial split decision at Madison Square Garden Bowl on Long Island, New York.

25 Goldmann Press publishes the novel *Fräulein Müller wird am Telefon verlangt* (*Telephone Call for Miss Müller, Please*), by Rudolf Presber.

28 Conductor Wilhelm Furtwängler warns in an essay published in Berlin newspaper *Mittag* that radio and recordings have the potential to destroy live music concerts.

JULY

1 The film drama *Mensch ohne Namen* (*Man without a Name*) premieres, directed by Gustav Ucicky, with Werner Krauss and Helen Thimig.

2 The institute for Theater History at University of Cologne opens the exhibition Goethe in the Theater at the Cologne Arts and Crafts Museum.

5 The Reich district court bans publication for three days of the Cologne newspaper *Kölnische Volkszeitung* on grounds of insulting the Reich chancellor; the same court bans the Social Democrat newsaper *Vorwärts* for five days.

7 Voegels Press publishes the National Socialist treatise *Der Marsch auf Berlin* (*The March on Berlin*), by Fritz Carl Roegels.

8 Reutlingen Press publishes the novel *Helen Jungs Liebe* (*The Love of Helen Jung*), by Hedwig Courths-Mahler.

9 The international reparations conference in Lausanne, Switzerland, agrees to terminate the demand for payments from Germany, provided that the German government comes up with a one-time payment of RM 3 billion ($710 million).

11 Atlantis Press publishes the monograph on Baron Karl von und zum Stein titled *Stein: Der Erwecker des Reichsgedankens* (*Stein: Inspiration of the Reich Concept*), by Ricarda Huch.

14 Shuttering of Berlin's 104th motion picture theater since the beginning of the year.

15 Campaign for the Reichstag elections officially begins; National Socialists renew innovative use of aircraft, radio broadcasts, billboard advertising, print media, and phonograph recordings to win votes.

17 The German Davis Cup tennis team defeats the Italian team in Berlin to win the European championship.

Street battles rage in the west Hamburg district of Altona between National Socialists and Communists, leaving 18 dead and scores wounded.

18 The film drama *Der falsche Tenor* (*The Wrong Tenor*) premieres, directed by Ludwig Beck, with Edgar Boltz and Tamara Oberländer.

The Reich interior ministry bans outdoor rallies and demonstrations until elections conclude at the end of the month.

Joseph Goebbels is granted air time for national radio broadcast on "The National Character as Foundation for a National Culture."

19 The crime film *Der Schuss im Morgengrauen* (*Gunfire at Dawn*) premieres, directed by Alfred Zeisler, with Theodor Loos and Peter Lorre.

20 Rowohlt Press publishes the travel book *Packt an, Kameraden!* (*Pitch in, Comrades!*), by Peter Martin Lampel.

21 A retrospective exhibition of paintings and graphic work by Max Liebermann opens at the Helbing Gallery in Berlin.

27 The oratorio *Das deutsche Sanktus* (*The German Sanctus*), by Karl Hasse, premieres at the Kreuz Church in Dresden.

31 Elections for German Reichstag give National Socialists 230 seats (37.4 percent of votes cast, the most of any party; second are the Social Democrats with 21.6 percent, followed by the Communists with 14.5 percent).

Ellen Braumüller from Berlin wins the silver medal for the women's javelin throw at the Summer Olympics in Los Angeles

AUGUST

1 Overnight street clashes between National Socialists and leftist militia groups leave 20 dead. Government officials admit that local police forces are undermanned and unprepared for the ongoing public violence among political groups.

3 Rowohlt Press publishes the collection of essays titled *Die Grenze* (*The Border*), by René Schickele.

6 The oratorio *Das jüngste Gericht* (*The Last Judgement*), by Otto Jochum, premieres at the Frankfurt am Main City Opera.

The first "Autobahn" opens in Germany, a 30-mile stretch of four-lane, limited-access highway between Cologne and Bonn.

8 The film comedy *Quick* premieres, directed by Robert Siodmak, with Hans Albers in the title role and Lilian Harvey.

9 The film melodrama *Nacht der Versuchung* (*Night of Temptation*) premieres, directed by Leo Lasko, with Elga Brink, Lotte Deyers, and Werner Füetterer.

12 The musical film biography *Johann Strauss, k. u. k. Hofkapellmeister* (*Johann Strauss, Royal and Imperial Court Musician*) premieres, directed by Conrad Wiene, with Michael Bohnen in the title role and Lee Parry.

13 National Socialist leader Adolf Hitler meets with Reich president von Hindenburg to demand appointment as Reich chancellor in view of his party's successes during recent elections; Hindenburg rejects demands and offers Hitler the post of vice-chancellor, which Hitler refuses.

15 Painter Adolf Bode is awarded the Georg Büchner Prize from the Hessian State Cultural Ministry.

17 The film comedy *Zwei glückliche Tage* (*Two Happy-Go-Lucky Days*) premieres, directed by Rudolf Walther-Fein, with Jakob Tiedtke and Ida Wüst.

18   Reich broadcast authorities release ownership figures of radio sets in Germany: now 64 radios per 1,000 inhabitants; comparable figures in Great Britain are higher with 94 per 1,000; the United States has the highest number, with 124 per 1,000.

The film opera *The Bartered Bride*, by Beidrich Smetana, premieres, directed by Max Ophüls, with Willy Domgraf-Fassbänder and Jarmila Novotna.

20   The Berlin premiere of a new production of the operetta *Das Dreimäderlhaus* (*Blossom Time*), by Heinrich Berté, based on melodies by Franz Schubert) opens at the Theater des Westens in Berlin, with Richard Tauber as Franz Schubert.

21   The "Goethe Festival" opens in Frankfurt am Main (Johann Wolfgang Goethe's birthplace) celebrating the 100th anniversary of his death in Weimar; several performances and readings of his work take place in Frankfurt during the coming week. Norwegian painter Edvard Munch is awarded the Frankfurt Goethe Medallion.

22   Workers renovating a small parish church in Hollberg discover a wood altar piece by Tilman Riemenschneider.[4]

23   The film melodrama *Wer zählt heute noch?* (*Who's Paying Today?*), directed by Heinz Hille, with Max Ehrlich and Hedi Heising, premieres.

30   Honorary president of the Reichstag Klara Zetkin opens a new session of the German parliament with a denunciation of the capitalist social order and pleads for a unified front against National Socialism; members of the Reichstag elect the leader of the National Socialist faction Hermann Goering as president of the Reichstag.

SEPTEMBER

1   The operetta *Eine Frau, die weiss, was sie will* (*A Woman Who Knows What She Wants*), by Oscar Straus, premieres at the Metropol Theater in Berlin.

Adolf Hitler assures his listeners at a packed Sports Palace in Berlin that "parliamentary democracy is obsolete; from now on, the state must be renewed by the people."

2   The military film romance *Drei von der Kavallerie* (*Three from the Cavalry*) premieres, directed by Carl Boese, with Fritz Kampers, Paul Hörbiger, and Paul Heidemann.

5   An outdoor rally of the Steel Helmet organization attracts 150,000 participants in Berlin, all of whom swear eternal vigilance against both Marxism and pacifism.

8 The historical film fantasy *Die Tänzerin von Sanssouci* (*The Dancer from Sans Souci Palace*) premieres, directed by Friedrich Zelnik, with Otto Gebühr as King Frederick the Great and Lil Dagover.

9 The film melodrama *Ich will nicht wissen, wer Du bist* (*I Don't Want to Know Who You Are*) premieres, directed by Geza von Bolvary, with Liane Haid and Gustav Fröhlich.

German Press Institute publishes two novels: *Menschen unter Zwang* (*People Under Constraint*), by Clara Viebig and *Der Fährmann Adrian Risch* (*Ferryman Adrian Risch*), by Ernst Zahn.

10 Staackmann Press publishes the novel *Das Lächeln der Marie Antoinette* (*The Smile of Marie Antoinette*), by Budolf Bartsch.

11 German race car driver Rudolf Caracciola wins the Grand Prix in Monza with an average speed of 107 mph over a 120-mile course.

12 The German premiere of spy film thriller *Mara Hari*, directed by George Fitzmaurice, with Greta Garbo in the title role and Ramon Novarro, opens.

Fischer Press publishes the treatise *Was wird aus Deutschlands Theater?* (*What Will Become of Germany's Theater?*), by theater critic Alfred Kerr.

15 Kipenheuer Press publishes the novel *Radetzkymarsch* (*The Radetzky March*), by Joseph Roth.

16 Rowohlt Press publishes the biography *Arthur Aronymus und seine Väter* (*Arthur Aronymus and His Forefathers*), by Else Lasker-Schüler.

17 The drama *Männer im Kampf* (*Men in Battle*), by Kurt Sommerer, premieres at the Düsseldorf Theater am Rhein.

19 Staackmann Press publishes the novel *Liebe kommt zur macht* (*Love Comes to Power*), by Friedrich Schreyvogl. Rothbarth Press publishes the novel *Die Herrin der Armada* (*The Mistress of the Armada*), by Hedwig Courths-Mahler.

20 The film operetta *Gräfin Mariza* (*Countess Mariza*) premieres, directed by Richard Oswald, with music by Fritz Friedmann-Frederich, with Dorothea Wieck in the title role with Hubert Marischka.

Reissner Press publishes the autobiography *Vom "Kintopp" zum Tonfilm: Ein Stück miterlebter Filmgeschichte* (*From Sideshow to Sound Film: My Experience of Film History*), by actress Henny Porten.

22 Kiepenheuer Press publishes the novel *Der Scharlatan* (*The Charlatan*), by Hermann Kesten.

The Reich office of nutrition reports that beer consumption among the German populace has dropped to 50 percent of its prewar levels; in the preceding

12-month period, Germans drank only 954 million gallons of beer, or about 14.35 gallons for every man, woman, and child in the country.

23 The film comedy *Ein blonder Traum* (*A Blonde Dream*) premieres, directed by Paul Martin, written by Billy Wilder, with Lilian Harvey and Willy Fritsch.

The operetta *Der Fürst der Berge* (*The Prince of the Mountains*), by Franz Lehar, premieres at the Theater am Nollendorf Platz in Berlin.

26 The drama *Christoph Columbus, oder die Entdeckung Amerikas* (*Christopher Columbus, or the Discovery of America*), by Walter Hasenclever, premieres at the Leipzig City Theater.

Cotta Press publishes the novel *Horst Wessel* by Hanns Heinz Ewers.

27 The film drama *Kiki* premieres, directed by Carl Lamac, with Edith d'Amara and Josef Eichheim.

29 The opera *Mister Wu* by Eugen d'Albert (who died six months earlier; the opera was completed by Leo Blech), premieres at the Dresden State Opera.

OCTOBER

1 The Eighth annual Max Reger Festival opens in Baden-Baden.[5]

Berlin city council approves a RM 180,000 subsidy to the Berlin Philharmonic Orchestra, despite the city's dire financial plight.

National Socialists stage a "Reich Youth Congress" in Potsdam, attracting more than 110,000 participants.

2 On the occasion of his 85th birthday, Reich president Paul von Hindenburg makes a nationwide radio address to thank Germans for their "loyalty and allegiance to the Fatherland." Several cities stage official celebrations in his honor.

3 The film biography about soldier-poet *Theodor Körner* premieres, directed by Carl Boese, with Willy Domgraf-Fassbänder in the title role with Dorothea Wieck.

4 The film drama *Eine von uns* (*One of Us*) premieres, directed by Johannes Meyer, with Britgitte Helm and Gustav Diessl.

The drama *Der Rattenfänger von Hameln* (*The Pied Piper of Hamelin*), by Joachim von der Goltz, premieres at the Baden-Baden City Theater.

5 The new Operetta Theater (formerly the City Theater) of Breslau claims to have the lowest admission prices of any theater in Germany; tickets in the upper balcony seats cost 30 pfennigs (about 7¢) each.

6 Zsolnay Press publishes the novel *Ein ernstes Leben* (*A Serious Life*), by Heinrich Mann.

7 The documentary film *Die steinernen Wunder von Naumburg* (*The Wonders in Stone at Naumburg*) premieres, directed by Curt Ortel.[6]

8 A meeting of Communist International in Moscow adopts a resolution supporting the suppression of free trade unions in Germany and the call for a general strike; both tactics are endorsed as instrumental in combating the growing strength of National Socialism.

10 Zsolnay Press publishes the treatise *Tragic America* by German-American author Theodor Dreiser, translated by Marianne Schön.

11 The Mendelssohn Prize is awarded to 19-year old violinist Siegfried Borries.

12 Georg L. Jochum is named music director of the Münster City Orchestra.

14 The drama *Kanzler in Not* (*Chancellor in Crisis*), by Karl Dankworth, premieres at the Bremen City Theater.

15 An exhibition of previously unseen work by painters Otto Dix, George Grosz, Paul Klee, August Macke, Emil Nolde, Karl Schmitt-Rottluff, and Erich Heckel opens at the Wallraf-Richartz Museum in Cologne.

17 Kiepenheuer Press publishes a collection of essays under title *Nach dem Nihilismus* (*After Nihilism*), by Gottfried Benn.

19 Fischer Press publishes the travel book *Eine Insel heisst Korsika* (*An Island Named Corsica*), by theater critic Alfred Kerr.

20 Propyläen Press publishes the novel *Der jüdische Krieg* (*The Jewish War*), by Lion Feuchtwanger.

The Thuringian culture ministry orders school children within its jurisdiction to memorize the German war guilt paragraph from the Versailles Treaty.

21 The new production of the opera *Salomé* by Richard Strauss, libretto by Hugo von Hofmannsthal, at the Wuppertal City Theater, is disrupted by National Socialists with tear gas, driving audience members and cast out of the building and onto the street.

The Communist Party directs its members to stage "spontaneous strikes" in an effort to disrupt voting during the new Reichstag elections scheduled for early November.

22 Universitas Press publishes the novel *Einer gegen alle* (*One against All*), by Oskar Maria Graf.

23 The film melodrama *Das erste Recht des Kindes* (*The Primary Right of a Child*) premieres, directed by Fritz Wendhausen, with Herta Thiele and Eduard Wesener.

The first "Amazon Stakes" is run at the track in Karlshorst, featuring only female jockeys.

24 The military film comedy *Husarenliebe* (*Aunt Gussie Commands*), directed by Carl Heinz Wolff, with Hansi Niesse as Aunt Gussie and Max Adalbert, premieres.

The operetta *Freut Euch des Lebens* (*Enjoy Life*) with music selections by Johann and Josef Strauss, libretto by Bernhard Grün, premieres at the Leipzig Operetta Theater.

25 Painters Paul Klee, Lyonel Feininger, Vassily Kandinsky, and Oskar Moll form an organization called Selektion to market their works.

26 Wolff Press publishes the biography *Cicero* by Herbert Eulenberg.

27 The military adventure film *Trenck* premieres, directed by Hans Paul, with Hans Stüver and Olga Chekhova.

28 The military comedy film *Annemarie, die Braut der Kompanie* (*Annemarie, the Bride of the Company*) premieres, directed by Carl Boese, with Lucie Englisch in the title role and Paul Heidemann.

29 The opera *Der Schmied von Gent* (*The Smith of Ghent*), by Franz Schreker, premieres at the Berlin City Opera; National Socialist partisans disrupt the performance, protesting composer Schreker's work as "cultural bolshevisim."

31 The film operetta *Friederike*, by Franz Lehar, premieres, directed by Fritz Friedemann-Frederich, with Mady Christians in the title role and Hans Heinz Bollmann as Johann Wolfgang Goethe.

Unemployment in Germany sinks to 5.1 million and prospects for improved business and industrial output improve.

NOVEMBER

1 Fischer Press publishes a collection of essays titled *Um Volk und Geist* (*On Ethnicity and Intellect*), by Gerhart Hauptmann, on the occasion of his upcoming 70th birthday.

2 Kipenheuer Press publishes the novel *Die Wandlung der Susanne Dasseldorf* (*The Transformation of Suzanne Dasseldorf*), by Joserph Breitbach.

3 The Berlin office of museum management closes all Berlin museums for the winter months; the city can no longer afford to heat the buildings.

5 The drama *Hardenberg* by Baron Hartmann von Richthofen, premieres at the Hannover City Theater.

6 Reichstag elections cause National Socialists to lose ground, receiving 33.1 percent of the votes; they remain the largest Reichstag faction, followed by the Social Democrats (20.4 percent) and Communists (16.9 percent).

The historic drama *Der Grosse Kurfürst bei Fehrbellin* (*The Great Elector at the Battle of Fehrbellin*), by Carl Albrecht Bernouilli, premieres at the Meiningen Regional Theater.

8 The courtroom drama *Meineid* (*Perjury*), by Erich Frey, premieres at the Theater am Schiffbaerdamm in Berlin.

Hirschfeld Press publishes a biography of the actor *Adalbert Matkowsky* by theater critic Julius Bab.

9 The opera *Der Kreidekreis* (*The Chalk Circle*, based on the play by Klabund), by Alexander von Zemlinsky, premieres at the State Opera in Berlin.

12 Playwrights Richard Billinger and Else Lasker-Schüler share the Kleist Prize.

The first Berlin Film Ball takes place, celebrating recent German films, performers, directors, and producers at the Adlon Hotel in Berlin.

13 The largely self-taught pianist Walter Gieseking performs a debut concert, playing an all-Beethoven program in Neuss.

14 An exhibition opens in Berlin Charlottenburg honoring playwright Gerhart Hauptmann on his 70th birthday.

15 Bagel Press publishes the posthumous memoirs of actress and theater manager Louise Dumont titled *Vermächtnisse* (*Legacies*), edited by her husband Gustav Lindemann.

16 The film drama *Blonde Venus* directed by Josef von Sternberg, with Marlene Dietrich, Cary Grant, and Herbert Marshall, holds its German premiere.

17 National Socialist students attack Jewish students and faculty members at the University of Breslau; officials close the university for two weeks.

18 The tragicomedy *Kasimir und Karoline* by Ödön von Horvath, premieres at the Leipzig City Theater.

20 The musical film romance *Grün ist die Heide* (*The Heath Is Green*) premieres, directed by Hans Behrendt, with Camilla Spira and Peter Voss.

21 The film romance *Ein Mann mit Herz* (*A Man with Heart*) premieres, directed by Geza von Bolvary, with Gustav Fröhlich and Gina Falckenberg.

22 The military film biography *Marschall Vorwärts* (*Marshal Forwards*, chronicling the career of Field Marshal Gebhard Leberecht von Blücher, a Prussian hero of the Napoleonic wars), directed by Heinz Paul, with Paul Wegener in the title role and Traute Carlsen, premieres.

23 The operetta *Glückliche Reise* (*Happy Journey*), by Eduard Künnecke, premieres at the Theater am Schiffbauerdamm in Berlin.

24 Reich president von Hindenburg offers Adolf Hitler the chancellorship if he can put together a cabinet approved by the Reichstag. Hitler offers to create a cabinet independent of the Reichstag, but von Hindenburg refuses the offer.

29 The historical film *Das Geheimnis um Johann Orth* (*The Secret about Johann Orth*) premieres, directed by Willi Wolff, with Karl Ludwig Diehl in the title role and Paul Otto as Emperor Franz I.

DECEMBER

1 The operetta based on the life and espionage career of exotic dancer Mata Hari titled *Die Spionin* (*The Spy*), by Theodor Meyer-Steinegg, premieres at the Magdeburg City Theater.

2 New staging of Goethe's *Faust I* opens at the State Theater in Berlin, with Gustav Gründgens, whose performance as Mephisto creates a sensation; few critics had heretofore realized the popular entertainer's capability as an actor in German classics.

The comic opera *The Golden Slippers*, by Peter Illych Tchaikowsky, has its German premiere at the Mannheim National Theater.

3 The comedy *Das neue Paradies* (*The New Paradise*), by Julius Hay, premieres at the Berliner Theater am Bülow Platz in Berlin.

Wolff Press publishes the biography *Cicero: Rechtsanwalt, Redner, Dernker, und Staatsmann* (*Cicero: Lawyer, Speaker, Thinker, and Statesman*), by playwright Herbert Eulenberg.

Reich president von Hindenburg names Kurt von Schleicher as the new Reich chancellor. National Socialists swear vengeance against Reichstag deputies who refuse to acknowledge Adolf Hitler as the politician most deserving of chancellorship.

6 Reichstag deputies re-elect National Socialist faction leader Herman Goering as president of the Reichstag.

7 Violent altercations among National Socialist, Social Democratic, and Communist deputies in the reception hall of the Reichstag building leave several seriously injured, with many taken to hospitals.

8 The film skiing romance *Abenteuer in Engadin* (*Slalom*) premieres, directed by Max Obal, with Guzzi Lantschner, Hella Hartwich, and Walter Riml.

9 The drama *Mensch aus Erde gemacht* (*Man Made of Earth*), by Friedrich Griese, premieres at the Stuttgart Regional Theater.

10 Professor Werner Heisenberg at University of Leipzig is awarded the Nobel Prize for Physics.[7]

11 The comedy *Der Mann, den es nicht gibt* (*The Man Who Never Was*), by Friedrich Gräbke, premieres at the Hannover City Theater.

13 The film drama *An heiligen Wassern* (*Sacred Waters*) premieres, directed by Erich Waschneck, with Karin Hardt and Eduard von Winterstein.

14 Zsolnay Press publishes fictional biography *Van Gogh: Roman eines Gottessuchers* (*Van Gogh: Novel of a Man in Search of God*), by Julius Meier-Gräfe.

15 Reich chancellor Kurt von Schleicher makes an inaugural nationwide radio address, promising to create new jobs.

19 Ullstein Press publishes the novel *Leben ohne Geheimnis* (*Life without Secrets*), by Vicki Baum.

20 The auto racing film *Kampf* (*Contest*) premieres, directed by Erich Schönfelder, with real-life racing car driver Manfred von Brauchitsch[8] and Josefine Dora.

21 The film romance *Wenn die Liebe Mode macht* (*When Love Sets the Fashion*) premieres, directed by Franz Wenzler, with Renate Müller and Georg Alexander.

22 Two action films premiere: *Der Rebell* (*The Rebel*), directed by Curtis Bernhardt, with Luis Trenker and Luise Ullrich; *F.P. 1 antwortet nicht* (*Floating Platform #1 Does Not Answer*), directed by Karl Hartl, with Hans Albers, Sybille Schmitz, and Peter Lorre.

23 The operetta *Ball am Savoy* (*The Savoy Ball*), by Paul Abraham, premieres at the State Theater in Berlin.

25 The detective film *Schiff ohne Hafen* (*Ship without Harbor*) premieres, directed by Harry Piel, with Charly Berger and Trude Berliner.

The comedy *Gold!!!*, by Hermann Lekisch and Kurt Sellnick, premieres at the Wiesbaden Regional Theater.

26 The drama *Die vier Musketiere* (*The Four Musketeers*), by Sigmund Graff, premieres at the Hamburg-Altona City Theater.

30 The operetta *100 Meter Glück* (*100 Meters of Fortune*), by Martin Spoliansky, premieres at the Metropol Theater in Berlin.

31 The comedy *Dr. med. Hiob Pretorius* (*Job Pretorius, Gynecologist*), by Curt Goetz, premieres at Württemberg Regional Theater in Stuttgart.

Nearly all indicators of economic activity in Germany show severe decline; automobile ownership, theater attendance, coal deliveries, salaries, wages, and use of electricity down by an average of 30 percent over previous year's figures. Paid-up memberships in National Socialist German Workers' Party in marked increase.

NOTES

1. Heinrich Schliemann (1822–1890) was the subject of several books by the time Ludwig's appeared, largely because Schliemann's "history" was so fantastic. It included his birth in Mecklenburg to an impoverished pastor's family, his beginnings as a grocery clerk, near death by shipwreck at age 24, and his mastery of several languages. Thereafter followed acquisition of great wealth as a banker during the California gold rush, career as a multi-millionaire German-American merchant with offices and estates in Russia and France, an earned doctorate at the University of Tübingen, and his subsequent career as an archeologist. At age 46, he discovered, or at least convinced the Victorian world he had discovered, the site of Homer's Troy and a trove of treasures that today remains stupefying.

2. *The Eternal Road* was the last "war comradeship drama" of the Weimar Republic. Graff (under the pseudonym "Carl Hintze") had written his reminiscences of World War I in book form during 1926. Witnessing the success of war plays like Sheriff's *Journey's End* and Stallings/Anderson's *What Price Glory?* (not to mention the overwhelming success of the film *All Quiet on the Western Front*), he turned the book into a play. It was rejected by managers throughout Germany, but when it attracted big audiences in London during the 1929–1930 season, the Aachen City Theater premiered it in 1930. It had more than 5,000 performances thereafter in numerous theatres, culminating in a lengthy Berlin run.

3. The term *kuhle wampe* can be translated from Berlin proletarian patois as "empty stomach," or simply "hungry," but it also refers to a geographical area near Müggelsee (Lake Müggel) on the eastern outskirts of Berlin.

4. Tilman Riemenschneider (1460–1531) is considered the most accomplished sculptor of the late 15th century, known particularly for his astonishingly detailed altar pieces, usually executed in lime wood, alabaster, or sandstone. His studio in Würzburg was one of the most successful in central Europe by the 1490s, receiving commissions from parish churches, small chapels, courts, and bishoprics. Figures in his altar pieces are known for intense facial expressiveness and for the figures' remarkably detailed clothing. The most notable examples of his work are found today in Rothenburg ob der Tauber, the Louvre Museum in Paris, the Metropolitan Museum of Art in New York, the Cleveland Museum of Art, and the Mainfränkisches Museum in Würzburg.

5. Several cities had Max Reger Festivals by the 1920s, a testimony both to the popularity of the composer and to his prolific output. The Baden-Baden festival in this year concentrated on Reger's works for piano, featuring soloist Rudolf Serkin.

6. The Naumburg St. Peter and Paul Cathedral remains one of the most impressive examples of late Romanesque architecture in Germany. Construction on it began sometime in the 12th century; during the second century of its construction, statues of its founders the Margrave Ekkehard and his wife Uta were completed, along with those of other influential men and women. Those figures are the central focus of Ortel's film. The church fell into Protestant hands during the Reformation and it remains an Evangelical Lutheran venue to this day.

7. Werner Heisenberg (1901–1976) received the Nobel Prize, according to the Nobel committee, for "the creation of quantum mechanics, the application of which has, among other things, led to the discovery of the allotropic forms of hydrogen." "Allotropes" (differing physical properties of the same element) had long been known, such as diamonds and graphite as forms of carbon. Heisenberg's theories about hydrogen allotropes, however, resulted from his rejection of the 19th-century concept of atomic structure, which featured discrete subatomic particles orbiting in prescribed paths around a nucleus. Ultimately, Heisenberg became best known for his *Unschärferelation* (sometimes called the *Unbestimmtheitsrelation*, or "uncertainty principle") formulated in 1927, which posited the impossibility of determining both the position and the velocity of an electron simultaneously. Heisenberg theorized that subatomic particles should therefore be described in terms of their intensity and frequency of radiation.

8. Manfred von Brauchitsch (1905–2003) was perhaps best known as the German teammate of the far more successful driver Rudolf Caracciola. Von Brauchitsch's success with the sleek, cigar-shaped "Silver Arrows" that Mercedes produced in the late 1920s prompted Carraciola to leave the Alfa Romeo team, however, and together they won several Grand Prix events with Mercedes cars. Yet von Brauchitsch was also known for losing several important races—often just as he seemed on the verge of winning, usually due to some minor technical snag or failure. He was also known for his bad luck with injuries; in one of his several crashes, he suffered several broken ribs, a broken arm, shoulder blade, collarbone, and fractured skull. Yet he kept driving, remaining one of the Mercedes team's legendary performers.

1933

JANUARY

1 Erika Mann, daughter of novelist Thomas Mann, opens cabaret in Munich called *Die Pfeffermühle* (*The Pepper Mill*).

The film musical comedy Die Herren vom Maxim (The Gentlemen from Maxim's) premieres, directed by Carl Boese, with Lee Parry, Oskar Karlweis, Leo Slezak, and Johannes Riemann.

American novelist Upton Sinclair is named to the honorary membership committee of the Prussian Academy of the Arts.

4 The comedy *Die Männer sind mal so* (*Men Are Simply Like That*), by Walter Kollo, premieres at the Schiller Theater in Berlin.

Eine Tür geht auf (*A Door Opens*) premieres, directed by Alfred Zeisler, with Erika Fiedler and Hjermann Spielmanns.

6 Readers of the weekly movie magazine *Lichtbühne* vote German-speaking English actress Lilian Harvey "most interesting film star" of 1932.

Violinist Siegfried Borries is named concert master of the Berlin Philharmonic Orchestra.

9 The drama *Die Expedition nach San Domingo* (*The Expedition to San Domingo*), by Karl Otten, premieres at the Alten City Theater.

12 Thalia Theater in Berlin declares bankruptcy and ceases operations.

13 The comedy *Die Laus im Pelz* (*The Louse in the Fur Coat*), by Hans Müller-Schlösser, premieres at the Krefeld City Theater.

14 Two dramas premiere: *Der driezehnte Juni* (*The Thirteenth of June*), by Fred A. Angermeyer at the Hamburg Thalia Theater, and *Die Marneschalcht* (*The Battle of the Marne*), by Joseph Paul Cremers at the Mannheim National Theater.

15 Communist Party activists stage a public ceremony in Berlin, honoring Karl Liebknecht and Rosa Luxemburg, both murdered in the January 1919 Spartacist Uprising in Berlin.

16 The operetta *Die Fahrt ins Abenteuer* (*Journey into Adventure*), by Will Tanta, premieres at the Breslau City Theater.

The film comedy *Madame wünscht keine Kinder* (*Madame Desires No Children Present*) premieres, directed by Hans Steinhoff, with Liane Haid and Georg Alexander.

20 The film comedy *So ein Mädel vergisst man nicht* (*You Don't Forget a Girl Like That*) premieres, directed by Fritz Kortner, with Dolly Haas and Willi Frost.

Rumors begin to circulate (and many newspapers begin to print them) that Reich chancellor Kurt von Schleicher will resign in favor of Adolf Hitler, provided the make-up of the Hitler Cabinet will have only two or three National Socialist members. At the Sports Palace in Berlin later in the evening, Hitler demands to be named Reich chancellor before a standing-room-only audience.

21 The film drama *Eine Stadt steht kopf* (*A City Upside Down*) premieres, directed by Gustaf Gründgens, with Jenny Jugo and Hermann Thimig.

22 A new staging of Goethe's *Faust II* opens at the State Theater in Berlin with Gustaf Gründgens continuing as Mephisto; many critics praise Gründgens as the most versatile German actor of the age.

24 The musical film *Kaiserwalzer* (*Emperor's Waltz*) premieres, directed by Fredrich Zelnik, with Martha Eggert and Paul Hörbiger.

26 The film drama *Großstadtnacht* (*A Night in the Big City*) premieres, directed by Fyodor Otsep, with Dolly Haas and Ivan Koval-Samborsky.

Reich president von Hindenburg assures the German Army Chief of Staff Baron Kurt von Hammerstein-Equord that he "would never consider appointing that Bohemian corporal [Adolf Hitler] as Reich chancellor."

28 Piano Concerto No. 2 in G major, by Bela Bartok, with the Frankfurt Radio Symphony Orchestra (and the composer himself at the piano), premieres at Frankfurt am Main.

Reich chancellor Kurt von Schleicher and his entire cabinet resign.

29 Gottfried von Cramm defeats Pierre Landry of France for the international indoor tennis championship at a match in Bremen.

30 Reich president Paul von Hindenburg names Adolf Hitler Reich chancellor at 11:00 a.m. "And now, gentlemen, forward with God's help," states von Hindenburg at the conclusion of the swearing-in ceremony. Later in the afternoon, Hitler enters the Reich chancellery proclaiming, "No power on earth will bring me out of here alive." At 5:00 p.m. following the conclusion of his first cabinet meeting, Hitler states, "This day millions of people in Germany will greet with joy." The Weimar Republic is dead.

About the Author

William Grange is Hixson-Lied Professor of Theatre and Film at the University of Nebraska. The author of five books, along with numerous scholarly articles, essays, book chapters, and reviews, Grange has received several awards and fellowships both in the United States and abroad. He was named to the Fulbright Distinguished Chair of Humanities and Cultural Studies at the University of Vienna (Austria) for 2007, and in 2006 he was awarded the Dorot Family Fellowship from the Harry J. Ransom Center for Research in the Humanities at the University of Texas. Prior to those awards he had received Fulbright fellowships for teaching and research at the University of Cologne and the Film Acting School of Cologne and Senior Fellowships from the German Academic Exchange Service for research at the Academy of the Arts in Berlin. The Research Council of the University of Nebraska, the Jane Robertson Layman Fund, and the Hixson-Lied Endowment supported his research for this volume.